Lecture Notes in Compu 5

Edited by G. Goos, J. Hartmanis, a

Springer

Berlin
Heidelberg
New York
Barcelona
Hong Kong
London
Milan
Paris
Singapore
Tokyo

Michael Butler   Luigia Petre Kaisa Sere (Eds.)

Integrated
Formal Methods

Third International Conference, IFM 2002
Turku, Finland, May 15-18, 2002
Proceedings

 Springer

Gerhard Goos, Karlsruhe University, Germany
Juris Hartmanis, Cornell University, NY, USA
Jan van Leeuwen, Utrecht University, The Netherlands

Volume Editors

Michael Butler
University of Southampton, Department of Electronics and Computer Science
Declarative Systems and Software Engineering
Highı eld, Southampton, SO17 1BJ, UK
E-mail: mjb@ecs.soton.ak.uk

Luigia Petre
Turku Centre for Computer Science
Lemminkäisenkatu 14A, 20520 Turku, Finland
E-mail: lpetre@abo.ı

Kaisa Sere
Åbo Akademi University, Department of Computer Science
Lemminkäisenkatu 14, 20520 Turku, Finland
E-mail: Kaisa.Sere@abo.ı

Cataloging-in-Publication Data applied for

Die Deutsche Bibliothek - CIP-Einheitsaufnahme

Integrated formal methods : third international conference ; proceedings /
IFM 2002, Turku, Finland, May 15 - 18, 2002. Michael Butler ... (ed.). -
Berlin ; Heidelberg ; New York ; Barcelona ; Hong Kong ; London ; Milan ;
Paris ; Tokyo : Springer, 2002
  (Lecture notes in computer science ; Vol. 2335)
  ISBN 3-540-43703-7

CR Subject Classiı cation (1998): F.3, D.3, D.2, D.1

ISSN 0302-9743
ISBN 3-540-43703-7 Springer-Verlag Berlin Heidelberg New York

Springer-Verlag Berlin Heidelberg New York
a member of BertelsmannSpringer Science+Business Media GmbH

http://www.springer.de

© Springer-Verlag Berlin Heidelberg 2002
Printed in Germany

Typesetting: Camera-ready by author, data conversion by Olgun Computergraı k
Printed on acid-free paper   SPIN 10869773   06/3142   5 4 3 2 1 0

Preface

The third in a series of international conferences on Integrated Formal Methods, IFM 2002, was held in Turku, Finland, May 15–17, 2002. Turku, situated in the south western corner of the country, is the former capital of Finland. The conference was organized jointly by Åbo Akademi University and Turku Centre for Computer Science.

The theme of IFM 1999 was the integration of state and behavioral based formalisms. For IFM 2000 this was widened to include all aspects pertaining to the integration of formal methods and formal notations. One of the goals of IFM 2002 was to further investigate these themes. Moreover, IFM 2002 explored the relations between formal methods and graphical notations, especially the industrial standard language for software design, the Unified Modeling Language (UML).

The themes of IFM 2002 reflect what we believe is a growing trend in the Formal Methods and Software Engineering research communities. Over the last three decades, computer scientists have developed a range of formalisms focusing on particular aspects of behavior or analysis, such as sequential program structures, concurrent program structures, data and information structures, temporal reasoning, deductive proof, and model checking. Much effort is now being devoted to integrating these methods in order to combine their advantages and ensure they scale up to industrial needs. Graphical notations are now widely used in software engineering and there is growing recognition of the importance of providing these with the formal underpinnings and formal analysis capabilities found in formal methods.

The invited speakers for the conference represent a range of academic and industrial research experience. Eran Gery is Vice President for Rhapsody product development at I-Logix Inc. He is involved in the UML 2.0 consortium, and was a member of the UML founding team. Shmuel Katz is Professor of Computer Science at the Technion in Israel and leads research into the integration of specification notations and verification tools. Stuart Kent is Senior Lecturer in Computer Science at the University of Kent, UK and also works with IBM UK Research Laboratories on model-driven development of e-business systems.

In total there were 46 submissions for IFM 2002. Of these, 18 were selected for publication in the proceedings and presentation at the conference. Each paper was independently reviewed by several members of the Program Committee or their colleagues. The selection of the final 18 papers was based on the reviews followed by electronic discussion between the reviewers. In these proceedings, the papers are grouped into the following themes:

- Integration, Simulation, Animation
- From Specification to Verification
- Statecharts and B: Integration and Translation
- Model Checkers and Theorem Provers

- Links between Object-Z and CSP
- Combining Graphical and Formal Approaches
- Refinement and Proof

We hope that these proceedings will be of benefit both to the conference participants and to the wider community of researchers and practitioners in the field. The production of these proceedings would not have been possible without the invaluable help of the program committee members as well as their external referees, and of all the contributors who submitted papers to the conference.

March 2002

Michael Butler
Luigia Petre
Kaisa Sere

Organization

Michael Butler, University of Southampton, UK (PC Co-chair)
Luigia Petre, Turku Centre for Computer Science, Finland
Kaisa Sere, Åbo Akademi University, Turku, Finland (PC Co-chair)

Program Committee

Didier Bert (Grenoble, France)
Jonathan Bowen (London, UK)
Michael Butler (Southampton, UK)
Jim Davies (Oxford, UK)
John Derrick (Kent, UK)
Jin Song Dong (Singapore)
John Fitzgerald (Manchester, UK)
Andrew Galloway (York, UK)
Chris George (Macao)
Wolfgang Grieskamp (Redmond, USA)
Henri Habrias (Nantes, France)
Susumu Hayashi (Kobe, Japan)
Maritta Heisel (Magdeburg, Germany)
Michel Lemoine (Toulouse, France)
Shaoying Liu (Tokyo, Japan)

Dominique Mery (Nancy, France)
Luigia Petre (Turku, Finland)
Thomas Santen (Berlin, Germany)
Steve Schneider (London, UK)
Wolfram Schulte (Redmond, USA)
Kaisa Sere (Turku, Finland)
Jane Sinclair (Warwick, UK)
Graeme Smith (Queensland, Australia)
Bill Stoddart (Teesside, UK)
Kenji Taguchi (Uppsala, Sweden)
W J (Hans) Toetenel (Delft, Holland)
Heike Wehrheim (Oldenburg,
Germany)
Jim Woodcook (Oxford, UK)

Referees

Christian Attiogbé
Mike Barnett
Christie Bolton
Marcello Bonsangue
Alessandra Cavarra
Orieta Celiku
Gabriel Ciobanu
Steve Dunne

Carla Ferreira
Andy Gravell
Steffen Helke
Jean-Yves Lafaye
Kung-Kiu Lau
Ivan Porres Paltor
Viorel Preoteasa
Rimvydas Ruksenas

Mauno Rönkkö
Andrew Simpson
Colin Snook
Jing Sun
Carsten Sühl
Koichi Takahasi
Dang Van Hung

Sponsoring Institution

Turku Centre for Computer Science, Turku, Finland

Table of Contents

Model Checkers and Theorem Provers

Links between Object–Z and CSP

Invited Talk: Stuart Kent

Combining Graphical and Formal Approaches

Refinement and Proof

Author Index

Rhapsody:
A Complete Life-Cycle Model-Based Development System

Eran Gery, David Harel, and Eldad Palachi

I-Logix, Inc.

Abstract. We discuss Rhapsody, a UML based software development tool, designed to support complete model-based iterative life-cycle. First, we identify several key inhibiting factors that prevent model-based approaches from being adopted as a mainstream practice. We then examine the requirements for allowing complete life-cycle model-based development and discuss how they are met by Rhapsody through its key enabling technologies, which include:
- *model-code associativity*
- *automated implementation generation*
- *implementation framework*
- *model execution*
- *model-based testing*

We explain why each of these features is instrumental to an effective development of production systems, based on a key observation that the modeling language does not replace the implementation platform, but should be integrated with it in a synergistic manner. This allows the use of modeling for expressing requirements and design abstractions, along with the use of the full power of an implementation language and its supporting platform to specify implementation details. While allowing this flexibility, Rhapsody facilitates full consistency of the modeling and implementation artifacts throughout the life-cycle, and it also supports a high level of automation in the implementation and validation of the developed system.

1   Introduction

Model-based development has been of interest in the software development industry almost since its inception. Nevertheless, model-based development is not yet mainstream practice. The emergence of the unified modeling language (UML) [7] as a ubiquitous practice across the software industry brings awareness to modeling and abstraction a step forward. Still, only a small percentage of software developers practice model-based development with UML.

A common usage pattern of models is the informal use-case, by which concepts and ideas are sketched in a model, and then followed by traditional implementation, without any formal consistency between the modeling artifacts and the implementation artifacts. As we explain below, despite its common practice this approach exposes some major weaknesses and actually limits the ability to benefit from the main advantages of model-based development.

M. Butler, L. Petre, and K. Sere (Eds.): IFM 2002, LNCS 2335, pp. 1–10, 2002.

Other paradigms (e.g. [10]) follow a translative approach, whereby implementation artifacts are generated from models but are not practically accessible to the developers. This approach represent the other extreme. On the one hand it is formal, meaning that model-semantics is fully compiled into the implementation artifact. But on the other hand it poses significant difficulties as a mainstream technique in the software industry, since it ignores the role and importance of interfacing the implementation platform itself.

Recently, the OMG emerged with the Model Driven Architecture initiative [8], which combines a set of technologies to achieve the construction of systems in a highly reusable, platform-independent manner. In it, model-based development serves as the key facilitator in achieving platform independence and a high level of reuse. The model-based development approach proposed in the MDA is consistent with what we describe here, in that it offers a formal and automated approach on the one hand, while realistically addressing implementation constraints the other.

In this paper we describe the concepts behind Rhapsody [3,4], a system designed to facilitate an effective model-based development life-cycle. In retrospect, Rhapsody realizes many of the ideas outlined in MDA, while focusing its applicability on real-time embedded systems. It addresses those deficiencies that prohibit the effective usage of model-based development, turning it into a mainstream tool for industry. Rhapsody is based on the idea of executable models, as described in [3], and it is fair to say that both of these pioneered the idea of formal model-based development with UML.

2 Iterative Development

Iterative development is the current mainstream approach for software development. In the UML context it is described as a generic process in [5]. A more specific process suited for the development of embedded systems is described in [1]. Iterative development addresses several key issues that can be viewed as the legacy of waterfall-based processes:

- Reduces risk by early detection of analysis, design and implementation issues.
- Is able to effectively trade off schedule and functionality in order to address competition and/or schedule slippage.
- Facilitates concurrent development to shorten development life-cycles.

It is crucial that a model-based development process effectively support iterative development. Iterative development is based on incremental steps, each of which goes through a complete analyze-design-implement-test cycle. Completion of increment n is the starting point for increment $n + 1$. Therefore, effective iterative development requires strong bi-directional traceability between all development artifacts. In addition, it is important to facilitate rapid iteration throughout the development life-cycle.

In the sequel we will analyze the key enabling technologies required to facilitate effective iteration and traceability.

3 Problems with Model-Based Development

There are several key inhibitors for the adoption of model-based development by software developers. Each of them results in a workflow deficiency that inhibits the synergy between iterative and model-based development.

A common deficiency is lack of implementation automation, resulting in the need for manual coding of the implementation or significant parts of it. This results in inherent *incosistency* between the modeling and implementation artifacts, as the manual implementation is error prone. In addition lack of automation also results in lower *productivity*, which is also an inhibitor to an effective process by itself.

The main reason for this deficiency is lack of support for model executability. Model executability requires complete semantic interpretation of the model, accompanied by algorithms for translating the model into artifacts that can be executed and support a run-time execution model, that facilitates *validation* of the model. In the absence of a model-execution facility, validation is done only to the implementation artifacts, resulting in late detection of inconsistencies with the specification, as well as the non-validated model remaining an informal artifact used only at the beginning of the process and not throughout the iterative life-cycle.

Another common deficiency is the *discontinuity* between the implementation artifacts and modeling artifacts representing the analysis and design stages. Iterative life-cycles require that the implementation artifacts created in the nth iteration are augmented and refined during the $n+1$ iteration. In the absence of proper traceability support, changes to the implementation during integration of iteration n, invalidate the model for iteration $n+1$.

The next inhibiting factor is *disintegration* with the implementation platform. Modeling languages offer rich semantic abstractions of structure and behavior, but they do not normally provide rich sets of operations at the detailed level. In contrast, implementation languages offer rich constructs at the detailed level, such as arithmetic, memory manipulations and other kinds of detailed level operations, but lack proper abstractions for concepts above these. The lack of proper integration between the two results in a compromise, either of usability or of efficiency of the resulting implementation.

4 Rhapsody's Key Enabling Technologies

Rhapsody embodies several principles that are instrumental for effective model-based development, and which address the common automation and traceability deficiencies. The key enabling technologies are *model-code associativity, automated implementation generation, implementation framework, model execution and back animation*, and *model-based testing*.

We now describe each of these in some detail.

4.1 Model-Code Associativity

Model-code associativity is a key enabler for software developers to effectively leverage the benefits of model-based approaches, but without compromising the benefits of direct access to the implementation language/platform. The fundamental principle here is that the model does not replace the implementation language, but rather being augmented by it in a synergistic manner, where abstractions are described and viewed by models, but detailed implementation is carried out by an implementation language.

To achieve this in Rhapsody, the model and code are viewed as two viable development artifacts of the system. This is done using the following design principles:

- Detailed behaviors (also known as "actions") are written in the target implementation language. This avoids unnecessary translation of detailed computational expressions from one language (the "action language") to another, although the two are essentially isomorphic. Using the implementation language as the action language also contributes to the readability of the resulting code, as well as to the expressiveness of low-level manipulation.
- The implementation language is augmented by an execution framework (see subsection 4.3 below), which provides additional semantic constructs not supported by the implementation language. The framework is essentially the interface between the implementation language and the modeling language abstractions.
- Code resulting from the model is intuitive and self-explanatory. This is achieved by using common translation patterns for UML's abstract constructs, and by attaching notes and constraints to the resulting code. In addition, using the implementation language as the action language, and the implementation framework itself, contribute to the readability of the implementation source code.
- Rhapsody supports online navigability between the model artifacts and their code counterparts, and vice versa. It is always possible to trace the code resulting from certain model elements and to trace the model element corresponding to a particular section of the code.
- Model and code are always synchronized: changes in the model are instantaneously reflected in the code view, and changes in the implementation code are "round-tripped" back, to be reflected in the model. This facility is instrumental to the entire idea of model-based development. It addresses the inherent discontinuity problem, whereby changing the code invalidates the model and thus also the entire model-based development workflow.

4.2 Automated Implementation Generation

The core of Rhapsody support for model executability is its implementation generator. The generator generates fully functional, production-ready implementations, employing all the behavioral semantics specified in the UML model. These include system construction, object life-cycle management (construction and destruction), object behavior as specified by statecharts or activity-graphs, as well as methods directly specified by the implementation language.

The implementation generator maps every model artifact into a set of implementation artifacts (source code, make-files) based on generation rules and a set of predefined parameters for each model element type (metaclass). The generation parameters may specify translation tradeoffs (size/speed, size/modularity) as well as code style. In addition, the parameters specify implementation domain objects to be reused in the translation. These may come from the Rhapsody execution framework or be defined by the user. All this enables the user to choose from a wide range of implementation strategies that realize the model semantics.

The implementation generator supports various implementation languages (C++, C, Java) and component frameworks (COM, CORBA).

4.3   The Execution Framework

The execution framework is an infrastructure that augments the implementation language to support the modeling language semantics. The framework based approach is an open architectural mode of work, providing a set of architectural and mechanistic patterns to support modelling abstractions like active objects, signal dispatching, state based behaviors, object relationships and life-cycle management.

The execution framework is given in several forms of APIs, based on the implementation language. These APIs are used by the modeler to perform manipulation at model abstraction level, including sending signals, creating composite objects, creating object relationships, and interacting with the state model.

The Rhapsody framework consists of 3 domains of architectural and mechanistic patterns:

- The active objects base framework: a set of architectural patterns that supports the active object set of semantics, including concurrency, signal dispatching, synchronization, and life-cycle management.
- The operating system abstraction layer (OSAL): a layer that encapsulates a set of basic services typically supported by an operating system, such as creation of threads, event queues, semaphores, memory management, etc. The OSAL needs to be implemented specifically for every targeted operating system. It allows easy retargeting of models to different platforms without any change to the model.
- Utilities for mechanistic design: a set of containers to implement the various relationships and life-cycle management between objects in the system.

The execution framework API serves as an abstraction layer used by the code-generator to facilitate model semantics in the context of a particular implementation language. Developers may specialize and augment the basic semantics by specializing or changing the implementation of the framework pattern. The latter is achieved by changing the open code generator mappings to use a different set of framework classes.

The set of patterns provided by the framework comprises common structural and behavioral patterns used by applications based on the active object paradigm; specifically, real-time embedded applications. The framework implies a high level of reuse of these validated pattern implementations, which contribute to the modularity and quality of the generated application. A fairly detailed description of the framework can be found in [6].

4.4   Model Execution (Model-Based Debugging)

Model execution is a key enabler for effective model-based development, as it facilitates the ability to effectively *validate* what has been constructed. The key theme behind model execution is expanding the specification model with a runtime model that provides the ability to trace and control the execution of the system at the same level of abstraction as that of the system specification.

There are two main approaches two model execution. The first, which is often referred to as *simulation*, is to construct an interpreter that executes the model based on the runtime semantics. The other one, which is manifested in Rhapsody, is to provide a runtime traceability link between the implementation execution and the runtime model. This technique is also called *model-animation*.

The fact that the model execution is linked to the actual implementation execution has several advantages. From a methodological point of view, it enables shorter iterations of model-implement-debug cycles, while maintaining full consistency between the model and its implementation. Another advantage is the ability to have concurrent source-level and model-level debugging by allowing the use of a code level debugger in the process. Such a combination also allows an easier mapping between the UML design and its source code implementation.

Figure 1 is a screen-shot of the runtime model, instantiated during a model execution session. The model consists of all instances of objects, their links and internal states. It also includes event queues and call-stacks for active objects, and also a trace that logs all the events in the system.

As shown in the figure, one can view individual instances, including their current state configuration, attributes values and association references. The system trace is reflected as instantiations of animated sequence diagrams. Other available views are an output window that can be used to textually trace the run, call-stack and event queue windows that relate to a specified "focus" thread, a browser view showing the instances of each class, and more. As for control capabilities, Rhapsody provides a set of animation commands that can be invoked using the animation toolbar. These include injecting events, setting focus threads, running step-by-step in different granularities (for example, "go event", which means run until the application is finished dealing with the current event in the queue) setting filters for the output window, logging the trace to external files, and more.

The architecture behind our model-execution technique consists of the following components: (1) Source code instrumentation hooks, inserted by the implementation generator; (2) A runtime trace framework, implemented in the implementation language, which provides a set of services to trace and control

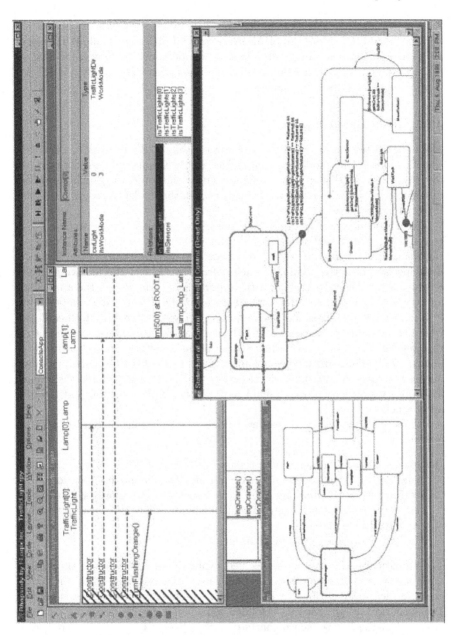

Fig. 1. Model execution using Rhapsody.

the application; (3) A trace and control communication protocol between the application and Rhapsody (implemented over TCP/IP), which allows Rhapsody to debug applications running on remote embedded devices using embedded operating systems; (4) A runtime model maintained within Rhapsody; (5) A set of runtime views, as described above.

4.5   Model-Based Testing

Model-based testing provides the ability to specify and run tests based on the specifications in the model, as well as the ability to pinpoint defects from the test results by visualizing points of failure within the model. A good model-based testing component also facilitate a trace between the modelled requirements and the constructed system.

Currently, most testing cycles have the following characteristic steps: write or record test scripts based on the specification documents and existing prototypes; run the scripts; review the results; report defects and/or confirm fixes. From the developer's perspective, handling such defects consists of the following: try to reproduce the defect by repeating the reported scenario; debug the application and try to diagnose the source of the failure; fix the defect and . . . hope for the best . . .. Usually, towards new releases, this cycle seems to repeat itself endlessly, where the number of defects constantly fluctuates, until the system meets the required level of quality according to the available set of tests. Another well-known fact is that using traditional approaches, most of the bugs are introduced during the early stages of the development, but are found towards the release. This observation is one of the main motivations for incremental and iterative approaches.

Rhapsody's model-based testing features the following canonical usage sequence:

1. Specify tests using scenarios specified in the model.
2. Run the tests. Rhapsody will drive and monitor the model execution.
3. Review results and pinpoint failures, by having the tool show the actual trace rendered as a sequence diagram that highlights where the scenario that was expected was violated.
4. Fix the defect and verify by rerunning the test.

The scenarios in clause 1 were specified explicitly as requirements throughout the analysis and design stages, or may have been recorded using the model execution feature described earlier to serve as a baseline for regression-testing. The scenarios are specified as extended sequence diagrams, following concepts proposed in the live sequence charts of [LSC]. Scenarios can be referred to as monitors or also drivers. Driver scenarios also provide stimuli to the system during test execution.

This approach to testing has the following main advantages:

– Abstract modeling concepts can be reused to specify tests, as an alternative to script files.

– The requirements from the model and execution traces can be reused as tests.
– Both black-box and white-box scenarios can be used for testing, unlike the traditional approach that executes only black-box scenarios. Also, one can easily elaborate a black-box into a white-box scenario by adding the relevant instances during the run, or offline, as part of the test specification.
– It is easier to diagnose the source of the defect, since the exact point of failure is shown by the tool using sequence diagram notation.
– Testers and developers alike can specify and execute tests: no specialized tools or knowledge of scripting languages is required.
– Earlier detection of bugs throughout the development process is possible: tests can be defined and executed as part of the development effort and then routinely executed from that point on.
– Consistency is maintained between requirements and tests: updating requirements automatically updates test criteria and in many cases the other way around too.

5 Conclusion

In this brief paper we have attempted to discuss the rationale behind the approach taken in designing the Rhapsody tool [3,4], and its main advantages in model-based system development. We talked about the problems Rhapsody was intended to solve, and its key enabling technologies.

Model-code associativity facilitates the seamless integration with the development platform and full associativity between the implementation and modeling artifacts, addressing the *discontinuity* and the *disintegration* inhibiting factors mentioned in Section 3. Automated implementation generation and the implementation framework address model to implementation consistency as well as the productivity factor. Model-execution addresses validation of the model throughout the iterative life-cycle and early detection of defects originating from requirements through design to detailed implementation. Model-based testing contributes to effective model-based development by maintaining consistency between model requirements and tests, by facilitating early testing throughout the iterative life-cycle, and by increasing the productivity of specifying tests and detecting defects.

References

1. B.P. Douglass Doing Hard Time. Addison-Wesley Object Technology Series, 1999.
2. W. Damm and D. Harel. LSCs: Breathing Life into Message Sequence Charts. *Formal Methods in System Design*, 19(1), 2001. (Preliminary version in *Proc. 3rd IFIP Int. Conf. on Formal Methods for Open Object-Based Distributed Systems* (*FMOODS'99*), (P. Ciancarini, A. Fantechi and R. Gorrieri, eds.), Kluwer Academic Publishers, 1999, pages 293–312.)

3. D. Harel and E. Gery. Executable Object Modeling with Statecharts. *IEEE Computer*, pages 31–42, July 1997. Also, *Proc. 18th Int. Conf. on Software Engineering*, Berlin, IEEE Press, March, 1996, pp. 246–257.)
4. Rhapsody's user guide. www.ilogix.com
5. I. Jacobson, G. Booch, J. Rumbaugh. The Unified Software Development Process. Addison-Wesley Object Technology Series, 1998.
6. E. Gery, R. Rinat, J. Ziegler. Octopus Concurrency Design with Rhapsody. www.ilogix.com
7. OMG Unified Modeling Language Specification, Version 1.4. OMG Document formal/01-09-67
8. OMG Architecture Board MDA Drafting Team. "Model Driven Architecture - A Technical Perspective". OMG Document ormsc/01-07-01
9. UML 1.4 with Action Semantics. OMG Document ptc/02-01-09, p. 2-209 - 2-349
10. http://www.projtech.com/prods/bp/info.html

An Integrated Semantics
for UML Class, Object and State Diagrams
Based on Graph Transformation*

Sabine Kuske, Martin Gogolla, Ralf Kollmann, and Hans-Jörg Kreowski

University of Bremen, Department of Computer Science
P.O.Box 330440, D-28334 Bremen, Germany
{kuske,gogolla,kollmann,kreo}@informatik.uni-bremen.de

Abstract. This paper studies the semantics of a central part of the
Unified Modeling Language UML. It discusses UML class, object and
state diagrams and presents a new integrated semantics for both on the
basis of graph transformation. Graph transformation is a formal technique having some common ideas with the UML. Graph transformation
rules are associated with the operations in class diagrams and with the
transitions in state diagrams. The resulting graph transformations are
combined into a one system in order to obtain a single coherent semantic description.

1 Introduction

In recent years, the Unified Modeling Language UML [4,38,33] has been widely
accepted as the standard language for modeling and documenting software systems. The UML offers a number of diagram forms used to describe particular
aspects of software artifacts. These diagram forms can be divided depending on
whether they are intended to describe structural or behavioral aspects. From
a fundamental point of view, class and state diagrams are the basic means for
system description, because class diagrams determine the fundamental object
structures and state diagrams can be employed for describing the fundamental
object behavior.

Graph transformation is a well-developed field [37,11,12] and has many application domains, among them questions related to graphical modeling languages
like UML [39,13,18,20,34,40], [14,25]. The basic idea of graph transformation is
to represent system states as graphs and system evolution steps as applications
of single graph transformation rules. We feel that this basic idea has many similarities with basic UML concepts. System states in UML can be regarded as
object diagrams which belong to certain class diagrams. Object diagrams are
essentially graphs. System evolution in UML may be described in various ways.

---

* This work was partially supported by the project Abstract Implementation of and
Documentation with UML (UML-AID) funded by the *Deutsche Forschungsgemein-
schaft* and the ESPRIT Working Group Applications of Graph Transformation
(APPLIGRAPH).

M. Butler, L. Petre, and K. Sere (Eds.): IFM 2002, LNCS 2335, pp. 11–28, 2002.
© Springer-Verlag Berlin Heidelberg 2002

One basic behavior description technique is the UML state diagram where each transition may be regarded as an atomic system evolution step transforming a system state, i.e. a graph, into another system state. Therefore, concepts of UML and graph transformation are closely related. Another advantage we see in regarding graphs as a semantic description technique is that graphs can be understood as visual entities like all diagrams in the UML. Explaining UML by graphs induces only a small gap between the language to be defined, namely the UML, and the language used as the target language, namely graphs.

The structure of the rest of the paper is as follows. Section 2 discusses the features of UML class and state diagrams we use in this paper. Section 3.1 explains how class diagrams can be translated to graph transformation and Sect. 3.2 does the same for state diagrams, in particular Sect. 3.2 shows how state transitions are expressed. Section 4 discusses how to integrate the resulting graph transformations from the class and state diagrams into a single transformation system. All concepts are explained by a single running example. Section 5 shortly touches related work. The paper closes in Sect. 6 with some final remarks.

2   Class and State Diagrams

Class and state diagrams are fundamental diagrams of the UML. In the following we shortly illustrate both diagram types. For further details, the reader is referred to e.g. [4,38,33].

Class diagrams are used to represent the static structure of object-oriented systems. They consist of classes and relationships where the latter are divided into associations, generalizations, and dependencies. Special kinds of associations are compositions and aggregations. A *class* consists of a name, a set of attributes and a set of operations possibly with parameters. Every class c specifies a set of objects called the *instances of c*. An *association end* is a language element of class diagrams which relates associations with classes and contains some information such as the *role* a class plays in the corresponding association or its *multiplicity*. A *class diagram* is a graph where the nodes are classes, and the edges are associations, generalizations, or dependencies. We here concentrate on binary associations. Some of the classes may be associations as well. These classes are called association classes.

Fig. 1 shows an example of a class diagram consisting of classes, binary associations, and an association class. It models a client-server system containing a class *DriveThrough* and a class *Client*. A drive-through can be visited by an ordered set of clients (client queue). Every client of a drive-through has a running number which indicates the place the client has in the client queue of the drive-through. Furthermore, there is a class *Order* which represents possible orders a client can give to a drive-through.

Object diagrams mainly differ from class diagrams in the sense that they contain objects instead of classes. Object diagrams are useful to represent the state of a system in a special moment. The nodes of an object diagram are objects and its edges are links. Analogously to class diagrams some objects may

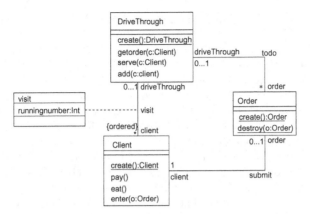

Fig. 1. A class diagram

be links as well. An example of an object diagram is shown in Fig. 2. It contains five objects: one drive-through *McD*, three clients *Ada*, *Bob*, and *Cher*, as well as one order *Shake*. The order is linked to the drive-through and to client *Ada*. Intuitively, this means that client *Ada* has submitted order *Shake* at the drive-through which in turn has to do the serving of this order. Moreover, the two *visit*-links signify that clients *Ada* and *Bob* are visiting the drive-through. The numbers beneath the links are the running numbers of the visits. Client *Cher* is not related to the drive-through.

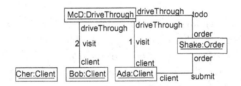

Fig. 2. An object diagram

An object diagram *fits* a class diagram if the objects are instances of the classes, the links can be mapped to the associations, and the multiplicity requirements of the class diagram are satisfied. For example the object diagram of Fig. 2 fits the class diagram in Fig. 1 but drawing an additional link from *Shake* to *Bob* would violate the specified multiplicities.

The dynamic behavior of object-oriented systems can be modeled with UML state diagrams which, in general, can be associated with classes in order to describe the behavior of the objects of the classes. A *state diagram* consists of a set of states and a set of transitions connecting them. The states are object states and the transitions specify state changes. In the following a simplified kind of UML state diagrams is considered that allows us to illustrate the basic ideas of defining an integrated semantics for UML class and state diagrams in a suitable way.

In this simplified model of state diagrams a *state* is just a name and a *transition* connects two states in a directed way. It is labeled with an event, a guard, and an action. A *guard* is an OCL expression (cf. [41,33]). OCL expressions may be logic formulas that evaluate either to *true* or to *false*. Events and actions can be of many types [38]. In the following we restrict ourselves to call events and a simple kind of call actions. A *(call) event* is of the form $op(p_1, \ldots, p_n)$ where op is a name (of an operation) and $p_1, \ldots, p_n$ are instantiated parameters. If op is an operation of a class c $op(p_1, \ldots, p_n)$ is called an *event of c*. A (call) action is of the form $o.e$ where o is an expression which specifies at run-time an object of some class and e is a call event of that class (see Fig. 3). To put it in another way, let us assume that there exists a class diagram CD containing a class c and that there is a state machine associated with c. Let $o.e$ be a call action in a transition of the state diagram associated with c. Then we require that o specifies an object of class c' in the context of class c. Moreover, e should be a call event of the class c' and we say that the action $o.e$ is a call action of the class c.

Fig. 3. Illustration of a call action

Examples of state diagrams for the classes *Client* and *DriveThough* of the above class diagram are depicted in Fig. 4. The objects of class *Client* can be in the state *ClientLife*, *HasOrderd*, or *hasPaid* and the transitions specify changes between those states. Analogously, any *DriveThrough* can be in the states *DriveThroughLife* or *ReceivedOrder*.

The firing of transitions is part of the execution semantics of state diagrams which is based on so-called run-to-completion steps. Let STD be a state diagram associated with some class c. Let o be an object of class c which is in state s [1]. We assume that the object o has an associated event queue q, and let e be the next event in q to be dispatched. Then in a run-to-completion step one transition with source s is chosen provided that it is labeled with event e and its guard can be evaluated to *true*. The firing of the transition includes the execution of e and sends the call event of a possible call action of the transition to the object specified in the call action. Afterwards STD is in the target state of the transition.

---

[1] Note that initially every object is in the target state of the transition which has the initial state as source. This means for our running example that every client is initially in the state *ClientLife* and every drive-through in the state *DriveThroughLife*.

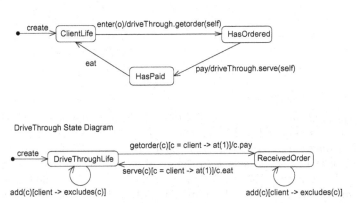

Fig. 4. State diagrams for *Client* and *DriveThrough*

As an example consider the state diagrams in Fig. 4. Roughly speaking, and considering the events of the transitions the life of a *Client* consists of entering orders, paying, and eating, and the life of a *DriveThough* consists of getting and serving orders. Assume that there exists a *Client* object *c* being in the state *ClientLife* and that the next event in the event queue of *c* is *enter*(*o*) where *o* is some order. Then the transition with source *ClientLife* can fire. This means that the call event *getorder*(*c*) is sent to the drive-through visited by *c*. Afterwards the client is in the state *HasOrdered*. Note that according to the UML specification a dispatched event is just deleted from the event queue if no transition can fire. In this case the state diagram remains in its previous state. Note that in the context of class *Client*, the OCL expression *driveThrough* (role name of visit) is of type *DriveThrough* (due to the multiplicity 0 . . . 1), and in the context of class *DriveThrough* the OCL expression *client* is of type *Sequence*(*Client*) (according to the multiplicity ∗ and the specification *ordered*).

3   Graph Transformation Rules for Class and State Diagrams

Graph transformation originated about thirty years ago as a generalization of the well-known Chomsky grammars to graphs. It is a theoretically well studied area with many potential application domains (see [37,11,12] for an overview). In the following we briefly present the basic concepts of graph transformation.

The basic operation of graph transformation consists of the local manipulation of graphs via the application of a rule. A *graph* consists of a set of (labeled) nodes and a set of (labeled) edges connecting them. Examples of graphs are the class diagram and the object diagram presented in the previous section where, roughly speaking, the nodes represent classes, resp. objects, and the edges associations, resp. links. A *graph transformation rule* mainly consists of two graphs,

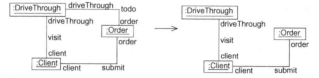

Fig. 5. Rule for *DriveThrough* :: *serve*(c : *Client*)

called *left-hand side* and *right-hand side* which have a common part. An example of a rule is depicted in Fig. 5. The left-hand side and the right-hand side are object diagrams. A rule (L, R) is applied to a graph G by choosing an image $g(L)$ of the left-hand side L in the graph G and by replacing $g(L)$ by the right-hand side R such that the common part is maintained. The rule in Fig. 5 can be applied to the object diagram of Fig. 2. It deletes the link between the drive-through and the order.

In the following we are going to illustrate with our running example how graph transformation rules can be associated with the operations of class diagrams and with the transitions of state diagrams. After that we will present in Section 4 how both diagram and rule types can be integrated into a graph transformation system which specifies the integrated semantics of class diagrams with associated state diagrams.

3.1 Associating Graph Transformation Rules with Class Diagrams

In general, the semantics of class diagrams can be defined as the set of all its object diagrams. Such an object diagram can be interpreted as a state of the system to be modeled, and the execution of operations of the class diagram may modify the state so that another object diagram is obtained. Clearly, this requires that additionally to the semantics of a class diagram, say CD, we specify a semantics for every operation in CD. This semantics is a binary relation on the semantics of CD, i.e. on the set of all object diagrams of CD. For example, we may specify that the operation *serve*(*Ada*) applied to the object diagram in Fig. 2 deletes the link between *Shake* and *McD*.

Fig. 5 shows the rule which implements the operation *serve*(c), i.e. the application of this rule to the above object diagram deletes the link between the *Order* and the *DriveThrough* object. Analogously we can assign a graph transformation rule to every other operation of our example class diagram (see Fig. 6 where *empty* denotes the empty graph). The rule *DriveThrough*::*create*(): *DriveThrough* creates an arbitrary object of type *DriveThrough*; the rule *Client*::*create*(): *Client* works analogously for clients. The rule *DriveThrough*::*getorder*(c: *Client*) requires that before executing the operation *getorder*(c) the client c is visiting a drive-through and has submitted an order. This is expressed by the left-hand side of the rule. After the execution of *getorder*(c) a *todo*-link must exist between the order and the drive-through. The rules for the remaining operations can be explained in an analogous way.

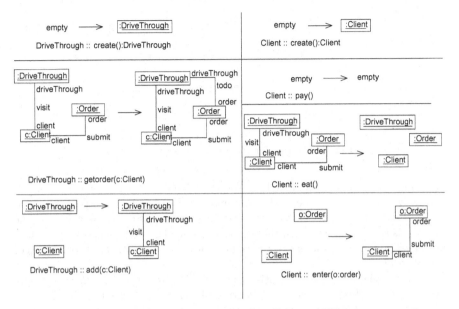

Fig. 6. Further rules for the class diagram of Fig. 1

Summarizing, the presented graph transformation rules provide a means which allows us to specify in a direct and intuitive way how object diagrams (i.e. system states) change after the execution of an operation. Moreover, it is possible to specify pre-conditions for the execution of the operations. In UML those pre- and post-conditions can be specified with OCL expressions.

The above consideration leads to the notion of *extended class diagrams* which consist of a class diagram CD and a mapping *mrule* which assigns a graph transformation rule to every operation of CD.

In general, one cannot assume that an operation can always be associated with a single graph transformation rule which specifies its semantics, because the operation may be too complicated. For those cases, more sophisticated concepts of graph transformation are needed such as, for example, *transformation units* that allow to encapsulate sets of graph transformation rules and which provide control mechanisms for the application process of its local rules (cf. [23,24]).

3.2 Representing Transitions as Graph Transformation Rules

The transitions of a state diagram STD can be also represented by means of graph transformation rules. The main idea associates a graph transformation rule with each transition. Let c be the class the state diagram STD is associated with, and let o be an object of class c. Let $t = (s, e, g, o'.e', s')$ be a transition of STD where s denotes the source state of t, e the event, g the guard, $o'.e'$ the call action, and s' the target state. Then the rule for t should model the dispatching of e in the event queue of o, the change of the state of o from s to s', and the insertion of e' in the event queue of the object specified by o'. For this

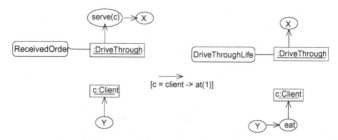

Fig. 7. The rule for the transition *serve* of Fig. 4

purpose the rule contains in its left- and right-hand side the object *o* (i.e. more precisely a variable of type *c*). It contains also the object or the path specified by *o'*. The state *s* is associated with *o* in the left-hand side of the rule, and the state *s'* is associated with *o* in the right-hand side. The event *e* is connected to *o* in the left-hand side whereas in the right-hand side *e'* is connected to the object specified by *o'*.

For example, the rule representing the transition from the state *ReceivedOrder* to *DriveThroughLife* in the state diagram of Fig. 4 is depicted in Fig. 7 where objects are denoted by rectangles, states by rectangles with rounded corners, and events by ellipses. The rule contains objects of class *Client* and *DriveThrough*. On the left-hand side of the graph transformation rule, the *DriveThrough* object is attached to the state *ReceivedOrder*. On the right-hand side, the state *DriveThroughLife* is attached to the *DriveThrough*. The *DriveThrough* on the left-hand side has a pointer to the event *serve(c)* of its event queue. Applying the rule, this event is deleted and the event *eat* is connected to the client on the right-hand side. The guard of the rule guarantees that the client is the first one in the client queue of the drive-through. The structure of this rule reflects the structure of the transition where *serve(c)* is the initiating event (left-hand side) and eat is the induced action (right-hand side). The rules of the remaining transitions are depicted in Fig. 8.

In general, the graph transformation rule for a transition $t = (s, e, g, o'.e', s')$ is constructed as indicated in Fig. 9 where $o1$ is an object of the class the state diagram containing t is associated with, and $o2$ is the object specified by o'. The guard g of the rule must be checked before its application.

4   Integrated Specifications and Their Semantics

Class and state diagrams can be integrated in such a way that every class is connected with the state diagram describing its behavior. The integrated dynamic semantics can be obtained based on the combination of the graph transformation rules associated with the class diagram and the graph transformation rules associated with the state diagram.

An *integrated diagram* is a pair $INTD = (CD, mstd)$ where CD is a class diagram and $mstd$ is a mapping assigning a state diagram $mstd(c)$ to every class c in CD such that $mstd(c)$ contains only events and call actions of class c.

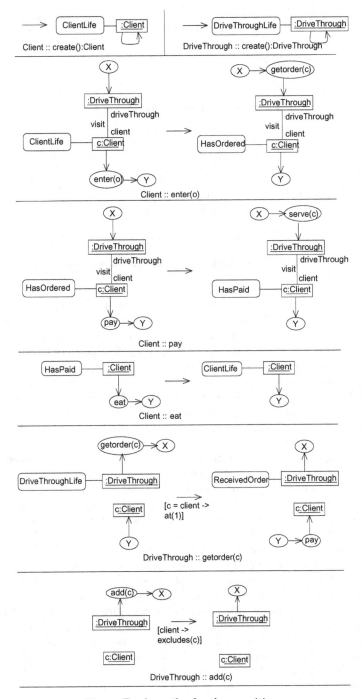

Fig. 8. Further rules for the transitions

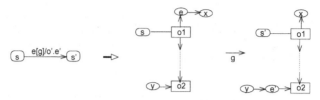

Fig. 9. The state changing rule schema

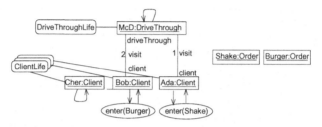

Fig. 10. An instance of an integrated diagram

Let $QUEUES$ denote the class of *event queues*. Then a *system state* of an integrated diagram $(CD, mstd)$ is an object diagram of CD where every object is connected with a state of the state diagram associated with the class of the object. Moreover every object has a pointer to the first entry of its event queue. For our concrete example we will use event queues that work according to the FIFO principle. The queues are represented as string graphs where the nodes (denoted by ellipses) are labeled with events. For technical reasons there will also be a pointer from the last entry of every event queue to the object it belongs to. Moreover, empty event queues will be represented as loops attached to the corresponding object.

An example of a system state of the integrated diagram composed of the above class diagram and state diagrams is presented in Fig. 10.

The execution semantics of integrated diagrams is given by a set of graph transformation rules obtained from the combination of the rules presented in the previous section. Roughly speaking, the transition rules of state diagrams are glued with the rules of the classes they are associated with by identifying common objects and links. For example, the combination of the rule in Fig. 7 and the class diagram rule in Fig. 5 results in the graph transformation rule depicted in Fig. 11. The left-hand side of the shown integrated rule is obtained by gluing together the left-hand sides of the rules in Fig. 5 and 7 in such a way that the drive-throughs and the clients of both graphs are identified. To put it in another way, the combined left-hand side can be obtained by performing first the disjoint union of the left-hand sides of Fig. 5 and 7 and identifying then the drive-through of Fig. 5 with the drive-through of Fig. 7 and the client of Fig. 5 with the client of Fig. 7. The right-hand side of the combined rule is obtained by gluing the right-hand sides of the rules in Fig. 5 and 7 analogously. The resulting rule models the serving of a client c provided that the drive-through visited by

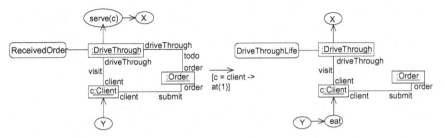

Fig. 11. The integrated rule for *serve*

c is in the state *ReceivedOrder* and has the event *serve*(c) as dispatched event. The application of the rule deletes the link between the order (which has been submitted to the drive-through by the client) and the drive-through. Moreover, it adds the event *eat* to the event queue of the client. Fig. 12 depicts further rules for our running example. The graph transformation rules which can be associated in the described way with an integrated diagram *INTD* are called *integrated rules for INTD*.

An *integrated specification* is a triple $IS = (INTD, I, R)$ where $INTD$ is an integrated diagram, I is a system state of $INTD$, called the *initial system state*, and R is a set of integrated rules for $INTD$. The *semantics* of an integrated specification consists of all graphs which can be obtained from I by applying rules of R.

An example of an integrated specification is $(INTD, I, R)$ where $INTD$ is composed of the class diagram in Fig. 1 and the state diagrams in Fig. 4 plus a state diagram for the class *Order* which just creates and destroys orders. The initial diagram is the empty graph and R consists of the rules presented in Fig. 12 plus some additional rules (for inserting events like *add*(c) in event queues, or creating orders). Fig. 13 illustrates how the different system states (i.e. system states of integrated diagrams) can be derived with the example specification. The derivation starts with the integrated diagram of Fig. 10 and applies at first the rule *Ada.enter*(*Shake*). This means that after dispatching the event *enter*(*Shake*) a *submit*-link is created between *Shake* and *Ada*. Additionally, the event *enter*(*Shake*) is deleted from the event queue of *Ada*, *getorder*(*Ada*) is inserted in the event queue of *McD*, and the state of *Ada* changes from *ClientLife* to *HasOrdered*. Afterwards *McD.getorder*(*Ada*) is applied which changes the state of *McD* to *ReceivedOrder*, deletes *getorder*(*Ada*) from its event queue, and inserts *pay* in the event queue of *Ada*. Moreover, a *todo*-link is created between *McD* and *Shake*. Afterwards the rules *Ada.pay*(), *McD.serve*(*Ada*), *Ada.eat*(), and *Bob.enter*(*Burger*) are applied in this order.

5 Related Work

In the last years much research has been done in the formalization of UML semantics so that in the framework of this paper it is impossible to refer to all

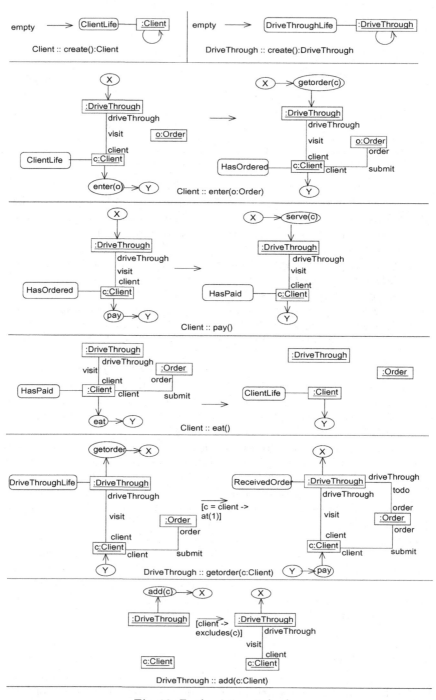

Fig. 12. Further integrated rules

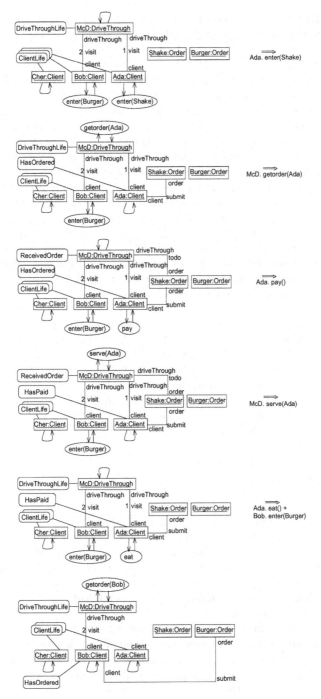

Fig. 13. A derivation

of them. Hence, in this section we mention only a selection of contributions on the formalization of UML semantics that are related to our work.

An approach to transform UML state diagrams into graphs to show the intended semantics is given in [21]. The expansion of nested states is explained by graph transformation. In [31] an operational semantics of statecharts is presented that is based on graph transformation. The work in [32] describes formalization of semantics of specification languages by means of graph rewriting, exemplified for state diagrams. In [29] state machines are modeled as conditional term rewrite systems. [27] uses rewrite rules and operational semantics for model checking of UML state diagrams. Another approach for a formal operational semantics for UML state diagrams is discussed in [28]. In [36] a semantics for active classes with associated state machines is given that is based on labeled transition systems. In [2] it is illustrated how state diagrams can be automatically translated into high-level Petri nets by using graph transformation rules. Another approach employs graph transformation units [24] to describe the execution semantics of state machines in a formal way [25]. [13] proposes a graphical approach to the operational semantics of behavioral diagrams. In [14] a methodology for the specification and verification of constraints for the UML is illustrated. The work in [13,14,8,16,19] discusses the specification of UML semantics on the metamodel level.

A graph-based semantics for OCL was developed by translating OCL constraints into expressions over graph rules [5]. A visualization of OCL expression with collaboration diagrams can be found in [6].

[3] concentrates on verification aspects in the context of relational semantics. [30] proposes a general framework for integrating UML within formal techniques. [1] discusses questions of making UML use cases more precise. [26] uses Catalysis concepts [10] for a comparison with UML. [17] gives a CSP-like view on real-time systems described with UML.

6   Conclusion

We have introduced graph transformations for central language features of UML class and state diagrams. Operations from class diagrams and transitions from state diagrams have been described by single graph transformation rules, respectively. The single rules have mainly operated on UML object diagrams representing system states. These rules have been combined to yield a coherent single graph transformation system representing the combined integrated semantics of the class and state diagram.

Up to now we considered class, object, and state diagrams. We have designed our approach however in such a way that it is possible to handle UML interaction diagrams, i.e. sequence and collaboration diagrams, as well. In the most basic case, sequence and collaboration diagrams may be regarded as test cases which require consistency with the graph transformation system specified by the class and state diagrams.

There remain some open questions to be worked out in the future:

- The presented integrated semantics does not cover all language features of class and state diagrams. Hence it has to be investigated how other langauge elements can be handled.
- In complex cases the integration of various UML diagrams may lead to large diagrams which are dificult to handle and to understand. Therefore, for practical use, structuring concepts for graphs should be incorporated in the presented approach (cf. e.g. [35,22,15,7,9]).
- For being able to use our approach in practice, adequate transformation tools are needed. It should be investigated in which way existing tools can be employed to achieve this aim.
- A further interesting question is how far the presented integration approach can be used for consistency checking of different diagrams.

References

1. Ralph-Johan Back, Luigia Petre, and Ivan Porres Paltor. Analysing UML use cases as contracts. In Robert France and Bernhard Rumpe, editors, *UML'99 - The Unified Modeling Language. Beyond the Standard. Second International Conference, Fort Collins, CO, USA, October 28-30. 1999, Proceedings*, volume 1723 of *LNCS*, pages 518–533. Springer, 1999.
2. Luciano Baresi and Mauro Pezzè. On formalizing UML with high-level Petri Nets. In G. Agha and F. De Cindio, editors, *Proc. Concurrent Object-Oriented Programming and Petri Nets*, volume 2001 of *Lecture Notes in Computer Science*, pages 271–300, 2001.
3. Christie Bolton and Jim Davies. Using relational and behavioural semantics in the verification of object models. In Scott F. Smith and Carolyn L. Talcott, editors, *Formal Methods for Open Object-Based Distributed Systems IV - Proc. FMOODS'2000, September, 2000, Stanford, California, USA*. Kluwer Academic Publishers, 2000.
4. Grady Booch, James Rumbaugh, and Ivar Jacobson. *The Unified Modeling Language User Guide*. Addison-Wesley, 1998.
5. Paolo Bottoni, Manuel Koch, Francesco Parisi-Presicce, and Gabriele Taentzer. Consistency checking and visualization of OCL constraints. In Andy Evans, Stuart Kent, and Bran Selic, editors, *UML 2000 - The Unified Modeling Language. Advancing the Standard. Third International Conference, York, UK, October 2000, Proceedings*, volume 1939 of *LNCS*, pages 294–308. Springer, 2000.
6. Paolo Bottoni, Manuel Koch, Francesco Parisi-Presicce, and Gabriele Taentzer. A visualization of ocl using collaborations. In Martin Gogolla and Cris Kobryn, editors, *UML 2001 – The Unified Modeling Language. Modeling Languages, Concepts, and Tools*, volume 2185 of *Lecture Notes in Computer Science*, pages 257–271, 2001.
7. Giorgio Busatto, Gregor Engels, Katharina Mehner, and Annika Wagner. A framework for adding packages to graph transformation systems. In Hartmut Ehrig, Gregor Engels, Hans-Jörg Kreowski, and Grzegorz Rozenberg, editors, *Proc. Theory and Application of Graph Transformations*, volume 1764 of *Lecture Notes in Computer Science*, pages 352–367, 2000.

8. Tony Clark, Andy Evans, and Stuart Kent. The metamodelling language calculus: Foundation semantics for UML. In Heinrich Hussmann, editor, *Fundamental Approaches to Software Engineering. 4th International Conference, FASE 2001 Held as Part of the Joint European Conferences on Theory and Practice of Software, ETAPS 2001 Genova, Italy, April 2-6. 2001 Proceedings*, volume 2029 of *LNCS*, pages 17–31. Springer, 2001.

9. Frank Drewes, Berthold Hoffmann, and Detlef Plump. Hierarchical graph transformation. *Journal of Computer and System Sciences*, 2002. To appear; short version in Proc. *FOSSACS 2000*, LNCS 1784.

10. Desmond D'Souza and Alan Wills. *Objects, Components and Frameworks With UML: The Catalysis Approach*. Addison-Wesley, 1998.

11. Hartmut Ehrig, Gregor Engels, Hans-Jörg Kreowski, and Grzegorz Rozenberg, editors. *Handbook of Graph Grammars and Computing by Graph Transformation, Vol. 2: Applications, Languages and Tools*. World Scientific, Singapore, 1999.

12. Hartmut Ehrig, Hans-Jörg Kreowski, Ugo Montanari, and Grzegorz Rozenberg, editors. *Handbook of Graph Grammars and Computing by Graph Transformation, Vol. 3: Concurrency, Parallelism, and Distribution*. World Scientific, Singapore, 1999.

13. Gregor Engels, Jan Hendrik Hausmann, Reiko Heckel, and Stefan Sauer. Dynamic meta modeling: A graphical approach to the operational semantics of behavioral diagrams in UML. In Andy Evans, Stuart Kent, and Bran Selic, editors, *UML 2000 – The Unified Modeling Language. Advancing the Standard*, volume 1939 of *Lecture Notes in Computer Science*, pages 323–337, 2000.

14. Gregor Engels, Reiko Heckel, and Jochen Malte Küster. Rule-based specification of behavioral consistency based on the UML meta-model. In Martin Gogolla and Cris Kobryn, editors, *UML 2001 – The Unified Modeling Language. Modeling Languages, Concepts, and Tools*, volume 2185 of *Lecture Notes in Computer Science*, pages 272–286, 2001.

15. Gregor Engels and Andy Schuerr. Encapsulated hierachical graphs, graph types, and meta types. In *SEGRAGRA'95, Joint COMPUGRAPH/SEMAGRAPH Workshop on Graph Rewriting and Computation*, volume 2 of *Electronic Notes in Theoretical Computer Science*. Elsevier, 1995.

16. Andy Evans and Stuart Kent. Core meta-modelling semantics of UML: The pUML approach. In Robert France and Bernhard Rumpe, editors, *UML'99 - The Unified Modeling Language. Beyond the Standard. Second International Conference, Fort Collins, CO, USA, October 28-30. 1999, Proceedings*, volume 1723 of *LNCS*, pages 140–155. Springer, 1999.

17. Clemens Fischer, Ernst-Rüdiger Olderog, and Heike Wehrheim. A CSP view on UML-RT structure diagrams. In Heinrich Hussmann, editor, *Fundamental Approaches to Software Engineering. 4th International Conference, FASE 2001 Held as Part of the Joint European Conferences on Theory and Practice of Software, ETAPS 2001 Genova, Italy, April 2-6. 2001 Proceedings*, volume 2029 of *LNCS*, pages 91–108. Springer, 2001.

18. T. Fischer, J. Niere, L. Torunski, and A. Zündorf. Story diagrams: A new graph transformation language based on UML and Java. In H. Ehrig, G. Engels, H.-J. Kreowski, and G. Rozenberg, editors, *Proc. Theory and Application to Graph Transformations (TAGT'98), Paderborn, November, 1998*, volume 1764 of *LNCS*. Springer, 1998.

19. Robert France, Andy Evans, and Kevin Lano. The UML as a formal modeling notation. In Haim Kilov, Bernhard Rumpe, and Ian Simmonds, editors, *Proceedings OOPSLA'97 Workshop on Object-oriented Behavioral Semantics*, pages 75–81. Technische Universität München, TUM-I9737, 1997.

20. Martin Gogolla. Graph transformations on the UML metamodel. In Jose D. P. Rolim, Andrei Z. Broder, Andrea Corradini, Roberto Gorrieri, Reiko Heckel, Juraj Hromkovic, Ugo Vaccaro, and Joe B. Wells, editors, *Proc. ICALP Workshop Graph Transformations and Visual Modeling Techniques (GVMT'2000)*, pages 359–371. Carleton Scientific, Waterloo, Ontario, Canada, 2000.
21. Martin Gogolla and Francesco Parisi-Presicce. State diagrams in UML: A formal semantics using graph transformations. In Manfred Broy, Derek Coleman, Tom Maibaum, and Bernhard Rumpe, editors, *Proc. ICSE'98 Workshop Precise Semantics of Modeling Techniques*, Technical Report TUM-I9803, pages 55–72, 1998.
22. David Harel. On visual formalisms. *Communications of the ACM*, 31(5):514–530, 1988.
23. Hans-Jörg Kreowski and Sabine Kuske. Graph transformation units with interleaving semantics. *Formal Aspects of Computing*, 11(6):690–723, 1999.
24. Sabine Kuske. *Transformation Units—A structuring Principle for Graph Transformation Systems*. PhD thesis, University of Bremen, 2000.
25. Sabine Kuske. A formal semantics of uml state machines based on structured graph transformation. In Martin Gogolla and Cris Kobryn, editors, *UML 2001 – The Unified Modeling Language. Modeling languages, Concepts, and Tools*, volume 2185 of *Lecture Notes in Computer Science*, pages 241–256, 2001.
26. J. Küster Filipe, K.-K. Lau, M. Ornaghi, K. Taguchi, A. Wills, and H. Yatsu. Formal specification of Catalysis frameworks. In Jing Song Dong, Jifeng He, and Martin Purvis, editors, *Proc. 7th Asia-Pacific Software Engineering Conference*, pages 180–187. IEEE Computer Society Press, 2000.
27. Gihwon Kwon. Rewrite rules and operational semantics for model checking UML statecharts. In Andy Evans, Stuart Kent, and Bran Selic, editors, *UML 2000 – The Unified Modeling Language. Advancing the Standard. Third International Conference, York, UK, October 2000, Proceedings*, volume 1939 of *LNCS*, pages 528–540. Springer, 2000.
28. Diego Latella, Istvan Majzik, and Mieke Massink. Towards a formal operational semantics of UML statechart diagrams. In *Proc. FMOODS'99, IFIP TC6/WG6.1 Third International Conference on Formal Methods for Open Object-Based Distributed Systems, Florence, Italy, February 15-18, 1999*. Kluwer, 1999.
29. Johan Lilius and Ivan Porres Paltor. Formalising UML state machines for model checking. In Robert France and Bernhard Rumpe, editors, *Proc. UML'99 – The Unified Modeling Language. Beyond the Standard*, volume 1723 of *Lecture Notes in Computer Science*, pages 430–445, 1999.
30. Jing Liu, Jin Song Dong, Kun Shi, and Brendan Mahony. Linking UML with integrated formal techniques. In Keng Siau and Terry Halpin, editors, *Unified Modeling Language: Systems Analysis, Design and Development Issues*, chapter 13, pages 210–223. Idea Publishing Group, 2001.
31. Andrea Maggiolo-Schettini and Adriano Peron. Semantics of full statecharts based on graph rewriting. In Hans-Jürgen Schneider and Hartmut Ehrig, editors, *Proc. Graph Transformation in Computer Science*, volume 776 of *Lecture Notes in Computer Science*, pages 265–279, 1994.
32. Andrea Maggiolo-Schettini and Adriano Peron. A Graph Rewriting Framework for Statecharts Semantics. In Janice E. Cuny, Hartmut Ehrig, Gregor Engels, and Grzegorz Rozenberg, editors, *Proc. 5th Int. Workshop on Graph Grammars and their Application to Computer Science*, volume 1073, pages 107–121. Springer-Verlag, 1996.
33. OMG. Unified Modeling Language specifcation, 2001. Available at http://www.omg.org//.

34. Dorina C. Petriu and Yimei Sun. Consistent behaviour representation in activity and sequence diagrams. In Andy Evans, Stuart Kent, and Bran Selic, editors, *Proc. UML 2000 – The Unified Modeling Language. Advancing the Standard*, volume 1939 of *Lecture Notes in Computer Science*, pages 359–368, 2000.
35. Terrence W. Pratt. Definition of programming language semantics using grammars for hierarchical graphs. In Volker Claus, Hartmut Ehrig, and Grzegorz Rozenberg, editors, *Proc. Graph Grammars and Their Application to Computer Science and Biology*, volume 73 of *Lecture Notes in Computer Science*, pages 389–400, 1979.
36. Gianna Reggio, Egidio Astesiano, Christine Choppy, and Heinrich Hussmann. Analysing UML active classes and associated state machines – A lightweight formal approach. In Tom Maibaum, editor, *Proc. Fundamental Approaches to Software Engineering (FASE 2000), Berlin, Germany*, volume 1783 of *Lecture Notes in Computer Science*, 2000.
37. Grzegorz Rozenberg, editor. *Handbook of Graph Grammars and Computing by Graph Transformation, Vol. 1: Foundations*. World Scientific, Singapore, 1997.
38. James Rumbaugh, Ivar Jacobson, and Grady Booch. *The Unified Modeling Language Reference Manual*. Addison-Wesley, 1998.
39. Andy Schürr and Andreas J. Winter. UML packages for PROgrammed Graph REwriting Systems. In Hartmut Ehrig, Gregor Engels, Hans-Jörg Kreowski, and Grzegorz Rozenberg, editors, *Proc. Theory and Application of Graph Transformations*, volume 1764 of *Lecture Notes in Computer Science*, pages 396–409, 2000.
40. Aliki Tsiolakis and Hartmut Ehrig. Consistency analysis of UML class and sequence diagrams using attributed graph grammars. In Hartmut Ehrig and Gabriele Taentzer, editors, *Proc. Joint APPLIGRAPH and GETGRATS Workshop on Graph Transformation Systems*, Report Nr. 2000-2, Technical University of Berlin, pages 77–86, 2000.
41. Jos Warmer and Anneke Kleppe. *The Object Constraint Language: Precise Modeling with UML*. Addison-Wesley, 1998.

Stochastic Process Algebras Meet Eden[*]

Natalia López, Manuel Núñez, and Fernando Rubio

Dept. Sistemas Informáticos y Programación
Universidad Complutense de Madrid, E-28040 Madrid, Spain
{natalia,mn,fernando}@sip.ucm.es

Abstract. Process algebras represent an appropriate mechanism to formally specify concurrent systems. In order to get a thorough knowledge of these systems, some *external* formalism must be used. In this paper we propose an integrated framework where a (non-trivial) process algebra is combined with a (concurrent) functional language. Specifically, we consider a stochastic process algebra featuring value passing where distributions are not restricted to be exponential. In order to study properties of these specifications, we *translate* them into functional programs written in Eden. This functional language is very suitable for concurrent programming. On the one hand, it presents the usual features of modern functional languages. On the other hand, it allows the execution of concurrent processes. We present an example showing how specifications can be translated into Eden and how quantitative properties can be studied.

Keywords: Process algebras, functional programming.

1 Introduction

Process algebras (see [2] for a good overview) are a very suitable formalism to specify concurrent systems because they allow to model them in a compositional manner. Process algebras have been extended to allow the specification of systems where not only functional requirements but also performance ones are included. Therefore, there have been several timed and/or probabilistic extensions of process algebras (e.g. [30,17,13,12,31,8,28,15,10,23,1]). An attempt to integrate time and probabilistic information has been given by introducing *stochastic process algebras* (e.g. [14,20,4]) where not only information about the period of time when the actions are enabled, but also about the probability distribution associated with these time intervals is included.

In order to study systems, *model checking* [9] represents a successful technique to check whether they fulfill a property. Nevertheless, current model checking techniques cannot be used to study systems where stochastic information is included. More exactly, model checking may deal with stochastic systems where probability distributions are restricted to be exponential, by using Markov chains techniques (see e.g. [18]). Unfortunately, this is not the case if probability distributions are *general* (a preliminary step has been given in [22] where semi-Markov

---

[*] Research supported in part by the CICYT projects TIC2000-0701-C02-01 and TIC2000-0738, and the Spanish-British Acción Integrada HB 1999-0102.

chains are considered). So, in order to analyze this kind of systems, a different approach should be used. Another possibility, that we will use in this paper, consists in the *simulation* of the specified system. Intuitively, in order to study a specification, we can *implement* it and simulate its performance. In this case, we can get *real* estimations of the *theoretical* performance of the system.

In this paper we provide an integrated framework that allows us to study systems containing stochastic information by simulating their behaviors in an appropriate language. In order to provide an expressive specification language we will consider a process algebra, that we call **VPSPA**, featuring value passing as well as the possibility to specify stochastic behaviors, where probability distributions are not restricted to be exponential, together with a notion of parallel composition. Let us note that value passing is not usually included in stochastic process algebras (to the best of our knowledge, [3] represents the only proposal for such a stochastic language). Anyway, the inclusion of value passing does not produce too many additional difficulties. However, in order to eliminate the restriction to exponential distributions we need a complicate semantic model[1].

Looking for an appropriate *simulation* language, we have found the functional paradigm to be very suitable for our purpose. First, due to the absence of side effects, functional programming allows to reason equationally about programs. In particular, it is possible to apply automatic transformations. Besides, it is easier to verify or even derive programs from their formal specifications. This is specially important for safety critical applications. Among the functional languages, Haskell [34] can be considered to be the current *standard*. Haskell represents the result of the joint effort of the (lazy evaluation) functional community to define a standard language to be used both for research and for real applications. Several Haskell compilers exist, being GHC (Glasgow Haskell Compiler) the most efficient and widely used. It is easily portable to different architectures, a COM interface allows to interact with programs written in other languages, and its sources are freely available.

Unfortunately, Haskell is based on a sequential evaluation strategy. Therefore, concurrent execution of programs cannot be defined. In the last years there have been some extensions of Haskell where concurrency has been included (see, e. g. [33]) but usually by means of very *low-level* concurrency primitives. On the contrary, the programming language Eden [7,6] is an adequate *high-level* concurrent extension of Haskell. Eden is the result of a joint research work between two groups in Germany and Spain with the support of the Scottish team who develops GHC. The first complete Eden compiler was finished recently, and heavy experimentation has been taken place since then (e.g. [32,24]). Eden aims at reusing the advantages of Haskell for reasoning about programs, but applying them also to both concurrent and parallel systems. The main goal of the language is to provide concurrency and parallelism at a high level of abstraction, without losing efficiency. In addition to these good properties, Eden includes

---

[1] The combination of a parallel operator and general distributions produce a lot of semantical difficulties. That is why stochastic models are usually based on (semi)-Markov chains.

a set of profiling utilities (called Paradise [19]) that facilitates the analysis of programs, so that it can also be used to study the real behaviour at runtime.

This combination of process algebras and functional languages allows us to profit from both the good properties of the former (as specification languages) and the ones of the latter (as implementation languages where formal reasoning can be performed easier than in other paradigms). In order to make a smooth transition from the specification to the implementation, we provide a mechanism to *translate* from one formalism into the other. Let us note that most of the features of functional languages are not needed to implement our specifications. Therefore, it is necessary to have only some knowledge of the functional paradigm, mainly to *optimize* the implementations that the translation produces. We have also adapted the profiling utilities of Eden to our stochastic framework. That is, we will be able to study quantitative properties of specifications by studying the behavior of the corresponding Eden programs.

Regarding related work, let us remark that the translation of process algebras into another programming language has been already done several times (e.g. considering LOTOS we have [29] among many others). In the stochastic process algebras area, [11] also studies the simulation and implementation of a stochastic process algebra. Even though a functional language is used (actually, Haskell) our approach differs in several points from that one. In that implementation, at each point of the execution, it is computed the set of all the possible next states of the whole system. So, it suffers from the inconvenience of state explosion. Moreover, our approach is a real concurrent implementation, where processes really evolve independently. In fact, we run the processes in parallel. Finally, our generated code is a usual program, so that a user with some command in functional languages may optimize it, if necessary, by hand.

The rest of the paper is organized as follows. In Section 2 we present our value passing stochastic process algebra. In Section 3 we present the basic features of Eden. We will mainly concentrate on the characteristics of the language that we will use along the paper. In particular, we will explain the way processes are defined in Eden. In Section 4 we present our methodology for translating from specifications to Eden programs. Finally, in Section 5 we introduce an example. We present its specification, the translation into Eden, and we study some quantitative properties.

2   A Stochastic Process Algebra with Value Passing

In this section we present our language and its semantics. Our model is based on [26] where we have introduced some important modifications. We have slightly simplified the model by removing probabilities associated with the choice operator. On the contrary, we have added some new features that add expressiveness to the language, even though they complicate the semantic model. First, we consider value passing. Second, a parallel operator is now included. This last addition leads to an involved definition of the operational semantics. However, we find extremely useful a parallel operator to model the systems that we are interested in. Moreover, despite of the complexity of the operational definition, the behavior of this operator is the *expected* in usual process algebras. Every process will be able to perform either actions for transmitting a message (output actions) or for receiving them (input actions), or stochastic actions (delays). These delays will be represented by random variables. We will suppose that the sample space (that is, the domain of random variables) is the set of real numbers $\mathbb{R}$ and that random variables take positive values only in $\mathbb{R}^+$, that is, given a random variable ξ we have $P(\xi \leq t) = 0$ for any $t < 0$. The reason for this restriction is that random variables are always associated with time distributions.

Definition 1. Let ξ be a random variable. We define its *probability distribution function*, denoted by F_ξ, as the function $F_\xi : \mathbb{R} \longrightarrow [0,1]$ such that $F_\xi(x) = P(\xi \leq x)$, where $P(\xi \leq x)$ is the probability that ξ assumes values less than or equal to x. □

Regarding *communication* actions, they can be divided into *output* and *input* actions. Next, we define our alphabet of actions.

Definition 2. We consider a set of *communication* actions $\mathsf{Act} = \mathsf{Input} \cup \mathsf{Output}$, such that $\mathsf{Input} \cap \mathsf{Output} = \emptyset$. We suppose that there exists a bijection $f : \mathsf{Input} \longrightarrow \mathsf{Output}$. For any *input* action $a? \in \mathsf{Input} \subseteq \mathsf{Act}$, $f(a?)$ is denoted by the *output* action $a! \in \mathsf{Output} \subseteq \mathsf{Act}$. If there exists a message transmission between $a?$ and $a!$ we say that a is the *channel* of the communication. We denote by $\mathcal{C}_{\mathsf{Act}}$ the set of channels in Act ($a, b, \cdots$ to range over $\mathcal{C}_{\mathsf{Act}}$). We consider a set of values *Val* representing the transmitted messages ($v, v', \ldots$ to range over *Val*) and a set of value variables $\mathcal{X}$ ($x, y, \ldots$ to range over $\mathcal{X}$) [2]. We define the set of *communications* as the set of input and output actions applied either to a value (output actions) or to a value variable (input actions), that is, $IO = \{c(x) \mid c \in \mathsf{Input}, x \in \mathcal{X}\} \cup \{c(v) \mid c \in \mathsf{Output}, v \in Val\}$. We define the channel of a communication action $c(m) \in IO$, denoted by $ch(c(m))$, as a if $c \in \{a?, a!\}$. □

We consider a denumerable set Id of process identifiers. In addition, we denote by $\mathcal{V}$ the set of random variables ($\xi, \xi', \psi, \cdots$ to range over $\mathcal{V}$). We also consider the *set of locations* $\mathrm{Loc} = \{loc_i \mid loc \in \{l, r\} \land i \in \mathbb{N}^+\}$ where l stands for left and r for right.

Definition 3. The set of processes, denoted by VPSPA, is given by the following set of expressions:

$$P ::= \mathsf{stop} \mid \xi; P \mid a?(x); P \mid a!(v); P \mid P+P \mid \mathsf{if}\ e\ \mathsf{then}\ P\ \mathsf{else}\ P \mid P \|_M P \mid P/A \mid X := P$$

where $X \in Id$ (the set of *process variables*), $\xi \in \mathcal{V}$, $a?, a! \in \mathsf{Act}$, $x \in \mathcal{X}$, $v \in Val$, $A \subseteq \mathcal{C}_{\mathsf{Act}}$, e is an expression such that $\mathsf{Eval}(e) \in Bool$ ($\mathsf{Eval}(e)$ represents the evaluation of e), and $M \subseteq (\mathcal{V} \times \mathbb{N}^+ \times \mathrm{Loc})$. □

---

[2] Sometimes we are not interested in transmitting a message because that communication is only a synchronization point. In this case, we *send* the value $-$.

We assume that all the random variables appearing in the definition of a process are independent. For the sake of clarity, if two delays are represented by the same random variable, this means that both delays are given by two independent random variables identically distributed. The term stop denotes a process that cannot execute any action. A process $\xi \, ; P$ waits a random amount of time (determined by the distribution function associated with ξ) and then it behaves as P. As we will show in the definition of the operational semantics, stochastic transitions are performed in two steps: start and termination. For each random variable ξ, we will denote by ξ^+ the start of the delay and by ξ^- its termination. As introduced in [5], this is one of the mechanisms to deal with general distributions in the context of parallel. The process $a?(x) \, ; P$ waits until it receives a value v on the input action $a?$, and after that P behaves as $P[v/x]$, where $P[v/x]$ denotes the substitution of all the free occurrences of x in P by v. Let us note that x is bound in $a?(x) \, ; P$. The process $a!(v) \, ; P$ transmits the value v on the output action $a!$ and after that it behaves like P. The process $P + Q$ behaves either like P or like Q. The process if e then P else Q behaves as P if the evaluation of the boolean expression e is true and as Q otherwise. The term $P \|_M Q$ can perform actions either from P or from Q asynchronously. Besides, if one of the processes is prepared to perform an input action and the other one an output action on the same channel, both actions can be performed synchronously, and some values can be exchanged from one process to the other. In order to avoid *undesirable* effects with some recursive processes, we assign indexes to delays. Specifically, problems may appear if we have several *starts* of the same delay in the context of a parallel operator. This is the case, for instance, in the process rec $X.(\xi \|_M a; X)$. Thus, for each start stochastic action ξ_i^+ there will be a unique termination action ξ_i^- associated with it. That information will be stored in M. Initially, we suppose $M = \emptyset$. Let us remark that, given the fact that we consider random variables (instead of probability distribution functions), indexes would not be needed if we restrict occurrences of the parallel computation in the scope of the recursive definitions. So, the parameter M could be removed. The process P/A expresses that P is restricted to perform only the communication actions that are not in A. Finally, $X := P$ denotes the definition of a (possible recursive) process.

The operational semantics for the language (presented in Figure 1) is inspired in [5]. We will use the following conventions: $P \xrightarrow{\omega} P'$ expresses that there exists a transition from P to P' labeled by the action ω; $P \xrightarrow{\omega}$ stands for there exists $P' \in$ VPSPA such that $P \xrightarrow{\omega} P'$; and we write $P \xrightarrow{\omega}\!\!\!\!\!/\,$ if there does not exist $P' \in$ VPSPA such that $P \xrightarrow{\omega} P'$. We consider that a special action τ denotes internal activity, that is, an internal communication between processes. Let us note that if a process is able to perform an internal action, then no stochastic transition will be allowed. This property is called *urgency* and it is a standard mechanism in stochastic process algebras. For that purpose the following predicate is defined to express the stability of a process. Intuitively, a process is *stable* if it cannot perform any internal communication.

$$\frac{}{a?(x);P \xrightarrow{a?(x)} P} \qquad \frac{}{a!(v);P \xrightarrow{a!(v)} P} \qquad \frac{}{\xi;P \xrightarrow{\xi_1^+} \xi_1^-;P} \qquad \frac{}{\xi_1^-;P \xrightarrow{\xi_1^-} P}$$

$$\frac{P \xrightarrow{\alpha} P'}{P+Q \xrightarrow{\alpha} P'} \qquad \frac{Q \xrightarrow{\alpha} Q'}{P+Q \xrightarrow{\alpha} Q'} \qquad \frac{P \xrightarrow{\xi_i^+} P',\ stab(Q)}{P+Q \xrightarrow{\xi_i^+} P'+Q} \qquad \frac{Q \xrightarrow{\xi_i^+} Q',\ stab(P)}{P+Q \xrightarrow{\xi_i^+} P+Q'}$$

$$\frac{P \xrightarrow{\xi_i^-} P',\ Q \xrightarrow{v^+}\!\!\!\not\rightarrow,\ stab(Q)}{P+Q \xrightarrow{\xi_i^-} P'} \qquad\qquad \frac{Q \xrightarrow{\xi_i^-} Q',\ P \xrightarrow{v^+}\!\!\!\not\rightarrow,\ stab(P)}{P+Q \xrightarrow{\xi_i^-} Q'}$$

$$\frac{P \xrightarrow{\alpha} P'}{P\|_M Q \xrightarrow{\alpha} P'\|_M Q} \qquad\qquad \frac{Q \xrightarrow{\alpha} Q'}{P\|_M Q \xrightarrow{\alpha} P\|_M Q'}$$

$$\frac{P \xrightarrow{a?(x)} P',\ Q \xrightarrow{a!(v)} Q'}{P\|_M Q \xrightarrow{\tau(v)} P'[v/x]\|_M Q'} \qquad\qquad \frac{P \xrightarrow{a!(v)} P',\ Q \xrightarrow{a?(x)} Q'}{P\|_M Q \xrightarrow{\tau(v)} P'\|_M Q'[v/x]}$$

$$\frac{P \xrightarrow{\xi_i^+} P',\ stab(P\|_M Q)}{P\|_M Q \xrightarrow{\xi_{n(M_\xi)}^+} P'\|_{M\cup\{(\xi,n(M_\xi),l_i)\}} Q} \qquad \frac{P \xrightarrow{\xi_i^-} P',\ Q \xrightarrow{v^+}\!\!\!\not\rightarrow,\ (\xi,j,l_i)\in M,\ stab(P\|_M Q)}{P\|_M Q \xrightarrow{\xi_j^-} P'\|_{M-\{(\xi,j,l_i)\}} Q}$$

$$\frac{Q \xrightarrow{\xi_i^+} Q',\ stab(P\|_M Q)}{P\|_M Q \xrightarrow{\xi_{n(M_\xi)}^+} P\|_{M\cup\{(\xi,n(M_\xi),r_i)\}} Q'} \qquad \frac{Q \xrightarrow{\xi_i^-} Q',\ P \xrightarrow{v^+}\!\!\!\not\rightarrow,\ (\xi,j,r_i)\in M,\ stab(P\|_M Q)}{P\|_M Q \xrightarrow{\xi_j^-} P\|_{M-\{(\xi,j,r_i)\}} Q'}$$

$$\frac{P \xrightarrow{\omega} P' \ (\omega\in V^+\cup V^-\cup IO_\tau \vee ch(\omega)\notin A)}{P/A \xrightarrow{\omega} P'/A} \qquad \frac{P[X/X:=P] \xrightarrow{\omega} P'}{X:=P \xrightarrow{\omega} P'}$$

$$\frac{\texttt{Eval}(e),\ P \xrightarrow{\omega} P'}{\texttt{if } e \texttt{ then } P \texttt{ else } Q \xrightarrow{\omega} P'} \qquad \frac{\neg\texttt{Eval}(e),\ Q \xrightarrow{\omega} Q'}{\texttt{if } e \texttt{ then } P \texttt{ else } Q \xrightarrow{\omega} Q'}$$

Fig. 1. Operational Semantics of VPSPA

Definition 4. Let P be a process. We define the *stability* of P, denoted by $stab(P)$, by structural induction as:

$$stab(\text{stop}) = stab(\xi\,;P) = stab(a?(x)\,;P) = stab(a!(v)\,;P) = \texttt{true}$$
$$stab(P+Q) = stab(\texttt{if } e \texttt{ then } P \texttt{ else } Q) = stab(P) \wedge stab(Q)$$
$$stab(P\,\|_M Q) = stab(P) \wedge stab(Q)$$
$$\wedge\ \not\exists a \in \texttt{Act}\!: (P \xrightarrow{a?(x)} \wedge Q \xrightarrow{a!(v)}) \vee (P \xrightarrow{a!(x)} \wedge Q \xrightarrow{a?(v)})$$
$$stab(P/A) = stab(P)$$
$$stab(X := P) = stab(P[X/X := P]) \qquad\qquad \square$$

In the definition of the operational semantics we have extended the set of communications with a set of internal communications $IO_\tau = \{\tau(v) \mid v \in Val\}$, as well as sets of starting actions $V^+ = \{\xi_i^+ \mid \xi \in V \wedge i \in \mathbb{N}^+\}$ and termination actions $\mathcal{V}^- = \{\xi_i^- \mid \xi \in \mathcal{V} \wedge i \in \mathbb{N}^+\}$. In that definition, we consider $a \in \mathcal{C}_{\text{Act}}$, $\xi \in \mathcal{V}$, $\alpha \in IO \cup IO_\tau$, $\omega \in IO \cup IO_\tau \cup \mathcal{V}^+ \cup \mathcal{V}^-$, and $A \subseteq \mathcal{C}_{\text{Act}}$. The first two rules of the operational semantics are the usual ones for the prefix operator for standard actions. The following two rules deal with stochastic transitions. An operational transition as $\xi \,;\, P \xrightarrow{\xi_1^+} \xi_1^- \,;\, P$ indicates the start of a delay given by ξ. Similarly, $\xi_1^- \,;\, P \xrightarrow{\xi_1^-} P$ denotes the termination of the delay. We consider that the start of a delay has higher priority than any termination action. So, a stochastic action cannot be *completed* if any stochastic action can be started. In order to index random variables we use dynamic names, that is, we assign to each random variable an index. This index will be the minimum natural number that it is not being currently used to label other occurrences of the same random variable. Once a stochastic transition is finished, its corresponding index is liberated. The following six rules represent the behaviour of the choice between processes. If one of the components of the choice can perform an action, then the choice can also perform it. If the action is stochastic, it has to be taken into account that the other process cannot evolve internally. Besides, if the stochastic action is a termination action, it is necessary to assure that the other process can perform neither a start action nor an internal action. The behaviour of the parallel operator is defined by the following eight rules. The first four rules represent the performance of communication actions. We briefly sketch how stochastic transitions are treated in the context of a parallel composition (the interested reader is pointed to [5] for additional details). If any of the processes of the composition can perform a start action and they cannot perform a communication, the composition can also perform it. However, we need to associate to that action a different index. It will be the minimum natural number not already used for this random variable in the scope of the corresponding parallel composition. This index is given by the following function:

Definition 5. Let $\xi \in \mathcal{V}$, $M \subseteq \mathcal{V} \times \mathbb{N}^+ \times \text{Loc}$. We define the *minimum value not used in* M *to index* ξ, denoted by $n(M_\xi)$, as

$$n(M_\xi) = \min\left(\{j \mid \not\exists(\xi, j, loc_i) \in M, loc \in \{l, r\}, i \in \mathbb{N}^+ \wedge 1 \le j \le mx\} \cup \{mx + 1\}\right)$$

where $mx = \max\{j \mid (\xi, j, loc_i) \in M, loc \in \{l, r\}, i \in \mathbb{N}^+\}$.   □

So, if the tuple $(\xi, n(M_\xi), l_i)$ is stored in M, this means that ξ^+ has been performed from the left hand side of the parallel operator due to P has performed ξ_i^+. If the termination action ξ^- with an index i can be performed by P and neither a communication action nor a start action can be performed, and there exists $(\xi, j, l_i) \in M$, then the parallel composition is able to perform the same termination action but indexed by j. The following two rules are the usual ones for the restriction operator and for recursive processes. The last two rules express the behaviour of the conditional operator. Moreover, even though our operational semantics has rules with negative premises, this does not cause any problem because a stratification in terms of [16] can be easily given, so the uniqueness of (stochastic) labeled transition systems is guaranteed.

Next we define the set of *input actions*, *output actions*, and *immediate output actions* that a process can perform. These notations will be necessary in Section 4.

Definition 6. We inductively define the set of *input actions* that a process P can perform, denoted by $\texttt{Inputs}(P)$, as:

$$\texttt{Inputs}(\text{stop}) = \emptyset \qquad\qquad \texttt{Inputs}(P + Q) = \texttt{Inputs}(P) \cup \texttt{Inputs}(Q)$$
$$\texttt{Inputs}(\xi\,;P) = \texttt{Inputs}(P) \qquad \texttt{Inputs}(P \parallel_M Q) = \texttt{Inputs}(P) \cup \texttt{Inputs}(Q)$$
$$\texttt{Inputs}(\tau\,;P) = \texttt{Inputs}(P) \qquad \texttt{Inputs}(P/A) = \texttt{Inputs}(P) - A$$
$$\texttt{Inputs}(a?(x)\,;P) = \texttt{Inputs}(P) \cup \{a\}\ \ \texttt{Inputs}(X := P) = \texttt{Inputs}(P)$$
$$\texttt{Inputs}(a!(v)\,;P) = \texttt{Inputs}(P) \qquad \texttt{Inputs}(\text{if } e \text{ then } P \text{ else } Q)$$
$$= \texttt{Inputs}(P) \cup \texttt{Inputs}(Q)$$

We denote by $\texttt{Outputs}(P)$ the set of *output actions* that P can perform. Formally:

$$\texttt{Outputs}(\text{stop}) = \emptyset \qquad\qquad \texttt{Outputs}(P + Q) = \texttt{Outputs}(P) \cup \texttt{Outputs}(Q)$$
$$\texttt{Outputs}(\xi\,;P) = \texttt{Outputs}(P) \qquad \texttt{Outputs}(P \parallel_M Q) = \texttt{Outputs}(P) \cup \texttt{Outputs}(Q)$$
$$\texttt{Outputs}(\tau\,;P) = \texttt{Outputs}(P) \qquad \texttt{Outputs}(P/A) = \texttt{Outputs}(P) - A$$
$$\texttt{Outputs}(a?(x)\,;P) = \texttt{Outputs}(P) \qquad \texttt{Outputs}(X := P) = \texttt{Outputs}(P)$$
$$\texttt{Outputs}(a!(v)\,;P) = \texttt{Outputs}(P) \cup \{a\}\ \ \texttt{Outputs}(\text{if } e \text{ then } P \text{ else } Q)$$
$$= \texttt{Outputs}(P) \cup \texttt{Outputs}(Q)$$

The set of *immediate output actions* P can perform, denoted by $\texttt{Imm\_Outputs}(P)$, is given by $\texttt{Imm\_Outputs}(P) = \{a \in \mathcal{C}_{\texttt{Act}} \mid \exists P' \in \textsf{VPSPA}, v \in \textit{Val} : P \xrightarrow{a!(v)} P'\}$. $\square$

3   The Concurrent Functional Language Eden

In this section we sketch the main features of Eden. Some knowledge of the functional paradigm is desirable, but is not essential. In particular, we will omit the description of the typing mechanism. Regarding the pure functional paradigm we will briefly explain a powerful mechanism to improve the quality of functional programs: Pattern Matching. Most of the programs written by using pattern matching can be rewritten by using **if then else** constructions, but the resulting programs are not so elegant. Then, we will concentrate on the concurrent features of Eden. A complete presentation of Eden can be found in [7].

A functional program consists in a list of function definitions. Each function can be defined in terms of several rules. Pattern matching is used to specify when a rule can be applied. A rule can be applied only if the arguments *match* the corresponding *pattern*. For instance, in the following example, the first rule is applied if its second input *matches* the *pattern* associated to the empty list, while the second rule is applied otherwise:

```
map f []     = []
map f (x:xs) = f x : map f xs
```

where [] denotes an empty list, and (x:xs) denotes a list whose head is x and whose tail is xs. As shown below, the map function can also be defined without using pattern matching. However, in general, pattern matching versions use to be shorter and clearer.

```
map f xs = if empty xs then []
                  else f x : map f xs
```

Eden extends Haskell by means of syntactical constructions to define and create (concurrent) processes. Eden distinguishes between *process abstractions* and *process instantiations*. The former are used to define the behavior of processes, but without actually creating them. The latter are used to create instances of processes. This distinction allows the creation of as many instances of the same process as needed. Eden includes a new expression process x -> e having x as input(s) and e as output(s). Process abstractions can be compared to functions. The main difference is that the former, when instantiated, are executed in a separate process. Besides, they perform communications by using the interface of that process. For example, the following process has two inputs and two outputs. It receives an integer and a string as inputs, and it produces a string and an integer as outputs.

```
p = process (n,s) -> (out1,out2)
  where (out1,out2) = f n s
        f 0 s = ("hello",length s)
        f n s = ("bye",length s)
```

The first thing this process needs to know is whether the first parameter is zero or not. So, it must synchronize on the first input channel until it receives a value. Afterwards, depending on that value, it will output either the string 'hello' and the length of the second input (if the input value is 0), or the string 'bye' and also the length of the second input (otherwise).

A *process instantiation* is achieved by using the predefined infix operator (#). Each time a binding outputs = p # inputs is found, a new process is created to evaluate the abstraction p. This new process will be able to receive values through the input channels associated to inputs, and send values through outputs. The actual readers of outputs and the actual producers of inputs will be detected by means of the data dependencies of processes. For instance, in the next example, p1 will be able to receive data both from the second output of p2 and from the first output of p3. The actual readers of both c and g will depend on the context in which process q is instantiated:

```
q = process () -> (c,g)
  where (a,b,c) = p1 # (e,f)
        (d,e)   = p2 # (h,b)
        (f,g,h) = p3 # (a,d)
```

In addition to process abstractions and instantiations, Eden provides a predefined function called merge that can be used to combine a list of lists into only one. This is useful to select from a list of alternatives. For instance, in case we want to select from two alternatives, the following `merge2` function can be used:

```
data Either a b = Left a | Right b
merge2 xs ys = merge [map Left xs, map Right ys]
```

After combining two lists `xs` and `ys`, we can use pattern matching over the merged list to know which inputs come from the *left* lists and which ones from the *right* list. This will be useful to choose between two different possible synchronizations:

```
... f (merge2 xs ys) ...
f (Left x : zs ) = ...
f (Right y : zs) = ...
```

Now we will present an Eden example. The following process defines the behavior of a simple timer. A timer receives as input a list of signals. When it receives a `Start`, the `timer` process waits t seconds, then it communicates a `TimeOut`, and after that it recursively starts again waiting for a new `Start`. The function `seq` is used to sequentially compose two actions, and `sleep` is a Haskell primitive for delaying a process. Notice that Eden does not include *send* or *receive* constructors: Communication and synchronization is automatic and only happens because of the data dependencies of the processes. Actually, this mechanism is close to the one for communication in process algebras.

```
timer t = process starts -> f starts
  where f (x:xs) = seq (sleep t) (TimeOut : f xs)
```

Let us note that the input of the `timer` process is a list of *start* messages, and the output is also a list. In fact, Eden processes use lists as both input and output channels. This enables to use the same Eden channel to communicate several times. Moreover, considering channels as lists will allow us to simulate a recursive process (of the process algebra) by using a unique Eden process. This Eden process will be defined by means of a recursive function. In this case, reading several times through the same channel corresponds to reading several elements of the corresponding input list; sending several times through an output channel corresponds to writing several elements to the output list. In the rest of the paper, we will assume that any Eden process communicates by using lists.

Finally, let us comment on the features that Eden includes to analyze quantitative properties. If we are interested in measuring different aspects of our programs, it is not enough (in general) to run them (several times). In order to know the *real* behavior of our programs, we need some extra feedback. We can obtain that feedback by using Paradise [19], an Eden profiler based on GranSim [25]. When using Paradise, the Eden program runs as usually but it also records, in a log file, all the relevant events happening during the execution: Creation of processes, communications of values, processes getting blocked, etc. After finishing the execution, several visualization tools can be used to analyze the log results. For instance, the evolution in time of the state, either running or blocked waiting for communication, of a process or set of processes can be viewed. It is also possible to combine log files corresponding to different executions in order to obtain statistics of properties about the behavior of the processes. This allows us to check whether the actual results really fit the theoretical predictions, and to obtain accurate statistics without performing complex theoretical studies.

4 From VPSPA to Eden

In this section we present how process algebraic specifications are translated into Eden programs. First, we need to define what a correct implementation is. We will consider that an Eden program implements a VPSPA specification if any (input, output, or internal) transition of the specification can be *simulated* by a channel of the Eden program, and any delay of the specification is reflected in that program. The formal definition is a little bit involved and can be found in [27]. The rest of this section is devoted to present our methodology for the translation of VPSPA specifications into Eden programs. Even though the translation can be done automatically, in order to optimize the generated code it is needed some command in functional programming, although not necessarily in Eden.

We suppose a specification written in VPSPA where we have a set of equations as:

$$X_1 := P_1 \qquad X_2 := P_2 \qquad \cdots \qquad X_n := P_n$$

We will impose the following restriction: Any occurrence of parallel operators in the processes P_j will be of the form: $X_{i_1} \|_\emptyset (X_{i_2} \|_\emptyset \cdots (X_{i_{j-1}} \|_\emptyset X_{i_j}) \cdots)$ where $\{X_{i_1}, \cdots, X_{i_j}\} \subseteq \{X_1, \cdots, X_n\}$. Intuitively, we consider that any occurrence of the parallel operator represents the composition of *real* processes (so, they have a *name*). Note that this is not a real restriction because $P \|_\emptyset Q$ can always be defined as $X := P$, $Y := Q$ and then $X \|_\emptyset Y$. This restriction simplifies the translation mechanism while we do not lose expressibility. Let us remark that our syntax allows to index parallel operators with any set of indexes. However, as we have already commented, non-empty sets of indexes are used only in the definition of the operational semantics. That is why we have assumed that all of them are (initially) empty. Let us also note that these indexes do not appear in the translation into Eden. This is so because every Eden process will manage its own delays. So, there cannot be any confusion, as it happens in the process algebra, regarding which process is delayed. For a similar reason, the distinction between start and termination actions appearing in the definition of the operational semantics is not needed.

First, we compute the sets of input and output channels of the VPSPA processes $P_1, \ldots, P_n$. For any $1 \leq j \leq n$ let $I_j = \{i_{j1}, \ldots, i_{js_j}\} = \texttt{Inputs}(P_j)$ and $O_j = \{o_{j1}, \ldots, o_{jr_j}\} = \texttt{Outputs}(P_j)$. We will generate n process abstractions in Eden. These process abstractions will have the same (number of) input and output channels as the corresponding process P_i:

```
F1 = process (i11,...,i1s1) -> (o11,...,o1r1)
  where (o11,...,o1r1) = f1 i11 ... i1s1 o11 ... o1r1
```

```
F2 = process (i21,...,i2s2) -> (o21,...,o2r2)
  where (o21,...,o2r2) = f2 i21 ... i2s2 o21 ... o2r1
  .....
Fn = process (in1,...,insn) -> (on1,...,onrn)
  where (on1,...,onrn) = fn in1 ... insn on1 ... onrn
```

In the special case where the output channels are independent we can use a different function for defining each of these channels. These functions will only depend on the inputs of the process:

```
F = process (i1,...,is) -> (o1,...,or)
  where o1 = f1 i1 ... is
        ....
        or = fr i1 ... is
```

Depending on the processes P_j, the functions f1,...,fr will be defined in a different way. If P_j = stop then we simply consider that there are no outputs. More exactly, empty lists are output through all of the output channels (let us recall that in Eden, input and output channels are considered to be lists). The three cases corresponding to prefixes are easy. If $P_j = a!(v)\,; P$ then we will have a process:

```
Fj = process (i1,...,is) -> (o1,...,v:oj,...,or)
  where (o1,...,oj,...,or) = translation(P)
```

where oj is the output channel corresponding to $a!$. In this case, we firstly output the value v through oj and then we follow with the translation of P. If $P_j := a?(x)\,; P$ we have:

```
Fj = process (i1,...,ij,...,is) -> (o1,...,or)
  where (o1,...,or)              = g i1 ... ij ... is
        g i1 ... Patternsj ... is = translation(P)
```

where ij is the input channel corresponding to $a?$. In this case, we define an auxiliary function g. This function is defined by pattern matching on the input ij: It will take different values according to the received value through the input channel ij. The different patterns will have to do with the occurrences of constructors if then else in P. If there are no such occurrences, we will have a unique pattern (that is, there is no distinction in P depending on the values taken by x); otherwise, the boolean conditions appearing in the definition of the if then else constructors will be taken into account to define the different Patterns.

Example 1. Let $P := a?(x)\,; $ if $(x = 1)$ then P_1 else P_2. The translation of P is given by:

```
FP = process (i1,...,is) -> (o1,...,or)
  where (o1,...,or) = g i1...is
        g 1 i2...is = translation(P1)
        g n i2...is = translation(P2)
```

where the inputs of the process are $\text{Inputs}(P_1) \cup \text{Inputs}(P_2) \cup \{a\} = \{\texttt{i1}, ..., \texttt{is}\}$, the outputs are $\text{Outputs}(P_1) \cup \text{Outputs}(P_2) = \{\texttt{o1}, ..., \texttt{or}\}$, and we suppose that the input channel corresponding to a? is $\texttt{i1}$.   □

If $P_j = \xi\,;P$ then we will have a process:

```
Fj = process (i1,...,is) -> (o1,...,or)
  where (o1,...,or) = seq (wait xi) (translation(P))
```

Let us remind that `seq` represents the sequential composition operator. Besides, (`wait xi`) interrupts the execution of the process by a random amount of time depending on the distribution given by `xi`. We have added `wait` to Eden, as no such operator was defined in the original compiler. The implementation of this operator is based on the primitive constructor `sleep` and on the generation of random delays. We have predefined in Eden the most common distributions. For instance, exponential distributions are translated as `wait(expo lambda)` and uniform distributions over the interval (a, b) are translated as `wait(unif a b)`. In this paper we will also use `wait(dirac a)` and `wait(poisson lambda)` for Dirac and Poisson distributions respectively. Obviously, more distributions can be added to Eden as needed. In this case, we would like to remark that functional languages (in particular Eden) are very suitable to define different distributions and to deal with them. Moreover, this is the case even if they depend on different numbers of parameters.

Analogously to the `if then else`, the choice operator can also be translated by using pattern matching, the difference being that `merge2` is used to decide which branch should be chosen. In order to choose between two alternatives, we merge the corresponding channels. The appropriate branch is selected by pattern matching on the left or right.

```
out = f (merge2 alt1 alt2)
f (Left alt1 : zs)  = ...
f (Right alt2 : zs) = ...
```

If P_j is the parallel composition of m process variables, that is, a process $P_j = Y_1 \parallel_\emptyset (Y_2 \parallel_\emptyset \cdots (Y_{m-1} \parallel_\emptyset Y_m) \cdots)$, where $\{Y_1, ..., Y_m\} \subseteq \{X_1, ..., X_n\}$, we will generate a process instantiation for each of the variables:

```
Fj = process (i1,...,is) -> (o1,...,or)
  where (out11,...,out1r1) = G1 # (in11,...,in1s1)
        (out21,...,out2r2) = G2 # (in21,...,in2s2)
        ........
        (outm1,...,outmrm) = Gm # (inm1,...,inmsm)
```

where for any $1 \le j \le m$ we have that `Gj` is the Eden process abstraction corresponding to Y_j, $\{\texttt{inj1}, ..., \texttt{injsj}\}$ is the set of input channels of `Gj`, and $\{\texttt{outj1}, ..., \texttt{outjrj}\}$ is its set of output channels. Let us note that, by the definition of the functions `Inputs` and `Outputs`, we have $\{\texttt{i1}, ..., \texttt{is}\} = \{\texttt{input} \mid \exists\, 1 \le k \le m,\ 1 \le l \le s_k : \texttt{input} = \texttt{inkl}\}$ (similarly for $\{\texttt{o1}, ..., \texttt{or}\}$).

It is rather easy to implement the restriction operator. The only externally visible actions of Fj will be those declared in its input an output lists (that is, i1...is, o1...or), while the remaining actions performed by the Gis are hidden. Thus, if the set of actions A is to be restricted, it is enough to define Inputs(Fj) = (⋃Inputs(P_i)) − A, and similarly for the outputs. Notice that each output (e.g. outij) of a process may correspond to an input (e.g. inkl) of another process. In that case, to enable the communication, it is enough to use the same name in the translation (e.g. a) for both the input and the output.

Example 2. Consider the process P given in Example 3, where $P_1 = c?(y) ; b!(1)$ and $P_2 = d!(0)$, and let $Q := a!(1) ;$ stop. Finally, let us take $(P \parallel_{\emptyset} Q)/\{a\}$. The translation of this last process is given by F below (the translation of Q is given by FQ).

```
FQ = process () -> a
   where a = [1]
F = process (c) -> (b,d)
   where (b,d) = FP # (a,c)
         a     = FQ # ()                                           □
```

5   An Example: The Token Ring

In this section we present a medium-size example. This relatively complex specification shows that our translation mechanism produces Eden programs *close enough* to the original specifications. Let us remark that in our specifications, for the sake of clarity, we use sometimes additional auxiliary processes. So, in some cases, auxiliary processes in the specification will be embedded into a unique Eden process. The pattern for the presentation of the example will be the following. First, we introduce the problem. Then we indicate the processes that we will use. Afterwards, for each specification we give the corresponding translation. Finally, we study some quantitative properties.

A token ring [21] is a network in which each station is only connected with two other stations. A station receives messages from the previous one and sends messages to the following. The last one sends messages to the first one, producing a ring structure. Each station can send its own generated messages but it can also forward the ones it receives.

A token circulates around the ring whenever all stations are idle. When a station needs to transmit a new message, it is required to seize the token and remove it from the ring before transmitting. As there is only one token, only one station can transmit at a given instant, solving the channel access problem.

Each station has two operating modes: *listen* and *transmit*. If the station is in listening mode, the input messages are simply forwarded to the output (after a short delay), unless the station is the actual receiver of the message. In that case, it just reads it without forwarding it. In the transmitting mode, which is only entered after the token is owned, the station is able to send its own generated messages. In this case, a queue is used to keep track of all the messages it needs to send. In order to guarantee fairness, a timer is used to control the maximum time a station can own the token. So, the station owning the token enters listening mode either if it has no more messages to transmit or if it receives a timeout from the timer. More specifically, after receiving a timeout the station is allowed to send a last message.

When traffic is light, the token circulates around the ring until a station seizes it, transmits a message, and releases the token again. When the traffic is heavy, as soon as a station releases the token, the following station seizes it and transmits new messages. Therefore, the network efficiency can approach 100%.

The token ring has been widely studied in the context of process algebras. Regarding stochastic process algebras, a study, similar to ours but restricted to exponential distributions, is given in [3].

The main processes of this system are: The $MsgGen$, the $Timer$, the $Queue$, the $MsgTrans$, the $Station$, and the $TokenRing$. In this example, we will consider that the addition operator fulfills the following condition: Given n, we have $i +_n 1 = i + 1$ for any $1 \leq i \leq n - 1$, and $n +_n 1 = 1$. For the sake of clarity, we use $+$ to denote this addition module n instead of $+_n$.

The $MsgGen$. This process generates messages. The generation of messages follows a Poisson distribution with parameter λ. After generating the message, it sends it to a queue, and then it is able to generate another message.

$$MsgGen_i := \xi_{po(\lambda)} ; generatedMsg_i!(msg) ; enqueue_i!(msg) ; MsgGen_i$$

To properly send messages, the generator needs to receive its identity and the size of the ring. Hence the two integer parameters appearing in the translation:

```
msgGen i n = process () -> enqueues    where
   enqueues   = f i n lambda
   f i n lambda= seq (wait(poisson lambda))(generateMsg i n :f i n lambda)
```

The $Timer$. It controls the time that a station owns the token. It will start its behavior when it receives a starting message. After an amount of time, given by a Dirac distribution, a timeout is generated, unless an interrupting message from the $MsgTrans$ ($intTimer$) is received.

$$Timer_i := startTimer_i?(y) ; (intTimer_i?(y') ; Timer_i +_{D(c)};timeOut_i!(-) ; Timer_i)$$

In the corresponding Eden process, we just need to merge the timeout messages and the stops. After that, if a timeout is produced, it is communicated to the $MsgTrans$. In case the timer is interrupted, we wait again until a new start message arrives.

```
timer = process (startsTimer,intsTimer) -> timeOuts
   where timeOuts = f startsTimer intsTimer
         f (x:xs) ys = g (merge2 ys [wait (dirac c)]) xs ys
         g (Left _ : _) xs (y:ys) = f xs ys
         g (Right _ : _)  xs ys   = TimeOut : f xs ys
```

The $Queue$. We use a parameter to store the messages created by the station.

$$Queue_i \quad := Queue_i'(<>)$$
$$Queue_i'(c) := \textbf{if} \ (c = x\#c') \ \textbf{then} \ enqueue_i?(y) \ ; Queue_i'(c\#y)$$
$$+ \ fetch_i?(y) \ ; dequeue_i!(x) \ ; Queue_i'(c')$$
$$\textbf{else} \ enqueue_i?(y) \ ; Queue_i'(c\#y)$$
$$+ \ fetch_i?(y) \ ; dequeue_i!(-) \ ; Queue_i$$

In Eden, we can reduce the number of cases because queuing a new element can be done regardless of the queue being empty or not. Let us note that we merge both input channels in order to be able to synchronize on them in any order.

```
queue = process (enqueues,fetchs) -> dequeues
  where dequeues = f Empty (merge2 enqueues fetchs)
        f q (Left msg : xs)    = f (addElem msg q) xs
        f Empty (Right fe : xs) = Nothing : f Empty xs
        f q (Right fe : xs)    = Just (first q) : f (extractFirst q) xs
```

The $MsgTrans$. It receives messages from the previous station. Then it checks whether it is the final receiver of the message. If so, it informs about its reception. Otherwise the message can be either the token or a message sent to another station. In the latter case, that message is automatically forwarded to the next station. In the former case, a timer is started, and messages are taken from the queue and sent to the next station. This is iterated until no more messages are available or until a timeout is received from the timer. In the latter case, the transmitter is allowed to send a last message. Notice that there are three possible states: *with* the token, *without* it, and *lastwith*. The last state denotes that it owns the token but that only one more message can be sent before releasing the token.

$$MsgTrans_{i,without} := transMsg_i?(msg);$$
$$\textbf{if} \ msg = (m,i) \ \textbf{then} \ read_i!(msg) \ ; MsgTrans_{i,without}$$
$$\textbf{else if} \ msg = token \ \textbf{then} \ MsgTrans_{i,with}$$
$$\textbf{else} \ \xi_{exp(\gamma)} \ ; transMsg_{i+1}!(msg) \ ; MsgTrans_{i,without}$$
$$MsgTrans_{i,with} \quad := startTimer_i!(-) \ ; fetch_i!(-) \ ; MsgTrans_{i,with2}$$
$$MsgTrans_{i,with2} \quad := dequeue_i?(msg) \ ; Sending_i(msg)$$
$$+timeOut_i?(x) \ ; MsgTrans_{i,lastwith}$$
$$Sending_i(msg) \quad := \textbf{if} \ msg = - \ \textbf{then} \ intTimer_i!(-) \ ; \xi_{U(a,b)};$$
$$transMsg_{i+1}!(token) \ ; MsgTrans_{i,without}$$
$$\textbf{else} \ \xi_{exp(\gamma)} \ ; transMsg_{i+1}!(msg);$$
$$fetch_i!(-) \ ; MsgTrans_{i,with2}$$
$$MsgTrans_{i,lastwith} := dequeue_i?(msg);$$
$$\textbf{if} \ msg = -$$
$$\textbf{then} \ \xi_{U(a,b)} \ ; transMsg_{i+1}!(token) \ ; MsgTrans_{i,without}$$
$$\textbf{else} \ \xi_{exp(\gamma)} \ ; transMsg_{i+1}!(msg) \ ; \xi_{U(a,b)};$$
$$transMsg_{i+1}!(token) \ ; MsgTrans_{i,without}$$

In the previous specification $exp(\gamma)$ denotes a random variable distributed as an exponential distribution with parameter γ. Besides $U(a,b)$ denotes a random variable distributed as a uniform distribution over the interval (a,b). The corresponding Eden process is shown below. The type Maybe is used to either receive a message `Just message` from the queue, or `Nothing` when the queue is empty. Let us remark that `inms` represents the messages received through $TransMsg_i$, while `outms` are the ones to be sent through $TransMsg_{i+1}$.

```
msgTrans i state =process(inms,dequeues,timeOuts) ->
                           (outms,reads,fetchs,startsTimer,intsTimer) where
  (outms,reads,fetchs,startsTimer,intsTimer)
    = f state inms (merge2 dequeues timeOuts)
  f Without (Token : inms') mts = f With inms' mts
  f Without (M m : inms') mts
   = if (isToMe m i) then (ys1,m:ys2,ys3,ys4,ys5)
                        else seq (wait(expo gamma))(M m:ys1,ys2,ys3,ys4,ys5)
    where (ys1,ys2,ys3,ys4,ys5) = f Without inms' mts
  f With xs ys = (y1,ys2,Fetch:ys3,StartTimer:ys4,ys5)
    where (ys1,ys2,ys3,ys4,ys5) = f With2 xs ys
  f With2 xs (Left Nothing : mts)
    = seq (wait (unif a b))(Token:ys1,ys2,ys3,ys4,IntTimer:ys5)
    where  (ys1,ys2,ys3,ys4,ys5) = f Without xs mts
  f With2 xs (Left (Just m): mts) = seq (wait (expo gamma))
                                    (M m:ys1,ys2,Fetch:ys3,ys4,ys5)
    where (ys1,ys2,ys3,ys4,ys5) = f With2 xs mts
  f With2 xs (Right _ : mts) = (ys1,ys2,ys3,ys4,ys5)
    where  (ys1,ys2,ys3,ys4,ys5) = f LastWith xs mts
  f LastWith xs (Left Nothing : mts)
    = seq (wait (unif a b))(Token:ys1,ys2,ys3,ys4,ys5)
    where  (ys1,ys2,ys3,ys4,ys5) = f Without xs mts
  f LastWith xs (Left (Just m) : mts)
    = seq (wait (expo gamma))
         (M m:(seq (wait (unif a b))(Token:ys1)),ys2,ys3,ys4,ys5)
    where  (ys1,ys2,ys3,ys4,ys5) = f Without xs mts
```

The *Station*. This process is a parallelization of the message generator, the queue to store the messages, the message transmitter, and the timer. The stations have an initial state representing the operating mode of each station at the beginning of the execution. It is either *listen* or *transmit*, depending on the possession of the token. Firstly, $Station_1$ has the token.

$$Station_{i,initstate} := (MsgGen_i \parallel_\emptyset Queue_i \parallel_\emptyset MsgTrans_{i,initstate} \parallel_\emptyset Timer_i)/S_i$$

where $S_i = \{enqueue_i, dequeue_i, fetch_i, startTimer_i, intTimer_i, timeOut_i\}$, and *initstate* is *with* for $Station_1$, and *without* for $Station_2 \ldots Station_n$.

The Eden implementation only needs to instantiate the corresponding processes, establishing the appropriate data dependencies:

```
station i n initState = process inms -> (outms,reads)
  where enqueues = (msgGen i n) # ()
        dequeues = queue # (enqueues,fetchs)
        timeOuts = timer # (startsTimer,intsTimer)
        (outms,reads,fetchs,startsTimer,intsTimer)
            = (msgTrans i initState) # (inms,dequeues,timeOuts)
```

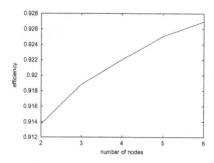 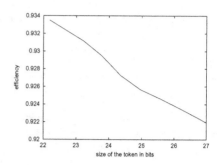

Fig. 2. Network efficiency depending on the number of stations (left) and on the token size (right)

The *TokenRing*. This process represents the whole system. The ring is a parallelization of n stations. Each station is communicated with the neighbor stations by sending messages from one to another through the action *transMsg*.

$$TokenRing := (Station_{1,with} \parallel_{\emptyset} Station_{2,without} \parallel_{\emptyset} \cdots \parallel_{\emptyset} Station_{n,without})/T$$

where $T = \{transMsg_i \mid 1 \leq i \leq n\}$.

The corresponding Eden program only needs to communicate all the stations in a ring fashion, and to initially assign the token to the first station. For doing that, we just need to create the appropriate dependencies. Our transformation rules can generate Eden code for a fix number of stations. For instance, in case we only have three stations, the following code will be used:

```
tokenRing 3 = merge [external1,external2,external3]    where
  (internal1,external1) = (station 1 3 With) # (internal3)
  (internal2,external2) = (station 2 3 Without) # (internal1)
  (internal3,external3) = (station 3 3 Without) # (internal2)
```

But the code can be optimized by hand to deal with a variable number of stations. This can be done by using a list comprehension and the **unzip** function which converts a list of pairs into a pair of lists:

```
tokenRing n = merge (external1:externals)    where
  (internal1,external1) = (station 1 n With) # (internals'!!n)
  (internals,externals)
    = unzip [(station i n Without)) # (internals'!!(i-1)) | i<-[2..n]]
  internals' = internal1 : internals
```

Finally, we use the profiling utilities of Eden to *measure* quantitative properties of our programs. In the Token Ring, we are interested in knowing the *efficiency* in the use of the network. We define efficiency as the time used for transmitting real messages divided by the total time transmitting messages (both messages and tokens). It was enough to profile the tokens and messages transmitted, and the graphics in Figure 2 were generated. The left one shows that the efficiency increases as the number of stations increases, because more messages are generated and transmitted. The right one shows that the efficiency is better when the token size is smaller. Thus, the token should be as small as possible, but there is a minimum size defined in terms of the size of the ring.

Acknowledgments

The authors thank Ismael Rodríguez and the anonymous referees for valuable comments on a previous version of this paper.

References

1. J.C.M. Baeten and C.A. Middelburg. Process algebra with timing: Real time and discrete time. In J.A. Bergstra, A. Ponse, and S.A. Smolka, editors, *Handbook of process algebra*, chapter 10. North Holland, 2001.
2. J.A. Bergstra, A. Ponse, and S.A. Smolka, editors. *Handbook of Process Algebra*. North Holland, 2001.
3. M. Bernardo. *Theory and application of extended markovian process algebra*. PhD thesis, Università di Bologna, 1999.
4. M. Bernardo and R. Gorrieri. A tutorial on EMPA: A theory of concurrent processes with nondeterminism, priorities, probabilities and time. *Theoretical Computer Science*, 202:1–54, 1998.
5. M. Bravetti and R. Gorrieri. The theory of interactive generalized semi-markov processes. To appear in Theoretical Computer Science., 2001.
6. S. Breitinger, U. Klusik, R. Loogen, Y. Ortega, and R. Peña. DREAM: the distributed Eden abstract machine. In *Implementation of Functional Languages. LNCS 1467.*, pages 250–269. Springer, 1998.
7. S. Breitinger, R. Loogen, Y. Ortega, and R. Peña. Eden: Language definition and operational semantics. Technical Report, Bericht 96-10, Philipps-Universität Marburg, Germany, 1998.
8. J. Bryans, J. Davies, and S. Schneider. Towards a denotational semantics for ET-LOTOS. In *CONCUR'95, LNCS 962*, pages 269–283, 1995.
9. E.M. Clarke, O. Grumberg, and D. Peled. *Model Checking*. MIT Press, 1999.
10. R. Cleaveland, Z. Dayar, S.A. Smolka, and S. Yuen. Testing preorders for probabilistic processes. *Information and Computation*, 154(2):93–148, 1999.
11. P.R. D'Argenio. *Algebras and Automata for Timed and Stochastic Systems*. PhD thesis, Department of Computer Science. University of Twente, 1999.
12. J. Davies and S. Schneider. A brief history of timed CSP. *Theoretical Computer Science*, 138:243–271, 1995.
13. R. van Glabbeek, S.A. Smolka, and B. Steffen. Reactive, generative and stratified models of probabilistic processes. *Information and Computation*, 121(1):59–80, 1995.
14. N. Götz, U. Herzog, and M. Rettelbach. Multiprocessor and distributed system design: The integration of functional specification and performance analysis using stochastic process algebras. In *16th Int. Symp. on Computer Performance Modelling, Measurement and Evaluation (PERFORMANCE'93), LNCS 729*, pages 121–146. Springer, 1993.

15. C. Gregorio and M. Núñez. Specifying and verifying the Alternating Bit Protocol with Probabilistic-Timed LOTOS. In *COST 247 International Workshop on Applied Formal Methods in System Design*, pages 38–50, 1996.
16. Jan Friso Groote. Transition system specifications with negative premises. *Theoretical Computer Science*, 118:263–299, 1993.
17. H. Hansson. *Time and Probability in Formal Design of Distributed Systems*. PhD thesis, Department of Computer Systems. Uppsala University, 1991.
18. H. Hermanns, J-P. Katoen, J. Meyer-Kayser, and M. Siegle. Towards model checking stochastic process algebra. In *IFM 2000, LNCS 1945*, pages 420–440. Springer, 2000.
19. F. Hernández, R. Peña, and F. Rubio. From GranSim to Paradise. In *Trends in Functional Programming*, pages 11–19. Intellect, 2000.
20. J. Hillston. *A Compositional Approach to Performance Modelling*. Cambridge University Press, 1996.
21. IEEE. 802.5: Token ring access method. IEEE, 1985.
22. G.G. Infante López, H. Hermanns, and J.-P. Katoen. Beyond memoryless distributions: Model checking semi-Markov chains. In *PAPM-PROBMIV 2001, LNCS 2165*, pages 57–70. Springer, 2001.
23. B. Jonsson, W. Yi, and K.G. Larsen. Probabilistic extensions of process algebras. In J.A. Bergstra, A. Ponse, and S.A. Smolka, editors, *Handbook of process algebra*, chapter 11. North Holland, 2001.
24. U. Klusik, R. Loogen, S. Priebe, and F. Rubio. Implementation skeletons in Eden: Low-effort parallel programming. In *Implementation of Functional Languages, IFL'00, LNCS 2011*. Springer, 2001.
25. H.W. Loidl. *GranSim User's Guide*. Department of Computing Science, Glasgow University, 1996.
26. N. López and M. Núñez. A testing theory for generally distributed stochastic processes. In *CONCUR 2001, LNCS 2154*, pages 321–335. Springer, 2001.
27. N. López, M. Núñez, and F. Rubio. Implementation relation between VPSPA and Eden, 2002. http://dalila.sip.ucm.es/ natalia/ifm02/appendix.ps.
28. G. Lowe. Probabilistic and prioritized models of timed CSP. *Theoretical Computer Science*, 138:315–352, 1995.
29. J.A. Mañas and T. de Miguel. From LOTOS to C. In *International Conference on Formal Description Techniques for Distributed Systems and Communications Protocols*, pages 79–84. Elsevier, 1988.
30. X. Nicollin and J. Sifakis. An overview and synthesis on timed process algebras. In *Computer Aided Verification'91, LNCS 575*, pages 376–398, 1991.
31. M. Núñez, D. de Frutos, and L. Llana. Acceptance trees for probabilistic processes. In *CONCUR'95, LNCS 962*, pages 249–263. Springer, 1995.
32. R. Peña and F. Rubio. Parallel Functional Programming at Two Levels of Abstraction. In *Principles and Practice of Declarative Programming (PPDP01)*, pages 187–198. ACM Press, 2001.
33. S.L. Peyton Jones, A. Gordon, and S. Finne. Concurrent Haskell. In *ACM Symp. on Principles of Prog. Lang. POPL'96*, pages 295–308. ACM Press, 1996.
34. S.L. Peyton Jones and J. Hughes, editors. *Report on the Programming Language Haskell 98*. Available at http://www.haskell.org, 1999.

From Implicit Specifications to Explicit Designs in Reactive System Development

K. Lano, D. Clark, and K. Androutsopoulos

Department of Computer Science, King's College London, Strand, London WC2R 2LS
kcl@dcs.kcl.ac.uk

Abstract. In this paper we describe how the RSDS method can be used as a bridge between implicit Z-style specifications of reactive systems, and explicit B AMN designs of these systems. We define the translation from RSDS to B and verify its correctness. We also define controller decomposition techniques, and a translation to SMV.

Keywords: B AMN, RSDS, Reactive Systems, UML, model-checking

1 Introduction

For critical systems the importance of identifying correct (and safe) requirements has been widely recognised. Incidents such as the Nagoya A300 crash [9] show that even systems correct with respect to their specifications may be unsafe if there are unforeseen consequences of these specifications. Therefore a language for formally expressing requirements must be as simple and as close to pure predicate logic as possible, without the need for a user to understand the complex syntax of a particular specification language such as Z or OCL [16]. RSDS [12] attempts to provide a suitable requirements formalisation notation, using predicate and CTL [5] logic, class diagrams and statemachines.

RSDS can be considered to be a subset of UML [16] with precise semantics. It also provides links to formal methods such as B [17,1] and the SMV model checker [3] to support validation and verification of reactive system specifications.

Section 2 gives an introduction to RSDS specifications, Section 3 shows how these specifications and design decompositions for RSDS can be generalised to object-oriented models. Section 4 covers the translation to B and its correctness. Section 5 describes the use of SMV for modular verification of temporal properties.

2 RSDS Specifications

RSDS (Reactive System Design Support) supports the specification of reactive systems using state machines, class diagrams and invariants. Its philosophy is to express such specifications in the simplest terms possible: no formal notation apart from these are used, and automated support for analysis, design and code generation is built into the RSDS tool.

M. Butler, L. Petre, and K. Sere (Eds.): IFM 2002, LNCS 2335, pp. 49–68, 2002.

An RSDS system is a tuple (*Sens*, *Invs*, *Conts*, *Acts*) where *Sens* is a set of named statemachines representing sensor components, *Invs* is a set of static, operational and temporal invariants involving the state variables and states of *Sens* and *Acts*, *Conts* is a set of named statemachines representing controller components, and *Acts* is a set of named statemachines representing actuator components. The class diagram of the system is represented by additional constraints in *Invs* expressing the association and inheritance relationships defined in the diagram.

2.1 Invariants

The use of invariants as the central means of specifying reactive control systems was suggested by the corresponding use of "transfer functions" in continuous control theory to express the required behaviour of a continuous controller [7]. This is also the approach used in Z specification [15], whereby a system state is specified in a state schema *Sys* which includes static (single-state) invariants to define the properties of the system. All operations on the system extend ΔSys, ie, they must implicitly preserve the invariants.

In a discrete event reactive control system the invariants expressed in a requirements specification are principally of three kinds:

1. Static (or 'safety') invariants: $P \Rightarrow Q$ where both P and Q consist only of constraints on the current states of sensors and actuators in the system. No temporal operators or event names are used. For example:

   sw = On & s2 = Off   =>   bm = On

   for the feed belt of the production cell [13], where $s2$ is the blank sensor at the end of the belt and bm the belt motor (Figure 1).

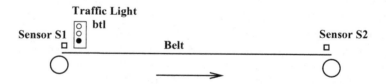

Fig. 1. Feedbelt of Fault-tolerant Production Cell

2. Action (or 'operational') invariants $\alpha \& P \Rightarrow AX(Q)$ where P and Q are single-state constraints as in 1, and α is an event of some sensor. AX is the branching temporal logic operator "in all next states". These invariants express the pre-post condition property "whenever α occurs in state P, the next state satisfies Q". For example

   swon & sw = Off & s2 = Off   =>   AX(bm = On)

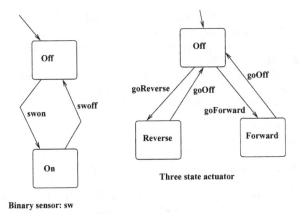

Fig. 2. Examples of Component Statemachines

3. Temporal invariants $P \Rightarrow AF(Q)$ or $P \Rightarrow AG(Q)$. AF is "in some future state" and AG is "in all future states". For example

```
s2 = Off & s1 = On & bm = On  =>  AF(s2 = On)
```

which expresses that blanks will eventually reach $s2$ from $s1$ if the belt motor is on.

Other temporal operators which are more rarely used are $EF(Q)$ "there exists a path on which Q eventually holds" and $EG(Q)$ "there exists a path on which Q always holds".

We also distinguish *system* invariants, which are requirements on the control system developer, from *environment* invariants, which are assumptions about the behaviour of the equipment under control. The static and action invariants above are examples of system invariants, the temporal is an example of an environment invariant.

2.2 Statemachines

Simple components Sm of a reactive system, such as a two-state sensor or three-state actuator (eg, a reversible motor) are represented in RSDS as statemachines (eg, Figure 2). Controllers may also be expressed as statemachines, whose transitions may have generations, defining the actuator or sub-controller events to be generated when the transition is taken. Each controller statemachine $S \in Conts$ has a set $receivers_{Sys}(S) \subseteq Conts \cup Acts$ of statemachines to which it can send events/commands.

2.3 Case Study: Fault Tolerant Production Cell

This system is a simple example of an automated manufacturing system, containing feed and deposit belts to move pieces into and out of the work cell, robot

arms for moving the pieces between the belts and a press, and a backup press
to be used if the primary press fails [13].

One subsystem of the production cell is the feedbelt control mechanism,
consisting of switch sw to initiate processing, sensor $s1$ at the start of the belt,
a belt traffic light, a sensor $s2$ at the end of the belt, and a motor bm to move
the belt (Figure 1). All of these are two-state devices with states On/Off. The
control invariants for the feedbelt are:

$$sw = Off \Rightarrow bm = Off$$
$$s2 = Off \ \& \ sw = On \Rightarrow bm = On$$
$$s2 = On \ \& \ (ts = Off \ \lor \ s3 = On) \Rightarrow bm = Off$$
$$sw = On \ \& \ s2 = On \ \& \ ts = On \ \& \ s3 = Off \Rightarrow bm = On$$

ts is the top position sensor of the elevating table subsystem which follows the
feedbelt, and $s3$ is the blank sensor of this subsystem. Blanks are transferred
from the feedbelt to the table only when the table is in the top position and
clear of a blank: $ts = On \ \& \ s3 = Off$. Thus the feedbelt controller needs to
know some information about the table state.

The table does not need to refer to the feedbelt state however. Its control
invariants are:

$$s3 = On \ \& \ bs = Off \Rightarrow tablemotor = down$$
$$s3 = On \ \& \ bs = On \Rightarrow tablemotor = Off$$
$$s3 = Off \ \& \ ts = Off \Rightarrow tablemotor = up$$
$$s3 = Off \ \& \ ts = On \Rightarrow tablemotor = Off$$

The *tablemotor* is a reversible motor, bs is the bottom position sensor of the
table and all sensors are two-state On/Off devices.

A static environmental assumption for the table is that not both of the top
and bottom table sensors are On simultaneously:

$$ts = On \Rightarrow bs = Off$$

Temporal environmental assumptions are that blanks are only added when the
table is in the top position: $s3on \Rightarrow ts = On$ and that if the table motor is
set to up, the table will eventually reach the top position: $tablemotor = up \Rightarrow
AF(ts = On)$.

A temporal required system property which we would like to deduce about
the table is that it regularly becomes available for receiving blanks if blanks are
regularly removed:

$$AGAF(s3 = Off) \Rightarrow AGAF(s3 = Off \ \& \ ts = On)$$

We will show that this can be proved in SMV, assuming the above environmental properties.

2.4   Controller Synthesis

Static invariants, of form 1 in Section 2.1, must hold in all *stable* states of the
complete system, ie, in the initial state and in all states where a reaction to an

input event has been completed and there are no pending actuator commands. This corresponds to the states of a B machine [10] specification, where the reaction to an event is completed in 'the same step' as the event itself, intermediate states (between input event occurrences and the sending of commands to actuators in reaction to these occurrences) not being visible. This is also the case in Z specifications.

Static invariants implicitly express requirements on the reactions to events which make their antecedents true. For the example invariant

```
sw = On & s2 = Off  =>  bm = On
```

events *swon* and *s2off* which make the antecedent of the invariant true must be reacted to by a command *bmSetOn*. The RSDS tool derives such a reaction by generating action invariants from static invariants, and then translating these into B or Java code. From this static invariant we get the action invariants

```
swon & sw = Off & s2 = Off  =>  AX(bm = On)
s2off & s2 = On & sw = On  =>  AX(bm = On)
```

and corresponding B code:

```
swon = ...
  IF sw = Off & s2 = Off
  THEN bmSetOn
  ELSE ...
  END


s2off = ...
```

Environmental assumptions are separated from system invariants by the RSDS tool and are not used to generate action invariants or control code (since they do not describe obligations on the control system to achieve particular functionality or states). Environmental assumptions of the forms $P \Rightarrow Q$ and $\alpha \Rightarrow Q$ where P, Q are sensor expressions and α is a sensor event, are used instead to generate fault detection code which is placed in a specialised fault detection controller *Fdc*. They are also used to reduce the state space of the generated controller state machine and the generated SMV modules.

Figure 3 shows how the RSDS process is applied, starting from statemachine descriptions of sensors and actuators of the equipment under control, and a set of static (single-state), action (pre/post) and temporal invariants defining the required controller behaviour and assumptions about the environment. From these a design is derived, consisting of a hierarchically organised set of controllers and control algorithms. The transformations of Section 3 can be used to achieve this. Verification of temporal properties can be carried out using SMV descriptions automatically generated from the RSDS design, and verification of static properties using B. Java code is also generated (C code may be generated by using the B Toolkit). Ladder logic designs [8] suitable for a PLC implementation can also be generated.

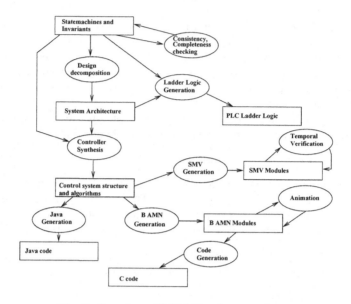

Fig. 3. Overview of RSDS Development Steps

3   RSDS Models

3.1   Semantics of Simple RSDS Systems

Simple components Sm of a reactive system are represented semantically by a CTL temporal logic theory Γ_{Sm} containing a single attribute $sm : States_{Sm}$ ranging over the states of the statemachine, and actions tr for each transition of the statemachine, and α ranging over its events. Axioms of Γ_{Sm} such as

$$AG(sm = s \land \alpha \ \Rightarrow \ tr)$$

where s is the source state of a transition tr, with trigger event α, define the state-transition behaviour of Sm [13].

A component translates directly into a B AMN machine. However this simple 'object-based' approach is inadequate for more general systems in which there may be several identically-structured copies of a component in a system, for example each floor in a lift control system will have a lift request button, and each request button will have a corresponding light to indicate if the request is awaiting service. To model such systems we parameterise the instance theory Γ_C of a component C by a constant type of object identities $@C$ for instances of C [2]. The resulting theory ΓC_C has attributes

$$att : @C \to T$$

for each attribute $att : T$ of C, and action symbol

$$\alpha : @C \ \to$$

for each action symbol α of C. In addition there is a new attribute $\overline{C} : \mathbb{F}@C$ representing the set of existing instances of C, and actions $new_C : @C \rightarrow$ and $kill_C : @C \rightarrow$ to add and remove elements of $@C$ from this set. Each axiom $AG\varphi$ of Γ_C becomes an axiom of ΓC_C in its parameterised form $AG(\forall a : \overline{C} \cdot \varphi(a))$. In addition there are sequentiality axioms for each action symbol α:

$$AG(\forall a : \overline{C}; \; b : \overline{C} \cdot \; a \neq b \; \wedge \; \alpha(a) \; \Rightarrow \; \neg \, \alpha(b))$$

where α is in $Events_C$. Similarly for actions α, β representing distinct transitions or distinct events:

$$AG(\forall a : \overline{C}; \; b : \overline{C} \cdot \; \alpha(a) \; \Rightarrow \; \neg \, \beta(b))$$

where α, β are distinct elements of $Events_C$.

There are standard axioms for new and $kill$:

$$AG(\forall x : \mathbb{P}(@C) \cdot \overline{C} = x \wedge new_C(a) \; \Rightarrow \; AX(\overline{C} = x \cup \{a\}))$$
$$AG(\forall x : \mathbb{P}(@C) \cdot \overline{C} = x \wedge kill_C(a) \; \Rightarrow \; AX(\overline{C} = x \setminus \{a\}))$$
$$AG\Big(\forall x : \mathbb{P}(@C) \cdot \overline{C} = x \; \Rightarrow \; \forall a : @C \cdot \neg \, new_C(a) \wedge \neg \, kill_C(a)$$
$$\Rightarrow \; AX(\overline{C} = x)\Big)$$

These axioms imply that new and $kill$ cannot co-occur.

If class D is a subclass of class C then $@D \subseteq @C$ and $AG(\overline{D} \subseteq \overline{C})$.

An association or aggregation from component (class) C to component (class) D is modelled as a mathematical relation

$$r : \overline{C} \leftrightarrow \overline{D}$$

ie, a set of pairs (c, d) of instances of C and D. r is considered as an attribute of ΓC_{Sys} and actions $link_r(c, d)$ to add and $unlink_r(c, d)$ to remove pairs from r are also included in this theory.

Such OO models can be directly expressed in B AMN, using variables to represent $\overline{C}$ and c, and a set to represent $@C$ [10].

3.2 Generalised Theory of an RSDS System

Let $Sys = (\{S_1, \ldots, S_n\}, Invs, Conts, \{A_1, \ldots, A_m\})$ be an RSDS system. At the initial specification stage, $Conts$ is empty.

The theory ΓC_{Sys} of Sys is the co-limit of the class theories ΓC of its components, extended with global axioms that express that only one instance $\alpha(a)$ of any sensor event may occur in any time step, and that any instance of an actuator event must co-occur with some instance of a sensor event.

Mutual exclusion of sensor events in ΓC_{Sys} is formally defined as the property

$$AG(\forall x_i \in \overline{S_i}; \; x_j \in \overline{S_j} \cdot \neg \, (\alpha(x_i) \wedge \beta(x_j)))$$

for each $1 \leq i \neq j \leq n$ and $\alpha \in Events_{S_i}$, $\beta \in Events_{S_j}$.

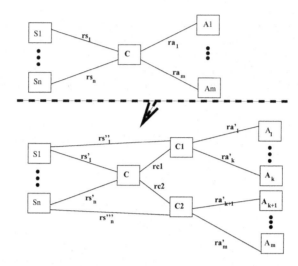

Fig. 4. Typical Initial RSDS Design and Horizontal Decomposition

Coverage of actuator events by sensor events is the property

$$AG(\forall z_i \in \overline{A_i} \cdot \alpha(z_i) \Rightarrow$$
$$\exists x_1 \in \overline{S_1} \cdot \bigvee_{\beta \in Events_{S_1}} \beta(x_1) \vee \ldots \vee \exists x_n \in \overline{S_n} \cdot \bigvee_{\beta \in Events_{S_n}} \beta(x_n))$$

for each $1 \leq i \leq m$ and $\alpha \in Events_{A_i}$.

The first design step is usually to introduce a *controller* component intermediate between the sensors and actuators of a system (top of Figure 4). The controller C has no attributes apart from $\overline{C}$ and has action symbols $kill_C$ and new_C, together with the union of the sets of action symbols for the events of each of the sensors.

3.3   Design Transformations

We can extend the RSDS design transformations of horizontal, phase, hierarchical and dynamic phase decompositions [11] to the OO framework, and verify their correctness, as shown in the following sections. We give the details for horizontal and phase decomposition. A refinement step from an RSDS system $Sys_1 = (Sens_1, Invs_1, Cons_1, Acts_1)$ to a system $Sys_2 = (Sens_2, Invs_2, Cons_2, Acts_2)$ is correct if there is a syntactic interpretation σ of Sys_1 in Sys_2 such that $\Gamma C_{Sys_2} \vdash \sigma(\varphi)$ for each axiom φ of ΓC_{Sys_1}. We say that ΓC_{Sys_2} is a *theory extension* [6] of ΓC_{Sys_1}.

Horizontal Decomposition. A typical general situation is shown in Figure 4, where controller C is decomposed into independent subcontrollers C_1 and C_2 which share the same set of sensors as C but have disjoint sets of actuators.

Assume that $\forall\, y \in \overline{C}\cdot\exists! y_1 \in \overline{C_1}\cdot(y, y_1) \in rc_1$ and $\forall\, y \in \overline{C}\cdot\exists! y_2 \in \overline{C_2}\cdot(y, y_2) \in rc_2$. Ie, each controller in C has unique C_1 and C_2 subcontrollers. Sys_1 is the subsystem consisting of $S_1, \ldots, S_n$, C_1 and A_1 to A_k. Sys_2 is the subsystem consisting of $S_1, \ldots, S_n$, C_2 and A_{k+1} to A_m. Sys_1 has all invariants of the original system Sys which refer only to components of Sys_1, Sys_2 has all invariants of Sys which refer only to components of Sys_2. There should be no other invariants of Sys not in these two sets.

Each rs_i'' relation is defined to be rs_i'; rc_1 in the first new submodel Sys_1 and rs_i''' is defined to be rs_i'; rc_2 in Sys_2.

rs_i in the original model Sys is interpreted by rs_i' in Sys_1, and ra_j is interpreted by rc_1; ra_j' (if $1 \le j \le k$) or by rc_2; ra_j' (if $k < j \le m$). This does yield a theory extension $Sys_1 \cup Sys_2$ of Sys provided that each axiom

$$(x_1, y) \in rs_1 \;\wedge\; \ldots \;\wedge\; (x_n, y) \in rs_n \;\wedge$$
$$(y, z_1) \in ra_1 \;\wedge\; \ldots \;\wedge\; (y, z_m) \in ra_m \;\Rightarrow\; \varphi(x_1, \ldots, x_n, z_1, \ldots, z_m)$$

of Sys is also an axiom of either the Sys_1 subsystem, in the form

$$(x_1, y_1) \in rs_1'' \;\wedge\; \ldots \;\wedge\; (x_n, y_1) \in rs_n'' \;\wedge$$
$$(y_1, z_1) \in ra_1' \;\wedge\; \ldots \;\wedge\; (y_1, z_k) \in ra_k' \;\Rightarrow\; \varphi(x_1, \ldots, x_n, z_1, \ldots, z_k)$$

or of the Sys_2 subsystem, in the form

$$(x_1, y_2) \in rs_1''' \;\wedge\; \ldots \;\wedge\; (x_n, y_2) \in rs_n''' \;\wedge$$
$$(y_2, z_{k+1}) \in ra_{k+1}' \;\wedge\; \ldots \;\wedge\; (y_2, z_m) \in ra_m' \;\Rightarrow\; \varphi(x_1, \ldots, x_n, z_{k+1}, \ldots, z_m)$$

depending on which set of actuators is involved in φ.

This holds because, if φ is of the first form, ie, involves only actuators from A_1 to A_k, then if

$$(x_1, y) \in rs_1' \;\wedge\; \ldots \;\wedge\; (x_n, y) \in rs_n' \;\wedge$$
$$(y, z_1) \in rc_1; ra_1' \;\wedge\; \ldots \;\wedge\; (y, z_k) \in rc_1; ra_k'$$

then there is a unique element y_1 such that (y, y_1) is in rc_1 so for this y_1:

$$(x_1, y_1) \in rs_1'' \;\wedge\; \ldots \;\wedge\; (x_n, y_1) \in rs_n''$$

and $(y_1, z_1) \in ra_1' \;\wedge\; \ldots \;\wedge\; (y_1, z_k) \in ra_k'$, so the result follows. Similarly for Sys_2 axioms. The global invariants of Sys_1 and Sys_2 together prove those of Sys: mutual exclusion of all sensor events holds since Sys_1 and Sys_2 have the same set of sensors and hence exclusion axioms as Sys. Also each actuator of Sys is either in Sys_1 and so its events are covered by some sensor event (of Sys_1 and hence Sys) or in Sys_2 (likewise).

Phase Decomposition. Figure 5 shows the typical situation in this case. Assume that Sen is the sensor on whose states we are going to split the controller into phases. For simplicity, assume $States_{Sen} = \{v_1, v_2\}$. Define

$$\overline{C1} = \{y : \overline{C} \mid (x, y) \in rsen \;\Rightarrow\; sen(x) = v_1\}$$
$$\overline{C2} = \{y : \overline{C} \mid (x, y) \in rsen \;\Rightarrow\; sen(x) = v_2\}$$

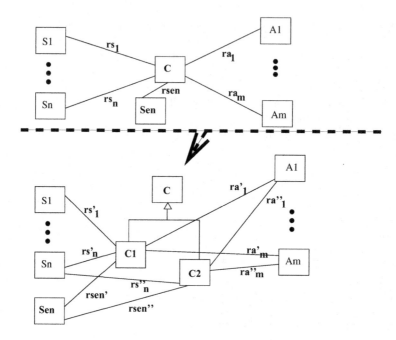

Fig. 5. Phase Decomposition

$rsen$ must be such that these two sets are non-empty and make up a partition of $\overline{C}$, this is the case if $rsen$ is surjective and $rsen^{-1}$ is a function, for example, if $\overline{Sen}$ has a unique element.

The system Sys_1 comprising $C1$ and the sensors and actuators must satisfy

$$(x, y) \in rsen' \ \wedge \ (x_1, y) \in rs'_1 \ \wedge \ \ldots \ \wedge \ (x_n, y) \in rs'_n \ \wedge$$
$$(y, z_1) \in ra'_1 \ \wedge \ \ldots \ \wedge \ (y, z_m) \in ra'_m$$
$$\Rightarrow \ (sen(x) = v_1 \ \Rightarrow \ \varphi(x, x_1, \ldots, x_n, z_1, \ldots, z_m))$$

for each invariant φ of the original system Sys. Similarly for Sys_2.

The interpretation of $rsen$ is $rsen' \cup rsen''$ and likewise for all other relations and $\overline{C}$, which is interpreted as $\overline{C1} \cup \overline{C2}$.

Then if $(x, y') \in rsen' \cup rsen''$ and

$$(x_1, y') \in rs'_1 \cup rs''_1 \ \wedge \ \ldots \ \wedge \ (x_n, y') \in rs'_n \cup rs''_n \ \wedge$$
$$(y', z_1) \in ra'_1 \cup ra''_1 \ \wedge \ \ldots \ \wedge \ (y', z_m) \in ra'_m \cup ra''_m$$

either $sen(x) = v_1$ and so $y' \in \overline{C1}$ and the above pairs are all in the Sys_1 relations, or $sen(x) = v_2$, $y' \in \overline{C2}$ and the pairs are all in the Sys_2 relations. In each case each invariant $\varphi(x, x_1, \ldots, x_n, z_1, \ldots, z_m)$ follows from the corresponding subsystem axiom, as required.

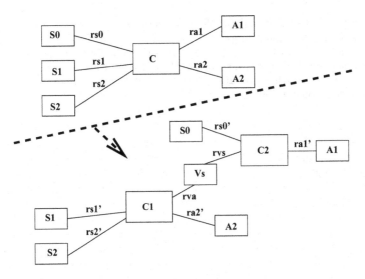

Fig. 6. Hierarchical Decomposition

Hierarchical Decomposition. Figure 6 shows a typical situation in this case, where a system Sys is split into two subsystems, and a new 'virtual sensor' component Vs is introduced as an interface between one system Sys_1 consisting of $S1$, $S2$, $C1$ and $A2$, and a subordinate system Sys_2 consisting of $S0$, Vs, $C2$ and $A1$.

The role of the controller $C1$ is to maintain some invariant between the states of Vs and the sensors which it conceals from $C2$ (in addition to carrying out its own control function for actuators it directly controls). For example Vs elements could express a "conjunction" of the states of these sensors:

$$vs(x) = On \iff s1(x1) = On \land s2(x2) = On$$

when x, $x1$ and $x2$ are connected to the same controller $c1 \in \overline{C1}$.

4   Translation of RSDS to B

The translation of RSDS to B AMN preserves the modules and structures of the RSDS specification:

- For each RSDS statemachine module M representing a sensor, actuator or controller, we generate a corresponding B machine $\mathcal{B}(M)$.
- If module $N \in receivers_{Sys}(M)$ then $\mathcal{B}(M)$ INCLUDES $\mathcal{B}(N)$. Because B does not allow two machines to INCLUDE a third [12], this means that only RSDS structures in which the sends/receives relation between modules is a tree can be translated into B. We assume this restriction in the following (this restriction is however not necessary for translation to SMV or Java).

We give the translation and proof of correctness for instances of components here, a similar proof for component classes can also be given [14].

We express the B machine $\mathcal{B}(M)$ in two parts, a basic interface $M0$ which has an operation for each transition of M, and a high-level interface $M1$ which INCLUDES $M0$ and has operations for each event of M. These operations then call the operations of $M0$.

```
MACHINE M0
INCLUDES N₁, ..., Nᵤ
VARIABLES m_state
INVARIANT m_state : StatesM
INITIALISATION m_state := initM
OPERATIONS
    t₁ = SELECT m_state = sr₁
         THEN m_state := tr₁ || act₁
         END;

    ⋮

    tₙ = ...
END
```

The t_i for $i : 1 .. N$ are all the transitions $t_i : sr_i \rightarrow tr_i$ of M, the generations of t_i are act_i, expressed as a $||$ combination of subordinate component events. These events must be from distinct components.

```
MACHINE M1
INCLUDES M0
OPERATIONS
    α = PRE m_state : { sr₁, ..., srₙ }
        THEN
            IF m_state = sr₁
            THEN t₁
            ELSE ...
            END
        END;

    ⋮

END
```

The $t_i : sr_i \rightarrow tr_i$, $i : 1 .. n$ are all the transitions of M which have event α, and t_i has generations act_i.

4.1   Correctness of B Translation

The correctness of the RSDS to B translation can be shown by giving a temporal logic semantics $Th(C)$ for each B component C, and then showing that the semantics $Th(\mathcal{B}(M))$ of the translation into B of an SRS module M establishes all the properties of the theory Γ_M of M [14].

Let $[S]P$ for a B generalised substitution S denote the usual weakest-precondition semantics of B AMN statements [10].

The theory $Th(C)$ of a B machine C has attributes $x : T$ for each variable x of C with typing T, axiom $AG(Inv_C)$ for the invariant of C (and similarly for C's constraints and properties), and axiom

$$(\neg [Init_C]\neg (v' = v))[v/v']$$

for the initialisation, where v is the tuple of all variables of C and its included machines, v' is a tuple of new variables of the same length as v, and

$$\forall v' \cdot AG(Pre \wedge op(p) \wedge v = v' \Rightarrow \neg [Def']\neg (v' = \bigcirc v))$$

for each operation

$$op(p) \quad = \quad PRE\ Pre\ THEN\ Def\ END$$

of C, where Def' is Def with each occurrence of x in v replaced by x'.

This axiom defines the overall effect of $op(p)$ in terms of the state change on the variables of C and the variables of machines included in C. We also need an axiom which expresses when the operations of included machines are invoked by an invocation of $op(p)$:

$$Pre \wedge op(p) \Rightarrow (\neg [Def]\neg (v' = v))[\bigcirc v/v']$$

where $\varphi(\bigcirc v)$ abbreviates $\exists w.(EX(w = v) \wedge \varphi(w)) \wedge \forall w.(EX(w = v) \Rightarrow \varphi(w))$ and in the conclusion we replace each formula $\neg [opx(q)]\neg Q$ "there is an execution of $opx(q)$ which establishes Q" by $opx(q)$.

There is also a locality axiom reflecting the fact that variables of a B machine may only be modified by operations of the same machine:

$$AG(\neg \exists p_1 \cdot op_1(p_1) \wedge \ \ldots \ \wedge \neg \exists p_k \cdot op_k(p_k) \wedge v = v' \Rightarrow AX(v = v'))$$

where v is the tuple of variables of C and the op_j are all operations of C.

For the $INCLUDES$ construct of B, there are the *coverage* axioms, for each operation op_N of a machine N, that:

$$AG(op_N(x) \Rightarrow \exists x_1 \cdot op_1(x_1) \vee \ldots \vee \exists x_p \cdot op_p(x_p))$$

where machine M INCLUDES N, and $op_1, \ldots, op_p$ are the operations of M which invoke this particular operation op_N.

We also include *sequentiality* axioms which express the purely sequential nature of B machines, that at most one instance of a given operation of a machine can be executing at any time, and that no two distinct operations of the same machine can co-execute:

$$AG(\forall a_i;\ a_j \cdot op_i(a_i) \Rightarrow \neg op_j(a_j))$$

for $i, j : 1 \ldots k$, $i \neq j$, where the operations of machine C are $op_1, \ldots, op_k$ and op_i has parameters a_i.

Similarly, for each $i : 1 .. k$:

$$AG(\forall\, a, b \cdot b \neq a \wedge op_i(a) \ \Rightarrow\ \neg\ op_i(b))$$

An important property of this semantics for B machines is that if a refinement MR refines a machine M, via a renaming of variables, and such that all the refinement operations and initialisation are terminating, then $Th(MR)$ is a theory extension of $Th(M)$. This follows from the result that if $[Def_{MR}]\neg\, [Def_M]\neg\, (v = v')$ where v and Def_M are the variables and initialisation/operation definitions of M, and v' and Def_{MR} the corresponding elements of MR, then:

$$\neg\, [Def_{MR}]\neg\, (v' = w) \ \Rightarrow\ \neg\, [Def_M]\neg\, (v = w)$$

where w does not occur in either Def_M or Def_{MR} [14].

It is direct to prove that each axiom of Γ_M is valid in $Th(M1)$ under the interpretation of m by m_state:

1. For each transition tr of M with source s, target t and trigger event α, the axioms

   $$AG(m\_state = s \ \wedge\ \alpha \ \Rightarrow\ tr)$$
   $$AG(tr \ \Rightarrow\ \alpha)$$
   $$AG(m\_state = s \ \wedge\ tr \ \Rightarrow\ AX(m\_state = t))$$

   hold because of the definition of α in $M1$ in the first case, because an operation in an INCLUDED machine can only occur if some operation in the INCLUDING machine which calls it occurs, in the second, and by definition of tr in $M0$, in the third case.
2. $m\_state = init_M$ in the initial state, by definition of the initialisation of $M0$.
3. That at most one transition of M can occur in a step:

   $$AG\neg\, (tr \wedge tr')$$

   for each pair of distinct transitions of M. This holds by the sequentiality axioms for $M0$. The corresponding axiom for events holds by the sequentiality axioms for $M1$.
4. That a transition can only occur if M is in its source state:

   $$AG(tr \ \Rightarrow\ m\_state = s)$$

   where $s = source_M(tr)$. This holds by definition of the operation for tr in $M0$, because of the use of $SELECT$.
5. Locality of M:

   $$AG(\neg\ tr_1 \wedge \ldots \wedge \neg\ tr_N \ \wedge\ m\_state = s \ \Rightarrow\ AX(m\_state = s))$$

   for each $s \in States_M$, where the tr_i are all transition action symbols of M. This holds by the locality axiom for $M0$.   □

At the system level, each static invariant I of an RSDS specification Sys is expressed in the controller B machine of the translation of Sys into B. Each operational invariant is translated into code in the B controller which ensures its truth in the theory of the B translation of Sys. Only temporal invariants of Sys are not expressed in the B translation.

There are additional global axioms in Sys:

1. At a system level we assume that only one sensor event occurs in each step:

$$AG\neg\, (tr \wedge tr')$$

for each pair of transitions tr of Sm, tr' of Sm' where Sm and Sm' are distinct sensor components. Similarly for events of distinct sensor components.

2. A "system locality" principle also states that each actuator event can only occur as a result of a reaction to some sensor event:

$$AG(\beta \;\Rightarrow\; \alpha_1 \vee \ldots \vee \alpha_n)$$

for each β which is an event of some actuator component, and where the α_i are all events of the set of sensor components.

These hold in the B translation because the set of all sensor events of the system are expressed as operations of the B controller, so two distinct events cannot co-occur. System locality follows from the coverage axioms of the actuator B machines, which are INCLUDED into the controller B machine.

The following theorem shows that refinement of control algorithms can either be carried out within the RSDS notation or within B AMN, depending on the preferences of the developer or the requirements of standards.

Theorem If M' and M are state machines, and M' is a refinement of M via an adequate abstraction map σ [13], then the translation of M' to a B refinement $\mathcal{B}(M')$ refines the translation $\mathcal{B}(M)$ of M.

Proof. The B machine for M has the form

```
MACHINE M
INCLUDES N₁, ..., Nᵤ
SETS Statesₘ = { s1, ..., sn }
VARIABLES stateₘ
INVARIANT stateₘ : Statesₘ ∧ Inv
INITIALISATION stateₘ := initₘ
OPERATIONS
    αₘ =
            PRE stateₘ : { sr₁, ..., srₓ }
            THEN
                    IF stateₘ = sr₁
                    THEN stateₘ := tr₁  ||  act
                    ELSE ...
            END

    ⋮

END
```

There is an operation for each member of $Events_M$, and operation definitions have a clause for each transition $t : sr_i \rightarrow tr_i$ for α in M. t has generations $\gamma_1 \frown \ldots \frown \gamma_m$. N_1 to N_u are the modules in the receivers $receivers(M)$ of M.

The structure of the B refinement component for M' is similar, the refinement relation is

$$state_M = \sigma(state_{M'})$$

Then the proof obligations for B refinement can be proved, as follows.

$$Inv_{M'} \wedge R \Rightarrow Inv_M$$

holds because of the typing of σ as a map $States_{M'} \rightarrow States_M$ which preserves Inv_M.

$$[Init_{M'}]\neg [Init_M]\neg R$$

holds because $init_M = \sigma(init_{M'})$.

$$Pre_{\alpha_M} \wedge R \Rightarrow Pre_{\alpha_{M'}}$$

holds because $state_M \in \{t \in Trans_M \wedge event_M(t) = \alpha \bullet source_M(t)\} \wedge R$ implies that for every $s' \in States_{M'}$ which has $\sigma(s') = state_M$, there is some transition t' in $Trans_{M'}$ with $source_{M'}(t') = s'$ and $\sigma(t') = t$ where $source_M(t) = state_M$ (the adequacy property of σ). But then for each possible $state_{M'} = s'$, $s' \in \{t' \in Trans_{M'} \wedge event_{M'}(t') = \alpha \bullet source_{M'}(t')\}$ as required.

$$Pre_{\alpha_M} \wedge R \Rightarrow [Def_{M'}]\neg [Def_M]\neg R$$

holds because the consequent is a conjunction of clauses of the form

$$state_{M'} = sr_i' \Rightarrow [state_{M'} := tr_i']\neg [Def_M]\neg R$$

In turn, the consequents of these can be broken down into a disjunction of clauses

$$state_M = sr_j \wedge tr_j = \sigma(tr_i')$$

But for each concrete transition $t' : sr_i' \rightarrow tr_i'$ in M' for α, $\sigma(t')$ is a transition $sr_j \rightarrow tr_j$ for α in M, for some j. This choice of j serves to validate the disjunction in the consequent of the conjunctive clause for this i. The $\|$-composition act of actions $\gamma_1, \ldots, \gamma_m$ is refined by any sequential composition act' of the same actions because the γ_i are operations of distinct sub-controllers or actuators. Thus the result follows.

5   Verification of Temporal Properties

SMV [3] is a model checker which uses CTL notation. If a formula such as $AG(s2 = Off \rightarrow AF(s2 = On))$ is valid in a model, SMV returns $true$ when run on this model with the formula written in a SPEC clause, otherwise it gives a counter-example sequence of events that reaches a state where the formula fails.

Translation of RSDS to SMV enables liveness properties to be verified which cannot be expressed or verified in Z or B. The approach of [1] to representing and proving temporal properties in B requires an extension of the language. In contrast, our approach separates the proof of temporal properties from the proof of static invariants. The former are carried out by model checking in SMV, and the latter in B.

The general form of the SMV modules generated from an RSDS specification is as follows. For the controller of a system consisting of sensors $S_1, \ldots, S_n$ we construct a controller state machine C whose states are all tuples $(x_1, \ldots, x_n)$ of states $x_1 \in States_{S_1}, \ldots, x_n \in States_{S_n}$ which satisfy the static system and environment invariants. The transitions of C are the transitions of the AND-composition (cartesian product) of $S_1, \ldots, S_n$. From the system invariants we derive the actuator settings which must hold in each state of C (the invariants of the RSDS specification are incomplete if there is not such a unique setting for each state of C).

The SMV module for C is then generated from its statemachine:

```
MODULE Controller
VAR
    global_state: { c1, ..., cm };  // Enumeration of (x1,...,xn) tuples
    con_event: { e1, ..., er };     // All sensor events
DEFINE
    CT1 := con_event = e1 & global_state = c1;
    ...
ASSIGN
    init(global_state) := c_init;  // Initial controller state

    next(global_state) :=
      case
        CT1: c2;
        ...
        1: global_state;
      esac;
```

The boolean CT variables represent all transitions of C, eg, a transition for $e_1 : c_1 \rightarrow c_2$ in the above case.

Sensors are represented by modules

```
MODULE S1(C)
VAR
    s1: { ss1, ..., ssp };
DEFINE
    s1T0 := C.con_event = e1 & s1 = ss1;
    ...
ASSIGN
    init(s1) := s1_init;

    next(s1) :=
      case
        s1T0: ss2;
        ...
        1: s1;
      esac;
```

Each controller event which is also an event of S_1 is used in a definition for the LHS of a case in the *next* statement. The corresponding RHS is the projection of the resulting global state onto S_1.

For actuators the same pattern is followed, except that the *next* statement uses the actuator settings which results from each global transition.

Finally there is a *main* module which combines the separate component modules and links them together:

```
MODULE main
VAR
  C: Controller;
  Ms1: S1(C);
  . .
SPEC AG(AG(Env) -> T1)
...
SPEC AG(AG(Env) -> Tr)
```

Env is the conjunction of (non-static) environmental assumptions. The T_i are all temporal system invariants. The SPEC clauses of *main* must evaluate to true for the specification to be correct.

For the elevating table, the generated SMV code is:

```
MODULE main
VAR
  C : Controller;
  Mbs : bs(C);
  Mts : ts(C);
  Ms3 : s3(C);
  Mtablemotor : tablemotor(C);
SPEC
  AG(AG(C.con_event = s3on -> Mts.ts = On) &
    AG(Mtablemotor.tablemotor = up -> AF(Mts.ts = On)) ->
          (Ms3.s3 = Off  ->  AF(Ms3.s3 = Off & Mts.ts = On)) )

MODULE Controller
VAR
  global_state : { Off_Off_Off, Off_Off_On, Off_On_Off, Off_On_On,
                  On_Off_Off, On_Off_On, On_On_Off, On_On_On };
  con_event : { bson, bsoff, tson, tsoff, s3on, s3off };
DEFINE
  CT0 := con_event = bson & global_state = Off_Off_Off;
  CT1 := con_event = bson & global_state = Off_Off_On;
  ...
  CT23 := con_event = s3off & global_state = On_On_On;
ASSIGN
  init(global_state) := Off_Off_Off;

  next(global_state) :=
    case
      CT0 : On_Off_Off;
```

```
CT1 : On_Off_On;
...
CT23 : On_On_Off;
1 : global_state;
esac;
```

The temporal properties expressed in *main* are verified by the SMV analysis tool, proving the required liveness property. The translation to SMV is highly modular and very similar in its structure to the RSDS module structure and generated B AMN designs, therefore enhancing the possibility of assessment and verification. The translation is significantly simpler than that of [4].

The correctness of this translation is proved by defining:

1. An axiomatic semantics of the subset of SMV that we use, so that for each SMV specification M there is a theory Λ_M which expresses the meaning of M, based on the temporal semantics of SMV given in [4].
2. An interpretation of the theory Γ_{Sys} of an RSDS specification Sys into the theory $\Lambda_{M(Sys)}$ which validates all of the axioms of Γ_{Sys}, where $M(Sys)$ is the SMV translation of Sys.

There is a similar translation for the fine-grain semantics. Details are in [14].

6 Conclusions

We have described the role of RSDS as a bridge between implicit Z-style specifications of a reactive system and explicit B AMN designs, and techniques by which this approach can be enhanced to deal with decomposition of object-oriented models and verification of temporal properties. An advantage of RSDS is the multiple analysis techniques that may be applied to specifications in the language: static invariant analysis using B AMN, temporal analysis using SMV, and consistency and completeness checks built into the RSDS tools. These analyses use a common semantic model (branching time temporal logic models) so that it is easy to relate the results of one analysis to another. For example, a counterexample trace produced from SMV defines a sequence $e_1, \ldots, e_n$ of sensor component events. This sequence corresponds to a possible history of the RSDS specification, and to a possible animation trace of the B translation of the specification in B AMN.

References

1. J. Abrial, L. Mussat, *Introducing Dynamic Constraints in B*, 2nd Conference on the B Method, LNCS 1393, pp. 83–128. Springer-Verlag, 1998.
2. J C Bicarregui, K C Lano, T S E Maibaum, *Objects, Associations and Subsystems: a hierarchical approach to encapsulation*, ECOOP 97, LNCS, 1997.
3. J R Burch, E M Clarke, K L McMillan, D L Dill, J Hwang, *Symbolic Model Checking: 10^{20} States and Beyond*, Proceedings of the Fifth Annual Symposium on Logic in Computer Science, 1990.

4. E. Clarke, W. Heinle, *Modular Translation of Statecharts to SMV*, CMU report, August 2000.
5. E. Emerson, J. Halpern, *'Sometimes' and 'Not never' revisited: On Branching versus Linear Time*, 10th ACM Symposium on Principles of Programming Languages, ACM Press, 1983.
6. J Fiadeiro and T Maibaum. Describing, Structuring and Implementing Objects, in de Bakker *et al.*, **Foundations of Object Oriented languages**, LNCS 489, Springer-Verlag, 1991.
7. S. Goldsack and J. Kramer, *Invariants in the Application-oriented Specification of Control Systems*, Automatica, Vol. 18, No. 2, pp. 71 – 76, 1982.
8. International Electrotechnical Commission. *IEC 61131: Programmable Controllers – Part 3: Programming Languages*, Geneva, 1993.
9. P. Ladkin, *The A300 Crash in Nagoya*, http://www.rvs.uni-bielefeld.de/publications/Incidents/DOCS/FBW.html.
10. K. Lano, *The B Language and Method: A Guide to Practical Formal Development*, Springer-Verlag, June 1996.
11. K. Lano, K. Androutsopoulos, D. Clark, *Structuring and Design of Reactive Systems using RSDS and B*, FASE 2000, LNCS, Springer-Verlag, 2000.
12. K. Lano, K. Androutsopolous, *Structuring Reactive System Specifications in B AMN*, ICFEM 2000, IEEE Computer Society Press, 2000.
13. K. Lano, D. Clark, K. Androutsopoulos, P. Kan, *Invariant-based Synthesis of Fault-tolerant Systems*, FTRTFT 2000.
14. K. Lano, *Semantic Foundations of RSDS*, Department of Computer Science, King's College London, Strand, London WC2R 2LS, 2001.
15. D. Lightfoot, *Formal Specification Using Z*, Palgrave, 2001.
16. Rational Software et al, *OMG Unified Modeling Language Specification Version 1.3*, June 1999.
17. H. Treharne, *Combining Control Executives and Software Specifications*, PhD Thesis, University of London, 2001.

Basic-REAL: Integrated Approach for Design, Specification and Verification of Distributed Systems

V.A. Nepomniaschy, N.V. Shilov, E.V. Bodin, and V.E. Kozura

Institute of Informatics Systems, Russian Academy of Sciences, Siberian Division,
6, Lavrentiev ave., 630090, Novosibirsk, Russia
{vnep,shilov,bodin,kozura}@iis.nsk.su

Abstract. We suggest a three-level integrated approach to design, specification and verification of distributed system. The approach is based on a newly designed specification language Basic-REAL (bREAL) and comprises (I) translation of a high-level design of distributed systems to executional specifications of bREAL, (II) presentation of high-level properties of distributed systems as logical specifications of bREAL, (III) problem-oriented compositional deductive reasoning coupled with model-checking. The paper presents syntax and semantics of bREAL in formal and informal levels, some meta-properties of this language (namely, stuttering invariance and interleaving concurrency), proof-principles and model-checking for progress properties. An illustrative example (Passenger and Vending Machine) is also presented.

1 Introduction

The standard formal description techniques (FDT) such as SDL are widely used in practice for design of distributed systems. Verification of FDT specifications, i.e., proving their safety, progress and other properties, is an actual research problem. Verification approaches are based on formal semantics of FDT specifications, suitable language for properties presentation and on feasible and sound verification techniques.

Concise formal semantics has been suggested for some particular fragments of SDL [5,11,12,19,22], though a complete formal semantics of SDL-96 has more than 500 pages. Due to lack of feasible formal semantics of SDL, a popular approach to verification of properties of SDL specifications comprises a property-conservative translation/simulation of the specifications to another intermediate formalism, and formal verification of the translated specifications against the desired properties [3,4], but soundness of this simulation is usually justified by informal or quasi-formal arguments.

Temporal logic is a popular formalism for presentation of the properties of SDL specifications. Different temporal logics have been suggested for representation of safety and progress properties: linear temporal logic LTL [3], branching temporal logic CTL [7,19], metric temporal logic MTL [16], temporal logic of actions TLA+ [13], etc. We would like to remark that these formalisms are external for SDL lead to complicated formulae for presentation of real-time properties.

M. Butler, L. Petre, and K. Sere (Eds.): IFM 2002, LNCS 2335, pp. 69–88, 2002.

Two techniques are mainly used for proving properties of the formal models of distributed systems, namely, model-checking and deductive reasoning. The standard model-checking has been successfully used for finite systems, while deductive reasoning is oriented to parameterized and infinite state systems. The automatic nature is the main advantage of the model-checking, while deductive reasoning implies a manual design of proof-outlines and the level of automatization is limited by proof-checking.

As follows from the above arguments, the intermediate formalism is a very critical issue for sound verification of SDL specifications. We suppose that a proper intermediate formalism should meet certain requirements, some of which are enumerated below:

1. SDL-like syntax and semantics,
2. modest blow up in size against SDL specifications,
3. integration with presentation of properties,
4. verification-oriented and human-friendly formal semantics,
5. opportunity for proving meta-level properties and reasoning,
6. support for a variety of verification techniques and their integration.

Let us discuss from viewpoint of these requirements some intermediate formalisms which have been used for SDL. A formal language φ^-SDL [1] is a limited version of SDL. Its semantics is based on process algebras [1]. This language does not cover all structural aspects of SDL, and it is not integrated with presentation of properties. Another intermediate language IF [4] is used for modeling static SDL specifications. It has a considerable expressive power and formal operational semantics, but its meta-level reasoning remains quasi-formal. Although the input language Promela of model-checker SPIN is a convenient formalism for presentation of static SDL specifications [3], and it is well-integrated with linear temporal logic, its complex semantics is not oriented to meta-level reasoning and it has been designed for model-checking temporal properties of finite-state systems only. Thus we can summarize that none of the discussed intermediate formalisms simultaneously meets the constraints listed above.

The aim of the paper is to present our approach to verification of distributed systems specified in SDL-like style. The approach is based on a new intermediate high-level specification language Basic-REAL (bREAL) and meets the requirements listed above. The rest of the paper consists of six sections. The main constructs of bREAL are informally explained in Section 2, while formal context-free syntax is presented in Appendix 1. Section 2 also presents an illustrative example "Passenger and Vending Machine", while the corresponding SDL specification and executional bREAL specification are presented in Appendices 2 and 3. The structural operational semantics of bREAL is sketched in Sections 3, 4 and 5. Two theorems about important meta-properties of bREAL semantics are given in Section 6. Verification techniques based on finite-state model-checking and deductive-like reasoning are discussed in Section 7. Logical specification and verification of the example "Passenger and Vending Machine" are presented in Section 8. In Conclusion the results and prospects of our approach are discussed.

2   Outline of Basic-REAL

Informal[1] introduction of syntax and semantics. bREAL has executional
and logical specifications. Logical specifications are used for properties presentation. They have hierarchical structure based on predicates. The predicates can
be grouped into formulae. Formulae, in turn, make up higher level formulae. Distributed systems are presented as executional specifications. They have a hierarchical structure based on processes. The processes can be grouped into blocks.
Blocks, in turn, make up higher level blocks. Channels are used for communication between such entities as processes, blocks, and the external environment.
From the viewpoint of a process, each of its channels is external (input or output
one). From the viewpoint of a block, each of its channels is inner if the channel
connects its subblocks. A channel is external (input or output one) for a block
if it connects a subblock with outside environment (for example, other blocks).

In general, a specification (executional or logical) consists of a head, a scale,
a context, a scheme, and subspecification(s). The head defines the specification
name and kind: an executional specification is either a process or a block, and
a logical one is either a predicate or a formula. Processes and predicates are
elementary specifications, blocks and formulae are composite specifications.

Every activity in bREAL has an associated time interval. Time intervals
are expressed in terms of time units. Every time unit is a tick of a special
clock. A collection of special clocks is a multiple clock. A scale is a finite set
of linear integer (in)equalities where time units are variables. A priory, ticks of
all clocks are asynchronous and have uninterpreted values, but scales introduce
some synchronization. For example, a scale { 60 *sec* = 1 *min*; 60 *min* =
1 *hour*; 24 *hour* = 1 *day*; } does not define any particular value for time units
sec, *min*, *hour* and *day*, but impose the standard relation between them.

A context of a specification consists of type definitions, variable and channel
declarations. Let us note that every variable can be declared as a program or a
quantifier variable but not both. The values of the quantifier variables can not be
changed in executional specifications, they can be varied by the (universal and
existential) quantifiers in logical specifications. The values of program variables
can be changed by assignments and parameter passing in executional specifications. Channels are intended for passing signals with possible parameters. They
can have different inner structures, viz., queues, stacks, bags.

A scheme of a logical specification consists of a diagram and a system list.
The system list consists of the name(s) of the executional (sub)specification(s)
whose properties are described by the logical specification. There are four kinds
of predicate diagrams: relations between values, locators of the control flow,
emptiness/overflow controllers for channels, checkers for signals in channels. A
diagram of a formula is constructed from name(s) of (sub)specification(s) by
propositional combinations, quantification over quantifier variables, and special
dynamic/temporal expressions. Dynamic/temporal expressions are bREAL for-

---

[1]   Formal definition of bREAL syntax can be found in [21]. The context-free syntax is
given in Appendix 1. Please refer for syntax details if necessary.

malism for reasoning about every/some fair behaviours of distributed systems and every/some time moment in temporal intervals. This formalism expands the branching temporal logic CTL [9] by means of explicit time intervals in terms of time units in temporal modalities and explicit references to executional specifications in action modalities in style of dynamic logic [14]. There are several reasons why we prefer the explicit style of dynamic logic instead of the implicit style of CTL. The main ones are opportunities for explicit transformations, optimizations, (bi)simulation and compositional reasoning for executional specifications to be verified.

A scheme of an executional specification consists of a diagram and a finite set of fairness conditions. Fairness conditions restrict a set of behaviours: bREAL considers only the "fair behaviours", i.e., the behaviours where every fairness condition holds infinitely often.

A block diagram consists of channel routes. A route connects a subblock with another subblock or (exclusively) with the (external) environment. In the last case the channel is called an *input* or *output* channel. Otherwise, the channel is called an *inner* channel. All sub-blocks of a block work in parallel, and they interact with each other and with the external environment by sending/reading signals with parameters via channels.

A process diagram consists of transitions. Every transition consists of a control state, a body, a time interval, and a (non-deterministic, maybe) jump to next control states. The body of a transition determines the following actions: to read a signal from an input channel (and to assign the values of the parameters to program variables); to write a signal into an output channel (with parameter passing by value); to clean an input or output channel; to execute a (non-deterministic, maybe) sequential program. Each of the actions is atomic, but it can happen only within the time interval specified for the transition. Each process is sequential. A process communicates with the other processes and the environment by means of input/output channels.

An Illustrative Example: "Passenger and Vending Machine". Let us consider the following example: a protocol Σ of serving a passenger by a vending-machine. The vending-machine keeps the money received from the passenger and has the following features: a keyboard with stations, return, and request buttons; a slot for coins; an indicator for showing a sum; a tray for change; a booking window. The passenger knows a desired destination, has enough money and can: press buttons on the keyboard; drop coins into the slot; see readings of the indicator; get coins from the change tray; get a ticket from the booking window. We consider a good passenger who has enough money to pay for the ticket and requests the ticket only when enough money has been paid. Vending machine and passenger can be time-independent (time-free case) or time-dependent (timed case). In the former case no time constraints are imposed on any activity or event, in the later case stricture constraints are imposed on every activity and event. Thus in timed case a slow passenger may not get the ticket after all.

An SDL specification of the time-free protocol is presented in Appendix 2. The top-level view is presented below:

This top-level view is also a block diagram for the corresponding bREAL specification. Appendix 3 presents other fragments of the corresponding bREAL specification. A complete bREAL specification can be assembled from these fragments and the block diagram by adding context and fairness conditions to the machine diagram and a context to the block diagram.

A protocol Σ is specified as a block which consists of two processes, namely, the process **passenger** and the process **machine**. These processes are connected by five channels. Two of them (**buttons** and **slot**) are directed from the passenger to the machine. The other three channels (**indicator**, **change**, and **booking**) are from the machine to the passenger. A behaviour of the process **machine** is fair if the process cannot stay forever in a state other than waiting for input signals. A behaviour of the process **passenger** is fair if the process cannot stay forever in a state other than waiting for input signals. It should be noted also that there are two different cases for $\Sigma - \Sigma_{fin}$ and Σ_{par}: in the former case of Σ_{fin}, ticket price is fixed; in the later case of Σ_{par}, ticket price is a parameter. The specification of the time-free protocol has explicit time intervals FROM NOW TILL FOREVER. This case is presented in [21]. The specification of timed protocol is a variation of time-free specification where time intervals are parameterized as FROM $const'$ TILL $const''$.

3   Foundations of Semantics of Basic-REAL

Data Domains and Channel Structures. A model with channel structures is a triple $M = (DOM, INT, CHS)$, where a non-empty set is the domain DOM of the model, INT is an interpretation of relation and operation symbols over DOM, and CHS is a collection of available data structures for channels. Moreover, DOM includes integers and INT provides the standard interpretation for integer arithmetic operations and relations. DOM includes arrays and INT provides the standard interpretation for array operations $UpDate$ and $Apply$. A data structure of a channel is a mapping which binds every channel with a set of possible contents. Every content is a finite oriented graph whose vertices are marked by signals with vectors of parameter values. For every particular channel structure $DAT \in CHS$, two monadic relations (EMP and FUL), two partial non-deterministic operations (PUT and GET) and one constant (INI) are defined. Let DOM^{PAR} be a set of parameter value vectors from DOM, dom and rng be the domain and range of the operations, and SIG be a finite set of all signals admissible for the channel. Then

$EMP = \{INI\}, PUT : (DAT \times SIG \times DOM^{PAR}) \rightarrow DAT,$
$dom(PUT) = (DAT \setminus FUL) \times SIG \times DOM^{PAR}, rng(PUT) = DAT \setminus EMP,$
$GET : DAT \rightarrow (DAT \times SIG \times DOM^{PAR}), dom(GET) = DAT \setminus EMP,$
$rng(GET) = ((DAT \setminus FUL) \times SIG \times DOM^{PAR}).$

If $graph \in DAT \setminus FUL$, $signal \in SIG$ and $vector \in DOM^{PAR}$, then the graph $PUT(graph, signal, vector)$ is constructed by adding a new vertex with several adjacent edges and by marking the new vertex by the pair $(signal, vector)$. If $graph \in DAT \setminus EMP$, then the triple $(graph', signal, vector)$ is in $GET(graph)$ iff $graph'$ results from removing some vertex with all adjacent edges. Standard (un)bounded queues, stacks, and multisets (bags) are compatible with this notion of CHS. For example, let us consider a channel with stack access discipline to data for three admissible signals $\{a, b, c\}$ with a single integer parameter. A particular structure $DAT \in CHS$ for this channel is the set of finite chains (including the empty chain Λ) $sig_1(int_1) \longleftarrow ...sig_n(int_n)$, where $n \geq 0$, and $sig_i \in \{a, b, c\}$, $int_i \in Int$ for all $i \in [1..n]$. Relation EMP holds on the empty chain only, while another relation FUL does not hold at all. PUT and GET operations are illustrated below:

$$\left(sig_1(int_1) \longleftarrow ... sig_n(int_n) , \ sig(int) \right)$$
$$GET \uparrow \qquad \downarrow PUT$$
$$sig_1(int_1) \longleftarrow ... sig_n(int_n) \longleftarrow sig(int)$$

Time and Clocks. Informally speaking, every time unit is a tact of a special clock. All clocks are used for measuring time after some fixed moment in the past. A scale is a set of linear (in)equalities with time units as variables. Scales are used for synchronization of speed of clocks. Formally speaking, a time measure is a positive integer solution of the scale as a system of (in)equalities. We will identify a time measure MSR with a mapping which associates each time $unit$ with its value $MSR(unit)$. With a fixed time measure MSR, an indication of a multiple clock T is a mapping of time units into integer numbers so that there exists an integer t such that for every time $unit$, we have: $T(unit) = [\frac{t}{MSR(unit)}]$. Just for example let us consider a scale $\{ 60\ sec = 1\ min;\ 60\ min = 1\ hour;\ 24\ hour = 1\ day; \}$. A possible time measure MSR is $\{ sec \mapsto 2,\ min \mapsto 120,\ hour \mapsto 7200,\ day \mapsto 172800 \}$. Then $T = \{ sec \mapsto 325,\ min \mapsto 5,\ hour \mapsto 0,\ day \mapsto 0 \}$ is a possible indication of the multiple clock $(sec, min, hour, day)$, since there exists an integer t (ex., 651) such that $T(sec) = 325 = [\frac{t}{2}] = [\frac{t}{MSR(sec)}]$, $T(min) = 5 = [\frac{t}{120}] = [\frac{t}{MSR(min)}]$, $T(hour) = 0 = [\frac{t}{7200}] = [\frac{t}{MSR(hour)}]$, $T(day) = 325 = [\frac{t}{172800}] = [\frac{t}{MSR(day)}]$. In contrast, another mapping $T = \{ sec \mapsto 0,\ min \mapsto 0,\ hour \mapsto 5,\ day \mapsto 325 \}$ can not be an indication for the time measure MSR.

Configurations. Let SYS be an executional specification the of bREAL language. Let us fix a model with structures for channels $M = (DOM, INT, CHS)$ and a time measure MSR. Let $PR^1, ... PR^k$ be all processes of SYS. An extended name (of a variable, a state or a channel) is the name itself preceded by the "path" of sub-block names in accordance with the nesting. A configuration CNF of SYS is a quadruple (T, V, C, S), where T is the indication of the multiple clock, V is the evaluation of variables, C is the contents of the channels, S is the control flow. The evaluation of variables is a mapping that maps every extended name of every variable of the processes $PR^1, ..., PR^k$ to its value from

DOM. The current flow is a pair (ACT, DEL) where ACT is a set of extended names of active states and DEL is a mapping that maps extended names of states of the processes PR^1, ..., PR^k to delays (the indication of a special local multiple clocks associated with states). For every individual process there is a single active state.

A *merge operation* $\mathcal{M}(CNF^1, ..., CNF^k)$ is said to be possible for the configurations $CNF^1 = (T^1, V^1, C^1, S^1)$, ..., $CNF^k = (T^k, V^k, C^k, S^k)$ of the processes PR^1, ..., PR^k iff $T^1 = ... = T^k$ and for every *channel* and for all processes PR^i and PR^j, which shared it as an input/output channel, $C^i(channel) = C^j(channel)$. If the merge is possible, then the result of the merge is a configuration $CNF = (T, V, C, S)$ of the executional specification SYS such that for every $0 \leq i \leq k$: $T = T^i$; the values V^i of the variables of the process PR^i coincides with the values V of their extended names; the contents C^i of the channels of the process PR^i coincides with the contents C of their extended names; the active state and the delays S^i for the states of the process PR^i coincides with the active states and delays for their extended name. When the sub-blocks are considered instead of the processes, the merge is defined in a similar way. If BLK is a sub-block of an executional specification SYS, and $CNF = (T, V, C, S)$ is the configuration of SYS, then the *projection of CNF to BLK* (denoted by CNF/BLK) is a configuration $CNF' = (T', V', C', S')$ of the sub-block BLK such that $T' = T$; for every *variable* $V'(variable) = V(BLK.variable)$; for every *channel* $C'(channel) = C(BLK.channel)$; for every *state* $state \in S'.ACT = BLK.state \in S.ACT$ and $S'DEL(state) = S.DEL(BLK.state)$. It is easy to prove by induction over the specification structure that a configuration of an executional specification is the merge of its projections to all its processes, i.e., $CNF = \mathcal{M}(CNF/PR^1, ..., CNF/PR^k)$.

4   The Semantics of Executional Specifications

Step Rules and Semantics of Blocks. The semantics of the executional specifications is defined in terms of events (EVN) and step rules. There are six kinds of events:

1. writing a signal with parameters into a channel (WRiTing),
2. reading a signal with parameters from a channel (ReaDiNg),
3. cleaning an input channel (CLeaNing INput),
4. cleaning an output channel (CLeaNing OUTput),
5. program execution (EXEcution),
6. invisible event (INVisible).

A *firing* is a triple $CNF1 < EVN > CNF2$. If $EVN \neq INV$, then the firing is said to be *active*. Otherwise, it is called *passive*. A step rule has the form CND $\models CNF1 < EVN > CNF2$, where $CNF1 < EVN > CNF2$ is a firing while CND is a condition on the configurations $CNF1$, $CNF2$ and the event EVN. An intuitive semantics of the step rule is as follows: if the condition CND holds, then the executional specification can transform the configuration $CNF1$ into the configuration $CNF2$ by means of the event EVN. In total, there exist twelve step rules for executional specifications. A countable sequence of configurations is a behaviour of a specification iff, for every successive pair of configurations $CNF1$ and $CNF2$ of this sequence, there exists an event EVN and a condition CND, such that CND $\models CNF1 < EVN > CNF2$ is an instance of a corresponding step rule. Below are presented some steps rules[2]. A behaviour of an executional specification is said to be fair iff each of the fairness conditions of the specification holds infinitely often in the configurations of this behaviour.

Semantics of blocks For blocks there is a single step rule, namely, the composition rule. Informally, a behaviour of a block is an interleaving merge of consistent behaviours of its sub-blocks. Let us fix a model with channel structures M, a scale MSR, and a block B, consisting of the sub-blocks $B_1, ..., B_k$.

RULE 0 (Composition)
$$\begin{pmatrix} \forall i \in [1..k] \ : \\ CNF1/B_i < EVN/B_i > CNF2/B_i \end{pmatrix} \models CNF1 < EVN > CNF2.$$

Semantics of Processes. The other eleven step rules deal with individual processes and the environment. For simplicity of presentation, let us fix a process and the two configurations, $CNF1 = (T1, V1, C1, S1)$ and $CNF2 = (T2, V2, C2, S2)$. Let us use meta-variables $state$, $state'$, $nextstate$, $signal$, $variable$, $variable'$, $channel$, $channel'$, $interval$, $program$ and $jumpset$ (for sets of states). Let us fix values of $state$, $nextstate$, $signal$, $variable$, $channel$, $program$ and $jumpset$ so that $nextstate \in jumpset$.

Process stuttering and stabilization. The first rule for a process is a stutter rule. Informally, it concerns the case when nothing changes in the process. This rule is essential for the interleaving merge of consistent behaviours of some processes with shared channels into a behaviour of a block.

The second rule deals with stabilization and it means that a process is in a state which does not mark any transition on the process diagram. Thus, the process stabilizes forever, and the configuration of the process cannot change and is called a stable configuration.

Signal reading and writing. The third and fourth rules deal with a process reading a signal with a parameter from an input channel and writing a signal with a parameter into an output channel, respectively. For simplicity let us present and discuss the rule for writing a signal with a single implicit parameter.

RULE 4 (Writing a signal)
$$\begin{pmatrix} \text{The diagram has the transition} \\ state \ \texttt{WRITE} \ signal(variable)\texttt{INTO} \ channel \ interval\texttt{JUMP} \ jumpset, \\ state \in ACT1, \ nextstate \in ACT2, \ DEL1(state) \in interval, \\ T1 = T2, (\forall state' \ : \ DEL2(state') = 0), \ V1 = V2, \\ PUT(C1(channel), signal, V1(variable)) = C2(channel), \\ (\forall channel' \neq channel \ : \ C1(channel') = C2(channel')) \end{pmatrix}$$
$$\models CNF1 < WRT(channel, signal, variable) > CNF2.$$

This rule can be commented as follows. The process can write the $signal$, if it has a corresponding transition, and a control state of this transition is active

---

[2] The complete semantics is given in [21].

($state \in ACT1$) for a time which is the range of the time interval of the transition ($DEL1(state) \in interval$). Writing is an instant action ($T1 = T2$) which resets delays for all states of the process ($\forall state' : DEL2(state') = 0$). This action does not change values of variables and content of channels other than a channel to which it writes ($V1 = V2$ and $\forall channel' \neq channel : C1(channel') = C2(channel')$). In contrast, the content of this channel absorbs the signal with a value of a variable as the parameter value in accordance with structure of the channel ($C2(channel) = PUT(C1(channel), signal, V1(variable))$). The action passes control to some next state ($nextstate \in ACT2$).

Impact of external environment. The fifth and the sixth rules deal with appearance of a new signal with a parameter in an input channel and with disappearance of a signal with a parameter from an output channel. The environment ENV is responsible for those actions. The process itself can only observe the appearance of a new signal in an input channel or that some signal disappears from an output channel. *Signal* and *parameter* are legal for an input (output) *channel* if there is a transition with body READ *signal*(*parameter*) FROM *channel* (resp. WRITE *signal*(*parameter*) INTO *channel*). In accordance with the composition rule, if a process is combined with other process(es) into a block, then appearance of a new signal in its input channel corresponds to writing this signal into this channel by the partner process. Similarly, if a process is combined with other process(es) into a block, then disappearance of a signal from its output channel corresponds to reading this signal from this channel by the partner process. For simplicity, let us present the rule for appearance of a signal with a single implicit parameter.

RULE 5 (Appearance of a signal in an input channel)

$$\left(\begin{array}{l} Signal \text{ and } parameter \text{ are legal for an input } channel, \\ T1 = T2, \ V1 = V2, \ ACT1 = ACT2, \ DEL1 = DEL2, \\ PUT(C1(channel), signal, parameter) = C2(channel), \\ (\forall channel' \neq channel : C1(channel') = C2(channel')) \end{array}\right)$$
$$\models CNF1 < INV > CNF2.$$

Channel cleaning and program execution. The seventh and the eighth rules are the rules of cleaning the input and the output channels. The ninth rule for a process is the rule of program execution.

Time progress and starvation. The tenth rule deals with time progress. It concerns the case when nothing has changed except the value of the multiple clock and the synchronous local multiple clock of every current delay, and there is a transition marked by the active state such that its current delay has not exceeded the right bound of the corresponding time interval.

RULE 10 (Time progress)

$$\left(\begin{array}{l} T1 < T2, \ V1 = V2, \ C1 = C2, \ ACT1 = ACT2, \\ (\forall state \in ACT1 : DEL2(state) = DEL1(state) + T2 - T1), \\ (\forall state \notin ACT1 : DEL2(state) = 0), \\ (\forall state \in ACT1 : \exists transition : transition \text{ is marked by } state, \text{ and} \\ DEL1(state) \text{ does not exceed the right bound of time interval of } transition) \end{array}\right)$$
$$\models CNF1 < INV > CNF2.$$

The eleventh rule deals with a starvation. It is similar to the time-progress rule, but in this case a current delay of an active state surpasses the right bounds of time intervals of all transitions marked by the active state. It means that the process failed to read or write a signal during the specified time interval.

RULE 11 (Starvation)

$$\begin{pmatrix} T1 < T2, \ V1 = V2, \ C1 = C2, \ ACT1 = ACT2, \\ (\forall state \in ACT1 \ : \ DEL2(state) = DEL1(state) + T2 - T1), \\ (\forall state \notin ACT1 \ : \ DEL2(state) = 0), \\ (\forall state \in ACT1 \ : \ \forall transition \ : state \text{ marks } transition \Rightarrow \\ DEL1(state) \text{ exceeds the right bound of time interval of } transition) \end{pmatrix}$$
$$\models CNF1 < INV > CNF2.$$

5   The Semantics of Logical Specifications

The semantics of logical specifications is defined in terms of validity in the configurations. For every configuration CNF and every logical specification SPC, $CNF \models SPC$ means that the configuration belongs to the truth set of the logical specification, and $CNF \not\models SPC$ means the negation of this fact. In order to shorten the description of the semantics, let us fix a model with channel structures M, a scale MSR, and a configuration $CNF = (T, V, C, S)$. Let the relation $CNF \models SPC$ be defined by induction on structure of the diagram of a logical specification SPC.

Semantics of Predicates. A predicate[3] can be a relation, a locator, a controller, or a checker. If SPC is a relation, then its diagram has the form $R(t1, \ldots, t2)$, where R is a relation symbol, and $t1$, $\ldots$, $t2$ are terms constructed from the operation symbols, variables and parameters of channels and $CNF \models SPC \Leftrightarrow$ $(VAL_{CNF}(t1), \ldots, VAL_{CNF}(t2)) \in INT(R)$, where evaluation VAL_{CNF} for terms is defined by the ordinary rules. If SPC is a locator, then its diagram has the form AT $state$ and $CNF \models SPC \Leftrightarrow state \in S.ACT$. If SPC is a controller, then its diagram has the form EMP $channel$ or FUL $channel$ and $CNF \models$ $SPC \Leftrightarrow$ EMP$(C(channel))$, $CNF \models SPC \Leftrightarrow$ FUL$(C(channel))$, respectively. If SPC is a checker, then its diagram has the form $signal$ IN $channel$ or $signal$ RD $channel$. In the former case, $CNF \models SPC$ iff there exists a $value$ from DOM, such that there exists a pair $(signal, value)$ in $C(channel)$. In the latter case, $CNF \models SPC$ iff there exists a $graph$ from DAT and a $value$ from DOM, such that $GET(C(channel)) = (graph, signal, value)$.

Semantics of Formulae. The diagram of a formula[3] can be a name of a predicate, a propositional combination of subformulae, a quantified subformula, or a dynamic expression.

If the diagram of SPC is a name of a predicate, then $CNF \models SPC \Leftrightarrow$ $CNF \models PRD$, where PRD is the predicate with this name. If the diagram of SPC is a propositional combination, then its value is determined in a natural way.

---

[3] Please refer the syntax definition in Appendix 1.

If the diagram of SPC is $\forall$ *variable DGR* or $\exists$ *variable DGR*, where DGR is a formula diagram, then $CNF \models SPC$ iff for every/some configuration CNF' which agrees with CNF everywhere but *variable*, the following holds: $CNF' \models SPDGR$, where $SPDGR$ is a formula with diagram DGR.

If the diagram of SPC is M_B SYS M_T I_T DGR, where M_B is a modality AB or EB, SYS is an executional specification, M_T is a modality AT or ET, I_T is a time interval, and DGR is a formula diagram, then we have the following. Prefix "AB/EB SYS" means "for every/some fair behaviour of SYS". Prefix "AT/ET I_T" means "for every/some time moment in I_T".

6 Some Meta-properties of Basic-REAL Semantics

In [15] a property of invariance under stuttering was introduced. It means that expressible properties are not affected by duplication of some configurations. The following definitions, Theorem 1 and Corollary 1 state that bREAL enjoys the invariance under stuttering.

Let us fix the model M with structures for channels and the time measure MSR. For all behaviours $SEQA$ and $SEQB$, $SEQB$ is said to be obtained from $SEQA$ by copying (configurations) (or $SEQB$ is a *copy-extension* of $SEQA$) iff some configurations in $SEQA$ are duplicated in $SEQB$, i.e., $SEQA = CNF_0 \ ... \ CNF_i \ ...,$ $SEQB = CNF_0...CNF_0 \ ... \ CNF_i...CNF_i \ ...$. For all sets of behaviours $SETA$ and $SETB$, $SETB$ is said to be obtained from $SETA$ by copying configurations (or $SETB$ is a *copy-extension* of $SETA$) iff

- every behaviour in $SETB$ is a copy-extension of a behaviour in $SETA$,
- for every behaviour in $SETA$ has a copy-extension in $SETB$.

Theorem 1. *Let SYS be an executional bREAL specifications. For all behaviours $SEQA$ and $SEQB$, if $SEQB$ is a copy-extension of $SEQA$, then $SEQB$ is a (fair) behaviour of SYS iff $SEQA$ is.*

Corollary 1. *For every set of configurations PRP and every interval I_T, for all sets of behaviours $SETA$ and $SETB$, if $SETB$ is a copy-extension of $SETA$, then dynamic/temporal expressions (M_B $SETB$ M_T I_T PRP) and (M_B $SETA$ M_T I_T PRP) are equivalent.*

An interleaving character of bREAL concurrency is stated in the following Theorem 2 and Corollary 2. It implies (in particular) an interleaving access to shared channels, i.e. impossibility of synchronous access to them.

Theorem 2. *Let SYS be an executional bREAL specification, let $CNF1$ and $CNF2$ be its configurations, and $PR^1,... PR^k$ be all its subprocesses, and EVN be an event.*

(2.1) $CNF1 < INV > CNF2$ is a firing of SYS iff $CNF1/PR^i < INV > CNF2/PR^i$ is a firing of PR^i for every i in $1..k$.

(2.2) $CNF1 < EVN > CNF2$ is an active firing of SYS iff there exists a single j in $1..k$ such that $CNF1/PR^j < INV > CNF2/PR^j$ an active firing of PR^j.

Corollary 2. *Let SYS be an executional bREAL specification and $PR^1, ... PR^k$ be all its subprocesses. The set of all behaviours of SYS is equal to the set of behaviours $CNF_0 ... CNF_n ... ...$ such that for every i in $1..k$ and for every $n \geq 0$ there exists an event EVN_n^i for which*
(1) $CNF_n/PR^i < EVN_n^i > CNF_{n+1}/PR^i$ is a firing of PR^i,
(2) $EVN_n^i \neq INV \Rightarrow EVN_n^j = INV$ for every $j \neq i$.

Proofs of Theorems 1 and 2 can be found in [21].

7   Verification Techniques

Problem-Oriented Deduction for Basic-REAL. Our deductive approach is inspirited by the problem-oriented approach adopted in [8,17,18]. This approach assumes

- classification properties into classes of problems with respect to their semantics and syntax;
- formulation and justification of problem-oriented proof principles for every problem class.

We would like to point out that in general the proof-principles are not inference rules, since they exploit some higher order notions like sets, partitions, well-foundness, etc.

Let us explain our problem-oriented approach to deductive reasoning by a class of time-free progress properties, i.e., the class of the properties which can be presented in the bREAL logical specification by means of formulae with diagrams ($A \Rightarrow$ AB SYS ET FROM NOW TILL FOREVER B), where A and B are subdiagrams and SYS is a fixed name of an executional specification. Let us denote diagrams of this kind by $A \mapsto B$. That is, for every configuration $CNF \models (A \mapsto B)$ iff $CNF \models A$ implies that for every fair behaviour of SYS that starts from CNF, there exists a configuration CNF' from this behaviour such that $CNF' \models B$.

To formulate the proof principles, let us fix the executional specification SYS. Let SET' and SET'' (with possible subscripts) denote sets of configurations of SYS. The semantics of the expression $SET' \mapsto SET''$ is as follows: for every fair behaviour of SYS, if this behaviour begins in SET', then it contains a configuration in SET''. Thus, if SET' and SET'' are the truth sets of logical specifications with the diagrams A and B, respectively, then $SET' \mapsto SET''$ is equivalent to $A \mapsto B$. Note that the following concept of a *fair firing* is used: a fair firing is a firing that begins a fair behaviour.

   1. Subset principle
$SET' \subseteq SET'' \vdash SET' \mapsto SET''$ or in the logical form $A \rightarrow B \vdash A \mapsto B$.

   2. Partition/Union principle
For every set of indices I
$\{SET_i' \mapsto SET_i'' \ : \ i \in I\} \vdash (U_{i \in I} SET_i') \mapsto (U_{i \in I} SET_i'')$
or in the logical form $\forall i \in I.(A_i \mapsto B_i) \vdash (\exists i \in I \ : \ A_i) \mapsto (\exists i \in I \ : \ B_i)$.

   3. Single step principle
$\vdash \{CNF'\} \mapsto \{CNF'' : \text{there exists a fair firing } CNF' < EVN > CNF''\}$.

4. Transitivity principle

$$SET' \mapsto SET, \ SET \mapsto SET'' \ \vdash SET' \mapsto SET''$$

or in the logical form $A \mapsto B, \ B \mapsto C \ \vdash \ A \mapsto C$.

5. Principle of mapping to a well-founded set

Let SET be a set of configurations. Let WFS be a well-founded set (i.e., a partially ordered set without infinite descending chains) and let MIN be the set of minimal elements of the set WFS. Let $f : SET \xrightarrow{\text{partial}} WFS$ be a partial function and let $f^- : WFS \xrightarrow{\text{partial}} \mathcal{P}(SET)$ be the inverse function such that $f^-(w) = \{CNF \in SET : f(CNF) = w\}$ for every $v \in WFS$. Then the principle of mapping to a well-founded set is as follows:

$$\left(\forall \ v \in WFS \setminus MIN \ : \ f^-(v) \mapsto \cup_{u < v} f^-(u) \right) \vdash f^-(WFS) \mapsto f^-(MIN).$$

Model-Checking for Basic-REAL. There are many opportunities to exploit model-checking for verification of bREAL specifications. Let us enumerate some of them:

1. overall verification of finite-space time-free specifications;
2. overall verification of infinite-space time-bounded specifications;
3. validation of conditions of above two types in deductive proofs.

The first case is classical problem domain for model-checking. In the second case, when we would like to verify the time-bounded properties (e.g., that nothing bad happens in, say, first ten hours), the model may be safely cut off when the specification clock exceeds a time limit. It is done by detecting that a special "time" variable reaches a given value.

In the last case, a proof is designed manually in terms of problem-oriented proof-principles with extensive finite-space/time-free or infinite-space/time-bounded conditions and then their correctness is model-checked. Thus we integrate model-checking and deductive reasoning neither as a tactics, nor as a decision procedure, but as a checker for applicability of proof principles (see example in the next section).

Our model-checking tool is implemented as an application programming interface (API) and consists of the following three modules: a model-constructor for executional specifications, a translator from logical specifications, a kernel model-checker. Let us note that the model is an extended finite automaton whose states are configurations of the executional specification, and whose transitions are the firings of the transitions of the executional specification. It should be noted also that the kernel model-checker has been developed on the base of the faster model-checking algorithm for the μ-Calculus in finite models [10]. A preliminary tool version for time-free properties only has been presented in [2].

8   Verification of the Example

Logical Specification. We would like to discuss both time-free and timed properties of the system "Passenger and Vending Machine" presented in Section 2. Let us give at first a logical specification of the following time-free property: a good passenger will eventually get the ticket to the desired station. Or, more formally, for all ticket prices, for every station, the condition A leads to the condition B where A is the conjunction of the five conditions: the machine is ready, the passenger wants to buy a ticket, no button is stuck, the indicator shows no information, the booking is empty, and B is the conjunction of the two conditions: there is a ticket in the booking window, and a station on the ticket is the needed one. Let us use the abbreviations "p" for "passenger" and "m" for "machine", respectively. The predicates for these (seven) conditions are st_mach, st_pass, no_comm, no_info, no_tick, tick_in, and prop_st, respectively. Let us denote the conjunction of the first five predicates by init: st_mach & st_pass & no_comm & no_info & no_tick. In this notation the time-free property can be expressed as a logical specification $SPEC1$ with diagram

$\forall$ m.expenses : $\forall$ p.station : $\big($init$\mapsto$tick_in & prop_st$\big)$.

Let us turn to timed property, namely: a quick passenger will eventually get the ticket to the desired station, a sluggish passenger either will never get the ticket to the desired station or may get it sometimes. Let $RushTime$ and $SlowTime$ be (parameterized) integers

$RushTime = Const1 * MaxPrice/MinCoin + Const2$,
$SlowTime = Const3 * MaxPrice/MinCoin + Const4$,

with MaxPrice for the maximal possible expenses, MinCoin for the smallest coin in use, $const1$–4 for parameters. Let $pFAST$ express the fact that the passenger is fast enough to drop coins in time, let $pSLOWEST$ mean that the passenger can't drop even the first coin because of a slow speed, and let $pSLOW$ express the intermediate case where the passenger may fail and may succeed. For each particular case only one of these predicates is true. Then let $SPEC2$ be a logical specification with the following diagram :

$\forall$ m.expenses : $\forall$ p.station :
((init & pFAST$\Rightarrow$ AB Σ ET FROM NOW TILL $RushTime$(tick_in & prop_st))&
(init & pSLOWEST$\Rightarrow$ AB Σ ET FROM NOW TILL $SlowTime$(AT m.retcoin))&
(init & pSLOW$\Rightarrow$ EB Σ ET FROM NOW TILL $SlowTime$(tick_in & prop_st))&
(init & pSLOW$\Rightarrow$ EB Σ ET FROM NOW TILL $SlowTime$ (AT m.retcoin)).

Coupling Deduction and Model-Checking. For the case Σ_{fin} (when expenses are fixed integers) the model-checking technique has been applied to both time-free and timed variants. For example, the μ-formula corresponding to the SPEC1 is:

(st_mach & st_pass & no_comm & no_info & no_tick
$\Rightarrow \mu$ x. ((tick_in & prop_st) & ($\langle a\rangle true$ & [a]x))).

For the time-free case Σ_{par} (when expenses are parameters), coupling model-checking with deductive technique from Section 7 has been applied. In this case a proof of progress property init $\mapsto$ (tick_in & prop_st) has been decomposed in [21] (according to the transitivity principle) onto proofs of some "local" progress properties: init $\equiv P \mapsto P1 \mapsto P2 \mapsto P3 \mapsto Q \equiv$ (tick_in&prop_st). The last local property $P3 \mapsto Q$ is due to the subset principle. The properties $P \mapsto P1$ and $P2 \mapsto P3$ have been proved using the model-checking. But the step $P1 \mapsto P2$ is essentially inductive, since it has an uninterpreted parameter, viz., the price of the required ticket. Details of a proof of this progress property using the principle of mapping to a well-founded set with aid of model-checking are given in [21].

9   Conclusion

We presented the distributed systems specification language Basic-REAL as a formalism for the description of asynchronous systems. It has not been designed with the aim to replace formal description techniques such as SDL, but as a intermediate representation for them (in particular, for SDL).

The bREAL meets constraints 1–6 mentioned in Section 1. Indeed, a static subset of SDL (i.e., without dynamic process generation) can be translated into executional bREAL specifications in a property- and structure-conservative manner [23]. We implemented a prototype SDL2REAL translator which generates operationally equivalent REAL specifications from SDL ones. Given the static nature of bREAL, this translation does not cover the dynamical features of SDL (e.g., creation of process instances). An optimization is also performed to reduce the state space size: the unreachable generated state are removed from the bREAL specification. Due to these reasons, the equivalent specifications have approximately the same size and the same safety/progress properties. A presentation of this translation is a subject of a forthcoming publication. The formal semantics of bREAL described in Sections 3, 4 and 5 is simple, and it can be used to derive the important meta-properties like properties formulated in Section 6. Automatic proof of these and some other meta-properties of bREAL (e.g., bisimulation of synchronous communication between processes, i.e., rendezvous) is a topic for forthcoming research. The verification techniques discussed in Section 7, demonstrate that bREAL is a language suitable for representation and verification of properties. Study of problem classes other than progress properties and corresponding problem-oriented proof-principles is also a topic for further research.

The bREAL has the following advanced features for specifying distributed systems and their properties:

- The new time concept based on uninterpreted time units extends expressiveness of the language, and the time intervals associated with transitions allow the shortcoming of the timer concept in SDL [3,6] to be overcome.
- The logical specification language is rather expressive due to the extension of real-time variants of CTL by time intervals and first order dynamic logic constructs.
- The expressive power of executional specifications is essentially increased by using fairness conditions and communication via channels with different structures (i.e., (un)bounded queues, stacks, bags, etc.).
- The formal semantics of bREAL provides the interaction of processes with the external environment, which simplifies specification and verification of distributed systems.

The project REAL is under development since 1991. Initial presentation of the project is in [20] where a sketch of formal semantics of language REAL was given. A complete definition of bREAL is presented in a technical report [21]. We intend to extend the bREAL language by dynamic process generation. The new REAL version — Dynamic-REAL — will increase the expressive power of bREAL and essentially extend the SDL subset which can be naturally translated to REAL.

Acknowledgements

The authors would like to thank the anonymous reviewers for valuable comments and suggestions.

References

1. Bergstra J.A., Middelburg C.A., Usenko Y.S. Discrete time process algebra and the semantics of SDL. Technical report SEN-R9809, CWI, June 1998.
2. Bodin E.V., Kozura V.E., Shilov N.V. Experiments with model checking for μ-calculus in specification and verification project REAL. Proc. of the Fifth New Zealand Formal Program Development Colloquium, IIMS Technical Report 99-1, 1999, 1–18.
3. Bošnački D. et al. Model checking SDL with Spin, TACAS/ETAPS 2000, Lect. Notes in Comp. Sci., 2000, 363–377.
4. Bozga M. et al. IF: An intermediate representation and validation environment for timed asynchronous systems, FM'99, Vol.I, Lect. Notes in Comp. Sci., 1999, v.1708, 307–327.
5. Broy M. Towards a formal foundation of the specification and description language SDL, Formal Aspects of Computing, v.3, n.1, 1991, 21–57.
6. Broy M., Grosu R. Klein C. Reconciling real-time with asynchronous message passing, Lect. Notes in Computer Sci., 1997, v.1313, 182–200.
7. Cavalli A.R., Horn F. Proof of specification properties by using finite state machines and temporal logic, Proc. of 7-th IFIP Conf. on Protocol Specifications, Testing, and Verification, 1987, 221–233.
8. Chandy K.M., Misra J. Parallel program design, Addison-Wesley, 1988.
9. Clarke E.M., Emerson E.A., Sistla A.P. Automatic verification of finite state concurrent systems using temporal logic specifications, ACM Trans. Programming Languages & Systems, 1986, **8, n. 2**, 244–263.
10. Cleaveland R., Klein M., Steffen B. Faster model checking for modal mu-calculus, Proceedings of CAV-92, Montreal, Canada, Lect. Notes in Comp. Sci., v.663, p.410-422.
11. Eschbach R. et al. On the formal semantics of SDL-2000: A compilation approach based on an abstract SDL machine, ASM 2000, Lect. Notes in Comp. Sci., 2000, v.1912, 242–265.
12. Gammelgaard A., Kristensen J.E. A correctness proof of a translation from SDL to CRL, Proc. of the 6th SDL Forum, 1993, 205–219.
13. Gibson P., Mery D. Telephone feature verification: translating SDL to TLA+, Report CRIN, Nancy, Dec. 1996.
14. Harel D. First-order dynamic logic, Lect. Notes in Comp. Sci., v.68, 1979.
15. Lamport L. Verification and specification of concurrent programs. - Lect. Notes in Comp. Sci., 1994, v.803, 347–374.
16. Leue S. Specifying real-time requirements for SDL specifications — A temporal logic-based approach, Proc. 15-th IFIP Intern. Symp. on Protocol Spec. Test. and Verif., 1995, Warsaw, p.19–34.

17. Manna Z., Pnueli A. The temporal logic of Reactive and Concurrent Systems. Springer-Verlag, Berlin/New York, 1991.
18. Manna Z., Pnueli A. Temporal verification of reactive systems: safety. Springer-Verlag, Berlin/New York, 1995.
19. Mery D., Mokkedem A. CROCOS: An integrated environment for interactive verification of SDL specifications, Lect. Notes in Comp. Sci., 1993, v.663, 343–356.
20. Nepomniaschy V.A., Shilov N.V. Real92: A combined specification language for systems and properties of real-time communicating processes, Proc. Int. Conf. on Formal Methods in Programming and Their Applications, Novosibirsk, 1993, Lect. Notes in Comp. Sci., v.735, 1993, 377-393.
21. Nepomniaschy V.A., Shilov N.V., Bodin E.V. A new language Basic-REAL for specification and verification of distributed system models, Report Nr. 65 of A.P. Ershov's Institute of Informatics Systems, Novosibirsk, 1999, 39 p. (also available at http://www.iis.nsk.su/preprints/shilov/bre99/)
22. Orava F. Formal semantics of SDL specifications, Proc. of 8-th IFIP Intern. Symp. on Protocol Spec. Test., and Verif., 1988, 143–157.
23. Valiullin R. Translation of static SDL specifications to Basic-REAL, Bachelor thesis. Novosibirsk State University, Department of Information Technologies, 2001 (in Russian).

Appendix 1. Formal Syntax of Basic-REAL

specification:: executional-specification | logical-specification
executional-specification:: process | block
logical-specification:: predicate| formula
process:: process-head scale context fairness-conditions process-diagram
block:: block-head scale context fairness-conditions block-diagram subblocks
predicate:: predicate-head scale context systems predicate-diagram
formula:: formula-head scale context systems formula-diagram subformulae
process-head:: name : PROCESS
block-head:: name : BLOCK
predicate-head:: name : PREDICATE
formula-head:: name : FORMULA
scale:: {linear-equality-over-time-units | linear-inequality-over-time-units }*
context:: {type-definition | object-declaration }*
type-definition:: TYPE type IS type-expression
type-expression:: predefined-type | enumerated-type |
    type-expression ARRAY OF type-expression |
    type-expression QUEUE OF type-expression |
    type-expression STACK OF type-expression |
    type-expression BAG OF type-expression
predefined-type:: INT | STR
enumerated-type::name | name, enumerated-type | name; enumerated-type
subblocks:: { executional-specification }*
subformulae:: { logical-specification }*
object-declaration:: variable-declaration | channel-declaration
variable-declaration:: location appointment VAR variable OF type

appointment:: QU | PR
channel-declaration:: location role organization CHN channel FOR signal {WITH PAR
parameter OF type-expression }*
role:: INP | OUT | INN
organization:: capacity structure | ELEMENTARY
capacity:: number-ELM | UNB
structure:: QUE | STACK | BAG
process-diagram:: { transition }*
transition:: state [:] body interval jump
body:: EXE program | READ signal-with-parameters-1 FROM channel |
    WRITE signal-with-parameters-2 INTO channel | CLEAN channel
program:: operator {; operator }*
operator:: variable :=expression | SKIP | ABRT | IF condition THEN program [ELSE
program] FI | WHILE condition DO program OD | CASE program [ALT program]
ESAC | LOOP program POOL
signal-with-parameters-1:: signal [(variable-list)
variable-list:: variable {, variable }*
signal-with-parameters-2:: signal [(value-list)
value-list:: expression {, expression }*
expression :: constant | variable | (expression) |expression operation-sign expres-
sion
operation-sign:: + | - | * | / | APPLY | UPDATE
interval:: left-bound linear-time-expression right-bound linear-time-expression
left-bound:: AFTER | FROM
right-bound:: UNTIL | UPTO
jump:: JUMP state-list.
state-list:: state {, state }*.
block-diagram:: { route }*
route:: source CHN channel destination
source:: name | ENV
destination:: name | ENV
predicate-diagram:: relation | locator | controller | checker
relation:: expression relation-sign expression
locator:: AT state
controller:: EMP channel | channel IS EMPTY | FUL channel | channel IS OVERFULL
checker:: signal IN channel | signal RD channel
formula-diagram:: name | (propositional-combination) |
    (quantifier variable formula-diagram) |
    (behavioural-modality system temporal-modality interval formula-diagram)
quantifier:: ∀ | ∃
behavioural-modality:: EACH | SOME | AB | EB
temporal-modality □ | ◇ | AT | ET
state:: name
channel:: name
parameter:: name

Appendix 2. SDL-Specification
of "Passenger and Vending Machine"

```
SYSTEM All;
BLOCK Passenger_and_Machine;
 SIGNAL coin (integer), light (integer), sigchange (integer),
  ticket (integer), sigstation (integer), request, return;
 SIGNALROUTE buttons FROM Passenger TO Machine
   WITH sigstation, return, request;
 SIGNALROUTE slot FROM Passenger TO Machine WITH coin;
 SIGNALROUTE indicator FROM Machine TO Passenger WITH light;
 SIGNALROUTE change FROM Machine TO Passenger WITH sigchange;
 SIGNALROUTE booking FROM Machine TO Passenger WITH ticket;
PROCESS Passenger;
  DCL sum, nominal, station, gotstation, gotsum integer;
  START; 'Initialize (constant) station';
   TASK decision := station;
   OUTPUT sigstation(decision); NEXTSTATE look;
  STATE look; INPUT light(sum); DECISION sum;
   (<=0): OUTPUT request; NEXTSTATE get;
   ELSE: /* choose a random coin from range 1..10 */
         TASK nominal := RANDOM(10);
         OUTPUT coin(nominal); NEXTSTATE look; ENDDECISION;
  ENDSTATE;
  STATE get; INPUT ticket(gotstation); INPUT sigchange(gotsum);
   STOP; ENDSTATE; ENDPROCESS;
PROCESS Machine;
  NEWTYPE price ARRAY (integer, integer) ENDNEWTYPE;
  DCL sum, nominal, station integer, expenses price;
  START; 'Initialize the (constant) expenses array';
  NEXTSTATE get_station;
  STATE get_station;
   INPUT sigstation(station); TASK sum := expenses(station);
   NEXTSTATE showcount;
  STATE showcount; OUTPUT light(sum); NEXTSTATE getcoin;
  STATE getcoin;
   INPUT coin(nominal); TASK sum := sum - nominal;
    NEXTSTATE showcount;
   INPUT return; OUTPUT sigchange(expenses(station) - sum); STOP;
   INPUT request; DECISION sum;
    (>0): OUTPUT light(sum); NEXTSTATE showcount;
    ELSE: OUTPUT ticket(station); OUTPUT sigchange( - sum );
     STOP; ENDDECISION;
  ENDSTATE; ENDPROCESS;
ENDBLOCK;
ENDSYSTEM;
```

Appendix 3. Basic-REAL Specification of "Passenger and Vending Machine"

Specification of the Process "passenger"

```
passenger : PROCESS
OUT CHN buttons FOR sigstation WITH PAR name OF 1..100,
     FOR return, FOR request ;
OUT CHN slot FOR coin WITH PAR nominal OF integer ;
INP CHN indicator FOR light WITH PAR sum OF integer ;
INP CHN change FOR sigchange WITH PAR value OF integer ;
INP CHN booking FOR ticket WITH PAR name OF 1..100' ;
PR VAR sum, nominal OF integer,
PR VAR decision, gottenstation, station OF 1..100 ;
   { Fairness conditions}
   ¬AT start ; ¬AT press ; ¬AT continue ;
   ¬AT request ; ¬AT chcoin ; ¬AT drop ;
start EXE decision := station JUMP press.
press WRITE sigstation(decision) INTO buttons JUMP look.
look READ light(sum) FROM indicator JUMP continue.
continue EXE (sum <= 0)? JUMP request.
continue EXE (sum > 0)? JUMP chcoin.
chcoin EXE nominal := RANDOM(10) ; JUMP drop.
drop WRITE coin(nominal) INTO slot JUMP look.
request WRITE request INTO buttons JUMP get.
get READ ticket(gottenstation) FROM booking JUMP getchange.
getchange READ sigchange(sum) FROM change JUMP satisfaction.
```

Diagram of the Process "machine"

```
start READ sigstation(station) FROM buttons JUMP defcount.
defcount EXE sum := expenses[station] JUMP showcount.
showcount WRITE light(sum) INTO indicator JUMP getcoin.
getcoin READ coin(nominal) FROM slot JUMP add.
getcoin READ return FROM buttons JUMP retcoin.
getcoin READ request FROM buttons JUMP check.
add EXE sum := sum - nominal ; JUMP showcount.
retcoin WRITE sigchange(expenses[station] - sum) INTO change
     JUMP finish.
check EXE (sum <= 0)? ; JUMP give.
check EXE (sum > 0)? JUMP showcount.
give WRITE ticket(station) INTO booking JUMP givechange.
givechange WRITE sigchange( - sum ) INTO change JUMP finish.
```

Assume-Guarantee Algorithms
for Automatic Detection of Software Failures

Mohammad Zulkernine and Rudolph E. Seviora

Bell Canada Software Reliability Laboratory
University of Waterloo
Waterloo, Ontario, Canada N2L 3G1
{mzulker,seviora}@uwaterloo.ca

Abstract. This paper presents an approach based on assume-guarantee style reasoning for automatic detection of software failures. Reasoning about failures requires knowing the expected behavior. The paper considers the case when the requirement specification of the behavior of the target system is available, and expressed in a formalism based on communicating finite state machines. The failure detector observes the external inputs and outputs, and receives partial information about the internal state of the target system. Using this information, it interprets the specification, and determines whether a failure has occurred. A key issue in the interpretation of the specification is the efficiency of handling of inherent nondeterminism present in the specification. The paper describes, in a step by step manner, a compositional approach for online failure detection which reduces the computational costs of dealing with non-determinism. The details of the algorithms required in each of the steps are provided. To evaluate the algorithms described, a prototype failure detector was used to detect failures of the control program of a small telephone exchange. We present some of the results obtained.

Keywords: Software reliability, online monitoring, failure detection, applied formal methods, compositionality.

1   Introduction

It is well accepted that the development of reliable software requires the use of rigorous and mathematically based development techniques [1,4]. Formal methods, in particular model checking and testing, is increasingly deployed to the artifacts that appear throughout the software life cycle. Model checking generally subjects a model rather than an implementation, and decides whether the model satisfies *certain* properties. Software testing usually depends on an *assumed* input distribution, and the predictions based on software testing can be disqualified if the input distribution is inaccurate or changes during the operational stage of the software. As a result, despite rigorous use of model checking, testing, and other technological innovations there exist faults which elude those detection efforts, and do not surface until the software is operational. A

M. Butler, L. Petre, and K. Sere (Eds.): IFM 2002, LNCS 2335, pp. 89–108, 2002.

number of studies have shown that even professionally written programs may contain between one and ten independently detectable faults per thousand lines of codes [1,2,3]. These faults may lead to serious software failures. The difficulty in releasing correct software is drawing a growing interest in the usefulness of operational stage monitoring.

A software failure detector is an online monitoring tool which passively observes the inputs, outputs, and stable state information of the target system, and reports the discrepancies between the behavior prescribed by the specification model and the observed behavior as failures[1]. There are several other advantages of this type of failure detector. It can be used as a test oracle which is able to detect and report a relatively complete set of failures. The detector can be used to assist in testing the sub-systems of a large software system during the development ("verify while develop" [4]), by attaching it to each of the sub-systems. It helps to detect errors before they manifest themselves as externally observable failures. At the field level, early error reporting helps the system operator to issue an advance warning, and attempt to take corrective actions before a serious system failure may occur.

To hide the complexity of real-time systems, and to provide more freedom in their implementation, most of the specification languages offer various types of nondeterminism in their syntax and semantics. In a concurrent system, if multiple transitions are triggered in different independent parallel processes, the execution order of those transitions is nondeterministic. As a consequence of these nondeterminisms, a target system may show different, nevertheless legal external behaviors for the same set of stimuli from the environment. A failure detector monitoring such a nondeterministically specified system must be able to consider all possible legal behavioral alternatives to avoid erroneous failure reports. This is one of the major challenges of failure detection as the number of behavioral alternatives required to be considered by the detector may be large resulting in a large detection time and space complexity. Due to the parallel composition of interacting process specifications, the size of the global model becomes exponential with respect to the number of concurrent processes[2]. Compositional reasoning is advocated to combat this state explosion [4]. Unfortunately compositional approaches have not been applied in the operational stage of software yet. Among the compositional approaches, assumption-commitment [5] (also called rely-guarantee [6]) model has been "more widely studied than actually used" [7]. According to this model, it is asserted that a component satisfies a guarantee G only as long its environment satisfies an assumption A.

This paper proposes a compositional approach to detecting software failures. It means that the correctness of the behavior actually observed for the whole system is proved without constructing a global state graph. We present a disciplined application and adaptation of assume-guarantee style automatic reasoning

---

[1] This characterization of failure is in accordance with the definitions of the IEEE [8] and the IFIP WG 10.4 [9].

[2] The global model is also nondeterministic, which further increases computational cost.

technique for failure detection of concurrent programs. The principle for failure detection is formalized. We provide generic algorithms and architecture for the detector based on that principle. The detection approach is described in a step by step manner by providing the details of the algorithms required in each of the steps. The operations are first described in general, which are followed by detailed structured pseudo-code and examples. A prototype implementation based on these algorithms is put into practice to detect failures of the control program of a private branch exchange (PBX). The proposed technique is applicable for concurrent, responsive, real-time, and failure sensitive but not safety critical systems. This work is based on the following hypotheses. The requirements specification of the target system is available, expressed in a formalism based on communicating finite state machines (CFSM). The target system traverses a set of stable global states infinitely often, and these states are visible to the detector along with the external messages.

The rest of the paper is structured as follows. The next section introduces the system specification, assume-guarantee model for failure detection, and an overview of the architecture and operation of the detector. Section 3 describes the algorithm for generating assumptions and guarantees. The details of the core algorithms for discharging assumptions are exposed in Section 4. Section 5 reports the evaluation results of a prototype implementation for detecting failures of a PBX control program. Finally, Section 6 discusses related work which is followed by some concluding remarks in Section 7.

2   Preliminaries

2.1   System Specification

The target system specification is expressed in a set of asynchronously communicating finite state machines. The behavior of each process is represented by a finite state machine (FSM). An FSM is a directed graph (V, E), where V is a set of states, and E is the set of edges or state transitions. The processes run in parallel at nondeterministic speeds. Each pair of communicating processes is connected by two simplex FIFO channels for incoming and outgoing messages. Processes which communicate with the system environment are also connected with the environment by two different channels. While the messages in a particular channel maintain a strict FIFO ordering, the orderings among the messages of different channels are nondeterministic.

The transition or execution of a system is represented by a sequence of global states, where each global state consists of the current states of all the processes. Consider a system consists of N communicating processes: $P_1, P_2, ...,$ and P_N, then formally a global state is defined as follows:

Definition 1 Global State. *A global state S is a tuple $< s_1, s_2, ..., s_N, C_1, C_2, ..., C_N >$, where s_j denotes the symbolic name of the current state of P_j, and C_j is the current contents of the P_j's input channels, i.e., $C_j =< c_{je}, c_{j1}, c_{j2}, ..., c_{jN} >$. Here, c_{je} represents the contents of the incoming channel from the* *system environment to P_j, while c_{ji} denotes the contents of the incoming channel of P_j from P_i, where $i \neq j$. Since for N communicating processes each C_j is an N-tuple, in a global state there are contents of N^2 channels.*

In some global states, the system waits for an external input i.e., input from the environment of the observed system, and no further progress can be made without any external input. Such states are called *stable* global states, and in these states there is no *enabling internal transition* since the incoming channels are empty. In the global states other than the stable ones, at least one of the component processes has internal input/output operations ready to be executed. Note that the initial global state is always stable since all the processes of the system are in their initial states, and all channels are empty.

Definition 2 Stable Global State. *A global state $< s_1, s_2, ..., s_N, C_1, C_2, ..., C_N >$ is called stable iff the channels of all the processes are empty, i.e., $C_1 = C_2 = ... = C_N = nil$. A stable global state is represented by an N-tuple $< \sigma_1, \sigma_2, ..., \sigma_N >$, and σ_j (symbolic state name) is called a stable state of P_j.*

2.2   Assume-Guarantee Paradigm for Failure Detection

In the assume-guarantee paradigm [5,6], one part of the specification defines the guaranteed behavior of a component, and the other part defines the assumed behavior of the environment of the component. This implies conditional specification for a process, usually written as $\{A_j\}P_j\{G_j\}$, where A_j is called the assumption, and G_j is called the guarantee of the process P_j. If A_j is satisfied by the environment then P_j will satisfy G_j. By combining the set of assume-guarantee behavior pairs (A_j, G_j) in an appropriate manner, it is possible to prove the correctness of the whole system. In the literature, there are several forms of specifications proposed for the assume-guarantee model in the context of different settings [4,5,6,7]. In many cases, they have been studied as an extension of Hoare Logic. In this view, the specification is a tuple $< p, A_j, G_j, q >$, where p and q are precondition and postcondition.

In this work, from the given CFSM based specification, an assume-guarantee style specification similar to the above one is derived with different interpretations of p and q. Here, p and q are state information of the process instead of the predicates on the state of a process. The predicates are implicitly implied to be true for a process if the process transfers from state p to q by a finite sequence of transitions. The specification is considered as a tuple of the following form $< \sigma_{j(i-1)}, A_j, G_j, \sigma_{ji} >$, where A_j and G_j are the assumptions and guarantees of the process P_j based on its interaction with the other component processes or the system environment. According to the hypotheses of this work, a process traverses a sequence of stable states, and $\sigma_{j(i-1)}$ and σ_{ji} represent two successive (i-th and $(i+1)$-th) stable states of P_j. These stable states have corresponding symbolic state names in the specification of P_j, and there may be zero or more specification states between a pair of successive stable states.

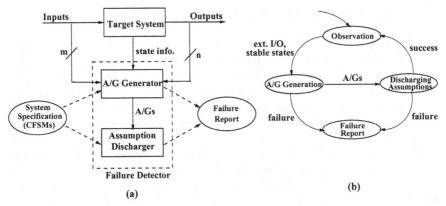

Fig. 1. (a) Major components and settings of the failure detector. (b) Detection cycle.

To provide a formal interpretation of the above specification tuple, we introduce the following definitions. Any process P_j can be regarded as a finite or infinite sequence of states $s_j = s_{j0}, s_{j1}, ..., s_{jk}, ...$, where s_{jk} represents the $(k+1)$-th state of P_j. The expression $P_j \models < \sigma_{j(i-1)}, A_j, G_j, \sigma_{ji} >$ denotes that the process P_j satisfies a specification $< \sigma_{j(i-1)}, A_j, G_j, \sigma_{ji} >$. Let $\sigma_{j(i-1)} = s_{jk}$, $\sigma_{ji} = s_{jl}$, and $s_j|_k^{l-1}$ denotes the finite sequence of states of length $(l-k)$ from s_{jk} to $s_{j(l-1)}$. Similarly, $s_j|_k^l$ denotes the sequence of states of length $(l-k+1)$ from s_{jk} to s_{jl}. Now, if $s_j|_k^{l-1} \models A_j$ then $s_j|_k^l \models G_j$.

2.3   Architecture and Operation of the Detector

The failure detector may be attached to either the entire system or a sub-system under observation. External inputs/outputs, and stable state information must be observable. As shown in Fig. 1(a), the detector has two principal components: A/G generator and assumption discharger. The A/G generator generates the individual process assumptions and guarantees, while the assumption discharger validates the assumptions made by the A/G generator. The dynamic nature of the failure detector is described by the cycle of operations depicted in Fig. 1(b). The detection cycle begins by observing the external I/O and a stable global state of the target system under observation. In the first phase, the detector generates the assumptions and guarantees of each process based on the observed I/O and stable states. If no assumptions or guarantees can be generated for a process, which has changed its stable state, a failure is reported. In the second phase, the assumptions made for each of the processes are validated. If all the assumptions made so far cannot be discharged the detector reports a failure and stops. Otherwise it waits for the next stable global state of the target system, and repeats the cycle.

3   Generation of Assumptions and Guarantees

Assumptions and guarantees (A/Gs) for a process are the set of inputs and outputs respectively due to the transitions of the process between a pair of successive stable states. The A/Gs are generated only for the set of *active* processes (P_{act}). An active process is the process which has changed its state since the previous stable global state of the target system. A process which makes transition(s) and returns to its previous stable state is also considered as an active process.

The individual process assumptions and guarantees are generated by employing a *cause-effect* analysis technique *within* the process specification. The internal message events are determined based on the external stimuli from the environment. The detector identifies one or more trajectories for a process using a process-level depth first reachability analysis technique [13]. A trajectory of a process is a sequence of states corresponding to the sequence of transitions between any pair of successive stable states of the process following its process specification.

Definition 3 Trajectory. *Suppose p and q are a pair of successive stable states of P_j. The k-th trajectory of the j-th process (trajectory$_{jk}$) with start state p and end state q is a finite sequence of states $p_0, p_1, ..., $ and p_n, where $p_0 = p$, $p_n = q$, and for all i, $1 \leq i \leq n$ there exists a triggering message event m_i for the i-th transition such that $p_{i-1} \overset{m_i}{\to} p_i$. One or more trajectories between the two stable states of a process constitute the trajectory set (Trajectories$_j$) of the process (i.e., trajectory$_{jk} \in Trajectories_j$).*

Each trajectory is traced forward independently for generating A/Gs (c.f. Algorithm 1). If any external message is required for a transition of a trajectory that message must have been observed. Otherwise no A/G is generated following that trajectory. If a transition requires an internal input, the transition is enabled based on the assumption of the occurrence of that input. The outputs due to the transition are computed, and the external outputs are compared with the observed outputs. If any computed output is different from the observed output that trajectory is rejected for the A/G generation. Otherwise the assumed/observed inputs and the computed outputs of a process are appended to the A/G list of the process as assumptions and guarantees respectively. The above procedure is followed for all the transitions of a trajectory. A list of message events (both internal and external) following a process trajectory constitutes an A/G list of the process. If for any process no A/G list can be generated, a failure is reported.

In some cases, the actual trajectory chosen by a process may not be inferred dynamically (c.f. Example 1). Each of the possible trajectories for this process contains the same sequence of start and end states, and same list of external I/O, while their interim states and messages are different. An alternative A/G list is derived for each trajectory. The alternative A/G lists of a process are mutually exclusive, and are grouped together to form the A/G set of the process. The lists of an A/G set are mutually exclusive.

Definition 4 A/G List. *The k-th A/G list of the j-th process ($A\_G\_List_{jk}$) is a finite sequence of input or output message events $m_1, m_2, ..., m_n$. If an event is external it must have been observed by the detector. One or more A/G lists of a process constitute the A/G set ($A\_G\_Set_j$) of the process (i.e., $A\_G\_List_{jk} \in A\_G\_Set_j$).*

Since a system contains more than one process, and each of these processes may have more than one possible A/G lists, each of the lists is assigned an identifier consisting of two parts. The first part denotes the process identifier, while the second part represents a trajectory identifier of the process. For example, the identifier $j.k$ refers to the k-th A/G list of the j-th process. In summary, an assumption or guarantee of an A/G list is a six-tuple of the following form: $< msgid, spid, rpid, t_{obs}, A\_G\_Type, A\_G\_List\_Id >$. Here, $msgid$ represents the message symbol, while $spid$ and $rpid$ are respectively the sender and receiver process identifier. Since there may be more than one process instance of a given CFSM with a certain name, pids are different from CFSM names of the specification. t_{obs} denotes the observation instant of the message. We omit the timing issues in this paper (c.f. [13] for real-time issues). The value of A_G_Type is "A" for an assumption, and "G" for a guarantee. $A\_G\_List\_Id$ is the identification of the A/G list.

Algorithm 1 Individual Process A/G Generation[3].

Input: *Trajectories of each active process ($Trajectories_j$) and observed I/O.*
Output: *Set of A/G lists for each active process ($A\_G\_Set_j$) or failure report.*

```
01. for each process P_j ∈ P_act
02.     fail_process ← true;
03.     for each trajectory_jk ∈ Trajectories_j
04.         fail_trajectory ← false;
05.         current state s ← the first state of trajectory_jk;
06.         for each transition s --m_i--> s' of trajectory_jk
07.             if (m_i is an external input but not observed)
08.                 then
09.                     fail_trajectory ← true;
10.                     break;
11.                 else trigger the transition using m_i;
12.             endif
13.             compute outputs m_o based on the transition;
14.             if (m_o is external but not observed)
15.                 fail_trajectory ← true;
16.                 break;
17.             endif
18.             append the assumed/observed m_i to A_G_List_jk as A;
19.             append the computed output(s) m_o to A_G_List_jk as G;
```

---

[3] Each notation used in different algorithms is explained only once in the paper.

```
20.          update s by the current state s';
21.      endfor
22.      if (fail_trajectory) continue;
23.      label each A/G of A_G_List_jk by the identifier j.k;
24.      insert A_G_List_jk into A_G_Set_j;
25.      fail_process ← false;
26.   endfor
27.   if (fail_process) report "failure" and exit;
28. endfor
```

Example 1. *A/G Lists Generation.* Consider that the failure detector observes the external I/O [4]: {?OFFHOOK, !FASTBUSY}, and obtains current stable state: offhook_fastbusy for a process instance $Phone_1$. Based on the CFSM specification (c.f. Fig. 2), $Phone_1$ might have reached to this state because either it was not granted a channel or it could not acquire a touch tone receiver (ttrx). The detector generates the following two mutually exclusive A/G lists which constitutes $A\_G\_Set_1$: $A\_G\_List_{11}$ = {?OFFHOOK, !req_chan, ?grant_chan, !req_ttrx, ?no_ttrx, !FASTBUSY}, and $A\_G\_List_{12}$ = {?OFFHOOK, !req_chan, ?no_chan, !FASTBUSY}.

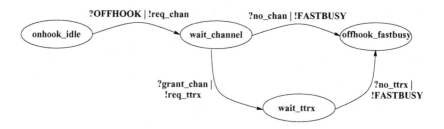

Fig. 2. Partial specification of a Phone process.

3.1   Address Determination

If a guarantee message sent by a process could be received by multiple possible receivers, the sender process cannot ascertain the receiver of the message from its process-level information only. The information derived from the interpretation of an individual process specification based on its stable states and the external input(s) destined to the process are referred to as *process-level information* of the process. Similarly, if an assumption message received by a process could be sent by more than one sender, the address of the sender process cannot be determined

---

[4] The symbols "!" and "?" denote the transmission and reception of a message respectively. The capitalized messages represent communications with the system environment, while the other messages are used for inter-process communications.

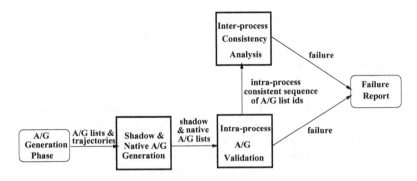

Fig. 3. The steps for discharging assumptions.

by the receiver certainly from the process-level information only. Based on the uncertainty over the sender/receiver addresses, the message events in an A/G list can be divided into the following two categories.

Identified A/G. A guarantee message in an A/G list of a sender (receiver) process is called identified if the receiver (sender) address of the event can be determined only from the process-level information of the sender (receiver). Note that the external I/Os are always identified A/Gs.

Anonymous A/G. A guarantee message of a process is called anonymous if the receiver address of the event cannot be determined by the sender from its process-level information only. Similarly, an assumption message is anonymous if the sender address is unknown to the receiver process.

This paper assumes a *pairwise process communication,* where for any message, either the destination address is known by the sender process or the source address is available to the receiver process.

Proposition 1 *The complementary event of an anonymous message event in a sender (receiver) process is an identified message event in the receiver (sender) process. Two events are complementary if they are the sending and receiving events of the same message communicated between a pair of processes.*

4 Discharging Assumptions

In the assume-guarantee style reasoning, discharging an assumption means to prove the existence of its complementary event in the premise of the logical implication rule used to discharge this assumption. It requires that all the A/Gs of the A/G lists generated in the A/G generation phase must be identified message events. A naive approach would be to replace an anonymous message event by its complementary identified message event from any of the other processes. However, this leads to a *problem of circularity* [7]. For example, if we use the value of

"a" to compute the value of "g", then using this value of "g" to discharge "a" is called circular reasoning. In the presence of any circular reasoning of this kind, assumptions cannot be discharged certainly.

In order to avoid this circularity, an indirect approach is followed here (c.f. Fig. 3). The complementary events of the identified message events of the A/G lists of a process are exported to the corresponding processes but are kept as a separate set of A/G lists of the importing processes. Then the imported A/G lists are validated by executing the individual process specifications. If for any process no execution trace is possible using these lists, or there are redundant message events, a failure is reported. Otherwise each of the possible execution traces of the processes are sent for inter-process consistency analysis in order to check the consistency in the composition of alternative A/G lists. In case of absence of any consistent composition of A/G lists, a failure is reported. The major steps of discharging assumptions (c.f. bold boxes in Fig. 3) are described in detail in the following subsections.

4.1   Shadow and Native A/G Generation

An external message to a process may cause (directly or indirectly) zero or more external/internal inputs/outputs not only in the process itself but also in other processes. The objective of this shadow and native A/G generation phase is to find out which message event was a causal factor in the occurrence of another message event, or which message event would occur in response to the occurrence of another message event. The cause or effect is determined based on the identified internal message events of the A/G lists. For each process two different sets of A/G lists are derived: *shadow A/G set* and *native A/G set*.

Algorithm 2 investigates each of the lists derived in the A/G generation phase as follows. The external message events are left unaltered, and becomes a part of the native A/G list of the process. Each identified internal message event of the list is appended to the corresponding sender or receiver process shadow A/G lists. The anonymous message events present in the original A/G lists are removed. As a result, after this step each process will contain only identified message events separated in two sets.

The lists in the native set of a process contain the message events derived from process-level information only, while the lists in the shadow set are built from message events imported from the other processes that communicate with this one. However, the lists in both the sets maintain the original A/G list identifiers ($A\_G\_List\_Id$) assigned in the A/G generation phase. The native lists of a process are always mutually exclusive, while the shadow lists of a process may or may not be mutually exclusive. Only the shadow lists derived from the same process are mutually exclusive.

Supplementary Definitions. $s\_A\_G\_List_{jk(i)}$: a shadow A/G list of the i-th process derived from the k-th list of P_j, where $s\_A\_G\_List_{jk(i)} \in S\_A\_G\_Set_j$. $n\_A\_G\_List_{jk}$: the k-th native list of P_j, where $n\_A\_G\_List_{jk} \in N\_A\_G\_Set_j$.

Algorithm 2 Shadow and Native A/G Generation.

Input: *Set of A/G lists of each active process ($A\_G\_Set_j$).*
Output: *Set of shadow and native A/G lists ($S\_A\_G\_Set_j$, $N\_A\_G\_Set_j$) of each active process.*

```
01. for each process P_j ∈ P_act
02.    N_A_G_Set_j ← A_G_Set_j;
03.    for each list A_G_List_jk ∈ A_G_Set_j
04.       for each message event m ∈ A_G_List_jk
05.          switch (A_G_Type of m)
06.             case A:
07.                if (m is an internal event, and spid is determined)
08.                   then append the complementary event of m
                           to s_A_G_List_jk(spid);
09.                   else remove m from n_A_G_List_jk;
10.                endif
11.                break;
12.             endcase
13.             case G:
14.                if (m is an internal event, and rpid is determined)
15.                   then append the complementary event of m
                           to s_A_G_List_jk(rpid);
16.                   else remove m from n_A_G_List_jk;
17.                endif
18.                break;
19.             endcase
20.          endswitch
21.       endfor
22.    endfor
23. endfor
```

Example 2. *Shadow and Native A/G Lists Generation.* Consider the following A/G lists for three Phone processes, where $Phone_1$ and $Phone_2$ attempt to call $Phone_3$. $Phone_1$ gets the connection with a RINGTONE, while $Phone_2$ is refused with a SLOWBUSY tone. The underlined messages are anonymous A/Gs.
$Phone_1$: $A\_G\_List_{11}$ = {?DIGIT, !con_req, ?available, !RINGTONE}.
$Phone_2$: $A\_G\_List_{21}$ = {?DIGIT, !con_req, ?not_available, !SLOWBUSY}.
$Phone_3$: $A\_G\_List_{31}$ = {?con_req, !available, !RINGGEN, ?con_req, !not_available}.

The shadow and native A/G lists generated using Algorithm 2 are as follows:
$Phone_1$: $n\_A\_G\_List_{11}$ = {?DIGIT, !con_req, ?available, !RINGTONE} and $s\_A\_G\_List_{11}$ = nil.

$Phone_2$: $n\_A\_G\_List_{21}$ = {?DIGIT, !con_req, ?not_available, !SLOWBUSY} and $s\_A\_G\_List_{21}$ = nil.

$Phone_3$: $n\_A\_G\_List_{31}$ = {!RINGGEN}, $s\_A\_G\_List_{11(3)}$ = {?con_req, !available}, and $s\_A\_G\_List_{21(3)}$ = {?con_req, !not_available}.

4.2 Intra-process A/G Validation

The shadow and native A/G lists generated for each of the active processes are validated in this step. A set of A/G lists (shadow or native) of a process is considered valid or intra-process consistent if the lists can be consumed or generated by executing the process specification based on the process trajectories. The A/G list identifiers of the A/Gs used to traverse a trajectory of a process completely is called a *consistent sequence* of the process. Note that in contrary to an *A/G list*, a consistent sequence is a *list of A/G list identifiers* ($A\_G\_List\_Id$). These identifiers were assigned to the alternative A/G lists in the A/G generation phase. Multiple consistent sequences may be derived for a process depending on the number of trajectories and the A/Gs in the shadow/native lists of the process. The consistent sequences derived for a process form the consistent sequence set for that process. If for any of the active processes, there is no such consistent sequence, or all the A/Gs in the shadow or native A/G lists cannot be consumed/generated by following the trajectories of the process, a failure is reported.

The complete validation procedure is presented in Algorithm 3. All the shadow and native A/G lists generated for a process in the previous step constitute the initial *available A/G set* ($Avail\_S\_N\_Set_j$) for the process. An assumption or guarantee from this set is chosen for execution based on the current state of the process specification. Since the A/Gs of a particular list maintains a total order in the list, an assumption or guarantee of an A/G list can be consumed if and only if all the previous A/Gs of that list have been consumed. However, due to the partial ordering among the A/Gs of different A/G lists, more than one A/G may be candidates for execution in a process state. The actual triggering assumption or a responding guarantee is selected for execution from the candidadte A/G set if the information (message name, sender/receiver addresses, time) in the A/G matches the information of the next allowabale message event at the current specification state. If more than one A/Gs in the candidate A/G set meet the above requirements, one of them is chosen for execution randomly. If there is no matching A/G in the candidate A/G set, and the current specification state is not the last state of the trajectory, the most recently executed A/G is undone for trying the other A/G lists to form a consistent sequence. In case of no matching A/G in the candidate set, and no excuted A/G to backtrack a failure is reported.

Supplementary Definitions. $a\_S\_N\_List_i$: a shadow or native A/G list available to execute the specification of P_j, where $a\_S\_N\_List_i \in Avail\_S\_N\_Set_j$. $c\_Id\_Seq_{jk}$: the k-th consistent sequence of P_j, where $c\_Id\_Seq_{jk} \in C\_Id\_Seq\_Set_j$. $next\_spec\_event$: the next message event to be executed. Its value is null when there is no event to execute following a trajectory. $next\_A\_G_i$: pointer to the A/G of $a\_S\_N\_List_i$. Its value is null when all the A/Gs of the i-th list have been used to execute the specification. $Cand\_A\_G\_Set$: a set of potential A/Gs of a process ready to be executed. $f\_state_j (l\_state_j)$: the first (last) state of $trajectory_{jk} \in Trajectories_j$.

Algorithm 3 Intra-process A/G Validation.

Input: *Shadow and native A/G sets* $(S\_A\_G\_Set_j, N\_A\_G\_Set_j)$, *and trajectories* $(Trajectories_j)$ *of each active process.*
Output: *A set of intra-process consistent sequences of A/G list identifiers for each active process* $(C\_Id\_Seq\_Set\_j)$ *or failure report.*

```
01. for each process P_j ∈ P_act
02.    Avail_S_N_Set_j ← S_A_G_Set_j ∪ N_A_G_Set_j;
03.    for each trajectory_jk ∈ Trajectories_j
04.       intialize: curr_state ← f_state_j, next_spec_event ← first
          event from curr_state, next_A_G_i points to the top A/G of
          a_S_N_List_i ∈ Avail_S_N_Set_j, and all A/Gs are unmarked;
05.       while (next_spec_event ≠ null)
06.       Cand_A_G_Set ← ∅;
07.       for each a_S_N_List_i ∈ Avail_S_N_Set_j
08.          if (next_spec_event is input and next_A_G_i is assumption)
09.             insert the assumption to Cand_A_G_Set;
10.          if (next_spec_event is output and next_A_G_i is guarantee)
11.             insert the guarantee to Cand_A_G_Set;
12.       endfor
13.       eliminate infeasible A/Gs from Cand_A_G_Set comparing
          to the next_spec_event (symbol, address, time);
14.       if (Cand_A_G_Set = ∅)
15.          then
16.             if (curr_state = l_state_j) break;
17.             if (no execution to undo)
18.                then report "failure" and exit;
19.                else undo the most recent execution, mark the
                      corresponding A/G, rollback next_A_G_i of the
                      A/G list, next_spec_event, and curr_state;
20.          endif
21.          else execute an unmarked A/G from Cand_A_G_Set,
                   unmark previously marked A/G (if any), advance
                   the next_A_G_i
                   of the A/G list, next_spec_event, and curr_state;
22.       endif
23.       endwhile
24.       if (next_A_G_i = null for all the lists of the executed A/Gs)
25.          remove the executed lists from Avail_S_N_Set_j;
26.          append the identifiers of the removed lists to c_Id_Seq_jk;
27.          insert c_Id_Seq_jk to C_Id_Seq_Set_j;
28.       endif
29.    endfor
30.    if ((Avail_S_N_Set_j ≠ ∅) ∨ (C_Id_Seq_Set_j = ∅))
31.       report "failure" and exit;
32. endfor
```

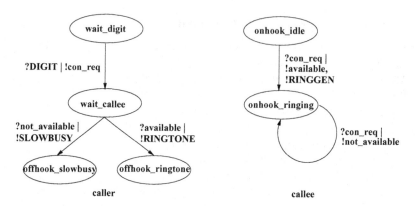

Fig. 4. Partial specification of a Phone process as caller and callee.

Example 3. *Intra-process A/G Validation.* Consider the shadow and native lists of Example 2. The initial available shadow and native A/G lists for the three Phone processes are as follows. For clarity the A/G list identifier of each list is written at the end of the list.

$Avail\_S\_N\_Set_1 = \{\{?DIGIT, !con\_req, ?available, !RINGTONE; 1.1\}\}$.
$Avail\_S\_N\_Set_2 = \{\{?DIGIT, !con\_req, ?not\_available, !SLOWBUSY; 2.1\}\}$.
$Avail\_S\_N\_Set_3 = \{\{!RINGGEN; 3.1\}, \{?con\_req, !available; 1.1(3)\}, \{?con\_req, !not\_available; 2.1(3)\}\}$.

The parts of the specification of a Phone process required to be executed for this example is shown in Fig. 4. Based on the above lists and the given specification, the consistent sequences obtained for the Phone processes are as follows: $c\_Id\_Seq_{11} = \{1.1\}$, $c\_Id\_Seq_{21} = \{2.1\}$, and $c\_Id\_Seq_{31} = \{1.1(3), 3.1, 2.1(3)\}$. Since, each process has one consistent sequence, and after deriving these sequences $Avail\_S\_N\_Set_j = \emptyset$, for $j = 1, 2$, and 3, no failure is reported.

We extend this example to explain a failure scenario where both callers get RINGTONE. The initial available A/G lists are as follows:

$Avail\_S\_N\_Set_1 = \{\{?DIGIT, !con\_req, ?available, !RINGTONE; 1.1\}\}$.
$Avail\_S\_N\_Set_2 = \{\{?DIGIT, !con\_req, ?available, !RINGTONE; 2.1\}\}$.
$Avail\_S\_N\_Set_3 = \{\{!RINGGEN; 3.1\}, \{?con\_req, !available; 1.1(3)\}, \{?con\_req, !available; 2.1(3)\}\}$.

The consistent sequences obtained for the Phone processes are as follows: $c\_Id\_Seq_{11} = \{1.1\}$, $c\_Id\_Seq_{21} = \{2.1\}$, and $c\_Id\_Seq_{31} = \{1.1(3), 3.1\}$. Here, each process has one consistent sequence, while $Avail\_S\_N\_Set_3 \neq \emptyset$ after the derivation of the sequences, a failure is reported.

4.3   Inter-process Consistency Analysis

The A/G list identifiers of an intra-process consistent sequence refer to the alternative execution possibilities of the process. Since the alternative A/G lists of the A/G set of a particular process generated in the A/G generation phase are mutually exclusive, the execution consideration of one alternative A/G list of the A/G set of a process invalidates the execution possibilities of the other alternative A/G lists of that set. This in turn implies constraints on the execution possibilities of the consistent sequences of the other processes. Inter-process consistency analysis procedure checks any violation of these constraints in composing the alternative A/G lists of different processes. In this step, the A/G list identifiers, not the actual A/Gs are analyzed for consistency.

The procedure presented in Algorithm 4 follows a breadth first, generate and test approach. The consistent sequences of all the active processes generated in the previous step constitutes the initial element (set) of a list called $Avail\_Queue$. $Avail\_Queue$ is a FIFO list of consistent sets, while a consistent set contains intra-process consistent sequences. Initially all the sequences of $Avail\_Queue$ are marked. Each time the first set of this list is removed to generate all the offsprings of this set. In the removed set, a process (P_L) is selected which has the lowest value of a metric called $execution$ $alternatives$ $metric$ or E^j_{metric}. In case of the processes with equal values of E^j_{metric}, one of them is chosen randomly.

Definition 5 E^j_{metric}. *The value of E^j_{metric} for a process P_j denotes the number of alternative execution possibilities of the process. More precisely, for a process, it is the number of intra-process consistent sequences generated in the intra-process A/G validation step. This is a dynamic metric.*

A sequence (candidate sequence) of the selected process is used (and unmarked) to find the possible sequences of the other processes consistent with the candidate sequence. A sequence is considered inconsistent with the candidate sequence if it contains identifiers *conflicting* with the identifiers of the candidate sequence. By *conflicting identifiers* we mean the identifiers of two separate A/G lists of the same process. Two identifiers $i.k$ and $j.l$ are conflicting if $i = j$ but $k \neq l$. A new set is created by taking only the sequences consistent with the candidate sequence. If this set contains at least one consistent sequence from each of the active processes, and all of them are unmarked then it is called an interprocess consistent set of sequences, and there is no failure. Otherwise this set is appended at the end of $Avail\_Queue$ for further analysis provided it contains at least one sequence from each of the processes. The same steps are followed using each sequence of the selected process as candidate sequence. This procedure is continued until we find an inter-process consistent set of sequences, or there is no set remaining for further analysis. In the latter case, a failure is reported.

Supplementary Definitions. $a\_Id\_Seq_i$: a consistent sequence, where $a\_Id\_Seq_i \in A\_Id\_Seq\_Set_k$. $Avail\_Queue$: a FIFO list of sets (of sequences) available for analysis, where $A\_Id\_Seq\_Set_k \in Avail\_Queue$. N: total number of processes in P_{act}. $p\_Id\_Seq_{jk}$: the k-th consistent sequence of P_j, where $p\_Id\_Seq_{jk} \in P\_Id\_Seq\_Set_j$. $Cand\_Id\_Set$: a set of sequences, which is subject to further analysis if it is not inter-process consistent.

Algorithm 4 Inter-process Consistency Analysis.

Input: *A set of intra-process consistent sequences (C_Id_Seq_Set$_j$) for each active process.*
Output: *Failure report or an inter-process consistent set.*

```
01.  Avail_Queue ← {∪ᴺⱼ₌₀C_Id_Seq_Setⱼ};
02.  for each A_Id_Seq_Setₖ ∈ Avail_Queue
        mark each a_Id_Seqᵢ ∈ A_Id_Seq_Setₖ;
05.  failure ← true;
06.  repeat
07.     remove the first set A_Id__Seq_Setf from Avail_Queue;
08.     group the sequences of A_Id_Seq_Setf so that P_Id_Seq_Setⱼ
           contains the sequence(s) of Pⱼ;
09.     identify Pₗ, where E^L_metric ≤ E^j_metric, for any j ≠ L,
           and each p_Id_Seq_Lk ∈ P_Id_Seq_Setₗ is marked;
10.     for each p_Id_Seq_Lk ∈ P_Id_Seq_Setₗ
11.        unmark and insert p_Id_Seq_Lk in Cand_Id_Set;
12.        for each a_Id_Seqᵢ ∈ A_Id_Seq_Setf
13.           if (a_Id_Seqᵢ does not contain A/G list ids conflicting
                  with the ids present in p_Id_Seq_Lk)
14.              Cand_Id_Set ← Cand_Id_Set ∪ {a_Id_Seqᵢ};
15.        endfor
16.        if (Cand_Id_Set contains sequence(s) for each Pⱼ ∈ P_act)
17.           if (all the sequences of Cand_Id_Set are unmarked)
18.              then
19.                 failure ← false;
20.                 break;
21.              else append Cand_Id_Set to Avail_Queue;
22.           endif
23.        endif
24.     endfor
25.  until((Avail_Queue ≠ ∅) ∨ (failure = false))
26.  if (failure) report "failure" and exit;
```

Example 4. *Inter-Process Consistency Analysis.* The inter-process consistency checking of three processes (P_1, P_2, and P_3) is shown in Fig. 5 using a tree structure. Each process has two intra-process consistent sequences for analysis. The "X" symbol under a sequence denotes that the sequence is marked. An inter-process consistent set {{1.1, 2.1, 3.2}, {1.1, 2.1}, {1.1, 2.1, 3.2}} is found for this example, and no failure is reported.

5   Case Study

In order to facilitate the evaluation of the proposed approach, a demonstration detector has been implemented and applied to monitor the behavior of the con-

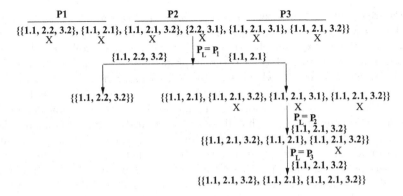

Fig. 5. Inter-process consistency analysis for three processes.

trol software of a PBX. The PBX is capable of serving 60 phones and 15 simultaneous two-way calls. The PBX control software is designed as a time-triggered system which periodically scans the state changes in the PBX hardware interface memory to determine the next course of executions. At the end of these execution tasks the PBX control program reports its current stable states. The interface memory is also shared by the detector to observe the external I/O.

The concepts presented in this paper are applicable in general to the systems, which are specified in a formalism based on communicating finite state machines. However, for the sake of notational convenience and widespread applications, we use the SDL (Specification and Description Language) - a standard of the International Telecommunication Union (ITU) for specifying communication protocols [16]. The SDL is being merged with the Unified Modeling Language (UML) of the Object Management Group (OMG) [17]. The specification used for this case study contained 60 instances of phone handler CFSMs, and two resource management related CFSMs, i.e., 62 concurrent processes in total.

A telephone traffic generator was used to produce inputs to the target system. The load generator simulates the typical, random Plain Old Telephone System (POTS) usage patterns based on Poisson distribution [18]. To characterize the failure detection capability, the exchange software has been seeded to generate unexpected external behaviors (missing message, incorrect message, redundant message). The failure detector has been able to detect and report all the occurrences of failures. In addition, the detector did not report any spurious failure when it was used to observe the original (correct) version of the software.

6   Related Research

In addition to online monitoring of software, the work described in this paper touches on compositional model checking and specification based testing. A survey related to the study of compositional paradigms can be found in [4].

Pasareanu *et al.* [12] present an application of assume-guarantee style model checking to verify the correctness properties of software components, written in Ada. They report experimental results of several possible implementations of assume-guarantee approaches for checking properties of software units in isolation using two popular model checking tools SPIN and SMV.

Barnett *et al.* [10,11] present a runtime monitor that uses executable specification to identify the behavioral discrepancies between a component and its specification. They are able to handle both deterministic [10] and nondeterministic [11] specifications. Their monitor snoops all the inter-component calls and returns, and does not need any instrumentation of the target system. Our detector observes only the messages to and from the system environment. However, we need a mechanism to obtain the state information when the target system reaches a stable condition.

The Observer approach [19] for online validation of distributed system reports failure based on Petri Nets models. In contrast to our approach, it observes all the messages exchanged between the components rather than the external I/0 only, and builds the observational model by composing the individual process specification. A variant of the Observer [20] investigated the advantages of using equivalent multiple binary (two-state) observers instead of a single large one. However, this one also requires the global state graph of the system to derive these small observers. Both of the above approaches are not compositional, and neither has explicitly considered the effect of specification nondeterminism.

The belief-based supervisors [14,15] maintain a collection of hypotheses called consistent belief sets, which are actually the sets of possible global states. They do not make the parallel composition of individual machines into a single one statically. Nevertheless, the number of beliefs or global states may grow exponentially as the nondeterminism increases. They observe the target system as a *complete* black box, i.e., only the external inputs and outputs are visible.

Passive testing [21,22] aimed at detecting failures in the same setting of the failure detector, where the inputs to the system cannot be controlled. They consider specification nondeterminism. However, in the case of collection of communicating finite state machines, they construct a composite machine to employ the same algorithms used for stand alone finite state machine. Test oracles [25] are capable of evaluating the outputs of the application software test cases. The difficulty of automatically detecting the failures is reduced by the control over the inputs to the program in testing. Specification nondeterminism is a consideration but it is generally avoided by judicious selection of inputs.

The work in runtime result checking [23,24], and software audit [26] deals with more constrained set of problems. The former ones are used for the verification of the results of the computation of mathematical functions. A software audit checks a data structure of a program periodically, and may detect a limited set of errors by comparing the data structure with a duplicate or by checking its consistency. It is an intrusive failure detector, which have access to the data structure of the main program. In all cases, specification nondeterminism and concurrency issues are out of their scopes.

7 Concluding Remarks

We have presented a novel approach for online detection of software failures of concurrent programs with respect to their specification. We have formalized an assume-guarantee style automatic reasoning technique in the context of failure detection. The detailed architecture and algorithms are provided for the detector. The algorithms have been implemented in order to monitor a PBX control program, which was specified in the SDL. The evaluation results endorse the efficacy of the proposed algorithms. The recent reconciliation between the ITU-SDL and the OMG-UML [17] suggests a smooth extension of this work for monitoring the systems specified in the UML.

This research advocates the use of the principles of compositionality in order to monitor the actual behavior of the end product of the software development process. The compositionality is achieved by separating the transitions of individual state machines into message receptions and transmissions. The presented detection approach incorporates the modularity and compositionality of verification techniques into the operational stage of software. This is particularly useful to avoid the state explosion problem in case of parallel composition of interacting processes. The process-level analysis also helps in localizing the faults in a system containing multiple processes.

We are aware of the fact that in the world of specifications there is no notion of complete correctness. We may not be absolutely sure about the correctness of the observed system unless the specification is assumed to be completely correct. Nevertheless, a failure report is important information for the user or operator of a system. In this approach, it is impossible to issue a completely *OK* verdict at any point of observation. Contrary to active testing we cannot control the inputs to the implementation under observation in order to cover all the transitions of the specification. As a result, when no failure is reported by the detector, it may happen that infrequent behaviors of the observed system remains unmonitored. There are two other research issues that deserve immediate attention: continuity of detection after the occurrence of a failure, and tradeoff analysis between the complexity of failure detection and the overhead for target system visibility.

References

1. C.A.R. Hoare, "How did software get so reliable without proof," *Lecture Notes in Computer Science,* vol. 1051, Springer-Verlag, 1996.
2. R. Glass, "Persistent Software Errors," *IEEE Transactions on Software Engineering,* 7(2), pp. 162-168, March 1981.
3. D. Kuhn, "Sources of Failure in the Public Switched Telephone Network," *IEEE Computer,* vol. 30, no. 4, pp. 31-36, April 1997.
4. W. P. de Roever, "The Need for Compositional Proof Systems: A Survey," *Lecture Notes in Computer Science,* vol. 1536, pp. 1-22, Springer-Verlag, 1997.
5. J. Misra and K. Chandy, "Proofs of Networks of Processes," *IEEE Transactions on Software Engineering,* 7(4), pp. 417-426, July 1981.
6. C. B. Jones, "Tentative steps towards a development method for interfering programs," *ACM Trans. on Programming Languages and Systems,* 5(4):596-619, 1983.

7. N. Shankar, "Lazy Compositional Verification," *Lecture Notes in Computer Science*, vol. 1536, Springer-Verlag, 1997.

8. IEEE, *Software Engineering: Customer and Terminology Standards*, vol. 1, IEEE, 1999.

9. J. C. Laprie, *Dependability: Basic Concepts and Terminology - In English, French, German, and Japanese*, Vienna, Springer-Verlag, 1992.

10. M. Barnett and W. Schulte, "Spying on Components: A Runtime Verification Technique in Specification and Verification of Component-Based Systems," *Proc. of the Workshop on Specification and Verification of Component Based Systems - OOPSLA '2001*, Tampa, Florida, USA, October, 2001.

11. M. Barnett, L. Nachmanson, and W. Schulte, "Conformance Checking of Components Against Their Non-deterministic Specifications," Technical Report MSR-TR-2001-56, Microsoft Research, June 2001.

12. C. Pasareanu, M. Dwyer, and M. Huth, "Assume-Guarantee Model Checking of Software: A Comparative Case Study," *Lecture Notes in Computer Science*, vol. 1680, Springer-Verlag, September 1999.

13. M. Zulkernine and R. Seviora, "Stable States Based Monitoring of Real-Time Software Systems," *Proc. of the 8th Intl. Conference on Real-Time Computing Systems and Applications*, Tokyo, Japan, March 2002.

14. T. Savor and R. Seviora, "Toward Automatic Detection of Software Failures," *IEEE Computer*, vol. 21, no. 8, pp. 68-74, August 1998.

15. J. Li and R. Seviora, "Automatic Failure Detection with Conditional Belief Supervisors," *Proc. of the 7th International Symposium on Software Reliability Engineering*, IEEE CS Press, pp. 4-13, October 1996.

16. ITU-T, *Recommendation Z.100, Specification and Description Language - SDL*, ITU-Telecommunication Standardization Sector, Geneva, Switzerland, 2000.

17. ITU-T, *Recommendation Z.109, SDL Combined with UML*, ITU-Telecommunication Standardization Sector, Geneva, Switzerland, 2000.

18. D. Bear, *Principles of Telecommunication-Traffic Engineering*, IEE Telecommunication Series 2, Peter Peregrinus Ltd., pp. 192-200, London, England, 1988.

19. M. Diaz, G. Juanole, and J. Courtiat, "Observer - a concept for formal on-line validation of distributed systems," *IEEE Transactions on Software Engineering*, vol. 20, no. 12, pp. 900-913, December 1994.

20. C. Wang and M. Schwartz, "Fault Detection with multiple observers," *IEEE/ACM Transactions on Networking*, vol. 1, no. 1, pp. 48-55, February 1993.

21. D. Lee, A Netravali, K. Sabnani, B. Sugla, and A. John, "Passive Testing and Applications to Network Management," *Proc. of the IEEE International Conference on Network Protocols*, pp. 113-122, October 1997.

22. M. Tabourier, A. Cavalli, and M. Ionescu, "A GSM-MAP Protocol Experiment Using Passive Testing," *Lecture Notes in Computer Science*, vol. 1708, pp. 915-934, Springer-Verlag, 1999.

23. S. Sankar and M. Mandal, "Concurrent runtime monitoring of formally specified programs," *IEEE Computer*, pp. 32-41, March 1993.

24. M. Blum and H. Wasserman, "Software Reliability via Run-Time Result-Checking," *Journal of the ACM*, vol. 44, no. 6, pp. 826-849, November 1997.

25. D. Brown, R. Roggio, J. Cross, and C. McCreary, "An Automated Oracle for Software Testing," *IEEE Trans. on Reliability*, vol. 41, no. 2, pp. 272-279, 1992.

26. John R. Connet, Edward J. Pasternak, and Brude D. Wagner, "Software Defenses in Real-time Control Systems," *Proc. of the IEEE Fault-Tolerant Computing Symposium*, pp. 94-99, June 1972.

Contributions for Modelling UML State-Charts in B

Hung Ledang and Jeanine Souquières

LORIA – Université Nancy 2 – UMR 7503
Campus scientifique, BP 239
54506 Vand÷uvre-lès-Nancy Cedex – France
{ledang,souquier}@loria.fr

Abstract. An appropriate approach for translating UML to B formal specifications allows one to use UML and B jointly in an unified, practical and rigorous
software development. We can formally analyse UML specifications via their derived B formal specifications. This point is significant because B support tools like
AtelierB are available. We can also use UML specifications as a tool for building
B specifications, so the development of B specifications become easier.
In this paper, we address the problem of modelling UML state-charts in B, which
has not been, so far, completely treated. We distinguish between event-related and
activity-related parts of UML state-charts. We propose deriving the B specification of the event-related part independently with the activity-related part. For this
purpose, a new approach for modelling events is proposed; the communication
among state-charts is also considered.

Keywords: UML, state-chart, event, activity, class operation, B method, B abstract
machine, B operation.

1 Introduction

The Unified Modelling Language (UML)[22] has become a de-facto standard notation
for describing analysis and design models of object-oriented software systems. The
graphical description of models is easily accessible. Developers and their customers intuitively grasp the general structure of a model and thus have a good basis for discussing
system requirements and their possible implementation. However, since the UML concepts have English-based informal semantics, it is difficult even impossible to design
tools for verifying or analysing formally UML specifications. This point is considered
as a serious drawback of UML-based techniques.

To remedy such a drawback, one approach is to develop UML as a precise modelling
language. The pUML[1] (precise UML) group has been created to achieve this goal.
However the main challenge [5] of the pUML is to define a new formal notation that has
been up to now an open issue. Furthermore, the support tool for such a new formalism
is perhaps another challenge.

In waiting for a precise version of UML and its support tool, the necessity to detect
semantic defects inside UML specifications should be solved in a pragmatic approach (cf.
[26,4]): formalising UML specifications by existing formal languages and then analysing
UML specifications via the derived formal specifications. In this perspective, using the B
language [1] to model UML specifications has been considered as a promising approach

---

[1] http://www.cs.york.ac.uk/puml/

M. Butler, L. Petre, and K. Sere (Eds.): IFM 2002, LNCS 2335, pp. 109–127, 2002.
© Springer-Verlag Berlin Heidelberg 2002

[13,25,18,20]. By formalising UML specifications in B, one can use B powerful support tools like AtelierB [27], B-Toolkit [3] to analyse and detect semantic defects inside UML specifications (cf. [14]). On the other hand, we can also use UML specifications as a tool to develop B specifications which can be refined automatically to the executable code [2,8].

This paper addresses the modelling in B of UML state-charts. Such a modelling has been previously done by Meyer, Nguyen and Lano [18,19,20,10,23]. However, their rules for mapping UML state-chart-related concepts into B have got followed shortcomings:

1. the modelling of the activity-related part (cf. [10]) in state-charts did not consider the interference of event-related part;
2. the modelling of events could not work if events trigger transitions with several sequential actions. This is the case in which a state entry/exit action must follow/precede actions of incoming/outgoing transitions of the state;
3. There has been no mechanised derivation procedure for UML state-charts due to ambiguities of modelling rules;
4. deferred events and the communication of UML state-charts have not been considered.

We propose to distinguish between activity-related and event-related parts of state-charts. The event-related part in state-charts relates to events. These elements comprise events, state, transition and actions. Remainders in state-charts constitute the activity-related part. Since activities do not affect states, it is natural to model the event-related part independently with respect to the activity-related part. However, the modelling of the activity-related part should take into account the interference of the event-related part.

This paper addresses only the modelling in B of the event-related part in UML state-charts. The interference of the event-related part to the activity-related part need a further investigation and is beyond the scope of the current paper. We propose a new approach for modelling events in which the different semantics of non deferred events and deferred events should be taken into account. Each non deferred events is modelled in two stages:

1. creating B abstract operations for non deferred events in which the event effect on the related data is directly specified;
2. implementing or refining the B operation in the first step by calling B operations for the triggered transition and actions.

In our opinion, this two-stages approach allows us to overcome the second shortcoming above. In addition, modelling non deferred events in two stages gives also possibilities to verify the conformance of the envisaged effects of an event with respect to its triggered actions. Deferred events are modelled in a similar manner, however, the queueing and dequeuing of those events should be taken into account. The approach for modelling deferred events can be extended to model the asynchronous communication among state-charts. Dealing with the synchronous communication among state-charts is another contribution in this paper. The idea is to avoid calling the B operation for *message receipt event* in the B operations of the event that send the message because both events are modelled in the same abstract machine. For this purpose, the content of the B operation for the message receipt event is inserted in the B operation of the event that send the message. Hence, our proposals together with previous proposals by Meyer, Nguyen and Lano for modelling states, transitions and actions give rise to a complete framework for deriving B specifications from the event-related part of UML state-charts.

In Section 2, basic concepts of UML state-charts and a UML specification example are presented. The example will be used through the whole presentation. In Section 3, previous work for modelling UML state-charts in B is presented. Section 4 presents a new approach to model non deferred events. The modelling of deferred events is presented in Section 5. In Section 6 we go on to present the modelling of the communication among UML state-charts. Section 7 presents an automatic integration procedure to derive B specifications from UML class diagrams and UML state-charts. Finally, in Section 8, concluding remarks complete our presentation.

2   UML State-Charts

2.1   Basic Concepts

State-chart diagrams are UML diagrams for modelling dynamic aspects of systems. State-charts were invented by Harel [7], the semantics and the notation of UML state-charts are substantially those of Harel state-charts with adaptations to the object-oriented context.

UML state-charts focus on the event-ordered behaviour of an object, a feature which is specially useful in modelling reactive systems. A state-chart shows the event triggered flow of control due to transitions which lead from state to state, i.e it describes the possible sequences of states and actions through which a model element can go during its lifetime as a result of reacting to discrete events. A state reflects a situation in the life of an object during which this object satisfies some condition, performs some action, or waits for some event.

Transitions are viewed in UML as relationships between two states indicating that an object in the first state will enter the second state and performs specific actions when a specified event occurs provided that certain conditions are satisfied.

The semantics of event processing in UML state-chart is based on the *run to completion* (rtc) assumption: events are processed one at a time and when the machine is in a stable configuration, i.e. a new event is processed only when all the consequences of the previous event have been exhausted. Therefore, an event is never processed when the state-chart is in some intermediate, unstable situation.

Events may be specified by a state as being possibly deferred. They are actually deferred if, when occurring, they do not trigger any transition. This will last until a state is reached where events are no more deferred or where events trigger a transition.

2.2   Example: A Lift Control System

This section presents the UML specification of a system that controls a set of lifts and buttons. The class diagram is shown in Figure 1. For a lift, we consider information about the current movement direction (dir $\in$ DIRECTION $\triangleq$ {*up,down*}), the next floor (curDestFloor $\in$ FLOOR $\triangleq$ *ground . . top*) where the lift will arrive and the lift door status (doorStatus $\in$ DOORSTATUS $\triangleq$ {*open,closed*}). Each button is attached to a floor.

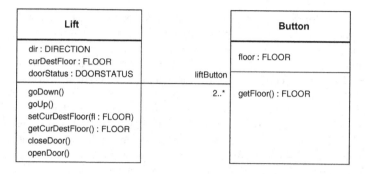

Fig. 1. Class diagram for the lift control system

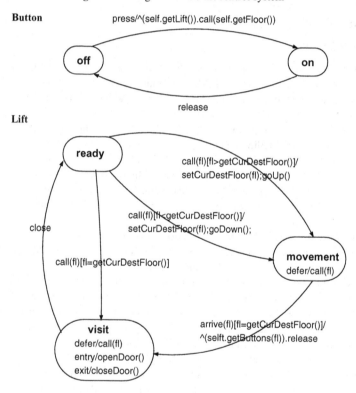

Fig. 2. State-charts for the lift control system

Given one lift and one floor, there are two buttons:the *indication button* is in the lift and the *call button* is at the given floor.

Figure 2 shows the state-charts of classes Button and Lift. Each button has two states *on* and *off* corresponding to the state of the button light. When the button is pressed, it is in the state *on*; when the floor of the button is visited, it returns to the state *off*. When a button in the state *off* is pressed, an event call is sent asynchronously to the lift associated to the button. The parameter of call is the floor of the button. Each lift has three states *ready*, *visit* and *movement*. It is only in the state *ready* that the lift serves an eventual call by changing into one of the states *visit* or *movement* depending on the calling floor. Because a lift should process all eventual events call, the event call is deferrable in states *visit* and *movement*. The door of a lift in the state *visit* should be open, meaning that openDoor() is the entry action of *visit*. The lift in the state *visit* should change to *ready* before process another event call. At the exit of the state *visit*, the lift door should be closed, hence closeDoor() is the exit action of *visit*. In the state *movement*, if the lift arrives at the destination floor (event arrive), the event release is sent synchronously for lighting off two buttons attached to the visited floor. Note also that a lift will not change its destination floor during the movement.

3   Modelling UML State-Charts in B: State-of-the-Art

This section recalls essential points in the work of Meyer, Nguyen and Lano for modelling UML state-charts in B. Those works are based on the UML state-chart concepts inherited from OMT state-chart [21]: state, sequential sub state, concurrent sub state, transition, action and non deferred event. Each of such elements is modelled by a derivation scheme. The B derivation of UML state-charts is integrated in the B derivation of class diagrams.

3.1   Derivation Schemes to B for UML Sate-charts

Derivation 1 (States) There has been derivation schemes for states, subs states, however, we recall here only, as an example, the derivation scheme for states.

For each state-chart attached to a class Class, we create a B enumerated set $STATE$ which gathers all the states of the diagram. The state of an object is recorded by a B variable $state$ defined as a function from the B variable $class$, which models the set of effective instances of Class, to $STATE$. Thus, the state of an object oo is defined as $state(oo)$. Transitions between states correspond to the modification of $state$. The initial state is set up in the instance creation operations as it is done for class attributes. Figure 3 presents the formalisation of the states assigned to the class Lift (cf. Section 2.2).

Let us recall that the special abstract machine $Types$ is used to model attribute types of classes. $Types$ is seen (link **SEES**) by abstract machines derived from classes in which we model the attributes. An interesting point of Meyer work is to model a class instance space by a constant. For example, the constant $LIFT$ models the instance space of Lift. $LIFT$ is considered as a subset of the set $OBJECTS$, which models instance space of all classes. $OBJECTS$ is also declared in $Types$. One can therefore model the multiple inheritance between class that could not be treated in the work of Nguyen and Lano in which the class instance space is modelled as a B deferred set.

Derivation 2 (Transitions) Each transition is formalised by a B operation which models the change of the state. Figure 4 shows the B operation $transVisitReady(...)$ modelling the transition from the state *visit* to *ready* in the state-chart Lift.

```
MACHINE Lift
/* the abstract machine Types declares OBJECTS and models attributes types */
SEES Types
CONSTANTS
    LIFT
PROPERTIES
    LIFT ⊆ OBJECTS
SETS
    LIFT_STATE = {ready, visit, movement}
VARIABLES
    lift, dir, curDestFloor, doorStatus, liftState
INVARIANT
    lift ⊆ LIFT ∧
    dir ∈ lift → DIRECTION ∧
    curDestFloor ∈ lift → FLOOR
    doorStatus ∈ lift → DOOR_STATUS
    liftState ∈ lift → LIFT_STATE
    ...
END
```

Fig. 3. B formalisation for states

```
MACHINE Lift
    ...
OPERATIONS
    transVisitReady(ll) =
    pre
        ll ∈ lift ∧ liftState(ll) = visit
    then
        liftState(ll) := ready
    end;
    closeDoor(ll) =
    pre
        ll ∈ lift
    then
        doorStatus(ll) := closed
    end;
    ...
END
```

Fig. 4. B formalisation for transitions and actions

Derivation 3 (Actions) Each action corresponds to a class operation. Thus, each action is naturally modelled as a B operation (cf. $closeDoor(...)$ in Figure 4).

Derivation 4 (Events) Each event is also formalised by a B operation. This operation is parameterised by target objects and eventual parameters of the event. Parameters are typed by a predicate in the precondition clause. The body of the B operation for an

```
...
OPERATIONS
    close(ll) =
    pre
        ll ∈ lift
    then
        select liftState(ll) = visit then
            transVisitReady(ll) ||
            closeDoor(ll)
        else skip end
    end;
...
```

Fig. 5. Current B formalisation for events

event constitutes invocations to B operations modelling the triggered transitions and their associated actions. Figure 5 shows the B operation $close(...)$ for the event close.

3.2 Observations

In our opinion, derivation schemes for states, transitions and actions have been well defined. Following observations are about the modelling of events. First of all, one cannot apply the event derivation scheme above for deferred events since the semantics of deferred events has not been considered. For non deferred events, at the first glance, the derivation scheme seems to be evident. However, at a close inspection, two problems can be raised:

1. **how to distribute B operations into abstract machines?** Considering the example in Figure 5. Because $close(...)$, $transVisitReady(...)$ and $closeDoor(...)$ are in abstract machines, the abstract machine for $close(...)$ should have a link **INCLUDES** to the abstract machine $Lift$ for $transVisitReady(...)$ and $closeDoor(...)$ (cf. Figure 4). However, calling two B operations from the same included abstract machine is not allowed according to [1,27]. The solution by Meyer to declare $transVisitReady(...)$ in the clause **DEFINITION** cannot deal with transitions from ready to movement in which several actions are attached to an individual transition;

2. **what about the action sequence?** The action sequences in transitions from ready to movement cannot be modelled in the abstract machine context since the sequential substitution ";" is not allowed.

The two above problems were justified by the fact that there has not been, so far, an appropriate solution to automatically map UML state-charts into B (cf. Self-evaluation of Meyer in section 6.2.3 of the chapter 6 in [18]). The prototype **Argo/UML+B** by Meyer works actually only with UML class diagrams. In [9], Laleau and Mammar have presented a support tool for generating B specifications from UML diagrams of data intensive applications. Although they considered UML state-charts, nothing new is added regarding the work of Nguyen. In the tool **U2B** by C. Snook and M. Butler [24], which implements a subset of Meyer derivation schemes for UML class diagrams, the modelling in B of UML state-chart could not deal with the action sequence. Furthermore, no mechanised way to organise B operations into abstract machines has been proposed (cf. [6]).

4   New Approach for Modelling Non-deferred Events in B

We distinguish between non deferred events and deferred events due to their different semantics. A non deferred event must be handled immediately just after its occurrence or it should be lost. A deferred event can occur at a state and can be handled afterward at another state. This section presents a way to model non deferred events. The modelling of deferred events will be discussed in the next section.

4.1   The Two-Stages Approach

As said earlier, we model each non deferred event by a B operation. However the B operation for each non deferred event is implemented or refined afterward. In other words, there are two B specifications for each non deferred event: the first is a B abstract operation; this abstract operation is then implemented or refined by the second. The expected effect of a non deferred event on related data is specified directly in the corresponding B abstract operation. It is only in the B implementation or refinement operation that we make explicitly invocations to B operations of the triggered transitions and actions. Building the abstract content and implementation or refinement content for B operations of non deferred events constitutes two stages in modelling non deferred events in B[2].

4.2   Creating B Abstract Operations for Non-deferred Events

In order to specify directly the effect of an event on its concerned data, we propose to group an event and related data in the same abstract machine. Thus, the problem of modelling events becomes one of how B substitutions can be used to express the pre-/post- of the event. This is similar to model actions or basic class operations that are local to one class. Figure 6 shows an abstract machine $System$, in which the B operation $close(...)$ models the event close. In the data declaration section (clauses **SETS**, **VARIABLES**...) of $System$ we notice the presence of the data derived from the class Lift. In addition, $System$ has link **SEES** to $Types$ because $System$ needs references to B types defined in $Types$ for modelling attribute types of Lift.

We propose to create an abstract machine ($System$) for all events; the reason is that an event can affect data from different classes (cf. the event arrive). Data of $System$ are derived from the whole class diagram. However, $System$ does not contain B operations for transitions and actions since those operations are used to implement or refine abstract operations of events as described in the following sections.

4.3   Solution 1: Implementing B Operations of Non-deferred Events

The first solution to deal with the relationship between non deferred events and their triggered transitions and actions is to use the B implementation construct and the B importation primitive. The abstract machine ($System$) for events is implemented by importing abstract machines for transitions and actions, so that B operations for events can be implemented by calling B operations of transitions and actions. In Figure 7(a), the B operation $close(...)$ of $System$ is implemented by calling operations $closeDoor(...)$ and $transVisitReady(...)$ of $Lift$.

---

[2] Similar ideas have been used in our previous work for modelling use cases and class operations [12,16,15].

```
MACHINE System
SEES Types
...
VARIABLES
    lift, liftState, doorStatus, ..., button, ...
...
OPERATIONS
    close(ll) =
    pre
        ll ∈ lift
    then
        select liftState(ll) = visit then
            doorStatus(ll) := closed ||
            liftState(ll) := ready
        else skip end
    end;
...
END
```

Fig. 6. New B formalisation for non deferred events

```
IMPLEMENTATION System_imp
REFINES System
SEES Types
IMPORTS Lift
OPERATIONS
    close(ll) =
    var bb in
        /* isVisit() is used to implement state */
        /* checking conditions in the substitution */
        /* select in System since the data in */
        /* Lift is not visible from operations in */
        /* System_imp */
        bb ← isVisit(ll);
        if bb = TRUE then
            closeDoor(ll);
            transVisitReady(ll)
        else skip end
    end;
...
END
```

```
REFINEMENT System_ref
REFINES System
SEES Types
INCLUDES Lift

OPERATIONS
    close(ll) =
    begin
        /* since the data in the Lift is visible */
        /* this time from operations in System_ref, */
        /* the operation isVisit() is not necessary */
        if liftState(ll) = visit then
            closeDoor(ll);
            transVisitReady(ll)
        else skip end
    end;
...
END
```

(a) Solution 1: using the B implementation construct

(b) Solution 2: using the B refinement construct

Fig. 7. B formalisation for the relationship between events, transitions and actions

As you can notice, both $System$ and $Lift$ contain some data with the same name and properties since those data are all derived from the same class (Lift). This identity acts as the implicit gluing invariant between $System$ and $Lift$ in $System\_imp$. In addition, the state checking expression $liftState(ll) = visit$ has been implemented by an auxiliary operation $isVisit(...)$. The reason is that data in $Lift$ is not visible in the operations of $System\_imp$ that imports $Lift$. The situation is similar for expressions that model eventual guard conditions of transitions. Those eventual auxiliary operations for the state checking and for guard conditions can be defined in abstract machines for classes or associations.

Remark 1

1. Since the B implementation construct allows sequence substitutions, the modelling of action sequence is enabled. Furthermore, since there is no restriction regarding operations in imported abstract machines to be called in the implemented operations, we are therefore free to arrange B operations of transitions and actions in different abstract machines or in one unique abstract machine.
2. The parallel substitution "||" is not allowed inside the B implementation construct so we can not model explicitly the parallelism of actions. However, since those actions affect different data (cf. page 434 in [22]), we can therefore simulate the parallelism of actions by the sequence without losing the total effect.

4.4   Solution 2: Refining B Operations of Non-deferred Events

The combination of the B refinement construct and the B inclusion primitive provides another way to deal with the relationship between non deferred events and their triggered transitions and actions (cf. Figure 7(b)). Both solutions for modelling the relationship between events and triggered transitions and actions are equivalent, however the use of the B refinement construct and the B inclusion primitive allows one to avoid auxiliary operations such as $isVisit(...)$ since the data in included abstract machines are visible in the operations of including refinement components. For this reason, the combination of the B refinement construct and the B inclusion primitive is preferred and will be referenced afterward.

5   Modelling Deferred Events in B

In some modelling situations, we may want to recognise some events but postpone a response to them until later. UML allows one to specify such situations by using deferred events. We therefore distinguish between the adding of deferred events in an internal buffer in some states and the handling them in another states. Deferred events are taken off the buffers as soon as the object enters a state that does not defer those events and the events become active.

5.1   Modelling Deferred Event Internal Buffers

The internal buffer is composed of items. Each item is a record of fields for receiver objects and arguments of the event. In the context of the state-chart Lift, the event call is deferred in the states *movement* and *visit*. The buffer call_Buffer for call contains records of two fields: (i) the reference to an object ll of the class Lift; and (ii) the argument fl of the type FLOOR. call_Buffer can be modelled as a B variable $call\_Buffer$ defined as followed:

$$\boxed{call\_Buffer \subseteq lift \times FLOOR}$$

Remark 2

If such a pair {ll, fl} can appear several times in call_Buffer, $call\_Buffer$ is defined as followed:

$$\boxed{call\_Buffer \in (lift \times FLOOR) \nrightarrow NAT}$$

where $call\_Buffer(ll, fl)$ is the occurrence number of {ll, fl} in call_Buffer.

5.2 B Abstract Operations for Deferred Events

As the case of non deferred events, we propose to model a deferred event by a B abstract operation and its refinement. In the B abstract operations we should model at the same time the buffering of the deferred events at states where they are deferrable and the handling them in states where they are not deferrable. Return to the event call; in the states *movement* and *visit*, call is deferred, it should be inserted in call_Buffer; in the state *ready*, call is no more deferred, it should be removed from call_Buffer (in case it was buffered previously) and triggers transitions (cf. Figure 8).

Remark 3

1. For the case where call_Buffer is a multi-set (cf. Remark 2), the buffering of an event call on the object ll is modelled by increasing $call\_Buffer(ll, fl)$ by 1. the removing of a call from call_Buffer is modelled by decreasing $call\_Buffer(ll, fl)$ by 1.
2. We have not yet considered the fact that call is asynchronously sent from the state-chart Button to the state-chart Lift, which will be discussed in Section 6.2.

5.3 B Refinement Operations for Deferred Events

In order to refine B abstract operations for deferred events, it is necessary to introduce B operations for inserting and removing deferred events. Such operations should be defined in a B abstract machine where the corresponding B variable for the internal buffer is defined. The refinement of B operations for deferred events is similar to the refinement of B operations for non deferred events (cf. Section 4.4).

6 Modelling the Communication among UML State-Charts in B

The solution in the works of Lano, Meyer and Nguyen for modelling the communication between state-charts can be applied in case of synchronous communication but not for the asynchronous communication. In addition, this solution could not deal with the case where a message is diffused to multiple objects. For this reason, the modelling in B of the communication between state-charts is discussed in this section.

MACHINE *System*
SEES *Types*
...
VARIABLES
 lift, button, ..., call_Buffer
INVARIANT
 ... $\wedge$ *call_Buffer* $\subseteq$ *lift* $\times$ *FLOOR*
INITIALISATION
 ... $\|$ *call_Buffer* := ϕ
...

OPERATIONS
 call(ll,fl) =
 pre
  ll $\in$ *lift* $\wedge$ *fl* $\in$ *FLOOR*
 then
  select *liftState(ll)* = *visit* **then**
   /* inserting call in call_Buffer */
   call_Buffer := *call_Buffer* $\cup$ $\{ll \mapsto fl\}$
  when *liftState(ll)* = *movement* **then**
   /* inserting call in call_Buffer */
   call_Buffer := *call_Buffer* $\cup$ $\{ll \mapsto fl\}$
  when *liftState(ll)* = *ready* $\wedge$ *fl* = *curDestFloor(ll)* **then**
   /* specifying effects of call on related data. */
   liftState(ll) := *visit* $\|$
   doorStatus(ll) := *open* $\|$
   /* removing call from call_Buffer. */
   call_Buffer := *call_Buffer* $-$ $\{ll \mapsto fl\}$
  when *liftState(ll)* = *ready* $\wedge$ *fl* > *curDestFloor(ll)* **then**
   /* specifying effects of call on related data. */
   liftState(ll) := *movement* $\|$
   curDestFloor(ll) := *fl* $\|$
   dir(ll) := *up* $\|$
   /* removing call from call_Buffer. */
   call_Buffer := *call_Buffer* $-$ $\{ll \mapsto fl\}$
  when *liftState(ll)* = *ready* $\wedge$ *fl* < *curDestFloor(ll)* **then**
   /* specifying effects of call on related data. */
   liftState(ll) := *movement* $\|$
   curDestFloor(ll) := *fl* $\|$
   dir(ll) := *down* $\|$
   /* removing call from call_Buffer. */
   call_Buffer := *call_Buffer* $-$ $\{ll \mapsto fl\}$
  else skip end
 end;
...
END

Fig. 8. B formalisation for deferred events

6.1 Modelling Synchronous Messages

The intuitive idea is to avoid calling the B operation of the *message receipt event* in the B operations of the event that sends the message, because both events are modelled in the same abstract machine (*System*). For this purpose, the content of B operation for the message receipt event is inserted in the B operation of the event that sends the message. Consider the example with the event arrive that send messages release to two objects Button (cf. Section 2). As you can notice, the effects of two events release are specified in the body of B operations for arrive (cf. Figure 9). Note also that the B operations for release are no longer needed.

6.2 Modelling Asynchronous Messages

Since B does not allow to model explicitly the asynchronous communication, we have to simulate it. The idea is similar to the management of deferred events, namely, we create for each signal type a buffer to store signals that have been sent but have not been treated by receiver state-chart. The buffer is written by sender state-chart and read by receiver state-chart. Generally, each item in the buffer should contain information about the receiver(s) objects, eventual parameters of the signals.

In the context of two state-charts for Lift and Button, the event call is no longer deferred in the states *visit* and *movement* but it is send asynchronously (message self.getLift().call(self.getFloor())) from the state-chart Button to the state-chart Lift. The signal buffer for call can be defined as followed:

$$call\_Signal\_Buffer \subseteq lift \times FLOOR$$

Remark 4

1. Remark 2 is still valid.
2. By introducing $call\_Signal\_Buffer$, we can model the sending of call in the B operations of the event press (cf. Figure 10).
3. Because call is no longer considered as deferred in the context of two state-charts Lift and Button, the B variable $call\_Buffer$ is no longer needed. As opposite to release, the B operations for call are needed and in those operations we model the effects of call as well as the removing of call from its signal buffer. For reason of space, the modified B operations for call is omitted.

7 Integrating UML State-Charts into B Specifications

This section presents the way to develop B specifications from UML class diagrams and the event-related part of UML state-charts.

7.1 Data in the B Specification

By definition (cf. [18]) the data in the B specification models the data in class and state-charts. Thus, the B data are derived from: (i) classes, association, attributes in

```
MACHINE System
SEES Types
...
OPERATIONS
    arrive(ll,fl) =
    pre
        ll ∈ lift ∧ fl ∈ FLOOR
    then
        select liftState(ll) = movement ∧ fl = curDestFloor(ll) then
            /* effects of arrive are effects of itself on the object Lift */
            liftState(ll) := visit ‖
            doorStatus(ll) := open ‖
            /* and effects of two events release on two objects Button. */
            any b1,b2 where
                b1 ∈ button ∧ b2 ∈ button ∧
                {b1,b2} = liftButton⁻¹[{ll}] ∩ floor⁻¹[{fl}]
            then
                buttonState := buttonState ⊲ {b1 ↦ off, b2 ↦ off}
            end
        else skip end
    end;
...
END

REFINEMENT System_ref
REFINES System
SEES Types
...
OPERATIONS
    arrive(ll,fl) =
    if liftState(ll) = movement ∧ fl = curDestFloor(ll) then
        transMovementVisit(ll);
        openDoor(ll);
        var b1,b2 in
            b1,b2 ← getButtons(ll,fl);
            if buttonState(b1) = on then
                transOnOff(b1)
            end;
            if buttonState(b2) = on then
                transOnOff(b2)
            end
        end
    else skip end
    end;
...
END
```

Fig. 9. B formalisation for synchronous messages

```
MACHINE System
SEES Types
VARIABLES
    lift,button,....,call_Signal_Buffer
INVARIANT
    ... ∧
    call_Signal_Buffer ⊆ lift × FLOOR
INITIALISATION
    ... ‖ call_Signal_Buffer := φ
OPERATIONS
    press(bt) =
    pre
        bt ∈ button
    then
      select buttonState(bt) = off then
        /* effects of press */
        buttonState(bt) := on ‖
        /* sending call */
        call_Signal_Buffer :=
            call_Signal_Buffer ∪ {liftButton(bt) ↦ floor(bt)}
      else skip end
    end;
    ...
END
```

Fig. 10. B formalisation for asynchronous messages

the class diagram; (ii) states, sub-states in the state-charts. According to Section 5.1 and Section 6.2, we can also have B data for modelling the buffers of eventual deferred events and signals. In our example, the B data come from: (i) two classes Lift and Button, their attributes and the association between Lift and Button; (ii) the states in the state-charts for Lift and Button and (iii) the buffer call_Signal_Buffer.

7.2 Operations in the B Specification

In general, the B operations are mainly used to model events[3], transitions, actions. However, according to Section 5, there are also B operations to model the inserting and removing of eventual deferred events and signals. In case using the B implementation construct, there should be B operations for the state checking and guarded conditions (cf. Section 4.3).

In our example, the B operations come from: (i) the transitions in state-charts for the classes Lift and Button; (ii) the class operations (they are basic); (iii) the events close,arrive,press and call but not release and the inserting and removing of call regarding the buffer call_Signal_Buffer.

---

[3] except the ones issued from the synchronous communication between state-charts

```
MACHINE Basic
SEES Types
...
VARIABLES
    lift,button, ...,
    call_Signal_Buffer
INVARIANT ...
INITIALISATION ...
OPERATIONS
    transOnOff(ll) = ...
    closeDoor(ll) = ...
    insertCall(ll,fl) = ...
...
END
```

(a) *Basic* models transitions, actions, deferred event and signal inserting/removing

```
MACHINE Basic
SEES Types
/* distributing B operations for transition, actions */
/* into abstract machines Lift, Button */
EXTENDS Lift, Button
VARIABLES
    call_Signal_Buffer
INVARIANT ...
INITIALISATION ...
OPERATIONS
    insertCall(ll,fl) = ...
...
END
```

(b) Decomposing *Basic* in abstract machines for classes and associations

Fig. 11. The abstract machine *Basic*

7.3   Structuring the Derived B Specification

The operations modelling events are grouped in an abstract machine called $System$ (cf. Figure 6 and Figure 8). Data in $System$ are described in Section 7.1.

We propose to create another abstract machine ($Basic$) to group B operations for transitions, actions and for inserting/removing eventual deferred events and signals (cf. Figure 11(a)). The data in $Basic$ are identical to the $System$ data. We refine $System$ by including $Basic$ so that we can refine B abstract operations for events in $System$ by calling B operations of transitions, actions in $Basic$. The identity of data of $Basic$ and $System$ acts as the implicit gluing invariant in $System\_ref$.

We can further structure $Basic$ by delegating B operations and related data of transitions and actions to abstract machines for classes and eventual abstract machines for associations. Consequently, there are links **EXTENDS** from $Basic$ to abstract machines for classes and eventual abstract machines for class associations; in $Basic$, we declare only data and operations for inserting and removing eventual deferred events and signals (cf. Figure 11(b)). Figure 12 shows the architecture of the B specification corresponding to the UML specification in Section 2.2. The abstract machine $Basic$, in this case, includes (clause **EXTENDS**) two abstract machines $Lift$ and $Button$ for classes Lift and Button. The association 1..(2..*) is expressed by the link **USES** from $Button$ to $Lift$; no abstract machine for this association is created. The B specification was developed with AtelierB and the code can be found in [11].

Remark 5

1. From experiences to develop the example in this paper, we have found that $LIFT$ must be defined once in $Types$. Otherwise, $LIFT$ should be defined twice, in $System$ and in $Lift$ but this situation is not allowed under AtelierB.

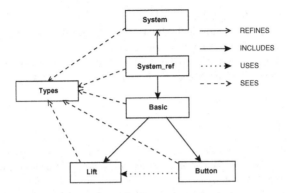

Fig. 12. The derived B specification architecture of the UML specification in Section 2.2

2. Furthermore, it is even possible to avoid the constants $LIFT$ and $BUTTON$. In that case, $lift$ that models the set of effective instances of Lift can be constrained directly to be a subset of $OBJECTS$.
3. Always under the AtelierB environment, $Basic$ is necessary and we cannot dispense it since in that case, $System\_ref$ must "**INCLUDES**" directly $Lift$ and $Button$, however this is impossible due to the link **USES** from $Button$ to $Lift$.

7.4 Generating B Operations' Body

We can presently automatically derive the architecture of B specifications. The data, the skeleton of B operations in the B specification are also automatically derived. According to Meyer [18], the B operations for transitions can be automatically derived. According to Section 5 the B operations for inserting and removing eventual deferred events and signals can also be automatically derived. For the purpose of a complete automation of the derivation, we propose to attach OCL-based specifications to events, actions and guard conditions. Hence, the of B abstract operations for events, actions can be derived by using OCL-B rules [17]. The B refinement operations for events can be derived from state-charts. The precise translation rules will be proposed at a later stage.

8 Conclusion

The contributions of our paper consist of a new approach for modelling non deferred events, the modelling of deferred events and the modelling of the communication between UML state-charts, which were not previously treated. Our proposals together with previous derivation schemes for states, actions, transitions give rise to a derivation procedure from the event-related part of UML state-chart in B (cf. Section 7).

Together with previous works [12,16,15] we are able to provide a complete framework for deriving B specifications from UML structure and behaviour diagrams. Hence, the conformance between two aspects (the structure and the behaviour) of UML specifications can be formally verified by analysing the corresponding B specification (cf. [14]).

For further study, the adaptation of OCL-B translation rules [17] in our work has been envisaged ; a study to translate UML state-charts into B implementation operations is also envisaged. As said earlier, the interference of event-related part to activity-related part which has not been treated so far, is also a subject to investigate. In addition, the prototype Argo/UML+B by Meyer is currently extended to take into account UML behavioural diagrams.

References

1. J.R. Abrial. *The B Book - Assigning Programs to Meanings.* Cambridge University Press, 1996. ISBN 0-521-49619-5.
2. A. Amelot and D. Dollé. Le raffinement automatique. Available at http://www3.inrets.fr/B@INRETS/Events/2001-ESTAS/actes/MTI-2001-ESTAS.*, 2001. Slides.
3. B-Core(UK) Ltd, Oxford (UK). *B-Toolkit User's Manual,* 1996. Release 3.2.
4. J.M. Bruel. Integrating Formal and Informal Specification Techniques. Why? How? In *the 2nd IEEE Workshop on Industrial-Strength Formal Specification Techniques,* pages 50–57, Boca Raton, Florida (USA), 1998. Available at http://www.univ-pau.fr/~bruel/publications.html.
5. J.M. Bruel, J. Lilius, A. Moreira, and R.B. France. Defining Precise Semantics for UML. In *Object-Oriented Technology,* LNCS 1964, pages 113–122, Sophia Antipolis and Cannes (F), June 12-16, 2000. ECOOP 2000 Workshop Reader.
6. C. Snook and M. Butler. Tool-Supported Use of UML for Constructing B Specifications. draft version.
7. D. Harel. Statecharts: A Visual Formalism for Complex Systems. *Science of Computer Programming,* 8:231–274, 1987.
8. R. Laleau and A. Mammar. A Generic Process to Refine a B Specification into a Relational Database Implementation. In *ZB 2000: Formal Specification and Development in Z and B,* LNCS 1878, York (UK), August/September 2000. Springer.
9. R. Laleau and A. Mammar. An Overview of a Method and its support Tool for Generating B Specifications from UML Notations. In *The 15st IEEE Int. Conf. on Automated Software Engineering,* Grenoble (F), September 11-15, 2000.
10. K. Lano. *The B Language and Method : A Guide to Practical Formal Development.* FACIT. Springer-Verlag, 1996. ISBN 3-540-76033-4.
11. H. Ledang. Case Study: *Lift Control System B Specification.* Available at http://www.loria.fr/~ledang/case-studies/Lift.zip, 2001.
12. H. Ledang. Des cas d'utilisation à une spécification B. In *Journées AFADL'2001: Approches Formelles dans l'Assistance au Développement de Logiciels,* Nancy (F), 11-13 juin, 2001. http://www.loria.fr/~ledang/publications/afadl01.ps.gz.
13. H. Ledang. Formal Techniques in the Object-Oriented Development: an Approach based on the B method. *PhDOOS2001: the 11th ECOOP Workshop for PhD Student in Object-Oriented Systems,* Budapest (Hu), http://www.st.informatik.tu-darmstadt.de/phdws/wstimetable.html, June 18-19, 2001. http://www.loria.fr/~ledang/publications/PhDOOS01.ps.gz.
14. H. Ledang and J. Souquières. Formalizing UML Behavioral Diagrams with B. In *the Tenth OOPSLA Workshop on Behavioral Semantics: Back to Basics,* Tampa Bay, Florida (USA), October 15, 2001. http://www.loria.fr/~ledang/publications/oopsla01.ps.gz.
15. H. Ledang and J. Souquières. Integrating UML and B Specification Techniques. In *the Informatik2001 Workshop on Integrating Diagrammatic and Formal Specification Techniques,* Vienna (Autria), September 26, 2001. http://www.loria.fr/~ledang/publications/informatik01.ps.gz.

16. H. Ledang and J. Souquières. Modeling Class Operations in B: Application to UML Behaviral Diagrams. In *ASE2001: the 16th IEEE International Conference on Automated Software Engineering, full paper*, Loews Coronado Bay, San Diego (USA), November 26-29, 2001. http://www.loria.fr/~ledang/publications/ase01.ps.gz.

17. R. Marcano and N. Lévy. Transformation d'annotations OCL en expressions B. In *Journées AFADL'2001: Approches Formelles dans l'Assistance au Développement de Logiciels*, Nancy (F), 11-13 juin, 2001.

18. E. Meyer. *Développements formels par objets: utilisation conjointe de B et d'UML*. PhD thesis, LORIA - Université Nancy 2, Nancy (F), mars 2001.

19. E. Meyer and J. Souquières. A systematic approach to transform OMT diagrams to a B specification. In *FM'99: World Congress on Formal Methods in the Development of Computing Systems*, LNCS 1708, Toulouse (F), September 1999. Springer-Verlag.

20. H.P. Nguyen. *Dérivation de spécifications formelles B à partir de spécifications semi-formelles*. PhD thesis, Conservatoire National des Arts et Métiers - CEDRIC, Paris (F), décembre 1998.

21. J. Rumbaugh, M. Blaha, W. Premerlani, F. Eddy, and W. Lorensen. *Object-Oriented Modeling and Design*. Prentice Hall Inc. Englewood Cliffs, 1991.

22. J. Rumbaugh, I. Jacobson, and G. Booch. *The Unified Modeling Language Reference Manual*. Addison-Wesley, 1998. ISBN 0-201-30998-X.

23. E. Sekerinski. Graphical Design of Reactive Systems. In D. Bert, editor, *B'98: Recent Advances in the Development and Use of the B Method - 2nd International B Conference*, LNCS 1393, Montpellier (F), April 1998. Springer-Verlag.

24. C. Snook and M. Butler. U2B: a tool for combining UML and B. Available at http://www.ecs.soton.ac.uk/~cfs98r/U2Bdownloads.htm.

25. C. Snook and M. Butler. Verifying Dynamic Properties of UML Models by Translation to the B Language and Toolkit. Technical Report DSSE-TR-2000-12, Declarative Systems & Software Engineering Group, Department of Electronics and Computer Science University of Southampton, September 2000.
Available at http://www.dsse.ecs.soton.ac.uk/techreports/2000-12.html.

26. C. Snook and R. Harrison. Practitioners Views on the Use of Formal Methods: An Industrial Survey by Structured Interview. *Information and Software Technology*, 43:275–283, March 2001.

27. STERIA - Technologies de l'Information, Aix-en-Provence (F). *Atelier B, Manuel Utilisateur*, 1998. Version 3.5.

Translating Statecharts to B

Emil Sekerinski and Rafik Zurob

McMaster University, Department of Computing and Software
Hamilton, Ontario, Canada
{emil,zurobrs}@mcmaster.ca

Abstract. We present algorithms for the translation of statecharts to the Abstract Machine Notation of the B method. These algorithms have been implemented in *iState*, a tool for translating statecharts to various programming languages. The translation proceeds in several phases. We give a model of statecharts, a model of the code in AMN, as well as the intermediate representations in terms of class diagrams and their textual counterpart. The translation algorithms are expressed in terms of these models. We also discuss optimizations of the generated code. The translation scheme is motivated by making the generated code comprehensible.

1 Introduction

Statecharts, an extension of finite state diagrams by *hierarchy*, *concurrency*, and *communication* were conceived as a visual formalism for the design of reactive systems [4]. Because of the appeal of the graphical notation, statecharts are now part of object-oriented modeling techniques [2,12,13].

In this paper we present algorithms for translating statecharts to the Abstract Machine Notation of the B method [1]. These algorithms have been implemented in *iState*, a tool for translating statecharts to various programming languages. While *iState* can generate code in various languages, AMN is used as a reference for several reasons: First, AMN supports nondeterminism. Nondeterminism between transitions can arise in statecharts, hence can be reflected directly in AMN. Secondly, AMN supports parallel (independent) composition of statements. This turns out to be essential for the translation of concurrent states. Additionally, invariants can be expressed in AMN, allowing statecharts to be analyzed for safety properties.

Our goal with *iState* is that the resulting code is not only executable, but is also comprehensible. The original motivation is its use for teaching statecharts. However, having comprehensible code allows us to get confidence in the translator and is a prerequisite for the generated code to be further analyzed.

A translation scheme for statecharts into AMN that supports hierarchy, concurrency and communication was proposed in [15]. In [14] the structure of its implementation in *iState* is discussed: a translation in phases is presented and the intermediate representations are formally defined and the notions of representable, normalized, and legal statecharts are introduced, see Figure 1. Normalized statecharts appear as an intermediate representation and code is generated only for legal statecharts. These classes of statecharts are defined in terms of an abstract representation given by class diagrams and in textual form. The refinement of this abstract representation is also discussed.

M. Butler, L. Petre, and K. Sere (Eds.): IFM 2002, LNCS 2335, pp. 128–144, 2002.

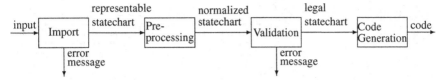

Fig. 1. Phases and intermediate representations of *iState*.

In this paper we present the translation algorithms. The algorithms are expressed in terms of an abstract representation of statecharts [14] and an abstract representation of AMN machines. Both abstract representations are given by class diagrams and in textual form. We also discuss the optimization done during and after the translation. To the best of our knowledge these algorithms are new.

An interpretation of statecharts in B for the purpose of structuring reactive systems was proposed by Lano et al [6]. In this approach concurrent states can only be on the outermost level such that each concurrent state can be mapped to a B machine. We allow arbitrarily composed statecharts and translate the statechart to a single B machine. Nguyen [11] studies the translation of both class diagrams and state transition diagrams to B. This generalizes our approach in specifying a state transition for every object of a class, but does not include nested and concurrent states. Laleau and Mammar [5] describe a tool for translating UML class diagrams, state diagrams, and collaboration diagrams to B. Building on [11], their approach is to define states in a state diagram by predicates over the attributes of an object, i.e. typically statechart states partition the states of objects. Our approach is to represent states directly by variables. Also, they do not mention nested or concurrent states.

Mikk et al. [10] and Lilius and Paltor [7,8] discuss the translation of statecharts to Promela, the input language of the Spin model checker. Promela is related to AMN in the sense that both are extensions of the guarded command language. The translation of Lilius and Paltor relies on a universal algorithm for each step. By comparison we generate code directly for each event. Also, they consider queuing of events according to UML whereas we follow Harel's statecharts in generating and consuming events instantaneously. In order to eliminate inter-level transitions, Mikk et al. use extended hierarchical automata as an intermediate step in the translation. In our translation scheme inter-level transitions do not cause any additional complications. In their translation scheme copies of the pre-state of all variables is kept in order to ensure that a state change is sensed only in the subsequent state. In our translation scheme this is done simply using the parallel composition of AMN (though a refinement of the generated machine may need to introduce such variables). In their translation scheme not only the states but also the events are represented by variables in order to maintain a set of simultaneously generated events. In our approach we do not introduce variables for the events but have the (syntactic) restriction that in any step an event cannot be broadcast simultaneously more than once. Our restriction is motivated by keeping the generated code simple and comprehensible.

Section 2 presents the abstract model of statecharts in terms of class diagrams and in textual form. Section 3 gives the normalization algorithms carried out on that model. Section 4 presents the abstract model of the AMN code in terms of class diagrams and

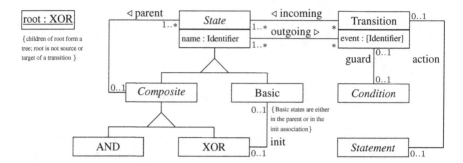

Fig. 2. Representable statecharts defined by a class diagram.

in textual form. Section 5 presents the translation algorithms and Section 6 discusses further processing. We conclude with a discussion in Section 7.

2   The Statechart Model

We define *representable* statecharts in two ways, graphically by the class diagram in Figure 2 and in an equivalent textual form. We follow the presentation of [14] but lift some restrictions. Our model is also related to the model of statecharts in [9]. Besides the difference in style which arises from starting with a graphical model and the fact that we do not consider entry and exit actions, the differences are that we do not introduce configurations and we do not consider sets of simultaneous events.

Let us introduce *Object* to be the set of all objects. The class of states is a subset of objects. Every *State* object has an attribute *name* of type *Identifier*. We let $S \rightarrow T$ denote the set of all total functions from S to T.

$State \subseteq Object$

$name \in State \rightarrow Identifier$

States are either composite states or basic states, but no state can be both basic and composite. Furthermore, *State* is an abstract class, meaning that all objects of class *State* must belong to one of its subclasses.

$Composite \subseteq State \land Basic \subseteq State$

$Composite \cap Basic = \emptyset \land Composite \cup Basic = State$

Likewise, composite states are either AND states or XOR states, but no state can be both an AND state and an XOR state. The class *Composite* is also abstract.

$AND \subseteq Composite \land XOR \subseteq Composite$

$AND \cap XOR = \emptyset \land AND \cup XOR = Composite$

Transitions are also objects. Each transition has an optional attribute *event* of type *Identifier*. Spontaneous transitions have no event name attached to them. We let $S \nrightarrow T$ denote the set of all partial functions from S to T.

$Transition \subseteq Object$

$event \in Transition \rightarrow Identifier$

Conditions and statements are objects as well.

$Condition \subseteq Object \land Statement \subseteq Object$

The *guard* association relates every transition to at most one condition. Likewise, the *action* association relates every transition to at most one statement. We do not require that every condition and every statement relate to exactly one transition, as conditions and statements may appear as part of other conditions and statements, respectively. We let $S \rightarrowtail T$ denote the set of partial, injective functions from S to T.

$guard \in Transition \rightarrowtail Condition$

$action \in Transition \rightarrowtail Statement$

The *outgoing* association relates every state to all the transitions leaving it. Any state may have zero or more transitions leaving it but every transition must have at least one state as origin. We let $S \leftrightarrow T$ denote the set of relations from S to T and $ran(R)$ the range of relation R.

$outgoing \in State \leftrightarrow Transition$

$ran(outgoing) = Transition$

The *incoming* association relates every transition to all the states to which it leads. Any state may have zero or more transitions leading to it but every transition must have at least one state as destination. We let $dom(R)$ denote the domain of relation R.

$incoming \in Transition \leftrightarrow State$

$dom(outgoing) = Transition$

The *init* association relates an XOR state to at most one basic state, which we call its *init* state. This is the state from which all the initializing transitions are leaving, the destinations of which are the initial states. *Init* states do not appear graphically in the statecharts, or perhaps just as fat dots. They are added here for allowing initializing and proper transitions to be treated uniformly. Not every XOR state must have an *init* state.

$init \in XOR \rightarrowtail Basic$

The *parent* association relates states to their parent states, which must be composite states. Every state has at most one parent and every composite state must have at least one child.

$parent \in State \rightarrow Composite$

$ran(parent) = Composite$

We define the relation *children* to be the inverse of the function *parent*. We let R^{-1} denote the inverse of relation R.

$children \mathrel{\widehat{=}} parent^{-1}$

All basic states are either in the *init* or *parent* association.

$ran(init) \cup dom(parent) = Basic$

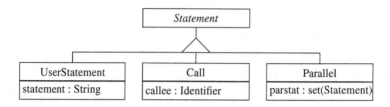

Fig. 3. Statements defined by a class diagram.

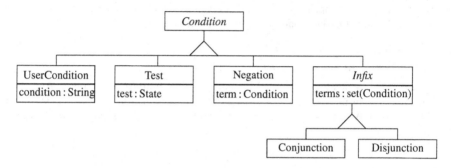

Fig. 4. Conditions defined by a class diagram.

The root state is an XOR state. Every composite state is a descendant of root. We let R^* denote the transitive and reflexive closure of relation R.

$$root \in XOR$$
$$Composite \subseteq children^*[\{root\}]$$

The root state must not be the source or target of a transition.

$$root \notin dom(outgoing)$$
$$root \notin ran(incoming)$$

This completes the textual definition of statecharts. Compared to [14] we do not require that every AND state has two children and all children of AND states are XOR states. While our tool enforces this in order to make the graphical and textual representation interchangeable, our translation algorithms can cope with the more general case. For brevity, we define the conditions of guards and the statements of actions only graphically by the class diagrams in Figures 3 and 4. Statements are either user defined, are broadcasts, or are compositions of statements. Broadcasts are referred to as calls and the composition is referred to as parallel.

3   Preprocessing

Normalization adds those transition arrows to representable statecharts that can be left out. Normalization is the first step to translation. A statechart is normalized if two conditions hold, *targetsProper* and *transitionsComplete*.

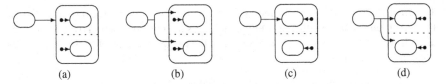

Fig. 5. (a) A statechart that violates *targetsProper*. (b) Normalization of the statechart in (a): the AND target of the transition is replaced by its two XOR children. (c) A statechart that violates *transitionsComplete*. (d) Normalization of the statechart in (c): the XOR child of the AND state that is not entered by the transition is added to its targets.

Targets of transitions must be either Basic or XOR states. If a target is an AND state, then that transition can be replaced by one that forks to all the children of that AND state, see Fig. 5(a).

$$targetsProper \ \widehat{=} \ ran(incoming) \subseteq Basic \cup XOR$$

If an AND state is entered by a transition, then all its children must be entered by that transition as well, see Fig. 5(b). We define the *closest common ancestor* of a set ss of states to be that state that is an ancestor of each state in ss and all other common ancestors are also its ancestor, where each state is also its own ancestor. We let $x \, R \, y$ denote that the pair of x and y is in relation R. For any $ss \subseteq State$ we define $cca(ss)$ by:

$$c = cca(ss) \Leftrightarrow \forall s \in ss \, . \, (c \, parent^* \, s \wedge \forall a \in State \, . \, (a \, parent^* \, s \Rightarrow a \, parent^* \, c))$$

The closest common ancestor exists for any set of states that consists of non-*init* states. The *path* from state s to a set ss of descendants of s is the set of all states that are on the paths from s to a state of ss. Formally, $path(s, ss)$ is defined as those states that are descendants of s and ancestors of states in ss, excluding s but including the states of ss. We let R^+ denote the transitive closure of relation R.

$$path(s, ss) \ \widehat{=} \ children^+[\{s\}] \cap parent^*[ss]$$

The set $to(tr)$ of transition tr is the set of all target states of that transition. Dually, the set $from(tr)$ is the set of all source states of tr:

$$to(tr) \ \widehat{=} \ outgoing^{-1}[\{tr\}]$$
$$from(tr) \ \widehat{=} \ incoming[\{tr\}]$$

Following [3], the *scope* of a transition is the state closest to the root through which the transition passes.

$$scope(tr) \ \widehat{=} \ cca(from(tr) \cup to(tr))$$

The states *entered* by a transition are all the states on the path from the scope of the transition to the targets of the transition. For symmetry, we define the states *exited* by a transition as all the states on the path from the scope of the transition to the sources of the transition.

$$entered(tr) \ \widehat{=} \ path(scope(tr), to(tr))$$
$$exited(tr) \ \widehat{=} \ path(scope(tr), from(tr))$$

This finally allows us to state the requirement that for all states entered by a transition, if the state is an AND state, then all children of that state must be entered by the transition as well. We let $R \triangleright S$ denote the restriction of the range of relation R to set S, formally defined as $R; id(S)$.

$$transitionsComplete \; \hat{=} \; (entered \triangleright AND); children \subseteq entered$$

We present an algorithm that makes all targets proper and all transitions complete. The algorithm iterates over all transitions. For each transition, a set vs of states to be visited is maintained. This is initially the set of all AND states entered by the transition. Each of these states is replaced by the set rs of all its children that are not entered by the transition. This continues until there are no more states to be visited. The children that are added in the replacement step can be either XOR, AND, or Basic states. Of these, the AND states have to be visited as well and are therefore added to vs. Assuming that the hierarchy is finite, the algorithm terminates and establishes $targetsProper$ and $transitionsComplete$. We let $x :\in e$ denote the nondeterministic assignment of an element of the set e to x. We write $R[S] := T$ for modifying the relation R such that all elements of S relate to all elements of T, formally $R := R \oplus (S \times T)$, where $\oplus$ stands for the relational overwrite.

```
procedure normalize
   for tr ∈ Transition do
      var vs : set(State) ;
      begin vs := entered(tr) ∩ AND ;
         while vs ≠ ∅ do
            var s : State, rs : set(State) ;
            begin s :∈ vs ; rs := children[{s}] − entered(tr) ;
               incoming[{tr}] := incoming[{tr}] − {s} ∪ rs ;
               vs := vs − {s} ∪ (rs ∩ AND)
            end
      end
```

Besides normalization, the preprocessing step also renames states with the same name but in different parts of the statechart by appending the names of the parent states. As states do not necessarily carry user-defined names, unique names are generated for those.

The validation step, which follows the preprocessing step, detects remaining name conflicts as well as a number of other errors: (1) Transitions must not be between concurrent states. (2) A transition can fork only to concurrent states. (3) A transition can join only from concurrent states. (4) There must not be a cycle in spontaneous transitions. (5) Every *init* state must have a transition leaving it. (6) The *init* transition must go to a child. (7) *init* states cannot be targets of transitions. (8) *init* transitions must not have an event or a guard. (9) No spontaneous transition can leave the target of an *init* transition. (10) Broadcasts don't lead to the same event being generated twice. These are further discussed in [14]. Violating these conditions would either cause the translation to fail or the generated code to be invalid.

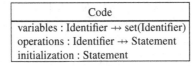

Fig. 6. Generated code defined by a class diagram.

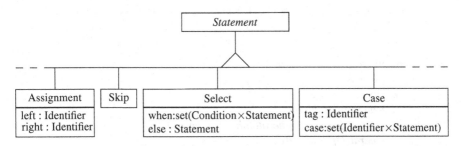

Fig. 7. Statements added to the class for the purpose of code generation.

4   The Code Model

The model of the code is given in Fig. 6. The attribute *variables* defines variables of enumerated set type by mapping variables to their possible values. The attribute *operations*
maps operations to their body. The generated operations have no parameters. The initialization is a statement. All identifiers in *variables* and the domain of *operations* have
to be distinct. In case the same state name appears in different parts of a statechart, this
is resolved by appending the name of the pare nt states, otherwise an error is reported.

In order to model the generated statements, we extend the class of statements by those
in Fig. 7. Generated statements may be of all the classes *UserStatement*, *Call*, *Parallel*,
Assignment, *Skip*, *Select*, and *Case*. In order to model the generated conditions, we
extend the class of conditions by the *Equality* as in Fig. 8. Generated conditions may
be of the classes *UserCondition*, *Negation*, *Conjunction*, *Disjunction*, and *Equality*, but
not of the class *Test*.

5   Translation

Assuming that the statechart is normalized and legal, code is generated for the variables,
for the initialization, and for the operations in sequence. We write $x :=$ **new** C for creating
a new object of class C. We assume that all classes are subtypes of class *Object*. If C is
in addition a subtype of classes $C_1, \ldots, C_n$, then $x :=$ **new** C is defined as $x :\notin Object$;
$Object := Object \cup \{x\}$; $C_1 := C_1 \cup \{x\}$; $\ldots$; $C_n := C_n \cup \{x\}$. Hence, we are identifying
a class with the set of all objects of that class. For example, $c :=$ **new** $Code$ is equivalent
to $c :\notin Object$; $Object := Object \cup \{c\}$; $Code := Code \cup \{c\}$.

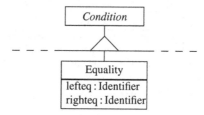

Fig. 8. Condition added to the class hierarchy for the purpose of code generation.

procedure *generate* : *Code*
  var *c* : *Code*
  begin *c* := **new** *Code* ;
    generateVariables(*c*) ;
    c.initialization := *generateInitialization*(*root*) ;
    generateOperations(*c*) ;
    return *c*
  end

For each composed state a variable is created. The values of this variable are the names of its children; we assume that in the preprocessing steps all states have been given a name. As the children may themselves be composed, new names have to be introduced. For example we could have:

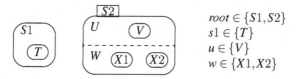

$$root \in \{S1, S2\}$$
$$s1 \in \{T\}$$
$$u \in \{V\}$$
$$w \in \{X1, X2\}$$

The variable declarations are generated by traversing all XOR states and generating a corresponding variable. If *a* is an attribute of an object *x* of class *C*, we write *x.a* instead of *a*(*x*).

procedure *generateVariables*(*c* : *Code*)
  begin *c.variables* := ∅ ;
    for *s* ∈ *XOR* **do**
      c.variables(*lc*(*s.name*)) := *UC*((*children* ; *name*)[{*s*}])
  end

The functions *lc*(*s*) and *uc*(*s*) convert an identifier represented as a string to lower case and upper case, respectively. For our purposes it suffices to assume that *lc*(*s*) ≠ *uc*(*s*) for any identifier *s*. The function *UC*(*ss*) converts all strings of the set *ss* to upper case.

For each event in the statechart an operation in the code is generated:

procedure *generateOperations*(*c* : *Code*)
   begin *c.operations* := $\emptyset$;
     for *eid* $\in$ *ran*(*event*) **do**
       c.operations(*eid*) := *generateTransition*(*eid*, *root*)
   end

There can be several transitions on the same event, including transitions leaving the same state, leading possibly to nondeterminism. All transitions on the same level are translated to a select statement. For example, assuming that *r* is the variable for the enclosing XOR state, we generate:

$E \ \hat{=}$ **SELECT** $r = S \wedge g$ **THEN** $r := U \parallel a$
       WHEN $r = R \wedge h$ **THEN** $r := V \parallel b$
       ELSE *skip*
       END

Transitions on outer levels have priority over transitions on the same event in inner levels. The procedure *generateTransitions*(*eid*, *s*) first generates the code for transition *tr* with *scope*(*tr*) = *s* and *event*(*tr*) = *eid* and then recursively code for the children of *s*.

procedure *generateTransitions*(*eid* : *Identifier*, *s* : *State*) : *Statement*
   var *sel* : *Select* ;
   begin *sel* := **new** *Select* ; *sel.when* := $\emptyset$;
     for *tr* $\in$ *scope*$^{-1}$[{*s*}] $\cap$ *event*$^{-1}$[{*eid*}] **do**
       sel.when := *sel.when* $\cup$ {(*generateGuard*(*tr*, *s*), *generateAction*(*tr*, *s*))} ;
     sel.else := *generateChildTransitions*(*eid*, *s*) ;
     return *sel*
   end

For generating the code for transitions in children, we have to distinguish the type of the children. If a child is a Basic state, then it cannot contain transitions and no code needs to be generated. If the child is an XOR state, a case analysis needs to be generated. For example, assuming that *r* is the variable for the enclosing XOR state, we generate:

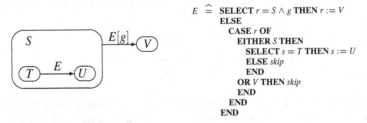

$E \ \hat{=}$ **SELECT** $r = S \wedge g$ **THEN** $r := V$
     ELSE
       CASE *r* **OF**
         EITHER *S* **THEN**
           SELECT *s* = *T* **THEN** *s* := *U*
         ELSE *skip*
         END
         OR *V* **THEN** *skip*
       END
     END
     END

Simplifications of the generated code are discussed in Sec. 6. If the child is an AND state, then a parallel composition is generated. In the following example state *S* is an AND state with two XOR children. Assuming that *r* is the variable for the enclosing XOR state, we generate:

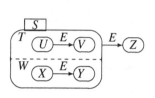

$$E \; \widehat{=} \; \textbf{SELECT } r = S \textbf{ THEN } r := Z$$
$$\textbf{ELSE}$$
$$\quad \textbf{CASE } t \textbf{ OF}$$
$$\qquad \textbf{EITHER } U \textbf{ THEN } t := V$$
$$\qquad \textbf{OR } V \textbf{ THEN } skip$$
$$\qquad \textbf{END}$$
$$\quad \textbf{END}$$
$$\quad \|$$
$$\quad \textbf{CASE } w \textbf{ OF}$$
$$\qquad \textbf{EITHER } X \textbf{ THEN } w := X$$
$$\qquad \textbf{OR } Y \textbf{ THEN } skip$$
$$\qquad \textbf{END}$$
$$\textbf{END}$$
$$\textbf{END}$$

The procedure *generateChildTransitions*(eid, s) generates code for transitions on event *eid* where the scope of the transition is a child of *s*.

procedure *generateChildTransitions*$(eid : Identifier, s : State) : Statement$
  if $s \in Basic$ **then return new** *Skip*
  else if $s \in XOR$ **then**
    var *ca* : *Case* ;
    begin *ca* := **new** *Case* ; *ca.tag* := *name*(s) ; *ca.cases* := $\emptyset$;
      for $cs \in children[\{s\}]$ **do**
        ca.cases := *ca.cases* $\cup \{(name(cs), generateTransitions(eid, cs))\}$;
      return *ca*
    end
  else
    var *pa* : *Parallel* ;
    begin *pa* := **new** *Parallel* ; *pa.parstat* := $\emptyset$;
      for $cs \in children[\{s\}]$ **do**
        pa.parstat := *pa.parstat* $\cup \{generateTransitions(eid, cs)\}$;
      return *pa*
    end

Making a step to a new state requires updating as many variables as XOR and Basic states are entered. In addition, the action associated with the transitions is executed. For example, assuming that r is the variable for the enclosing XOR state, we generate:

$$E \; \widehat{=} \; \textbf{SELECT } r = S \textbf{ THEN}$$
$$\quad r := T \parallel t := U \parallel a$$
$$\textbf{ELSE } skip$$
$$\textbf{END}$$

Procedure *generateAction*(tr, s) generates the parallel composition of assignment statements needed to move from the state s to the targets of the transition tr. Using parallel composition ensures that the new state is sensed only in the next step. If an XOR state is a target, the initialization of it is generated recursively. If the transition has an associated action, that action is added to the parallel composition without translation: broadcasting an event in the statechart is interpreted as calling the operation of that event in AMN.

The composition of user defined action and broadcasts in statecharts is interpreted as their parallel composition in AMN.

> **procedure** *generateAction*(tr : *Transition*, s : *State*) : *Statement*
>   **var** *pa* : *Parallel* ;
>   **begin** *pa* := **new** *Parallel* ; *pa.parstat* := $\emptyset$;
>   **for** $t \in$ *entered*(tr) $-$ *children*[*AND*] **do**
>   **var** *as* : *Assignment* ;
>   **begin** *as* := **new** *Assignment* ;
>   *as.left* := *lc*(*name*(*parent*(t))) ; *as.right* := *uc*(*name*(t)) ;
>   *pa.parstat* := *pa.parstat* $\cup$ {*as*} ;
>   **if** $t \in$ *XOR* $\wedge$ $t \in$ *to*(tr) **then**
>   *pa.parstat* := *pa.parstat* $\cup$ {*generateInitialization*(t)}
>   **end** ;
>   **if** $tr \in$ *dom*(*action*) **then**
>   *pa.parstat* := *pa.parstat* $\cup$ {*action*(tr)} ;
>   **return** *pa*
>   **end**

Making a step out of a state requires testing as many variables as XOR and Basic states are exited. In addition, the guard associated with the transition needs to be tested. For example, assuming that r is the variable for the enclosing XOR state, we generate:

$$E \;\widehat{=}\; \textbf{SELECT}\; r = S \wedge s = T \wedge g \;\textbf{THEN}$$
$$r := U$$
$$\textbf{ELSE}\; skip$$
$$\textbf{END}$$

Procedure *generateGuard*(tr, s) generates the conjunction of state tests needed for transition tr to leave state s. If the transition has an associated guard, that is added to the conjunction.

> **procedure** *generateGuard*(tr : *Transition*, s : *State*) : *Condition*
>   **var** *co* : *Conjunction* ;
>   **begin** *co* := **new** *Conjunction* ; *co.terms* := $\emptyset$;
>   **for** $t \in$ *exited*(tr) $-$ *children*[*AND*] **do**
>   *co.terms* := *co.terms* $\cup$ {*generateTest*(t)}
>   **if** $tr \in$ *dom*(*guard*) **then**
>   *co.terms* := *co.terms* $\cup$ {*generateCondition*(tr, *guard*(tr))} ;
>   **return** *co*
>   **end**

Procedure *generateTest*(s) generates the code for testing whether the parent of s is in s.

> **procedure** *generateTest*(s : *State*) : *Condition*
>   **var** *eq* : *Equality* ;
>   **begin** *eq* := *newEquality* ;
>   *eq.lefteq* := *lc*(*name*(*parent*(s))) ;
>   *eq.righteq* := *uc*(*name*(s)) ;
>   **return** *eq*
>   **end**

A state test requires testing a concurrent state. If that is nested, its parents have to be tested as well, up to (but excluding) the AND state that is the closest common ancestor of the source states of the transition with the state test and the state being tested. However, tests are only necessary for XOR states that are not children of AND states. For example, assuming that r is the variable for the enclosing XOR state, we generate after some simplifications:

$$E \; \hat{=} \; \textbf{IF } r = S \wedge t = U \wedge w = X \wedge x = Y \textbf{ THEN}$$
$$t := V$$
$$\textbf{END}$$

Procedure *generateCondition*(tr, c) transforms conditions as they appear in statecharts to conditions in AMN. It does so by recursively traversing the condition and only replacing state test with a conjunction of equalities.

procedure *generateCondition*$(tr : Transition, c : Condition) : Condition$
  if $c \in UserCondition$ **then return** c
  else if $c \in Test$ **then**
    var $co : Conjunction, s : State$;
    begin $co :=$ **new** $Conjunction$; $co.terms := \emptyset$;
    $s := cca(from(tr) \cup \{c.test\})$;
    for $t \in path(s, \{c.test\}) - children[AND]$ **do**
      $co.terms := co.terms \cup \{generateTest(t)\}$;
    return co
    end
  else if $c \in Negation$ **then**
    var $ne : Negation$;
    begin $ne :=$ **new** $Negation$; $ne.term := generateCondition(tr, c.term)$;
    return ne
    end
  else
    var $in : Infix$;
    begin $in :=$ **new** $Infix$; $in.terms := \emptyset$;
    for $d \in c.terms$ **do**
      $in.terms := in.terms \cup \{generateCondition(tr, d)\}$;
    return in
    end

Finally, procedure *generateInitialization*(s) generates the initialization of an XOR state by first determining the single transition leaving its *init* state.

procedure *generateInitialization*$(s : XOR) : Statement$
  return *generateAction*$(outgoing(init(s)), s)$

The restriction to only a single *init* transition can be lifted if instead a nondeterministic assignment is generated.

6   Further Processing

The generated code can in many cases be further simplified. The simplifications include:

- Intra-level transitions may generate code of the form **SELECT ELSE** S **END** which is simplified to S.
- If there is only a single transition on a level for an event, the generated code of the form **SELECT** C **THEN** A **ELSE** B **END** can be simplified to **IF** C **THEN** A **ELSE** B **END**.
- Case statements can be simplified by leaving out all alternatives with body *skip* and adding **ELSE** *skip* instead.
- Case statements with a single alternative after above simplification can be rewritten as if statements.
- An if statement of the form **IF** C **THEN** A **ELSE** *skip* **END** can be simplified to **IF** C **THEN** A **END**.

Currently all the simplifications are done during code generation. Here is the original and simplified code of the example in Sec. 5. It also illustrates how the testing of guards is moved:

```
E ≙  SELECT r = S ∧ g THEN r := V           E ≙  IF r = S THEN
     ELSE                                          IF g THEN r := V
        CASE r OF                                  ELSE
           EITHER S THEN                              IF s = T THEN s := U
              SELECT s = T THEN s := U                END
              ELSE skip                           END
              END                              END
           OR V THEN skip
           END
        END
     END
```

Another example of simplified code is given in [14]. Further optimizations like merging nested if and select statements are left as future work.

AMN does not allow calls of operations within the same machine. As broadcasting of events is translated to calling of operations, auxiliary definitions are generated for the called operations and these auxiliary definitions are "called" instead. For this, the call dependency is analyzed and the operations are first topologically sorted. In case of circular dependencies an error is reported.

Transitions without an event are *spontaneous* as they can be taken without that an event is generated, but may have a guard and action associated. Our code generator implements a run-to-completion of transitions: if a state is reached that has an outgoing spontaneous transition that can be taken it is taken. This is repeated for further spontaneous transitions. Circularities in spontaneous transitions are detected and reported as an error.

7   Discussion

A number of tools support code generation from statecharts, including xjCharts, with-Class, and Rhapsody. Compared to translation schemes used by other tools, ours can be characterized as *event-centric* rather than *state-centric*, as the main structure of the code is that of events, rather than classes for states. Our scheme is suitable for those kind of reactive systems where events are processed quickly enough so that no queuing of events is necessary and where blocking of events is undesirable. To our experience so far, the resulting code is not only comprehensible, but compact and efficient as well.

Our semantics of statecharts comes close to that of Mikk et al. [10], with the main difference being that we do not support sets of simultaneous events. Also, we currently do not support event parameters, enter and exit actions, histories, timed events, overlapping states, and sync states. These remain the subject of ongoing work.

An interesting consequence of our use of parallel composition and the restriction to operations that are not mutually recursive is that many problematic situations for which statecharts are known are ruled out. Here is an example with two concurrent states. On event E, one may argue whether state S ends up in T or U. To the right we give the code to which that would correspond. As the code would contain mutual recursion, the statechart is rejected as illegal:

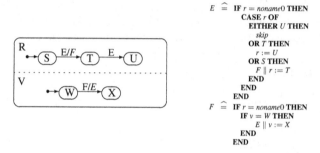

```
E ≙ IF r = noname0 THEN
        CASE r OF
        EITHER U THEN
            skip
        OR T THEN
            r := U
        OR S THEN
            F ∥ r := T
        END
        END
     END
F ≙ IF r = noname0 THEN
        IF v = W THEN
            E ∥ v := X
        END
     END
```

In the following statechart one can argue whether on event E a transition from S to T or to U is made. The translation would contain two assignments to variable r in parallel, which is not allowed.

```
E ≙ IF r = S THEN
        r := T ∥ F
     END
F ≙ IF r = S THEN
        r := U
     END
```

In the next example the event G is broadcast twice when the transition on event E is taken. The translation would contain $G\|G$, which is illegal.

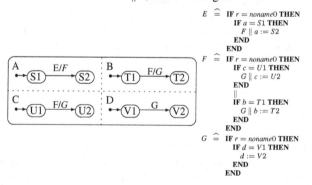

```
E ≙ IF r = noname0 THEN
        IF a = S1 THEN
            F ∥ a := S2
        END
     END
F ≙ IF r = noname0 THEN
        IF c = U1 THEN
            G ∥ c := U2
        END
        ∥
        IF b = T1 THEN
            G ∥ b := T2
        END
     END
G ≙ IF r = noname0 THEN
        IF d = V1 THEN
            d := V2
        END
     END
```

However, if G would be broadcast only once, the statechart would be valid. Finally, here is an example that is legal and illustrates that the parallel composition leads to state changes being sensed only after the transition. Hence, the transition on event F is not taken.

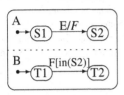

$$E \;\widehat{=}\; \textbf{IF } r = noname0 \textbf{ THEN}$$
$$\textbf{IF } a = S1 \textbf{ THEN}$$
$$F \parallel a := S2$$
$$\textbf{END}$$
$$\textbf{END}$$
$$F \;\widehat{=}\; \textbf{IF } r = noname0 \textbf{ THEN}$$
$$\textbf{IF } b = T1 \wedge a = S2 \textbf{ THEN}$$
$$b := T2$$
$$\textbf{END}$$
$$\textbf{END}$$

Acknowledgement

We are grateful to the reviewers for their comments.

References

1. J.-R. Abrial. *The B Book: Assigning Programs to Meaning.* Cambridge University Press, 1996.
2. D. Harel and E. Gery. Executable object modeling with statecharts. *IEEE Computer*, 30(7):31–42, 1996.
3. D. Harel and A. Naamad. The STATEMATE semantics of statecharts. *ACM Transactions on Software Engineering and Methodology*, 5(5):293–333, 1996.
4. D. Harel. Statecharts: A visual formalism for complex systems. *Science of Computer Programming*, 8:231–274, 1987.
5. R. Laleau and A. Mammar. An overview of a method and its support tool for generating B specifications from UMl notations. In *15th IEEE International Conference on Automated Software Engineering, ASE 2000*, Grenoble, France, 2000. IEEE Computer Socitey Press.
6. K. Lano, K. Androutsopoulos, and P. Kan. Structuring reactive systems in B AMN. In *3rd IEEE International Conference on Formal Engineering Methods*, York, England, 2000. IEEE Computer Socitey Press.
7. J. Lilius and I. P. Paltor. Formalising UML state machines for model checking. In R. France and B. Rumpe, editors, *UML'99 – The Unified Modeling Language Beyond the Standard*, Lecture Notes in Computer Science 1723, pages 430–445, Fort Collins, Colorado, 1999. Springer-Verlag.
8. J. Lilius and I. Paltor. vUML: a tool for verifying UML models. In *14th IEEE International Conference on Automated Software Engineering, ASE'99*, Cocoa Beach, Florida, 1999. IEEE Computer Socitey Press.
9. E. Mikk, Y. Lakhnech, C. Petersohn, and M. Siegel. On the formal semantics of statecharts as supported by statemate. In *BCS-FACS 2nd Northern Formal Methods Workshop*, Ilkley, 1997. Springer-Verlag.
10. E. Mikk, Y. Lakhnech, M. Siegel, and G. J. Holzmann. Implementing statecharts in Promela / Spin. In *Second IEEE Workshop on Industrial-Strength Formal Specification Techniques*, Boca Raton, Florida, 1998. IEEE Computer Society Press.
11. H. P. Nguyen. *Dérivation De Spécifications Formelles B à Partir De Spécifications Semi-Formelles.* Doctoral thesis, Centre d'Études et de Recherche en Informatique du CNAM, 1998.

12. J. Rumbaugh, M. Blaha, W. Premerlani, F. Eddi, and W. Lorensen. *Object-Oriented Modeling and Design*. Prentice-Hall, 1991.
13. J. Rumbaugh, I. Jacobson, and G. Booch. *The Unified Modeling Language Reference Manual*. Addison-Wesley, 1999.
14. E. Sekerinski and R. Zurob. iState: A statechart translator. In M. Gogolla and C. Kobryn, editors, *UML 2001 – The Unified Modeling Language, 4th International Conference*, Lecture Notes in Computer Science 2185, Toronto, Canada, 2001. Springer-Verlag.
15. E. Sekerinski. Graphical design of reactive systems. In D. Bert, editor, *2nd International B Conference*, Lecture Notes in Computer Science 1393, Montpellier, France, 1998. Springer-Verlag.

A Framework
for Translating Models and Specifications*

Shmuel Katz and Orna Grumberg

Computer Science Department
The Technion
Haifa, Israel
{katz,orna}@cs.technion.ac.il

Abstract. The reasons for translating a description of a model in one
notation into another are reviewed. This includes both translating entire models and describing different aspects of a system using different
notations.
In order to demonstrate the ideas, the VeriTech framework for translation
is described. A system being analyzed is seen as a collection of versions,
along with a description of how the versions are related. The versions are
given in different notations connected through a core notation by compilers from and to the notations of existing tools and specification methods.
The reasons that translations cannot always be exact are analyzed, based
on experience with over ten separate compiler translations among formal
methods notations. Additional information gathered during translation
is described, to facilitate optimizations, error tracing, and analysis.
The concept is presented of a *faithful* relation among models and families
of properties true of those models. In this framework families of properties are provided with uniform syntactic transformations, in addition
to the translations of the models. This framework is shown appropriate
for common instances of relations among translations previously treated
in an ad hoc way. The classes of properties that can be faithful for a
given translation provide a measure of the usefulness of the translation.
Open research directions are suggested concerning faithful transformations, additional information, error tracing, and optimizing translations.

1 Introduction

In this survey paper we present the possible uses of (direct or indirect) translations among model descriptions, show some of the difficulties that must in-
evitably arise during translation, describe the design of the VeriTech translation
framework and how it can alleviate some of the obstacles to translation, and provide a theoretical basis to quantify the quality of such translations in a formal
framework using *faithful* translations and syntactic transformations of properties. Material is included from [22,11,24] and [3].

---

* This research was partially supported by the Fund for the Support of Research at the
Technion and by the Bar-Nir Bergreen Software Technology Center of Excellence.

M. Butler, L. Petre, and K. Sere (Eds.): IFM 2002, LNCS 2335, pp. 145–164, 2002.

1.1   Existing Translations

Translations among notations for representing models and hardware designs have
become common, although often there is no available documentation. Such translations exist from SMV [8,27], to PVS[29], from Murphi[20] to PVS, from SMV
to Spin[18,19], from several notations into Cospan[25], from automata-based
notation into Petri nets, and among many other tools. Moreover, individual verification tools often have multiple input formats for models, and internal source-
to-source translations. For example, the STeP system [4] and the exposition in
[26] allow presenting designs either in a simple C-like programming language, or
using a modular collection of textual transitions, and internally translates from
the former representation to the latter. In addition to translations among formal methods tools, there is increasing interest in translating standard hardware
design notations such as Verilog or VHDL (or internal industrial notations) to
and from the notations of existing model-checking tools.

Translations are used also in the context of *software verification*. The Ban-
dera tool set [15] translates Java source code to the model checking tools SMV,
Spin, and dSpin [10] and also to the Java PathFinder software verification tool
(JPF) [16,7] which has its own translation to Spin.

Recently, the VeriTech project has been developed as a general framework for
translation through a simple intermediate notation [11]. The VeriTech project
defines a core design language (CDL) in which modules can be combined in
synchronous, asynchronous or partially synchronous manners, and each module
is a set of first-order transitions. The VeriTech project provides translations
between existing notations and the core language, in both directions. At present,
VeriTech includes translations between SMV, Murphi, Spin, STeP, Petri-nets[31]
and the core design language, and work is underway to incorporate, among
others, PVS and LOTOS[6]. Other such frameworks include the SAL system [2],
and the Model Checking Kit[28].

1.2   Why Translate?

Translations among model notations can be used in a variety of ways, and these
influence what needs to be true about a translation. Most obviously, a particular
property to be verified can be attacked with different tools. For example, if an
initial attempt to model check a temporal logic property of a system should
fail because of the size of the state space, it is possible to translate the model
(perhaps in stages, through an intermediate notation) to a BDD-based model
checker that can handle the problem. Alternatively, the source could be a model
description in the SMV language, but for which attempts to verify a property
have failed, and the target could be a description appropriate for a tool with
a theorem-proving approach like PVS or STeP. Of course, proving the desired
property in such a target requires using inductive methods and is not automatic,
but at least is not sensitive to the size of the data domain and will not suffer from
the state-explosion problem. We shall also see that in many relevant translations
the property to be proven in target models will not be identical to the property

asserted about the original source model. Nevertheless, a *back-implication* is desired: a property should necessarily hold in the source whenever the related property holds in the target.

In addition, unrelated properties can each be established for a system using a different verification tool, choosing the most convenient tool for each property. This should encourage using different verification tools for various aspects of the same system. For example, a propositional linear-time temporal property might be proven for a finite-state model of the system using a linear-time model checker like Spin. The system model can then be translated to a branching-time model checker like SMV for properties of that type. It can also be translated to a language with real-time notation, such as STeP, or to a theorem proving environment like PVS to treat infinite domains and first-order temporal properties. In this case, we would like to *import* some variant of the properties proven about the source into the target, so that they can be assumed there and used to help prove the new desired property.

Translation is also useful when an infinite or large finite model needs to be reduced prior to applying model checking. For methods like abstraction [9] and convenient executions [21] the system can first be modeled in full and sent to a theorem prover in which the abstraction or the choice of convenient executions is shown 'correct'. That is, the reduced version is shown to preserve the properties of interest, so that if the reduced version satisfies them, so does the original. The reduced version of the model (i.e., the abstraction or the convenient executions) can then be translated to a model checking tool that will verify temporal properties. Here again we would like to have back implication that is an essential link in guaranteeing the correctness of the proved temporal properties for the full model.

As already noted, there are also many translations to and from design notations that do not have associated verification tools. For hardware these include Verilog and VHDL, and for software, Bandera, JPF, and Statecharts [13,14] (which provides a hierarchical graphical state-transformation software design notation). Translating from such a notation to one with associated model-checking or other verification tools allows checking properties of existing designs, while a translation in the other direction can introduce a verified high-level design into a development process.

1.3   Semantic Issues

The quality of a translation depends on guaranteeing a close relation between the properties true of the source and those true of the target. This can be used to define the 'correctness' of a model translation. As seen above, the relation among properties can be used in either direction: we may want to 'import' versions of properties already guaranteed true of the original model into the resulting one (so they can be used in showing additional properties without being themselves reproven) or we may want to know that properties shown about the resulting model imply related properties in the original model.

Ideally, the semantic models (e.g., the execution trees) underlying the notations would be identical, making the question trivial in either direction. However, we demonstrate that this is often impossible. In the broader framework proposed here, a translation and transformation of properties will be faithful with respect to families of properties represented as classes of formulas in some temporal logic so that if property X is true of one model, then property Y will be true of the other.

The quality of translations also is related to the modularity and readability of the target model. That is, a desirable property of a translation is that it maintain the modularity of the source, and not lead to an explosion in the number of lines of code, relative to the source. Identifying inherent differences, and minimizing their influence, is crucial to effective translation among notations for describing models.

Investigation of these relations can be seen as a step in the research direction proposed in [17], to unify theories of programming. Here those theories used to describe models for formal verification tools are emphasized, rather than full-fledged programming languages.

1.4   Organization of the Paper

In Section 2 the design of the VeriTech project is described, as an example of a general translation framework, and one way to treat the many translation issues that arise. In Section 3 the semantic assumptions we use to compare source and target models are defined, based on fair execution trees as a common underlying semantics. In Section 4, we identify the translation issues that prevent a system and its translation from having identical semantics and thus satisfying the exact same properties. Translations also can lead to loss of the modular structure of the original in translation, and to a 'code explosion' problem, where the number of lines of code increases radically during translation. The added information that can alleviate these difficulties is described in Section 5.

The notion of a faithful relation among models and specifications is defined formally in Section 6, with three variants. We then demonstrate in Section 7 how such a faithful transformation looks for a common example of the inherent model incompatibilities seen in the translation issues. In the Conclusions, some research directions in this area are suggested.

2   The Design of VeriTech and CDL

The VeriTech project facilitates translations of problem statements from one formal specification notation to another. A key element in the design of this project is an intermediate *core design language* denoted CDL, described below. Each notation has compiler-like translation programs to and from CDL, thus requiring only $2n$ translations in order to achieve all of the possible n^2 relations among n different notations.

The core description should facilitate textual analysis and information gathering, transformations to alternative forms, and translations to and from other notations. The core actually has multiple versions of a system, and additional information connecting the versions, but discussion of those parts will be postponed to Section 5, after the semantics and differences among notations are considered.

In CDL emphasis is put on a variety of synchronization methods and possibilities for instantiating declarations of modules with different parameters. On the other hand, internal control structures common in programming languages (conditionals, looping statements, etc.) are not included in CDL, and will be encoded using program counter variables.

The core design language of VeriTech is based on collections of textual transitions, organized in modules. The modular transition system for the core incorporates ideas from state transition systems (especially the internal representation in the STeP system [4]), Z schemas [30], and LOTOS [5,6] composition operators. It is intended to deal with the issues outlined above, and to facilitate translations. Note that it is not particularly intended for direct human interface.

A system in CDL is composed of global declarations of types, constants, and variables, and declarations of the components of the system, which are called *modules*. A simple two place buffer example is given in Figure 1, and is explained below. The syntax and semantics of the globally declared types, constants, and variables are entirely standard. Module declarations are at the top level of a system, and are not nested. One module has the special designation SYSTEM (the COMB module in the example) to indicate that it defines the entire system. Each module declaration has a name, formal parameters, variable declarations, and a body that defines a collection of textual transitions, as described below. Local variables and their types can be declared for each module. Every variable name appearing within the body of a module declaration should be declared globally, declared as a local variable of the module, or be a formal parameter. The basic element of the body of a module is a *transition* defined as a triple $\tau = \langle I, P, R \rangle$, where I is an identifier (called the *name* of the transition), P is a predicate over states called the *precondition* or *enabling condition*, and R is a relation between states called the *transition relation*. The relation R is written as a logical formula including unprimed and primed versions of state variables. It is also optionally possible to write the relation as an assignment to the primed versions in terms of the unprimed ones, when appropriate. As will be explained in Section 3, the intuitive interpretation of a transition is that if the system is in a state that satisfies the transition's precondition, then it can be activated, which means that the state before and the state after the activation satisfy the transition relation, where the unprimed versions of variables relate to the state before the activation, and the primed versions represent the state afterwards.

The relation R should be total for the states of the system satisfying P. That is, if state s satisfies P then there exists a state s' such that the pair (s, s') satisfies R. This is guaranteed by automatically adding to the precondition of each transition the requirement that there exist values so that the relation can be satisfied. Otherwise, the transition is not enabled in the state.

A module body can be most simply specified by listing such transitions within a pair of brackets (as in the three first modules of the example).

HOLD_PREVIOUS
MODULE SENDER (a: INT) {
    VAR readys: BOOL INIT false
    TRANS produce:
        enable: $\neg$ readys
        relation: (a' = 0 $\vee$ a' = 1) $\wedge$ readys' = true
    TRANS send:
        enable: readys
        relation: readys' = false
}
MODULE BUFFER(c,d: INT) {
    VAR cok: BOOL INIT true, dok: BOOL INIT false
    TRANS get:
        enable: cok
        relation: cok' = false
    TRANS move:
        enable: $\neg$cok $\wedge$ $\neg$dok
        relation: d' = c $\wedge$ cok' = true $\wedge$ dok' = true
    TRANS put:
        enable: dok
        relation: dok' = false
}
MODULE RECEIVER(b: INT) {
    VAR vr: INT
        readyr: BOOL INIT true
    TRANS consume:
        enable: $\neg$ readyr
        relation: vr' = b $\wedge$ readyr' = true
    TRANS receive:
        enable: readyr
        relation: readyr' = false
}
MODULE COMB () {
    SYSTEM
    VAR s,t: INT
    (SENDER(s) |(send,get)| (BUFFER(s,t) |(put,receive)| RECEIVER(t)))
}

Fig. 1. A buffer system in CDL

One module can be defined in terms of others (as in the COMB module), by using instantiations of modules, but the definitions cannot be recursive. An instantiation of a module is created by listing the name of the module with actual parameters (variable names) in place of the formal ones, in the body of another module. In this case, it is as if a version of the module with the actuals substituted for the formals has been created. If this creates any conflicts between the actual parameters and local variable names, a systematic renaming is made of the local variables. Note that the effect of a variable common to two module instantiations, but not global to the system, can be attained by using the same actual parameter for two module instantiations in the same body (as is done with s in the instantiations of SENDER and BUFFER inside the body of COMB).

There are three composition operators used in combining instantiations of modules.

$P|||Q$ is called *asynchronous composition*, and is defined semantically as the union of the transitions in P and in Q, where P and Q are instantiations of modules with actual parameters. As noted above, a variable common to the instantiations is defined by using the same actual parameter in both instantiations.

$P||Q$ is called *synchronous composition* and is defined as the cross product of the transitions in P and in Q. The cross product of two transitions has a precondition of the conjunction of their preconditions, and a relation that is the intersection of the two relations (the conjunction of the relations written as logical formulas). From the definition of a transition, it follows that elements in the cross product for which the precondition is *false*, or for which the relation cannot be satisfied when the precondition holds, cannot be activated as transitions, and thus can be removed.

$P|s\_set|Q$ is *partial synchronization*, where the synchronization set s_set is a set of pairs of names of transitions, with the first from P and the second from Q. The module is defined as the cross products of the pairs of transitions in the list, plus the union of the other transitions from P and Q that do not appear in the list.

The COMB module has partial synchronization between the *send* and *get* transitions of the SENDER and BUFFER modules, respectively. The two transitions can be jointly executed when both of the enabling conditions of those transitions are true, and the result is the intersection of the results of those transitions. Otherwise those specific transitions cannot be taken. Another system could be defined by SENDER(s) ||| BUFFER(s,t) ||| RECEIVER(t). In this case each transition remains independent, and the SENDER can repeatedly 'produce' and 'send' s values, while the BUFFER occasionally decides to 'get' and then later actually moves the most recently sent value (losing the previous ones). (Similar effects would occur between the BUFFER and the RECEIVER). Thus the component modules can be combined in a variety of ways, giving some of the advantages of process algebra along with the simplicity of a collection of transitions.

3   The Semantics of Systems and Modules

In order to compare a model in one notation and its translation to a different notation, a uniform semantic basis is required. We will assume that for each notation for describing models a *fair execution tree semantics* can be derived.

Consider the case of a system model given in CDL as a collection of textual transitions, each with an applicability condition and a state transformation. As seen, such a collection defines a module, and such modules can be composed into new modules synchronously, asynchronously, or with partial synchronization (handshaking). The semantics of such a system and of a module can be defined in two stages. First, for semantic purposes only, each definition of a module can be shown equivalent to a textually expanded ("flattened") version, where the module is a list of transitions, replacing instantiations of modules by the collections of transitions they define (including substitution of actual parameters in place of formal ones, and renaming local variables when necessary to avoid conflicts).

Now we can define the semantics of such a 'flat' module with transitions given explicitly, by considering the execution sequences (also called *traces*) that it defines. A state of such a system clearly contains the constants and variables declared globally, and also those that follow from the instantiations of modules and their local variables.

Turning to the textual transitions, recall that each is a triple $\langle I, P, R \rangle$ with an *identifier* I, a *precondition* P over states, and a *relation* R between pairs of states. The intended semantics is that a transition can be activated in a state s if s satisfies P, and such an activation can be seen as constructing a new system state s' from the existing state s of the system, where the pair (s, s') satisfies R. For a system or module defined by a collection of transitions, the possible execution sequences are defined by the sequences of states reached by successive activations of transitions, starting from an initial state.

The initial state has all variable values undefined (e.g., equal to a special value $\bot$), except those with initial values given in their declaration.

The execution sequences are organized into an execution tree, where each state is the parent of the states reachable from it by activation of an enabled transition. If all sequences have the same initial state, that is the root of the tree. Otherwise, a root node with all variables undefined is added, and the possible initializations are the only transitions enabled in that state. (An alternative view would see the semantics as a forest of trees, each with its own initialization, but the single-tree view has the advantage of treating the initializations like other transitions, which can be helpful in some translations. The single-tree view has the disadvantage that usual temporal logic assertions –including invariants– are not intended to hold in the root if all its values are undefined.) Some of the paths in this tree can be declared irrelevant due to an additional *fairness* restriction that can remove infinite paths (criteria for which restrictions are reasonable can be found in [1]). This tree, with fairness restrictions, is the semantic interpretation of a system or module.

Other notations can also be given an execution tree semantics, allowing comparisons among translations. The correctness of a translation is defined relative to such trees, and this semantics is sufficient for the specification languages considered here.

Note that a richer semantics is possible, e.g., one that includes what is known as *partial-order* information. For example, if it is possible to ask which execution sequences are equivalent to which other ones under independence of operations in distributed processes, then semantic information on independence of operations is needed [23,21]. This possibility is not considered further here.

In any case, it is important to note that the properties that are to be shown about a system can influence how much of the information in an execution tree is relevant. According to various possible conventions, the tree of a system is 'equivalent' to reduced versions that, for example, eliminate nonessential variables, or remove hidden transitions, without otherwise affecting the system. Moreover, if only linear-time temporal properties will be proven, then the set of traces can be considered, and their organization into a tree structure is irrelevant. Furthermore, if only invariants are of interest, then it is sufficient to consider the set of reachable states. Such considerations will be crucial in understanding the relations needed among models, as will be seen in the continuation.

As part of the specification, additional restrictions can be added to define which traces are relevant. We have already seen that fairness assumptions can be added on the semantic level. There are also contexts in which an assumption of finiteness of the traces is appropriate, excluding the infinite ones.

For specific notations, particularly those defining finite-state systems, it will be convenient to consider also a finite representation of the execution tree by means of a finite state machine. In fact, an (equivalent) alternative semantic basis could be the fair transition system notation used by [26].

4   Issues in Translation

Translating between different modeling paradigms requires finding suitable solutions for those modeling aspects that are available in one model but not in the other. Translations generally attempt to keep the translated representation of the model as similar as possible in structure and size to the original system, and in addition to define the relation among the underlying semantic models so that wide categories of properties will be related in the two models.

Even when there is a blow-up in the model representation (the 'program text'), this does not necessarily imply a blow-up in the size of the model (given as an execution tree or a state machine). Below we consider some of the key issues in translation that make it impossible to always maintain the same semantic tree or state machine for a model and the result of its translation.

4.1   Synchrony and Asynchrony

Notations for describing models commonly use three types of composition operators between system modules: synchronous, asynchronous and partially synchronous (for example, in generally asynchronous composition of processes with handshaking communications). Translating among models with the same type of synchrony avoids the specific class of problems of this subsection.

However, we have to resolve cases in which the source model originates from a system with one type of composition while the resulting target model is in a notation that uses a different one.

Assume that we want to translate a synchronous system into an asynchronous tool. In a tool like Murphi, where no synchronization mechanism is available, the translation is done by constructing a Murphi rule for each pair of transitions to be synchronized. In SPIN, on the other hand, the original partition into modules can be preserved and synchronous execution of two transitions is simulated using handshaking communication (via a zero-length buffer, thus adding to the statespace).

Translating from an asynchronous model into a synchronous model (like SMV, in its most common mode of operation) should guarantee that, at each step, at most one module executes a transition while all the others are idle. This can be done by adding a self-loop on each state and a mechanism (a shared variable like **running** in SMV or an additional process) that enables the transitions of one module at a time. In this case the modules correspond to processes. Various fairness constraints can be added to eliminate traces in which all processes are idling forever, one process idles forever (starvation), or all processes idle at the same step (so the global state repeats).

4.2   Unenabled Transitions

In a typical transition system representation, each transition consists of an enabling condition, an optional assignment, and a relation that should hold among values of variables before and after the execution of the transition.

The semantics of the typical transition system notation seen earlier guarantees that a transition is executed only if its enabling condition holds and if its final values satisfy the relation. A precise translation should identify the values for which the enabling condition and the relation hold and construct a transition for these values only. This, however, may not be possible as an atomic operation in the target notation.

One possible solution to this problem is to introduce a special *fail* state in the target program. Transitions in the target program are extended with a conditional statement that results in the original final values if these values satisfy the needed relation, and otherwise results in the *fail* state. Assuming this is the only change caused by the translation, the resulting semantic model has transitions to the *fail* state added to the execution tree, and that state is a leaf (or sink, if we view the addition as adding just one such state).

4.3   Atomicity of Transitions

In many notations, transitions are considered atomic. This means that each transition is performed in isolation, with no interference.

In Murphi each transition (called a *rule*) is also considered atomic. However, there a transition can be defined by any C program. When such a complex transition is translated into a notation with a finer grain of atomicity (e.g., where each transition can be a single assignment to the state), it must be partitioned into a sequence of steps. A *visible* flag (or its equivalent) is typically used to indicate that the intermediate states do not occur in the original model, and are an unavoidable result of the difference in the possible grain of atomicity.

In other tools, like SPIN and LOTOS atomic actions are generally more restricted. SPIN, however, includes a mechanism to define a sequence of statements as atomic. Thus, it is straightforward to maintain the atomicity of Murphi transitions within SPIN. On the other hand, LOTOS does not have such a mechanism. As a result, a translation from any notation with large-grained transitions to LOTOS requires providing a mutual exclusion mechanism that enables the translation of a transition to run from start to end with no intermediate execution of actions from other transitions.

4.4 Variables with Unspecified Next Values

Models of computation differ also by their convention concerning variables whose next-state value has not been specified by the executed transition. One convention, usually taken by asynchronous models, assumes that such variables keep their previous values. This is natural in software, where an assignment to one variable leaves the others unchanged. Another convention, common to synchronous models, assumes that the unassigned variables can nondeterministically assume any value from their domain. This is common in hardware descriptions, because then all options are left open for a variable not updated in one component to be changed in a parallel (synchronously executed) component, and still obtain a consistent result.

If the first convention has been taken and we translate the program into a model where the second holds, then for every transition the resulting program will have to contain an explicit assignment of the previous value for every variable not already explicitly redefined. For the other direction (from a model with any value as a default to one that keeps the previous value), we could use nondeterministic assignments, if they are available in the target model. Otherwise, the resulting program could contain a choice among all possible explicit assignments, for each of the possible values in the domain. Here the blow-up in the size of the resulting program is unavoidable, and auxiliary variables are often needed, but at least the semantics does not otherwise change.

4.5 Partitioning into Components

Partitioning into components (modules, processes, etc.) differs conceptually among languages because they are driven by diverse concerns. In many notations oriented towards programming languages, a component is task-oriented, and a task can change the values of several variables. In hardware description languages like SMV, however, it is more common to collect all possible changes to a single variable into one component. A component then describes, for example, all possible changes to a given register. Such differences sometimes make it difficult to maintain the modular structure of the original system, and may force introducing variables or operations that are global under the partitioning advocated by the target notation.

4.6 State Extensions

The addition of a *visible* flag, or the need to globally declare variables that originally were local in a notation with local modules, or the addition of an explicit mutual exclusion mechanism to simulate differences in the grain of atomicity all mean that the state of the translated program must often be extended. Another common problem is that the target notation may not have the sequencing options of the source. Then the control flow of the original computation is sometimes maintained by adding a program counter as an explicit part of the state, and using it in the enabling condition of the transitions.

Such extensions to the state add variables that are needed to express the model, but usually are not part of the original assertions in the specification of the source. Such variables are called *nonessential* for the purposes of assertions about the model, even though they are needed to express the model itself. Of course, translations can also eliminate such variables, as when explicit control variables are replaced by the sequencing of translated steps, in a notation that does have expressive control commands.

5 Versions and Additional Information

In order to deal with the difficulties seen in the previous section, the core of VeriTech does not simply include the result of a translation from one of the component notations. Instead, it has information about multiple versions of the system being considered, as well as information gathered during the translation process, which is often not reflected in the translated code. Some of the information that connects the source and target codes of a translation are:

- **state correspondences and extensions.** The variables in the target are connected to the variables in the source to which they correspond. When the translation has extended the statespace by adding variables not in the original, this information is recorded.
- **hidden transitions.** When atomic steps in the source are translated to a collection of steps in the target, the intermediate states should be identified as internal, or *hidden*. This is because invariant properties corresponding to those of the source are not expected to hold in such intermediate states.
- **operation correspondences.** When modularity has to be destroyed or redefined, the components that are the source of a combined action in the translation should be identifiable, to facilitate error analysis and retranslation. Thus when separate actions of components that are composed synchronously in the source have to be made into a single step of the target, because the target language does not support such composition, the fact that this action came from two parts of the source should be recorded.

Some of the information above is recorded in the target code itself, by using naming conventions and special predefined flags. Other parts of the added information can be in a *log* file. Inclusion in the code is indicated when the assertions to be made about the target model depend on the presence of such conventions. This will be explained further when the faithful correspondence between properties of the source and of the target is discussed, in Section 6.

Note that the added information is useful both for translations into the core language CDL, and for translations from CDL to a specific notation. The information added in the translations between CDL and Petri nets can be found in [24].

For CDL, the simplest naming convention is that identifiers (variable names) beginning in '&' are considered *nonessential*, because they were not in the source program for which this CDL program is the target, but were rather generated during the translation. This means that any translation from CDL or equivalent core representation that eliminates such variables or updates them differently is acceptable, as long as the other parts of the state are not affected in any way. Since those variables are generated during the translation process of VeriTech, and are not in the original system, they will not appear in any assertion about the source system, and can be ignored for analysis purposes, except as they affect the other variables.

Another convention is intended to aid in the treatment of control statements in various notations. CDL itself does not have explicit control constructs. Variables called *control counters* enable ordering the enabling conditions of transitions to implement sequential control, conditional, or loop statements from other notations. Such variables are assumed to begin with the characters '&PC'. This convention helps in the analysis and translation of CDL programs with such variables.

It is possible to extend every state of a CDL system automatically with (boolean) *flags*. Here we consider only two possibilities relevant to our discussion. The *visible* flag can both appear in the precondition and be changed by the relation. Only states for which *visible* is *true* will be considered as having to satisfy specification formulas. Other states are considered to be *hidden*. This will allow defining different grains of atomicity, and use what has been called *mini-steps* [13] in defining more complex transitions.

The core handles the issue of unspecified next values by allowing both of the possible defaults discussed earlier. The HOLD_PREVIOUS flag remains globally constant in the model, and is used to define the next-state value of a variable when it is not assigned by a transition. If HOLD_PREVIOUS is false, then such a variable is assumed by default to have arbitrary values. Thus if part of the state is to be unchanged, that should be listed explicitly, as in $x' = x$. Recall that this assumption is appropriate for modules that are composed synchronously. On the other hand, maintaining the previous value is the natural default for asynchronous compositions of modules. Thus if HOLD_PREVIOUS is true, unassigned variables are understood to maintain the previous value in all transitions of the system, as in the example.

Note that states which are hidden (i.e., for which the flag *visible* is *false*) are also nonessential–but the overall change of a series of transitions among hidden states beginning and ending in a visible state must be the same as if there were a single transition with the cumulative effect of the series but directly between the visible states.

Above we showed that the source, the target, and additional information gathered during the translation are needed, and thus should be recorded. There also can be multiple CDL versions of a system, for example, where one could be an abstraction of another. Such situations occur when an infinite state program, say including integers, is abstracted to one with only boolean variables, or when some other form of reduction has been performed.

Besides the additional information gathered during translation, there is additional semantic information that can only be obtained through a deeper analysis and understanding of the models. In particular, for each version, we also are interested in the properties known to hold for them, say in temporal logic, and in transformations among classes of properties that ensure faithfulness among translations, as will be seen in Section 6. Just like the other information, this can be useful in optimizing translations, in tracing error analyses, and in deciding which properties to check for different versions of the model. These semantic issues are treated below.

6   Faithful Translations

Translations would ideally fully preserve the semantics of the translated system, thus guaranteeing that the source and the target satisfy exactly the same properties. However, as already seen, the semantics of the translated model cannot always be identical to that of the original.

Therefore we loosen the connection between the properties true of the source and those true of the target. Assume we are given two models, M_1 and M_2, possibly defined within two different verification tools. Further assume that the models are related via some model-translation relation. We identify a set of assertions about M_1 and a property-translation relation that connects the assertions in the set of assertions about M_1 to assertions about M_2.

One relation among the translations is that for every assertion in the set, if M_1 satisfies the assertion then M_2 satisfies the translated version of that assertion. The translation is then called *import faithful* with respect to those models and families of properties. We may alternatively establish that if the translated assertion is true of M_2, then the original assertion must have been true about M_1. This translation is then called *back-implication faithful*.

Of course, we may instead require a *strongly faithful* translation that satisfies both of the conditions above.

We require faithfulness to be transitive so that a series of translations can be considered. In particular, for general translation through a core notation, as in VeriTech, it is sufficient that the translations of models and of families of properties are faithful between different tool notations and the core (in both directions, perhaps for different families of properties). The faithfulness of the translation from one tool to another will then result from transitivity arguments.

Formally, let $\mathcal{M}_1$, $\mathcal{M}_2$ be two classes of models and $\mathcal{L}_1$, $\mathcal{L}_2$ be sets of properties expressed as formulas in an assertion language for $\mathcal{M}_1$ and $\mathcal{M}_2$, respectively. Let $TR \subseteq \mathcal{M}_1 \times \mathcal{M}_2$ be a *model-translation* relation indicating that a model $M_1 \in \mathcal{M}_1$ is translated to a model $M_2 \in \mathcal{M}_2$. Similarly, $tr \subseteq \mathcal{L}_1 \times \mathcal{L}_2$ is a *property-translation* relation that is total over $\mathcal{L}_1$ (i.e., so that each formula of $\mathcal{L}_1$ is in the relation tr).

TR and tr are *import faithful* for $\mathcal{M}_1$, $\mathcal{M}_2$, $\mathcal{L}_1$, and $\mathcal{L}_2$ if $\forall M_i \in \mathcal{M}_i$ and $f_i \in \mathcal{L}_i, i = 1, 2$, whenever $TR(M_1, M_2)$ and $tr(f_1, f_2)$, then $M_1 \models f_1 \Longrightarrow M_2 \models f_2$.

TR and tr are *back-implication faithful* for $\mathcal{M}_1$, $\mathcal{M}_2$, $\mathcal{L}_1$, and $\mathcal{L}_2$ if $\forall M_i \in \mathcal{M}_i$ and $f_i \in \mathcal{L}_i, i = 1, 2$, whenever $TR(M_1, M_2)$ and $tr(f_1, f_2)$, then $M_2 \models f_2 \Longrightarrow M_1 \models f_1$.

TR and tr are *strongly faithful* for $\mathcal{M}_1$, $\mathcal{M}_2$, $\mathcal{L}_1$, and $\mathcal{L}_2$ if $\forall M_i \in \mathcal{M}_i$ and $f_i \in \mathcal{L}_i, i = 1, 2$, whenever $TR(M_1, M_2)$ and $tr(f_1, f_2)$, then $M_1 \models f_1 \Longleftrightarrow M_2 \models f_2$.

A relation (rather than a function) is defined among the models in the definitions of faithfulness because internal optimizations or 'don't care' situations can lead to nondeterministic aspects in the translation. Thus, a single source model may be translated to any one of several target programs, or different source models can be translated to the same target. Similar considerations hold for the assertion transformations. Note that it follows from the definitions that if tr is a function, it is total over $\mathcal{L}_1$.

In this paper, we consider families of properties expressed as sublanguages of various temporal logics, although other modes of expression are possible. In particular, various forms of automata with infinite acceptance conditions are reasonable alternatives. The sets of languages for which we define faithfulness are not necessarily subsets of the specification languages used by the tools. For example, a compiler translation from Spin into SMV (so we have $TR(Spin, SMV)$) could be back-implication faithful for a transformation tr of properties expressible in linear-time temporal logic. In words, if a linear-time temporal logic property that is the second component in a pair satisfying tr is shown of an SMV model that is the result of activating the compiler on a Spin source model, then the first component will necessarily hold for the Spin source. This holds even though the specification language of SMV is the (restricted) branching-time logic CTL, which cannot express everything expressible in linear-time temporal logic. In such a situation, model checking (in SMV) of a transformed property in the intersection of CTL and linear-time temporal logic will be meaningful for the original Spin model and the appropriate source of the checked property. Clearly, properties not in the range of tr are irrelevant for back-implication. Although they may hold of the target model, they give no information about the source model.

On the other hand, if we show that the translation from Spin to SMV is import faithful for a transformation of all linear temporal logic safety properties of Spin, then we can assume that the SMV model satisfies the transformed versions of all safety properties already shown about the original model in Spin.

To establish that a (TR, tr) pair is faithful for two model notations and subsets of temporal logic properties, semantic abstractions must be established. Of course, the source and target models are given as code in different model description languages, and the translation works on the level of those codes. In the abstract level we need, the semantic models of the source notation and the target notation must be described, as must an abstraction of the model translation. The translation abstraction must show the changes introduced to the semantic model of the source in going to the target, as a transformation on the semantic trees. Two examples of such changes could be that a single transition in the source tree is replaced by a sequence of transitions in the target, or that some of the infinite paths of the source are replaced by finite paths that end in a specially designated *fail* state.

The transformation of temporal logic properties is given syntactically, where the family of properties is also defined by a syntactic structure. For this purpose the hierarchy of properties defined for normal forms of linear temporal logic in [26] can be used. For example, safety properties are characterized as being equivalent to a linear assertion $\mathbf{G}p$, where p only has past operators or is a property of a state with no modalities. Similarly, classes of properties seen in branching-time logics can be useful (e.g., 'forall' CTL* that uses only A and not E [12]). Then it must be shown that the transformed assertion is necessarily true of the target execution tree whenever the original is true of the source tree (for importation) or that the original assertion is necessarily true of the source tree whenever the transformed assertion is true of the target tree (for back-implication).

As seen, extensions to the state add variables that are needed to express the model, but usually are not part of the original assertions in the specification of the source. Such variables can be directly used in expressing the transformation of assertions, as will be seen for the *visible* flag, in the following section. This is but one example of how the additional information can be used in defining the property transformation and the relevant families of properties.

7   Using Faithful Translations

Below we present an example of a model-translation relation TR and a property transformation tr that are faithful for given models and families of specifications.

Consider a translation where a single action in the source is divided into several target actions, due to different grains of atomicity. Translations in this family are called 'refinement translations'. Thus the target model will contain intermediate states between the states of the original model. Also we assume that the result program has the additional flag (state component) called *visible* which is turned on when the system is in a state from the original model[1], and turned off when it is in one of the intermediate states.

---

[1] We refer to a state from the original model, and the corresponding state in the result model as the same state, although they are not exactly the same - in this example, the state from the result has the additional *visible* flag, which is *true*.

<u>Definition.</u> A path where all the states except the first and the last have a *false* value for their *visible* flag, will be called an <u>intermediate path.</u>

In a generic translation which does such <u>refinement</u>, the result model is characterized by having:

all of the state variables from the original model, plus an additional *visible* flag;
all the states of the original model, with a *true* value for the *visible* flag;
additional states, which have a *false* value for their *visible* flag.

The result model satisfies the following conditions:

1. For every two states which were connected by an edge in the original model, there exists at least one intermediate path between them in the result model.
2. For every two states which were <u>not</u> connected by an edge in the original model, there is no intermediate path between them in the result model.
3. There are no loops of only non-visible states (and thus there cannot be an infinite sequence of only non-visible states in the model paths).
4. In the paths of the result model the non-visible states always must appear as a finite sequence <u>between</u> visible states and not at the end of a path (This demand is a consequence of the previous one when the result model contains only infinite paths).

Note that we do not demand here that the non-visible intermediate paths for different pairs of states are distinct. Different intermediate paths can share the same non-visible states. Also, there can be several intermediate paths instead of one original edge.

The Property Transformation: We define a property transformation for CTL* that is strongly faithful for all refinement translations. The transformation, tr, will be defined by an induction on the structure of the formula.

* for ϕ=p an atomic proposition: $tr(p)$=p
* $tr(\neg\phi_1) = \neg tr(\phi_1)$
* $tr(\phi_1 \vee \phi_2)=tr(\phi_1) \vee tr(\phi_2)$
* $tr(\phi_1 \wedge \phi_2)=tr(\phi_1) \wedge tr(\phi_2)$
* $tr(X \phi_1)=X[\neg visible \text{ U } (visible \wedge tr(\phi_1))]$
* $tr(G \phi_1)=G[visible \rightarrow tr(\phi_1)]$
* $tr(\phi_1 \text{ U } \phi_2)=[visible \rightarrow tr(\phi_1)] \text{ U } [visible \wedge tr(\phi_2)]$
* $tr(A \phi_1)=A tr(\phi_1)$
* $tr(E \phi_1)=E tr(\phi_1)$

The proof that this transformation is indeed strongly faithful for operation refinements as defined above, is by induction on the structure of the formulas, and appears in [3].

However, this is not always an acceptable transformation. Often the tool of the target specification language can only operate for some sub-language of CTL*. If this is the case then we will not be able to use back-implication for all the properties in the source language of the transformation, but only those with a transformation result in the language of properties on which the tool of the target specification language can operate.

Assume we are using a property transformation tr defined for a source language L_1 (for simplicity, we assume here that tr is a function), together with a translation to some model specification language with a verification tool that can verify properties from some language L_*. We will define the *effective source language* to be all the properties ϕ from L_1 such that $tr(\phi) \in L_*$.

When using a transformation with a translation to a specific language, then often, what we really want to maximize is not the source language of the transformation, but the effective source language.

It may be the case that we have two different strongly faithful transformations for the same translation, with different source languages (groups of properties). Now we see that the one with the larger source language is not necessarily the better one, because it may have a smaller effective source language.

For LTL, the transformation given for CTL^* is effective, because if we begin with an LTL formula, the transformation will result in one too. However, if the target only can verify properties in CTL, then the given transformation is not optimal. For many properties, the result will not be in CTL, and thus cannot be verified in the target. A better transformation in this case would be to replace an innermost AGp, where p is atomic, with $AG(visible \rightarrow p)$ and an innermost AFp, again where p is atomic, by $AF(visible \wedge p)$. This will yield a larger effective source language when the target is CTL.

Other generic translations can also be analyzed to produce generic property transformations that can be proven faithful. Moreover, the property transformations that correspond to the composition of numerous translation steps can be treated uniformly, to treat more complex translations.

8   Conclusions

Translations among models are already common, and their use is growing rapidly. The ability to easily move among models, properties of interest, and tools extends the practical applicability of formal methods, and reduces the dependence on a single tool. Basic issues in translation, such as the differing grains of atomicity, synchronization primitives, treatment of failures, finiteness or infinity of the state space of the model, often force the models and structure of translations to differ from the original. Thus the framework of a faithful translation between both models and properties is essential to express necessary relations among models and properties of those models.

In practice, many translations involve more than one of the types of differences among models that were presented. Thus combinations of the transformations of properties are needed to guarantee faithful relations for interesting classes of properties. For example, one version of a model could concentrate on a particular group of variables, abstracting other parts of the system, while another model could concentrate on different variables. These models are *siblings* where neither is an abstraction of the other, but both are different refinements of some (perhaps implicit) abstraction. Such models should be related by faithful classes of transformed properties, even though in other frameworks they are not comparable.

The additional information gathered during translation and from semantic analysis of faithful transformations also needs to be further developed. In particular, much work remains to be done in understanding how such information can be exploited to aid in later translations, in connecting slightly changed versions, and in tracing errors discovered in the target program back to errors in the source.

References

1. K. R. Apt, N. Francez, and S. Katz. Appraising fairness in languages for distributed programming. *Distributed Computing*, 2:226–241, 1988.
2. Saddek Bensalem, Vijay Ganesh, Yassine Lakhnech, César Muñoz, Sam Owre, Harald Rueß, John Rushby, Vlad Rusu, Hassen Saïdi, N. Shankar, Eli Singerman, and Ashish Tiwari. An overview of SAL. In C. Michael Holloway, editor, *LFM 2000: Fifth NASA Langley Formal Methods Workshop*, pages 187–196, Hampton, VA, June 2000. Available at http://shemesh.larc.nasa.gov/fm/Lfm2000/Proc/.
3. M. Berg and S. Katz. Property transformations for translations. Technical Report CS-2002-05, Computer Science Department, The Technion, 2002.
4. N. Bjorner, A. Browne, E. Chang, M. Colon, A. Kapur, Z. Manna, H.B. Simpa, and T.E. Uribe. Step: The stanford temporal prover - user's manual. Technical Report STAN-CS-TR-95-1562, Department of Computer Science, Stanford University, November 1995.
5. T. Bolognesi and E. Brinksma. Introduction to the ISO specification language LOTOS. *Computer Networks and ISDN Systems*, 14:25–59, 1987.
6. T. Bolognesi, J.v.d. Legemaat, and C.A. Vissars (eds.). *LOTOSphere: software development with LOTOS*. Kluwer Academic Publishers, 1994.
7. G. Brat, K. Havelund, S. Park, and W. Visser. Model checking programs. In *In IEEE International Conference on Automated Software Engineering (ASE)*, September 2000.
8. J.R. Burch, E.M. Clarke, K.L. McMillan, D. Dill, and L.J. Hwang. Symbolic model checking: 10^{20} states and beyond. *Information and Computation*, 98:142–170, 1992.
9. E.M. Clarke, O. Grumberg, and D.A. Peled. *Model Checking*. MIT press, December 1999.
10. C. Demartini, R. Iosif, and R. Sisto. dSPIN: A dynamic extension of SPIN. In *SPIN*, pages 261–276, 1999.
11. O. Grumberg and S. Katz. VeriTech: translating among specifications and verification tools–design principles. In *Proceedings of third Austria-Israel Symposium Software for Communication Technologies*, pages 104–109, April 1999. http://www.cs.technion.ac.il/Labs/veritech/.
12. O. Grumberg and D.E. Long. Model checking and modular verification. *ACM Trans. on Programming Languages and Systems*, 16(3):843–871, 1994.
13. D. Harel. Statecharts: a visual formalism for complex systems. *Science of Computer Programming*, 8:231–274, 1987.
14. D. Harel, H. Lachover, A. Naamad, A. Pnueli, M. Politi, R. Sherman, A. Shtull-Trauring, and M. Trakhtenbrot. Statemate: a working environment for the development of complex reactive systems. *IEEE Trans. on Software Eng.*, 16(4):403–414, April 1990.

15. J. Hatcliff and M. Dwyer. Using the bandera tool set to model-check properties of concurrent java software. In *International Conference on Concurrency Theory (CONCUR)*, June 2001. Invited tutorial paper.
16. K. Havelund and T. Pressburger. Model checking JAVA programs using JAVA PathFinder. *International Journal on Software Tools for Technology Transfer*, 2(4):366–381, 2000.
17. C.A.R. Hoare and He Jifeng. *Unifying Theories of Programming*. Prentice-Hall, 1998.
18. G. Holzmann. *Design and Validation of Computer Protocols*. Prentice-Hall International, 1991.
19. G.J. Holzmann and D. Peled. The state of SPIN. In *Proceedings of CAV96*, volume 1102 of *LNCS*, pages 385–389. Springer-Verlag, 1996.
20. C.N. Ip and D.L. Dill. Better verification through symmetry. *Formal Methods in System Design*, 9:41–75, 1996.
21. S. Katz. Refinement with global equivalence proofs in temporal logic. In D. Peled, V. Pratt, and G. Holzmann, editors, *Partial Order Methods in Verification*, pages 59–78. American Mathematical Society, 1997. DIMACS Series in Discrete Mathematics and Theoretical Computer Science, vol. 29.
22. S. Katz. Faithful translations among models and specifications. In *Proceedings of FME2001: Formal Methods for Increasing Software Productivity*, volume 2021 of *LNCS*, pages 419–434. Springer-Verlag, 2001.
23. S. Katz and D. Peled. Interleaving set temporal logic. *Theoretical Computer Science*, 75:263–287, 1990. Preliminary version appeared in the 6th ACM-PODC, 1987.
24. K. Korenblat, O. Grumberg, and S. Katz. Translations between texual transition systems and petri nets. In *Third international conference on Integrated Formal Methods (IFM'02)*, Turku, Finland, May 2002.
25. R.P. Kurshan. *Computer-aided Verification of Coordinating Processes*. Princeton University Press, 1994.
26. Z. Manna and A. Pnueli. *The Temporal Logic of Reactive and Concurrent Systems: Specification*. Springer-Verlag, 1992.
27. K. L. McMillan. *Symbolic Model Checking: An Approach to the State Explosion Problem*. Kluwer Academic Publishers, 1993.
28. http://wwwbrauer.informatik.tu-muenchen.de/gruppen/theorie/KIT/.
29. Sam Owre, John Rushby, Natarajan Shankar, and Friedrich von Henke. Formal verification for fault-tolerant architectures: Prolegomena to the design of PVS. *IEEE Transactions on Software Engineering*, 21(2):107–125, February 1995.
30. B. Potter, J. Sinclair, and D. Till. *An introduction to Formal Specification and Z*. Prentice Hall, 1991.
31. W. Reisig. *Elements of Distributed Algorithms– Modeling and Analysis with Petri Nets*. Springer-Verlag, 1998.

Model Checking Object-Z Using ASM

Kirsten Winter and Roger Duke

Software Verification Research Centre
School of Information Technology and Electrical Engineering
University of Queensland
Phone: +61 7 3365 1656   Fax: +61 7 3365 1533
kirsten@svrc.uq.edu.au, rduke@itee.uq.edu.au

Abstract. A major problem with creating tools for Object-Z is that
its high-level abstractions are difficult to deal with directly. Integrating Object-Z with a more concrete notation is a sound strategy. With
this in mind, in this paper we introduce an approach to model-checking
Object-Z specifications based on first integrating Object-Z with the Abstract State Machine (ASM) notation to get the notation OZ-ASM. We
show that this notation can be readily translated into the specification
language ASM-SL, a language that can be automatically translated into
the language of the temporal logic model checker SMV.

Keywords: Object-Z, Abstract State Machines, language transformation, model checking, automated tool support.

1 Introduction

High level declarative specification languages such as Z [20] and Object-Z [3,19]
are ideally suited for capturing state-based system properties. A major obstacle
to the wider adoption of such languages, however, is the lack of tool support.
If the full potential of such languages is to be realised, they need to be supple-
mented with software tools to assist with the more taxing mathematical aspects
such as the detection of specification errors and the verification of system properties.

In this paper we introduce an approach to model-checking Object-Z specifications based on first integrating Object-Z with the Abstract State Machine
(ASM) notation [8] and then, through an automated process, translating this integrated notation (which we call OZ-ASM) into the temporal logic model checker
SMV [16].

We chose this integrated approach for several reasons. First, when faced with
the task of model checking Object-Z specifications it seemed wise to see if we
could make maximum use of existing model-checker technology rather than re-
inventing the wheel.

Next, the problem with Object-Z by itself is that, based as it is on logical
predicates and set theory, its high-level abstractions are difficult to deal with
directly. Most model checking tools do not provide a language that is expressive

M. Butler, L. Petre, and K. Sere (Eds.): IFM 2002, LNCS 2335, pp. 165–184, 2002.

enough to represent the operators and data structures that can be used in Object-Z. An automatic transformation of the full language of Object-Z into a simple model checker language would be hard to achieve. However, if we re-use an existing interface from ASM to the SMV language [1] we only need to provide a transformation from Object-Z into ASM in order to automatically generate SMV code from Object-Z models.

Third, for an algorithmic transformation from Object-Z into ASM, we have to ensure that operation predicates are given in a canonical form: the transition relation that relates pre- and post-states must be given in such a way that primed variables (denoting post-state values) depend only upon unprimed variables (denoting pre-state values). To provide this canonicity, we integrate Object-Z with ASM syntax. The resulting integrated language is easy to read and understand for anybody who is familiar with Object-Z.

Our work has similarities to that of Valentine [21] who introduces a restricted version of Z, called Z--, which has a similar canonicity of predicates. However, Valentine aims to provide a computational subset of Z, and the language restrictions required to do this are stronger than those required for model checking. In contrast to Valentine's approach, we use the concept of language integration to give a simple definition for the restricted scope of the language.

Based on Jackson's work on the automatic analysis of a subset of Z [12], Jackson et. al. have developed a new language, Alloy [13], which can be automatically analysed through SAT solvers. The language Alloy, created to avoid working with an 'ad hoc restriction' of Z, satisfies the necessary conditions for being translated into boolean formulae (a format that SAT solvers can deal with). In accordance with the SAT solver approach, Alloy is a declarative language. In contrast, our language focuses on operational models as required for model checkers.

The use of SMV to model check Z specifications has been suggested by Jacky and Patrick [14]. Their approach is to translate the Z specification directly into SMV, a process that involves considerable simplification of the specification. In contrast, our approach is to first integrate Object-Z with ASM. The OZ-ASM notation that results can be readily translated into the specification language ASM-SL and this can be automatically translated into SMV. Furthermore, ASM-SL is an ideal starting point for the application of other tools (although in this paper we will consider only SMV model checking).

Other researchers have approached the problem of model-checking Object-Z using tools based on process algebras such as FDR [6] or SPIN [11]. For example, Fischer and Wehrheim [5] integrate Object-Z with CSP and apply the model-checker FDR. Kassel and Smith [15] investigate an alternative approach for plain Object-Z but also exploit the CSP semantics for their mapping into CSP_M (the language of FDR). Although CSP_M is sufficiently expressible to cover many language constructs provided for Object-Z predicates, neither object referencing nor operation operators are supported. Moreover, the compilation effort within the FDR tool is enormous even for small examples. Similarly, Zave [25] has looked at model-checking Z by combining Z with Promela [10] (the language of SPIN).

However, although Promela is designed for model checking, it is not suited for representing system state or for manipulating global data.

Yet another approach to the checking of Z is to animate the specification. Essentially, Valentine's work mentioned previously [21] follows this strategy. Another computational approach is given by Grieskamp [7] who constructs a computational model for Z that allows the combination of the functional and logical aspects of Z.

In this paper we begin (in Section 2) by introducing the OZ-ASM specification notation integrating Object-Z and ASM. It is specifications written in OZ-ASM that we will be model checking. We emphasise, however, that we do not see OZ-ASM as yet another independent formal specification notation. Our underlying wish is to model-check Object-Z specifications, and ideally a first step in fulfilling such a wish would be to convert an Object-Z specification into the OZ-ASM notation. In practice, however, although such a conversion is in most cases straightforward, as it involves (among other things) various non-deterministic choices about the cardinality of underlying set structures, it would be difficult if not impossible to perform such a conversion automatically. For this reason, in this paper we take the OZ-ASM notation as our starting point.

Specifications written in ASM-SL can be automatically translated to SMV for model checking [1]. In our case the starting notation is OZ-ASM rather than ASM-SL, but the process of translation to SMV is essentially the same. In Section 3 we outline the principle issues behind the conversion from OZ-ASM into ASM-SL. Once this conversion is completed, the translation into SMV is automatic. We believe that it would be straightforward to automate the conversion from OZ-ASM into ASM-SL; we leave that for future work.

In Section 4 we illustrate how to apply the given transformation rules to convert a complex OZ-ASM operation into ASM-SL code. We discuss future directions and conclude the paper in Section 5.

2   The Integrated Language OZ-ASM

Object-Z [3,19] is a high-level specification language based on Z [20]. It supports object-orientation through the concept of class, inheritance between classes and object referencing. Object-Z models of complex systems can be nicely structured into a set of smaller sub-systems or components. Each component is modelled as a class that contains its local definitions: a state, an initialisation and operations. Object instances are accessed through referencing.

Most of these concepts are not supported by a simple model checker language, which is in most cases designed to describe hardware circuits, and a transformation from Object-Z into a model checker language is difficult to build. In order to ease this task we propose to make use of an existing transformation, the interface from the high-level language ASM to the SMV language ([1]). In doing so, it only remains to develop a transformation from Object-Z into ASM, a task that is easier to achieve since most Object-Z concepts can be simulated with ASM.

ASM [8] is a formal specification language that models state transition systems at a high level of abstraction. However, object orientation with its benefits for modular design is not facilitated. The concept of classes and, especially, the reuse of classes via inheritance and object instantiation is not supported.

The transition relation of an ASM model is given through a set of transition rules for which ASM provides a minimal set of rule constructors. These rule constructors are sufficient to model any kind of state machine or (sequential) algorithm [9]. The core concept of an ASM transition rule involves *locations* which become *updated* in a transition step, i.e. $loc := val\_term$. Similar to guarded command languages, updates can be conditional in the sense that the update is fired only if the corresponding guard is satisfied in the current state, i.e. if $guard$ then $loc := val\_term$. Clearly, a location resembles a state variable and the concept of guarded updates coincides with the notion of a transition relation in the model checker languages we are targeting. Note, however, that the two terms, $guard$ and val_term, depend only on the evaluation of terms in the current state; no next-state value can occur.

Whilst the structuring mechanisms of Object-Z are very close to concepts of object-oriented programming languages, the modelling paradigm for operations is essentially the same as in Z. That is, operations are modelled in a declarative way rather than operationally. The model represents *what* are the requirements of a system. The set of acceptable behaviours is thus specified implicitly by means of predicates that define a relation between pre- and post-states. However, in many cases, an operational modelling approach is adopted in which operations are seen as a transition in a state machine that describe an actual step, or sequence of steps, between pre- and post-states. The specification can present some information on *how* the requirements are met by the system. The user of Object-Z is basically free to choose a modelling style and the degree of abstraction of the model. No restrictions are given by the language.

If we want to provide an interface between Object-Z and ASM, we have to transform the definition of operations (i.e. the relation between pre- and post-states) into the canonical form of a transition relation that is supported by ASMs, i.e. each primed variable depends only on unprimed variables. For arbitrary Z or Object-Z predicates this transformation would be difficult (if not impossible) to perform automatically. Therefore, we restrict the appearance of predicates in an operation schema to a form that can be treated algorithmically. To do so, we integrate Object-Z with ASM.

For our integration of Object-Z and ASM, which we call OZ-ASM, we borrow the following ASM transition rule constructors[1]:

− skip

   The skip rule specifies an empty transition in which the state does not change.

---

[1] We do not allow the use of import or extend rules since these cannot be treated by the model checking approach ([1]).

- `loc := val_term`
  A simple update rule that specifies the assignment of a value to a location. `val_term` is a term whose value depends only on the current state.

- `if` *guard* `then` R_0 `else` R_2
  The if-then-else rule specifies a boolean expression *guard* (which may include also existential and universal quantification) and a rule that is to be fired in the case when the guard is satisfied, i.e. the *then-case*, as well as an optional rule for the case when the guard is not satisfied, i.e. the *else-case*.

- `block` R_1 R_2 ... R_n `endblock`
  The block rule allows the user to combine several rules into one. All rules $R_1, R_2, \ldots, R_n$ contained in the block rule are fired simultaneously.

- `do forall` v `in` A `[ with` G `]` $R(v)$ `enddo`
  The do-forall rule allows the user to parameterise a transition rule. The inner rule R is instantiated for all specified values v in set A and all rule instances are fired simultaneously. The optional boolean expression G allows the user to further restrict the possible values for v.

- `choose` v `in` A `[ with` G `]` $R(v)$ `endchoose`
  The choose rule allows the user to model non-determinism.

The listed ASM rule constructors replace ordinary predicates within operation schemas of OZ-ASM. Primed state variables do not occur anymore. Instead we use the variable assignment ':=' with a next-state variable as its left hand side. Thus, the use of predicates and their appearance in operation schemas is restricted in the intended way. The restriction, however, is only syntactical since any operation predicate (we could think of) can be 'simulated' by an ASM rule construct. Naturally, some expressions become more verbose but the semantics, adopted from Object-Z, will essentially be the same. The only significant semantic distinction between Object-Z and OZ-ASM is to do with the occurence of operations. In Object-Z an operation can occur if and only if it is applicable, i.e. its pre-conditions are satisfied and there exists a valid post-state. In OZ-ASM however, an operation can always occur; if it is not applicable (i.e. if the guard on the update rule is not true or if there is no valid next state) then the operation can skip, i.e. do nothing. Both non-occurrence and skip, however, have the same effect; they do not change the state of the systems.

As a consequence, operations that contain only a guard (i.e. a predicate over non-primed variables, e.g. *accessGranted* of class *Key* in the example on the following page) have the same effect if they are applicable or not. They do not change the state in both cases. These operations only become meaningful when combined with other operations (e.g. operation *insertKey* in class *KeySystem*). They restrict the applicability of the overall operation since their guard contributes to the overall guard (which is a conjunction of the guards of combined operations, see Section 3).

The benefit we gain from the syntactical adaption of ASM rules is a simpler language definition. Instead of listing a set of rules that define the predicates we can support, we provide (for Object-Z users) a new syntax of transition rules. These rule constructs will be easier to learn (and to keep in mind while modelling) than restrictions on predicates.

As an illustration of OZ-ASM we specify a simple key system (for the original Object-Z specification see [3] Chapter 3). This system consists of a set of keys and a set of rooms. Each key has access rights to (i.e. can unlock) a subset of the rooms, and these access rights can be modified, either by extending the access rights of a key to a room which the key cannot currently access, or by rescinding access rights to a room which the key can currently access. A key can attempt to access a room; if that room is locked and the key has access rights to the room, the room unlocks, otherwise nothing happens. An unlocked room can non-deterministically lock (in practice this would probably be realised by a timeout).

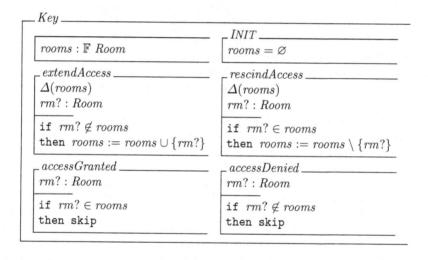

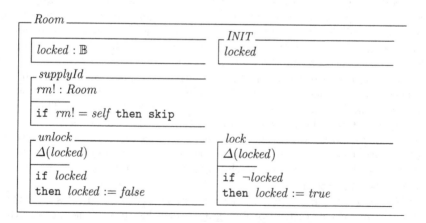

```
┌─ KeySystem ──────────────────────────────────────────────────
│  ┌─────────────────────────────┐  ┌─ INIT ──────────────────┐
│  │ keys : 𝔽 Key                │  │ ∀ k : keys • k.INIT     │
│  │ rooms : 𝔽 Room              │  │ ∀ r : rooms • r.INIT    │
│  └─────────────────────────────┘  └─────────────────────────┘
│  ┌──────────────────────────────┐
│  │ ∀ k : keys • k.rooms ⊆ rooms │
│  └──────────────────────────────┘
│  extendAccess ≙ [k? : keys] • k?.extendAccess
│  rescindAccess ≙ [k? : keys] • k?.rescindAccess
│  lock ≙ [] r : rooms • r.lock
│  insertKey ≙ [r? : rooms; k? : keys] •
│                  r?.suppyId ‖ (k?.accessGranted ∧ r?.unlock
│                                    [] k?.accessDenied)
└───────────────────────────────────────────────────────────────
```

Note that apart from predicates in operation schemas all the other constructs of Object-Z are not affected by our integration. State schema, state invariants, initialisation schema, and the definition of operations by means of operation operators can be used in OZ-ASM as in Object-Z. We claim that these constructs can be automatically mapped into a canonical representation that can be model checked. This mapping will be introduced and discussed in the next section.

3 Mapping OZ-ASM into ASM-SL

Castillo and Winter [1,23] have shown that ASM models in general can be automatically transformed into a simple intermediate format for transition systems (namely, ASM-IL) which can in turn be readily mapped into languages like the SMV language ([16]). In particular, this transformation has been implemented for ASM-SL which is a specification language that provide a machine readable syntax for ASM[2].

Our intention is to make use of this existing work by mapping OZ-ASM into ASM-SL. Because of the existing automatic transformation from ASM-SL into SMV, effectively we will have a transformation from OZ-ASM into SMV code. In the following we use the symbols ⇒ and ⇓ to denote the mapping from OZ-ASM into ASM-SL expressions that provides the basis of the transformation algorithm to be implemented.

3.1 Types

Since the model checking approach that is utilised here is limited to systems with a finite state space, we have to assume that all types of an OZ-ASM system are finite. Moreover, any given type needs to be enumerated, i.e.

---

[2] ASM-SL is supported by the ASM-Workbench ([2]) and the transformation from ASM-SL into SMV code implements an interface from the ASM-WB to the SMV model checker.

$$[GivenType] \;\Rightarrow\; \texttt{datatype}\;\; GivenType == \{e_1, \ldots, e_n\} \qquad (1)$$

where the number n of elements is explicitly defined. An approach for checking systems with given types is proposed in [24] but so as to be able to make use of an existing model checking tool we follow here the simpler approach introduced in [1].

3.2 Classes

As a general and readily implemented approach for simulating OZ-ASM by ASM-SL, we propose here a transformation that flattens the modular structure of OZ-ASM. In OZ-ASM, the concept of class provides a local name space for attributes and operations. These local name spaces are 'simulated' in an ASM-SL specification by identifiers that include the class name. Any types, constants or attributes that are local within a class are mapped into corresponding types or functions whose identifiers are extended by the class name. The use of functions allows us to deal easily with object referencing. For example, an attribute $attr$ in a class A which is of type $AttrType$ becomes a function $A\_attr : AType \rightarrow AttrType$. Referencing of the attribute $attr$ of an object a is then realised by the function application $A\_attr(a)$. To achieve this we have to generate an ASM type for each class. Note that the number of instances of a class must be finite and fixed if we want to apply model checking.

Since ASM-SL is a strongly typed language we need to distinguish between types and sets. Types are used in the declaration of functions; sets, modelled as static functions, are used within terms. Due to this restricted use of declared types, we have to introduce for each OZ-ASM class both a type and a constant set, with both containing the same elements.

$$
\begin{array}{|l|}
\hline
A \underline{\hspace{6cm}} \\
\;\ldots \\
\hline
\end{array}
$$

$$\Downarrow \qquad\qquad\qquad\qquad (2)$$

$$
\begin{aligned}
&\texttt{datatype}\;\; AType == \{obj_1, \ldots, obj_n\} \\
&\texttt{static function}\;\; A == \{obj_1, \ldots, obj_n\}
\end{aligned}
$$

Constant attributes are mapped into static functions in ASM-SL. All attributes that are declared in the state schema are mapped into dynamic functions. Input attributes become external functions (which in ASM-SL correspond to the notion of input). Instead of the '?' decoration we add the extension '_in' to the name of the corresponding external function; similarly, the decoration '!' is replaced by the extension '_out'.

Suppose in the following that $Type_2$, $Type_3$, and $Type_4$ are already declared types and $AType$ is given as above. Then the class A and its attributes as given below are mapped in the following way:

$$
\begin{array}{l}
\underline{A} \\[-2pt]
\hline
Type_1 \;::=\; t_1 \mid t_2 \mid \ldots \mid t_m \\
\mid\; attr_1 : Type_2 \\
\hline
attr_2 : Type_3 \rightarrow Type_4 \\
\hline
\end{array}
$$

$$\Downarrow \tag{3}$$

```
datatype  A_Type₁ == {A_t₁,..., A_tₘ}
static function  A_attr₁ : AType → Type₂
dynamic function  A_attr₂ : AType → (Type₃ → Type₄)
```

Attributes of a set type are mapped into a characteristic function which maps each element that is a member of the set to *true* and each element that is not a member of the set to *false*.

$$
\begin{array}{l}
\underline{A} \qquad\qquad\qquad\qquad\qquad \underline{INIT} \\[-2pt]
\hline
attr_3 : \mathbb{F}\ Type_2 \qquad\qquad\qquad \ldots \\
\hline
\end{array}
$$

$$\Downarrow \tag{4}$$

```
dynamic function  A_attr₃ : AType → (Type₂ → BOOL)
     initially {...}
```

The initialisation of a dynamic function is derived from the *INIT* schema of the OZ-ASM model. We give an example:

$$
\begin{array}{l}
\underline{Room} \qquad\qquad\qquad\qquad\qquad \underline{INIT} \\[-2pt]
\hline
locked : \mathbb{B} \qquad\qquad\qquad\qquad\quad locked \\
\hline
\end{array}
$$

$$
\begin{array}{l}
\underline{Key} \qquad\qquad\qquad\qquad\qquad\qquad \underline{INIT} \\[-2pt]
\hline
rooms : \mathbb{P}\,Room \qquad\qquad\qquad\quad rooms = \varnothing \\
\hline
\underline{extendAccess} \\
\Delta(rooms) \\
rm? : Room \\
\hline
\ldots \\
\hline
\end{array}
$$

$$\Downarrow \quad \text{via } (2),\ (3),\ (4)$$

```
datatype RoomType == {r₁,...,r₄}
datatype KeyType == {k₁,...,k₅}
static function Room == {r₁,...,r₄}
static function Key == {k₁,...,k₅}
dynamic function Room_locked : RoomType → BOOL
      initially MAP_TO_FUN {r ↦ true | r ∈ Room}
dynamic function Key_rooms : KeyType → (RoomType → BOOL)
      initially MAP_TO_FUN {(k,r) ↦ false |
                      Union ({{(k,r) | k ∈ Key} | r ∈ Room})}
external function Key_rm_in : KeyType → RoomType
```

3.3 Operations

When mapping OZ-ASM into ASM-SL we have to take into account that the underlying semantics of operation execution in OZ-ASM is different to the semantics of running an ASM program. In ASM all transitions fire simultaneously; in OZ-ASM one operation is selected for execution by angelic choice. This provides an asynchronous execution model.

As the target language SMV supports the notion of asynchronous processes, a semantic-preserving mapping from OZ-ASM into the SMV language can be given by the following scheme. Each OZ-ASM operation is transformed into a single-step ASM which we call the corresponding *operation*-ASM. An operation-ASM consists of one (possibly nested) transition rule that 'simulates' the operation.

Figure 1 illustrates the mapping from OZ-ASM operations into a set of operation-ASMs. Applying the results from [23], each operation-ASM can in turn be automatically transformed into an SMV process. In the corresponding SMV code all processes are tied together asynchronously by using the keyword **process** (see [16]). Semantically, in each state exactly one of the asynchronous processes is active and can proceed with one state change (or no state change if no progress is possible).

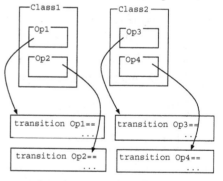

Fig. 1: The mapping schema

In the remainder of this section we introduce how OZ-ASM operations are mapped into operation-ASMs (in ASM-SL). We describe a mapping for operation schemas, the conjunction operator, the general choice operator, and the treatment of state invariants. The mapping for all the other operation operators, namely •, ∥!, ∥, and ⅋, can be derived from these basic operators (see [3,19] for definitions)[3]. However, in order to show the transformation on an example (see

---

[3] The sequential operator ⅋ , however, should be restricted to the composition of two operations only.

Section 4), we extend this section by outlining the rules for promotion, scope enrichment, and parallel composition.

We assume in the following that the state space for any resulting operation-ASM has already been generated by making appropriate use of the global definitions described above.

Mapping Set Expressions. Since in OZ-ASM operation predicates are expressed in the syntax of ASM transition rules, the mapping of these OZ-ASM transitions into ASM-SL is reduced to a mapping of expressions and locations that occur within the transitions. We introduce the function $\langle\!\langle . \rangle\!\rangle$ as a shorthand for the results of the transformation application, i.e. $\langle\!\langle A \rangle\!\rangle \equiv B$ holds if $A \Rightarrow B$, and give an (incomplete) set of rules for handling expressions. Assume that E, E_1, E_2, E_3 are sets where $E_1 \subset E$, $E_2 \subset E$, and $E_3 \subset E$. χ_{Ei} (for $i \in \{1, 2, 3\}$) denotes the characteristic function for the set E_i.

$$\langle\!\langle \text{if } g \text{ then } upds \rangle\!\rangle \equiv \text{if } \langle\!\langle g \rangle\!\rangle \text{ then } \langle\!\langle upds \rangle\!\rangle \tag{5}$$

$$\langle\!\langle e \in E \rangle\!\rangle \equiv \chi_E(e) = true \tag{6}$$

$$\langle\!\langle E_1 \subset E_2 \rangle\!\rangle \equiv \texttt{forall } e \texttt{ in } E : \tag{7}$$
$$\chi_{E1}(e) \texttt{ implies } \chi_{E2}(e)$$

$$\langle\!\langle E_1 := E_2 \rangle\!\rangle \equiv \texttt{block} \tag{8}$$
$$\texttt{do forall } e \texttt{ in } E$$
$$\texttt{with } (\chi_{E2}(e) = true)$$
$$\chi_{E1}(e) := true$$
$$\texttt{enddo}$$
$$\texttt{do forall } e \texttt{ in } E$$
$$\texttt{with } (\chi_{E2}(e) = false)$$
$$\chi_{E1}(e) := false$$
$$\texttt{enddo}$$
$$\texttt{endblock}$$

$$\langle\!\langle E_1 := E_1 \cup \{e\} \rangle\!\rangle \equiv \chi_{E1}(e) := true \tag{9}$$

$$\langle\!\langle E_1 := E_1 \setminus \{e\} \rangle\!\rangle \equiv \chi_{E1}(e) := false \tag{10}$$

$$\langle\!\langle E_1 := E_2 \cap E_3 \rangle\!\rangle \equiv \texttt{block} \tag{11}$$
$$\texttt{do forall } e \texttt{ in } E$$
$$\texttt{with } (\chi_{E2}(e) = true \texttt{ and } \chi_{E3}(e) = true)$$
$$\chi_{E1}(e) := true$$
$$\texttt{enddo}$$
$$\texttt{do forall } e \texttt{ in } E$$
$$\texttt{with } not(\chi_{E2}(e) = true \texttt{ and } \chi_{E3}(e) = true)$$
$$\chi_{E1}(e) := false$$
$$\texttt{enddo}$$
$$\texttt{endblock}$$

Although this set of rules is incomplete, it illustrates how set operations and expressions in OZ-ASM can be transformed into ASM-SL transition rules and expressions over characteristic functions. Similarly, rules for operators on other data types, such as sequences, can be defined.

Following the results in [23], all ASM rule constructs (apart from the extend and import rules) can be mapped into a set of simple rules of the form 'if guard then updates'. For such a straightforward rule we can readily determine its guard, its locations and its updates. The guard is simply a boolean expression over variables, while locations are the variables that are changed by the rule (i.e. the left hand sides of updates). For updates we consider a set of assignment expressions of the form $loc := val$. We reference these entities in the following discussion with $guard(rule)$, $locs(rule)$ and $upds(rule)$ respectively.

Operation Schema. Given the mapping for OZ-ASM transitions, we can now define rules for mapping OZ-ASM operations into operation-ASMs (in ASM-SL). We start with the rule for mapping operations that are defined simply in terms of an OZ-ASM operation schema. Due to the integration of ASM syntax into OZ, this rule is straightforward:

$$
\boxed{
\begin{array}{l}
A \\[4pt]
\boxed{
\begin{array}{l}
op \\
\hline
\Delta(\textit{attributes}) \\
\hline
\textit{transition}
\end{array}
}
\end{array}
}
$$

$$\Downarrow \qquad\qquad (12)$$

$$\texttt{transition}\ A\_op == \langle\!\langle \textit{transition} \rangle\!\rangle$$

Similarly, this rule applies to any operation definition, i.e. $op \mathrel{\widehat{=}} op_1 \Rightarrow$ transition $op == \langle\!\langle op_1 \rangle\!\rangle$.

Conjunction Operator. In OZ-ASM the conjunction $op_1 \land op_2$ of two operations is applicable if the preconditions of both op_1 and op_2 are satisfied and for both operations there exists a valid post-state. The precondition is given by the conjunction of the guards of the mapped operations $\langle\!\langle op_1 \rangle\!\rangle$ and $\langle\!\langle op_2 \rangle\!\rangle$ together with any given state invariant that affects the operation.

The effect of the conjoined operation is basically given as the union of the updates $upds(\langle\!\langle op_1 \rangle\!\rangle)$ and $upds(\langle\!\langle op_2 \rangle\!\rangle)$, assuming that no conflicts occur. No conflict occurs if for any location that is addressed in both operations the different updates deterministically assign the same value to the location, or if the updates are non-deterministic but the intersection of both sets of possible update-values is not empty. No conflict occurs also in the mixed case, i.e. if the assigned value of a deterministic update falls into the range of a non-deterministic update.

In Object-Z, examples of the second situation arise quite frequently, e.g. $(n' \in \{1..10\}) \land (n' \in \{5..15\})$. The result of this conjunction is clearly $(n' \in \{5..10\})$, i.e. n' is a member of the intersection of both update-ranges. In OZ-ASM we model such non-deterministic updates by means of the choose-rule: $\texttt{choose}\quad v$ $\texttt{in}\quad \{1..10\} \cap \{5..15\}\ n := v\ \texttt{endchoose}$. The possible update-values of this rule are given as the range of v.

Let the function upd_vals provide for each rule R and each location loc that is addressed within R the set of possible update values that can be assigned to *loc*. For a deterministic update, $upd\_vals(R, loc)$ is a singleton that contains exactly the right hand side of the update, i.e. *val* for the update $loc := val$. (Note that *val* is the evaluation of the right hand side expression in the current state.) For a non-deterministic update we get more than one possible update value, so $upd\_vals(R, loc)$ is a set. For example, for the rule

> **transition** $R ==$
> **choose** v **in** $\{1, \ldots, 10\}$
> $n := v + 1$
> **endchoose**

we get $upd\_vals(R, n) = \{1 + 1, \ldots, 10 + 1\} = \{2, \ldots, 11\}$.

In general, we can conjoin two operations that address the same location by selecting as the update value an element from the intersection of all the update-value sets for that location. All other updates that address locations that are not referenced in both operations can be fired simultaneously.

We denote the set of conflicting updates by means of a function *conflict_upds*:

$$(\text{if } g \text{ then } loc := exp) \in conflict\_upds(\langle\!\langle\!\langle op_1 \rangle\!\rangle\!\rangle, \langle\!\langle\!\langle op_2 \rangle\!\rangle\!\rangle)$$
$$\Leftrightarrow \quad loc \in (locs(\langle\!\langle\!\langle op_1 \rangle\!\rangle\!\rangle) \cap locs(\langle\!\langle\!\langle op_2 \rangle\!\rangle\!\rangle))$$
$$\wedge \ (\text{if } g \text{ then } loc := exp) \in (upds(\langle\!\langle\!\langle op_1 \rangle\!\rangle\!\rangle) \cup upds(\langle\!\langle\!\langle op_2 \rangle\!\rangle\!\rangle))$$

The set of non-conflicting updates of operations op_1 and op_2 is then determined by $(upds(\langle\!\langle\!\langle op_1 \rangle\!\rangle\!\rangle) \cup upds(\langle\!\langle\!\langle op_2 \rangle\!\rangle\!\rangle)) \setminus conflict\_upds(\langle\!\langle\!\langle op_1 \rangle\!\rangle\!\rangle, \langle\!\langle\!\langle op_2 \rangle\!\rangle\!\rangle)$.

Putting this all together we get the following rule for the conjunction of operation ASMs. (Note that sets of updates denote the simultaneous firing of these updates. The treatment of state invariants is discussed later in this section.)

$$op_1 \ \wedge \ op_2$$
$$\Downarrow \tag{13}$$

```
if  guard(⟨⟨⟨op₁⟩⟩⟩) and  guard(⟨⟨⟨op₂⟩⟩⟩) and  ⟨⟨state_invariants⟩⟩
then
    if forall loc in (locs(⟨⟨⟨op₁⟩⟩⟩) intersect locs(⟨⟨⟨op₂⟩⟩⟩))
        (upd_vals(op₁, loc) intersect upd_vals(op₂, loc)) ≠ emptyset
    then
        (upds(⟨⟨⟨op₁⟩⟩⟩) ∪ upds(⟨⟨⟨op₂⟩⟩⟩)) \ conflict_upds(⟨⟨⟨op₁⟩⟩⟩, ⟨⟨⟨op₂⟩⟩⟩)
        do forall loc in (locs(⟨⟨⟨op₁⟩⟩⟩) intersect locs(⟨⟨⟨op₂⟩⟩⟩))
            choose val in (upd_vals(op₁, loc) intersect upd_vals(op₂, loc))
                loc := val
            endchoose
        enddo
    else skip
    endif
endif
```

Choice Operator. The choice operator models an angelic choice between two operations. That is, depending on the applicability of the operations, either one or the other is executed. Only if both operations are not applicable in the current state is the choice operation not applicable.

We map a choice operation $op1 \; [] \; op2$ into an ASM that models the same behaviour. Generally, an operation-ASM is applicable if its guard is satisfied and the state invariant is satisfiable in the next state (see the discussion of state invariants later in this section). If operations $op1$ and $op2$ in OZ-ASM are both applicable then one of them is chosen non-deterministically. This choice is simulated in the corresponding operation-ASM by a toggle variable $which\_op$. If only one of the operations is applicable, the ASM chooses that one. If none of the operations is applicable the ASM does nothing, i.e. skips.

$$op_1 \; [] \; op_2$$

$$\Downarrow \qquad\qquad\qquad\qquad\qquad (14)$$

```
if  guard(⟪op₁⟫) and  guard(⟪op₂⟫) and  ⟪state_invariants⟫
then
  choose which_op in {first_op, scd_op}
      if which_op = first_op
      then upds(⟪op₁⟫)
      else if which_op = scd_op
              then upds(⟪op₂⟫)
              endif
      endif
  endchoose
else if  guard(⟪op₁⟫) and  ⟪state_invariants⟫
      then  upds(⟪op₁⟫)
      else if  guard(⟪op₂⟫) and  ⟪state_invariants⟫
              then  upds(⟪op₂⟫)
              endif
      endif
endif
```

Operation Promotion. A class may contain an operation that models the application of an operation of an object instance of another class. For example, $a.op$ invokes the operation op on the object a. Assume that op is already mapped into an operation-ASM, then the invocation $a.op$ effects that the first parameter in all dynamic/external functions that are declared in op are instantiated with object a. These functions are local to the object a.

$$a.op \Rightarrow \langle\!\langle op \rangle\!\rangle(a) \qquad\qquad\qquad (15)$$

Scope Enrichment. Scope enrichment, $op_1 \bullet op_2$, introduces an additional level of scope for the operation op_2. As the modular structure of OZ-ASM is flattened in our mapping, a new ASM-SL function is introduced for each attribute. These functions are globally accessible within each operation-ASM. Therefore, scope enrichment can be reduced to the conjunction of both operations.

$$op1 \bullet op2 \Rightarrow \langle\!\langle op1 \; \wedge \; op2 \rangle\!\rangle \tag{16}$$

Parallel Operator. The parallel composition operator is similar to the conjunction operation, but additionally models communication between both operations. $op_1 \parallel op_2$ models an operation that executes op_1 and op_2 in parallel and matches similarly named (i.e. matching apart from the '?' or '!' decoration) input and output variables of both classes. Additionally, all input/output name-matched variables of the composed operation are hidden. Hiding of a variable means that it is not visible to the environment.

The mapping of this operator is defined by its semantical definition as introduced in [19]. It is given in terms of the conjunction operator that is defined earlier (see mapping 13) plus an additional renaming of the matching input and output variables and hiding of the latter. Hiding of variables in Object-Z can be simulated in ASM by means of fresh variables that do not occur elsewhere in the specification.

Assume, we have functions $in(op)$ and $out(op)$ that provide, with the '?' or '!' decoration removed, all name-matching input and output variables of an operation. We introduce new variables, $z_1, \ldots z_{n+m}$, that do not appear as free variables elsewhere in the OZ-ASM model. These are used as hidden output variables. Since we do not distinguish in ASM between output variables and internal variables, the z_i are declared, as is usual, as dynamic functions. We get

$$op_1 \parallel op_2$$

$$\Downarrow \tag{17}$$

$$\langle\!\langle \; \big(op_1[x_1!/x_1?, \ldots, x_n!/x_n?] \; \wedge \; op_2[y_1!/y_1?, \ldots, y_m!/y_m?] \big) \\ [z_1/x_1!, \ldots, z_n/x_n!, z_{n+1}/y_1!, \ldots, z_{n+m}/y_m!] \; \rangle\!\rangle$$

where $in(op1) \cap out(op2) = \{x_1, \ldots, x_n\}$
        $in(op2) \cap out(op1) = \{y_1, \ldots, y_m\}$

State Invariants. OZ-ASM state invariants enable system behaviour to be modelled abstractly. Invariants allow certain states to be avoided without having to explicitly include the required constraints in the specification of the operations.

Basically, invariants involve attributes and are predicates that need to be satisfied by the pre- and post-state of any operation. One of their effects is to help determine if an operation is applicable or not.

If we can show that the specified initial state satisfies the invariant then it is sufficient to show that for each operation the invariant is not violated in the post-state. If this is guaranteed, we can be sure that all pre-states (i.e. all reachable states) satisfy the invariant too.

To guarantee that the post-state of an operation satisfies the invariant, we add an extra guard to each operation-ASM. In both Object-Z, and OZ-ASM, this extra condition is implicitly expressed in terms of pre-values (unprimed) and post-values (primed) of attributes; however, within the operation-ASM any guard that models the extra condition may not depend on post-values. Therefore, we simply substitute each primed attribute with the update-value that will be assigned when the transition is fired. This is illustrated in the following example:

```
┌─ A ─────────────────────────────────────────────────────────────
│  ┌──────────────────────────────┐  ┌─ increase ──────────────────
│  │  n : ℕ                        │  │  Δ(n)
│  ├──────────────────────────────┤  ├─────────────────────────────
│  │  n < 10                       │  │  n := n + 1
│  └──────────────────────────────┘  └─────────────────────────────
└─────────────────────────────────────────────────────────────────
```

The invariant on the post-state of every operation is given as $(n' < 10)$. Each primed variable has to be substituted by its post-state evaluation, i.e. $(n' < 10)[n + 1/n'] = (n + 1 < 10)$. Therefore, we get

$$\textbf{transition } \textit{increase} ==$$
$$\textbf{if } (n + 1 < 10)$$
$$\textbf{then } n := n + 1$$
$$\textbf{endif}$$

In general, we get an additional guard for each operation in the class (in the example above the extra guard is $(n + 1 < 10)$). In the next section we illustrate the application of the mapping rules introduced above.

4   The Operation Transformation, an Example

In this section, we show how the given mapping rules can be applied to transform OZ-ASM operations (which are defined via operation operators) into an operation-ASM. As an example we use the operation $insertKey$ of class $KeySystem$ that is introduced in Section 2. We assume that an algorithm for substitution is given and that the variable $self$ within a class is equal to the object it refers to, i.e. $\langle\!\langle obj.self \rangle\!\rangle = self(obj) = obj$.

To begin, we show how to map the state invariant of the class $KeySystem$, namely $\forall k : keys \bullet k.rooms \subseteq rooms$. This invariant can be transformed into the following ASM-SL expression:

```
forall k in Key :
```
$$Key\_rooms(k, r) = true \textbf{ implies } KeySystem\_rooms(r) = true$$

As discussed in Section 3, it is sufficient to show that the invariant is satisfied in the initial state and for all post-states of the operations. The operation $insertKey$ comprises the operations $supplyId$ and $unlock$ of class $Room$ and operations $accessGranted$ and $accessDenied$ of class Key. Of these only the operation $unlock$

has a non-empty update, namely $lock := false$. Since this update does not affect the state invariant given above, we do not have to add an additional guard to the operation-ASM $insertKey$ to ensure the satisfiability of the invariant.

For the sake of readability, in the following we omit the brackets $\langle\!\langle . \rangle\!\rangle$ within the intermediate steps of the transformation.

$$insertKey \mathrel{\widehat{=}} [r? : rooms;\ k? : keys]\ \bullet$$
$$r?.supplyId$$
$$\|\ (k?.accessGranted\ \wedge\ r?.unlock$$
$$[]\ k?.accessDenied)$$

$$\Downarrow \qquad\qquad\qquad\qquad \text{via (17)}$$

$$insertKey \mathrel{\widehat{=}} [r? : rooms;\ k? : keys]\ \bullet$$
$$r?.supplyId$$
$$\wedge\ (k?.accessGranted\ \wedge\ r?.unlock$$
$$[]\ k?.accessDenied)[rm!/rm?]$$

$$\Downarrow \qquad\qquad\qquad\qquad \text{via (15), (12)}$$

$$insertKey \mathrel{\widehat{=}} [r? : rooms;\ k? : keys]\ \bullet$$
$$\texttt{if}\ rm! = self(r?)\ \texttt{then skip}$$
$$\wedge\ (k?.accessGranted\ \wedge\ r?.unlock$$
$$[]\ k?.accessDenied)[rm!/rm?]$$

$$\Downarrow \qquad\qquad\qquad\qquad \text{via } (self(x) = x)$$

$$insertKey \mathrel{\widehat{=}} [r? : rooms;\ k? : keys]\ \bullet$$
$$\texttt{if}\ rm! = r?\ \texttt{then skip}$$
$$\wedge\ (k?.accessGranted[rm!/rm?]\ \wedge\ r?.unlock[rm!/rm?]$$
$$[]\ k?.accessDenied[rm!/rm?])$$

$$\Downarrow \qquad\qquad \text{via (15), (12), (substitution)}$$

$$insertKey \mathrel{\widehat{=}} [r? : rooms;\ k? : keys]\ \bullet$$
$$\texttt{if}\ rm! = r?\ \texttt{then skip}$$
$$\wedge\ ((\texttt{if}\ key\_rooms(k?, rm!) = true\ \texttt{then skip}$$
$$\wedge\ \texttt{if}\ room\_locked(rm!) = true\ \texttt{then}\ room\_locked := false)$$
$$[]\ (\texttt{if}\ key\_rooms(k?, rm!) = false\ \texttt{then skip}\ ))$$

$$\Downarrow \qquad\qquad\qquad\qquad \text{via (13)}$$

$$insertKey \mathrel{\widehat{=}} [r? : rooms;\ k? : keys]\ \bullet$$
$$(\texttt{if}\ rm! = r?\ \texttt{and}$$
$$key\_rooms(k?, rm!) = true\ \texttt{and}\ room\_locked(rm!) = true$$
$$\texttt{then}\ room\_locked := false)$$
$$[]$$
$$(\texttt{if}\ rm! = r?\ \texttt{and}$$
$$key\_rooms(k?, rm!) = false$$
$$\texttt{then skip}\ )$$

$$\Downarrow \qquad\qquad \text{via (3), (12), (16), (14)}$$

```
external function k_in : KeyType
   with k_in in Key
external function r_in : RoomType
   with r_in in Room

transition insertKey ==
      if rm_out = r_in and
      key_rooms(k_in, rm_out) = true and room_locked(r_in) = true
         and key_rooms(k_in, rm_out) = false
      then
       choose which_op in {first_op, scd_op}
          if which_op = first_op
          then room_locked(r_in) := false
          else if which_op = scd_op
                then skip
                endif
          endif
       endchoose
      else if rm_out = r_in and
              key_rooms(k_in, rm_out) = true and room_locked(r_in) = true
           then room_locked(r_in) := false
           else if rm_out = r_in and
                   key_rooms(k_in, rm_out) = false
                then skip
                endif
           endif
      endif
```

5   Conclusion and Future Work

We have shown in this paper how language integration can be used to define a
subset of a specification language in order to tailor it for automated tool support.
We introduced the integrated language OZ-ASM, which combines Object-Z with
ASM transition rules. OZ-ASM enables the user to model systems in a state
transition based fashion, a style that can also be adopted by Object-Z users
if operation predicates are modelled in a canonical form. The syntax of ASM
transition rules provides a clear definition of this canonical form, which ensures
that primed attributes (i.e. variables in the next state) depend only on non-
primed attributes (i.e. variables in the current state). State transition systems
can interface with various analysis tools, such as state transition based model
checkers like SMV.

We showed by means of a set of mapping rules how OZ-ASM can be transformed into a set of ASMs which in turn can be automatically compiled into
SMV code. The interface from ASM and the ASM Workbench tool environ-

ment to the SMV model checker is already available. Therefore, the results of this paper provide the theoretical basis for an interface from the integrated language OZ-ASM to the model checker SMV. Clearly, the interface needs to be implemented in order to provide automated tool support; this is future work.

Our approach complements the work of others in which either a process-algebra based model checker or SAT solvers are interfaced with a Z-based language. Each of these approaches have their special merits for particular applications.

Future work involves the completion of the list of mapping rules for operation operators (e.g. the distributed operation operators) and OZ-ASM expressions and data structures (e.g. sequences). Based on the mapping rules, a transformation algorithm needs to be implemented. We will also investigate the use of other analysis tools that deal with state transition systems. Especially, other model checkers could be interfaced using ASM as an intermediate language (e.g.NuSMV [18], VIS [22], MDG-Tool [17])[4]. Abstraction and decomposition techniques have to be developed which target the limitations of model checking with respect to the model size. Furthermore, we will attempt to develop (informal or formal) rules for mapping Object-Z into OZ-ASM so that model checking based on transition systems can be directly available for Object-Z.

Acknowledgements

Thanks to Graeme Smith for his initial inspiration of this work and his useful comments on earlier drafts of this paper.

References

1. G. Del Castillo and K. Winter. Model checking support for the ASM high-level language. In S. Graf and M. Schwartzbach, editors, *Proc. of 6th Int. Conference for Tools and Algorithms for the Construction and Analysis of Systems, (TACAS 2000)*, vol. 1785 of LNCS, Springer-Verlag, 2000.
2. G. Del Castillo. The ASM Workbench. PhD thesis, Department of Mathematics and Computer Science of Paderborn University, Germany, 2000.
3. R. Duke and G. Rose. *Formal Object-Oriented Specification Using Object-Z*. Macmillan Press, 2000.
4. E. A. Emerson. Temporal and Modal Logic. In J. van Leeuwen, editor, *Handbook of Theoretical Computer Science*, pages 996–1072. Elsevier Science Publishers, 1990.
5. C. Fischer and H. Wehrheim. Model-checking CSP-OZ specifications with FDR. In K. Araki, A. Galloway and K. Taguchi editors, *Proceedings of the 1st International Conference on Integrated Formal Methods (IFM'99)*, pages 315–334. Springer-Verlag, 1999.
6. Formal Systems (Europe) Ltd. *Failures-Divergence Refinement: FDR2 User Manual*, Oct 1997.

---

[4] As shown in [23], the transformation from ASM-SL into the SMV language can be easily adapted to interface other tools that are based on transition systems.

7. W. Grieskamp. A computation model for Z based on concurrent constraint resolution. In *ZB2000 - International Conference of Z and B Users*, September, 2000.
8. Y. Gurevich. May 1997 Draft of the ASM Guide. Technical report, University of Michigan EECS Department, 1997.
9. Y. Gurevich. Sequential abstract state machines capture sequential algorithms. *ACM Transactions on Computational Logic*, 2000.
10. G. Holzmann. Design and validation of protocols: A tutorial. In *Computer Networks and ISDN Systems*, volume XXV, pages 981–1017, 1993.
11. G. Holzmann. The SPIN model checker. *IEEE Transactions on Software Engineering*, 23(5):279–295, May 1997.
12. D. Jackson. Nitpick: A checkable specification language. In *Proc. of the First ACM SIGSOFT Workshop on Formal Methods in Software Practice*, pages 60–69, 1996.
13. D. Jackson, I. Schechter and I. Shlyakhter. Alcoa: the Alloy constraint analyser. In *Int. Conf. on Software Engineering*, 2000.
14. J. Jacky and M. Patrick. Modelling, checking and implementing a control program for a radiation therapy machine. In R. Cleaveland, D. Jackson, editors, *Proc. of the First ACM SIGPLAN Workshop on Automated Analysis of Software(AAS'97)*, pages 25–32, 1997.
15. G. Kassel and G. Smith. Model checking Object-Z classes: Some experiments with FDR. In *8th Asia-Pacific Software Engineering Conference (APSEC 2001)*, IEEE Computer Society Press, 2001 (to appear).
16. K. McMillan. *Symbolic Model Checking*. Kluwer Academic Publishers, 1993.
17. F. Corella, Z. Zhou, X. Song, M. Langevin and E. Cerny. Multiway Decision Graphs for automated hardware verification. In *Formal Methods in System Design*, 10(1), 1997.
18. A. Cimatti, E.M. Clarke, F. Giunchiglia and M. Roveri. NuSMV: a new Symbolic Model Verifier. In N. Halbwachs and D. Peled, editors, *11th Conference on Computer-Aided Verification (CAV'99)*, vol. 1633 of LNCS, Springer-Verlag, 1999.
19. G. Smith. *The Object-Z Specification Language*. Kluwer Academic Publishers, 2000.
20. J.M. Spivey. *The Z Notation - A Reference Manual*. Prentice Hall, 1992.
21. S. Valentine. The programming language Z--. *Information and Software Technology*, volume 37, number 5-6, pages 293–301, May-June, 1995.
22. The VIS Group. VIS: A System for Verification and Synthesis. In R. Alur and T. Henzinger, editors, *8th Int. Conf. on Computer Aided Verifaction, (CAV'96)*. vol. 1102 of LNCS, Springer-Verlag, 1996.
23. K. Winter. *Model Checking Abstract State Machines*. PhD thesis, Technical University of Berlin, Germany, http://edocs.tu-berlin.de/diss/2001/winter_kirsten.htm, 2001.
24. K. Winter. Model checking with abstract types. In S. Stoller and W. Visser, editors, *Electronic Notes in Theoretical Computer Science*, volume 55. Elsevier Science Publishers, 2001.
25. P. Zave. Formal description of telecommunication services in Promela and Z. In *Calculational System Design, Proc. of the Nineteenth International NATO Summer School*. IOS Press, 1999.

Formalization of Cadence SPW Fixed-Point Arithmetic in HOL

Behzad Akbarpour, Abdelkader Dekdouk, and Sofiène Tahar

Dept. of Electrical & Computer Engineering, Concordia University
1455 de Maisonneuve W., Montreal, Quebec, H3H 1M8, Canada
{behzad,adekdouk,tahar}@ece.concordia.ca

Abstract. This paper addresses the formalization in higher-order logic of fixed-point arithmetic based on the SPW (Signal Processing WorkSystem) tool. We encoded the fixed-point number system and specified the different rounding modes in fixed-point arithmetic such as the directed and even rounding modes. We also considered the formalization of exceptions detection and their handling like overflow and invalid operation. An error analysis is then performed to check the correctness of the rounding and to verify the basic arithmetic operations, addition, subtraction, multiplication and division against their mathematical counterparts. Finally, we showed by an example how this formalization can be used to enable the verification of the transition from the floating-point to fixed-point algorithmic levels in the design flow of signal processors.

Keywords: Fixed-point, Floating-point, Signal Processing, Theorem-Proving, HOL, SPW

1 Introduction

Modern signal processing chips, such as integrated cable modems and wireless multimedia terminals, are described with algorithms in floating-point precision. Often, the architectural style with which these algorithms are implemented is precision-limited, and relies on a fixed-point representation. This requires a translation of the specification from floating- to fixed-point precision (see Figure 1). This implementation is optimized following some application specific trade-offs such as the speed, cost, area and the power consumption of the chip. The optimization task is tedious and error prone due to the effects of quantization noise introduced by the limited precision of fixed-point representation.

Usually the conformance of the fixed-point implementation with respect to the floating-point specification is verified by simulation techniques which cannot cover the entire input space described by floating-point representation. The objective of this work is to formalize the fixed-point arithmetic in higher-order logic as a basis for checking the correctness of higher level algorithmic descriptions of DSP designs modeled in floating- and fixed-point representations. Contrary to the floating-point arithmetic which is standardized in IEEE-754 [13] and IEEE-854 [14], the fixed-point arithmetic description depends on the tool we use to design the DSP (Digital Signal Processor) chip. In this paper, we consider Cadence SPW [22] fixed-point arithmetic.

M. Butler, L. Petre, and K. Sere (Eds.): IFM 2002, LNCS 2335, pp. 185–204, 2002.
© Springer-Verlag Berlin Heidelberg 2002

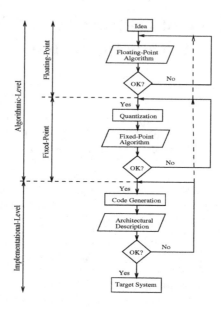

Fig. 1. DSP Design Flow

In higher-order logic, the fixed-point number is encoded by a pair composed of a boolean stream, and a triple indicating the stream length, the length of the integer portion and the sign format. Then we formalize the concepts of valuation and rounding as functions that convert respectively a fixed-point number to a real and vice versa, taking into account different rounding and overflow modes. Arithmetic operations are formalized as functions performing operations on the real numbers corresponding to the fixed-point operands and then applying the rounding on the real result. Finally, we prove different lemmas regarding the error analysis of the fixed-point quantization and correctness of the basic operations like addition, multiplication, and division. The higher-order logic formalization and proof were done using the HOL theorem prover [8].

The organization of this paper is as follows: Section 2 gives a review on the related work. Section 3 describes the SPW fixed-point arithmetic including the format of the fixed-point numbers, arithmetic operations, exceptions detection and their handling, and the different rounding modes. Section 4 describes in detail their formalization in HOL. In Section 5, we discuss the verification of the SPW basic arithmetic operations. Section 6 presents an illustrative example on how this formalization can be used through the modeling and verification of an Integrator circuit. Finally, Section 7 concludes the paper.

2   Related Work

There exist several related works in the open literature on the formalization and verification of IEEE standard based floating-point arithmetic. For instance,

Barett [2] specified parts of the IEEE-754 standard in Z, and Miner [18] formalized the IEEE-854 floating-point standard in PVS. The latter defined the relation between floating-point numbers and real numbers, rounding, and some arithmetic operations on both finite and infinite operands. He used this formalization to verify abstract mathematical descriptions of the main operations and their relation to the corresponding floating-point implementations. His work was one of the earliest in formalization of floating-point standards using theorem proving.

Carreno [4] formalized the same IEEE-854 standard in HOL. He interpreted the lexical descriptions of the standard into mathematical conditional descriptions and organized them in tables; then these tables were formalized in HOL. He discussed different standard aspects such as precisions, exceptions and traps, and many other arithmetic operations such as addition, multiplication and square-root of floating-point numbers.

Harrison [9] defined and formalized real numbers using HOL. He then developed a generic floating-point library [11] to define and verify the most fundamental terms and lemmas of the IEEE-754 standard. This former library was used by him to formalize and verify floating-point algorithms against behavioral specification such as the square root and the exponential function [10].

Moore et al. [19] have verified the AMD-K5 floating-point division algorithm using the ACL2 theorem prover. Also, Russinoff [21] has developed a library for ACL2 prover and applied it successfully to verify the K5 square root, and the Athlon multiplication, division, square root, and addition algorithms.

More recently, Daumas et al. [7] have presented a generic library for reasoning about floating-point numbers within the Coq system. Berg et al. [3] have formally verified a theory of IEEE rounding presented in [20] using the theorem prover PVS, and then used the theory to prove the correctness of a fully IEEE compliant floating-point unit used in the VAMP processor. They have used a formal definition of rounding based on Miners formalization of standard.

Aagaard and Seger [1] combined BDD based methods and theorem proving techniques to verify a floating-point multiplier. Chen and Bryant [6] used word-level SMV to verify a floating-point adder. Miner and Leathrum [17] verified a general class of subtractive division algorithms with respect to the IEEE-754 standard in PVS. Leeser et al. [15] verified a radix-2 square root algorithm and its hardware implementation using theorem proving methods. Cornea-Hasegan [5] used iterative approaches and mathematical proofs to verify the correctness of the IEEE floating-point square root, division and remainder algorithms. O'Leary et al. [16] reported on the verification of the Intel's FPU at the gate level using a combination of model-checking and theorem proving.

While the above works are all concerned with floating-point representation and arithmetic, there is no machine-checked formal development on properties of fixed-point arithmetic. Therefore, the formalization presented in this paper is to our best knowledge, the first of its kind. Our formalization of the fixed-point arithmetic has been inspired mostly by the work done by Harrison [10] and Carreno [4] on the floating-point formalization. Harrison's work was more oriented to verification purposes. Indeed we used an analogous set of lemmas to his work, to check the validity of operation results and to do the error analysis on our definition of the fixed-point rounding. For exception handling which is not covered by Harrison, we followed Carreno who formalized exceptions and their handling in more details.

3   SPW Fixed-Point Arithmetic

In this section we describe SPW (Signal Processing WorkSystem) based fixed-point arithmetic. SPW is an integrated framework that provides a unified graphical interface for all aspects of system design, simulation, and implementation for developing DSP based products. It graphically represents a system as a network of functional blocks. SPW design flow supports different abstraction levels starting from floating-point algorithmic description, converting that to an optimized fixed-point specification from which an RTL (Register Transfer Level) implementation (in VHDL or Verilog) is generated (Figure 1).

3.1   Fixed-Point Numbers

A fixed-point number in SPW has a fixed number of binary digits and a fixed position for the decimal point with respect to that set of digits. Fixed-point numbers can be either unsigned (always positive) or signed (in two's complement representation). For example, consider the case of four bits being used to represent signal values. If the numbers are unsigned and if the decimal point or, more properly, the binary point is fixed at the position after the second digit (XX.XX), the representable real values range from 0.0 to 3.75. In two's complement format, the most significant bit is the sign bit. The remaining bits specify the magnitude. If four bits represent signal values, and the binary point is fixed at the position after the second digit following the sign bit (SXX.X), the real values range from -4.0 to +3.5.

Fixed-point signal values are expressed as a binary stream and a set of attributes, *Stream < Set of Attributes >*. The attributes specify how the binary stream is interpreted. Generally, the attributes are specified in the following format:

$$< \#bits, \#integer\_bits, sign\_format >$$

- **#bits:** The total number of bits used to represent the fixed-point stream, including integer bits, fractional bits, and sign bit, if any. The total number of bits must be in the range of 1 to 256.
- **#integer_bits:** The number of integer bits (the number of bits to the left of the binary point, excluding the sign bit, if any). If this number is negative, repeated leading sign bits or zeros are added to generate the equivalent binary value. If this number is greater than the total number of bits, trailing zeroes are added to generate the equivalent binary value.
- **sign_format:** A letter specifying the sign format: "u" for unsigned, "t" for two's complement.

For example the signal value -0.75 is represented by $111101 < 6, 3, t >$. If we consider the same bit string with unsigned attributes ($111101 < 6, 3, u >$), then the equivalent number is 111.101 or $+7.625$. $1111 < 4, -1, u >$ represents the value $.01111$ which is 0.46875.

3.2 Fixed-Point Operations

The SPW library includes basic fixed-point signal processing blocks such as adders, multipliers, delay blocks, and vector blocks. It also supports fixed-point hardware blocks such as multiplexers, buffers, inverters, flip-flops, bit manipulation and general-purpose combinational logic blocks. These blocks accurately model the behavior of fixed-point digital signal processing systems. In this paper we will focus on the arithmetic and logic operations, but the idea can be generalized to the remaining operations. In addition to the parameters corresponding to the input operands and output result, the arithmetic operations take two specific parameters defining the overflow and rounding (loss of precision) modes.

Fixed-point arithmetic that does not compute and return an exact result resorts to an exception-handling procedure. This procedure is controlled by the exception flags. There are three kinds of exceptions that can be tested:

- **Loss of Sign:** The result was negative but the result storage area was unsigned. Zero is stored.
- **Overflow:** The result was too big to be represented in the result storage area. The overflow mode determines the returned value.
- **Invalid:** No result can be meaningfully represented (e.g., divide by zero). This error can also occur if the fixed-point number itself is invalid.

The overflow-handling parameter is used to indicate how to handle overflow errors. The parameter is a string that should be set to:

- **Wrap:** Overflow bits are ignored, or
- **Clip (default):** Values are saturated. The closest representable value to the true result is returned.

The loss of precision handling parameter determines the rounding mode. The parameter names are patterned after the IEEE standards for floating-point arithmetic [13]. The loss of precision parameter values are:

- **Round (default):** The block uses the nearest representable value on either side of the original value. If the original value is exactly halfway between the two nearest representable values, the block rounds toward plus infinity.
- **Round_To_Zero:** The block uses the nearest representable value towards zero.
- **Round_To_Plus_Infinity:** The block uses the nearest representable value towards plus infinity.
- **Truncate or Round_To_Minus_Infinity:** The block discards the trailing bits or equivalently, uses the nearest representable value towards minus infinity. Both parameter settings result in the same behavior, so we can use them interchangeably.

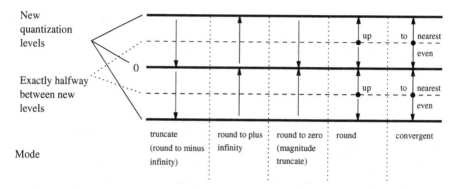

Fig. 2. Loss of Precision Modes

- **Convergent_Round:** The block uses the nearest representable value on either side of the original value. If the original value is exactly halfway between
  the two nearest representable values, the block uses the "even" value (the
  value having zero as the least significant bit). Figure 2 summarizes the loss
  of precision modes.

For example, consider a block that serves as a primitive fixed-point multiplier
that truncates the results when loss of precision occurs and wraps the result
when overflow occurs. We can make the multiplier routine by calling the function
fxpMul (Wrap | Truncate, In1, In2, Out).

4   Formalizing Fixed-Point Arithmetic in HOL

In this section, we present the formalization of SPW based fixed-point arithmetic
in higher-order logic, based on the general purpose HOL theorem prover [8].
The system supports both forward and backward proofs. The forward proof
style applies inference rules to existing theorems to obtain new theorems and
eventually the desired theorem. Backward or goal oriented proofs start with the
goal to be proven. Tactics are applied to the goal and subgoals until the goal is
decomposed into simpler existing theorems or axioms. The system basic language
includes the natural numbers and boolean type. It also includes other specific
extensions like John Harrison's reals library [9] which proved to be essential for
our fixed-point arithmetic formalization. Table 1 summarizes some of the HOL
symbols used in this paper and their meanings.

4.1   Fixed-Point Numbers Representation

The actual fixed-point numbers are represented by a pair of elements representing
the binary stream and the set of attributes. The extractors for the two fields of
a fixed-point number are defined as follows:

Table 1. HOL Symbols

Standard symbol	HOL notation	Meaning
ε	@	Hilbert choice
(none)	&	Natural map $\aleph \rightarrow \Re$
(none)	$c \rightarrow a \mid b$	if c then a else b
$-x$	$\neg x$	Unary negation of x
$x^{-}1$	inv (x)	Multiplicative inverse of x
$\mid x \mid$	$abs\ (x)$	Absolute value of x
x^n	x pow n	Real x raised to natural number power n

$\vdash_{def}$ **stream (v,a)** = v
$\vdash_{def}$ **attrib (v,a)** = a

The binary stream is treated as a boolean word (type: bool word). For example, the bit string 1010 is represented by WORD [T; F; T; F]. In this way, we use the definitions and theorems already available in the HOL word library [23] to facilitate the manipulation of binary words. The attributes are represented by a triple of natural numbers for the total number of bits, the integer bits and the sign format.

In HOL, we define functions to extract the primitive parameters for arbitrary attributes:

$\vdash_{def}$ **streamlength (b,ib,st)** = b
$\vdash_{def}$ **intbits (b,ib,st)** = ib
$\vdash_{def}$ **signtype (b,ib,st)** = st

We define predicates partitioning the fixed-point numbers into signed and unsigned numbers:

$\vdash_{def}$ **is_signed (X)** = (signtype (X) = 1)
$\vdash_{def}$ **is_unsigned (X)** = (signtype (X) = 0)

The number of digits of a fixed-point number in the right hand side of the binary point is defined as *fracbits*. It can be derived as the difference between the total number of the bits and the number of integer bits, considering the sign bit in the case of signed numbers.

$\vdash_{def}$ **fracbits X** = (is_unsigned X $\rightarrow$ (streamlength X $-$ intbits X) |
    (streamlength X $-$ intbits X $-$ 1))

Two useful derived predicates test the validity of a set of attributes and a fixed-point number based on the definition in Section 3.1. In a valid set of attributes, the *streamlength* should be in the range of 1 and 256, the *signtype* can be either 0 or 1, and the number of integer bits is less than or equal to the *streamlength*. A valid fixed-point number must have a valid set of attributes and the length of the binary stream must be equal to *streamlength*.

$\vdash_{def}$ `validAttr X = (streamlength X > 0) ∧ (streamlength X < 257) ∧`
       `(signtype X < 2) ∧ (intbits X < (streamlength X + 1))`

$\vdash_{def}$ `is_valid (a: (bool word,(num,num,num))) = (validAttr (attrib a)) ∧`
       `(WORDLEN (stream a) = streamlength (attrib a))`

4.2 Fixed-Point Type

Now we define the actual HOL type for fixed-point numbers. The type is defined to be in bijection with the appropriate subset of *bool word* $\times \, \aleph^3$, with the bijections written in HOL as $Fxp : (bool\ word\, , \ (num\, , \ num\, , \ num)) \to fxp$ and $deFxp : fxp \to (bool\ word\, , \ (num\, , \ num\, , \ num))$:

$\vdash_{def}$ `fxp_tybij =`
      `(∀ a. Fxp (deFxp a) = a) ∧`
      `(∀ r. is_valid r = (deFxp (Fxp r) = r))`

We specialize the previous functions and predicates to the *fxp* type, e.g:

$\vdash_{def}$ `Stream (a: fxp) = stream (deFxp a)`
$\vdash_{def}$ `Issigned (a:fxp) = is_signed (Attrib a)`
$\vdash_{def}$ `Isvalid (a:fxp) = is_valid (deFxp a)`

Note that we start the name of the functions manipulating fixed-point numbers by capital letters to distinguish them from the ones taking pairs and triples as argument.

4.3 Valuation

Now we specify the real number valuation of fixed-point numbers. We use two separate formulas for signed and unsigned numbers:

    Unsigned:

$$(1/2^M) * \left(\sum_{n=0}^{N-1} 2^n * v_n \right)$$

    Signed:

$$(1/2^M) * \left[-2^{N-1} * v_{N-1} + \sum_{n=0}^{N-2} 2^n * v_n \right]$$

where v_n represents n^{th} bit of the binary stream in fixed-point number[1], M and N are respectively *fracbits* and *streamlength*. In HOL, we define the valuation function *value* that returns the corresponding real value of a fixed-point number.

$\vdash_{def}$ `value (a: fxp) =`
      `Isunsigned a ⟹  & (BNVAL (Stream a)) / (&2 pow Fracbits a) |`
      `(& (BNVAL (Stream a)) − &(((BV (MSB (Stream a)))) *`
      `(2 EXP (Streamlength a)))) / (&2 pow Fracbits a)`

---

[1] We adopt the convention that bits are indexed from the right hand side.

BNVAL is a predefined function of HOL *word* library which returns the numeric value of a boolean word. *BV* is a function for mapping between a single bit and a number, and *MSB* is a constant for most significant bit of a word.

We also define the real value of the smallest (*MIN*) and largest (*MAX*) representable numbers for a given set of attributes. The maximum is defined for both signed and unsigned numbers using the following formula:

$$MAX = 2^a - 2^{-b}$$

where a is the *intbits* and b the *fracbits*. The minimum value for unsigned numbers is zero and for signed numbers is computed using the following formula:

$$MIN = -2^a$$

So, we obtain the corresponding functions in HOL.

$\vdash_{def}$ MAX (X) = &2 pow intbits (X) $-$ inv (&2 pow fracbits (X))
$\vdash_{def}$ MIN (X) = is_unsigned (X) $\rightarrow$ &0 | ¬(&2 pow (intbits (X))))

The constants for the smallest (*bottomfxp*) and largest (*topfxp*) representable fixed-point numbers for a given set of attributes can be defined as follows:

$\vdash_{def}$ topfxp X =
    (is_unsigned (X) $\rightarrow$ Fxp (WORD (REPLICATE (streamlength (X)) T),X) |
    Fxp (WCAT ((WORD [F]),
    (WORD (REPLICATE ((streamlength (X)) $-$ 1) T))),X))

$\vdash_{def}$ bottomfxp X =
    (is_unsigned (X) $\rightarrow$ Fxp (WORD (REPLICATE (streamlength (X)) F),X) |
    Fxp (WCAT ((WORD [T]),
    (WORD (REPLICATE ((streamlength (X)) $-$ 1) F))),X))

WCAT, the concatenation of two words, is a predefined HOL function.

4.4   Exception Handling

Operations on fixed-point numbers can signal exceptions as a result of performing the operation. Exceptions are described in Section 3.2 and declared as a new HOL data type:

$\vdash_{def}$ Exception = no_except | overflow | invalid | loss_sign

no_except is reserved for the case without exception.

Two overflow modes are also represented via an enumerated type definition:

$\vdash_{def}$ overflowmode = Wrap | Clip

According to the definition of overflow modes in Section 3.2 for clipping, if the number is greater than *MAX* or less than *MIN*, we return *topfxp* and *bottomfxp*, as the closest representable values to the right result, respectively. For wrapping, we must first convert the real number to binary format, and then discard the extra bits according to the output attributes.

4.5   Rounding

Rounding takes an infinitely precise real number and converts it into a fixed-point number. Five rounding modes are specified in Section 3.2 according to SPW documentation, which we formalize using the following datatype.

$\vdash_{def}$ roundmode =
      Round | To_zero | To_plus_infinity | Truncate | Convergent

The rounding operation is defined by a family of functions which are defined case by case on the rounding modes. The functions take as arguments a real number, rounding and overflow modes, and output attributes. They return a fixed-point number and an exception flag. The real number value may be outside the representable range of finite fixed-point numbers. In this case, the rounding function must check for overflow and return an overflow exception flag if detected. Similar to the floating-point case [10], its definition is based on the following predicate meaning that a is an element of the set s that provides a best approximation to x, assuming a valuation function v:

$\vdash_{def}$ is_closest v s x a = a IN s $\land$
      ($\forall$b. b IN s $\implies$ abs(v(a) $-$ x) $\leq$ abs(v(b) $-$ x))

However, we still need to define a function that picks out, using the Hilbert choice operator, a best approximation in case there are more than one closest number, based on a given property like *even*.

$\vdash_{def}$ closest v p s x = @a. is_closest v s x a $\land$
      (($\exists$b. is_closest v s x b $\land$ p(b)) $\implies$ p(a))

Finally, we define the actual rounding function for an arbitrary fixed-point output attributes. We only show the clause for *Convergent* rounding mode[2].

$\vdash_{def}$ (fxp_round (X) Convergent mode x =
      (x > MAX X) $\land$ (mode = Clip) $\rightarrow$ (topfxp (X) , overflow) |
      (x < MIN X) $\land$ (mode = Clip) $\rightarrow$ (bottomfxp (X) , overflow) |
      (x > MAX X) $\land$ (mode = Wrap) $\rightarrow$ (Wrapp (X) x , overflow) |
      (x < MIN X) $\land$ (mode = Wrap) $\rightarrow$ (Wrapp (X) x , overflow) |
      (closest (value) (λ a. LSB (Straem a) = F)
      {(a: fxp) | Isvalid a $\land$ (Attrib a = X)} x, no_except))

4.6   Arithmetic Operations

In accordance with the SPW description of fixed-point arithmetic functions, operations such as addition or multiplication take two fixed-point input signals and store their result into a third. The attributes of the inputs and output need not match one another. Both unsigned and two's complement inputs and output

---
[2] see Appendix A

are allowed. The result is formatted into the output as specified by the output attributes and by the overflow and loss of precision mode parameters. In our formalization, we first deal with exceptional cases such as invalid operation and loss of sign. If any of the input numbers is invalid then the result is *Null* and an exception flag *invalid* is raised.

Null is a constant that represents the result of an invalid operation, as follows:

$\vdash_{def}$ Null = @ (a : fxp). ¬(Isvalid a)

If the result is negative but the output is unsigned then zero is returned and exception flag is *loss_sign*. Also in the case of division by zero, the output value is forced to zero and the *invalid* flag is raised. Otherwise, we take the real value of the input arguments, perform the operation as infinite precision, then round the result according to the desired rounding and overflow modes. Formally, the operations for addition and multiplication are defined as follows:

$\vdash_{def}$ fxpAdd (X) rnd over a b =
    ¬(Isvalid a ∧ Isvalid b) → (Null,invalid) |
    (value a + value b < &0) ∧ (is_unsigned X) →
    (Fxp (WORD (REPLICATE (streamlength X) F), X), loss_sign) |
    (fxp_round (X) rnd over (value a + value b))

$\vdash_{def}$ fxpMul (X) rnd over a b =
    ¬(Isvalid a ∧ Isvalid b) → (Null,invalid) |
    (value a * value b < &0) ∧ (is_unsigned X) →
    (Fxp (WORD (REPLICATE (streamlength X) F), X), loss_sign) |
    (fxp_round (X) rnd over (value a * value b))

5   Verification of SPW Arithmetic Operations

According to the discussion in Section 4.3 each fixed-point number has a corresponding real number value. The correctness of a fixed-point operation can be specified by comparing its output with the true mathematical result, using the valuation function *value* which converts a fixed-point to an infinitely precise number. For example, the correctness of a fixed-point adder *fxpAdd* is specified by comparing it with its ideal counterpart +. That is, for each pair of fixed-point numbers a b, we compare *value* (a) + *value* (b) and *value* (*fxpAdd* a b). In other words, we check if the diagram in Figure 3 commutes. In following, we discuss the addition operation. Other operations can be handled similarly[3].

For this purpose we define the error resulting from rounding a real number to a fixed-point value:

$\vdash_{def}$ fxperror (X) rnd over x
    = (value (FST (fxp_round (X) rnd x over))) − x)

and then establish the correctness theorem as follows:

---

[3] see Appendix C

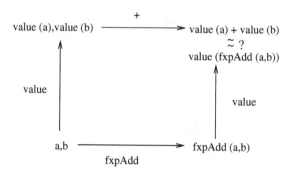

Fig. 3. Correctness Criteria in Fixed-Point Addition

Theorem 1: FXP_ADD_THM
```
⊢ (Isvalid a) ∧ (Isvalid b) ∧ validAttr (X) ⟹
  (Isvalid (FST (fxpAdd (X) Convergent Clip a b))) ∧
  (value (FST (fxpAdd (X) Convergent Clip a b)) = value (a) + value (b) +
  (fxperror (X) Convergent Clip (value (a) + value (b)))))
```

The theorem is composed of two parts. The first part is about the validity of fixed-point addition output and states that if the input fixed-point numbers and the output attributes are valid then the result of fixed-point addition is valid. The second part of the theorem relates the result of fixed-point addition to the real result based on the corresponding error function. To prove this main theorem, a number of lemmas have been established[4].

The following ensures the existence of the best approximation to a given real number in a finite non empty set of fixed-point numbers:

Lemma 1: FXP_IS_CLOSEST_EXISTS
```
⊢ FINITE (s) ⟹ ¬(s = EMPTY) ⟹ ∃ (a: fxp). is_closest v s x a
```

Next lemma states that the chosen best approximation satisfying a property p is itself the best approximation of a given real number:

Lemma 2: FXP_CLOSEST_IS_CLOSEST
```
⊢ FINITE (s) ⟹ ¬(s = EMPTY) ⟹ is_closest v s x (closest v p s x)
```

Then we prove that the set of all valid fixed-point numbers with a given attributes is finite:

Lemma 3: FINITE_VALID_ATTRIB
```
⊢ FINITE {(a: fxp) | Isvalid a ∧ (Attrib a = X)}
```

Finally, the following lemma establishes the validity of the rounding result:

Lemma 4: IS_VALID_ROUND_CONV_CLIP
```
⊢ (validAttr (X)) ⟹ Isvalid (FST (fxp_round X Convergent Clip x))
```

---
[4] For a complete list of lemmas refer to Appendix B.

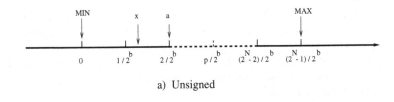

a) Unsigned

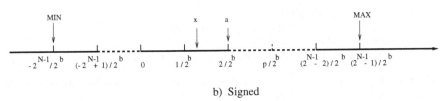

b) Signed

Fig. 4. Fixed-Point Values on the Real Axis

The validity of the rounding directly implies the validity of fixed-point addition output, and this completes the proof of the first part of the theorem. The second part of the theorem is proved using the properties of real arithmetic in HOL and rewriting with the definitions of *fxpAdd* and *fxperror* functions.

The second main theorem on error analysis concerns bounding the rounding error. The error can be absolutely quantified as follows:

Theorem 2: FXP_ERROR_BOUND_THM
⊢ (validAttr X) ∧ ¬(x > MAX (X)) ∧ ¬ (x < MIN (X)) ⟹
  abs (fxperror (X) Convergent Clip x) ≤ inv (&2 pow fracbits X)

According to this theorem, the error in rounding a real number which is in the range representable by a given set of attributes X is less than the quantity $1 / 2^{fracbits\ (X)}$.
To explain the theorem, we consider the following fact which relates the definition of the fixed-point numbers to the rationals.

An N-bit binary word, when interpreted as an unsigned fixed-point number, can take on values from a subset P of the non-negative rationals given by:

$$P = \{p/2^b \mid 0 \le p \le 2^N - 1, p \in Z\}$$

Similarly, for signed two's complement representation:

$$P = \{p/2^b \mid -2^{N-1} \le p \le 2^{N-1} - 1, p \in Z\}$$

Note that P contains 2^N elements and b represents the fractional bits in each case.
Based on this fact, we can depict the range of values covered by each case as shown by Figure 4.

Thereafter, the representable range of fixed-point numbers is divided into 2^N equispaced quantization steps with the distance between two successive steps equal to $1 / 2^b$. Suppose that $x \in \Re$ is approximated by a fixed-point number *a*. The position of these values are labeled in the figure. The error $| x - a |$ is hence less than the length of one interval, or $1 / 2^b$, as mentioned in the second theorem.

In HOL we first proved that the rounding result is the nearest value to a real number and the corresponding error is minimum comparing to the other fixed-point numbers:

Lemma 5: FXP_ERROR_AT_WORST_LEMMA
⊢ (validAttr X) ∧ ¬(x > MAX (X)) ∧ ¬(x < MIN (X)) ∧
  (Isvalid a) ∧ (Attrib a = X) ⟹
  abs (fxperror X Convergent Clip x) ≤ abs (value a − x)

Then we proved that each representable real value x can be surrounded by two successive rational numbers:

Lemma 6: FXP_ERROR_BOUND_LEMMA1
⊢ (validAttr X) ∧ ¬(x > MAX (X)) ∧ ¬(x < MIN (X)) ⟹
  ∃k. (k < 2 EXP streamlength X) ∧ (&k / (&2 pow fracbits X) ≤ x) ∧
  (x < (&(SUC k) / (&2 pow fracbits (X))))

Also we proved that the differnce between the real number and the surrounding rationals is less than $1 / 2^{fracbits\ (X)}$:

Lemma 7: FXP_ERROR_BOUND_LEMMA2
⊢ (validAttr X) ∧ ¬(x > MAX (X)) ∧ ¬(x < MIN (X)) ⟹
  ∃k. (k ≤ 2 EXP streamlength X) ∧
  abs (x − &k / (&2 pow (fracbits (X)))) ≤ inv (&2 pow (fracbits (X)))

Finally, we proved that for each real value we can find a fixed-point number with the required error characteristics.

Lemma 8: FXP_ERROR_BOUND_LEMMA3
⊢ (validAttr X) ∧ ¬(x > MAX (X)) ∧ ¬(x < MIN (X)) ⟹ ∃(w: bool word).
  abs (value (Fxp (w,X)) − x) ≤ inv (&2 pow (fracbits X)) ∧
  (WORDLEN w = streamlength X)

Since the rounding produces the minimum error as stated in *Lemma 5*, the proof of the second theorem (FXP_ERROR_BOUND_THM) is a direct consequence of *Lemma 8*. In these proofs, we have treated the case of signed and unsigned numbers separately since they have different definitions for *MAX*, *MIN*, and *value* functions. For signed numbers a special attention needs also to be paid for dealing with the negative numbers. Although the two main theorems in this section are proved for *Convergent* and *Clip* modes, the proof for other modes can be handled in a similar manner.

6 The Integrator Example

In this section we demonstrate how the formalization presented in the previous sections can be used for the verification of the transition from floating-point to

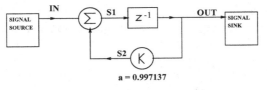

a = 0.997137

a) Floating-Point Design

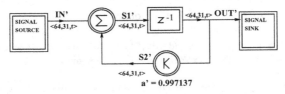

a' = 0.997137

b) Fixed-Point Design

Fig. 5. SPW Design of an Integrator

fixed-point algorithmic levels in SPW. As an example consider the case of an *Integrator* as shown in Figure 5. The *Integrator* is first designed and simulated using predefined floating-point blocks and parameters (Figure 5(a)). The design is composed of *Add, Gain* (multiply by a constant), and *Delay* blocks together with signal source and sink elements. Figure 5(b) shows the converted fixed-point design in which each block is replaced with the corresponding fixed-point block. Fixed-point blocks are shown by double circles and squares to distinguish from the floating-point blocks. The attributes of all fixed-point block outputs are set to $< 64, 31, 1 >$ to ensure that overflows and quantization do not affect the system operation.

We first model the design in each level as predicates in higher-order logic. The predicates corresponding to the floating-point design are as follows:

$\vdash_{def}$ Float_Gain_Block a b c = ($\forall$n. c n = a n float_mul b)
$\vdash_{def}$ Float_Delay_Block a b = ($\forall$ n. b n = a (n - 1))
$\vdash_{def}$ Float_Add_Block a b c = ($\forall$ n. c n = a n float_add b n)

$\vdash_{def}$ Float_Integrator_Imp a IN OUT =
    $\exists$ S1 S2.
    Float_Add_Block IN S2 S1 $\wedge$
    Float_Delay_Block S1 OUT $\wedge$
    Float_Gain_Block OUT a S2

In these definitions we have used Harrison's formalization of floating-point arithmetic [10]. Floating-point data types are stored in SPW as standard IEEE 64 bit double precision format.

The corresponding predicates for the fixed-point implementation are as follows:

$\vdash_{def}$ Fxp_Gain_Block a' b' c'
= ($\forall$n. c' n = a' n fxp_mul b') $\vdash_{def}$ Fxp_Delay_Block a' b' = ($\forall$ n.
b' n = a' (n − 1)) $\vdash_{def}$ Fxp_Add_Block a' b' c' = ($\forall$ n. c' n = a'
n fxp_add b' n)

$\vdash_{def}$ Fxp_Integrator_Imp
a' IN' OUT' = $\exists$ S1' S2'. Fxp_Add_Block IN' S2' S1' $\land$ Fxp_Delay_Block
S1' OUT' $\land$ Fxp_Gain_Block OUT' a' S2'

The functions *fxp_add* and *fxp_mul* are defined as follows:

$\vdash_{def}$ a' fxp_add b' = FST (fxpAdd (64,31,1) Convergent Clip a' b')
$\vdash_{def}$ a' fxp_mul b' = FST (fxpMul (64,31,1) Convergent Clip a' b')

In the next step, we describe each design as a difference equation relating
the input and output samples.

$\vdash_{def}$ FLOAT_Integrator_Spec a IN OUT =
    $\forall$n. OUT n = (IN (n − 1) float_add (OUT (n − 1) float_mul a))
$\vdash_{def}$ FXP_Integrator_Spec a' IN' OUT' =
    $\forall$n. OUT' n = (IN' (n − 1) fxp_add (OUT' (n − 1) fxp_mul a'))

The following lemmas ensure that the implementation at each level satisfies
the corresponding specification:

Lemma 9: FLOAT_INTEGRATOR_IMP_SPEC
$\vdash$ Float_Integrator_Imp a IN OUT $\Longrightarrow$ Float_Integrator_Spec a IN OUT

Lemma 10: FXP_INTEGRATOR_IMP_SPEC
$\vdash$ Fxp_Integrator_Imp a' IN' OUT' $\Longrightarrow$ Fxp_Integrator_Spec a' IN' OUT'

Based on the theorems FXP_ADD_THM and FXP_MUL_THM and the corresponding ones in floating-point theory [10], we prove the following theorem that
states the error between the real values of the floating and fixed-point precision
output samples.

Theorem 3: INTEGRATOR_THM
$\vdash$ Float_Integrator_Imp a IN OUT $\land$ Fxp_Integrator_Imp a' IN' OUT' $\land$
    Finite IN (n − 1) $\land$ Finite OUT (n − 1) $\land$ Finite a $\land$
    Isvalid IN'(n − 1) $\land$ Isvalid OUT' (n − 1) $\land$ Isvalid a' $\land$
    abs (Val OUT (n − 1) * Val a) < threshold float_format $\land$
    abs (Val (IN (n − 1)) + Val (OUT (n − 1) float_mul a)) <
    threshold float_format $\land$
    (value (OUT' (n − 1)) * value a') $\leq$ MAX (64,31,1) $\land$
    (value (OUT' (n − 1)) * value a') $\geq$ MIN (64,31,1) $\land$
    (value (IN' (n − 1)) + value (OUT' (n − 1) fxp_mul a'))
        $\leq$ MAX (64,31,1) $\land$
    (value (IN' (n − 1)) + value (OUT' (n − 1) fxp_mul a')) $\geq$ MIN (64,31,1)
    $\Longrightarrow$

```
Finite (OUT n) ∧ Isvalid (OUT' n) ∧
(Val (OUT n) − value (OUT' n)) =
(Val (IN (n − 1)) − value (IN' (n − 1))) +
((Val (OUT (n − 1)) * Val a) − (value (OUT' (n − 1)) * value a')) +
error (Val (OUT (n − 1)) * Val a) +
error (Val (IN (n − 1)) + Val (OUT (n − 1) float_mul a)) +
fxperror (64,31,1) Convergent Clip (value (OUT' (n − 1)) * value a') +
fxperror (64,31,1) Convergent Clip
(value (IN' (n − 1)) + value (OUT' (n − 1) fxp_mul a'))
```

As shown by this theorem, three sources of error can be distinguished: errors due to the quantization of input samples, errors due to the rounding in arithmetic operations, and errors due to quantization of coefficients. The assumptions are set to guarantee the validity of output samples. The errors are already quantified using the second theorem in this paper (FXP_ERROR_BOUND_THM) and the corresponding theorems for error analysis in floating-point case.

7   Conclusions

In this paper, we proposed the formalization of SPW based fixed-point arithmetic in the HOL theorem prover. We started first by encoding the fixed-point arithmetic in HOL considering different rounding and overflow modes and exception handling, then we proved two main theorems stating that the operations on fixed-point numbers are closely related to the corresponding operations on infinitely precise values, considering some error. The error is bounded to a certain absolute value which is a function of the output precision. We also showed by an example how these theorems can be used as a basis for analysis of the quantization errors in the design of fixed-point DSP systems. The formalization presented in this paper can be considered as a complement to the floating-point formalizations which are widely available in the literature. Our future work will focous on the verification of the transition from the floating-point algorithmic level to RTL or gate level implementations in DSP applications.

References

1. M. D. Aagaard, and C.-J. H. Seger, The formal Verification of a Pipelined Double-Precision IEEE Floating-Point Multiplier, In ICCAD, pages 7-10. IEEE, Nov. 1995.
2. G. Barrett, "Formal Methods Applied to a Floating Point Number System", IEEE Transactions on Software Engineering, SE-15(5): 611-621, May 1989.
3. C. Berg and C. Jacobi, "Formal Verification of the VAMP Floating Point Unit", Proc. 11th Advanced Research Working Conference on Correct Hardware Design and Verification Methods, CHARME 2001:325-339.
4. V. A. Carreno, "Interpretation of IEEE-854 Floating-Point Standard and Definition in the HOL System", NASA Technical Memorandum 110189, September 1995.

5. M. Cornea-Hasegan, "Proving the IEEE Correctness of Iterative Floating-Point Square Root, Divide, and Remainder Algorithms", Intel Technology Journal, Q2, 1998.
6. Y.-A. Chen and R. E. Bryant, "Verification of Floating Point Adders", In CAV'98, Volume 1427 of LNCS, 1998.
7. M. Daumas, L. Rideau, L. Théry, "A Generic Library for Floating-Point Numbers and Its Application to Exact Computing", Proc. TPHOLs'2001:169-184, November 2001.
8. M. J. C. Gordon and T. F. Melham, "Introduction to HOL: A Theorem Proving Environment for Higher-Order Logic." Cambridge University Press, 1993.
9. J. R. Harrison, "Theorem Proving with the Real Numbers", Technical Report Number 408, University of Cambridge Computer Laboratory, December 1996.
10. J. R. Harrison, "Floating-Point Verification in HOL Light: The Exponential Function", Technical Report Number 28, University of Cambridge Computer Laboratory. UK, June 1997.
11. J. R. Harrison, "A Machine-Checked Theory of Floating-Point Arithmetic", Proc. TPHOLs'99, August 1999.
12. G. Huet, G. Kahn, and C. Paulin-Mohring, "The Coq Proof Assistant: A Tutorial: Version 6.1" Technical Report 204, INRIA, 1997.
13. IEEE, "IEEE Standard for Binary Floating-Point Arithmetic", 1985. ANSI/IEEE Std 754-1985.
14. IEEE, "IEEE Standard for Radix-Independent Floating-Point Arithmetic", 1987. ANSI/IEEE Std 854-1987.
15. M. Leeser, and J. O'Leary, "Verification of a Subtractive Radix-2 Square Root Algorithm and Implementation", Proc. ICCD'95, October 1995.
16. J. O'Leary, X. Zhao, R. Gerth, and C. H. Seger, "Formally Verifying IEEE Compliance of Floating-Point Hardware", Intel Technology Journal, 1999.
17. P. S. Miner, and J. F. Leathrum, "Verification of IEEE Compliant Subtractive Division Algorithms", In FMCAD-96, Volume 1166 of LNCS, pages 64-, November 1996.
18. P.S. Miner, "Defining the IEEE-854 Floating-Point Standard in PVS", Technical Memorandum 110167, NASA, Langley Research Center, Hampton, VA 236810001, USA, June 1995.
19. J. S. Moore, T. Lynch, and M. Kaufmann, "A Mechanically Checked Proof of the AMD5K86 Floating Point Division Program", IEEE Transactions on Computers, 47(9):913-926, 1998.
20. S. M. Mueller and W. J. Paul, "Computer Architecture. Complexity and Correctness", Springer 2000.
21. D. M. Russinoff, "A Case Study in Formal Verification of Register-Transfer Logic with ACL2: The Floating Point Adder of the AMD Athlon Processor", In Proceedings of FMCAD-00, volume 1954 of LNCS. Springer, 2000.
22. "Signal Processing WorkSystem (SPW) User's Guide", Cadence Design Systems, Inc., July 1999.
23. W. Wong, "The HOL word Library", University of Cambridge, Computer Laboratory, May 1993.

A   Rounding to Fixed-Point Values

```
floor = ⊢  ∀ x. floor x = @n. &n ≤ abs x ∧ ∀i. &i ≤ abs x ⟹ i ≤ n
fraction = ⊢  ∀x. fraction x = x − &(floor x)
BDIG = ⊢  ∀n a. BDIG n a = (VB ((a DIV (2 EXP n)) MOD 2))
BDIGFUN = ⊢  ∀a. BDIGFUN a = λ n. BDIG n a
BWORD = ⊢  ∀n m. BWORD n m = WORD (GENLIST (BDIGFUN n) m)
TWOEXPONENT = ⊢  ∀x. TWOEXPONENT x = @n. &(2 EXP n) ≥ abs x ∧
∀m. (& (2 EXP m) ≥ abs x) ⟹ n ≤ m
POSITIVE = ⊢  ∀x. POSITIVE x = &(2 EXP (TWOEXPONENT x)) + x
Wrapp = ⊢  ∀X x. Wrapp (X) x = (x ≥ 0 → fxp (WCAT ((BWORD (floor x)
(intbits X)),(BWORD (floor (& (2 EXP fracbits X)*(fraction (POSITIVE x))))
(fracbits X))), X)) | fxp (WCAT (((BWORD (floor (POSITIVE x)) (intbits X))
WOR (BWORD ((2 EXP (TWOEXPONENT x))) (intbits X))), (BWORD (floor (& (2 EXP
fracbits X) * (fraction (POSITIVE x)))) (fracbits X))), X))
fxp_round = ⊢  ∀X x mode.
         (fxp_round (X) Convergent mode x =
              (x > MAX X) ∧ (mode = Clip) → (topfxp X, overflow) |
              (x < MIN X) ∧ (mode = Clip) → (bottomfxp X , overflow) |
              (x > MAX X) ∧ (mode = Wrap) → (Wrapp X x , overflow) |
              (x < MIN X) ∧ (mode = Wrap) → (Wrapp X x , overflow) |
              (closest (value) (λ a. LSB (Stram a) = F)
         {(a: fxp) | Isvalid a ∧ (Attrib a = X)} x, no_except)) ∧
   (fxp_round (X) To_zero mode x =
              (x > MAX X) ∧ (mode = Clip) → (topfxp X, overflow) |
              (x < MIN X) ∧ (mode = Clip) → (bottomfxp X , overflow) |
              (x > MAX X) ∧ (mode = Wrap) → (Wrapp X x , overflow) |
              (x < MIN X) ∧ (mode = Wrap) → (Wrapp X x , overflow) |
              (closest (value) (λ a. T) {a | Isvalid a ∧ (Attrib a = X) ∧
         abs (value a) ≤ abs x} x, no_except)) ∧
   (fxp_round (X) To_plus_infinity mode x =
              (x > MAX X) ∧ (mode = Clip) → (topfxp X, overflow) |
              (x < MIN X) ∧ (mode = Clip) → (bottomfxp X , overflow) |
              (x > MAX X) ∧ (mode = Wrap) → (Wrapp X x , overflow) |
              (x < MIN X) ∧ (mode = Wrap) → (Wrapp X x , overflow) |
              (closest (value) (λ a. T)
         {a | Isvalid a ∧ (Attrib a = X) ∧ (value a ≥ x)} x, no_except)) ∧
   (fxp_round (X) Truncate mode x =
              (x > MAX X) ∧ (mode = Clip) → (topfxp X, overflow) |
              (x < MIN X) ∧ (mode = Clip) → (bottomfxp X , overflow) |
              (x > MAX X) ∧ (mode = Wrap) → (Wrapp X x , overflow) |
              (x < MIN X) ∧ (mode = Wrap) → (Wrapp X x , overflow) |
              (closest (value) (λ a. T)
         {a | Isvalid a ∧ (Attrib a = X) ∧ (value a ≤ x)} x, no_except)) ∧
   (fxp_round (X) Round mode x =
              (x > MAX X) ∧ (mode = Clip) → (topfxp X, overflow) |
              (x < MIN X) ∧ (mode = Clip) → (bottomfxp X , overflow) |
              (x > MAX X) ∧ (mode = Wrap) → (Wrapp X x , overflow) |
              (x < MIN X) ∧ (mode = Wrap) → (Wrapp X x , overflow) |
              (closest (value) (λ a. value (fxp (Stream a, X)) ≥ x)
         {a | Isvalid a ∧ (Attrib a = X)} x, no_except))
```

B   Lemmas for Analyzing the Fixed-Point Rounding Operation

```
FXP_IS_CLOSEST_EXISTS = ⊢ ∀v x s.
FINITE (s) ⟹  ¬(s = EMPTY) ⟹  ∃(a: fxp). is_closest v s x a
FXP_CLOSEST_IS_EVERYTHING = ⊢ ∀v p x s.
FINITE (s) ⟹  ¬(s = EMPTY) ⟹  is_closest v s x (closest v p s X) ∧
((∃b. is_closest v s x b ∧ p b) ⟹  p (closest v p s X))
FXP_CLOSEST_IN_SET = ⊢ ∀v p x s.
FINITE (s) ⟹  ¬(s = EMPTY) ⟹  (closest v p s X) IN s
FXP_CLOSEST_IS_CLOSEST = ⊢ ∀v p x s.
FINITE (s) ⟹  ¬(s = EMPTY) ⟹  is_closest v s x (closest v p s X)
MAINFINITE =
⊢ FINITE {a | (FST (SND a) < 257) ∧ (FST (SND (SND a)) < (FST (SND a) +
1)) ∧ (SND (SND (SND a)) < 2) ∧ (WORDLEN (FST a) = FST (SND a))}
FINITE_VALID_ATTRIB = ⊢ ∀X. FINITE {a | Isvalid a ∧ (Attrib a = X)}
IS_VALID_NONEMPTY = ⊢ ∀X.
validAttr X ⟹  ¬({a | Isvalid a ∧ (Attrib a = X)} = EMPTY)
IS_VALID_CLOSEST = ⊢ ∀v p X x.
validAttr X ⟹  Isvalid (closest v p {a | Isvalid a ∧
((Attrib a) = X)} x)
IS_VALID_TOPFXP = ⊢ ∀X. Isvalid topfxp X
IS_VALID_BOTTOMFXP = ⊢ ∀X. Isvalid bottomfxp X
IS_VALID_WRAPP = ⊢ ∀X x. Isvalid Wrapp X x
IS_VALID_ROUND_CONV_CLIP = ⊢ ∀X x.
validAttr X ⟹  Isvalid (FST (fxp_round X Convergent Clip x))
```

C   Rounding Error in Fixed-Point Arithmetic Operations

```
FXP_SUB_THM
⊢ (Isvalid a) ∧ (Isvalid b) ∧ validAttr (X) ⟹
  (Isvalid (FST (fxpSub X Convergent Clip a b))) ∧
  (value (FST (fxpSub X Convergent Clip a b)) = value (a) − value (b) +
  (fxperror X Convergent Clip (value a − value b)))
FXP_MUL_THM
⊢ (Isvalid a) ∧ (Isvalid b) ∧ validAttr (X) ⟹
  (Isvalid (FST (fxpMul X Convergent Clip a b))) ∧
  (value (FST (fxpMul X Convergent Clip a b)) = (value a * value b) +
  (fxperror X Convergent Clip (value a * value b)))
FXP_DIV_THM
⊢ (Isvalid a) ∧ (Isvalid b) ∧ validAttr (X) ⟹
  (Isvalid (FST (fxpDiv X Convergent Clip a b))) ∧
  (value (FST (fxpDiv X Convergent Clip a b)) = (value a / value b) +
  (fxperror X Convergent Clip (value a / value b)))
```

Formally Linking MDG and HOL
Based on a Verified MDG System

Haiyan Xiong[1], Paul Curzon[1], Sofiène Tahar[2], and Ann Blandford[3]

[1] School of Computing Science, Middlesex University, London, UK
{h.xiong,p.curzon}@mdx.ac.uk
[2] ECE Department, Concordia University, Montreal, Canada
tahar@ece.concordia.ca
[3] UCL Interaction Centre, University College of London, London, UK
a.blandford@ucl.ac.uk

Abstract. We describe an approach for formally linking a symbolic state enumeration system and a theorem proving system based on a verified version of the former. It has been realized using a simplified version of the MDG system and the HOL system. Firstly, we have verified aspects of correctness of a simplified version of the MDG system. We have made certain that the semantics of a program is preserved in those of its translated form. Secondly, we have provided a formal linkage between the MDG system and the HOL system based on importing theorems. The MDG verification results can be formally imported into HOL to form a HOL theorem. Thirdly, we have combined the translator correctness theorems and importing theorems. This allows the MDG verification results to be imported in terms of a high level language (MDG-HDL) rather than a low level language. We also summarize a general method to prove **existential theorems** for the design. The feasibility of this approach is demonstrated in a case study that integrates two applications: hardware verification (in MDG) and usability verification (in HOL). A single HOL theorem is proved that integrates the two results.

Keywords: hardware verification, hybrid verification systems, deductive theorem proving, symbolic state enumeration, usability verification.

1 Introduction

Deductive theorem proving and symbolic state enumeration are complementary approaches to formal verification. In the former, the correctness condition for a design is represented as a theorem in a mathematical logic, and a mechanically checked proof of this theorem is generated using a general-purpose theorem prover. In symbolic state enumeration systems, the design being verified is represented as a decision diagram. Techniques such as reachability analysis are used to automatically verify given properties of the design or machine equivalence. Much of this work is based on Binary Decision Diagrams (BDD) [2].

Deductive theorem proving systems often use interactive proof methods. The user interactively constructs a formal proof which proves a theorem stating the

M. Butler, L. Petre, and K. Sere (Eds.): IFM 2002, LNCS 2335, pp. 205–224, 2002.

correctness of an implementation. Theorem proving systems allow a hierarchical verification method to be used to model the overall functionality of designs with complex datapaths. They are very general in their application. Theorems cannot only be used to formalize a specific design but also can be abstracted as a general situation of this class of design. Theorem proving systems are semi-automated. To complete a verification, experts with good knowledge of the internal structure of the design are required to guide the proof searching process. This enables the designer to gain greater insight into the system and thus achieve better designs. However, the learning curve is very steep and modeling and verifying a system is very time-consuming. This is a major problem for applying theorem proving systems in industry.

In contrast, symbolic state enumeration systems are automated decision diagram approaches. In this kind of approach, an implementation and its behavioral specification are represented as decision diagrams. A set of algorithms is used to efficiently manipulate the decision diagrams so as to get the correctness results. The symbolic state enumeration verification approach can be viewed as a black-box approach. During the verification, the user does not need to understand the internal structure of the design. The strength of this approach is its speed and ease of use. However, it does not scale well to complex designs since it uses non-hierarchy state-based descriptions of the design. An increase in the number of design components can result in the state space growing exponentially.

Recently, there has been a great deal of work concerned with combining theorem proving and symbolic state enumeration systems to gain the advantages of both. A common approach to combining proof tools is to use a symbolic state enumeration system as an oracle to provide results to the theorem proving system. The issue in such work is to guarantee that the results provided by external tools are theorems within the theory of the proof system. In other words, an oracle is used to receive problems and return answers. For example, the HOL system provides approaches for tagging theorems that are dependent on the correctness of external verification tools. An oracle can be built in the HOL system and viewed as a plug-in. This process brings about two questions.

1. Can we ensure the automated verification system produces correct results?
2. Have the verification results from an automated verification system been correctly converted into a valid theorem in the theorem proving system?

We investigate the answers to the above two questions. Some symbolic state enumeration based systems such as MDG [6] consist of a series of translators and a set of algorithms. Higher level languages such as hardware description languages are used to describe the specification and implementation of the design. The specification and implementation are then translated into the decision diagrams via intermediate languages. The algorithms in the system are used to efficiently and automatically deal with the decision diagrams so as to obtain the correctness results. We need to verify the translators and algorithms in order to get the answer to the first question. To solve the second question, we can formally justify the correctness results obtained from the symbolic state enumeration system in a theorem prover.

The main contribution of this paper is that we describe an approach that provides a formal linkage between a theorem proving system and a symbolic state enumeration system based on a verified symbolic state enumeration system, to ensure the correctness of the theorem creation process. We partly realize the methodology with the HOL system and a simplified version of the MDG system. We prove the correctness of aspects of the simplified MDG system. We also provide a formal linkage between the HOL system and the simplified MDG system based on importing theorems [22]. Most importantly, we combine the translator correctness theorems with the importing theorems. This combination allows the low level MDG verification results to be imported into HOL in terms of the semantics of a high level language (MDG-HDL). Lessons from the work are applicable to other related systems. We chose HOL and MDG because this work is part of a large project in collaboration with the Hardware Verification group at Concordia University. They are developing a hybrid system (MDG-HOL) [17] which combines the MDG system and the HOL system.

The structure of the rest of this paper is as follows: in Section 2, we review related work. In Section 3 we briefly introduce the MDG and HOL systems. The main body of the paper is described in Section 4. Finally, our conclusion and ideas for further work are presented in Section 5.

2 Related Work

Many different technologies have been used to link systems. We will briefly review some related techniques here.

Joyce and Seger [16] presented a hybrid verification system: HOL-Voss. Several predicates were defined in the HOL system, which presented a mathematical link between the specification language of the Voss system (symbolic trajectory evaluation) [14] and that of the HOL system.

Aagaard et al. developed the Forte verification system [1]. Forte is a combined model checking (in Voss via symbolic trajectory evaluation) and theorem proving system (ThmTac)[1]. Both specification and implementation language are fl which has been deeply embedded in itself so as to be lifted. In other words, the system can execute fl functions in Voss and reason about the behavior of fl functions in ThmTac.

Rajan et al. [20] proposed an approach for the integration of model checking with PVS [7]: the Prototype Verification System. The μ-calculus, which consists of quantified boolean formula and predicates defined by means of the least and greatest fixpoint operators, was used as a medium for communicating between PVS and a model checker.

The PROSPER toolkit [10] provides a uniform way of linking HOL with external proof tools. The specification of its integration interface has been implemented in several languages allowing components written in these languages to be used together. A range of different external proof tools can access the

---

[1] ThmTac is written in fl and is an LCF style implementation of a higher order classical logic.

toolkit and act as servers to a HOL client. It also tags theorems produced by its plug-in with a label which can be used in the HOL system. The MDG-HOL system [17] used the PROSPER/Harness Plug-in Interface to link the HOL system and the MDG system.

Gordon [12] integrated the BDD based verification system BuDDY into HOL by implementing BDD-based verification algorithms inside HOL building on top of primitives provided. Since "LCF-Style" general infrastructure was provided, by implementing BDD primitives in HOL – as long as they are correct – not only could the standard state algorithms be efficiently and safely programmed in HOL, but it also made it possible to achieve the advantages of both theorem proving tools and state algorithms.

Hurd [15] used a different method to combine the strengths of two theorem-prover systems – Gandalf and HOL. He wrote functions to simulate the Gandalf proof according to the Gandalf logged file so reconstructing the proof in HOL to form the HOL theorems. As a result, the Gandalf proof results need not be tagged into HOL and the degree of trust is high.

We take a different approach. We focus on the verification of a symbolic state enumeration system (the MDG system) and provide a theoretical underpinning to the formal linkage of a symbolic state enumeration system and a theorem proving system (MDG and HOL). We verify the correctness of translators of the MDG system by using the HOL system and prove theorems that formally convert the MDG verification results of MDG's different applications into the traditional HOL hardware verification theorems. By combining the translator correctness theorems with the importing theorems, the MDG verification results can be imported into HOL in terms of the MDG input language (MDG-HDL). The feasibility of this approach is demonstrated in a case study that integrates two distinct applications: hardware verification (in MDG) and usability verification (in HOL). A single HOL theorem is proved that integrates the two results.

3   The MDG and HOL Systems

The MDG system is a hardware verification system based on Multiway Decision Graphs (MDGs). MDGs subsume the class of Bryant's Reduced Ordered Binary Decision Diagrams (ROBDD) [3] while accommodating abstract sorts and uninterpreted function symbols. The system combines a variety of different hardware verification applications implemented using MDGs [25]. The applications developed include: combinational verification, sequential verification, invariant checking and model checking.

The input language of MDG is MDG-HDL [25], which is a Prolog-style hardware description language that allows the use of abstract variables for representing data signals. In MDG, a circuit description file declares signals and their sort assignment, components network, outputs, initial values for sequential verification and the mapping between state variables and next state variables. In the components network, there is a large set of predefined components such as logic gates, flip-flops, registers, constants, etc. Among the predefined components there is a special component constructor known as a table which is used to describe a functional block in an implementation or specification. The TABLE constructor is similar to a truth table but allows first-order terms in rows. It also allows the description of high-level constructs as ITE (If-Then-Else) formulas and CASE formulas. A table is essentially a series of lists, together with a single final default value. The first list contains variables and cross-terms. The last element of this first list is the output of the table which must be a variable (either concrete or abstract). The other variables in the list must be concrete variables. For example, a two input AND gate can be described as

$$\text{table}([[\text{x1, x2, y}], [0, *, 0], [1, 0, 0] | 1]) \tag{1}$$

where "*" means "don't care". It states that if x1 is false and x2 is don't care then the output y is equal to false, if x1 is equal to true and x2 is equal to false then the output y is equal to false, otherwise the output y is equal to true.

HOL [13] uses higher-order logic to model and verify a system. There are two main proof methods used: forward and backward proof. In forward proof, the steps of a proof are implemented by applying inference rules chosen by the user, and HOL checks that the steps are safe. It is an LCF [11] style proof system: all derived inference rules are built on top of a small number of primitive inference rules. In backward proof, the user sets the desired theorem as a goal. Small programs written in SML [19] called tactics and tacticals are applied that break the goal into a list of subgoals. Tactics and tacticals are repeatedly applied to the subgoals until they can be proved. A justification function is also created mapping a list of theorems corresponding to subgoals to a theorem that solves the goal. In practice, forward proof is often used within backward proof to convert a goal's assumptions to a suitable form.

Theorems in the HOL system are represented by values of the ML abstract type thm. In a pure system (where mk_thm which creates arbitrary theorems is not used), a theorem is only obtained by carrying out a proof based on the primitive inference rules and axioms. More complex inference rules and tactics must ultimately call a series of primitive rules to do the job. In this way, the ML type system protects the HOL logic from the arbitrary construction of a theorem, so that every computed value of the type representing theorems is a theorem. The user can have a great deal of confidence in the results of the system provided mk_thm and new axioms are not used.

HOL has a rudimentary library facility which enables theories to be shared. This provides a file structure and documentation format for self contained HOL developments. Many basic reasoners are given as libraries such as mesonLib, simpLib, decisionLib and bossLib. These libraries integrate rewriting, conversion and decision procedures that automate a proof. They free the user from performing low-level proof.

4   Formally Linking a Verified MDG and HOL System

The intention of our work is to explore a way of increasing the degree of trust of the MDG system and provide a formal linkage between the HOL system and the

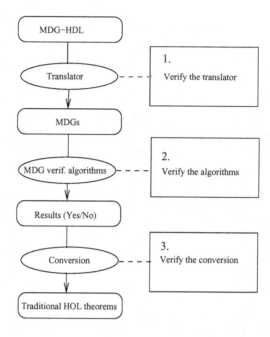

Fig. 1. Overview of the Verification Project

MDG system in terms of the MDG input language as shown in Figure 1. This work can be divided into three steps. (a) We must verify the correctness of the MDG system using the HOL system. It consists of two phases: (1) verification of the translators [23] and (2) verification of the algorithms. (b) We then must prove theorems (step 3), which formally convert the verification results of the MDG applications into traditional HOL hardware verification theorems [22]. (c) By combining the correctness theorems (theorems obtained from step 1 and step 2) of the verification of the MDG system with the importing theorems (obtained from step 3), the MDG verification results can be formalized in terms of MDG-HDL.

During this study, we concentrate on the verification of the translation phase of the MDG system (see step 1 in Figure 1) using the HOL theorem prover and importing the MDG results into HOL to form the HOL theorems (see step 3 in Figure 1) [22]. Step 2 is similar to Chou and Peled's work [5] which verifies a partial-order reduction technique for model checking. Verifying the algorithms is beyond the scope of this paper: we are primarily concerned with the linkage and how it could be combined with the correctness theorems and importing theorems. We outline the overall methodology and emphasize the importation process of the hybrid system. We not only verify the correctness of aspects of the MDG system in HOL, but also formally import the MDG results into HOL to form HOL theorems based on the semantics of the high level MDG input language (MDG-HDL) [25] rather than the semantics of the low level MDG results. Since we use a

$$\text{MDG–HDL} \xrightarrow{\quad (1) \quad} \text{core MDG–HDL} \xrightarrow{\quad (2) \quad} \text{MDGs}$$

Fig. 2. Overview of the MDG Translation Phases

deep embedding semantics, the separate translator correctness theorems can be combined with themselves and the importing theorems. The combination allows the low level MDG results to be converted into a form that can be easily reasoned about in HOL based on the semantics of MDG-HDL. We also summarize the general method about proving the `existential theorem`. This theorem is needed for importing sequential verification result into the theorem proving system.

In the remainder of this section, we will briefly introduce the individual steps that we have undertaken: verifying the translator correctness theorems, proving the general importing theorems, combining the translator correctness theorems with the importing theorems in terms of deep embedding semantics, proving the `existential theorem` and implementing our method in a case study that integrates two different applications.

4.1   Verifying the MDG Translators

In the MDG system, most of the components in the MDG-HDL library are compiled into their own core MDG-HDL tabular code first. The core MDG-HDL program can then be compiled into an internal MDG. Some components, such as registers, are implemented directly in terms of an MDG. However, in theory these components also could be implemented as tables which provides a general specification mechanism. We assume the MDG-HDL program is firstly translated into a core MDG-HDL program. The core MDG-HDL program is then translated into the MDG. In this situation, the MDG system could be specified as in Figure 2.

Adopting this approach makes the translation phase more amenable to verification. We are not verifying the actual MDG implementation. Rather our formalization of the translator is a specification of it. Once combined with a translator from core MDG-HDL to the MDG, it would be specifying the output required from the implementation. This would be used as the basis for verifying such an implementation. We thus split the problem of verifying the translator into the two problems of verifying that the implementation meets a functional specification, and that the functional specification then meets the requirement of preserving semantics. We are concerned with the latter step here. This split between implementation and specification correctness was advocated by Chirica and Martin [4] with respect to compiler correctness.

The MDG system is based on Multiway Decision Graphs which extend ROB-DDs with concrete sorts, abstract sorts and uninterpreted function symbols. We define a deep embedding semantics for a subset of the MDG-HDL language. This subset is all of MDG except three predefined components (Multiplexer, Driver and constant) and the Transform construct used to apply functions. These components are omitted from our subset as they have non-boolean inputs or outputs.

We consider this subset since our aim is to explore the feasibility of this method. However, this subset allows a program to contain concrete sorts. In other words, the inputs and outputs of a `table` could be boolean sorts and concrete sorts. The concrete sort of boolean values is treated separately as it is predefined in MDG and used with most components. It is therefore treated as a special case. To cope with different types in one list, we define a new type `Mdg_Basic` in HOL. The value of the type can be either a boolean value or a string. In the rest of this paper, we will refer to the simplified version of the MDG system as "the MDG system".

We verified the first translation step of the MDG system (see phase 1 in Figure 2) based on the syntax and semantics of the MDG input language and the core MDG-HDL language using the HOL theorem prover. The syntax and the semantics of the subset MDG-HDL and core MDG-HDL are defined. A set of functions, which translate the program from MDG-HDL to core MDG-HDL is then defined. For each program in MDG-HDL, the compilation operators are defined as functions, which return their core MDG-HDL code. Translation function `TransProgMC` is applied to each MDG-HDL program so that the corresponding core MDG-HDL program is established. In other words, the relations of the translations can be represented as below:

$$\forall \ \text{p. TransProgMC p} = \textit{Corresponding core MDG-HDL program}$$

The standard approach to prove a translator between two languages is in terms of the semantics of the languages. Essentially the translation should preserve the semantics of the source language. This has the traditional form of compiler specification correctness used in the verification of a compiler [4]. An analogous method has been used in the specification and verification of the MDG system. For the translation to core MDG-HDL, the correctness theorem has been proved:

$$\vdash_{thm} \forall \ \text{p. SemProgram (p)} = \text{SemProgram\_Core (TransProgMC p)} \tag{2}$$

where `SemProgram` and `SemProgram_Core` are semantic functions for the MDG-HDL program and core MDG-HDL program. This theorem states that the semantics of the low level core MDG-HDL program is equal to the semantics of the high level MDG-HDL (the MDG input language). For a subset of MDG without concrete sorts we have also verified translation to a lower level formula language of decision diagrams. More details can be found in [21].

4.2   The Importing Theorems

Generally, when we use HOL to verify a design, the design is modeled as a hierarchy structure with modules divided into submodules. The submodules are repeatedly subdivided until the logic gate level is eventually reached. Both the structural and the behavioral specifications of each module are given as relations in higher-order logic. The verification of each module is carried out by proving a theorem asserting that the implementation (its structure) implements (implies) the specification (its behavior). They have the very general form:

$$\text{implementation} \supset \text{specification} \tag{3}$$

PSEQ

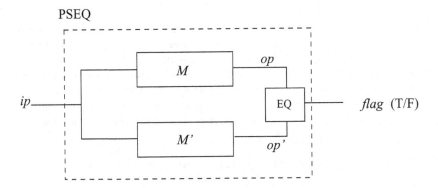

Fig. 3. The Product Machine used in MDG Sequential Verification

The correctness theorem for each module states that its implementation down to the logic gate level satisfies the specification. The correctness theorem for each module can be established using the correctness theorems of its submodules. In this sense the submodule is treated as a black-box. A consequence of this is that different technologies can be used to address the correctness theorem for the submodules. In particular, we can use the MDG system instead of HOL to prove the correctness of submodules.

In order to convert the MDG verification results into HOL, we formalized the results of the MDG verification applications in HOL. These formalizations have different forms for the different verification applications, i.e., combinational verification gives a theorem of one form, sequential verification gives a different form and so on. However, the most natural and obvious way to formalize the MDG results does not give theorems of the form that HOL needs if we are to use traditional HOL hardware verification techniques. Therefore, we have to convert the MDG results into a form that can be used. In other words, we proved a series of translation theorems (one for combinational verification and one for sequential verification, etc.) that state how an MDG result can be converted into the traditional HOL form:

```
Formalized MDG result ⊃

      implementation ⊃ specification          (4)
```

We have formally specified the correctness results produced by several different MDG verification applications and given general importing theorems. These theorems do not explicitly deal with the MDG-HDL semantics or multiway decision graphs. Rather they are given in terms of general relations on inputs and outputs. The theorems proved could be applied to other verification systems with similar architectures based on reachability analysis or equivalence checking.

For example, the behavioral equivalence of two abstract state machines (Figure 3) is verified by checking that the machines produce the same sequence of outputs for every sequence of inputs. The same inputs are fed to the two machines M and M' and then reachability analysis is performed on their product machine using an invariant asserting the equality of the corresponding outputs in all reachable states. This effectively introduces new "hardware" (see Figure 3) which we refer to here as PSEQ (the Product machine for SEQuential verification). PSEQ has the same inputs as M and M', but has as output a single boolean signal (flag). The outputs op and op' of M and M' are input into an equality checker. On each cycle, PSEQ outputs true if op and op' are identical at that time, and false otherwise. The result that MDG proves about PSEQ is that the flag output is always true. This can be formalized as

$$\forall \text{ ip op op' flag. PSEQ ip flag op op' M M'} \supset (\forall \text{ t. flag t = T)} \quad (5)$$

The corresponding importing theorem which converts MDG results to the appropriate HOL form has been obtained:

$$\vdash_{thm} \forall \text{ M M'.}$$
$$((\forall \text{ ip op op' flag.}$$
$$\text{PSEQ ip flag op op' M M'} \supset \forall \text{ t. flag t = T)} \land$$
$$(\forall \text{ ip. } \exists \text{ op'. M' ip op')}) \supset$$
$$(\forall \text{ ip op. M ip op} \supset \text{M' ip op}) \quad (6)$$

However, the MDG results can be imported into HOL when an additional assumption ($\forall$ ip. $\exists$ op'. M' ip op') is proved. We summarize a general method to prove the additional assumption of the design in Section 4.4.

4.3   Combining the Translator Correctness Theorems with the Importing Theorems

In this section, we introduce the basic idea about how to combine the translator correctness theorems with importing theorems based on a deep embedding semantics. This combination allows MDG results to be reasoned about in HOL in terms of the MDG input language (MDG-HDL). Ultimately in HOL we want a theorem about input language artifacts. However, the MDG verification result is obtained based on a low level data structure – an MDG representation: that is what the algorithms apply to. Therefore, the formalization of the MDG verification results in the importing theorems ought to be based on the semantics of the MDG representations. Moreover, the theorem about the translator's correctness can be used to convert the result MDG proves about the low level representation to one about the input language (MDG-HDL). By combining the translator correctness theorems with the importation theorems, we obtain the new importing theorems which convert the low level MDG verification results into HOL to form the HOL theorems in terms of the semantics of MDG-HDL. In other words, we are not only able to import the MDG result into HOL based on a verified MDG system, but also the MDG verification results can be converted directly from the MDG input files to the theorems of HOL naturally.

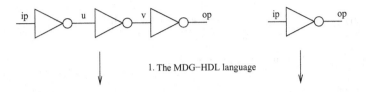

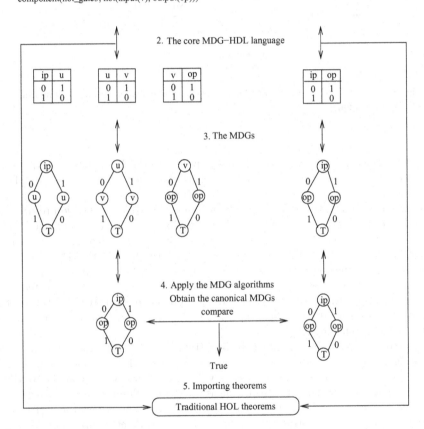

Fig. 4. The MDG Verification Process

For example, if we check that three NOT gates are equivalent to a single NOT gate, the whole MDG verification process and the importing process can be illustrated in Figure 4. In Figure 4, step (1) gives the main part of the two circuit description files (the MDG-HDL input language), which are translated into the core MDG-HDL (tabular representations) language as shown in step (2). The core MDG-HDL languages are then translated into the MDG language

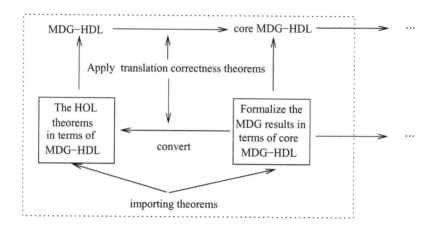

Fig. 5. Combining the Translator Correctness Theorems with Importing Theorems for a Subset Language

(step (3)). The MDG algorithm is then applied to the MDG in order to obtain two canonical MDGs and the MDG tool checks whether the two canonical MDGs are identical and returns true or false (step (4)).

In our example the MDG tool returns true. The MDG verification results are obtained based on the low level MDGs rather than the high level language MDG-HDL. However, the translator correctness theorems state that the semantics of the low level MDG is equal to the semantics of the high level MDG-HDL (the MDG input language). By combining the low-level MDG result with the translator correctness theorems, the MDG verification results can be imported into HOL based on the semantics of the MDG input language (MDG-HDL). Therefore, the traditional HOL theorem can be obtained in terms of the semantics of the MDG input language.

In our work, we have verified the first translator. In order to demonstrate the combination of the translator correctness theorems and the importing theorems, the formalization of the MDG results will be in terms of the core MDG-HDL (see Figure 5). In fact, the principle is the same. Similar conversion can be done for further verified translators. By combining the translator correctness theorem with the importation theorems, we obtain the new importing theorems which convert the low level MDG verification results into HOL to form the HOL theorems in terms of the semantics of MDG-HDL. The combination also allows the additional assumption for sequential verification to be proved in terms of the semantics of MDG-HDL and the conversion theorem to be obtained in terms of the semantics of MDG-HDL.

Therefore, the different MDG verification applications are formalized in a way that corresponds to the semantics of the low level program (core MDG-HDL) and converted into HOL to form the HOL theorem in terms of the semantics of MDG-HDL. We have obtained theorems for both combinational verification and sequential verification. They state that a verification result about a circuit based on a low level program is equivalent to a HOL theorem based on the semantics of the high level language (MDG-HDL), i.e., that the structural specification implements the behavioral specification. For example, the new sequential verification importing theorem is obtained by instantiating (SemProgram_Core (TransProgMC SPEC)) and (SemProgram_Core (TransProgMC IMP)) for the machine M and M' in the general importing theorem (6) and using the translator correctness theorem (2).

$$\vdash_{thm} \forall \text{ IMP SPEC.}$$

$$(\forall \text{ ip op op' flag.}$$

$$\text{PSEQ ip op op' flag}$$

$$\text{(SemProgram\_Core (TransProgMC SPEC))}$$

$$\text{(SemProgram\_Core (TransProgMC IMP))}$$

$$\supset (\forall \text{ t. (flag t = T))}) \wedge$$

$$(\forall \text{ ip. } \exists \text{ op'. SemProgram SPEC ip op')} \supset$$

$$(\forall \text{ ip op. SemProgram IMP ip op} \supset$$

$$\text{SemProgram SPEC ip op)} \qquad (7)$$

4.4   Proving the Existential Theorem

We proved the importing theorem for sequential verification. It has the form:

$$\vdash_{thm} \text{ Formalized MDG result } \wedge$$
$$\forall \text{ ip. } \exists \text{ op. SPECIFICATION ip op} \supset$$
$$(\forall \text{ ip op. (IMPLEMENTION ip op} \supset \text{ SPECIFICATION ip op))}$$

where SPECIFICATION represents the behavioral specification and IMPLEMENTATION represents the structural specification. The first assumption is discharged by the MDG verification. However, for importing the sequential verification results into HOL, a user of the hybrid system strictly needs to prove the additional assumption (an existential theorem) to ensure the correct HOL theorem can be made. This theorem states that for all possible input traces, the behavioral specification SPECIFICATION can be satisfied for some outputs:

$$\vdash_{thm} \forall \text{ ip. } \exists \text{ op. SPECIFICATION ip op} \qquad (8)$$

When we convert the MDG results into HOL to form the HOL theorems, the theorems actually state that the implementation of the design implements its specification as shown in (9).

$$\vdash_{thm} \forall \text{ ip op. IMPLEMENTATION ip op} \supset \text{ SPECIFICATION ip op} \qquad (9)$$

This representation might meet an inconsistent model that trivially satisfies any specification. We need to verify a stronger consistency theorem against the implementation as suggested in [18], which has the form:

$$\vdash_{thm} \forall \text{ ip. } \exists \text{ op. IMPLEMENTATION ip op} \qquad (10)$$

This means that for any set of input values ip there is a set of output values op which is consistent with it. This shows that the model does not satisfy a specification merely because it is inconsistent.

We have investigated a way of proving the additional assumption and the stronger consistency theorem based on the syntax and semantics of the MDG input language [23]. As we mentioned above, we prove the additional assumption because we want to make the linking process easier and remove the burden from the user of the hybrid system. We prove the stronger consistency theorem because we want to avoid an inconsistent model occurring. The above two theorems actually have the same form. We call them existential theorems. If we use C to represent any specification or implementation of a circuit, ip and op to represent the external inputs and outputs, the existential theorem should have the form:

$$\vdash_{thm} \forall \text{ ip. } \exists \text{ op. C ip op} \tag{11}$$

In fact, the stronger consistency theorem (10) is an existential theorem for the structural specification, whereas the additional assumption (8) for the importing theorem is an existential theorem for the behavioral specification.

The existential theorem is existentially quantified. We can remove hidden lines in goals of this form using the HOL tactic EXISTS_TAC, which strips away the leading existentially quantified variable and substitutes term for each free occurrence in the body. This term is called the existential term. An existential term of a variable is determined by one or several output representations of the corresponding MDG-HDL components. An output representation of a component represents an output function of this component, which depends on its input value and output value at the current time or an earlier time instance.

We prove the existential theorems based on the syntax and semantics of MDG-HDL [23] [9]. We provide the output representation for each component (mainly logic gates and flip-flops). The existential term of a design, which reduces the goal ∃ x. t to t[u/x], is determined in terms of the corresponding output representations. This is very important for verifying the existential theorem, since as long as we find the existential term of the design, the corresponding theorem will be proved. We also provide HOL tactics for expanding the semantics of the circuit and proving the existential theorem. More detail can be found in [21] [24].

4.5   Case Study: Integrated Hardware and Usability Verification

So far, we have discussed how to prove translator correctness theorems and importing theorems. We have combined the translator correctness theorems with the importing theorems. The combination allows the MDG verification results to be formalized and reasoned about in HOL in terms of the semantics of MDG-HDL. We now consider a simple case study to show that this method works in practice. We show how an actual MDG verification result can be imported into HOL to form a traditional HOL theorem. Moreover, we show that the importing theorems can be practically used in HOL. In particular, we apply our approach to a simple example, integrating MDG hardware verification and HOL usability verification for a vending machine. This example was originally used to verify the absence of a common class of user errors known as post-completion errors (users missing completion tasks such as taking change after their goal, such as getting chocolate, is achieved) within the framework of a traditional hardware verification by Curzon and Blandford [8]. In this work, it was proved that the implementation of the vending machine meets its specification. A usability theorem that a usability property holds about post-completion errors based on its specification was then proved. By combining the above two theorems, the usability theorem based on its implementation was proved. In the original work all the verification was done in HOL.

We closely followed their steps. However, we used the MDG system to verify the correctness of the vending machine and imported it into HOL using the theorem (7). We then proved the specification based usability theorem in the HOL system. By combining those two theorems, first the correctness theorem of the vending machine which is verified in MDG (the importing theorem), second the specification based usability theorem which is proved in HOL, we obtained the implementation based usability theorem. Therefore, the importing theorem (the correctness theorem) cannot only be imported into HOL but also can be used in HOL.

We first did a hardware verification of the vending machine in MDG. The theorem about the formalization of the MDG verification result can be tagged into HOL in terms of the semantics of core MDG-HDL.

$$\vdash_{thm} \forall \texttt{ ip flag op op'}.$$

$$\texttt{PSEQ ip flag op op'}$$

$$\texttt{(SemProgram\_Core (TransProgMC } \mathit{Vend\_Imp\_Syn}))$$

$$\texttt{(SemProgram\_Core (TransProgMC } \mathit{Vend\_Spe\_Syn}))$$

$$\supset (\forall \texttt{ t. (flag t = T)}) \tag{12}$$

where $\mathit{Vend\_Imp\_Syn}$ and $\mathit{Vend\_Spe\_Syn}$ stand for syntax of the implementation and specification of the vending machine in terms of MDG-HDL. As stated in Section 4.3, the importing theorem for the vending machine can be obtained by instantiating theorem (7) with the syntax of its implementation and specification ($\mathit{Vend\_Spe\_Syn}$ and $\mathit{Vend\_Imp\_Syn}$). We obtain theorem Import_Vend_Thm

$$\vdash_{thm} (\forall \texttt{ ip flag op op'}.$$

$$\texttt{PSEQ ip flag op op'}$$

$$\texttt{(SemProgram\_Core (TransProgMC } \mathit{Vend\_Imp\_Syn}))$$

$$\texttt{(SemProgram\_Core (TransProgMC } \mathit{Vend\_Spe\_Syn}))$$

$$\supset (\forall \texttt{ t. (flag t = T)})) \wedge$$

$$\forall \texttt{ ip. } \exists \texttt{ op'. SemProgram } \mathit{Vend\_Spe\_Syn} \texttt{ ip op'} \supset$$

$$(\forall \texttt{ ip op. SemProgram } \mathit{Vend\_Imp\_Syn} \texttt{ ip op} \supset$$

$$\texttt{SemProgram } \mathit{Vend\_Spe\_Syn} \texttt{ ip op}) \tag{13}$$

We then prove the **existential theorem** for the behavioral specification in terms of the semantics of MDG-HDL.

$$\vdash_{thm} \;\; \forall \; \texttt{ip.} \; \exists \; \texttt{op'.} \; (\texttt{SemProgram} \; \textit{Vend\_Spe\_Syn} \; \texttt{ip op'}) \tag{14}$$

Finally, the conversion theorem can be obtained by discharging the formalization theorem (12) and the existential theorem (14) from the importing theorem (13). This theorem states that the implementation implies the specification.

$$\vdash_{thm} \; \forall \; \texttt{ip} \;\; \texttt{op.} \; \texttt{SemProgram} \; \textit{Vend\_Imp\_Syn} \; \texttt{ip op} \; \supset$$
$$\texttt{SemProgram} \; \textit{Vend\_Spe\_Syn} \; \texttt{ip op} \tag{15}$$

We then prove the **specification** based usability theorem in the HOL system. The general user model for a vending machine is defined as CHOC_MACHINE_USER ustate op ip. This specifies a simple form of rational user behaviour. We prove that if a user behaves in this rational way, they will not make post completion errors with the particular vending machine in question (though they may with other poorer designs). It specifies concrete types for the machine and user state, a list of pairs of lights and the actions associated with them, history functions that represent the possessions of the user, functions that extract the part of the user state that indicates when the user has finished and has achieved their main goal and an invariant that indicates the part of the state that the user intends to be preserved after the interaction. The details of the user model are not important for our main argument here about integrating the results: the interested reader should refer to [8].

```
⊢def CHOC_MACHINE_USER ustate op ip =
  USER
  [(CoinLight,InsertCoin); (ChocLight,PushChoc);
   (ChangeLight,PushChange)]
  (CHOC_POSSESSIONS UserHasChoc GiveChoc CountChoc UserHasChange
   GiveChange CountChange UserHasCoin InsertCoin CountCoin)
  UserFinished
  UserHasChoc
  (VALUE_INVARIANT (CHOC_POSSESSIONS UserHasChoc GiveChoc CountChoc
   UserHasChange GiveChange CountChange
   UserHasCoin InsertCoin CountCoin))
  ustate op ip
```

The usability of a vending machine is defined as CHOC_MACHINE_USABLE ustate op ip in terms of a user-centric property. It states that if at any time, t, a user approaches the machine when its coin light is on, then they will at some time, t1, have both chocolate and change: they will not make post-completion errors.

```
⊢def CHOC_MACHINE_USABLE ustate op ip =
  ∀ t. ~ (UserHasChoc ustate t) ∧
       ~ (UserHasChange ustate t) ∧
       (UserHasCoin ustate t) ∧
       (VALUE_INVARIANT (CHOC_POSSESSIONS UserHasChoc GiveChoc
             CountChoc UserHasChange GiveChange CountChange
             UserHasCoin InsertCoin CountCoin) ustate t) ∧
```

```
((CoinLight op t)= BOOL T) ⊃
    ∃ t1. (UserHasChoc ustate t1) ∧
             (UserHasChange ustate t1)
```

The `specification` based usability theorem states that if all the external inputs and outputs are boolean, a user acts rationally and the machine behaves according to its specification, then the usability property will hold.

$\vdash_{thm}$ ∀ ustate op ip.

Boolean ip op ∧

CHOC_MACHINE_USER ustate op ip ∧

CHOC_MACHINE_SPEC ip op ⊃

CHOC_MACHINE_USABLE ustate op ip   (16)

where predicate `Boolean` checks if all the external wires are boolean values. This is because the inputs of a `TABLE` could be either a concrete type variable or a boolean variable. This predicate ensures the external wires have proper values.

The `implementation` based usability theorem can be proved in terms of the above theorems (15) and (16). It (17) states that if the inputs and outputs are boolean, a user acts rationally according to the user model and the machine behaves according to its `implementation`, then the usability property will hold.

$\vdash_{thm}$ ∀ ustate op ip.

Boolean ip op ∧

CHOC_MACHINE_USER ustate op ip ∧

CHOC_MACHINE_IMPL ip op ⊃

CHOC_MACHINE_USABLE ustate op ip   (17)

From this example, we have shown that a system can be verified in two parts. One part of the proof can be done in MDG and the other part of the proof can be done in HOL. The division allows MDG to be used when it would be easier than obtaining the result directly in HOL. We have provided a formal linkage between the MDG system and the HOL system, which allows the MDG verification results to be formally imported into HOL to form the HOL theorem. We do not simply assume that the results proved by MDG are directly equivalent to the result that would have been proved in HOL. The linkage is based on the importing theorems giving a greater degree of trust. We have made use of the importing theorem. In other words, the MDG verification result not only can be imported into HOL to form the HOL theorem, it also can be used as part of a compositional verification in HOL. We have also shown that two different applications (hardware verification and usability verification) suited to two different tools can be combined together.

5   Conclusions

We have described a methodology which provides a formal linkage between a symbolic state enumeration system and a theorem proving system based on a verified symbolic state enumeration system. The methodology involves the following three steps. The first step is to verify correctness of the symbolic state enumeration system in an interactive theorem proving system. Some symbolic state enumeration based systems such as MDG consist of a series of translators and a set of algorithms. We need to prove the translators and algorithms to ensure the correctness of the system. We have not verified the algorithms in this work, but concentrated on the translators. For verifying the translators, we need to define the deep embedding semantics and translation functions. We have to make certain that the semantics of a program is preserved in those of its translated form. This work increases our trust in the results of the symbolic state enumeration system.

The second step of the methodology is to prove importing theorems in the proof system about the results from the symbolic state enumeration system. We need to formalize the correctness results produced by different hardware verification applications using the theorem proving system. The formalization is based on semantics of the low level language (decision graph). We need to prove a theorem in each case that translates them into a form usable in the theorem proving system. In other words, we need to provide the theoretical justification for linking two systems.

The third step is to combine the translator correctness theorems with the importing theorems. This combination allows the verification results from the state enumeration system to be formalized in terms of the semantics of a low level language that the algorithms manipulate, and the result is strictly about, and imported in terms of, the semantics of a high level language (HDL). Therefore, we are able to import the result into the theorem proving system based on the semantics of the input language of a verified symbolic state enumeration system.

We have implemented this methodology on a simplified version of the MDG system and the HOL system, and provided a formal linkage by using the above mentioned steps. We have verified aspects of correctness of a simplified version of the MDG system. We have provided a formal linkage between the MDG system and the HOL system based on importing theorems [22]. Most importantly, we have combined the translator correctness theorems with the importing theorems. This combination allows the low level MDG verification results to be imported into HOL in terms of the semantics of a high level language (MDG-HDL). We have also summarized a general method which is used to prove the **existential theorem** for the specification and implementation of the design [24]. This work makes the linking process easier and removes the burden from the user of the hybrid system. The feasibility of this approach has been demonstrated in a case study: integrating hardware verification and usability verification for a vending machine. However, for importing the MDG verification result into HOL, we have to prove the **existential theorem** for the specification of the design. The behaviour specifications must be in the form of a finite state machine or table description.

In ongoing work we are verifying the translator from core MDG-HDL to MDGs. This has already been done, and integrated with the importing theorems, for a smaller subset of the language (only using boolean sorts). We will also prove importing theorems for other MDG applications, verify more complex examples and use our method in a combined system. In the longer term we will verify the MDG algorithms and so integrate them with the existing work.

Acknowledgments

This work is funded by EPSRC grant GR/M45221, and a studentship from the School of Computing Science, Middlesex University. Travel funding was provided by the British Council, Canada.

References

1. M. D. Aagaard, R. B. Jones, R. Kaivola, and C. J. H. Seger. Formal verification of iterative algorithms in microprocessors. *DAC*, June 2000.
2. R. Bryant. Graph-based algorithms for boolean function manipulation. *IEEE Transactions in Computers*, 35(8):677–691, August 1986.
3. R. E. Bryant. Symbolic boolean manipulation with ordered binary-decision diagrams. *ACM Computer Surveys*, 24(3), September 1992.
4. L. M. Chirica and D. F. Martin. Toward compiler implementation correctness proofs. *ACM Transactions on Programming Languages and Systems*, 8(2):185–214, April 1986.
5. C. T. Chou and D. Peled. Formal verification of a partial-order reduction technique for model checking. In T. Margaria and B. Steffen, editors, *Tools and Algorithms for the Construction and Analysis of Systems*, number 1055 in Lecture Notes in Computer Science, pages 241–257, 1996.
6. F. Corella, Z. Zhou, X. Song, M. Langevin, and E. Cerny. Multiway decision graphs for automated hardware verification. *Formal Methods in System Design*, 10(1):7–46, 1997.
7. J. Crow, S. Owre, J. Rushby, N. Shankar, and M. Srivas. A tutorial introduction to PVS. http://www.dcs.gla.ac.uk/prosper/papers.html, 1999.
8. P. Curzon and A. Blandford. Using a verification system to reason about post-completion errors. In *Participants Proceedings of DSV-IS 2000: 7th International Workshop on Design, Specification and Verification of Interactive Systems, at the 22nd International Conference on Software Engineering*.
9. P. Curzon, S. Tahar, and O. Aït-Mohamed. Verification of the MDG components library in HOL. In Jim Grundy and Malcolm Newey, editors, *Theorem Proving in Higher-Order Logics: Emerging Trends*, pages 31–46. Department of Computer Science, The Australian National University, 1998.
10. L. A. Dennis, G. Collins, M. Norrish, R. Boulton, K. Slind, G. Robinson, M. Gordon, and T. Melham. The PROSPER toolkit. In *The Sixth International Conference on Tools and Algorithms for the Construction and Analysis of Systems*, number 1785 in Lecture Notes in Computer Science. Springer Verlag, 2000.
11. M. J. Gordon, R. Milner, and C. P. Wadsworth. Edinburgh LCF: A mechanised logic of computation. Number 78 in Lecture Notes in Computer Science, 1979.
12. M. J. C. Gordon. Reachability programming in HOL98 using BDDs. In Mark Aagaard and John Harrison, editors, *Theorem Proving in Higher Order Logics*, number 1869 in Lecture Notes in Computing Science, pages 179–196. Springer-Verlag, Aug. 2000.

13. M. J. C. Gordon and T. F. Melham. *Introduction to HOL: A Theorem Proving Environment for Higher-order Logic*. Cambridge University Press, 1993.
14. S. Hazelhurst and C. J. H. Seger. *Symbolic trajectory evaluation*. Springer Verlag. New York, 1997.
15. J. Hurd. Integrating GANDALF and HOL. Technical Report 461, University of Cambridge, Computer Laboratory, April 1999.
16. J. Joyce and C. Seger. Linking BDD-based symbolic evaluation to interactive theorem-proving. In *the 30th Design Automation Conference*, 1993.
17. S. Kort, S. Tahar, and P. Curzon. Hierarchical verification using an MDG-HOL hybrid tool. In T. Margaria and T. Melham, editors, *11th IFIP WG 10.5 Advanced Research Working Conference (CHARME'2001)*, number 2144 in Lecture Notes in Computer Science, pages 244–258, Livingston, Scotland, UK, September 2001. Springer-Verlag.
18. T. F. Melham. *Higher Order Logic and Hardware Verification*. Cambridge Tracts in Theoretical Computer Science 31. Cambridge University Press, 1993.
19. L. C. Paulson. *ML for the Working Programmer*. Cambridge University Press, 1991.
20. S. Rajan, N. Shankar, and M. K. Srivas. An integration of model-checking with automated proof checking. In Pierre Wolper, editor, *Computer-Aided Verification*, number 939 in Lecture Notes in Computer Science, pages 84–97. Springer-Verlag, 1995.
21. H. Xiong. *Providing a Formal Linkage between MDG and HOL Based on a Verified MDG System*. School of Computing Science, Middlesex University, January 2002. Ph.D. thesis.
22. H. Xiong, P. Curzon, and S. Tahar. Importing MDG verification results into HOL. In *Theorem Proving in Higher Order Logics*, number 1690 in Lecture Notes in Computer Science, pages 293–310. Springer-Verlag, September 1999.
23. H. Xiong, P. Curzon, S. Tahar, and A. Blandford. Embedding and verification of an MDG-HDL translator in HOL. In *TPHOLs 2000 Supplemental Proceedings*, Technical Reprot CSE-00-009, pages 237–248, August 2000.
24. H. Xiong, P. Curzon, S. Tahar, and A. Blandford. Proving existential theorems when importing results from MDG to HOL. In Richard J. Boulton and Paul B. Jackson, editors, *TPHOLs 2001 Supplemental Proceedings*, Informatic Research Report EDI-INF-RR-0046, pages 384–399, September 2001.
25. Z. Zhou and N. Boulerice. *MDG Tools (V1.0) User Manual*. University of Montreal, Dept. D'IRO, 1996.

Refinement in Object-Z and CSP

Christie Bolton and Jim Davies

Oxford University Computing Laboratory
Wolfson Building, Parks Road
Oxford OX1 3QD
{christie,jdavies}@comlab.ox.ac.uk

Abstract. In this paper we explore the relationship between refinement
in Object-Z and refinement in CSP. We prove with a simple counter-
example that refinement within Object-Z, established using the standard
simulation rules, does not imply failures-divergences refinement in CSP.
This contradicts accepted results.

Having established that data refinement in Object-Z and failures refinement in CSP are not equivalent we identify alternative refinement orderings that may be used to compare Object-Z classes and CSP processes.
When reasoning about concurrent properties we need the strength of the
failures-divergences refinement ordering and hence identify equivalent
simulation rules for Object-Z. However, when reasoning about sequential
properties it is sufficient to work within the simpler relational semantics
of Object-Z. We discuss an alternative denotational semantics for CSP,
the *singleton failures* semantic model, which has the same information
content as the relational model of Object-Z.

1 Introduction

Refinement is a crucial component in the production of provably reliable software. During the step-wise hierarchical process of program development a software engineer may use refinement to prove formally that each model satisfies the
properties of the previous, more abstract, description of the system. If each successive model is a refinement of the previous model then it follows automatically
that the final implementation will be a refinement of the original specification.

In the specification and development of large, complex systems various models may be built, each model describing a different aspect of the design. Furthermore, for clarity and concision, it may be desirable to use more than one
specification language; some languages are more suitable for describing certain
properties or behaviours than others. In this paper we focus on two formal specification languages: Object-Z [8,19], an object-oriented extension of the state-based
specification language Z [21]; and the process algebra CSP [11,15], a behavioural
specification language. We explore the relationship between established refinement orderings within these languages.

The contribution of the paper is two-fold. Firstly we prove with a simple
counter example that data refinement in Object-Z is not equivalent to failures

M. Butler, L. Petre, and K. Sere (Eds.): IFM 2002, LNCS 2335, pp. 225–244, 2002.

refinement [15] within CSP. Data refinement records availability on an operation-by-operation basis whereas the stable failures refinement ordering of CSP records availability of combinations of events[1]. Secondly we discuss the information content and applicability of each of these refinement orderings. We present an alternative set of simulation rules for Object-Z and show that these are sound and jointly complete with respect to Roscoe's failures-divergences refinement ordering. Furthermore we describe an alternative semantic model for CSP, presented in full in [3]. This newly proposed refinement ordering coincides precisely with data refinement in Object-Z.

We begin the paper with introductions to Object-Z and CSP and then prove that data refinement in Object-Z does not imply failures refinement in CSP. We discuss the information content of each of these refinement orderings, why the implication does not hold, and we show how Object-Z and CSP descriptions may be compared both for concurrent and sequential systems. We conclude the paper with a literature survey.

2   Object-Z

The Z Notation [21] is a formal specification language that is used to model systems, describing the behaviour of the system in terms of its state. A characteristic feature of Z is the schema, a pattern of declaration and constraint. The name of a schema can be used anywhere that a declaration, constraint or set could appear.

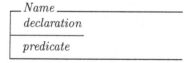

One of the strengths of the schema notation is the level of abstraction and factorisation it allows. The schema calculus allows specification and analysis to be conducted at the level of schemas; we can refer to the collection of identifiers in a particular schema without introducing a named instance of that schema type. If S is a schema, then θS denotes the characteristic binding of S in which each declared component is associated with its current value.

Object-Z is an object-oriented extension of Z adding notions of classes, objects, inheritance and polymorphism, constructs that facilitate specification in an object-oriented style. A class is represented by a named box containing local types and constant definitions along with schemas describing the state, initialisation and all operations on the class. The optional visibility list restricts external access to constants, variables and operations defined within the class. Attributes, operations and visibility lists are inherited from super classes; state schemas are merged and shared operation schemas conjoined.

---

[1] In this paper we consider only divergence-free systems and hence may use the stable-failures and failures-divergences refinement orderings interchangeably.

Class Name [*generic parameters*]

> *visibility list and inherited classes*
> *local type and constant definitions*
> *state schema*
> *initial state schema*
> *operations*

Within Object-Z, schemas modelling operations that might alter the state contain a Δ-list in the declaration. This list identifies all those components of the state that may be changed by the operation. All components of the state that are not included in this list are left unchanged by the operation. Within the predicate, components of the state decorated with a prime describe the state after the operation; undecorated components describe the state before the operation.

Object-Z has a reference-based semantics. Given a class C and given a declaration $c : C$ identifying c as a reference to an object of that class, the predicate $c.INIT$ is true if object c satisfies the constraints described in class C's initialisation schema. Similarly, if OP is an operation defined on class C then $c.OP$ is an operation on the object referenced by c. This operation changes the state of c according to the constraints defined by OP.

Example 1. A simple yo-yo. Given the type *Position* which has three distinct values, *up*, *down* and *spin* we can model a yo-yo in Object-Z as shown. The yo-yo goes down and up repeatedly until it starts spinning. After that no more *Up* or *Down* operations may occur; the system deadlocks.

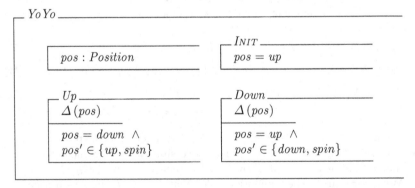

The yo-yo has a single state variable that records its position. It is either in the up position or in the down position or it has started spinning. Initially it is in the state *up*, and whenever it is in this state it may perform the operation *Down* and the state will non-deterministically be set either to *down* or to *spin*. If it is in the state *down* it may perform the operation *Up* and the state will non-deterministically be set either to *up* or to *spin*. If the position of the yo-yo has become the state *spin* then neither operation is enabled and the system deadlocks.

Refinement and simulation. Each Object-Z class effectively defines an abstract data type; it includes schemas describing the state, initialisation and operations on the data type. We can prove that one such data type is refined by another – that is every possible behaviour of the second data type is a possible behaviour of the first – if we can prove that the first *simulates* [12] the second. We do this by identifying a retrieve relation from the state space of one of the data types to the state space of the other and proving that a set of *simulation rules* hold. For clarity and brevity we consider the simulation rules that do not explicitly handle input and output.

There are two distinct sets of simulation rules for Object-Z: the forwards or downwards rules and the backwards or upwards rules. One Object-Z class *downwards* simulates another if some of the non-determinism in the first has been resolved and one Object-Z class *upwards* simulates another if some of the non-determinism has been postponed. Furthermore, simulation is transitive; it may be the case that one Object-Z class neither forwards nor backwards simulates another but we can find a third class that is simulated by the first and simulates the second.

If A and C are Object-Z classes with the same set of operation names X, then given a retrieve relation *Retr* relating the state spaces of the two classes, the forwards/downwards and backwards/upwards simulation rules for Object-Z, as presented in [20,6], are respectively as follows[2]:

$$\forall\, C.STATE \bullet C.INIT \Rightarrow (\exists\, A.STATE \bullet A.INIT \wedge Retr) \qquad (\mathrm{F_r}1)$$

$$\forall\, Op : X;\ A.STATE;\ C.STATE \bullet Retr \Rightarrow (\text{pre } A.OP \Leftrightarrow \text{pre } C.OP) \qquad (\mathrm{F_r}2)$$

$$\forall\, Op : X;\ A.STATE;\ C.STATE;\ C.STATE' \bullet \qquad (\mathrm{F_r}3)$$
$$Retr \wedge C.OP \Rightarrow \exists\, A.STATE' \bullet Retr' \wedge A.OP$$

$$\forall\, A.STATE;\ C.STATE \bullet C.INIT \wedge Retr \Rightarrow A.INIT \qquad (\mathrm{B_r}1)$$

$$\forall\, Op : X;\ C.STATE \bullet \exists\, A.STATE \bullet Retr \wedge (\text{pre } A.OP \Rightarrow \text{pre } C.OP) \qquad (\mathrm{B_r}2)$$

$$\forall\, Op : X;\ A.STATE';\ C.STATE;\ C.STATE' \bullet \qquad (\mathrm{B_r}3)$$
$$Retr' \wedge C.OP \Rightarrow \exists\, A.STATE \bullet Retr \wedge A.OP$$

These rules are sound and jointly complete with respect to the relational semantics given to Object-Z: see [6]. If the above simulation rules hold and class A simulates (and hence is refined by) class C then we write $A \sqsubseteq_{\mathcal{R}} C$.

We observe from the simulation rules that Object-Z employs a *behavioural* or *blocking* semantic model in which operations are blocked outside their preconditions. Within this semantic model an operation may be refined only by strengthening its post-conditions. Unlike the *contract* or *non-blocking* model, the domain of each operation cannot not be extended.

---

[2] The reason for tagging these simulation rules with the subscript r will become apparent in Section 5.

3   CSP

A *process*, as defined in [11], is a pattern of communication. We may use processes to represent components in terms of their communicating behaviour, building up descriptions using the standard operators of the CSP language. In this section we present a subset of the CSP syntax: those operators with which we will be concerned throughout the rest of the paper.

Syntax. Processes are defined in terms of *events*: synchronous, atomic communications between the process and its environment. The atomic process *Stop* denotes deadlock. Parameters may be used to represent aspects of the process state, and may appear in *guards*: we write *bool* & *P* to denote the process that behaves as *P* if Boolean *bool* is true, and can perform no events otherwise. The most basic operator is the *prefix operator*; if *P* is a process and *a* is an event then $a \rightarrow P$ denotes a process that is initially ready to engage in *a*. If this event occurs then subsequent behaviour will be that of *P*.

There are two types of *choice operators* in CSP: one denoting internal choice and the other denoting external choice. An *internal choice* is resolved between the processes involved without reference to the environment whereas an *external choice* may be influenced by the environment and is resolved by the first event to occur. These operators each come in two forms: the binary operator; and the choice over an indexed set of processes. Given processes *P* and *Q* and a set of processes $R(i)$ indexed over some set *I*, the following processes are as described:

$P \sqcap Q$	an internal choice between *P* and *Q*;
$P \square Q$	an external choice between *P* and *Q*;
$\sqcap i : I \bullet R(i)$	an internal choice over the indexed set of processes;
$\square i : I \bullet R(i)$	an external choice over the indexed set of processes.

Descriptions of large systems may be built up from smaller components using parallel composition and hiding. In the combination $P \,_X\|_Y\, Q$, the two processes must synchronise upon every event from the set $X \cap Y$, but may perform all others independently. If *P* is a process and *A* is a set of events then $P \setminus A$ is a process that behaves as *P*, except that both the requirement to synchronise upon and the ability to observe events from the set *A* has been removed.

Processes may be defined by sets of mutually-recursive equations; these equations may be indexed to allow parameterised definitions and may be defined locally using the "let ... within ..." construct.

Denotational semantics. A *trace* records a history of communication between a process and the environment. It is expressed as a sequence of events in which the process has engaged up to a particular point in time with the head of the sequence being the first event that was communicated. Given a process *P* the set $\mathcal{T}[\![P]\!]$ is the set of all possible finite traces of *P*. If *Event* is the (finite) set of all possible events then, defining *Trace* to be all possible sequences of events (*Trace* == seq *Event*), the semantic domain of the traces model is the set

$\mathbb{P}$ *Trace.* Whilst the set of all possible traces of a process carries a great deal of information, it does not record the availability of events. We may preserve this information in *refusal sets*, sets of events from which a process may refuse to communicate anything no matter how long it is offered.

Given a process P the set *refusals*(P) is the set of P's initial refusals. For instance, the process $a \rightarrow P$ may initially refuse any set of events that does not contain the event a; the process $a \rightarrow P \square b \rightarrow Q$ may initially refuse any set of events that contains neither a nor b whereas the process $a \rightarrow P \sqcap b \rightarrow Q$ may initially refuse any set of events that does not contain both a and b. The process *Stop* can refuse any set of events. More formally,

$$
\begin{aligned}
\textit{refusals}(\textit{Stop}) &= \mathbb{P}\,\textit{Event} \\
\textit{refusals}(a \rightarrow P) &= \{\textit{ref} : \textit{Refusal} \mid a \notin \textit{ref}\} \\
\textit{refusals}(a \rightarrow P \square b \rightarrow Q) &= \{\textit{ref} : \textit{Refusal} \mid \{a, b\} \cap \textit{ref} = \emptyset\} \\
\textit{refusals}(a \rightarrow P \sqcap b \rightarrow Q) &= \{\textit{ref} : \textit{Refusal} \mid \{a, b\} \not\subseteq \textit{ref}\}
\end{aligned}
$$

where *Refusal* is the set of all possible sets of events: $\textit{Refusal} == \mathbb{P}\,\textit{Event}$.

A *failure* is a pair in which the first element is the trace of a process and the second is a refusal set of the process after the given trace. Given a process P and the set *Event* of all possible events, the set of failures of P, $\mathcal{F}[\![P]\!]$, is formally defined as follows:

$$
\mathcal{F}[\![P]\!] = \{\textit{tr} : \textit{Trace}; \ \textit{ref} : \textit{Refusal} \mid \textit{tr} \in \mathcal{T}[\![P]\!] \wedge \textit{ref} \in \textit{refusals}\,(P \,/\, \textit{tr})\}
$$

where $P \,/\, \textit{tr}$ is the process that models the behaviour of P after trace $\textit{tr}$ has been completed. The semantic domain of the failures model is then the set $\mathbb{P}(\textit{Trace} \times \textit{Refusal})$.

A *divergence* is the possibility of a process entering into an infinite sequence of internal actions. Divergence is most commonly introduced into a process by hiding.

Refinement. Roscoe introduces three refinement orderings on CSP: the traces model $(\mathcal{T})$; the stable failures model $(\mathcal{F})$; and the failures-divergences model $(\mathcal{N})$. In this paper we are concerned only with divergence-free processes. Hence refinement within the stable failures model is equivalent to refinement within the failures-divergences model.

For any given processes P and Q, event a and sets of events X and Y, the function $\mathcal{F}$ satisfies the laws given below. The process *Stop* will never interact with its environment and can initially refuse any set of events. The process $a \rightarrow P$ can initially refuse any set of events not containing a. If event a does occur then subsequent behaviour is that of P. The failures model can distinguish between internal and external choice. The process $P \square Q$ can initially refuse only those sets of events that could be refused initially by *both* P and Q whereas the process $P \sqcap Q$ can initially refuse all sets of events that could be refused by *either* P or Q. After the first event has occurred their behaviour is equivalent.

$$\mathcal{F}[\![Stop]\!] = \{ref : Refusal \bullet (\langle\rangle, ref)\}$$

$$\mathcal{F}[\![a \rightarrow P]\!] = \{ref : Refusal \mid a \notin ref \bullet (\langle\rangle, ref)\}$$
$$\cup$$
$$\{tr : Trace;\ ref : Refusal \mid (tr, ref) \in \mathcal{F}[\![P]\!] \bullet (\langle a\rangle \frown tr, ref)\}$$

$$\mathcal{F}[\![P \square Q]\!] = (\mathcal{F}[\![P]\!] \cap \mathcal{F}[\![Q]\!]) \cap \{tr : Trace;\ ref : Refusal \mid tr = \langle\rangle\}$$
$$\cup$$
$$(\mathcal{F}[\![P]\!] \cup \mathcal{F}[\![Q]\!]) \cap \{tr : Trace;\ ref : Refusal \mid tr \neq \langle\rangle\}$$

$$\mathcal{F}[\![P \sqcap Q]\!] = \mathcal{F}[\![P]\!] \cup \mathcal{F}[\![Q]\!]$$

$$\mathcal{F}[\![P \ _X\|_Y\ Q]\!] = \{tr : \text{seq } Trace;\ ref, ref_P, ref_Q : Refusal \mid$$
$$\text{ran } tr \subseteq X \cup Y$$
$$\wedge$$
$$ref \cap (X \cup Y) = (ref_P \cap X) \cup (ref_Q \cap Y)$$
$$\wedge$$
$$(tr \restriction X, ref_P) \in \mathcal{F}[\![P]\!] \wedge (tr \restriction Y, ref_Q) \in \mathcal{F}[\![Q]\!] \bullet (tr, ref)\}$$

$$\mathcal{F}[\![P \setminus X]\!] = \{tr : Trace;\ ref : Refusal \mid$$
$$(tr, X \cup ref) \in \mathcal{F}[\![P]\!] \bullet (tr \setminus X, ref)\}$$

The refinement ordering induced by the stable failures model is based upon reverse containment; one process is failures-refined by another if every failure of the second is also a failure of the first. Furthermore, we define two processes to be equivalent if each refines the other. Given processes P and Q we write

$$P \sqsubseteq_\mathcal{F} Q \ \Leftrightarrow\ \mathcal{F}[\![Q]\!] \subseteq \mathcal{F}[\![P]\!]$$

$$P \equiv_\mathcal{F} Q \ \Leftrightarrow\ P \sqsubseteq_\mathcal{F} Q \wedge Q \sqsubseteq_\mathcal{F} P$$

4   Data Refinement in Object-Z Is Not Equivalent to Failures Refinement in CSP

In this section we explore the relationship between data refinement in Object-Z and stable failures refinement in CSP. We consider only Object-Z classes with no internal operations, thereby avoiding the possibility of divergence: for divergence-free processes Roscoe's stable failures refinement ordering is equivalent to his failures-divergences refinement ordering [15]. Furthermore for clarity we will prove that data refinement is not equivalent to failures refinement for Object-Z classes whose operations have no inputs and outputs. Obviously the result extends to those classes with operations requiring inputs and giving outputs.

The semantic link between Object-Z and CSP is obtained by identifying each operation in the Object-Z class with an event in the alphabet of the corresponding CSP process: for more details see [17]. The CSP process is then parametrised by the state variables of the Object-Z class and the availability of each event is determined by the pre-conditions of the corresponding operation. We illustrate this correspondence below.

Example 2. In Example 1 we gave an Object-Z description of a yo-yo. The yo-yo has a single state variable *pos* that takes three values: *up*, *down* and *spin*; it is initially in the state *up*. The yo-yo has two operations: *Up* and *Down*. The precondition of *Up* is that *pos* is equal to *down* and the precondition of *Down* is that *pos* is equal to *up*. The postcondition of *Up* is that *pos* is equal to *up* or *spin* and the postcondition of *Down* is that *pos* is equal to *down* or *spin*. We see this reflected in the corresponding process $YoYo_P$.

$$YoYo_P = \text{let}$$
$$Y(pos) = (pos == up) \ \& \ Down \ \rightarrow \ (Y(down) \sqcap Y(spin))$$
$$\square$$
$$(pos == down) \ \& \ Up \ \rightarrow \ (Y(up) \sqcap Y(spin))$$
$$\square$$
$$(pos == spin) \ \& \ Stop$$
$$\text{within}$$
$$Y(up)$$

Having shown in Example 2 above how the CSP process corresponding to an Object-Z class may be constructed, we now prove with a simple counter example that data refinement does not imply stable failures refinement. We identify two Object-Z classes and prove that the first simulates the second but that the process corresponding to the first is not refined by the process corresponding to the second.

Given $State == 0 \ldots 4$, let Object-Z classes P and Q be defined as follows.

```
┌─ P ──────────────────────────────────────────────────────────

    ┌─────────────────────┐      ┌─ INIT ──────────────┐
    │  s : State          │      │  s ∈ {1,2}          │
    └─────────────────────┘      └─────────────────────┘

    ┌─ a ─────────────────┐      ┌─ b ─────────────────┐
    │  Δ(s)               │      │  Δ(s)               │
    ├─────────────────────┤      ├─────────────────────┤
    │  s = 1 ∧ s′ = 0     │      │  s ∈ {2,3} ∧ s′ = 0 │
    └─────────────────────┘      └─────────────────────┘

    ┌─ c ─────────────────┐
    │  Δ(s)               │
    ├─────────────────────┤
    │  s ∈ {2,4} ∧ s′ = 0 │
    └─────────────────────┘

└──────────────────────────────────────────────────────────────
```

$$
\begin{array}{|l}
\hline Q \\
\hline
\quad
\begin{array}{|l} \hline\ s : State \\ \hline \end{array}
\qquad
\begin{array}{|l} \hline\ INIT \\ \hline\ s \in \{1,3,4\} \\ \hline \end{array}
\\[2em]
\quad
\begin{array}{|l} \hline\ a \\ \hline\ \Delta\,(s) \\ \hline\ s = 1 \ \wedge\ s' = 0 \\ \hline \end{array}
\qquad
\begin{array}{|l} \hline\ b \\ \hline\ \Delta\,(s) \\ \hline\ s \in \{2,3\} \ \wedge\ s' = 0 \\ \hline \end{array}
\\[2em]
\quad
\begin{array}{|l} \hline\ c \\ \hline\ \Delta\,(s) \\ \hline\ s \in \{2,4\} \ \wedge\ s' = 0 \\ \hline \end{array}
\\[1em]
\hline
\end{array}
$$

Both classes share the operations a, b and c and have the same state space. The difference lies in their initial states. An object of class P can initially be in states 1 or 2 whereas an object of class Q can initially be in states 1, 3 or 4.

Lemma 1. *Class P is refined by class Q where P and Q are as defined above.*

Proof. Defining retrieve relation T as follows:

$$
\begin{array}{|l}
\hline T \\
\hline
P.\text{STATE} \\
Q.\text{STATE} \\
\hline
(\,Q.s = 0 \wedge P.s = 0\,) \ \vee \\
(\,Q.s = 1 \wedge P.s = 1\,) \ \vee \\
(\,Q.s = 2 \wedge P.s = 2\,) \ \vee \\
(\,Q.s = 3 \wedge (\,P.s = 1 \vee P.s = 2\,)) \ \vee \\
(\,Q.s = 4 \wedge (\,P.s = 1 \vee P.s = 2\,)) \\
\hline
\end{array}
$$

we prove that the upwards simulation rules presented in Section 2 hold and hence that P is refined by Q. Rule $B_r 1$ reduces to

$$\forall\, p, q : State \ \bullet$$
$$((\,q = 1 \wedge p = 1\,) \ \vee ((\,q = 3 \vee q = 4\,) \wedge (\,p = 1 \vee p = 2\,))) \ \Rightarrow$$
$$(\,p = 1 \vee p = 2\,)$$

which is equivalent to true. In the case of operation a, rule $B_r 2$ reduces to

$$\forall\, q : State \ \bullet$$
$$\exists\, p : State \ \bullet$$
$$((\,q = 0 \wedge p = 0\,) \ \vee (\,q = 1 \wedge p = 1\,) \ \vee (\,q = 2 \wedge p = 2\,) \ \vee$$
$$(\,q = 3 \wedge (\,p = 1 \vee p = 2\,)) \ \vee (\,q = 4 \wedge (\,p = 1 \vee p = 2\,)))$$
$$\wedge$$
$$p = 1 \Rightarrow q = 1$$

which in turn reduces to

$$\forall\, q : State \;\bullet\; (\,(\,q = 0 \;\Rightarrow\; \exists\, p : State \bullet p = 0\,) \;\wedge$$
$$(\,q = 1 \;\Rightarrow\; \exists\, p : State \bullet p = 1\,) \;\wedge$$
$$(\,q = 2 \;\Rightarrow\; \exists\, p : State \bullet p = 2\,) \;\wedge$$
$$(\,q = 3 \;\Rightarrow\; \exists\, p : State \bullet p = 2\,) \;\wedge$$
$$(\,q = 4 \;\Rightarrow\; \exists\, p : State \bullet p = 2\,)\,)$$

which is equivalent to true. In the case of operation b, rule $B_r\,2$ reduces to

$$\forall\, q : State \;\bullet$$
$$\exists\, p : State \;\bullet$$
$$(\,(q = 0 \wedge p = 0) \;\vee\; (q = 1 \wedge p = 1) \;\vee\; (q = 2 \wedge p = 2) \;\vee$$
$$(q = 3 \wedge (p = 1 \vee p = 2)) \;\vee\; (q = 4 \wedge (p = 1 \vee p = 2)))$$
$$\wedge$$
$$(p = 2 \vee p = 3) \;\Rightarrow\; (q = 2 \vee q = 3)$$

which reduces to

$$\forall\, q : State \;\bullet\; (\,(\,q = 0 \;\Rightarrow\; \exists\, p : State \bullet p = 0\,) \;\wedge$$
$$(\,q = 1 \;\Rightarrow\; \exists\, p : State \bullet p = 1\,) \;\wedge$$
$$(\,q = 2 \;\Rightarrow\; \exists\, p : State \bullet p = 2\,) \;\wedge$$
$$(\,q = 3 \;\Rightarrow\; \exists\, p : State \bullet p = 1 \vee p = 2\,) \;\wedge$$
$$(\,q = 4 \;\Rightarrow\; \exists\, p : State \bullet p = 1\,)\,)$$

which is equivalent to true. Furthermore, by symmetry, we see that rule $B_r\,2$ must also be equivalent to true in the case of operation c.

We have shown that rule $B_r\,1$ holds and that rule $B_r\,2$ holds for each of the operations on the data types. Next we consider the third rule. In the case of operation a rule $B_r\,3$ reduces to

$$\forall\, p', q, q' : State \;\bullet$$
$$(\,q = 1 \wedge q' = 0 \wedge p' = 0\,) \;\Rightarrow$$
$$\exists\, p : State \;\bullet\; p = 1 \wedge p' = 0 \wedge (\,q = 1 \vee q = 3 \vee q = 4\,)$$

which is equivalent to true. In the case of operation b, this rule reduces to

$$\forall\, p', q, q' : State \;\bullet$$
$$(\,q = 2 \vee q = 3\,) \wedge q' = 0 \wedge p' = 0$$
$$\Rightarrow$$
$$\exists\, p : State \bullet p = 2 \wedge p' = 0 \wedge (\,q = 2 \vee q = 3 \vee q = 4\,)$$
$$\vee$$
$$p = 3 \wedge p' = 0 \wedge false$$

which is also equivalent to true. Once again we call upon symmetry to prove that rule $B_r\,3$ is equivalent to true in the case of operation c.

Given Object-Z classes P and Q, we have identified a retrieve relation T such that the upwards simulation rules hold. We have proved that P simulates, and hence is refined by, Q.

Lemma 2. *The process corresponding to P is not refined within the stable failures model by the process corresponding to Q where Object-Z classes P and Q are as defined above.*

Proof. The processes P_P and Q_P corresponding respectively to Object-Z classes P and Q are given below.

$P_P = $ let

$$Proc(s) = (s == 0) \ \& \ Stop$$
$$\square$$
$$(s == 1) \ \& \ a \rightarrow Proc(0)$$
$$\square$$
$$(s == 2) \ \& \ b \rightarrow Proc(0) \ \square \ c \rightarrow Proc(0)$$
$$\square$$
$$(s == 3) \ \& \ b \rightarrow Proc(0)$$
$$\square$$
$$(s == 4) \ \& \ c \rightarrow Proc(0)$$

within
$$\sqcap s : \{1, 2\} \bullet Proc(s)$$

$Q_P = $ let

$$Proc(s) = (s == 0) \ \& \ Stop$$
$$\square$$
$$(s == 1) \ \& \ a \rightarrow Proc(0)$$
$$\square$$
$$(s == 2) \ \& \ b \rightarrow Proc(0) \ \square \ c \rightarrow Proc(0)$$
$$\square$$
$$(s == 3) \ \& \ b \rightarrow Proc(0)$$
$$\square$$
$$(s == 4) \ \& \ c \rightarrow Proc(0)$$

within
$$\sqcap s : \{1, 3, 4\} \bullet Proc(s)$$

Observe that process P_P may initially, non-deterministically, be in state 1 in which case event a may occur or may be in state 2 in which case we may choose between events b and c. Observe also that process Q_P may initially, non-deterministically, be in state 1 in which case event a may occur or may be in state 3 in which case event b may occur or may be in state 4 in which case event c may occur. Furthermore, after any event has occurred both processes will be in state 0 and hence behave as *Stop*.

It follows from these observations that processes P_P and Q_P are respectively equivalent to *ProcP* and *ProcQ* as defined below:

$$ProcP = (a \rightarrow Stop) \ \sqcap \ ((b \rightarrow Stop) \ \square \ (c \rightarrow Stop))$$
$$ProcQ = (a \rightarrow Stop) \ \sqcap \ (b \rightarrow Stop) \ \sqcap \ (c \rightarrow Stop)$$

Both *ProcP* and *ProcQ* can initially individually refuse the events a, b and c. The difference is that process *ProcP* cannot initially refuse the *combinations* of both a and b or of both a and c whereas the process $ProcQ$ can refuse both of these combinations. If $Event == \{a, b, c\}$ then the failures of these processes are as follows:

$$\mathcal{F}[\![\,ProcP\,]\!] \;=\; \{(\langle\rangle, \emptyset), (\langle\rangle, \{a\}), (\langle\rangle, \{b\}), (\langle\rangle, \{c\}), (\langle\rangle, \{b, c\})\}$$
$$\cup$$
$$\{e : Event;\; ref : Refusal \bullet (\langle e\rangle, ref)\}$$

$$\mathcal{F}[\![\,ProcQ\,]\!] \;=\; \{(\langle\rangle, \emptyset), (\langle\rangle, \{a\}), (\langle\rangle, \{b\}), (\langle\rangle, \{c\}), (\langle\rangle, \{b, c\})\}$$
$$\cup$$
$$\{(\langle\rangle, \{a, c\}), (\langle\rangle, \{a, b, \})\}$$
$$\cup$$
$$\{e : Event;\; ref : Refusal \bullet (\langle e\rangle, ref)\}$$

Observe that $\mathcal{F}[\![\,ProcQ\,]\!]$ is the disjoint union of $\mathcal{F}[\![\,ProcP\,]\!]$ and the set $\{(\langle\rangle, \{a, c\}), (\langle\rangle, \{a, b, \})\}$. Since the failures set of $ProcQ$ is not a subset of the failures set of $ProcP$ it follows that $ProcP$ is not refined by $ProcQ$. Hence, since $ProcP$ is equivalent to P_P and $ProcQ$ is equivalent to Q_P, it follows that P_P is not refined by Q_P.

$$\mathcal{F}[\![\,ProcQ\,]\!] \not\subseteq \mathcal{F}[\![\,ProcP\,]\!] \;\Rightarrow\; P_P \not\sqsubseteq_{\mathcal{F}} Q_P$$

Theorem 1. *Data refinement is not equivalent to stable failures refinement.*

Proof. We have identified two Object-Z classes P and Q. In Lemma 1 we proved that P is data refined by Q and in Lemma 2 we proved that the process corresponding to P is not refined within the stable failures semantic model by the process corresponding to Q. From this it follows that data refinement does not imply stable failures refinement: data refinement and stable failures refinement are not equivalent.

In Theorem 1 above we proved that data refinement within Object-Z is not equivalent to failures refinement within CSP. This is because the stable failures refinement ordering records which *combinations* of events might be refused whereas data refinement in Object-Z records refusal information only on an operation-by-operation basis.

If we wish to compare data types and processes we must adopt an alternative refinement ordering either for Object-Z or for CSP. Our choice will be determined by the nature of the system or property about which we are reasoning. If the system or property is sequential then it is sufficient to adopt the simpler relational model; we retain the simulation rules presented in Section 2 and adopt an alternative semantic model for CSP. We discuss this approach further in Section 6. If, on the other hand, we wish to reason about concurrency we must adopt a failures-divergences model. In this case we retain the stable failures semantic model for CSP (or equivalently the failures-diverges model since we are concerned only with divergence-free processes) and adopt a matching semantic model for Object-Z. We discuss this approach further in Section 5 below.

5 Reasoning about General Concurrent Properties

Josephs [13] presents a set of simulation rules for state transition systems that are both sound and jointly complete with respect to the failures-divergences semantic model in CSP. It had been thought [20,4,9,6] that these rules were equivalent to those presented in Section 2. This is not however the case as we have proved in Theorem 1. Josephs' simulation rules record the availability of combinations of operations whereas the simulation rules presented in Section 2 record availability on an operation-by-operation basis. The simulation rules of Josephs are correctly translated below. We tag them with the label c (denoting concurrent) to distinguish between this set of simulation rules and those presented in Section 2, derived from the relational semantics of Object-Z and tagged with the label r. If A and C are Object-Z classes with the same set of operation names X, then given a retrieve relation $Retr$ relating the state spaces of the two classes, the concurrent versions of the forwards/downwards and backwards/upwards simulation rules are respectively as follows.

$$\forall\, C.STATE \bullet C.INIT \Rightarrow (\exists\, A.STATE \bullet A.INIT \wedge Retr) \qquad (\text{F}_c\,1)$$

$$\forall\, Op : X;\; A.STATE;\; C.STATE \bullet Retr \Rightarrow (\text{pre } A.Op \Leftrightarrow \text{pre } C.Op) \qquad (\text{F}_c\,2)$$

$$\forall\, Op : X;\; A.STATE;\; C.STATE;\; C.STATE' \bullet \qquad (\text{F}_c\,3)$$
$$Retr \wedge C.Op \Rightarrow \exists\, A.STATE' \bullet Retr' \wedge A.Op$$

$$\forall\, A.STATE;\; C.STATE \bullet C.INIT \wedge Retr \Rightarrow A.INIT \qquad (\text{B}_c\,1)$$

$$\forall\, C.STATE \bullet \exists\, A.STATE \bullet \qquad (\text{B}_c\,2)$$
$$\forall\, Op : X \bullet Retr \wedge (\text{pre } A.Op \Rightarrow \text{pre } C.Op)$$

$$\forall\, Op : X;\; A.STATE';\; C.STATE;\; C.STATE' \bullet \qquad (\text{B}_c\,3)$$
$$Retr' \wedge C.Op \Rightarrow \exists\, A.STATE \bullet Retr \wedge A.Op$$

If the above simulation rules hold and class A simulates (and hence is refined by) class C then we write $A \sqsubseteq_C C$.

Theorem 2. *The concurrent simulation rules presented above are sound and jointly complete with respect to the failures-divergences semantic model of CSP.*

Proof. This follows directly from Josephs' corresponding result.

These rules are very similar to those for establishing the refinement of sequential systems. Indeed five out of the six rules are identical. The only rule that is different is the second backwards simulation rule, concerning the applicability of operations. The difference lies in the scope of the quantifications. In rule B_r2 we have the universal quantification of all operations over the existential quantification of all abstract states ($\forall\, Op : X \bullet \exists\, A.STATE \bullet \ldots$) whereas in rule B_c2 we have a stronger predicate, the existential quantification of all abstract states over the universal quantification of all operations ($\exists\, A.STATE \bullet \forall\, Op : X \bullet \ldots$).

The former provides information about the availability of individual operations but the latter provides information about the availability of combinations of operations.

In Theorem 1 we identified two Object-Z classes P and Q and their corresponding processes $ProcP$ and $ProcQ$. We showed that Q is a data refinement of P using the sequential simulation rules presented in Section 2 but that $ProcQ$ is not a stable failures refinement of $ProcP$. We have now presented a set of concurrent simulation rules that are sound and complete with respect to the failures-divergences refinement ordering of CSP. In Observation 1 below we confirm that, using the retrieve relation identified in Lemma 1, and adopting these concurrent rules, P does not simulate Q [3].

Observation 1 *Simulation rule B_c2 does not hold for classes P and Q and retrieve relation T as defined in Lemma 1.*

Proof. Given P, Q and T, simulation rule B_c2 reduces to

$$\forall\, q : State \, \bullet$$
$$\exists\, p : State \, \bullet$$
$$\quad ((q = 0 \wedge p = 0) \vee (q = 1 \wedge p = 1) \vee (q = 2 \wedge p = 2) \vee$$
$$\quad (q = 3 \wedge (p = 1 \vee p = 2)) \vee (q = 4 \wedge (p = 1 \vee p = 2)))$$
$$\wedge$$
$$\quad ((p = 1 \Rightarrow q = 1) \wedge$$
$$\quad (p \in \{2,3\} \Rightarrow q \in \{2,3\}) \wedge (p \in \{2,4\} \Rightarrow q \in \{2,4\}))$$

which in turn reduces to

$$\forall\, q : State \, \bullet \, ((\, q = 0 \, \Rightarrow \, \exists\, p : State \bullet p = 0\,) \, \wedge$$
$$(\, q = 1 \, \Rightarrow \, \exists\, p : State \bullet p = 1\,) \, \wedge$$
$$(\, q = 2 \, \Rightarrow \, \exists\, p : State \bullet p = 2\,) \, \wedge$$
$$(\, q = 3 \, \Rightarrow \, \exists\, p : State \bullet \text{false}\,) \, \wedge$$
$$(\, q = 4 \, \Rightarrow \, \exists\, p : State \bullet \text{false}\,))$$

which is equivalent to false.

It is interesting to note that the failures-divergences refinement ordering for Object-Z is *defined* by the above sets of simulation rules whereas the simulation rules presented in Section 2 are *derived* to reflect the relational, behavioural (blocking) semantic model that may be given to Object-Z.

6   Reasoning about Sequential Properties

We observed at the end of Section 4 that if the system or property about which we are reasoning is inherently a sequential one, and hence it can be characterised in

---

[3] Note that Observation 1 does not *prove* that P does not simulate Q, rather it confirms that the second backwards simulation rule no longer holds. We could present a proof that no retrieve relation exists but this result does not merit the space it would take.

terms of event-by-event refusal, then it is sufficient to adopt the simpler relational model. We may retain the simulation rules presented in Section 2 but must define a corresponding semantic model for CSP. This semantic model must record *some* refusal information – within the relational semantics we record the fact that an operation might be refused after a given trace – but this refusal information must only be on an event-by-event basis. We note that it is significantly easier to identify the appropriate retrieve relation and establish simulation for the relational model than for the concurrent model.

The singleton failures model. The semantic model that we are looking for is essentially[4] a projection of the stable failures model, recording only those trace-refusal pairs in which the cardinality of the refusal set is at most one. We call this model the *singleton failures semantic model* and have formally and fully defined it in [3]. The semantics presented here is a simplification tailored to the needs of this paper. Given $Refusal_1$, the subset of $Refusal$ containing sets of events of cardinality at most one

$$Refusal_1 == \emptyset \cup \{e : Event \bullet \{e\}\}$$

the semantic function $\mathcal{S}$ that defines the singleton failures model is as follows:

$$\mathcal{S}\,[\![Stop]\!] = \{ref : Refusal_1 \bullet (\langle\rangle, ref)\}$$

$$\mathcal{S}\,[\![a \rightarrow P]\!] = \{ref : Refusal_1 \mid ref \neq \{a\} \bullet (\langle\rangle, ref)\}$$
$$\cup$$
$$\{tr : Trace;\ ref : Refusal_1 \mid (tr, ref) \in \mathcal{S}\,[\![P]\!] \bullet (\langle a \rangle \frown tr, ref)\}$$

$$\mathcal{S}\,[\![P \,\square\, Q]\!] = \{ref : Refusal_1 \mid (\langle\rangle, ref) \in \mathcal{S}\,[\![P]\!] \cap \mathcal{S}\,[\![Q]\!] \bullet (\langle\rangle, ref)\}$$
$$\cup$$
$$\{tr : Trace;\ ref : Refusal_1 \mid (tr, ref) \in \mathcal{S}\,[\![P]\!] \cup \mathcal{S}\,[\![Q]\!] \wedge tr \neq \langle\rangle\}$$

$$\mathcal{S}\,[\![P \sqcap Q]\!] = \mathcal{S}\,[\![P]\!] \cup \mathcal{S}\,[\![Q]\!]$$

$$\mathcal{S}\,[\![P_X \,\|\,_Y Q]\!] = \{tr : \text{seq } Trace;\ ref, ref_P, ref_Q : Refusal_1 \mid$$
$$\text{ran } tr \subseteq X \cup Y$$
$$\wedge$$
$$ref \cap (X \cup Y) = (ref_P \cap X) \cup (ref_Q \cap Y)$$
$$\wedge$$
$$(tr \upharpoonright X, ref_P) \in \mathcal{S}\,[\![P]\!] \wedge (tr \upharpoonright Y, ref_Q) \in \mathcal{S}\,[\![Q]\!]$$
$$\bullet (tr, ref)\}$$

The process *Stop* will never interact with its environment and can initially refuse any event. The process $a \rightarrow P$ can initially refuse any event other than a. If event a does occur then subsequent behaviour is that of P. The process $P \,\square\, Q$ can initially refuse only those events that could be refused by both components

---

[4] The exception is the hiding operator.

whereas the process $P \sqcap Q$ can initially refuse those that could be refused by either component. After the first event has occurred their behaviour is equivalent. In the parallel combination P $_X\|_Y$ Q, process P can influence the occurrence (or refusal) only of those events in set X. Similarly process Q can influence the occurrence (or refusal) only of those events in set Y. Furthermore, any possible sequence of interaction restricted to those events in the set X must be a possible trace of P and any possible sequence of interaction restricted to those events in the set Y must be a possible trace of Q.

We have excluded the hiding operator from our definitions above for two reasons. Firstly, in this paper we are working only in the context of Object-Z classes with no internal operations, and so do not require a hiding operator. And secondly, the hiding operator is not distributive with respect to the internal choice operator within the singleton failures model and this causes problems. The interested reader may discover more about the whole semantic model and the properties that *are* preserved by hiding in [3]. For the time being it is sufficient to observe that all the properties within the stable failures semantic model that concern only the operators given above are preserved within the singleton failures semantic model.

Theorem 3. *Any algebraic property in the failures model that involves only the process Stop and the operators* $\rightarrow$, $\sqcap$, $\square$ *and* $_X\|_Y$ *will be preserved within the singleton failures semantic model.*

Proof. For each such algebraic property, this result follows directly from the fact that for each of these operators $\mathcal{S}$ is a simple projection of $\mathcal{F}$. If P is a process constructed using only the operators $Stop$, $\rightarrow$, $\sqcap$, $\square$, and $_X\|_Y$ then its semantics under $\mathcal{S}$ will be a simple projection of its semantics under $\mathcal{F}$:

$$\mathcal{S}[\![P]\!] \;=\; \mathcal{F}[\![P]\!] \cap (Trace \times Refusal_1).$$

Refinement within the singleton failures model, as with both the traces and the stable failures model, is based upon reverse containment. Given two processes P and Q, expressible in terms of the process $Stop$ and the operators $\rightarrow$, $\sqcap$, $\square$ and $_X\|_Y$, P is refined by Q within this model if every singleton failure of Q is also a singleton failure of P. Once more we say that two processes are equivalent if each refines the other.

$$P \sqsubseteq_S Q \;\Leftrightarrow\; \mathcal{S}[\![Q]\!] \subseteq \mathcal{S}[\![P]\!]$$

$$P \equiv_S Q \;\Leftrightarrow\; (P \sqsubseteq_S Q \wedge Q \sqsubseteq_S P)$$

Theorem 4. *Singleton failures refinement is equivalent to data refinement of Object-Z classes as described in Section 2. Given Object-Z classes A and C with no internal operations, and their corresponding CSP processes ProcA and ProcC,*

$$A \sqsubseteq_{\mathcal{R}} C \;\Leftrightarrow\; ProcA \sqsubseteq_S ProcC$$

Proof. The proof for this result is presented in [3].

In Observation 2 below we confirm that for classes P and Q and their corresponding processes *ProcP* and *ProcQ* as described in Theorem 1,

$$ProcP = (\, a \rightarrow Stop \,) \sqcap ((\, b \rightarrow Stop \,) \ \Box \ (\, c \rightarrow Stop \,))$$
$$ProcQ = (\, a \rightarrow Stop \,) \sqcap (\, b \rightarrow Stop \,) \sqcap (\, c \rightarrow Stop \,)$$

the singleton failures refinement ordering is consistent with the sequential simulation rules presented in Section 2.

Observation 2 *Process ProcP is refined by process ProcQ within the singleton failures semantic model.*

Proof. If $Event == \{a, b, c\}$ then the singleton failures of processes *ProcP* and *ProcQ* are as follows:

$$\mathcal{S} [\![\, ProcP \,]\!] \ = \ \{(\, \langle \rangle \,, \emptyset), (\, \langle \rangle \,, \{a\}), (\, \langle \rangle \,, \{b\}), (\, \langle \rangle \,, \{c\})\}$$
$$\cup$$
$$\{e : Event; \ ref : Refusal_1 \bullet (\langle e \rangle, ref)\}$$

$$\mathcal{S} [\![\, ProcQ \,]\!] \ = \ \{(\, \langle \rangle \,, \emptyset), (\, \langle \rangle \,, \{a\}), (\, \langle \rangle \,, \{b\}), (\, \langle \rangle \,, \{c\})\}$$
$$\cup$$
$$\{e : Event; \ ref : Refusal_1 \bullet (\langle e \rangle, ref)\}$$

Since the singleton failures of *ProcQ* is a subset of the singleton failures of *ProcP* it follows that *ProcP* is refined by *ProcQ* within the singleton failures model. This is consistent with the fact that Q is a data refinement of P.

7   Discussion

The motivation behind the work presented in this paper is to provide a means for comparing state-based and behavioural descriptions of systems. This is becoming increasingly important as semi-formal specification languages such as UML [16], languages that model all aspects of the system from different perspectives, are increasingly being adopted by companies and individuals within the industry. But combining state-based and behavioural formalisms is by no means a new area of research: these issues have been addressed for well over a decade.

In [13] Josephs adopts a state-based approach to the refinement and specification of non-divergent CSP processes; Morgan [14] defines a correspondence between action systems [1] and CSP by expressing the traces, failures and divergences of CSP processes as weakest pre-condition formulae [7]; Butler [5] addresses the issue of unbounded nondeterminism and extends Morgan's correspondence [14] to the infinite traces model; and He [10], like Josephs, expresses CSP processes as labelled transition systems and presents sets of sound and complete simulation rules. In each case refinement within the state-based formalism is shown to be equivalent either to the stable failures refinement or the failures-divergences refinement of CSP.

We showed in Section 5 that refinement within a state-transition system may be equivalent to the failures-divergences refinement ordering only if we can reason about the availability of combinations of operations. Josephs [13] achieves this using the *next* operator. For state transition system P and state σ, the set $next_P(\sigma)$ contains all those events in which the state transition system P is able to engage from state σ. Given retrieve relation U, his simulation rule that corresponds to the critical rule $B_c 2$ for Object-Z is as follows:

$$\forall \sigma_C \in S_C \ . \ \exists \sigma_A \in S_A \ . \ \sigma_C U \sigma_A \ \wedge \ next_{P_A}(\sigma_A) \subseteq next_{P_C}(\sigma_C).$$

This rules requires that every concrete state (σ_C) must correspond to an abstract state (σ_A) that lies outside the domain of *every* transition that the more concrete state lies outside the domain of. He [10] achieves the same effect by referring to the domains of the operations. His simulation rules are defined in terms of concrete and abstract state transition systems P and Q both with operations A. Given retrieve relation u the relevant, and equivalent, upwards simulation rule is as follows:

$$\forall s \in P\Sigma \ . \ \exists s' \in Q\Sigma \ . \ (s \, u \, s' \wedge \ \forall a \in A \, . \, (s' \in \mathrm{dom} \, Q_a \Rightarrow s \in \mathrm{dom} \, P_a) \,).$$

This rule states that every concrete state (s) must correspond to an abstract state (s') that does not lie in the domain of any operation on the more abstract transition system if the first state (s) lies outside the domain of the operation on the more concrete transition system.

Similarly in [22], Woodcock and Morgan's corresponding backwards simulation rules for action systems give information about combinations of operations. Given retrieve relation I, for all sets of action names *ref*, the relevant backwards simulation rule is as follows:

$$\neg \, (gd_C \ ref) \ \Rightarrow \ \exists a \bullet I \wedge \neg \, (gd_A \ ref).$$

where, for action system P with associated set of actions A, $gd_P \, X$ denotes the disjunction of the guards of the actions drawn from set $X \subseteq A$. The above rule states that any concrete state that lies outside the preconditions of a given *set* of operations must correspond to an abstract state that also lies outside the preconditions of the given set of operations.

Combining data types. In the specification and development of large systems it will often be desirable to reason at various levels of abstraction. For instance the initial description of a system may involve just a few components and their interactions, but as we approach an implementation-level description of the system it may be convenient to break these components down into subcomponents and indeed to break the subcomponents down into subsubcomponents. Having broken down components into their subcomponents it is vital that we are able to verify that these descriptions are consistent: that the combined behaviour of a collection of subcomponents satisfies the description of the behaviour of the component that they combine to form.

However, care must be taken when comparing Object-Z and CSP models of such systems. Since the singleton failures semantics is not a congruence, hiding may cause problems when comparing models of sequential systems. Refinement is preserved by hiding only if the hiding operator is applied at the outermost level. Furthermore difficulties arising from the non-deterministic choice of outputs may arise when putting in parallel systems (both concurrent and sequential) that handle communications explicitly. These issues are discussed further in [3] and [2].

Summary. There are two means of establishing refinement within Object-Z: by considering either the histories of the classes involved, or by showing that one class simulates the other. Smith [17,18] shows that refinement established by considering the histories is equivalent to failures-divergences refinement within CSP. In Section 4 we proved that refinement established using the standard simulation rules is *not* equivalent to failures-divergences refinement. We cannot compare Object-Z classes using the standard Object-Z simulation rules with CSP processes in the context of either the stable failures or failures-divergences refinement orderings. In order to compare Object-Z classes and CSP processes we must adopt a either a different refinement ordering for our CSP processes or a different set of simulation rules for our Object-Z classes.

If we wish to reason about concurrent properties we must retain the stable failures (or failures-divergences) model for CSP processes and must use an equivalent set of simulation rules for our Object-Z classes. We presented such a set of simulations rules in Section 5. Alternatively, if we wish to reason about sequential properties, even of a concurrent system, we may use the simpler simulation rules presented in Section 2 but must use an equivalent refinement ordering for CSP. In Section 6 we presented such a refinement ordering, the *singleton failures* refinement.

Acknowledgements

We would like to thank John Derrick, Michael Goldsmith, Gavin Lowe and Graeme Smith for their helpful and insightful comments.

References

1. R. J. R. Back and R. Kurki-Suonio. Decentralisation of process nets with centralised control. In *In 2nd ACM SIGACT-SIGOPS Symposium on Principles of Distributed Computing*, 1983.
2. C. Bolton. *On the refinement of state-based and event-based models.* PhD thesis, University of Oxford, January 2002. Submitted for examination.
3. C. Bolton and J. Davies. A singleton failures semantics for communicating sequential processes, 2001. Submitted to Formal Aspects of Computing.
4. C. Bolton, J. Davies, and J. Woodcock. On the refinement and simulation of data types and processes. In K. Araki, A. Galloway, and K. Taguchi, editors, *Proceedings of Integrated Formal Methods (IFM'99)*. Springer, 1999.

5. M. J. Butler. *A CSP approach to action systems*. PhD thesis, University of Oxford, 1992.
6. J. Derrick and E. Boiten. *Refinement in Z and Object-Z*. Springer, 2001.
7. E. W. Dijkstra. *A discipline of Programming*. Prentice Hall, 1976.
8. R. Duke, G. Rose, and G. Smith. Object-Z: a specification language advocated for the description of standards. *Computer Standards and Interfaces*, 17, 1995.
9. C. Fischer. *Combination and implementation of processes and data: from CSP-OZ to Java*. PhD thesis, University of Oldenburg, 2000.
10. J. He. Process refinement. In J. McDermid, editor, *The theory and practice of refinement*. Butterworths, 1989.
11. C. A. R. Hoare. *Communicating Sequential Processes*. Prentice Hall, 1985.
12. C. A. R. Hoare, J. He, and J. W. Sanders. Prespecification in data refinement. *Information Processing Letters*, 1987.
13. M. B. Josephs. A state-based approach to communicating processes. *Distributed Computing*, 3:9–18, 1988.
14. C.C. Morgan. Of wp and CSP. In W.H.J. Feijen, A.J.M. van Gasteren, D. Gries, and J. Misra, editors, *Beauty is our business: a birthday salute to Edsger W. Dijkstra*. Springer-Verlag, 1990.
15. A. W. Roscoe. *The Theory and Practice of Concurrency*. Prentice Hall Series in Computer Science, 1998.
16. J. Rumbaugh, I. Jacobson, and G. Booch. *The Unified Modeling Language Reference Manual*. Addison-Wesley, 1997.
17. G. Smith. A fully abstract semantics of classes for Object-Z. *Formal Aspects of Computing*, 7, 1995.
18. G. Smith. A semantic integration of Object-Z and CSP. In J. Fitzgerald, C. B. Jones, and P. Lucas, editors, *Proceedings of Formal Methods Europe (FME '97)*, volume 1313 of *Lecture Notes in Computer Science*. Springer Verlag, 1997.
19. G. Smith. *The Object-Z specification language*. Kluwer Academic Publishers, 2000.
20. G. Smith and J. Derrick. Refinement and verification of concurrent systems specified in Object-Z and CSP. In M. Hinchey and Shaoying Liu, editors, *Proceedings of First IEEE International Conference on Formal Engineering Methods (ICFEM '97)*. IEEE Computer Society, 1997.
21. J. M. Spivey. *The Z notation: a reference manual*. Prentice Hall, 1992.
22. J. C. P. Woodcock and C. C. Morgan. Refinement of state-based concurrent systems. In D. Bjørner, C. A. R. Hoare, and H. Langmaack, editors, *VDM and Z: Formal methods in software development*. Springer, 1990.

Combining Specification Techniques
for Processes, Data and Time*

Jochen Hoenicke and Ernst-Rüdiger Olderog

Fachbereich Informatik, Universität Oldenburg
26111 Oldenburg, Germany
Fax: +49-441-798-2965
{hoenicke,olderog}@informatik.uni-oldenburg.de

Abstract. We present a new combination CSP-OZ-DC of three well
researched formal techniques for the specification of processes, data and
time: CSP [18], Object-Z [37], and Duration Calculus [40]. The emphasis
is on a smooth integration of the underlying semantic models and its
use for verifying properties of CSP-OZ-DC specifications by a combined
application of the model-checkers FDR [29] for CSP and UPPAAL [1]
for Timed Automata. This approach is applied to part of a case study
on radio controlled railway crossings.

Keywords: CSP, Object-Z, Duration Calculus, transformational semantic, real-time processes, model-checking, FDR, UPPAAL

1 Introduction

Complex computing systems exhibit various behavioural aspects such as communication between components, state transformation inside components, and
real-time constraints on the communications and state changes. Formal specification techniques for such systems have to be able to describe all these aspects.
Unfortunately, a single specification technique that is well suited for all these
aspects is yet not available. Instead one finds various specialised techniques that
are very good at describing individual aspects of system behaviour. This observation has led to research into the combination and semantic integration of
specification techniques. In this paper we combine three well researched specification techniques: CSP, Object-Z and Duration Calculus.

Communicating Sequential Processes (CSP) were originally introduced by
Hoare in [17] and developed further in [18]. The central concepts of CSP are
synchronous communication via channels between different processes, parallel
composition and hiding of internal communication. For CSP a rich mathematical theory comprising operational, denotational and algebraic semantics with
consistency proofs has been developed [30]. Tool support comes through the
FDR model-checker [29]. The name stands for Failure Divergence Refinement
and refers to the standard semantic model of CSP, the failures divergence model,
and its notion of process refinement.

---

* This research is partially supported by the DFG under grant Ol/98-2.

M. Butler, L. Petre, and K. Sere (Eds.): IFM 2002, LNCS 2335, pp. 245–266, 2002.
© Springer-Verlag Berlin Heidelberg 2002

Z was introduced in the early 80's in Oxford by Abrial as a set-theoretic and predicate language for the specification of data, state spaces and state transformations. The first systematic description of Z is [38]. Since then the language has been published extensively (e.g. [39]) and used in many case studies and industrial projects. In particular, Z schemas and the schema calculus enable a structured way of presenting large state spaces and their transformation. *Object-Z* is an object-oriented extension of Z [37]. It comprises the concepts of classes, inheritance and instantiation. Z and Object-Z come with the concept of data refinement. For Z there exist proof systems for establishing properties of specifications and refinements such as Z/EVES [31] or HOL-Z [19]. For Object-Z type checkers exist. Verification support is less developed except for an extension of HOL-Z [32].

Duration Calculus (DC for short) originated during the ProCoS (Provably Correct Systems) project [15] as a new logic and calculus for specifying the behaviour of real-time systems [40,12]. It is based on the notion of an observable *obs* interpreted as a time dependent function $obs_{\mathcal{I}} : Time \rightarrow D$ for some data domain D. A real-time system is described by a set of such observables. This links up well to the mathematical basis found in classical dynamic systems theory [20] and enables extensions to cover hybrid systems. Duration Calculus was inspired by the work on interval temporal logic [23,24] and thus specifies interval-based properties of observables. Its name stems from its ability to specify the *duration* of certain states in a given interval using the integral. By choosing the right set of observables, real-time systems can be described at various levels of abstraction [27,26,33,6]. Verification support for the general DC is provided by [35,13] using theorem provers, and for a more specialised application of DC by [5] using a translation into timed automata for model-checking with UPPAAL [1].

It is well known that a consistent combination of different specification techniques is difficult [16]. Very popular is currently UML, the Unified Modeling Language [2]. It collects all the widespread specification techniques for object-oriented systems in one language. There is even an extension UML-RT [34] intended to cover real-time systems. However, a closer examination shows that this extension is just able to deal with reactive systems. A problem with UML is the so far missing semantic basis for this huge language. It is still a topic of ongoing research to provide a semantics for suitable subsets of UML.

We believe that the best chances for a well founded combination are with specification techniques that are well researched individually. An example of a clear combination of two specification techniques is CSP-OZ [9,10]. In this paper we extend CSP-OZ by the aspect of continuous real-time. This is done by combining it in a suitable way with DC. The resulting specification language we call CSP-OZ-DC. The paper is organised as follows. Section 2 introduces the main constructs of CSP-OZ-DC. Section 3 describes the semantics of the combination. Section 4 shows how this semantics can be utilized for a partially automatic verification of properties of CSP-OZ-DC specifications, and applies this approach to an example of a radio controlled railway crossing. Finally, we conclude with section 5.

2   The Combination CSP-OZ-DC

In this section we introduce the new combined formalism with some examples taken from a case study of radio controlled railway crossings[1], see Fig. 1. The main issue in this study is to remotely operate points and crossings via radio based communication while keeping the safety standard.

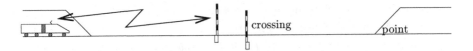

Fig. 1. Case study: radio controlled railway crossings

Fig. 2 surveys the controller architecture for a small part of this case study dealing with the safety of a level crossing. The diagram shows several components connected by communication channels. We discuss here the *cross controller* whose purpose is to secure the crossing upon requests issued by trains via the *radio controller*. We consider a multi-track level crossing where a request can be made for each track with the *set* communication. A request can be withdrawn at any time via the *clear* communication. The cross controller starts its securing cycle when at least one request was given. It continues through that cycle even if the request is withdrawn at a later time. When the crossing is secured it can communicate *secured* events to all requested tracks. When the train passes the crossing a *wheel counter* will notice that and trigger the *passed* communication. When no more requests are pending the crossing can be released.

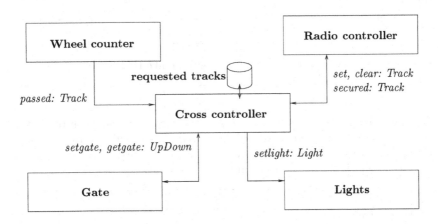

Fig. 2. Controller architecture

---
[1] This case study is part of the priority research program "Integration of specification techniques with applications in engineering" of the German Research Council (DFG) (http://tfs.cs.tu-berlin.de/projekte/indspec/SPP/index.html).

To specify the cross controller several concepts must be handled, as described in the following. The cross controller communicates with other components, e. g. the *radio controller*. The order of these communications can be easily specified with CSP using mutually recursive process equations. The main equation is distinguished by the process identifier `main`. For the cross controller we have

$$\texttt{main} \stackrel{c}{=} \mathit{assigned} \rightarrow \mathit{setlight!yellow} \rightarrow \mathit{setlight!red}$$
$$\rightarrow \mathit{setgate!down} \rightarrow \mathit{getgate.down} \rightarrow \mathit{Secure}$$
$$\mathit{Secure} \stackrel{c}{=} \mathit{secured?t} \rightarrow \mathit{Secure}$$
$$\Box \; \mathit{free} \rightarrow \mathit{setgate!up} \rightarrow \mathit{setlight!off} \rightarrow \mathit{getgate.up}$$
$$\rightarrow \mathit{wait} \rightarrow \texttt{main}$$

The symbol $\stackrel{c}{=}$ is used instead of an ordinary equals symbol to distinguish between CSP process equations and Z equations. The communication *assigned* will be local and enabled only when a request for the crossing is pending (see Fig. 3). The crossing is secured in three steps: switch on first the yellow and then the red light, and afterwards close the gate. Next the process waits for a confirmation *getgate.down* form the *gate* that it is indeed closed. Then the crossing has reached a secure state and its further behaviour is modelled by the process *Secure*. Here it waits until all requests are either cleared or the corresponding train has passed the gate. Afterwards the gate opens again and the lights are switched off.

The cross controller should work for multi-track crossings. It therefore needs to remember the set of *requested tracks*. Handling such data and state information can be easily done with Object-Z (OZ). The state space is denoted by an unnamed schema:

$$\boxed{\; r : \mathbb{P} \; \mathit{Track} \;}$$

The initial state is described by an `Init` schema like this:

_Init_____
$$r = \varnothing$$

When a communication event like *set* is received from the radio controller, the Z state needs to be updated. In CSP-OZ it is very easy to link a data operation to a communication by writing a Z-schema with the name `com_set` specifying the operation associated with that communication event:

_com_set_____
$$\Delta(r)$$
$$t? : \mathit{Track}$$
$$t? \notin r \wedge r' = r \cup \{t?\}$$

The Δ in the first line of this schema declares that this operation may (only) change r. The next line declares a parameter t, decorated with ? to signify that

t is an input parameter. Notice that this naming convention of Z corresponds nicely with the naming conventions of CSP: the output of t along channel *set* synchronises with the input of t in the Z schema. In Z a state transformation is expressed by a predicate relating the state before and the state after the transformation. The second state is distinguished from the first one by decorating it with a prime. In this case the predicate states that the element $t?$ is added to the set r of requested tracks.

For embedded controllers another important aspect are real-time constraints. In our case study we want communication events to occur within certain time bounds. On the other hand, some events must not occur too early. This means we need timed progress and stability constraints. For specifying such real-time constrains, we use the Duration Calculus (DC). In DC *state assertions* P describe time dependent properties of observables $obs : Time \rightarrow D$. *Duration terms* describe interval-based real values. The name of the calculus stems from terms of the form $\int P$ measuring the *duration* of a state assertion P, i.e. the accumulated time that P holds in the considered interval. The simplest duration term is the symbol ℓ abbreviating $\int 1$ and thus denoting the *length* of the given interval. *Duration formulae* F, G describe interval-based properties. For example, $\lceil P \rceil$ abbreviates $\int P = \ell \wedge \ell > 0$ and thus specifies that P holds (almost) everywhere on a non-point interval. Sequential behaviour is modelled by the *chop* operator "; ": the formula $F ; G$ specifies that first F and then G holds. The formula $\Diamond F$ abbreviates $true; F; true$ and thus expresses that on some subinterval F holds. The dual $\Box F$ abbreviates $\neg \Diamond \neg F$ and thus states that F holds on all subintervals.

A subset of the DC are the so-called *implementables* due to [28], which make use of the following idioms where $t \in Time$:

$$
\begin{array}{lll}
F \longrightarrow \lceil P \rceil & == & \Box \neg (F; \lceil \neg P \rceil) & \text{[followed-by]} \\
F \xrightarrow{t} \lceil P \rceil & == & (F \wedge \ell = t) \longrightarrow \lceil P \rceil & \text{[leads-to]} \\
F \xrightarrow{\leq t} \lceil P \rceil & == & (F \wedge \ell \leq t) \longrightarrow \lceil P \rceil & \text{[up-to]}
\end{array}
$$

Intuitively, $F \longrightarrow \lceil P \rceil$ expresses that whenever a pattern given by the formula F is observed, it will be "followed by" an interval where P holds. In the "leads-to" form the pattern is required to have a length t and in the "up-to" form it is bounded by a length "up to" t.

In this paper we also consider variants of the above formulae where we check an event ev by counting its number of occurrences:

$$
F \xrightarrow[ev]{t} G == F \wedge \lceil ct(ev) = n \rceil \xrightarrow{t} G \wedge \lceil ct(ev) > n \rceil
$$

For the cross controller we require for example the progress constraint

$$
\lceil en(assigned) \rceil \xrightarrow[assigned]{1} \lceil true \rceil
$$

stating that whenever the communication *assigned* is enabled it has to occur within 1 second. As an example for a stability constraint consider the DC formula

$$
\lceil \neg\, en(setlight.red) \rceil; \lceil en(setlight.red) \rceil \xrightarrow{\leq 4} \lceil en(setlight.red) \rceil
$$

stating that the *setlight.red* communication should stay enabled for at least 4 seconds before it can actually occur.

The basic building block in our combined formalism CSP-OZ-DC is a class. Its syntax is as in CSP-OZ [9,10] except for the new DC part: see Fig. 3 for the complete specification of the *CrossController* class. First, the communication channels of the class are declared. Every channel has a type restricting the values that it can communicate. There are also local channels that are visible only inside the class and used for the interaction of the CSP, Z and DC parts. Second, the CSP part follows; it is given by a system of (recursive) process equations. Third, the Z part is given which itself consists of the state space, the Init schema, and communication schemas specifying how the state changes when the corresponding communication event occurs. Finally, below a horizontal line the DC part is stated.

To describe architectures as in Fig. 2 classes can be combined into larger specifications by CSP operators like parallel composition, hiding and renaming.

3   Semantics

Each class of a CSP-OZ-DC specification denotes a time dependent process. In this section we describe how to define this process in a transformational way.

3.1   Semantics of the Constituents

We begin by recalling the semantic domains of the constituent specification techniques. The standard semantics of untimed CSP is the $\mathcal{FD}$-semantics based on failures and divergence [30]. A *failure* is a pair (s, X) consisting of a finite sequence or *trace* $s \in$ seq *Comm* over a set *Comm* of communications and a so-called *refusal set* $X \in \mathbb{P}$ *Comm*. Intuitively, a failure (s, X) describes that after engaging in the trace s the process can refuse to engage in any of the communications in X. Refusal sets allow us to make fine distinctions between different nondeterministic process behaviour; they are essential for obtaining a compositional definition of parallel composition in the CSP setting of synchronous communication when we want to observe deadlocks. Formally, we define the sets

$Traces == $ seq *Comm* and $Refusals == \mathbb{P}$ *Comm*,
$Failures == Traces \times Refusals.$

A *divergence* is a trace after which the process can engage in an infinite sequence of internal actions. The $\mathcal{FD}$-*semantics* of CSP is then given by two mappings

$\mathcal{F} : $ CSP $\rightarrow \mathbb{P}$ *Failures* and $\mathcal{D} : $ CSP $\rightarrow \mathbb{P}$ *Traces*.

For a CSP process P we write $\mathcal{FD}[\![P]\!] = (\mathcal{F}[\![P]\!], \mathcal{D}[\![P]\!])$. Certain well-formedness conditions relate the values of $\mathcal{F}$ and $\mathcal{D}$ (see [30], p.192). The $\mathcal{FD}$-semantics

$Track == 0..1$
$Color ::= off \mid yellow \mid red$
$UpDown ::= up \mid down$

CrossController

chan $set, clear, passed, secured : [t? : Track]$
chan $setlight : [color! : Color]$
chan $setgate : [status! : UpDown]$
chan $getgate : [status? : UpDown]$
local_chan $assigned, free, wait$

$\mathbf{main} \stackrel{c}{=} assigned \rightarrow setlight!yellow \rightarrow setlight!red$
$\qquad \rightarrow setgate!down \rightarrow getgate.down \rightarrow Secure$

$Secure \stackrel{c}{=} secured?t \rightarrow Secure$
$\qquad \Box\, free \rightarrow setgate!up \rightarrow setlight!off \rightarrow getgate.up$
$\qquad \rightarrow wait \rightarrow \mathbf{main}$

Init

$r : \mathbb{P}\, Track$ | $r = \varnothing$

com_secured

$t? : Track$

$t? \in r$

com_set

$\Delta(r)$
$t? : Track$

$t? \notin r$
$r' = r \cup \{t?\}$

com_clear

$\Delta(r)$
$t? : Track$

$t? \in r$
$r' = r \setminus \{t?\}$

com_passed

$\Delta(r)$
$t? : Track$

$t? \in r$
$r' = r \setminus \{t?\}$

com_assigned

$r \neq \varnothing$

com_free

$r = \varnothing$

$(\lceil en(assigned)\rceil \xrightarrow[assigned]{1} \lceil true\rceil) \quad \wedge \quad (\lceil en(free)\rceil \xrightarrow[free]{1} \lceil true\rceil)$

$\lceil en(setlight.yellow)\rceil \xrightarrow[setlight.yellow]{1} \lceil true\rceil$

$\lceil \neg\, en(setlight.red)\rceil; \lceil en(setlight.red)\rceil \xrightarrow{\leq 4} \lceil en(setlight.red)\rceil$
$\lceil en(setlight.red)\rceil \xrightarrow[setlight.red]{5} \lceil true\rceil$

$\lceil \neg\, en(setlight.off)\rceil; \lceil en(setlight.off)\rceil \xrightarrow{\leq 1} \lceil en(setlight.off)\rceil$
$\lceil en(setlight.off)\rceil \xrightarrow[setlight.off]{2} \lceil true\rceil$

$\lceil \neg\, en(setgate.down)\rceil; \lceil en(setgate.down)\rceil \xrightarrow{\leq 2} \lceil en(getgate.down)\rceil$
$\lceil en(setgate.down)\rceil \xrightarrow[setgate.down]{3} \lceil true\rceil$

$\lceil en(setgate.up)\rceil \xrightarrow[setgate.up]{1} \lceil true\rceil$

$\lceil \neg\, en(wait)\rceil; \lceil en(wait)\rceil \xrightarrow{\leq 30} \lceil en(wait)\rceil$
$\lceil en(wait)\rceil \xrightarrow[wait]{31} \lceil true\rceil$

Fig. 3. A multi-track level crossing

induces a notion of *process refinement* denoted by $\sqsubseteq_{\mathcal{FD}}$. For CSP processes P and Q this relation is defined as follows:

$$P \sqsubseteq_{\mathcal{FD}} Q \text{ iff } \mathcal{F}[\![P]\!] \supseteq \mathcal{F}[\![Q]\!] \text{ and } \mathcal{D}[\![P]\!] \supseteq \mathcal{D}[\![Q]\!]$$

Intuitively, $P \sqsubseteq_{\mathcal{FD}} Q$ means that Q refines P, i.e. Q is more deterministic and more defined than P.

Instead of the negative information of refusal sets one can also use positive information about the future process behaviour in terms of so-called *acceptance sets*. For a trace s an acceptance set $A \in \mathbb{P}\,Comm$ describes a set of communications that are possible after s. The set of all initial communications after s is the largest acceptance set after s. Acceptance sets are due to Hennessy and De Nicola [14,25] who developed an approach to testing of processes that resulted in a process model equivalent to the failures divergence model but with acceptance sets instead of refusal sets. Acceptance sets satisfy certain closure properties (see [14], p.77). For example, they are closed under union. Formally, let

$$Acceptances == \mathbb{P}\,Comm$$

and $\mathcal{A}$ be the process semantics

$$\mathcal{A} : \text{CSP} \rightarrow \mathbb{P}(\,Traces \times Acceptances)$$

based on acceptance sets instead of refusal sets. $\mathcal{AD}$-semantics is the process semantics based on $\mathcal{A}$ and $\mathcal{D}$. We write $\mathcal{AD}[\![P]\!] = (\mathcal{A}[\![P]\!]\,,\,\mathcal{D}[\![P]\!])$ for a CSP process P. Then the following proposition on process refinement can be proved:

Proposition 1. $P \sqsubseteq_{\mathcal{FD}} Q$ iff $\mathcal{A}[\![P]\!] \supseteq \mathcal{A}[\![Q]\!]$ and $\mathcal{D}[\![P]\!] \supseteq \mathcal{D}[\![Q]\!]$

Thus we do not lose any process information by taking acceptance sets instead of refusal sets. Since for our approach to verification will be based on acceptance sets, we shall represent here the semantics of untimed CSP on $\mathcal{A}$ and $\mathcal{D}$.

Object-Z (OZ) describes state spaces as collections of typed variables, say x of type D_x, and their possible transformation with the help of action predicates $A(x, x')$, for example $x' \geq x + 1$, where the decorated version x' represents the value of x after the transformation. The language comes with the usual notion of *data refinement* [39].

Duration Calculus (DC) specifies properties of observables obs interpreted as *finitely varying* functions of the form $obs_I : Time \rightarrow D$ for a continuous time domain $Time$ and a data domain D. Finitely varying means that obs_I can assume only finitely many different values within a finite time interval [12]. When modelling real-time systems in DC, refinement boils down to logical implication.

3.2   Untimed Semantics of CSP-OZ Classes

The untimed semantics of the combination CSP-OZ is defined in [9,10]. The idea is that each CSP-OZ class denotes a process in the semantic model of CSP. This is achieved by transforming the Z part of such a class into a CSP process that runs in parallel and communicates with the CSP part of the class.

Consider a CSP-OZ class

```
┌─ U ─────────────────────────────────────────────────
│  I                                        [interface]
│  L                                   [local channels]
│  P                                         [CSP part]
│  Z                                          [Z part]
└─────────────────────────────────────────────────────
```

also written horizontally as $U \hateq \text{spec } I\ L\ P\ Z \text{ end}$ with a Z part of the form

```
┌─ Z ─────────────────────────────────────────────────
│  st                                     [state space]
│  Init(st)                         [initial condition]
│  ...com_c(st, in?, out!, st')...
│                    [one communication schema for each c in I or L]
└─────────────────────────────────────────────────────
```

where the notation $com\_c(st, in?, out!, st')$ indicates that this communication schema relates the state st to the successor state st' and has input parameters $in?$ and output parameters $out!$.

The Z part of the class is transformed into a CSP process $ZMain$ defined by the following system of (parametrised) recursive equations for $ZPart$ using (indexed) CSP operators for internal choice ($\sqcap$) and alternative composition ($\square$):

$$ZMain = \bigsqcap\nolimits_{st \text{ with } Init(st)} ZPart(st)$$

$$ZPart(st) = \square_{c \text{ in } I \text{ or } L;\ in? : Inputs(c)} \atop \text{with } \exists\, out! : Outputs(c);\ st' \bullet com\_c(st, in?, out!, st')$$

$$\bigsqcap\nolimits_{out! : Outputs(c);\ st'} \atop \text{with } com\_c(st, in?, out!, st') \quad c.in?.out! \to ZPart(st')$$

Informally, $ZMain$ can start in any state st satisfying $Init(st)$. Then $ZPart(st)$ is ready for every communication event $c.in?.out!$ along a channel c in I or L where for the input values $in?$ the communication schema $com\_c(st, in?, out!, st')$ is satisfiable for some output values $out!$ and successor state st'. For given input values $in?$ any such $out!$ and st' can be internally chosen to yield $c.in?.out!$ and the next recursive call $ZPart(st')$. Thus input and output along channels c are modelled by a subtle interplay of the CSP alternative and choice.

$ZMain$ runs in parallel with the explicit CSP process P of the class:

$$proc_U = P \parallel Events(I \cup L) \parallel ZMain$$

Here the parallel composition synchronises on all events in I and L. In [9,10] the semantics of the class U is then defined by

$$\mathcal{FD}[\![U]\!] = \mathcal{FD}[\![proc_U \setminus Events(L)]\!]$$

where all events along local channels L are hidden. Hiding in untimed CSP makes communications occur autonomously without delay. Thus hiding can cause non-determinism and divergence.

By the above process semantics of CSP-OZ, the refinement notion $\sqsubseteq_{\mathcal{FD}}$ is immediately available for CSP-OZ. One of our guidelines for combining specification techniques is *refinement compositionality*, i.e. refinement of the parts should imply refinement of the whole. For CSP-OZ this is shown in [10]:

Theorem 2. *Process refinement $P_1 \sqsubseteq_{\mathcal{FD}} P_2$ implies refinement in CSP-OZ:*

$$\textsf{spec } I\ L\ P_1\ Z\ \textsf{end}\quad \sqsubseteq_{\mathcal{FD}}\quad \textsf{spec } I\ L\ P_2\ Z\ \textsf{end}$$

Data refinement $Z_1 \sqsubseteq_R Z_2$ for a refinement relation R implies refinement in CSP-OZ:

$$\textsf{spec } I\ L\ P\ Z_1\ \textsf{end}\quad \sqsubseteq_{\mathcal{FD}}\quad \textsf{spec } I\ L\ P\ Z_2\ \textsf{end}$$

3.3 Timed Semantics of CSP-OZ-DC Classes

The semantic idea of the combination CSP-OZ-DC is that each class denotes a timed process. To this end, we lift the semantics of CSP and OZ onto the level of time dependent observables. In the timed setting the behaviour of internal actions has to be studied carefully. We distinguish between internal τ actions inherited form the untimed CSP setting and internal *wait* actions induced by hiding communications with a certain timing behaviour. Whereas internal τ actions do not take time and can thus be eliminated in accordance with the $\mathcal{FD}$-semantics, possibly inducing nondeterminism or divergence, internal *wait* actions let time pass before the next visible communication can occur. Whereas an infinite sequence of τ actions is equivalent to divergence, an infinite sequence of wait actions is equivalent to deadlock.

For simplicity, we do not consider the case where the untimed part diverges. Thus the semantics of CSP-OZ-DC will associate with each specification of the combined language a timed process consisting of a set of time dependent traces and time dependent acceptances:

$$\mathcal{A}_{Time} : \text{CSP-OZ-DC} \to \mathbb{P}((\text{Time} \to \text{Traces}) \times (\text{Time} \to \text{Acceptances}))$$

For a CSP-OZ-DC specification S its semantics $\mathcal{A}_{Time}[\![S]\!]$ will be described by a DC formula in the observables tr and Acc interpreted as finitely varying functions

$$tr_{\mathcal{I}} : \text{Time} \to \text{Traces} \quad \text{and} \quad Acc_{\mathcal{I}} : \text{Time} \to \text{Acceptances}.$$

This DC formula denotes the set of all interpretations of tr and Acc that make the formula true; thus it will be identified with $\mathcal{A}_{Time}[\![S]\!]$.

We explain the details first for a CSP-OZ-DC class C, which augments the untimed CSP-OZ class U by an additional timing part T expressed in DC:

$$\begin{array}{|l|}\hline \rule{0pt}{2.5ex}\_C\_\\ \hline U \qquad\qquad\qquad\qquad\qquad\qquad\qquad\qquad\qquad\qquad\text{[untimed components]}\\ \hline T \qquad\qquad\qquad\qquad\qquad\qquad\qquad\qquad\qquad\qquad\qquad\text{[DC part]}\\ \hline\end{array}$$

We shall also expand C horizontally into

$$C \mathrel{\widehat{=}} \text{spec } I \ L \ P \ Z \ T \text{ end.}$$

The semantics of C is obtained by taking the CSP process $proc_U$ defined for the CSP-OZ class U but interpreting it in the setting of the time dependent observables tr and Acc, and then conjoining it with the time dependent restrictions expressed in the DC part T. Since $proc_U$ is still an untimed process, its semantics in terms of tr and Acc will allow any time dependent behaviour. More precisely, given the untimed acceptance semantics of $proc_U$ assumed to be divergence free,

$$\mathcal{A}[\![proc_U]\!] : \mathbb{P}(\mathit{Traces} \times \mathit{Acceptances}) \quad \text{with} \quad \mathcal{D}[\![proc_U]\!] = \varnothing,$$

we define its timed semantics as the DC formula

$$\mathcal{A}_{\mathit{Time}}[\![proc_U]\!] \Leftrightarrow \mathcal{F}_U \wedge \mathcal{F}_1 \wedge \mathcal{F}_2 \wedge \mathcal{F}_3$$

in the observables tr and Acc with subformulae $\mathcal{F}_U, \mathcal{F}_1 - \mathcal{F}_3$ given as follows:

$$\mathcal{F}_U : \Box \lceil (tr, Acc) \in \mathcal{A}[\![proc_U]\!] \rceil$$

requires that the values of the observables tr and Acc are taken from the untimed acceptance semantics of $proc_U$.

$$\mathcal{F}_1 : \lceil\rceil \vee \lceil tr = \langle\rangle \rceil; \ \mathit{true}$$

requires that initially the trace is empty.

$$\mathcal{F}_2 : \Box \forall h, h' \bullet (h \neq h' \wedge \lceil tr = h \rceil; \ \lceil tr = h' \rceil) \Rightarrow \exists c, v \bullet h' = h \mathbin{^\frown} \langle c.v \rangle$$

requires that the trace can only grow and that one communication event occurs at a time. The modality $\Box$ quantifies over all subintervals of a given time interval, and ; is the chop operator of interval temporal logic used in DC [40,12]. The subformula $\lceil tr = h \rceil; \ \lceil tr = h' \rceil$ holds in any time interval where on a first non-point interval tr assumes the value h and on a second non-point interval the value h'. By $\mathcal{F}_2$, h' can differ from h only by one communication event. Together with the restriction to finite variability, we thus require that only finitely many communication events occur within a finite time interval and that one communication event occurs at a time. Consequently in our semantics a non-zero time passes between successive events. Finally,

$$\mathcal{F}_3 : \Box \forall h, c, v \bullet (\lceil tr = h \rceil; \ \lceil tr = h \mathbin{^\frown} \langle c.v \rangle \rceil \Rightarrow$$
$$(\lceil tr = h \rceil \wedge (\mathit{true}; \ \lceil c.v \in Acc \rceil)); \ \lceil tr = h \mathbin{^\frown} \langle c.v \rangle \rceil)$$

requires that every communication $c.v$ can occur only with prior appearance in an acceptance set.

Only the DC part T can actually restrict this behaviour in a time dependent manner. To this end, T has limited access to the observables tr and Acc via the expressions $ct(X)$ and $en(X)$ where X is a set of communication events. By definition,

$$\left|\begin{array}{l} ct : \mathbb{P}\ Comm \to \mathbb{N} \\ \hline \forall X : \mathbb{P}\ Comm \bullet ct(X) = \#(tr \triangleright X) \end{array}\right.$$

Thus $ct(X)$ counts the number of occurrences of events from X in the trace tr. Next

$$\left|\begin{array}{l} en : \mathbb{P}\ Comm \to \mathbb{B} \\ \hline \forall X : \mathbb{P}\ Comm \bullet en(X) \Leftrightarrow X \subseteq Acc \end{array}\right.$$

Thus $en(X)$ records whether all events from X can be accepted next. It is for this definition of enabledness that acceptance sets are easier to use than refusals. This motivated our choice of the semantic representation. For a single communication event $c.v$ we write $ct(c.v)$ and $en(c.v)$ instead of $ct(\{c.v\})$ and $en(\{c.v\})$. Using these expressions we can specify timing constraints for the visible communications.

Altogether the semantics of the timed class C is given by the formula

$$\mathcal{A}_{Time}[\![C]\!] \Leftrightarrow \text{hide } L \bullet (\mathcal{F}_U \wedge \mathcal{F}_1 \wedge \mathcal{F}_2 \wedge \mathcal{F}_3 \wedge T)$$

where all communications along the local channels in L are hidden. For a DC formula F in the observables tr and Acc we define

$$\text{hide } L \bullet F \Leftrightarrow \exists tr_0, Acc_0 \bullet ((\lceil\rceil \vee \lceil tr = squash(tr_0 \triangleright L) \wedge Acc = Acc_0 \setminus L]) \wedge$$
$$F[tr_0/tr, Acc_0/Acc])$$

Thus hide $L \bullet F$ is a DC formula in the observables tr and Acc, and their values are linked via the substitution $F[tr_0/tr, Acc_0/Acc]$ to the original values of these observables in F. It describes the timed semantics of the CSP hiding operator.

3.4   Timed Semantics of System Specifications

System specifications S are obtained by combining class specifications with the CSP operators for parallel composition, hiding and renaming. Thus a typical specification could be of the form

$$S = (C_1[R_1] \parallel C_2[R_2]) \setminus L.$$

The parallel composition $\parallel$ can be modelled by an *alphabetised parallel* $_A \parallel_B$ where A and B are the sets of interface events of $C_1[R_1]$ and $C_2[R_2]$. For DC formulae F_1 and F_2 in the observables tr and Acc the semantics of the parallel composition can be expressed, similarly to [33], by the following DC formula:

$$F_1 \ _A\|_B \ F_2 \Leftrightarrow \exists \, tr_1, tr_2, Acc_0, Acc_1, Acc_2 \bullet$$
$$((\lceil\rceil \vee \lceil tr \in \text{seq}(A \cup B) \wedge tr \upharpoonright A = tr_1 \wedge tr \upharpoonright B = tr_2 \wedge$$
$$Acc_0 \cap (A \cup B) = \varnothing \wedge$$
$$Acc = (Acc_1 \cap Acc_2 \cap A \cap B) \cup$$
$$(Acc_1 \setminus B) \cup (Acc_2 \setminus A)\rceil) \wedge$$
$$F_1[tr_1/tr, Acc_1/Acc] \wedge F_2[tr_2/tr, Acc_2/Acc])$$

Hiding, denoted by $\setminus L$, is used to make the communication events in L internal. Semantically, hiding is defined using the operator **hide** $L \bullet F$ introduced above. Renaming, denoted by $[R]$ for a relation R between events, is used to rename communication events. The semantic definition is straightforward.

The *refinement* relation between classes or between specifications of the same interface is modelled by (reverse) logical implication in the semantic domain: a class C_2 *refines* a class C_1, abbreviated by

$$C_1 \sqsubseteq C_2, \text{ if } \mathcal{A}_{Time}[\![C_2]\!] \Rightarrow \mathcal{A}_{Time}[\![C_1]\!]$$

holds. We show that *refinement compositionality* holds also for CSP-OZ-DC.

Theorem 3. *(a) Process refinement* $P_1 \sqsubseteq_{\mathcal{FD}} P_2$ *implies refinement in CSP-OZ-DC:*   spec I L P_1 Z T end $\sqsubseteq$ spec I L P_2 Z T end

(b) Data refinement $Z_1 \sqsubseteq_R Z_2$ *for a refinement relation R implies refinement in CSP-OZ-DC:*   spec I L P Z_1 T end $\sqsubseteq$ spec I L P Z_2 T end

(c) Time constraint refinement $T_2 \Rightarrow T_1$ *implies refinement in CSP-OZ-DC:* spec I L P Z T_1 end $\sqsubseteq$ spec I L P Z T_2 end

Proof. Statements (a) and (b) are immediate consequences of Theorem 2 and the monotonicity of $\mathcal{F}_U$ w.r.t. refinements of the untimed class U. Statement (c) follows from the conjunctive form of $\mathcal{A}_{Time}[\![C]\!]$.   □

By this theorem, it is possible to reuse verification techniques for the components of a CSP-OZ-DC specification to prove refinement results for the whole specification. However, when the desired property of the whole specification depends on the semantic interplay of the components, more sophisticated verification techniques are needed. In the following we develop one such a technique.

4   Verification

We exploit the above style of semantics for a partially automatic verification of properties of CSP-OZ-DC specifications that satisfy the following restrictions: the CSP part represents a finite-state process, the OZ data types are finite, and the DC part obeys certain patterns described below. Then the idea is as follows. Given a class $C \cong$ spec I L P Z T end we proceed in four steps:

(1) Represent the untimed process $U = \text{spec } I \ L \ P \ Z \text{ end}$ in FDR-CSP, the input language of the FDR model-checker [29,11] for CSP.

(2) Use the FDR model-checker to output a transition system TS_U for U with acceptance sets.

(3) Transform this transition system TS_U into a timed automaton $\mathcal{A}_C$ representing all the timing restrictions of the DC semantics.

(4) Verify properties of the class C by applying the model-checker UPPAAL [1] to $\mathcal{A}_C$.

Step(1) follows an approach of [8]. While steps (1) and (4) currently require user interaction, steps (2) and (3) proceed fully automatic.

The DC patterns for timing restrictions that can be handled in step (3) are new variants of the DC implementables [28] introduced next. An event set X appearing as a subscript of the chop operator or the followed-by operator (cf. section 2) indicates that an event from X happens at the corresponding chop point. Formally:

$$F \underset{X}{;} G == (F \land \lceil ct(X) = n \rceil); \ (G \land \lceil ct(X) > n \rceil)$$
$$F \xrightarrow[X]{t} G == (F \land \lceil ct(X) = n \rceil) \xrightarrow{t} (G \land \lceil ct(X) > n \rceil)$$

The following formula states that while a stability constraint applies, events from the set X *must not* happen:

$$F \xrightarrow[/X]{\leq t} G == (F \land \lceil ct(X) = n \rceil) \xrightarrow{\leq t} (G \land \lceil ct(X) = n \rceil)$$

A tool for step (3) developed by C. Ohler supports the following DC patterns:

$$\lceil P \rceil \underset{X}{;} \lceil Q \rceil \xrightarrow[Y]{t} \lceil R \rceil \qquad\qquad\qquad \text{[chop-leads-to]}$$
$$\lceil P \rceil \underset{X}{;} \lceil Q \rceil \xrightarrow[/Y]{\leq t} \lceil R \rceil \qquad\qquad\qquad \text{[chop-up-to]}$$
$$\lceil Q \rceil \xrightarrow[X]{t} \lceil R \rceil \qquad\qquad\qquad\qquad\quad \text{[leads-to]}$$
$$\lceil Q \rceil \xrightarrow[/Y]{\leq t} \lceil R \rceil \qquad\qquad\qquad\qquad\quad \text{[up-to]}$$

Here $t \in Time$ and P, Q, R are state assertions. The event sets X, Y are optional and can be omitted. Also the upper bound t in the *up-to* formulas can be omitted.

The tool implements an algorithm that applies given DC formulae of the above patterns one after the other to transform the transition system produced in step (2) into a timed automaton. As an example we show in Fig. 4 the pseudo code for the leads-to pattern. In step 1 the algorithm adds a new clock to measure the time the transition system stayed in a Q-state without executing an event from X. While being in a Q-state this clock must not grow beyond t because otherwise the DC formula would be violated. Therefore we add in step 2 a corresponding state invariant to all Q-states. The clock needs to be reset when a Q-state is entered from outside (step 3.a) or when an event from X occurs

```
Pattern:  ⌈Q⌉  ──t──→  ⌈R⌉
               X
1. Introduce new clock c
2. To all states s ∈ Q add invariant c ≤ t
3. For each transition tr : s ──ev──→ s' do:
   a. if s ∉ Q, s' ∈ Q
      add reset c := 0 to tr
   b. if s ∈ Q, s' ∈ Q, ev ∈ X
      add reset c := 0 to tr
   c. if s ∈ Q, (s' ∉ R ∨ ev ∉ X)
      add guard c < t   to tr
```

Fig. 4. Algorithm for the leads-to pattern

and the control stays in Q (step 3.b). All outgoing events that do not lead into an R-state or do not communicate an event from X must happen before time t has elapsed. Therefore a corresponding guard is added in step 3.c.

Besides enriching the transition system generated by FDR our tool also adds a timed *supervisor* automaton running in parallel. The supervisor serves two purposes: first, it ensures that – in agreement with the DC semantics defined in section 3.3 – a non zero time passes between successive events, and second, it hides the local channels that should not be visible to other processes.

4.1   Case Study

We now apply the above verification procedure to the case study introduced in section 2. The result of the manual step (1) is given in Fig. 5. It shows the FDR-CSP specification using the input language of the FDR model-checker and representing the CSP and Z part of the combined cross controller specification in Fig. 3. The representation of the constant declaration, the channel declaration and the CSP part is straightforward. Only at a few locations the syntax needs to be adapted to FDR. The transformation of the Z part into a CSP process *ZPart* was described in section 3.2: *ZPart* takes the complete Z state, here r, as a parameter. It offers an external choice over all communications that had corresponding Z schemas in the original specification. For readability we applied some simplifications to this part. The CSP and Z part are put in parallel and synchronize over their common alphabet.

The next two steps are performed automatically by our tool. In step (2) it uses the FDR model-checker to create a compact finite transition system from the specification of Fig. 5. The result is sketched in Fig. 6. The graph contains 40 states and 160 transitions. To make it more readable not all transitions are labelled. The whole graph is shaped as a cycle that corresponds to the cyclic behaviour of securing the crossing and releasing it.

Every CSP state is expanded into four substates corresponding to the four possible values of the variable r in the Z part. A closer view of the top left part of the graph is given in Fig. 7. The *passed* transitions are still omitted; they are in the same places as the *clear* transitions. Note that the initial state (the top most

```
-- Constants
Track   = {0..1}
datatype Color  = off | yellow | red
datatype UpDown = up | down

-- Channels
channel set, clear, secured, passed : Track
channel setlight                    : Color
channel setgate, getgate            : UpDown
channel assigned, free, wait

-- Class CrossController
CrossController =
  let
    -- CSP part
    main = assigned -> setlight!yellow -> setlight!red
              -> setgate!down -> getgate!down -> Secure
    Secure = secured?t -> Secure
           [] free -> setgate!up -> setlight!off -> getgate!up
              -> wait -> main

    -- Z part
    ZPart(r) =
        ([] t : diff(Track, r) @ set.t -> ZPart(union(r, {t})))
      [] ([] t : r @ clear.t -> ZPart(diff(r, {t})))
      [] ([] t : r @ passed.t -> ZPart(diff(r, {t})))
      [] ([] t : r @ secured.t -> ZPart(r))
      [] r != {} & assigned -> ZPart(r)
      [] r == {} & free -> ZPart(r)

  within  -- Put CSP and Z part in parallel
    main [| {| secured, assigned, free |} |] ZPart({})
```

Fig. 5. FDR-CSP specification for the cross controller

in the detailed graph) has no outgoing *assigned* transition. This is because the Z part blocks this transition when r is empty. Since all transitions are deterministic in our case study, every state has only one acceptance set, which contains all outgoing events.

In step (3) the DC formulae are applied one after the other. For each DC formula a new clock is introduced and new guards and resets are added to the transition. The tool starts with the first DC formula

$$\lceil en(assigned) \rceil \xrightarrow[assigned]{1} \lceil true \rceil \ .$$

This is an instance of the leads-to pattern. The states where *en(assigned)* holds are only the three states in Fig. 7 that have an outgoing *assigned* transition.

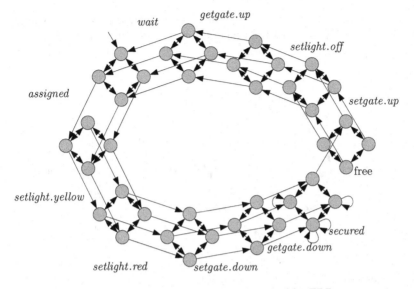

Fig. 6. Transition system generated by FDR

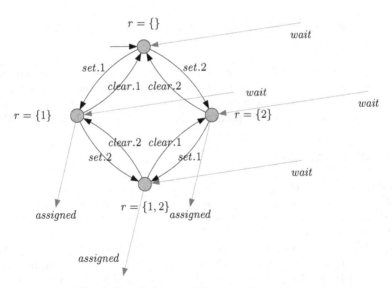

Fig. 7. Detailed view of the transition system

Thus only the transitions depicted in the detailed view are changed. Applying the algorithm in Fig. 4 yields the timed automaton depicted in Fig. 8.

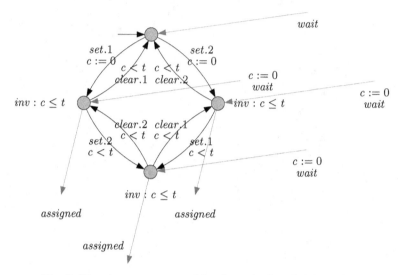

Fig. 8. Timed automaton resulting from the first DC formula

After applying all DC formulae step (3) terminates with a timed automaton representing the complete CSP-OZ-DC class. Altogether the algorithm adds 12 clocks and a lot of resets and guards. So the complete graph is not easily readable but we can verify that certain properties hold with the model-checker UPPAAL.

4.2   Model-Checking

We consider the following real-time property: Whenever a train requests a track and it does not clear the request or passes the crossing it can get a *secured* communication within a certain time t. We wish to determine the exact value of t experimentally.

To verify this property we build a test automaton. This is a small timed automaton that communicates with the cross controller over some of the channels we defined in our CSP-OZ-DC specification. As the identity of the track does not matter, we assume that our test automaton deals with track 0. Therefore we link it over the *set*.0, *clear*.0, *passed*.0 and *secured*.0 communication events. We instruct the tool to hide all other communications, so that they can occur at any time.

The test automaton is given in Fig. 9. In its initial state *idle* the automaton is able to communicate any event. When communicating *set*.0 it resets a clock *c_waiting* and switches to the *busy* state. In this state it waits until it can communicate *secured.0*. Then it returns to the *idle* state. This automaton is put in parallel with the cross controller.

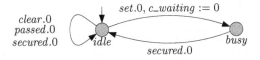

Fig. 9. Test automaton

We ask UPPAAL whether for all reachable states the test automaton is in the *idle* state or its clock is smaller than t, where t is an integer constant. This query can be expressed in the UPPAAL syntax as follows:

$$Property_t \Leftrightarrow A \square \ TestAutomaton.idle \ \text{or} \ c\_waiting < t$$

Applying this to the cross controller, UPPAAL quickly generates a counter example showing that the property does not hold. The trace contains the CSP events so it is possible to compare it to the CSP-OZ-DC specification. It turns out that the property is violated because we do not have enough progress conditions.

We need the assumptions that the gate will actually close or open within a certain time bound, say 15 seconds, and that the train will actually receive the *secured* communication within a certain time. Note that these are assumptions about the *environment* of the controller. However, for simplicity we add them to our specification. The formulae we add are:

$$\lceil en(getgate.down) \rceil \xrightarrow[getgate.down]{15} \lceil true \rceil$$
$$\lceil en(getgate.up) \rceil \xrightarrow[getgate.up]{15} \lceil true \rceil$$
$$\lceil en(secured.0) \rceil \xrightarrow[secured.0]{1} \lceil true \rceil$$

Now we can run UPPAAL again to check $Property_t$ for different values of t. If we choose a value for t smaller than 75 UPPAAL finds a counter example within a few seconds. For $t = 75$ the property is satisfied.

4.3 Experimental Results

The table in Fig. 10 gives some timings for these steps. The times were measured on an UltraSPARC-II with 296 MHz. Steps (2) and (3) of the verification procedure are quite fast. For the cross controller step (2) needs less than a second, and step (3) needs 1.8 seconds to apply the twelve DC formulae from the original specification plus the three formulae from the environment to the transition system generated by step (2). Model-checking in step (4) is most time consuming when no counter example exists, this is the reason for the difference in the last two columns. For $t = 74$ there is a counter example, but for $t = 75$ UPPAAL has to investigate the complete state space.

Consider now a larger system with more tracks. Adding a track doubles the Z state space and thus the resulting automaton states, and it yields almost three times as many transitions. As shown in Fig. 10, the steps take more time by a factor between two and three.

Number of tracks	step (2)	step (3)	step (4) with $t = 74$	step (4) with $t = 75$
2	0.3	1.8	16.4	1662
3	0.4	3.6	43.5	4379
4	0.6	10.4	101.5	10979

Fig. 10. Verification time (in seconds).

5   Conclusion

Related work. Closest to our way of combining specification techniques is Real-Time Object-Z [36]. Classes in this combination look similar to ours but lack the CSP and DC part. As we have seen in the case study, the CSP part is convenient for specifying sequencing constraints on the communications events. Furthermore, CSP offers parallel composition and hiding that can well be used for the structuring of larger CSP-OZ-DC specifications. In Real-Time Object-Z the timing properties are specified in an interval-based set-theoretic notation [7]. We also use an interval-based approach but in terms of the well researched Duration Calculus [40,12]. The semantics of Real-Time Object-Z is given in terms of time dependent traces [36] whereas we consider also time dependent acceptances due to the presence of CSP.

Another related work is TCOZ, a combination of Timed CSP [3] with Object-Z [21,22]. Obviously, DC is not involved in this combination. So the constructs of Timed CSP are used to specify time dependencies between communications. Besides this difference, the semantic integration of CSP with Object-Z differs from ours. In TCOZ an Object-Z operation schema denotes a process whereas in CSP-OZ-DC it specifies the effect of a communication event on the state.

Verification. We have shown how to exploit the transformational semantics of CSP-OZ-DC for a partially automatic verification of properties of combined specifications. To this end, we have developed a novel, systematic transformation of CSP-OZ-DC classes into timed automata that can be model-checked by the UPPAAL tool. This poses the question whether the timed automata semantics produced by the algorithm described in section 4 is *equivalent* to the DC semantics of section 3. A proof of such an equivalence is left for future work. We notice, however, that similar equivalence proofs between timed automata and DC semantics are given in [4].

Perspectives. Automatic verification works only for finite data types in the Z part and certain patterns of timing constraints in the DC part. For infinite data and more general DC formula one will need interactive verification techniques.

In this paper the DC part restricts only the timing of the communications. In general one would also like to restrict the timed behaviour of the class state. To this end, we pursue the idea that the current state of the Z part is made observable by a special communication.

Acknowledgement

Christian Ohler implemented the algorithm transforming FDR transition systems and DC patterns into UPPAAL timed automata.

References

1. J. Bengtsson, K.G. Larsen, F. Larsson, P. Pettersson, and Wang Yi. Uppaal – a tool suite for automatic verification of real-time systems. In R. Alur, T.A. Henzinger, and E.D. Sonntag, editors, *Hybrid Systems III – Verification and Control*, volume 1066 of *LNCS*, pages 232–243. Springer, 1997.
2. G. Booch, J. Rumbaugh, and I. Jacobson. *The Unified Modeling Language User Guide*. Object Technology Series. Addison Wesley, 1999.
3. J. Davies and S. Schneider. A brief history of Timed CSP. *Theoretical Computer Science*, 138:243–271, 1995.
4. H. Dierks, A. Fehnker, A. Mader, and F.W. Vaandrager. Operational and Logical Semantics for Polling Real-Time Systems. In A.P. Ravn and H. Rischel, editors, *FTRTFT'98*, volume 1486 of *LNCS*, pages 29–40. Springer, 1998.
5. H. Dierks and J. Tapken. Modelling and verifying of a 'cash point service' using MOBY/PLC. *Formal Aspects of Computing*, 12:220–221, 2000.
6. H. Dierks. PLC-Automata: A New Class of Implementable Real-Time Automata. *Theoretical Computer Science*, 253(1):61–93, 2001.
7. C.J. Fidge, I.J. Hayes, A.P. Martin, and A.K. Wabenhorst. A set-theoretic model for real-time specification and reasoning. In J. Jeuring, editor, *Mathematics of Program Construction*, volume 1422 of *LNCS*, pages 188–206. Springer, 1998.
8. C. Fischer and H. Wehrheim. Model-checking CSP-OZ specifications with FDR. In K. Araki, A. Galloway, and K. Taguchi, editors, *Integrated Formal Methods*, pages 315–334. Springer, 1999.
9. C. Fischer. CSP-OZ: A combination of Object-Z and CSP. In H. Bowman and J. Derrick, editors, *Formal Methods for Open Object-Based Distributed Systems (FMOODS'97)*, volume 2, pages 423–438. Chapman & Hall, 1997.
10. C. Fischer. *Combination and Implementation of Processes and Data: From CSP-OZ to Java*. PhD thesis, Bericht Nr. 2/2000, University of Oldenburg, April 2000.
11. Formal Systems (Europe) Ltd. *Failures-Divergence Refinement: FDR 2*, Dec. 1995.
12. M.R. Hansen and C. Zhou. Duration calculus: Logical foundations. *Formal Aspects of Computing*, 9:283–330, 1997.
13. S. Heilmann. *Proof Support for Duration Calculus*. PhD thesis, Dept. Inform. Technology, Tech. Univ. Denmark, June 1999. Tech. Report IT-TR: 1999-030.
14. M. Hennessy. *Algebraic Theory of Processes*. MIT Press, 1988.
15. J. He, C.A.R. Hoare, M. Fränzle, M. Müller-Olm, E.-R. Olderog, M. Schenke, M.R. Hansen, A.P. Ravn, and H. Rischel. Provably correct systems. In H. Langmaack, W.-P. de Roever, and J. Vytopil, editors, *Formal Techniques in Real-Time and Fault Tolerant Systems*, volume 863 of *LNCS*, pages 288–335. Springer, 1994.

16. C.A.R. Hoare and J. He. *Unifying Theories of Programming.* Prentice Hall, 1997.
17. C.A.R. Hoare. Communicating sequential processes. *CACM*, 21:666–677, 1978.
18. C.A.R. Hoare. *Communicating Sequential Processes.* Prentice Hall, 1985.
19. Kolyang. *HOL-Z – An Integrated Formal Support Environment for Z in Isabelle/HOL.* PhD thesis, Univ. Bremen, 1997. Shaker Verlag, Aachen, 1999.
20. D.G. Luenberger. *Introduction to Dynamic Systems. Theory, Models & Applications.* Wiley, 1979.
21. B.P. Mahony and J.S. Dong. Blending Object-Z and Timed CSP: an introduction to TCOZ. In K. Futatsugi, R. Kemmerer, and K. Torii, editors, *The 20th International Conference on Software Engineering (ICSE'98)*, pages 95–104. IEEE Computer Society Press, 1998.
22. B.P. Mahony and J.S. Dong. Sensors and actuators in TCOZ. In J.M. Wing, J. Woodcock, and J. Davies, editors, *FM'99 – Formal Methods*, volume 1709 of *LNCS*, pages 1166–1185. Springer, 1999.
23. B. Moszkowski. A temporal logic for multi-level reasoning about hardware. *IEEE Computer*, 18(2):10–19, 1985.
24. B. Moszkowski. *Executing Temporal Logic Programs.* Cambridge Univ. Press, 1986.
25. R. De Nicola and M. Hennessy. Testing equivalences of processes. *Theoretical Computer Science*, 34:83–133, 1983.
26. E.-R. Olderog, A. P. Ravn, and J. U. Skakkebæk. Refining system requirements to program specifications. In C. Heitmeyer and D. Mandrioli, editors, *Formal Methods for Real-Time Computing*, pages 107–134. Wiley, 1996.
27. A.P. Ravn, H. Rischel, and K.M. Hansen. Specifying and verifying requirements of real-time systems. *IEEE Trans. Software Engineering*, 19(1):41–55, 1993.
28. A.P. Ravn. Design of embedded real-time computing systems. Technical Report ID-TR: 1995-170, Tech. Univ. Denmark, 1995. Thesis for Doctor of Technics.
29. A.W. Roscoe. Model-checking CSP. In A.W. Roscoe, editor, *A Classical Mind – Essays in Honour of C.A.R.Hoare*, pages 353–378. Prentice-Hall, 1994.
30. A.W. Roscoe. *The Theory and Practice of Concurrency.* Prentice-Hall, 1997.
31. M. Saaltink. The Z/EVES system. In J. Bowen, M. Hinchey, and D. Till, editors, *ZUM'97*, volume 1212 of *LNCS*, pages 72–88. Springer, 1997.
32. T. Santen. *A Mechanized Logical Model of Z and Object-Oriented Specification.* PhD thesis, Tech. Univ. Berlin, Juli 1999. Shaker Verlag, Aachen, 2000.
33. M. Schenke and E.-R. Olderog. Transformational design of real-time systems – Part 1: from requirements to program specifications. *Acta Inform.*, 36:1–65, 1999.
34. B. Selic and J. Rumbaugh. Using UML for modeling complex real-time systems. Technical report, ObjecTime, 1998.
35. J.U. Skakkebæk. *A Verification Assistent for a Real-Time Logic.* PhD thesis, Dept. Comp. Sci., Tech. Univ. Denmark, Nov. 1994. Tech. Report ID-TR: 1994-150.
36. G. Smith and I. Hayes. Towards real-time Object-Z. In K. Araki, A. Galloway, and K. Taguchi, editors, *Integrated Formal Methods*, pages 49–65. Springer, 1999.
37. G. Smith. *The Object-Z Specification Language.* Kluwer Academic Publisher, 2000.
38. J.M. Spivey. *The Z Notation: A Reference Manual.* Prentice-Hall International Series in Computer Science, 2nd edition, 1992.
39. J. Woodcock and J. Davies. *Using Z – Specification, Refinement, and Proof.* Prentice-Hall, 1996.
40. C. Zhou, C.A.R. Hoare, and A.P. Ravn. A calculus of durations. *Information Processing Letters*, 40(5):269–276, 1991.

An Integration of Real-Time Object-Z and CSP for Specifying Concurrent Real-Time Systems

Graeme Smith

Software Verification Research Centre, University of Queensland, Australia
smith@svrc.uq.edu.au

Abstract. Real-Time Object-Z is an integration of the object-oriented formal specification language Object-Z with a timed trace notation suitable for modelling timing constraints and continuous variables. This extends the applicability of Object-Z to real-time and embedded systems. In this paper, we enhance the ability of Real-Time Object-Z to specify concurrent real-time and embedded systems by semantically integrating it with the process algebra CSP. The approach builds on the existing work on the integration of (standard) Object-Z and CSP.

1 Introduction

Object-Z [16,3] is an object-oriented specification language based on Z [21]. It extends Z with a notion of *classes*, used to encapsulate a state schema with its initial state schema and associated set of operations, and *objects*, instances of classes used to specifying systems. The enhanced structuring provided by classes and associated techniques such as *inheritance*, which enables definitions of one class to include those of another, and *polymorphism*, which enables the construction of a type corresponding to a collection of classes, makes Object-Z well-suited to modelling large-scale systems with complex data structures.

When modelling interaction in concurrent systems, however, Object-Z specification can become unwieldy. This is due to the necessity to explicitly specify all concurrent occurrences of operations [16, Chapter 5]. This shortcoming led to the development of Object-Z/CSP [15,17,2,18], a semantic integration[1] of Object-Z and CSP [9,12] in which Object-Z classes are identified with CSP processes so that interaction between instances of them can be specified using CSP operators.

In order to model real-time and embedded systems, Object-Z has also been semantically integrated with the timed trace notation of Fidge et al. [5] in which variables are modelled as (possibly continuous) functions defining their values over all time. The integrated notation, referred to as Real-Time Object-Z [19,20], suffers from the same shortcomings with respect to modelling concurrent systems as standard Object-Z.

---

[1] A semantic integration is one in which language constructs of the constituent languages are semantically identified and usually involves no change to the syntax of either language [6].

M. Butler, L. Petre, and K. Sere (Eds.): IFM 2002, LNCS 2335, pp. 267–285, 2002.

To overcome this problem with Real-Time Object-Z, Smith and Hayes [20], developed a simple parallel composition operator. This operator, which identifies common-named inputs, outputs and operations of instances of combined classes, provides a concise means of modelling concurrency. However, it is overly restrictive since it requires synchronising operations to have the same start and end times. Furthermore, it provides only a limited means for constructing concurrent systems. For example, there is no support for combining instances of classes which do not synchronise on common-named operations nor any means of renaming or hiding operations.

In this paper, we provide an alternative approach to concurrency in Real-Time Object-Z. Building on the work on Object-Z/CSP, we semantically identify Real-Time Object-Z classes with CSP processes allowing instances of them to be combined with the full range of CSP operators. We begin by providing an overview of Object-Z/CSP (in Section 2) and Real-Time Object-Z (in Section 3). We then show how a failures/divergences semantics (the semantics of CSP processes) can be given to Real-Time Object-Z classes by associating CSP events with (instantaneous) observations of operations and process parameters with continuous variables (in Section 4). We discuss alternative approaches for specifying real-time concurrent systems based on Object-Z (in Section 5) before concluding (in Section 6).

2   Overview of Object-Z/CSP

Object-Z/CSP [15,17,2,18] is an integration of Object-Z [16,3] and CSP [9,12] motivated by the need to model both complex data structures and process interaction in the specification of concurrent and distributed systems. Object-Z classes are used to model data structures, comprising a state and collection of operations, and CSP operators are used to model the interactions between instances of these classes.

The integration is *semantic* in the sense that a common semantics is given to the two languages and hence to the overall specifications. This approach has two main advantages. Firstly, the individual notations are syntactically unchanged and clearly separated in specifications. This makes the specifications more accessible to users already familiar with the languages, and the use of existing tool support and verification and refinement methods possible [8,17,18]. Secondly, there is no need to define a new semantics for the integration. Adopting the existing semantics of one of the languages is possible. The semantics adopted for Object-Z/CSP is the existing failures/divergences semantics of CSP.

To illustrate Object-Z/CSP, we specify a simple case study. The case study is based on a proposed system to help farmers in outback Australia keep track of the condition of their cattle[2]. Due to the large size of cattle properties, it is not always possible for farmers to be aware of the condition of their cattle, and hence to know whether additional food needs to be brought to them in

---

[2] The author worked on the implementation of this system while an undergraduate student. He is not aware whether it is still in use.

times of drought. To overcome this, weighbridges can be installed around fenced waterholes. As the cattle enter and leave the area around the waterhole, their weight is recorded and trends in weight loss or gain can be noticed by the farmer.

Typically, the system would comprise several weighbridges, each with its own *weigh unit*, and a central *store unit* (see Fig. 1).

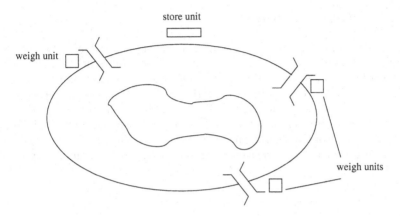

Fig. 1. Aerial view of cattle weighing system

The weigh units calculate the weight of individual cattle from a continuous signal input from the weighbridge (see Fig. 2).

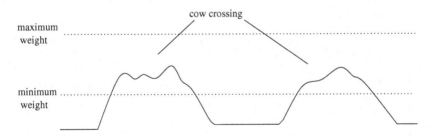

Fig. 2. Typical weighbridge signal

These weights are then transmitted to the store unit which stores them along with the day they were recorded.

To specify such a system in Object-Z/CSP, we would begin by specifying its components, weigh units and store units, as Object-Z classes. As a preliminary, we specify the set of non-negative real numbers $\mathbb{R}_+$ for representing weights and the constants *MinWeight* and *MaxWeight* denoting the minimum weight that should be detected as a cattle crossing and the maximum weight the system needs to be able to deal with respectively.

$$\mathbb{R}_+ == \{r : \mathbb{R} \mid r \geqslant 0\}$$

$$
\begin{array}{|l}
\hline
Min\,Weight, Max\,Weight : \mathbb{R}_+ \\
\hline
Min\,Weight < Max\,Weight \\
\end{array}
$$

A weigh unit is specified as having a single state variable: *data* comprising recently recorded data not yet transmitted to the store unit. Initially, there is no recorded data. An operation *Weigh* allows a new weight, input as *weight?*, to be added to the data, and an operation *SendData* allows the recorded data to be output, as *data!*, and cleared. Note that the input *weight?* of the former operation is an abstraction of the actual continuous signal from the weighbridge. It (informally) corresponds to the average value of the weighbridge signal over an interval of time where the signal is greater than the level "minimum weight" (see Fig. 2).

$$
\begin{array}{l}
\hline
\textit{WeighUnit} \\
\hline
\quad
\begin{array}{l}
\hline
data : \text{bag}\,\mathbb{R}_+ \\
\hline
\end{array} \\
\quad
\begin{array}{l}
\hline
\textit{INIT} \\
\hline
data = [\![\,]\!] \\
\hline
\end{array} \\
\quad
\begin{array}{l}
\hline
\textit{Weigh} \\
\hline
\Delta(data) \\
weight? : \mathbb{R}_+ \\
\hline
Min\,Weight \leqslant weight? \leqslant Max\,Weight \\
data' = data \uplus [\![weight?]\!] \\
\hline
\end{array} \\
\quad
\begin{array}{l}
\hline
\textit{SendData} \\
\hline
\Delta(data) \\
data! : \text{bag}\,\mathbb{R}_+ \\
\hline
data! = data \\
data' = [\![\,]\!] \\
\hline
\end{array} \\
\hline
\end{array}
$$

A store unit is specified as having two variables: *day* denoting the day of operation of the system (incremented every 24 hours), and *record* denoting the data received from the weigh units each day. Initially, *day* is set to 1 and there is no received data. An operation *RecData* allows data to be received and added to any other data received for that day. An operation *UpdateDay* allows the day to be incremented.

$$
\begin{array}{|l}
\hline
\_StoreUnit _____ \\
\hline
day : \mathbb{N} \\
record : \mathbb{N} \to \text{bag}\,\mathbb{R}_+ \\
\hline
\_INIT_____ \\
day = 1 \\
\forall\, n : \mathbb{N} \bullet record(n) = [\![\,]\!] \\
\hline
\_RecData_____ \\
\Delta(data) \\
data? : \text{bag}\,\mathbb{R}_+ \\
\hline
record' = record \oplus \{\, day \mapsto record(day) \uplus data? \,\} \\
\hline
\_UpdateDay_____ \\
\Delta(day) \\
\hline
day' = day + 1 \\
\hline
\end{array}
$$

To specify systems of components, Object-Z/CSP views such classes as processes which can be combined using the operators of CSP. In particular, operations are identified with events and, to synchronise, must have the same name and parameters with the same basenames (i.e., apart from the ? or !) and values. In the case study, we want $RecData$ of $StoreUnit$ to synchronise with $SendData$ of $WeighUnit$. Hence, we specify new classes SU and WU which inherit $StoreUnit$ and $WeighUnit$, respectively, applying appropriate renaming.

$$
\begin{array}{|l}
\hline
\_SU_____ \\
\hline
StoreUnit[ComData/RecData] \\
\hline
\end{array}
$$

We also need to refer to multiple instances of $WeighUnit$. This is facilitated by adding a constant to the class so that distinct weigh units can be assigned unique numbers. Given the specification below, $WU_{\{number \mapsto i\}}$ denotes an instance of WU with $number = i$ [15].

$$
\begin{array}{|l}
\hline
\_WU_____ \\
\hline
WeighUnit[ComData/SendData] \\
\mid number : \mathbb{N} \\
\hline
\end{array}
$$

The weighing system is specified as a parameterised system. The parameter denotes how many weigh units are present. The weigh units are combined with each other using the CSP interleaving operator $|||$ (i.e., they do not synchronise with each other on any events) and with the store unit using the CSP parallel operator $\|$ (i.e., the store unit performs the (renamed) operation $SendData$ only when one of the weigh units can synchronise with it).

$$WeighingSystem(n) = (\|\|_{i=1}^{n} \ WU_{\{number \mapsto i\}}) \ X\|_Y \ SU$$

where $X = \{| \ Weigh, SendData \ |\}$ and $Y = \{| \ SendData, UpdateDay \ |\}$.

The preceding specification of the cattle weighing system has several short-comings. Firstly, the interpretation of the *weight?* inputs is informal. Additionally, the fact that the *Weigh* operations occur every time their associated weigh-bridge signals are greater than the level "minimum weight", is not specified.

There are also some timing constraints which are not formalised. Firstly, the fact the *UpdateDay* operation occurs regularly at an appropriate time is not formalised. Secondly, the fact that the information recorded by the weigh units is transmitted to the store unit on the same day they are recorded is similarly omitted. Both of these timing constraints are crucial to the information in the store unit being of use to the farmer.

3   Overview of Real-Time Object-Z

Real-Time Object-Z [19,20] is an integration of Object-Z with the timed trace notation of Fidge et al. [5]. It allows the specification of complex data structures which behave according to real-time constraints and interact with a continuously changing environment. A type $\mathbb{T} == \mathbb{R}$ is introduced to model absolute time. In this paper, we assume its units are seconds and use constants min=60 and hour=60*60 to allow us to write times in minutes or hours respectively.

Classes are divided into two parts by a horizontal line. The part above the line is essentially standard Object-Z with the addition of an implicit variable τ of type $\mathbb{T}$ denoting the current time. The part below the line contains two timed trace predicates denoting an assumption on the class's environment and an effect the class achieves when that assumption is met.

Using Real-Time Object-Z, the class *WeighUnit* can be modified as follows. A timed trace constant *weight?*, denoting the continuous signal from the weigh-bridge over all time, replaces the need for the input *weight?* of the operation *Weigh*. The ? decoration on this constant denotes that it is an input from the environment (a ! decoration would similarly denote an output). The fact that such an input is continuous (and smooth) is specified using the function symbol $\leadsto$ [4]. A timed trace assumption predicate is added to the class restricting the value of *weight?* to always be less than or equal to *MaxWeight*.

The operation *Weigh* uses this environmental input to calculate the weight of a cow. It adds to *data* the average value of the signal between its start time τ and end time τ' [3]. To ensure this operation occurs when necessary (and not otherwise), we add an effect predicate which states that the operation occurs precisely when *weight?* is at least *MinWeight*.

The predicate uses the notation $\langle P \rangle$ to denote the set of intervals of time in which a predicate P holds. In general, any timed trace constants and variables

---

[3] In practice, some error, due to sampling and time delays, would be introduced in the calculation of the average weight. For simplifying the presentation, however, we ignore this and other such errors in this paper.

in such a predicate P may be *lifted* to their range types [5], i.e., a constant or variable of type $\mathbb{T} \to T$ is treated as if it were a variable of type T (e.g., *weight?* in the predicate below). Such a predicate P may also include the names of operations denoting Boolean variables which are true precisely when the operation is occurring (e.g., *Weigh* in the predicate below).

The frequency of occurrence of the operation *SendData* is also constrained by a timed trace effect predicate. This predicate use the operator ';' for concatenating sets of time intervals [5]. It specifies that in any time interval of at least 10 minutes duration, the operation *SendData* must occur. This is done using the reserved symbol δ which denotes the duration of an interval. Similarly, α and ω are reserved symbols denoting the start and end times of an interval, and ϕ is a reserved symbol denoting the interval itself.

__*WeighUnit* _____

$weight? : \mathbb{T} \nrightarrow \mathbb{R}_+$

$data : \text{bag}\,\mathbb{R}_+$

__*INIT* _____

$data = \langle\,\rangle$

__*Weigh* _____

$\Delta(data)$

$data' = data \uplus [\![(\int_\tau^{\tau'} weight?)/(\tau' - \tau)]\!]$

__*SendData* _____

$\Delta(data)$
$data! : \text{bag}\,\mathbb{R}_+$

$data! = data$
$data' = [\![\,]\!]$

---

assumption $\forall\, t : \mathbb{T} \bullet weight?(t) \leqslant MaxWeight$

effect $\langle Weigh \rangle = \langle weight? \geqslant MinWeight \rangle$
$\langle \delta \geqslant 10 * \min \rangle \subseteq \langle true \rangle ; \langle SendData \rangle ; \langle true \rangle$

The class *StoreUnit* is extended with a variable *last_update* denoting the last time the day was updated. Initially, this value is equal to the current time. The operation *UpdateDay* is extended to set this variable to its start time and to only occur when this time is 24 hours since the time held by the variable.

By itself, the precondition of *UpdateDay* only prevents the operation from happening at times other than 24 hours after *last_update*. It does not ensure that the operation occurs when its precondition is satisfied. To specify this, we add an effect predicate which states that the operation occurs in every 24 hour interval of time.

```
┌─ StoreUnit ──────────────────────────────────────────────────
│
│  ┌──────────────────────────────────────────────────────────
│  │ day : ℕ
│  │ record : ℕ ⇸ bag ℝ₊
│  │ last_update : 𝕋
│  ├──────────────────────────────────────────────────────────
│  │ ┌─ INIT ──────────────────────────────────────────────
│  │ │ day = 1
│  │ │ ∀ n : ℕ • record(n) = [[ ]]
│  │ │ last_update = τ
│  │
│  │ ┌─ RecData ───────────────────────────────────────────
│  │ │ Δ(data)
│  │ │ data? : bag ℝ₊
│  │ ├──────────────────────────────────────────────────────
│  │ │ record' = record ⊕ {day ↦ record(day) ⊎ data?}
│  │
│  │ ┌─ UpdateDay ─────────────────────────────────────────
│  │ │ Δ(day, last_update)
│  │ ├──────────────────────────────────────────────────────
│  │ │ τ − last_update = 24 ∗ hour
│  │ │ day' = day + 1
│  │ │ last_update' = τ
│  │
│  ├──────────────────────────────────────────────────────────
│  │ assumption    true
│  ├──────────────────────────────────────────────────────────
│  │ effect        ⟨δ = 24 ∗ hour⟩ ⊆ ⟨true⟩ ; ⟨UpdateDay⟩ ; ⟨true⟩
```

The above classes overcome the shortcomings identified at the end of Section 2. The interpretation of the input to the *Weigh* operation is formalised as are the constraints on the occurrence of *Weigh*, *UpdateDay* and *SendData*. To specify the weighing system, however, we would like to be able to combine these classes in a manner similar to that in Section 2.

4   Semantic Integration of Real-Time Object-Z and CSP

To enable instances of Object-Z classes to be combined with CSP operators in Object-Z/CSP, classes are given a failures/divergences semantics, i.e., the semantics of processes in CSP. This semantics is derived from the existing history semantics of Object-Z [14].

A history of a class is a possible sequence of states an instance of the class can pass through, together with the associated sequence of operations that cause the state changes. A state is an assignment of values to a set of identifiers representing its variables and the constants it can refer to. The states S of a class are hence defined as

$$S \subseteq Id \nrightarrow Value$$

An operation comprises the operation's name and an assignment of values to the operations parameters. The operations O of a class are defined as

$$O \subseteq Id \times (Id \nrightarrow Value)$$

Therefore, the set of histories of a class is represented by a set[4]

$$H \subseteq S^\omega \times O^\omega$$

such that

$$(s, o) \in H \Rightarrow s \neq \langle \rangle \tag{H1}$$
$$(s, o) \in H \wedge s \in S^* \Rightarrow \#s = \#o + 1 \tag{H2}$$
$$(s, o) \in H \wedge s \notin S^* \Rightarrow o \notin O^* \tag{H3}$$
$$(s_1 \frown s_2, o_1 \frown o_2) \in H \wedge \#s_1 = \#o_1 + 1 \Rightarrow (s_1, o_1) \in H \tag{H4}$$

These properties capture the fact that the sequence of states is non-empty (H1) and is one longer than the sequence of operations (H2) (except when both are infinite (H3)), and that the set of histories is prefix-closed (H4).

To relate Object-Z classes and CSP processes, we identify Object-Z operations with CSP events. In order that common-named operations synchronise and communicate via parameters with common basenames, we define a function *event* which, given an operation (n, p), where n is the operation's name and p is an assignment of values to its parameters, returns the event $n.p'$ where p' is p with all parameters replaced by their basenames (i.e., with the ? and ! decorations removed).

The failures of an Object-Z class C with constants $\vec{c}$ assigned values $\vec{v}$ are then derived from its histories as follows: (tr, X) is a failure of $C_{\{\vec{c} \mapsto \vec{v}\}}$ if

- there exists a finite history of C whose initial state is satisfied by the assignment of $\vec{v}$ to $\vec{c}$,
- the sequence of operations of the history correspond to the sequence of events in tr, and
- for each event in X, there does not exist a history which extends the original history by an operation corresponding to the event.

$$
\begin{aligned}
failures(C_{\{\vec{c} \mapsto \vec{v}\}}) = \{(tr, X) \mid \exists (s, o) \in H \bullet \\
s \in S^* \wedge \\
\{\vec{c} \mapsto \vec{v}\} \subseteq s(1) \wedge \\
\#tr = \#o \wedge \\
(\forall i \in 1 .. \#tr \bullet tr(i) = event(o(i))) \wedge \\
(\forall e \in X \bullet (\nexists st \in S, op \in O \bullet \\
e = event(op) \wedge (s \frown \langle st \rangle, o \frown \langle op \rangle) \in H))\}
\end{aligned}
$$

---

[4] S^ω and S^* denote the set of (possibly infinite) sequences and set of finite sequences, respectively, of elements from the set S.

This definition assumes classes do not have liveness constraints (since it only refers to finite histories) and that outputs of class instances are angelic, i.e., for the purpose of specification they can be influenced by the environment [15]. Alternative semantics also exist which support liveness constraints [7] and demonic outputs [18]. Operations are also assumed to be *blocked* outside their preconditions, i.e., they do not behave chaotically. Hence, the set of divergences of a class instance $C_{\{\bar{c} \mapsto \bar{v}\}}$ is empty.

$$divergences(C_{\{\bar{c} \mapsto \bar{v}\}}) = \varnothing$$

Problems due to unbounded nondeterminism are avoided by restricting hiding of unbounded sequences of events [15].

To similarly integrate Real-Time Object-Z with CSP, we need means of encoding both timing constraints and continuous variables in CSP process definitions. There are a number of approaches to the former. For example, start and end times could be associated with events. That is, an operation Op starting at time t_1 and ending at time t_2 could be represented by an event $Op.t_1.t_2$. Alternatively, the operation could be associated with two events, $Op_S.t_1$ and $Op_E.t_2$, denoting the start and end of the operation respectively.

The problem with these approaches is that they restrict the way in which synchronisations can occur between processes. The first approach forces two synchronising events to have the same start and end times (since they have to agree on the values t_1 and t_2). The second approach forces synchronisation to occur at the start or end times of the operations, or at the start time of one and the end time of the other. In general, synchronising operations may simply overlap and not have any common start or end times (see Fig. 3).

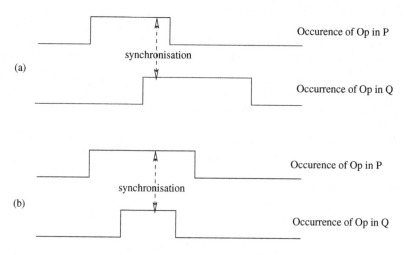

Fig. 3. Possible operation synchronisations

A more general approach, which we adopt in this paper, is to represent an operation occurrence by a single event and a single time during the occurrence.

In this case, the event corresponds to an instantaneous observation of the time-consuming operation. For example, if an operation Op starts at time 10 and ends at time 15, it is represented by a single event $Op.t$ where $10 \leqslant t \leqslant 15$. This enables operations to synchronise whenever they overlap, i.e., have at least one point in time in common.

Since continuous variables in Real-Time Object-Z are class constants, they can be assigned values when an instance of the class is used in a specification (cf., the constant *number* of class WU in Section 2). The resulting failures of the class instance depend on the value assigned. For example, the times of events related to the operation $Weigh$ of $WeighUnit$ depend directly on the value assigned to the continuous variable $weight?$ (see Fig. 4).

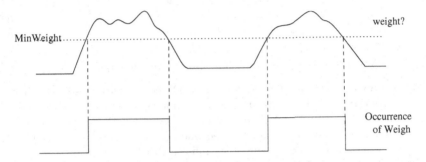

Fig. 4. Dependence of *Weigh* operations on *weight?*

When a class instance is used in a specification, the values of any continuous variables need to be supplied as additional parameters. For example, given the definitions of $WeighUnit$ and $StoreUnit$ of Section 3 together with the definitions of WU and SU of Section 2, the weighing system can be specified as

$$WeighingSystem(n, w_1, \ldots, w_n) = (\|\|_{i=1}^{n} \; WU_{\{weight? \mapsto w_i, number \mapsto i\}}) \; X\|_Y \; SU$$

where $X = \{| \; Weigh, SendData \; |\}$ and $Y = \{| \; SendData, UpdateDay \; |\}$.

To formalise this approach, we need to translate the semantics of Real-Time Object-Z to appropriate failures and divergences. The semantics as given by Smith and Hayes [19,20] models a class as a set of *real-time histories*. A real-time history extends a standard Object-Z history with

- start and end times of each operation,
- timed trace representations of all constants and variables, and
- a set of time intervals for each operation denoting the operation occurrences.

Since the latter can be derived from the start and end times of operations [19,20], we do not need to include them explicitly as part of the semantics. Similarly, since the timed trace representation of constants and variables can be derived from the sequence of states [19,20][5], we do not need to explicitly include them either.

---

[5] Note that since continuous variables are modelled as constants, their value (over all time) is available in any state.

The start times are represented by a sequence of times equal in length to the number of operations (or infinite when the number of operations are infinite). Similarly, the end times are represented by a sequence of times. The first end time denotes the time at which initialisation occurred. Hence, the length of the sequence is one greater than the number of start times (or infinite when the number of start times is infinite).

Therefore, the real-time histories of a class are represented by a set

$$R \subseteq S^\omega \times O^\omega \times \mathbb{T}^\omega \times \mathbb{T}^\omega$$

such that

$$
\begin{aligned}
&(s, o, t_s, t_e) \in R \Rightarrow s \neq \langle \rangle \wedge (\forall i \in 1 \mathinner{..} \#t_s \bullet t_e(i) \leqslant t_s(i) \leqslant t_e(i+1)) && \text{(R1)} \\
&(s, o, t_s, t_e) \in R \wedge s \in S^* \Rightarrow \#s = \#o + 1 = \#t_s + 1 = \#t_e && \text{(R2)} \\
&(s, o, t_s, t_e) \in R \wedge s \notin S^* \Rightarrow o \notin O^* \wedge t_s \notin \mathbb{T}^* \wedge t_e \notin \mathbb{T}^* && \text{(R3)} \\
&(s_1 \frown s_2, o_1 \frown o_2, t_{s1} \frown t_{s2}, t_{e1} \frown t_{e2}) \in R \\
&\quad \wedge \#s_1 = \#o_1 + 1 = \#t_{s1} + 1 = \#t_{e1} \Rightarrow (s_1, o_1, t_{s1}, t_{e1}) \in R && \text{(R4)}
\end{aligned}
$$

These properties extend those for standard Object-Z histories so that there is an appropriate ordering on start and end times of operations (R1), and the sequences of start and end times are of the same length as the sequence of operations, and one more than the sequence of operations, respectively (R2) (except when each of the sequences are infinite (R3)).

The integration of Real-Time Object-Z and CSP is formalised via the following derivations of failures. (The set of divergences of a class is empty as for Object-Z/CSP. Problems with unbounded nondeterminism are avoided by an identical restriction on hiding.)

(tr, X) is a failure of $C_{\{\vec{c} \mapsto \vec{v}\}}$ if

- there exists a finite real-time history of C whose initial state is satisfied by the assignment of $\vec{v}$ to $\vec{c}$,
- each event in tr represents the corresponding operation in the history together with a time of occurrence between the corresponding start and end times, and
- for each event in X, there does not exist a real-time history which extends the original real-time history by an operation corresponding to the event.

$$
\begin{aligned}
failures_{rt}(C_{\{\vec{c} \mapsto \vec{v}\}}) = \{ (tr, X) \mid \exists (s, o, t_s, t_e) \in R \bullet \\
s \in S^* \wedge \\
\{\vec{c} \mapsto \vec{v}\} \subseteq s(1) \wedge \\
\#tr = \#o \wedge \\
(\forall i \in 1 \mathinner{..} \#tr \bullet (\exists t \in \mathbb{T} \bullet \\
t_s(i) \leqslant t \leqslant t_e(i+1) \wedge \\
tr(i) = event(o(i)).t)) \wedge \\
(\forall e \in X \bullet (\not\exists st \in S, op \in O, t, t_1, t_2 \in \mathbb{T} \bullet \\
t_1 \leqslant t \leqslant t_2 \wedge e = event(op).t \wedge \\
(s \frown \langle st \rangle, o \frown \langle op \rangle, t_s \frown \langle t_1 \rangle, t_e \frown \langle t_2 \rangle) \in R)) \}
\end{aligned}
$$

For Real-Time Object-Z classes to be combined using CSP operators, the set of failures F derived for a class must satisfy the following properties [12].

$$(\langle\rangle, \varnothing) \in F \tag{F1}$$
$$(tr_1 \frown tr_2, \varnothing) \in F \Rightarrow (tr_1, \varnothing) \in F \tag{F2}$$
$$(tr, X) \in F \land Y \subseteq X \Rightarrow (tr, Y) \in F \tag{F3}$$
$$(tr, X) \in F \land (\forall y \in Y \bullet (tr \frown \langle y \rangle, \varnothing) \notin F) \Rightarrow (tr, X \cup Y) \in F \tag{F4}$$

These properties hold for the definition of $failures_{rt}$ as shown below.

Proof of $F1$.

$C_{\{\vec{c} \mapsto \vec{v}\}}$ is regarded as well-defined by Smith [15] only if there exists a possible initial state of C satisfying the assignment of values to constants, $\{\vec{c} \mapsto \vec{v}\}$. Hence, if a failures semantics is given to $C_{\{\vec{c} \mapsto \vec{v}\}}$ then $\exists(s, o, t_s, t_e) \in R \bullet \{\vec{c} \mapsto \vec{v}\} \subseteq s(1)$.
By $R4$, therefore, it follows that $(\langle s(1) \rangle, \langle\rangle, \langle\rangle, \langle t \rangle) \in R$, for some $t : \mathbb{T}$.
Since $\langle s(1) \rangle \in S^*$, the trace of events corresponding to the operation sequence $\langle\rangle$ is $\langle\rangle$, and $\forall e \in \varnothing \bullet P$ is true for any predicate P, it follows that $(\langle\rangle, \varnothing) \in failures_{rt}(C_{\{\vec{c} \mapsto \vec{v}\}})$. □

Proof of $F2$.

If $(tr_1 \frown tr_2, \varnothing) \in failures_{rt}(C_{\{\vec{c} \mapsto \vec{v}\}})$ then, by the definition of $failures_{rt}$,
$\exists(s, o, t_s, t_e) \in R \bullet \{\vec{c} \mapsto \vec{v}\} \subseteq s(1) \land (\forall i \in 1 .. \#(tr_1 \frown tr_2) \bullet (\exists t \in \mathbb{T} \bullet t_s(i) \leqslant t \leqslant t_e(i+1) \land (tr_1 \frown tr_2)(i) = event(o(i)).t)).$
If $s = s_1 \frown s_2$, $o = o_1 \frown o_2$, $t_s = t_{s1} \frown t_{s2}$ and $t_e = t_{e1} \frown t_{e2}$ such that $\#o_1 = \#tr_1 = \#t_{s1}$ and $\#s_1 = \#o1 + 1 = \#t_{e1}$ then $(s_1, o_1, t_{s1}, t_{e1}) \in R$ by $R4$.
Since $s_1(1) = s(1)$ it follows that $\{\vec{c} \mapsto \vec{v}\} \subseteq s_1(1)$. Also, $s_1 \in S^*$ and $(\forall i \in 1 .. \#tr_1 \bullet (\exists t \in \mathbb{T} \bullet t_{s1}(i) \leqslant t \leqslant t_{e1}(i+1) \land tr_1(i) = event(o_1(i)).t))$. Hence, since $\forall e \in \varnothing \bullet P$ is true for any predicate P, it follows that $(tr_1, \varnothing) \in failures_{rt}(C_{\{\vec{c} \mapsto \vec{v}\}})$. □

Proof of $F3$.

Since $(\forall e \in X \bullet P) \Rightarrow (\forall e \in Y \bullet P)$ for any predicate P when $Y \subseteq X$, if $(t, X) \in failures_{rt}(C_{\{\vec{c} \mapsto \vec{v}\}})$ and $Y \subseteq X$ then $(t, Y) \in failures_{rt}(C_{\{\vec{c} \mapsto \vec{v}\}})$. □

Proof of $F4$.

If $(tr, X) \in failures_{rt}(C_{\{\vec{c} \mapsto \vec{v}\}})$ then, by the definition of $failures_{rt}$,
$\exists(s, o, t_s, t_e) \in R \bullet s \in S^* \land \{\vec{c} \mapsto \vec{v}\} \subseteq s(1) \land \#tr = \#o \land (\forall i \in 1 .. \#tr \bullet (\exists t \in \mathbb{T} \bullet t_s(i) \leqslant t \leqslant t_e(i+1) \land tr(i) = event(o(i).t)).$
Since $\forall e \in \varnothing \bullet P$ is true for any predicate P, it then follows that $(tr \frown \langle y \rangle, \varnothing) \in failures_{rt}(C_{\{\vec{c} \mapsto \vec{v}\}})$ unless $\nexists st \in S, op \in O, t, t_1, t_2 \in \mathbb{T} \bullet t_1 \leqslant t \leqslant t_2 \land y = event(op).t \land (s \frown \langle st \rangle, o \frown \langle op \rangle, t_s \frown \langle t_1 \rangle, t_e \frown \langle t_2 \rangle) \in R$.
Therefore, if $\forall y \in Y \bullet (tr \frown \langle y \rangle, \varnothing) \notin failures_{rt}(C_{\{\vec{c} \mapsto \vec{v}\}})$ then $(tr, X \cup Y) \in failures_{rt}(C_{\{\vec{c} \mapsto \vec{v}\}})$. □

5   Alternative Approaches Based on Object-Z

The integration of Real-Time Object-Z and CSP enables specifications of concurrent systems with real-time properties which interact with continuous variables in their environment. Having Object-Z as the basis of the integration enables complex data structures and data manipulations within the components of such systems to be constructed incrementally. Both inheritance and polymorphism are useful in this respect.

For example, suppose that the weigh units need to additionally control a gate at the end of the weighbridge to separate cows of different weight. This would be necessary, for instance, to remove older calves from their mothers. In times of drought, calves are known to drink milk from their mother for extended periods of time often to the detriment of the mother's health.

To avoid complicating the specification of the *WeighUnit* class, this aspect of the weighbridge could be added via inheritance as follows. We assume there are two gates, identified by the numbers 1 and 2, and that cows whose weights lie above $W_1 : \mathbb{R}_+$ but below $W_2 : \mathbb{R}_+$ should go through gate 1. All others should go through gate 2.

```
┌─ GateControlUnit ──────────────────────────────────────
│  WU
│  ┌────────────────────────────────────────────────────
│  │ gate : {1, 2}
│  ├────────────────────────────────────────────────────
│  │ ┌─ Weigh ──────────────────────────────────────────
│  │ │ Δ(gate)
│  │ ├──────────────────────────────────────────────────
│  │ │ gate' = 1 ⇔ W₁ < (∫ weight?)/(τ' − τ) < W₂
└──┴─┴──────────────────────────────────────────────────
```

$$gate' = 1 \Leftrightarrow W_1 < \left(\int_\tau^{\tau'} weight?\right)/(\tau' - \tau) < W_2$$

The class inherits *WU*, i.e., the class *WeighUnit* extended with a number as in Section 2, and adds a state variable *gate* denoting the gate which is currently opened. If desired, this variable could be related via a timed trace predicate to continuous output variables representing signals to the gate mechanisms. The operation *Weigh* is extended so that *gate* will be set to 1 when the recorded weight is in the range $W_1 \ldots W_2$, and set to 2 otherwise.

If we then wanted to specify a system where weighbridges may optionally be connected to gates, we could use polymorphism as follows.

$$WeighingSystem(n, w_1, \ldots, w_n) = (\|\|_{i=1}^n \downarrow WU_{\{weight? \mapsto w_i, number \mapsto i\}}) \; {}_X\|_Y \; SU$$

where $X = \{| \; Weigh, SendData \; |\}$ and $Y = \{| \; SendData, UpdateDay \; |\}$. The notation $\downarrow WU$ denotes the class *WU* or any class inherited from *WU* (in this case, the class *GateControlUnit*). The actual class of each instance is chosen nondeterministically.

Given the usefulness of these structuring concepts for larger-scale systems, we focus our discussion, in this section, on alternative approaches to specifying concurrent real-time systems which are based on Object-Z.

5.1   Other Approaches Using Real-Time Object-Z

The issue of concurrency in Real-Time Object-Z is addressed by Smith and Hayes [20]. One option explored is the use of object instantiation (as in standard Object-Z). Given an object a of a class C (declared as $a : C$), we can refer to a variable or constant x of the object by the notation $a.x$. Similarly, we can state that the object satisfies its class's initial condition or undergoes operation Op of its class by $a.\textsc{Init}$ and $a.Op$ respectively. Adopting this approach, we might specify the weighing system as follows.

$\_\_$ *WeighingSystem* $_____$

$\quad$ $wu : \mathbb{P}\ WU$
$\quad$ $su : SU$

$\quad$ $\forall\, a, b : wu \bullet a.number = b.number \Rightarrow a = b$

$\quad$ $\_\ \textsc{Init}\ _____$
$\quad\quad$ $\forall\, a : wu \bullet a.\textsc{Init}$
$\quad\quad$ $su.\textsc{Init}$

$\quad$ $Weigh \mathrel{==} [a : wu] \bullet a.Weigh$
$\quad$ $SendData \mathrel{==} [a : wu] \bullet a.SendData \parallel su.RecData$
$\quad$ $UpdateDay \mathrel{\widehat{=}} su.UpdateDay$

This class comprises a set of objects of class WU, each with a unique number, and an object of class SU. We assume that the real-time properties of the objects' classes are implicitly maintained. The initial condition and operations of the class are constructed from those of the component classes using Object-Z operation operators [16, Chapter 3].

Synchronisation, including communication, is explicitly modelled using the $\parallel$ operator. This operator conjoins its argument operations and equates any inputs in one with outputs in the other when they have common basenames. Similarly, concurrent occurrences of operations (whether as part of synchronisation or not) are explicitly specified via the conjunction of operations.

As pointed out by Smith and Hayes, however, this approach is undesirable for two reasons.

— Explicitly stating all combinations of operations which can occur concurrently may become unwieldy for large systems comprising many components.
— Conjoined operations are forced to have the same start and end times. Hence, the partial overlap of operations cannot be specified.

An alternative approach explored by Smith and Hayes is the definition of a parallel composition operator for combining classes. This operator is similar to the CSP operator in that it ensures the synchronisation of common-named operations. However, any synchronising operations must still have the same start and end times.

A more fundamental problem with this approach is that the single operator introduced hinders direct specification of many systems. For example, the
weighing system specification in this paper makes use of CSP's interleaving op-
erator $|||$. Using parallel composition alone, in this case, would require *Weigh*
and *SendData* operations to include the weigh unit's number as a parameter (to
avoid weigh units synchronising on these operations).

The approach could be extended with an interleaving operator, as well as
other operators such as renaming and hiding found in CSP. However, the result
would not improve on an integration with CSP itself as detailed in this paper.
Furthermore, the introduction of new notations, as opposed to the integration
of existing notations, result in an approach which is both less familiar and less
amenable to use with existing tools and verification and refinement techniques.

5.2   Integrating Object-Z/CSP with the Timed Trace Notation

An alternative to integrating Real-Time Object-Z with CSP would be to integrate Object-Z/CSP with the timed trace notation giving a timed trace semantics to specifications. In such an approach, timed trace predicates could be
used to restrict the time of occurrence of events within an Object-Z/CSP system
specification.

For example, given the Object-Z/CSP specification of the weighing system in
Section 2, the following effect predicates might be added to ensure the *UpdateDay*
event occurs as required.

$$\langle \delta = 24 * \text{hour} \rangle \subseteq \langle true \rangle \ ; \ \langle UpdateDay \rangle \ ; \ \langle true \rangle$$
$$\langle UpdateDay \rangle \ ; \ \langle \neg \ UpdateDay \rangle \ ; \ \langle UpdateDay \rangle \subseteq \langle \delta = 24 * hours \rangle$$

The first predicate (identical to that in the Real-Time Object-Z specification
in Section 3) ensures that *UpdateDay* occurs at least once in every 24 hours.
The second predicate ensures that the separation between *UpdateDay* events
is precisely 24 hours. (Note that the intervals $\langle UpdateDay \rangle$ here correspond to
event occurrences and hence comprise a single point of time only.)

One problem with this approach is that because we are constraining CSP
processes, rather than Object-Z classes, we can only specify timing constraints
on operation occurrences. However, it is also often desirable to specify timing
constraints on state variables as evidenced by the case studies by Smith and
Hayes [19,20].

A more serious problem becomes obvious if we try to specify the timing
constraints on the events *Weigh* and *SendData*. These constraints need to be
specified for each weigh unit and not just for the system as a whole. For example,
we need to ensure that *each* weigh unit performs *SendData* every 10 minutes.
This can only be done if we can distinguish *Weigh* events from individual weigh
units at the system level. This could be done only by adding their number, or
some other unique identifier, as a parameter to the event.

In general, however, we cannot, in this approach, add timing constraints
to components of a specification before composing them. This would give the
components a timed trace semantics and hence invalidate the use of standard

CSP operators. Therefore, the approach is not compositional in the sense that a system specification, together with timing constraints, could not be used as a component in the specification of another system. This limits the use of such an approach for specifying larger-scale systems.

5.3 Integrating Object-Z with Timed CSP

A final alternative is to integrate Object-Z with Timed CSP [1]. Timed CSP extends CSP with operators for modelling delays, timeouts and timed interrupts. The approach in this case would be to associate a Timed CSP process definition with each Object-Z class in order to control the timing of events associated with operations. Such an approach has been adopted in RT-Z [22], an integration of Z and Timed CSP, and TCOZ [11], an integration of Object-Z and Timed CSP.

Since CSP (and, hence, Timed CSP) processes are conceptually driven by their environment, the timing operators are limited in order that the maximum or exact time between events cannot be specified. Otherwise, a process could restrict its environment. Therefore, the timing properties on the operations *Weigh* and *UpdateDay* of the classes *WeighUnit* and *StoreUnit*, respectively, cannot be readily captured with this approach.

They can be captured, however, if we can guarantee the event in question is not refused by the process's environment. One way of doing this is to make the event internal to the process by hiding it. For example, the constraint on *StoreUnit* is captured by the following process.

$$SU_{Behav} = (\mu\, R \bullet RecData?\, data \rightarrow R)$$
$$|||$$
$$(\mu\, U \bullet Wait\ 24 * hour;\ UpdateDay \rightarrow U)$$
$$\setminus \{ UpdateDay \}$$

This process allows *RecData* events to occur as often as necessary, and each *UpdateDay* event to occur only after a delay of 24 hours. Since the latter event is internal and cannot be refused by the environment, it occurs immediately after the 24 hour delay.

This approach is not suitable for the timing constraint on *SendData* of class *WeighUnit* however. This event cannot be hidden since it needs to synchronise with the corresponding event of *StoreUnit*. To specify this constraint, we could complement the process description with explicit predicates on the (timed) failures of the process. Alternatively, we could place a constraint on the environment of *WeighUnit* stating that it never refuses a *SendData* event. The use of such environmental constraints is discussed by Schneider [13].

Another approach is to introduce additional operators, such as the "deadline" command of TCOZ [10], to model the fact that events must occur before or at particular times. The use of such additional operators, however, goes against our desire to integrate existing notations for reasons of familiarity and reuse of existing tools and techniques. In particular, the addition of a dealine command changes the specification paradigm of Timed CSP to one in which processes are able to "force" synchronising events in their environment to occur. This makes it unlikely that methods of compositional refinement developed for Timed CSP would be applicable. In contrast, our approach uses untimed CSP and time is represented simply as an event parameter. Hence, CSP refinement methods are still applicable.

Timed CSP also differs from the approach of this paper in that it does not support modelling constraints on continuous variables. In addition, the style of specification is fundamentally different. Timing constraints are modelled in a very operational fashion via delays, timeouts and interrupts. This can sometimes be cumbersome. In contrast, using the timed trace notation of Real-Time Object-Z, timing constraints can be modelled declaratively as predicates on time intervals. The approach is more abstract resulting in more concise specifications.

6   Conclusion

In this paper, we have brought together two tracks of research on integrating formal methods (Object-Z/CSP and Real-Time Object-Z) and, in doing so, three modelling paradigms: state-based (Object-Z), event-based (CSP) and trace-based (the timed trace notation). The result is a specification notation that is capable of modelling complex data structures, concurrency, real-time constraints and continuous variables.

By developing a semantic integration where the individual notations are separated in specifications, we have aimed at increasing the accessibility of the approach to specifiers already familiar with one or more of the notations, and the amenability of using existing tools and verification and refinement techniques with the approach. The latter is an area of future work.

Acknowledgements

Thanks to Ian Hayes and Kirsten Winter for comments on an earlier draft of this paper. Thanks also to Jim Davies, Steve Schneider and Carsten Sühl for improving my understanding of Timed CSP. This work is funded by Australian Research Council Large Grant A49801500, *A Unified Formalism for Concurrent Real-Time Software Development*.

References

1. J. Davies and S. Schneider. A brief history of Timed CSP. *Theoretical Computer Science*, 138(2):243–271, 1995.
2. J. Derrick and G. Smith.   Structural refinement in Object-Z/CSP.   In W. Grieskamp, T. Santen, and B. Stoddart, editors, *2nd International Conference on Integrated Formal Methods (IFM'00)*, volume 1945 of *Lecture Notes in Computer Science*, pages 194–213. Springer-Verlag, 2000.
3. R. Duke and G. Rose.   *Formal Object-Oriented Specification using Object-Z*. MacMillan, 2000.
4. C.J. Fidge, I.J. Hayes, and B.P. Mahony. Defining differentiation and integration in Z. In J. Staples, M.G. Hinchey, and Shaoying Liu, editors, *IEEE International Conference on Formal Engineering Methods (ICFEM '98)*, pages 64–73. IEEE Computer Society Press, 1998.

5. C.J. Fidge, I.J. Hayes, A.P. Martin, and A.K. Wabenhorst. A set-theoretic model for real-time specification and reasoning. In J. Jeuring, editor, *Mathematics of Program Construction (MPC'98)*, volume 1422 of *Lecture Notes in Computer Science*, pages 188–206. Springer-Verlag, 1998.

6. C. Fischer. How to combine Z with a process algebra. In J.P. Bowen, A. Fett, and M.G. Hinchey, editors, *11th International Conference of Z Users*, volume 1493 of *Lecture Notes in Computer Science*, pages 5–23. Springer-Verlag, 1998.

7. C. Fischer and G. Smith. Combining CSP and Object-Z: Finite or infinite trace semantics? In T. Higashino and A. Togashi, editors, *Formal Description Techniques and Protocol Specification, Testing, and Verification (FORTE/PSTV '97)*, pages 503–518. Chapman and Hall, 1997.

8. C. Fischer and H. Wehrheim. Model-checking CSP-OZ specifications with FDR. In K. Araki, A. Galloway, and K. Taguchi, editors, *1st International Conference on Integrated Formal Methods*, pages 315–334. Springer-Verlag, 1999.

9. C.A.R. Hoare. *Communicating Sequential Processes*. Prentice Hall, 1985.

10. B.P. Mahony and J.S. Dong. Sensors and actuators in TCOZ. In J. Wing, J.C.P. Woodcock, and J. Davies, editors, *World Congress on Formal Methods (FM'99)*, volume 1709 of *Lecture Notes in Computer Science*, pages 1166–1185. Springer-Verlag, 1999.

11. B.P. Mahony and J.S. Dong. Timed Communicating Object Z. *IEEE Transactions on Software Engineering*, 26(2):150–177, 2000.

12. A.W. Roscoe. *The Theory and Practice of Concurrency*. Prentice Hall, 1998.

13. S. Schneider. *Concurrent and Real-Time Systems: The CSP Approach*. John Wiley & Sons, 1999.

14. G. Smith. A fully abstract semantics of classes for Object-Z. *Formal Aspects of Computing*, 7(3):289–313, 1995.

15. G. Smith. A semantic integration of Object-Z and CSP for the specification of concurrent systems. In J. Fitzgerald, C.B. Jones, and P. Lucas, editors, *Formal Methods Europe (FME'97)*, volume 1313 of *Lecture Notes in Computer Science*, pages 62–81. Springer-Verlag, 1997.

16. G. Smith. *The Object-Z Specification Language*. Advances in Formal Methods. Kluwer Academic Publishers, 2000.

17. G. Smith and J. Derrick. Refinement and verification of concurrent systems specified in Object-Z and CSP. In M.G. Hinchey and Shaoying Lui, editors, *First International Conference on Formal Engineering Methods (ICFEM '97)*, pages 293–302. IEEE Computer Society Press, 1997.

18. G. Smith and J. Derrick. Specification, refinement and verification of concurrent systems – an integration of Object-Z and CSP. *Formal Methods in System Design*, 18(3):249–284, 2000.

19. G. Smith and I.J. Hayes. Towards real-time Object-Z. In K. Araki, A. Galloway, and K. Taguchi, editors, *1st International Conference on Integrated Formal Methods (IFM'99)*, pages 49–65. Springer-Verlag, 1999.

20. G. Smith and I.J. Hayes. Structuring Real-Time Object-Z specifications. In W. Grieskamp, T. Santen, and B. Stoddart, editors, *2nd International Conference on Integrated Formal Methods (IFM'00)*, volume 1945 of *Lecture Notes in Computer Science*, pages 97–115. Springer-Verlag, 2000.

21. J.M. Spivey. *The Z Notation: A Reference Manual*. Prentice Hall, 2nd edition, 1992.

22. C. Sühl. RT-Z: An integration of Z and timed CSP. In K. Araki, A. Galloway, and K. Taguchi, editors, *1st International Conference on Integrated Formal Methods (IFM'99)*, pages 29–48. Springer-Verlag, 1999.

Model Driven Engineering

Stuart Kent

University of Kent, Canterbury, UK
sjhk@ukc.ac.uk
http://www.cs.ukc.ac.uk

Abstract. The Object Management Group's (OMG) Model Driven Architecture (MDA) strategy envisages a world where models play a more direct role in software production, being amenable to manipulation and transformation by machine. Model Driven *Engineering* (MDE) is wider in scope than MDA. MDE combines *process* and *analysis* with architecture. This article sets out a framework for model driven engineering, which can be used as a point of reference for activity in this area. It proposes an organisation of the modelling 'space' and how to locate models in that space. It discusses different kinds of mappings between models. It explains why process and architecture are tightly connected. It discusses the importance and nature of tools. It identifies the need for defining families of languages and transformations, and for developing techniques for generating/configuring tools from such definitions. It concludes with a call to align metamodelling with formal language engineering techniques.

1 Introduction

This article describes a conceptual framework for the model driven engineering (MDE) of software intensive systems. It begins, in section 2, with an overview of the OMG's Model Driven Architecture (MDA), and identifies a number of aspects of the model driven approach which MDA has yet to address. The remainder of the article discusses those aspects. Section 3 identifies various dimensions of the modelling space other than the platform independent (PI)/platform specific (PS) distinction made by MDA. Section 4 discusses mappings between models, including mappings from PI models (PIMs) to PS models (PSMs). Section 5 explains why process can not be divorced from architecture, and why, therefore, definition of process is just as central to the model driven approach. Section 6 discusses the importance of tools to MDE, and considers various kinds of tooling. Section 7 argues that MDE requires meta techniques and technology that allow us to define families of languages and of processes, and tooling to boot. Section 8 discusses what technologies exist and what they may become.

2 Model Driven Architecture

A detailed description of the OMG's MDA strategy is provided in [16]. This begins as follows:

M. Butler, L. Petre, and K. Sere (Eds.): IFM 2002, LNCS 2335, pp. 286–298, 2002.

"The OMG's mission is to help computer users solve integration problems by supplying open, vendor-neutral interoperability specifications. The Model Driven Architecture (MDA) is OMG's next step in solving integration problems."

On page 2, [16] further elaborates on the problem:

"There are limits to the interoperability that can be achieved by creating a single set of standard programming interfaces. Computer systems have lives measured in decades, and not all ancient systems written in obsolete programming languages can be modified to support standards. Furthermore, the increasing need to incorporate Web-based front ends and link to business partners who may be using propietary interface sets can force integrators back to the low-productivity activities of writing glue code to hold multiple components together. When these systems in their turn need modifying and integrating with next year's hot new technology (and they will) the result is the kind of maintenance nightmare all computer users fear."

Then on page 3, section 2.1, it indicates how MDA aims to solve the problem:

"The MDA defines an approach to IT system specification that separates the specification of system functionality from the specification of the implementation of that functionality on a specific technology platform. [] The MDA approach and the standards that support it allow the same model specifying system functionality to be realized on multiple platforms through auxiliary mapping standards, or through point mappings to specific platforms, and allows different applications to be integrated by explicitly relating their models, enabling integration and interoperability and supporting system evolution as platform technologies come and go."

This identifies the key distinction made in MDA, between platform independent and platform specific models (PIMs and PSMs). Much of the rest of [16] is an attempt to explain this distinction. The claim is that by abstracting away from platform-specific detail (pages 7 & 8) "it is easier to validate the correctness of the model", "it is easier to produce implementations on different platforms while conforming to the same essential and precise structure and behaviour of the system", and "integration and interoperability across systems can be defined more clearly in platform-independent terms, then mapped down to platform specific mechanisms".

So what are PIMs and PSMs? The definition is given in [16] on page 6: "A PIM is a formal specification[1] of the structure and function of a system that abstracts away technical detail." A PSM is not a PIM, but is also not an implementation. It is a "specification model of the target platform". These

---

[1] [16] page 3: "A specification is said to 'formal' when it is based on a language that has a well-defined form ("syntax"), meaning ("semantics"), and possibly rules of analaysis, inference, or proof for its constructs. [] The semantics might be defined, more or less formally, ..."

specification models may have different bindings to particular implementation language environments (like CORBA). The functionality specified in a PIM is realized in a platform-specific way in the PSM, which is derived from the PIM via some transformation.

On page 13, [16] expands on different kinds of mappings that might be involved in MDA: PIM to PIM (refinement of designs), PIM to PSM, which has already been discussed, PSM to PSM (refinement of platform models) and PSM to PIM (mining of existing implementations for useful PI abstractions). However. most of the paper focuses on the PIM to PSM mapping.

It is worth noting that there may be many PIMs which may take different viewpoints or perspectives on the system and which may be more or less abstract. This is acknowledged by [16]. However MDA itself, at least as defined in [16], is reasonably quiet about how that space might be structured, other than distinguishing between PIMs and PSMs. One goal of this article is to provide a more general characterisation of the modelling space.

A clear goal of MDA is to provide a framework which integrates the existing OMG standards. Thus it comes as no surprise that it is intended that all PIMs and PSMs be expressed in the Unified Modeling Language (UML), using its profile mechanism to specialise and extend the language for different contexts (it is unlikely that exactly the same language will fulfill all the needs of every kind of PIM and PSM). The Meta Object Facility (MOF) will be used to define the UML and its profiles not only in a formal way, but also in a way that supports the generation/configuration of tools directly from the definitions. The OMG has recently issued requests for proposals for the revision of MOF so (a) that it is a subset of UML itself (true metamodelling) and (b) that it has facilities for defining transformations between metamodels. We will revisit MOF in the final section of this article, where we discuss the kinds of meta technologies required to realise Model Driven Engineering.

Although MDA does not insist that the mappings between PIMs and PSMs be automated, it is clear that this is the intention. [16] page 13 talks about how mappings might be executed using, for example, scripts in CASE tools or external tools such as XSLT on XMI files[2]; and a more detailed discussion of code generation possibilities is provided on page 15. Pages 24 and 25 discuss the place of existing OMG standards in the context of MDA. XMI and MOF are most relevant to tooling. XMI "adds *Modeling* and *Architecture* to the world of XML", and XML, of course, delivers models in a machine-processable form. Note that XMI is focussed on a representation of the abstract syntax of models, not just surface representation. MOF "defines programmatic interfaces for manipulating models and their instances []. These are defined in IDL and are being extended to Java."

To summarise, MDA focuses on architecture, on artefacts, on models. It aims to exploit the usefulness of models as tools for abstraction, for summarising, and for providing alternative perspectives. Although it acknowledges there might be

---

[2] XMI is the OMG standard which stipulates how UML and MOF models are rendered in XML.

a richer modelling space, it chooses to focus on just one dimension, the dichotomy between platform independent and platform specific models. It claims that UML is up to the task of defining all PIMs and PSMs, though acknowledges a need for UML profiles to tailor UML to particular modelling contexts. MOF will be used to define languages (chiefly UML profiles) and transformations between languages. A clear goal is that transformations between models should at least be partially automated, thereby reducing the burden of keeping models in step to the point that their intrinsic benefits outweigh the costs of their maintenance.

The remainder of this article explores all those aspects of a model driven approach largely ignored by MDA: dimensions of the modelling space other than the PIM/PSM distinction; transformations or mappings between models including mappings from PIMs to PSMs; the close relationship between process and architecture; various kinds of tools. The article concludes with a discussion of language engineering technologies required to support this vision, which will include some assessment of MOF and UML.

3   Modelling Dimensions

In general, when one produces a model, one needs to take account of the perspective that model is intended to take. One way to structure the modelling space is to categorise perspectives. MDA does this, but it just has two categories: PIMs and PSMs. A more general way to categorise perspectives is to identify the orthogonal criteria which can be used to distinguish between one perspective and another. These criteria can be thought of as different dimensions in an n-dimensional space [22], and a perspective is then at the intersection of different positions along those axes. So what are these dimensions?

Clearly there is the platform specific/platform independent dimension. One could view this as an example of the more general abstract/concrete dimension. In which case we can only talk about whether a model is abstract (platform independent) with respect to some other model. One could imagine a UML specification of an e-business system that abstracted away from details of a specific platform (e.g. J2EE), but which was viewed as a concrete realisation of part of a more abstract model of a business or business process. Perhaps one key feature of the PIM/PSM distinction is that the models are likely to be expressed in different languages[3]. This is not necessarily the case for models which bear an abstract/concrete relationship. For example, refinement is typically a relationship between models in the same language, where the difference between the models is one of granularity of action.

Various dimensions of concern have already begun to be identified in the area of Aspect Oriented Software Development (AOSD) [1]. One dimension of concern is *subject area*, for example the area of the system dealing with customers, or that concerned with processing of orders. Separation of concern by subject area has been proposed in Subject-Oriented Programming [11] and Catalysis [9]. Another dimension of concern has been called *aspect*, for example concurrency control

---
[3] Here we count different UML profiles as different languages

and distribution. A notable feature of these two dimensions is that often it does not make sense to define mappings directly between models at different locations along a dimension, but rather their relationship is better expressed by showing how they map into one single integrated model. Interestingly, the AOSD community, though accepting that these dimensions may be applied at different levels of abstraction, do not seem to regard the abstract/concrete dimension as just another dimension of the whole space.

A third category of dimension is less concerned with the technical aspects of a system, and more with the managerial and societal aspects. Such dimensions include *authorship*, *version* (as in version and configuration control), *location*, in case the system development is distributed across sites, and *stakeholder*, such as business expert or programmer.

[22] points out that for any particular software development project, one will need to state the dimensions that need to be considered, which includes defining the points of interest along those dimensions. Some of those dimensions are likely to be standard across projects, for example authorship, version and location, only needing to decide whether the dimension needs to be included or not. The subject area dimension is likely always to be present, and that will require the subject areas to be identified. Similarly one will need to decide the relevant points on the aspect dimension, for example whether points are required for concurrency or distribution, for information and data, and so on. One will also need to define the stakeholders involved; and the levels of abstraction are of interest. In MDA, one may choose that the only two points of interest are PIM and PSM along this dimension.

Then, when building a model, one identifies at what intersection of the dimensions the model should be placed. In theory, there could be a different language for describing models at each different intersection. In practice, the language used at a particular point of intersection will be determined by one (or a small subset) of the dimensions that determine that point. For example, a subject area may be defined from the perspective of many different aspects, and the language used will be determined by the aspect being described. It may also be that the level of abstraction and/or stakeholder will influence the language to be used. With regard to the latter, a business expert and programmer are likely to need to see the specification of a system in different languages, even though the two renderings would be isomorphic – they are at the same level of abstraction, looking at the same aspect and subject area.

4   Mappings

We have seen that models can take on different perspectives, and that different perspectives often, but not always, require modelling languages with different properties. Thus, when engineering a particular system, it is possible, in theory, that there may be many models of that system taking different perspectives, and that these models will not necessarily be expressed in the same language (though some might be).

Perspectives on their own are more use than if they can be related, and this requires mappings to be defined. In MDA, the main mapping is between PIM and PSM, and this is often associated with code generation. However, this is not the only kind of mapping required.

There is a distinction between *model translation* and *language translation*. One can define mappings between models in the same language (model translation) and mappings between models in different languages (language translation). Model translations should be expressable in the language (or an extension of the language) in which the models are expressed. Language translation needs to be expressed in terms of the definitions of the languages themselves. Interestingly, if the definitions of the languages are also thought of as models (in terms of OMG standards they would be MOF models, or metamodels) then it should be possible to express language translations in an extension of the language used to define languages, the metamodeling language, which, in OMG MDA, is MOF. Indeed, a request for proposals is soon to be issued by the OMG for just such an extension to MOF. In short, language translation is just (meta-)model translation.

In a model driven approach, it is not enough to leave these mappings implicit, as vague sets of rules. To make it worth the effort of maintaining models other than the target implementation, the burden of keeping models in step needs to be considerably reduced than in current (manual) practice. If models (e.g. target code) can be generated from other models, so much the better. The question, then, is how to define model and language translations so they can be used for the practical purpose of maintaining consistency between models and, where feasible and desirable, generating one model from another.

It is not the aim of this article to come up with a solution to this problem, but it is worth considering what factors need to be take into account. Is the definition intended to be machine processed? If so what kind of processing? Is it to be used to generate one model from another, or to maintain consistency between models? Or should the definition be in a form suitable for mathematical analysis (for example, whether or not it is isomorphic). Another factor to consider is whether or not it is easy to comprehend and/or write, and this depends, of course, on the audience and/or author. For example, one might consider using XSLT, which is machine processable, but might be regarded as difficult to comprehend especially since the models will have to be converted first to XML.

Another option is to try and use the same language (or an extension thereof) as that used to define the models being mapped, in model translation, or the languages being mapped, in language translation. The advantage of this approach is that it is not necessary for the modeller/language designer to learn a new language for writing out mappings. This will be discussed further in section 8.

5   Process

Models and transformations are artefacts. For any given project, a particular set of models providing chosen perspectives on the system will be constructed, and appropriate mappings between these models will be defined. This determines the essential architecture of the artefacts to be constructed during the project. However, this only constitutes part of what is required. Specifically, there needs to be some process, at the very least some guidelines on the order in which models should be produced, how the work should be divided between teams and so on.

There are macro and micro processes associated with the engineering of the different models. Macro processes concern the order in which models are produced and how they are coordinated. Micro processes amount to guidelines for producing a particular model.

A simple example will suffice to illustrate the close relationship between process and architecture. A common approach to software development is to use *use cases*. A use case explores scenarios associated with a particular part, indeed subject area, of the system. Identifying different use cases corresponds to identifying different subject areas. It is possible to define a use case in increments, with the first increment making many simplifying assumptions, and each subsequent increment relaxing assumptions [13]. Defining use cases in this way can help to organise the management of the project. If one adopts an iterative approach to software development, then each iteration can correspond to the completion of a use case or use case increment. The ordering of iterations can be determined by ranking the relative importance of use cases, and by ordering of increments on use cases. In this way, the number of iterations and their ordering is determined by the use cases. Furthermore, the tasks associated with each iteration will be determined to some extent by the choice of models that it has been determined need to be produced in each iteration. It will still be necessary, in addition, to define the micro processes associated with the manipulation of each kind of model in an iteration, and macro processes governing how the development of individual models are to be coordinated.

Thus in general, the definition of the artefacts or models developed by a particular process are intrinsic to the definition of that process. The reverse is also true – it is difficult to see how one can identify the artefacts one needs for a particular project or family of projects, without defining the process within which they are intended to be used. Further, the content of the models (e.g. use cases) can directly influence how the process progresses when it is invoked.

6   Tools

In mainstream practice, models, apart from the code, tend only to get sketched out, sometimes after the fact for documentation, at varying levels of abstraction, and with largely unwritten rules used to (loosely) relate the models to themselves and to the code. This is certainly true for a typical OO development.

In a model driven approach, the vision is that models become artefacts to be maintained along with the code. This will only happen if the benefit obtained from producing the models is considerably more and the effort required to keep them in line with the code is considerably less than current practice. Models are valuable as tools for abstraction, for summarising, and for providing alternative perspectives. The value is greatly enhanced if models become tangible artefacts that can be simulated, transformed, checked etc., and if the burden of keeping them in step with each other and the delivered system is considerably reduced.

Tooling is essential to maximise the benefits of having models, and to minimise the effort required to maintain them. Specifically, more sophisticated tools are required than those in common use today, which are in many cases just model editors. What might these tools be? Here are some examples.

Tools to check/enforce well formedness constraints on models.
That is, type/static semantics checking. It still amazes me that many commercially available modelling tools do not do this in any systematic way. This may be because the definitions of languages, such as UML, only pay lip service to these rules.

Support for working with *instances of models*. These include checking the validity of instances against a model, generation of instances from a model, both with and without user interference, and (partial) generation of models from instances. An example is the USE tool [20] which provides some support for working with snapshots and filmstrips [9] which may be viewed as instances of a restricted subset of UML. The tool allows one to create snapshots and filmstrips by hand, then check their validity against a class diagram, annotated with invariants and pre-post conditions in OCL.

These tools are important not least to explore the validity of a model. They provide a means of establishing examples and counter examples for a model, and it is much easier both to elicit and explain a model (e.g. to a customer) in terms of examples. Of course the language(s) used to render examples must be appropriate for the stakeholders for which it is intended.

Tools to support mappings between models. There are a family of different tools here. There are, of course, tools that generate one model from another, the most cited example probably being code generation.

However, there is also a need for *coordination tools*, which would be responsible for coordinating the mappings between different models, by flagging inconsistencies and trying to correct them automatically. For example, such a tool could be used to monitor a refinement relationship (which must be established by the developer as it involves taking design decisions) and checking that the relationship is always a true refinement, or at least maintaining a list of verification conditions that need to be discharged. Another example, would be the translation between PIMs and PSMs. In today's world, many PSMs integrate existing (legacy) code with new code, and this usually requires some parts of the system to be hand coded. Therefore the PSM is being interfered with directly and can not be completely generated. It is therefore necessary to maintain both PIM and PSM, and coordinate their relationship.

A third example is where models are not at different levels of abstraction but still provide alternative perspectives. In that case, each model is likely only to define a part of the system, and needs to be kept in step with the other viewpoints, possibly via some underlying integrated model. We need look no further than this proceedings to see a body of work focusing on this topic. Much of the work on *viewpoints* [15] is also relevant here.

Tools to support *model driven testing.* Here platform specific tests and test data are derived from platform independent models and instances of those models. This could be particularly relevant in the development of today's e-business systems, which often involves the integration of existing systems with themselves and new systems, usually using some kind of messaging infrastructure such as the Java Messaging Service (JMS) or IBM's Message Queuing platforms. In this environment, it would at least be desirable to establish a PIM which provides a definition of the information structures being passed around, and the (invariant) constraints they can obey, which abstracts away from the detail of the component-specific renderings of that information. And then one will need to check that the system does not violate the abstract information model, in particular the invariant constraints. This could be done by monitoring messages that go in and out of ports, then mapping these up to instances of the abstract model, using an appropriate retrieval function, and then checking that the instances satisfy the abstract model. In this case a tool is required to generate abstract instances from concrete instances, which are obtained through probes on the running system.

***Dashboard* applications.** The state of the system is still monitored through probes and mapped to abstract instances, but this time the abstract model is aimed at business experts, and abstract instances are presented in a form that allows those stakeholders to monitor the ongoing business processes which the system implements.

Tools for version control and distributed working. The challenge here is to integrate these tools with multiple modelling and coordination tools.

Tools for managing the software process. For example directing developers in the artefacts they should produce and when, making assessments of the level of quality assurance being adhered to (possibly using data, such as consistency checking results, from other tools) and so on.

An important aspect of realising such tools, is to ensure that they remain flexible and configurable. Observation of practice [14] seems to suggest that developers prefer small, flexible tools that can easily be configured to interwork with other tools. A natural architecture for this tooling would be to follow the architecture of models and mappings between models being used in the project. Frameworks are now beginning to emerge (e.g. Eclipse [17]), which could make this possible. Further, more and more UML modelling tools export models in XML format (actually XMI), which at least allows models to be interchanged with other tools.

7   Roll Your Own: Families of Languages and Processes

A model driven engineering approach must specify the modelling languages, models, translations between models and languages, and the process used to coordinate the construction and evolution of the models. To ensure that the burden of maintaining more than one formal model does not outweigh the considerable benefits of models as tools for abstraction, summarising and providing alternative perspectives, powerful tool support is required.

On the other hand, it is unlikely that the same set of models, mappings and process will fit all domains, all organisations or all projects. There will be variations. This is already evident in standardisation work going on in the OMG. Numerous so-called UML Profiles have been or are being defined for particular domains. See [2] for a complete list. Many may have you believe that these are just slight variations on UML, but don't be fooled. For example, in both the Enterprise Application Integration (EAI) and Enterprise Distributed Object Computing (EDOC) profiles, UML notation is used to notate a fundamentally different computational paradigm than the traditional OO programming language heritage of UML. The paradigm in question is one of components which communicate by passing messages or events, through channels connected to their input and output ports. Channels are generally asynchronous and can be used to broadcast the same message to many components. Although such a framework can be implemented on top of an OO programming language, the paradigm is conceptually very different to the basis of OOPLs. However, there is some commonality between the languages. For example, object-oriented structuring, as depicted by class diagrams, can also also be used to structure the information delivered by messages. It is this commonality that suggests it may be possible do define families of languages. Doing so, could considerably ease the burden of developing tools to support different languages.

It is barely necessary to make the point that different processes, involving different model architectures, will be required in different domains, often in different organisations, and sometimes in different projects. Indeed some have argued (e.g. [14]) that nearly every project needs the flexibility to "roll their own"; and in MDE this also means identifying the kind of models they are going to maintain, and the tools for developing and coordinating those models. As there is commonality between languages, there is also commonality between processes and it follows that it may be possible to define families of processes, with the desirable result of making it easier to develop/configure tools to different processes.

But this could make MDE (and MDA) untenable as a widespread approach. I have argued quite strongly that tools are essential to reduce the burden in maintaining many different, related models to a level that outweighs the benefits of abstraction that models can provide. Building tools by hand is resource intensive, and certainly could not be done for every process "rolled" for a project. Of course standard forms of MDE could be established for the development of particular kinds of system, by picking a particular process and particular kinds of models to be maintained, and then hand-building tools to support that package. It is unlikely that such 'solutions' would be very configurable and there is a great danger that developers would be forced into too much of a straightjacket.

An alternative is to work out how to generate and/or configure tools from definitions of processes and languages. This is the topic of the next and concluding section of this article.

8   Going Meta

Somehow we need a way to go "meta". We need to be able to feed language and mapping definitions into tools that will then either generate other tools or configure themselves according to that definition. This is, in a sense, applying MDE/MDA to itself. Language definitions are just models, possibly models with mappings defined between them (e.g. mapping of concrete notation(s) to abstract syntax). Is there a PIM language good for defining languages from which tools (PSMs) can be generated?

Technologies are beginning to emerge that are allowing this to happen in practice, for example the Extensible Markup Language (XML) and (more importantly, in my view) the OMG's Meta-Object Facility (MOF). XML is gaining widespread use in industry as a means of interchaging information that conforms to a particular structure. In other words, interchanging expressions of a precisely defined language. XML forces the information to be structured as a tree, though it does offer adhoc devices to break that structure when necessary, and its syntax is only just about human readable. On the other hand, there are plenty of tools to support XML, such as parsers, checkers (to check well-formedness) and transformation technology in the form of XSLT. Furthermore, these tools are meta-tools in the sense that they work with expressions of any XML-defined language, provided they have access to the definition of that language in the form of an XML-schema.

MOF is a language used for metamodelling. In general useage, this has come to mean the use of an object-oriented modelling language for the definition of languages. Typically the language used is MOF, or an appropriate subset of UML. All OMG standards are now defined in this way; in particular a goal in the development of MOF version 2 [6], is to make MOF *the* subset of UML used for metamodelling.

The advantage of using MOF to define languages is that, like, XML, MOF definitions are machine processable. Specifically, the MOF standard dictates how MOF models and instances of MOF models (languages and language expressions) may be rendered in XML format (schemas and XML documents, respectively), and how interfaces to repositories for models can be derived from MOF definitions of the languages in which those models are expressed. There is work in the pipeline to add a capability in MOF to express transformations between MOF models, that is language translations.

Metamodelling has only really been used to define the abstract syntax of a modelling language. However, there is recent work to show that concrete syntax and semantics can be defined using a metamodelling approach [3,8,4,19,18]. In this work, it is proposed that concrete notation is defined as another metamodel, as is the mapping to abstract syntax. Semantics is defined using a denotational approach, where a metamodel definition of the semantics domain (or instances of models) is provided, together with a metamodel definition of what it means for an instance to satisfy a model. If MOF is extended with a specialised language for expressing mappings, and this language is both rich enough and is supported by tools implementing those mappings, then there is a chance that some of the tools described in section 6, in particular those concerned with the relationship between instance and model, could be derived automatically from language definitions. Similarly, it should be possible to derive tools that transform concrete to abstract syntax an vice-versa.

One question here is whether the transformation language can be made expressive enough in a way that does not break the ability to derive tools from the definition. This is certainly an interesting topic for research, which could build on much of the work done in formal language theory. In particular, one promising source of inspiration could be graph grammars [10].

Another question concerns the richness of the semantics that can be expressed in this way. It would be very interesting to explore the relationship between standard, mathematical approaches to giving semantics and this approach. Could the metamodelling approach provide a pathway through which mathematical style semantics could be be used to generate automated or semi-automated analysis tools?

An area where MOF is weak is in its support for well-formedness rules. Although OCL is recommended as a (semi-)formal way of expressing these rules, MOF tools tend to ignore them. If well-formedness rules are to be checked and/or enforced then constraints need to find their way into repositories generated from MOF definitions. This should not be that difficult to do. For example, there are already Java libraries that allow OCL constraints to be monitored [12].

There is a clear need in the OMG for metamodelling techniques to support the definition of families of languages, but there are no explicit plans to properly support this within MOF. However, we have been working on this problem. Initial ideas are reported in [3,8], and these are being developed further in a submission to the UML 2 RFPs [5], latest versions of which are available from the 2U submission team's website [21].

With regard to defining processes, there is also a UML profile for defining software development processes, called the *Software Process Engineering Management (SPEM) UML Profile* [7]. This is an initial attempt at defining a language, which shares some of UML's constructs, for defining software engineering processes. The language is being implemented; for example, Rational's Unified Process tool is intended to be configurable with SPEM definitions. There is a considerable amount of work to do in integrating SPEM with MOF, and generating process coordination tools that integrate with modelling tools from SPEM definitions.

Acknowledgements

I would like to thank Tony Clark, Steve Cook, Andy Evans and Alan Wills for many useful discussions on ideas presented in this paper. This work was partially supported by a Royal Society Industry Fellowship.

References

1. Aspect oriented software design (AOSD) home page. http://www.aosd.net.
2. Catalog of OMG modeling specifications.
   http://www.omg.org/technology/documents/modeling_spec_catalog.htm.
3. Clark A., Evans A., Kent S., Brodsky S., and Cook S. A feasibility study in rearchitecting UML as a family of languages using a precise OO meta-modeling approach. Available from www.puml.org, September 2000.

4. J. M. Alvarez, A. Clark, A. Evans, and P. Sammut. An action semantics for MML. In C. Kobryn and M. Gogolla, editors, *Proceedings of The Fourth International Conference on the Unified Modeling Language (UML'2001)*, LNCS. Springer, 2000.
5. OMG Analysis and Design Task Force. UML 2.0 requests for proposals. Available from http://www.omg.org/techprocess/meetings/schedule/, 2001.
6. OMG Analysis and Design Task Force. MOF 2.0 requests for proposals. Available from http://www.omg.org/techprocess/meetings/schedule/, 2002.
7. OMG Analysis and Design Task Force. SPEM final adopted specification. OMG document number ptc/02-01-23, available from [2], 2002.
8. A. Clark, A. Evans, and S. Kent. Engineering modelling languages: A precise meta-modelling approach. In *Proceedings of ETAPS 02 FASE Conference*, LNCS. Springer, April 2002.
9. D. D'Souza and A. Wills. *Objects, Components and Frameworks With UML: The Catalysis Approach.* Addison-Wesley, 1998.
10. H. Ehrig, G. Engels, H-J. Kreowski, and G. Rozenberg, editors. *Handbook Of Graph Grammars And Computing By Graph Transformation. Volume 2: Applications, Languages and Tools.* World Scientific, October 1999.
11. W. Harrison and H. Ossher. Subject-oriented programming (a critique of pure objects). In *Proceedings of the Conference on Object-Oriented Programming: Systems, Languages, and Applications*, pages 411–428. ACM, September 1993.
12. Heinrich Hussmann, Birgit Demuth, and Frank Finger. Modular architecture for a toolset supporting OCL. In Andy Evans, Stuart Kent, and Bran Selic, editors, *UML 2000 - The Unified Modeling Language. Advancing the Standard. Third International Conference, York, UK, October 2000, Proceedings*, volume 1939 of *LNCS*, pages 278–293. Springer, 2000.
13. C. Larman. *Applying UML and Patterns: An Introduction to Object-Oriented Analysis and Design.* Prentice Hall, 1997.
14. A. Lauder. *A Productive Response To Legacy System Petrification.* PhD thesis, Department of Computer Science, University of Kent, UK, January 2002.
15. B. Nuseibeh, J. Kramer, and A. Finkelstein. A framework for expressing the relationships between multiple views in requirements specifications. *IEEE Transactions on Software Engineering*, 20(10):760773, October 1994.
16. OMG Architecture Board ORMSC. Model driven architecture (MDA). OMG document number ormsc/2001-07-01, available from www.omg.org, July 2001.
17. Eclipse Project. Home page. http://www.eclipse.org.
18. G. Reggio. Metamodelling behavioural aspects: the case of the UML state machines (complete version). Technical Report DISI-TR-02-3, DISI, Universit di Genova, Italy, 2001.
19. G. Reggio and E. Astesiano. A proposal of a dynamic core for UML metamodelling with MML. Technical Report DISI-TR-01-17, DISI, Universit di Genova, Italy, 2001.
20. M. Richters and M. Gogolla. Validating UML models and OCL constraints. In A. Evans and S. Kent, editors, *The Third International Conference on the Unified Modeling Language (UML'2000), York, UK, October 2-6. 2000, Proceedings*, LNCS. Springer, 2000.
21. 2U Submitters. Home page. http://www.2uworks.org.
22. P. Tarr, H. Ossher, W. Harrison, and Jr. S. M. Sutton. N degrees of separation: Multidimensional separation of concerns. In *Proceedings of the 21st International Conference on Software Engineering (ICSE'99)*, pages 107–119, May 1999.

The Design of a Tool-Supported Graphical Notation for Timed CSP

Phillip J. Brooke[1,*] and Richard F. Paige[2]

[1] School of Computing, University of Plymouth, Drake Circus, Plymouth,
Devon, PL4 8AA, UK
philb@soc.plym.ac.uk
[2] Department of Computer Science, University of York, Heslington, York, YO10 5DD, UK
paige@cs.york.ac.uk

Abstract. A graphical notation for representing Timed CSP (TCSP) specifications is presented. The notation, which integrates features from a number of existing specification languages, including Statecharts, is aimed at providing the means for more easily constructing and managing large TCSP specifications, with the intention of forming the basis for tools and a methodology for applying TCSP in the large. The graphical notation extends TCSP by allowing specifications to be both processes and arbitrary predicates, thus increasing the expressiveness and applicability of the notation. An extendible tool framework, designed for the graphical notation and to be integrated with other tools, is outlined. We discuss the features of this framework, especially how it aims to support reasoning about TCSP specifications.

Keywords: Timed CSP, process algebra, graphical notation, tool support.

1   Introduction

The general theme of this paper is the usability of formal specification languages, particularly as they apply to large-scale software development. Our aim is to improve the usability of one formal specification language – Timed CSP – in this domain, in part by integrating techniques that have proven successful, and by providing an extendible basis for tool support, for reasoning about and validating specifications.

Timed CSP (TCSP) [23] has been proposed as a specification language for modelling and reasoning about concurrent, communicating systems that must obey explicit timing constraints. The notation of TCSP is based on the process algebra CSP [13]. The syntax of TCSP and related notations may be unpopular with system engineers, especially those with little experience with formal specification languages and mathematical notations in general. Moreover, TCSP is generally difficult to use in modelling and describing large systems, in part because of its limited support for a notion of module, and also because of its design: as it stands, it is well-suited to capture the behaviour of small, yet critical components of software systems, and to support reasoning about them. As well, limited methodological support exists for TCSP; this arises typically through use

---

* Corresponding author.

M. Butler, L. Petre, and K. Sere (Eds.): IFM 2002, LNCS 2335, pp. 299–318, 2002.

of tools such as FDR [8] (although issues arise with using these tools when working in the timed domain [4]). Methodological support is vital if languages and tools are to be usable for development in the large.

In this paper, we propose a graphical notation for Timed CSP, designed to make TCSP more appealing to system engineers, to make the notation more appropriate and usable for large-scale modelling, and to provide a foundation for further tool support. Tool support will be particularly vital for drawing models and for generating textual representations of TCSP specii cations (and encodings of TCSP specii cations in other languages, such as PVS [28] or FDR). The graphical notation is constructed by integrating proven techniques from other notations, particularly textual TCSP and Harel's Statecharts [12].

We discuss design criteria for the graphical notation in Section 2. To give an overview, the notation has a formal syntax and semantics, is designed to be simple, usable, scalable, and, we claim, intuitive. Our intention is that this notation will appeal to systems engineers with less experience of formal methods, while providing the necessary formality of syntax and semantics that can be exploited with automated tools such as FDR and PVS. At the same time, we do not desire to introduce a graphical notation that will require developers experienced with textual TCSP to overcome a substantial learning curve to deal with in order to work with the new notation.

The notation will also extend the expressive power and applicability of TCSP by integrating predicates with the language, thus allowing specii cations to be both processes and predicates. This is particularly desirable for modelling in the large, in part because it allows, in certain cases, simpler specii cations to be written, and also because it makes it easier for TCSP to be integrated with other formal specii cation languages and their tools.

1.1   Overview

We start by briei y examining the desirable characteristics of our graphical notation – and similar notations in general – based on work in [4, 19]. We also discuss the related work upon which our notation and its supporting tools are founded. Then we summarise the syntax for Timed CSP. (In this paper, we do not concern ourselves with the semantics of TCSP, but only with the meaning of the notations we describe. Effectively, the semantics of graphical TCSP will be given in terms of TCSP programs.) From there, we propose our graphical notation, give an example, and explain the semantics of the graphical notation, which is constructed via a mapping from the grammar of the graphical notation to its semantic domain. The syntax and semantics of the graphical notation are not described via a metamodel, as is currently common in the object-oriented realm [6, 20]; rather the syntax is captured via integrating context-free grammars with graphical terms, and by dei ning a precise mapping from sentences generated by the grammar to sentences in textual TCSP.

We explain the extension of the notation to predicate specii cations, and the benei ts obtained from doing this. We then outline an extendible tool framework for supporting the graphical notation. The framework is designed to be integrated with a variety of additional tools, including pretty-printers, documentation generators, model checkers, and theorem provers. We describe how this tool integration works, and we end with a discussion of ongoing and future work, and some conclusions.

2 Background and Design Goals

We give a short overview of related work, and particularly discuss design criteria for the graphical notation.

2.1 Related Work

There has been much related work on graphical notations for modelling and building software systems. These languages have been used in particular for constructing new systems (e.g. to capture requirements or architectural designs), and for describing existing systems (e.g. via reverse-engineered models such as UML diagrams or architectural interconnection diagrams). Our particular focus in this paper is on the former class of languages, particularly those suitable for formal reasoning. As well, we are particularly focused on the development of graphical notations for existing textual notations.

Statecharts [12] is a formal language for modelling real-time and reactive systems. It is a tool-supported graphical language based on ı nite state machines. It possesses extra notation for managing and packaging large speciı cations, and for capturing timing constraints and triggers for allowing transitions to be taken. Statecharts possesses a formal semantics and is supported by the Statemate tool, which can be used for simulation, code generation, and automated reasoning. A number of formal semantics have been proposed for Statecharts, including the ofı cial semantics provided by the Statemate tool.

The Uniı ed Modelling Language (UML) [3] is a language for visualising systems of all kinds from a variety of different perspectives, including static structure, behaviour, and user interactions. The UML is not a formal language; it does not possess a formal semantics. A variety of tools are available for producing UML speciı cations, and for validating them against well-formedness constraints. Tools such as Rational Rose and Together/J are particularly useful for visualising programs, e.g. in Java or C++. UML proı les [6] can be used for deı ning speciı c dialects of UML that are more appropriate for visualising programs in speciı c languages.

The work of Baresi and Pezzè et al. [1] has focused on providing a formal semantics for Structured Analysis diagrams, e.g. data ı ow diagrams. Their work showed that the numerous different interpretations of data ı ow diagrams could be carefully structured and classiı ed, so that the diagrams should actually be considered a family of languages. In other words, data ı ow diagrams are semantically fragmented, and formalisation of such diagrams involves selecting a member of the family of interest and using a specially crafted formalisation appropriate for that family member. This discovery provides further motivation for UML proı les, and is also the same problem that has arisen with Statecharts. It also illustrates some of the complications with providing a formal semantics to a notation after the notation has been put into widespread use.

Dong et al. [7] have recently considered visualising Timed Communicating Object-Z speciı cations on the web, via use of XML/XMI, and by using UML diagrams as projected views. This work is similar in intent to our own: the construction of lightweight tools to support formal methods. This project emphasises visualisation, as well as the use of Z and Object-Z. While we also emphasise visualisation, we focus strictly on TCSP, and we also desire to support automated reasoning via tool integration; reasoning is not yet considered in Dong's work [7]. However, Dong's use of XML as an infrastructure suggests that it should be possible for their toolset to be extended to support interfacing with a variety of reasoning tools. We also do not require nor desire the use of UML diagrams for visualisation, as we do not need object-oriented modelling features for capturing TCSP. We also desire to avoid the semantic problems associated with UML, such as its imprecise semantics for state machines.

SOFL [17] integrates data ﬂow diagrams, Petri Nets and VDM. This work is, like earlier examples, concerned with visualisation. In contrast to the work below, we concentrate on the visualisation of a single notation, rather than integration of approaches and providing a methodology. Both SOFL and our work have hierarchical elements and support the notion of concurrency.

Our work is most closely related to that on G-LOTOS, the graphical syntax extension for LOTOS [2]. The aims of the language are to improve the readability of the notation, as a basis for tool support, and to facilitate teaching. G-LOTOS inherits the formal semantics of LOTOS: it is viewed as an extension of the syntax of LOTOS. As in our work, it places restrictions on the graphical notation in order to properly generate valid LOTOS.

There is an increasing amount of work on the subject of *visualisation* [9, 10, 21] of information, programs, and systems. One general conclusion from this work is that the utility of a notation is entirely dependent on context. A further inference is that for reasoning and programming, textual notations are invariably preferable (since for this type of work, details are relevant and needed), whereas for other tasks such as architectural design, analysis, and explanation of systems, graphical notations are often preferable.

2.2   Design Goals

Timed CSP, being textually based, is not entirely appropriate for describing large-scale systems. While it does provide support for abstraction – a necessary mechanism in modelling languages – it does not provide large-scale structuring mechanisms such as modules, class, components, or packages. Graphical notations are generally considered to be suitable, though certainly not suﬃcient, for large-scale modelling and development, in part because of their capabilities at abstraction, because of their readability and usability, and because of their ability of being able to present many critical architectural aspects of systems succinctly and quickly.

Textual notations are essentially one dimensional. Indenting of programs can make their interpretation easier. Similarly, formulæ can be structured in a manner to assist the reader, as in Lamport's work [15], or using the structured calculational proof style [11]. On the other hand, graphical notations have two dimensions, and there are several ways in which the notations can be structured. Two common types of structuring are graphs or trees and nested boxes. In each case, the nodes, arcs or boxes can be decorated with textual symbols, dashes, arrows, etc. We can also combine both mechanisms of structuring, which is what is done in Statecharts, and also in several of the diagrams of UML, e.g., packages.

A desirable graphical notation will not use colours and subtly distinct decorations or annotations, since they may be difi cult to print (in the case of monochrome printers) in the former case, or difi cult to hand-draw in the latter case. Similarly, we rule out the use of fonts and font styles on the grounds that they are difi cult for humans to draw. For example, UML allows use of italic font to indicate that classes are abstract (i.e. they cannot be instantiated). This is clearly useful only when tools are available; for hand-drawn models, textual annotations are preferable (and are, in fact, what UML users typically apply in this particular case).

In general, specii cations written using a graphical language will take up more space than specii cations written using a similar textual language. It is undesirable for a graphical notation to be explosive, in that its specii cations tend to grow rapidly in size (measured in terms of amount of space taken on the screen or on a piece of paper) as further elements are added to the specii cation.

We have the following specii c design goals for our graphical notation for TCSP. For a detailed overview of general design goals for modelling language, the reader is referred to [19], where principles for designing languages are discussed. Leveson et al. have also described desirable design criteria for graphical languages [16]. The following list of requirements is also partially based on these criteria.

1. *Usability in the large.* It should be possible to structure and manage large TCSP specii cations. This ability will arise by being able to omit details of a specii cation where necessary, and focus on presentation of architectural details. For TCSP, this means being able to focus on selected process connectors, e.g. nondeterministic choice, parallel composition, etc. This is analogous to modelling languages like UML where it is possible to describe the abstractions and connectors in a system without describing the details of the abstractions at the same time.

2. *Simplicity.* The notation should be simple to draw, both by hand and by automated tool. It should require use of a minimum number of marks and graphical cues in order to distinguish between the different TCSP elements graphically. It should provide a unique way of describing each TCSP construct, following the *principle of uniqueness* described by Meyer [18].

3. *Tool-supportable.* The graphical syntax should be dei ned so as to be easy to support by automated tools. In particular, it is desirable to have a GUI-based tool for constructing the graphical TCSP specii cations. As well, it is desirable to be able to use an assortment of automated tools, such as model checkers (e.g. FDR) and theorem provers (e.g. PVS) for reasoning about the specii cations. At the same time, it is difi cult to predict the exact types of different reasoning that will be need on TCSP specii cations, and thus it is desirable to have an extendible *tool framework* in which different reasoning tools can be integrated or removed as the need arises. This is discussed further in the sequel.

4. *Suitable for use without tools.* Though the notation must be supportable by tools, we also desire that it be easy to hand-draw, since many developers will want to use a graphical language as a rough-sketch tool.

5. *Clear relationship with textual TCSP.* The relationship between elements of the graphical TCSP and the textual TCSP should be obvious, so as to reduce the learn-

ing curve for the new syntax, to improve *traceability*, and to de ne a clear and precise mapping between a graphical TCSP speci cation and its formal semantics.

6. *Seamlessness and reversibility.* A graphical TCSP speci cation will eventually be transformed into textual TCSP, so as to make use of tools and to produce executable code. The mapping from graphical TCSP to textual TCSP should be seamless [18]: the same abstractions should be used in each syntax, and a precise mapping should be de ned between them. The mapping should also be reversible, so that it should be possible to automatically produce graphical TCSP speci cations from textual TCSP speci cations, thus enabling round-trip engineering [18].

7. *Semantically consistent.* A diagram should be interpreted in exactly and only one way. This is essential for a language that is to be used for formal speci cation and reasoning.

The issue of traceability, in point 5 above, is a critical one, especially when considered in parallel with point 4. The concept of a tool framework discussed in point 3 suggests a graphical front-end with which different back-end tools can be integrated, e.g. FDR. Back-end reasoning tools will in general require text-based input, and will produce text-based feedback. It should be possible to easily map concepts in the graphical notation to concepts in textual TCSP - and vice versa - so that feedback from tools can be more easily integrated into speci cations.

Point 1 above discusses usability, particularly in the large. Whether or not a particular notation is usable or aesthetically pleasing is a subjective matter. Graphical notations are generally considered more appropriate for capturing large amounts of information, and for presenting it in such a way so that details can be ignored where needed. However, graphical notations, by virtue of using their layout for imparting information, rather than textual symbols, suffer more from *secondary notation*, such as layout and typographic cues, than textual notations [22]. It is this secondary notation that sometimes appeals to users, and causes confusion in interpreting such notations. We aim to avoid use of secondary notation in the design of our graphical notation.

3   Overview of Timed CSP

We will now describe the textual notation of Timed CSP. Timed CSP has a simple grammar, as follows (P_T represents a sentence in Timed CSP).

$$P_T ::= \quad Stop \mid Skip \mid Wait\ t \mid a \to P_T \mid P_T;\ P_T \mid P_T \,\square\, P_T \mid P_T \sqcap P_T$$
$$\mid a : A \to P_{T_a} \mid P_T \rhd_t P_T \mid P_T \triangle P_T \mid P_T \oslash_t P_T \mid f(P_T) \mid l : P_T$$
$$\mid P_T \backslash A \mid \|_A P_T \mid P_T {}_A\|_A P_T \mid P_T \,\|\|\, P_T \mid P_T \|_A P_T \mid \mu X \bullet F(X)$$

A description of the meaning of each operator and terminal now follows:

Stop This will never engage in any external communication; it is the broken program.
Skip Do nothing except terminate (event ✔); it is ready to terminate immediately.
Wait t This does nothing, but is ready to terminate after delay t.
$a \to P$ This program is initially prepared to engage in event a; it then behaves as P. It is right associative, i.e., $a \to b \to P \equiv a \to (b \to P)$.

$P;\ Q$ Sequential composition transfers control from P to Q when P performs ✔. Right associative.

$P \square Q$ The environment is offered a choice between the programs P and Q. If the environment will cooperate with both, then the choice is nondeterministic. Right associative.

$P \sqcap Q$ The outcome between P and Q is a nondeterministic (internal) choice. Right associative.

$a : A \rightarrow P_a$ This program offers an external choice of events drawn from the (possibly ini nite) set A.

We can use this to build the channel notation: for a channel c carrying values of type T and $P'_{c.v} \equiv P_v$
- $c?x : T \rightarrow P_x \equiv a : \{v : T \mid c.v\} \rightarrow P'_a$
- $c!v \equiv c.v$

$P \triangleright_t Q$ (Timeout.) After delay t, if no communications have occurred, then control is passed to Q. If the ı rst communication with P occurs at exactly t, then the result is nondeterministic. This is internal choice in the untimed model.

$P \triangle Q$ (Interrupt.) This behaves as P until the ı rst event of Q, when control passes to Q.

$P \otimes_t Q$ (Transfer.) Control passes from P to Q after the delay t has passed. The ı rst program is interrupted at some nondeterministic point in the untimed model.

$f(P)$ Observable events in P are renamed according to the function f.

$l : P$ This program behaves as P, except all events a in P are renamed $l.a$.

$P \backslash A$ This program behaves as P, except that events in A are hidden. Hidden events no longer require the cooperation of the environment, and occur as soon as P is ready to perform them.

$\|_{A_i} P_i$ Network parallel, where the program P_i has interface A_i: every pair of programs must cooperate on the intersection of their interface sets.

$P_A\|_B Q$ (Simple binary parallel.) P may only perform events in A; Q may only perform events in B. They must agree on events in $A \cap B$.

$P \mid\mid\mid Q$ (Interleave.) Both P and Q evolve concurrently without interacting, except that they must both agree on termination. Right associative.

$P\|_C Q$ (Hybrid parallel.) P and Q must synchronise on the events in C and agree on termination; they interleave on other events. Right associative.

$\mu X \bullet P(X)$ This deı nes X to be P, possibly recursively. For a well-deı ned semantics, P must be guarded:
- untimed model: each free occurrence of X in P must be preceded by at least one observable event
- timed model: each free occurrence of X in P must be preceded by a non-zero time delay

Timed CSP has a well-understood semantics [23]. We will not repeat them here.

4 Graphical Timed CSP

4.1 Initial Discussion of the Design

The graphical notation that we introduce in Section 4.3 uses a syntax similar, but not identical to the textual syntax of TCSP. Indeed, initially, we attempted to construct a graphical notation with the same grammar structure as for the textual notation. Hence the graphical notation would be interchangeable with the textual notation and vice versa, and the semantics of the graphical notation would be easily determined via the textual notation.

Using the graphical notation with the identical syntax, we soon ran into problems: the diagrams generated by such a syntax are not intuitive. For example, external choice does not run directly onto the prei x statements. More concretely, we might like the program $a \rightarrow P \square b \rightarrow Q$ to be rendered something like

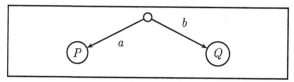

But then, how should we treat $P \square Q$? Using the same syntax structure, we would have

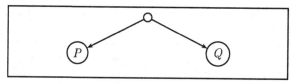

This is not intuitive; there are no labels on the node, but for the program to progress, the environment must choose the leading event of either P or Q.

After this failed attempt at mimicking the grammar of the textual syntax for the graphical notation, we considered a number of options.

1. Conclude that graphical representations of textual notations are undesirable, and should never be used as replacements. However, work on reverse engineering and program understanding [26] suggests that this is not an appropriate conclusion.
2. Design a restricted graphical syntax. For example, in the case illustrated above, the operands of an external choice operator would be restricted to being programs which start with a prei x. This is the approach that we adopt in the next section. Moreover, we soon concluded that it would be useful if textual grammar terms and predicates could be 'plugged in' to a graphical specii cation. Doing this increases the expressiveness of the language, improves extendibility – particularly by making it easier to dei ne linkages to other language and tools – and does not increase the complexity of using the language.
3. Some users will want to draw 'pretty pictures' in a tool which will thereafter generate code. Such users often do not understand the semantics of the graphical notation. Thus, a third option is to educate the users so that they understand the underlying assumptions of the language's semantics further.

Generally, whichever approach is adopted, the users need to understand what they're designing. Of course, it may then be the case that once the users are familiar with the language (graphical or textual), that they may then prefer the textual notation – it is often quicker to write, and easier to manipulate during reasoning. Obviously, we chose approach 2; elements of approach 3 are also desirable.

4.2 Proposal for a Graphical Notation for TCSP

We now propose our graphical notation for Timed CSP. We desire to satisfy the requirements discussed in Section 2. Typically, when the syntax of a graphical notation is presented, the syntax is described informally by example (and by cataloguing the available constructs), or by providing a metamodel, a list of rules that valid specifications written in the language must obey.

Instead of taking this approach, we present the syntax of graphical TCSP using a context-free grammar, where terminal symbols in the grammar are graphical constructs. This is useful for several reasons: the presentation of the grammar is formal, and can be implemented more straightforwardly using tools than an informal presentation; and the grammar allows substitution of equivalent textual constructs where graphical constructs are expected (thus permitting an integration of textual TCSP and graphical TCSP). Moreover, it simplifies traceability: the structure of the grammar for graphical TCSP mimics much of the structure of the grammar for textual TCSP, and as such it is straightforward to see the textual equivalent of a graphical TCSP specification, and vice versa. The metamodelling approach to defining the syntax and semantics of a language is appropriate for a complex family of languages like UML, where different views of the same system are constructed and need to be verified, but for a relatively simple language like TCSP, it is excessive.

4.3 Grammar for Graphical TCSP

We present the context-free grammar for graphical TCSP. In the grammar, P_G refers to a term in the graphical language, and P_T is a term in the textual language. We further add P_P as a process defined by a (textual) predicate; we will return to this point later. It is the mechanism by which predicate specifications can be integrated into TCSP. This desirable from the point of view of extendibility, expressiveness, and with an eye towards future tool integration.

We first define terms in the graphical language. Each graphical term is annotated with a comment in the right-most column, indicating the textual TCSP term that it depicts.

$$P_G ::= \qquad \otimes \qquad\qquad \text{Stop}$$

$$| \qquad \oslash \qquad\qquad \text{Skip}$$

$$| \qquad \bullet \xrightarrow{\text{Wait } t} P_G \qquad\qquad \text{Wait}$$

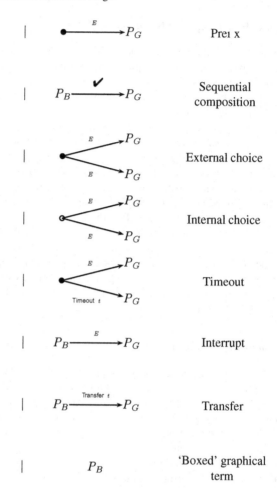

Prei x	
Sequential composition	
External choice	
Internal choice	
Timeout	
Interrupt	
Transfer	
'Boxed' graphical term	

Although not explicitly stated in the grammar, the external and internal choices can both be generalised from 2-way to n-way; the prototype tool support described in Section 6 includes this concept (i.e. that multiple arcs leaving a node can be included). Note that the choice must be entirely external or entirely internal; it cannot be a mixture.

The last production above refers to a 'boxed' graphical term. We use *boxes* as our modularisation construct. They introduce scoping, and optionally, naming. P_B representing boxed graphical terms, is as follows.

$$P_B ::=$$

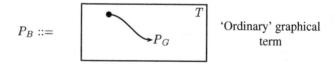

'Ordinary' graphical term

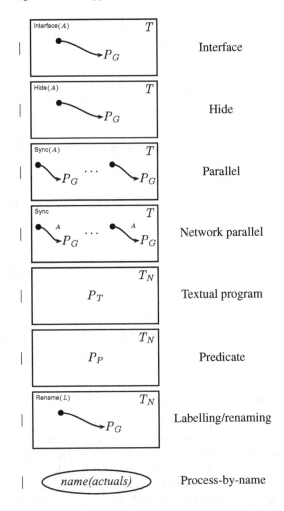

	Interface
	Hide
	Parallel
	Network parallel
	Textual program
	Predicate
	Labelling/renaming
	Process-by-name

The last section of the grammar 1 lls in all the remaining details, by adding annotations for boxes (i.e., names, local variables, parameters), as well as events and renaming functions. For now, we do not specify the details of the renaming function. We envisage it working in the same way as FDR's renaming function [8].

$$T ::= \qquad [T_N][T_L][T_P] \qquad \text{Annotations}$$

$T_N ::=$	*name*	Naming
$T_N ::=$	Local(*locals*)	Local variables
$T_P ::=$	Params(*parameters*)	Parameters
$E ::=$	$c/e : a$	condition-event-action
$\vert$	e	(simple) event
$L ::=$	(a renaming function)	condition-event-action

4.4   Semantics

The semantics of a graphical TCSP diagram can be found by trivially translating the diagram into a TCSP program. From there, we use the standard semantics for TCSP. The translation operates on the structure of the grammar for graphical TCSP. Each terminal in the graphical grammar is translated into an equivalent terminal in the textual grammar. Each operator in the graphical grammar (and thus, each production) is translated into the equivalent operator (and production) in the textual grammar. This translation can be formally expressed as a function $\mathcal{M} : P_G \rightarrow P_T$, and can be deı ned inductively over the structure of the grammar. A partial deı nition of this function is as follows:

If $P =$ ✗   then $\mathcal{M}(P) = Stop$

If $P =$ ✓   then $\mathcal{M}(P) = Skip$

If $P =$ ●———Wait t———▶Q then $\mathcal{M}(P) = Waitt;\ \mathcal{M}(Q)$

If $P =$ ●———e———▶Q then $\mathcal{M}(P) = e \rightarrow \mathcal{M}(Q)$

If $P =$ Q———✔———▶R then $\mathcal{M}(P) = \mathcal{M}(Q);\ \mathcal{M}(R)$

If $P =$ ●<$\begin{smallmatrix} e \nearrow Q \\ f \searrow R \end{smallmatrix}$ then $\mathcal{M}(P) = (e \rightarrow \mathcal{M}(Q))\ \square\ (f \rightarrow \mathcal{M}(R))$

If $P =$ ○<$\begin{smallmatrix} e \nearrow Q \\ f \searrow R \end{smallmatrix}$ then $\mathcal{M}(P) = (e \rightarrow \mathcal{M}(Q))\ \sqcap\ (f \rightarrow \mathcal{M}(R))$

If $P =$ ●<$\begin{smallmatrix} e \nearrow Q \\ \text{Timeout } t \searrow R \end{smallmatrix}$ then $\mathcal{M}(P) = (e \rightarrow \mathcal{M}(Q)) \vartriangleright_t \mathcal{M}(R)$

If $P =$ Q———e———▶R then $\mathcal{M}(P) = \mathcal{M}(Q)\triangle(e \rightarrow \mathcal{M}(R))$

If $P =$ Q———Transfer t———▶R then $\mathcal{M}(P) = \mathcal{M}(Q)\ \varnothing_t\ \mathcal{M}(R)$

If $P =$ [●↘Q]   then $\mathcal{M}(P) = (\mathcal{M}(Q))$

If $P =$ [Interface(A) ●↘Q]   then $\mathcal{M}(P) = (\mathcal{M}(Q)\backslash(\alpha(Q)\backslash A))$

If $P =$ [Hide(A) ●↘Q]   then $\mathcal{M}(P) = (\mathcal{M}(Q)\backslash A)$

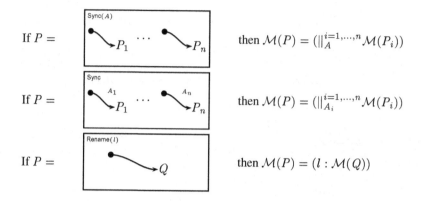

If $P =$ [Sync(A) diagram with $P_1 \cdots P_n$] then $\mathcal{M}(P) = (\|_A^{i=1,\ldots,n} \mathcal{M}(P_i))$

If $P =$ [Sync diagram with $A_1, \ldots, A_n$ and $P_1 \cdots P_n$] then $\mathcal{M}(P) = (\|_{A_i}^{i=1,\ldots,n} \mathcal{M}(P_i))$

If $P =$ [Rename(l) diagram with Q] then $\mathcal{M}(P) = (l : \mathcal{M}(Q))$

Textual programs are included easily. Since the graphical grammar already includes productions from nonterminal P_T, they can be included in graphical specii cations, and their semantics is produced simply by dei ning $\mathcal{M}$ on textual terms to be the identity map.

If $P =$ [$Q : P_T$] then $\mathcal{M}(P) = (Q)$

The graphical grammar includes general predicate specii cations. Their semantics is included by treating them, informally, as the most general program that satisi es the predicate. More precisely, predicates are dei ned on a set of observations: depending on the semantic domain, this may be, for example untimed traces; timed traces; untimed failures; or timed failures.

A predicate S is dei ned as a function with domain equal to the semantic domain, and a range of $\{true, false\}$. Given an observation of any process, it either satisi es the predicate or it does not. The textual program we use has to be a program, R, such that R generates all observations accepted by S while not generating any observations that are not accepted by S. (For now, we ignore the possibility of unsatisi able predicates: we would envisage some part of the tool support reporting that it cannot satisfy this predicate.)

If $P =$ [$S : P_P$] then $\mathcal{M}(P) = ($a process that satisi es $S)$

Note that in a theorem proving environment which uses the observations of a process, we would simply use S directly as a predicate on those observations.

The graphical syntax P_G constrains the choice constructs: they are *not* general choice as is usual in TCSP. By requiring that they are labelled, we solve our problem from Section 4.1 at the expense of a loss of expression. We consider that this is a reasonable trade-off, since we are keeping intuitiveness of meaning. If the original form of general choice was required, then a user can always use the normal textual form (which is still available, by design).

This limitation aside, the rest of the graphical syntax mirrors the textual syntax: the graphical syntax is almost as expressive as the textual syntax.

5 Examples

Our 1 rst example is a simple two-state process. Although our grammar does not insist on it, we would expect there to be an outermost box in most cases.

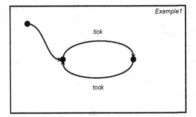

This example de1 nes the process

$$Example1 = tick \rightarrow tock \rightarrow Example1$$

However, we might have been more comfortable de1 ning this in terms of a predicate over untimed traces:

$$\forall tr : 1 \geq \#tick - \#tock \geq 0$$

The predicate in the box means: for all possible traces that may be observed of *Example1*, the difference between the number of *tick*s and the number of *tock*s can only be 0 or 1.

Our second example builds on the 1 rst: it describes a process that engages in two *bong* events after every *tock*.

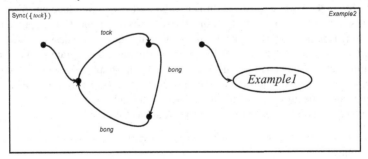

We might write this as

$$Example2 = (\mu\, X \bullet tock \rightarrow bong \rightarrow bong \rightarrow X) \parallel_{\{tock\}} Example1$$

Finally, we could have used *Example1* anonymously by copying it (the innermost box is not necessary; we have included it to illustrate that it can be done):

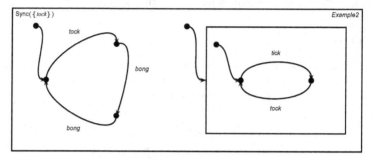

Alternatively, we could include the 1 rst example as the predicate given earlier:

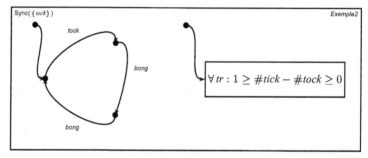

6   Tool Support

The graphical notation has been designed with tool support in mind. We desire to pro-vide support for drawing and constructing TCSP specii cations, and also for reason-ing about them. Our underlying philosophy is to produce a notation (and tool support) that is compatible with and can be integrated with other existing notations and tools, e.g. TCSP, FDR, PVS, and ACL2. In particular, rather than produce our own reason-ing tools, we desire to use existing tools. However, as it is impossible to predict which forms of reasoning support will be useful in all circumstances, we desire to provide tool support for graphical TCSP that makes it straightforward to integrate with other tools. This approach is schematically illustrated in Fig. 1. The graphical notation, and its sup-port tools, will be used in loose integration with reasoning tools such as FDR and PVS, as well as documentation preparation facilities such as LATEX.

The ongoing objectives in this line of work are as follows:

- Dei ne a simple machine-readable language (MRL) that describes programs in the graphical notation.

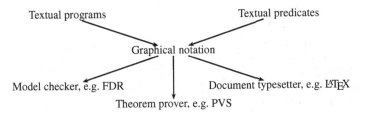

Fig. 1. Tool framework

- Write a drawing tool that produces programs in the MRL, and which will draw programs expressed in the MRL.
- Write a converter that takes MRL programs and transforms them into some other notation, e.g. FDR or PVS input, thus obtaining a loose integration of the drawing tool with reasoning tools.

The 1 rst and third items are mostly complete; we have a prototype tool constructed. The second item is in the design phase, but it should only be started when we are convinced that both the graphical notation and the MRL are stable and useful. The existing prototype can be viewed as a compiler: it reads in a 1 le written in the current MRL, and then generates output code. At this time, it has a lex/yacc front end, which is used to produce a parse tree. The tree is then walked to produce output as requested by the user (i.e. PVS, FDR, or LATEX output).

The current MRL is a simple declarative language, where graphical elements are given an internal name to identify them as nodes; these internal names are used as the end-points of arcs. The notation is textual, and in the case of boxes, uses BOX. . . ENDBOX constructs for scoping. For example, the MRL for the 1 rst two examples in the previous section are of the form:

```
i1 BOX
    NAME Example1
    i2 NODE
    i3 NODE
    INITIAL_ARC i2
    ARC i2 -> i3 ; tick
    ARC i3 -> i2 ; tock
ENDBOX
```

for *Example1* graphically;

```
i4 BOX
    NAME Example1
    i5 PREDICATE forall tr : 1 >= #(tick,tr) - #(tock,tr) >= 0
ENDBOX
```

for *Example1* as a predicate; and

```
i6 BOX
   NAME Example2
   PARALLEL {tock}
   i7 NODE
   i8 NODE
   i9 NODE
   INITIAL_ARC i7
   ARC i7 -> i8 ; tock
   ARC i8 -> i9 ; bong
   ARC i9 -> i7 ; bong
   i10 PROCESS Example1()
   INITIAL_ARC i10
ENDBOX
```

Note that we explicitly name the nodes and other entities within the graph that arcs may need to connect to. We are considering converting this to use XML; this may make future interoperability easier than with a one-off MRL.

The i rst theorem provers we are considering supporting in the near future is PVS. This generates an additional requirement: to generate input for PVS, we need an embedding of TCSP into PVS. We envisage building on one of the author's doctoral work [4] to achieve this. This work used PVS: for a given semantic domain, processes are dei ned by the observations that they admit. The meaning of the various syntactic constructs is dei ned by the resulting observations that may be admitted.

7 Future Work and Summary

This paper has presented a graphical notation for Timed CSP. We have given a rationale, and outlined the process by which we came to this notation. We claim that it has the major benei ts of combining both graphical and textual notations in an intuitive and relatively simple fashion. We also allow textual notations to encompass both process and predicate approaches to dei ning processes. Additionally, we have extendible tool support for this approach as a partially-completed prototype.

We believe that this notation makes the use of formal notations easier to introduce into projects, while allowing a path towards using textual notations when proi ciency with textual TCSP is achieved. Moreover, the graphical notation can stand as a useful illustrative tool, particularly for rough-sketch modelling.

Related work beyond the elements of tool construction discussed in the previous section includes

- A discussion of when it is appropriate to use textual processes, textual predicates, and graphical notations.
- Better expressions, ideally using an identical notation to FDR.
- Evaluation: Have we achieved the goals we set out in Section 2.2?
- Other language targets for TCSP, e.g. ACL2.

Acknowledgements

We thank the three anonymous referees for their constructive and useful comments.

References

[1] L. Baresi and M. Pezzè. Towards Formalizing Structured Analysis. *ACM Trans. Software Engineering and Methodology* 7(1), January 1998.

[2] T. Bolognesi, E. Najm, and P. Tilanus. G-LOTOS: a graphical language for concurrent systems. *Computer Networks and ISDN Systems*, 26(9):1101–1127, 1994.

[3] G. Booch, J. Rumbaugh, and I. Jacobson. *The UML User Guide*. Addison-Wesley, 1999.

[4] P. Brooke. A Timed Semantics for A Hierarchical Design Notation. DPhil thesis, Department of Computer Science, University of York; also issued as YCST 99/08.

[5] P. Brooke, J. Jacob, and J. Armstrong. An analysis of the four-slot mechanism. In *Proceedings of the BCS-FACS Northern Formal Methods Workshop*, electronic Workshops in Computing. Springer-Verlag, 1996.

[6] S. Brodsky, T. Clark, S. Cook, A. Evans, and S. Kent. Feasibility Study in Rearchitecting the UML as a Family of Languages using a Precise Meta-Modeling Approach. Technical Report of pUML Group, September 2000. Available at www.puml.org.

[7] J. Sun, J.S. Dong, J. Liu, and H. Wang. Z Family on the Web with their UML Photos. Technical Report TR-A1-01, School of Computing, National University of Singapore, January 2001.

[8] Formal Systems (Europe) Ltd. Failures-Divergence Re nement: FDR 2. http://www.formal.demon.co.uk/, December 1995.

[9] T. Green and R. Navarro. Programming plans, imagery and visual programming. In *Proceedings of INTERACT '95*, 1995.

[10] T. Green and M. Petre. When visual programs are harder to read than textual programs. In G.C. van der Veer, M.J. Tauber, S. Bagnarola, and M. Antavolits, editors, *Human-Computer Interaction: Tasks and Organisation. Proceedings of ECCE6 (6th European Conference on Cognitive Ergonomics)*. CUD, 1992.

[11] J. Grundy, R.Back, and J. von Wright. Structured Calculational Proof. *Formal Aspects of Computing* 9(5-6), 1997.

[12] D. Harel. Statecharts: A visual formalism for complex systems. *Science of Computer Programming*, 8:231–274, 1987.

[13] C. Hoare. *Communicating Sequential Processes*. Prentice-Hall International UK, 1985.

[14] i-Logix. *Statemate: Semantics of Statecharts*.

[15] L. Lamport. How to write a long formula. Technical Report 119, DEC SRC, December 1993.

[16] N. Leveson, M. Heimdahl, H. Hildreth, and J. Reese. Requirements speci cation for process-control systems. *IEEE Transactions on Software Engineering*, 20(9):684–707, September 1994. Also Technical Report 92-106 (University of California).

[17] S. Liu, A.J. Offutt, C. Ho-Stuart, Y. Sun, and M. Ohba. SOFL: A formal engineering methodology for industrial applications. *IEEE Transactions on Software Engineering*, 24(1):24–45, January 1998.

[18] B. Meyer. *Object-Oriented Software Construction* (Second Edition). Prentice-Hall, 1997.

[19] R. Paige, J. Ostroff, and P. Brooke. Principles of Modelling Language Design. *Information and Software Technology*, 42(10):665-675, June 2000.

[20] R. Paige and J. Ostroff. Metamodelling and Conformance Checking with PVS. In *Proc. Fundamental Aspects of Software Engineering 2001*. LNCS 2029, Springer-Verlag, April 2001.

[21] M. Petre, A. Blackwell, and T. Green. Cognitive questions in software visualisation. In J. Stasko, J. Domingue, B. Price, and M. Brown, editors, *Software Visualisation: Programming as a Multi-Media Experience*. MIT Press, 1997.

[22] M. Petre. Why looking isn't always seeing: Readership skills and graphical programming. *Communications of the ACM*, 38(6):33–44, June 1995.

[23] S. Schneider. *Concurrent and Real-time Systems*. Wiley, 2000.

[24] H. Simpson. Four-slot fully asynchronous communication mechanism. *IEE Proceedings*, 137 Part E(1):17–30, January 1990.

[25] H. Simpson. Correctness analysis for class of asynchronous communication mechanisms. *IEE Proceedings*, 139 Part E(1):35–49, January 1992.

[26] T. Systa, P. Yu, and H. Muller. Analyzing Java Software by Combining Metrics and Program Visualization. In *Proc. CSMR-2000*, IEEE Press, Feb. 2000.

[27] M. von der Beeck. A comparison of Statecharts variants. In H. Langmaack, W.P. de Roever, and J. Vytopil, editors, *Proceedings of the 3rd International Symposium on Formal Techniques in Real-Time and Fault-Tolerant Systems*, volume 863 of *Lecture Notes in Computer Science*, pages 128–148. Springer-Verlag, 1994.

[28] S. Owre, N. Shankar, J. Rushby, and D. Stringer-Calvert. *PVS System Guide*. Computer Science Laboratory, SRI International, September 1998.

Combining Graphical and Formal Development of Open Distributed Systems[*]

Einar B. Johnsen[1,3], Wenhui Zhang[2], Olaf Owe[1], and Demissie B. Aredo[2,4]

[1] Dept. of Informatics, University of Oslo, Norway
{einarj,olaf}@ifi.uio.no
[2] Institute for Energy Technology, Halden, Norway
[3] BISS, FB3, University of Bremen, Germany
einar@tzi.de
[4] Norwegian Computing Center, Oslo, Norway
aredo@nr.no

Abstract. A specification of a software system involves several aspects. Two essential aspects are convenience in specification and possibility for formal analysis. These aspects are, to some extent, exclusive. This paper describes an approach to the specification of systems that emphasizes both aspects, by combining UML with a language for description of the observable behavior of object viewpoints, OUN. Whereas both languages are centered around object-oriented concepts, they are complementary in the sense that one is graphical and semi-formal while the other is textual and formal. The approach is demonstrated by a case study focusing on the specification of an open communication infrastructure.

1 Introduction

In order to develop open distributed systems, we need techniques and tools for specification, design, and code generation. For the specification of such systems, it can be desirable to use graphical notations, so that specifications are intuitive and easy to understand, and misunderstandings and mistakes thereby hopefully avoided. On the other hand, it is also desirable for the specification technique to have a formal basis which supports rigorous reasoning about specifications and designs. As there is no single existing method that covers all the desired aspects adequately, we have chosen to extend, adapt, and combine existing formal methods and tools into a platform for specification, design, and refinement of open distributed systems. In this approach, we integrate the Unified Modeling Language (UML) [20,6] modeling techniques, the Oslo University Notation (OUN) specification language [12,21], and the Prototype Verification System (PVS) specification language [22] in a common platform [26].

UML is a comprehensive notation for creating a visual model of a system. It is a dynamic specification language based on a combination of popular modeling

---

[*] This work is financed by the Research Council of Norway under the research program for Distributed IT-Systems.

M. Butler, L. Petre, and K. Sere (Eds.): IFM 2002, LNCS 2335, pp. 319–338, 2002.

languages [5, 10, 24] and has become a widely used standard for object-oriented software development. As a modeling language, UML allows a description of a system in great detail at any level of abstraction. UML does not rely on a specific development process, although it facilitates descriptions and development processes that are case-driven, architecture centric, iterative, and incremental. It provides notations needed to define a system with any particular architecture and does so in an object-oriented way. The graphical notation of UML includes class diagrams, object diagrams, use case diagrams, interaction diagrams (including sequence diagrams and collaboration diagrams), statechart diagrams, activity diagrams, component diagrams, and deployment diagrams. These diagrams allows us to describe central *aspects* of the overall system. However, rigorous reasoning in UML is difficult as the language lacks a formal semantics.

OUN is a high-level object-oriented design language which supports the development of open distributed systems. The language is designed to enable formal reasoning in a convenient manner. In particular, reasoning control is based on static typing and proofs, and generation of verification conditions is based on static analysis of program or specification units. A system design in OUN consists of classes, interfaces, and contracts, however in this paper we will only consider specification by means of interfaces. An object in OUN can support a number of interfaces and this number can change dynamically.

In contrast to OCL [27], OUN lets us capture aspects of the *observable behavior* of objects in terms of input and output. For open systems, implementation details of components may not be available, but the behavior of a component can be locally determined by its interaction with the environment [1]. OUN objects may have internal activity and run in parallel. They communicate asynchronously by means of remote methods calls and exchange object identities. Object interaction is recorded in *communication traces* [8, 14, 23], so the semantics of the language is trace-based. In OUN, the observable behavior of an object can be specified by several interfaces that represent aspects of the object's behavior. An interface is specified syntactically by an alphabet and semantically by predicates on traces. Hence, an interface identifies a set of finite traces reflecting possible communication histories of a component (or object) at different points of time. Requirement specifications of interfaces consider observable behavior in the form of an input/output-driven assumption guarantee paradigm; invariant predicates about output are guaranteed when assumption predicates about input are respected by the communication environment. For these predicates, we may use patterns that describe the traces of the system in a graphical style reminiscent of message sequence charts.

PVS is a specification language based on higher-order logic. It has a rich type system including predicate subtypes and dependent types. These features make the language very expressive, but type checking becomes undecidable. In addition, there are type constructors for functions, tuples, records, and abstract data types. PVS specifications are organized into theories and modularity and reuse are supported by means of parameterized theories. PVS has a powerful verification tool which uses decision procedures for simplifying and discharging proofs, and provides many proof techniques such as induction, term rewriting, backward proofs, forward proofs, and proof by cases, for interactive user intervention.

The purpose of the integration of the techniques is to exploit the advantages of UML for high-level specification with graphical notations, the formal notation provided by OUN for specification of additional aspects concerning the observable behavior of objects or components, and the theorem-proving capabilities of PVS for verification of correctness requirements. The system development process in our approach consists of the following steps: informal specification of user requirements; partial specifications in UML; extension of the UML interface specifications into OUN specifications; translation of the partial specifications into a PVS specification; verification and validation of the specification with PVS tools; and code generation (for instance towards Java). The emphasis here is on specification, verification aspects are briefly considered at the end of the paper.

This approach is demonstrated by a case study. We consider a specification of the **SoftwareBus** system[1], an object-oriented data exchange system developed at the OECD Halden Reactor Project [2]. The system itself is not safety critical, but, depending on the user applications of the system, it may have safety implications. For instance, the PLASMA plant safety monitoring and assessment system [7] is based on the **SoftwareBus** communication package. Important functions of the system include: providing the current safety status of the plant, online monitoring of the safety function status trees, displaying the pertinent emergency operating procedures, and displaying the process parameters which are referenced in the procedures. Another application of the **SoftwareBus** system is data communication mechanism in the SCORPIO core surveillance system [16], a system supporting control room operators, reactor physicists, and system supervisors. The SCORPIO system has two modes: monitoring and predicting, and the main purpose of the system is to increase the quality and quantity of information and enhance plant safety by detecting and preventing undesired core conditions. Correctness and reliability of such systems are important, e.g. presentation of wrong information may lead to wrong control actions and trigger safety protection actions, which could contribute to the possibility of failure with safety consequences. Consequently, rigorous specification and formal analysis of the underlying communication framework are important.

The paper is organized as follows. In Section 2, the functionality of the **SoftwareBus** system is described and a possible system architecture proposed. In Section 3, a specification of the **SoftwareBus** system is presented, using the UML modeling techniques. In Section 4, we extend the UML interface specifications into OUN and show how graphical patterns are used to capture the observable behavior of the components. Section 5 considers robustness issues and illustrates how fault-tolerance can be added to the system in OUN. In Section 6, we discuss the usefulness of our approach.

---

[1] As the purpose of this paper is to illustrate our approach to system development, considerable simplifications have been made. Readers interested in the system are referred to the web-page `http://www.ife.no/swbus` for detailed documentation.

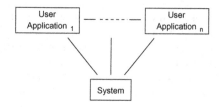

Fig. 1. Basic structure of the **SoftwareBus** system with user applications.

2   Functionality of the Software Bus

The main motivation for constructing distributed systems considered in this paper arises from the need for surveillance and control of processes in power plants. For this purpose, data collected from processes have to be processed and presented. As the same set of data may be a basis for presentation in different forms at different locations, data sharing among user applications is a necessity.

To begin with, we may think of a *system* with an unknown number of potential user applications connected to it, as shown in Figure 1. The user applications communicate with the system in order to carry out necessary data processing tasks. These include the creation of variables, the assignment of values to variables, accessing the values of variables, and the destruction of variables.

The **SoftwareBus** system is an object-oriented system in which classes, functions, and variables are treated as **SoftwareBus** objects, i.e. as manipulatable units in the **SoftwareBus** system. A **SoftwareBus** object can be identified in two ways. First, by its identifier: In the implementation of the **SoftwareBus** system, an object identifier identifies a row in a table where object information is stored. Second, by the object's name and its parent's identifier, as objects are organized in a hierarchy where the top level represents the local application or proxy objects representing remote applications. A pointer type is used for the contents of objects, i.e. pointers to places in user applications where the contents of objects are stored, and another type is used for codes of functions. In addition, variables holding references to remote applications are grouped as a type. Therefore, we have the following basic types: **SbTName** for object names, **SbTSti** for local object identifiers, **SbTContents** for contents of objects, **SbTCode** for code of functions, and **SbTApplication** for references to applications. **SbTSti** is a general type for identifying **SoftwareBus** objects. We classify different objects or objects used in different contexts into subtypes of **SbTSti**.

2.1   System Interfaces

With the system architecture of Figure 1, we only need to consider one interface, which is the interface the system provides towards user applications. This interface includes operations for initializing user applications, establishing logical connections with other applications, and manipulating **SoftwareBus** objects:

Name   sb_initialize
Arguments   name: **SbTName**
Return Value none
Description   signals that a calling user application enters the system.

Name   sb_exit
Arguments   none
Return Value none
Description   signals that the calling user application leaves the system.

Name   sb_connect_appl
Arguments   appl_name: **SbTName**
Return Value appl_ref: **SbTApplication**
Description   establishes a logical connection with *appl_name*.

Name   sb_disconnect_appl
Arguments   appl_ref: **SbTApplication**
Return Value none
Description   destroys the logical connection to *appl_ref*.

Name   sb_id
Arguments   name: **SbTName**
                  parent_ref: **SbTStiParent**
Return Value obj_ref: **SbTSti**
Description   obtains the reference of (a proxy of) the object identified
                  by *name* and *parent_ref*.

Name   sb_delete_obj
Arguments   obj_ref: **SbTSti**
Return Value none
Description   deletes the object identified by *obj_ref*.

The operations **sb_initialize** and **sb_exit** are invoked by a user application in order to enter and leave the **SoftwareBus** system, respectively. The operations **sb_connect_appl** and **sb_disconnect_appl** concern the logical connections between processes. To establish a logical connection, the remote application (identified by *appl_name*) must have entered the system prior to the method invocation. The operations **sb_id** and **sb_delete_obj** are for object manipulation. For brevity, other object manipulation operations (e.g. for creating subclasses, modifying classes, creating instances of classes, using attributes and methods of such instances) are not described here. The parameter *parent_ref* of the operation **sb_id** identifies either the local application, an object in the local application, a remote application, or a proxy of an object of a remote application. A proxy needs to be created if *name* identifies a remote object without a proxy in the local application. **SbTStiParent** is a subtype of **SbTSti** that represents **SoftwareBus** objects used as parent objects in given contexts.

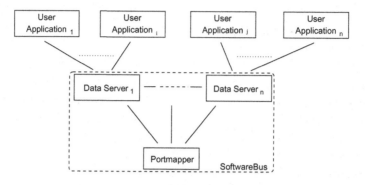

Fig. 2. Decomposition of **SoftwareBus**.

2.2 Decomposition of the System

A centralized system architecture is not the best choice for a distributed computing environment with respect to efficiency, communication overhead, and reliability. A better solution is to keep as much data as possible in or near the user applications that possess the data, and provide a mechanism for data sharing. Figure 2 shows a decomposition of the system based on this principle.

With this architecture, the system consists of a central unit and a set of data servers. The purpose of the central unit is to maintain information about the data servers and their user applications, while the purpose of the servers is to store data that is shared among user applications. In this system, a user application communicates with a data server in order to carry out necessary data processing tasks. Depending on requests from the user application, the data server may communicate directly with another data server to fulfill the requests or communicate with the central unit if information about other servers is requested or needed. The number of data servers and their locations is not predetermined. Data servers may be started at any location, whenever necessary.

Two interfaces need to be specified. One is the interface of the central unit towards data servers and the other is the interface of a data server to other data servers. To be consistent with the terminology of the **SoftwareBus** documentation [2], we call the central unit a **portmapper** in the sequel. The interface provided by the portmapper to data servers includes the following operations: **pm_initialize**, **pm_exit**, **pm_connect_appl**, and **pm_disconnect_appl**.

These operations are the internal equivalents of the data server operations starting with **sb**, except that the internal operations have an additional input parameter of type **SbTApplication**. Think that all calls from user applications to the system are delivered by a data server. Upon receipt of a call **sb_m** (with m being one of **initialize**, **exit**, **connect_appl**, and **disconnect_appl**) from a user application, the data server forwards the call to the portmapper by calling **pm_m**. The additional input parameter is used to identify the calling user application in order to ensure that returns to calls are transmitted correctly.

The operations of the interface provided by data servers to other data servers are similar (with respect to the functionality) to the interface provided by the system to user applications, if we omit the operations associated with the portmapper, i.e. the operations **sb_initialize**, **sb_exit**, **sb_connect_appl**, and **sb_disconnect_appl**. When a user application calls an operation of the system, these four operations are forwarded to the portmapper while the other operations are handled by a data server. The data server may issue a corresponding call to another data server when necessary.

3 UML Specification

In this section, we present a specification of the **SoftwareBus** system using UML modeling techniques. First, we give static structural descriptions of the major system components such as interfaces, classes (or objects), and relationships among them, as outlined in the previous section. For this purpose, we model basic elements like classes, components, and the interfaces that they provide to each other. Then, the static structure and the dynamic behavior of the system can be specified by putting together the basic elements into UML diagrams.

3.1 External Interfaces

The external interface of the **SoftwareBus** specifies operations available to user applications. These operations can be grouped into two: those concerned with object manipulations and those dealing with communication between user applications and the **SoftwareBus** system. Accordingly, we decompose the interface towards external user applications into two subinterfaces: **SB_SoftwareBusData** and **SB_SoftwareBusConnections**. The operations of these interfaces have been discussed in the previous section. Here, we describe the interfaces and their relationships to the **SoftwareBus** system using the UML graphical notation.

For the purpose of this paper, the interface **SB_SoftwareBusData** includes at least the operations **sb_id** and **sb_delete_obj**. In the actual **SoftwareBus** system, several other operations are provided for object manipulation. The specification, given as a UML interface, is as follows.

```
┌─────────────────────────────────┐
│          ≪interface≫            │
│       SB_SoftwareBusData         │
├─────────────────────────────────┤
│                                 │
├─────────────────────────────────┤
│ sb_id( name,parent_ref; obj_ref )│
│    sb_delete_obj( obj_ref )      │
│               ⋮                 │
│                                 │
└─────────────────────────────────┘
```

The interface **SB_SoftwareBusData** consists of operations for object manipulation. The interpretation of operation signatures is as follows. In the list of parameters, values that occur before the symbol ";" are *input* parameters, whereas the remaining values are *output* parameters. The types of the parameters are as specified in the previous section.

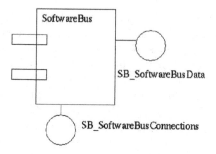

Fig. 3. SoftwareBus interfaces.

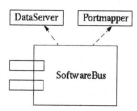

Fig. 4. The **SoftwareBus** component and its classes.

The interface **SB_SoftwareBusConnections** consists of operations that handle connections between the system and the user applications. The specification, given as a UML interface, is as follows.

≪interface≫ SB_SoftwareBusConnections
sb_initialize(name)   sb_exit()   sb_connect_appl(appl_name; appl_ref)   sb_disconnect_appl(appl_ref)

The relationships between the **SoftwareBus** system and its external interfaces are depicted in a UML class diagram in Figure 3.

3.2   Internal Interfaces

By "internal" interfaces, we mean the interfaces that the different parts of the **SoftwareBus** system provide to each other, in contrast to the interfaces that are available to the user applications. The internal structure of the **Software-Bus** system consists of a portmapper with a set of data servers. A description of the **SoftwareBus** system in terms of its classes is shown in Figure 4. We consider two interfaces **SB_Portmapper** and **SB_DataServer**, provided by the portmapper to data servers and by data servers to other data servers, respectively. SB_Portmapper resembles SB_SoftwareBusConnections, specified as follows:

≪interface≫
SB_Portmapper
pm_initialize(name;user_ref) pm_exit(user_ref) pm_connect_appl(user_ref,server_name; server_ref) pm_disconnect_appl(user_ref,server_ref)

The interface **SB_DataServer** is similar to SB_SoftwareBusData, so the description is omitted. The class diagram given in Figure 5 shows the classes and internal interfaces of the **SoftwareBus** system and relationships among them.

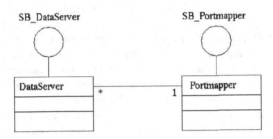

Fig. 5. SoftwareBus class diagram.

Remarks on Implementation Issues. In theory, a user application may communicate with the system by contacting any data server. However, this complicates the communication pattern. A possible solution is a one-to-one mapping between user applications and data servers. With such a mapping, parameters to method calls can be simplified, as the identity of the user application at the source of a call is given by its corresponding data server. In this paper, we have adopted a more general solution, where several applications can use the same data server. For simplicity, we nevertheless assume that an application does not employ several data servers during the same session (i.e. without exiting the **SoftwareBus** and reconnecting via the new server). In practice, a user application and its corresponding data server are often implemented in one component [2].

4   OUN Specification

OUN allows the specification of observable behavior by means of interfaces. Thus, an object considered through an interface represents a specific viewpoint to the services provided by the object. There may be several interfaces associated with an object, which give rise to supplementary behavioral specifications of the same object. Proof obligations arise in order to verify that objects of a given class actually fulfill the requirements of the interfaces they claim to implement [21]. In this section, we semantically restrict the UML interfaces of Section 3 to obtain OUN interfaces that express the *behavior* of the **SoftwareBus** interfaces.

In OUN, the interfaces of an object do not only contain syntactic method declarations, they also specify aspects of the observable behavior of that object, i.e. the possible communication histories of the object when a particular subset of its alphabet is taken into account. The alphabet of an interface consists of a set of communication events reflecting the relevant method calls for the currently considered role of the object. Say that a method "m" is implemented by some object o and it is called by another object o' with parameters $p_1, \ldots, p_n$ and returns with values $v_1, \ldots, v_m$. The call is represented by two distinct communication events: first, $o' \rightarrow o.m(p_1, \ldots, p_n)$ reflects the *initiation* of the method call and then, $o' \leftarrow o.m(p_1, \ldots, p_n; v_1, \ldots, v_m)$ reflects the *completion* of the call.

The aspect of an object's behavior that is specified by an interface is given by (first-order) predicates on finite sequences of such communication events. For each interface there are two (optional) predicates, an assumption and an invariant. The assumption states conditions on objects in the environment of the object, so it is a predicate that should hold for sequences that end with input events to the object. The assumption predicate should be respected by every object in the environment; we consider communication with one object at a time. The invariant guarantees a certain behavior when the assumption holds, so the invariant is given by a predicate on the sequences ending with output from the object. When an assumption or an invariant predicate is omitted in the specification of an interface, we understand it as "true".

For the specification of the boundary between users and the **SoftwareBus** system, two interfaces are introduced: **SB_SoftwareBus** and **SB_User**. The first interface is offered by the **SoftwareBus** to its users. The second interface is an "empty" interface used to identify users. OUN objects are always considered through interfaces, so all objects need interfaces, even if they do not contain methods that are accessible to the environment. In the next section, we consider requirements on the OUN objects that provide the SB_SoftwareBus interface.

4.1   External Interfaces

In OUN, an interface may inherit other interfaces. Using inheritance, the interface of the **SoftwareBus** can be specified as follows.

```
interface SB_SoftwareBus
    inherits SB_SoftwareBusData,
             SB_SoftwareBusConnections
begin
end
```

Here, SB_SoftwareBusData and SB_SoftwareBusConnections are as discussed in the previous section, without any semantic restrictions. Operations are inherited automatically from the UML interface specifications via the Integrator [26]. In this section, we extend the interfaces with behavioral constraints.

SB_SoftwareBusData. This interface considers object manipulation between applications in the **SoftwareBus**. (For remote object manipulation, logical connections between applications are established via the SB_SoftwareBusConnections interface.) After initialization, the user application may talk to the **SoftwareBus** in order to create new objects and manipulate existing objects. It is assumed that no objects are known a priori to a user. References to objects are obtained from the **SoftwareBus** before they are passed on as arguments in method invocations. Knowledge of an object reference is obtained either through the creation of that object by the user or by a call to **sb_id** with the appropriate parameters. We capture knowledge of object references by a predicate on the history. Let $known(x, y, r, h)$ express that the object reference r is known by the application x, where h is its history of communication with the **SoftwareBus** y, defined as follows for the operations considered in this paper:

$$known(x, y, r, \varepsilon) = \textbf{false}$$
$$known(x, y, r, h \vdash x{\leftarrow}y.\text{sb\_id}(\_, \_; r)) = \textbf{true}$$
$$known(x, y, r, h \vdash x{\leftarrow}y.\text{sb\_delete\_obj}(r)) = \textbf{false}$$
$$known(x, y, r, h \vdash \text{others}) = known(x, y, r, h)$$

Here, cases are considered in the order listed (à la ML), so we recursively inspect the history until one of the cases apply. The symbols "ε" and "$\vdash$" denote the empty trace and the *right append* operation, respectively. Furthermore, we represent by "$\_$" an uninteresting parameter in parameter lists. In the last case, "others" will match any event. When the history is empty, the object reference has not been obtained and the predicate returns "false". Likewise, if an object has been deleted, it cannot have a reference. If the reference has been obtained by means of the method sb_id, the predicate returns "true". As we consider the last event first, we normally do not need to inspect the entire history.

The communication environment of the **SoftwareBus** is dynamic as objects may be (remotely) created and destroyed at run-time. We want to capture by a function on the history the requirement that objects are referred to only when they are known to the user application. If a method call refers to i objects, the references to all i objects must be checked. (In this simplified version of the **SoftwareBus**, we only consider methods with one reference to check.) Define a predicate $correctObjRef(x, y, h)$ to express that all object references that are passed as parameters to events between the user application x and the **SoftwareBus** y in the history h are known to x, as follows:

$$correctObjRef(x, y, \varepsilon) = \textbf{true}$$
$$correctObjRef(x, y, h \vdash x{\rightarrow}y.\text{sb\_id}(\_, r; \_))$$
$$= known(x, y, r, h) \wedge correctObjRef(x, y, h)$$
$$correctObjRef(x, y, h \vdash x{\rightarrow}y.\text{sb\_delete\_obj}(r))$$
$$= known(x, y, r, h) \wedge correctObjRef(x, y, h)$$
$$correctObjRef(x, y, h \vdash \text{others}) = correctObjRef(x, y, h)$$

The methods of SB_SoftwareBusData should only be available to users, i.e. access should be restricted to objects that provide the SB_User interface, which is an empty interface in the sense that it contains no methods. This is done by a WITH-clause in the specification of SB_SoftwareBusData. In the interface below, we denote by "this" the object specified by the interface and by "caller" an object offering the SB_User interface.

> **interface** SB_SoftwareBusData
> **begin**
>   **with** SB_User
>   [operations as in the UML specification]
>   **asm** $correctObjRef$(caller,this,h)
> **end**

In the specification, **asm** is the keyword preceding assumptions. Assumptions are requirements on the environment, i.e. they are expected to hold for histories ending with input to "this" object. Inputs to an object x are either initiations of calls to methods declared in x or completions of calls made by x to other objects. It is implicit in the formalism that assumption predicates must hold for output as well as input, as the trace sets of interfaces are prefix-closed [11]. An object may not break its own assumption. Although no particular invariant predicate is specified for SB_SoftwareBusData, we still get as invariant the assumption predicate, but for histories that end with output from "this" object.

SB_SoftwareBusConnections. The sequence of events expected to hold between the **SoftwareBus** and a particular application is described by an assumption, naturally expressed by a prefix of a pattern.

Let p be an OUN object which offers the SB_SoftwareBusConnections interface (i.e. p is the **SoftwareBus**). Let h be the history of p. The sequence of events in the alphabet of the **SoftwareBus** that reflect calls from some user application a can be described by the following predicate (for convenience, we write c_a for *connect_appl* and d_a for *disconnect_appl*).

$$correctComSeq(a, p, h) =$$
$$h \; \mathbf{prp} \; [a{\hookrightarrow}p.\text{sb\_initialize}() \; [a{\hookrightarrow}p.\text{sb\_c\_a}(\_; \_) \; a{\hookrightarrow}p.\text{sb\_d\_a}(\_)]^*$$
$$a{\hookrightarrow}p.\text{sb\_exit}()]^*$$

In the specifications, $h \; \mathbf{ptn} \; P$ denotes that the trace h adheres to the pattern P, which is a regular expression extended with simple pattern matching [11]. Subpatterns may be enclosed in square brackets. The prefix predicate $h \; \mathbf{prp} \; P$ expresses *invariant properties*; it is true if there is an extension h' of h such that $hh' \; \mathbf{ptn} \; P$, where hh' is the concatenation of the two traces h and h'. The notation $o_1{\hookrightarrow}o_2.m(\ldots)$ is shorthand for the initiation event $o_1{\to}o_2.m(\ldots)$ immediately succeeded by the completion $o_1{\leftarrow}o_2.m(\ldots)$. This corresponds to synchrony if the two events are perceived as immediately succeeding each other by both parties. For brevity, the same notation used in sets represents both the initiation and the completion event. Using projection on the history, the more graphical style of behavioral constraints given by patterns can also be used to capture specific aspects of the behavior, rather than the more state-resembling predicates previously encountered. Denote by h/S a trace h restricted to events of a set S. The following predicate determines whether an application a is registered in the **SoftwareBus** system with portmapper p after history h:

$$up(a, p, h) =$$
$$h/\{a{\leftrightarrow}p.\text{sb\_initialize}(), a{\leftrightarrow}p.\text{sb\_exit}()\}$$
$$\textbf{ptn } [a{\leftrightarrow}p.\text{sb\_initialize}() \ a{\leftrightarrow}p.\text{sb\_exit}()]^* \ a{\leftrightarrow}p.\text{sb\_initialize}().$$

The **SoftwareBus** may receive requests from an application a_1 for the reference of another application a_2 (known to a_1 only by name) in order to establish a logical connection. Before such a connection is possible, both a_1 and a_2 must already be registered in the system. The following predicate determines whether a_1 has a logical connection to a_2:

$$connection(a_1, a_2, p, h) =$$
$$h/\{a_1{\leftrightarrow}p.\text{sb\_c\_a}(\_; a_2), a_1{\leftrightarrow}p.\text{sb\_d\_a}(a_2)\}$$
$$\textbf{ptn } [a_1{\leftrightarrow}p.\text{sb\_c\_a}(\_; a_2) \ a_1{\leftrightarrow}p.\text{sb\_d\_a}(a_2)]^* \ a_1{\leftrightarrow}p.\text{sb\_c\_a}(\_; a_2).$$

Using these predicates, the requirement that connections are only opened to applications that have registered with the **SoftwareBus** and that only those connections are closed that are currently open, is expressed by a predicate on the history, checking that up holds before $\text{sb\_c\_a}(a_2)$ is called and that $connection$ holds before $\text{sb\_d\_a}(a_2)$ is called.

$$cn(p, \varepsilon) = \textbf{true}$$
$$cn(p, h \vdash a_1{\leftarrow}p.\text{sb\_c\_a}(\_; a_2)) = cn(p, h) \wedge up(a_1, p, h) \wedge up(a_2, p, h)$$
$$cn(p, h \vdash a_1{\leftarrow}p.\text{sb\_d\_a}(a_2)) = cn(p, h) \wedge connection(a_1, a_2, p, h)$$
$$cn(p, h \vdash others) = cn(p, h)$$

With these predicates, the interface SB_SoftwareBusConnections can be specified as follows:

```
interface SB_SoftwareBusConnections
begin
    with SB_User
        [operations as in the UML specification]
    asm correctComSeq(caller,this, h)
    inv cn(this, h)
end
```

In the specification, **inv** is the keyword preceding invariant predicates. Invariants are guaranteed by the object offering the interface, provided that the assumption is not broken by *any* object in the environment. Invariant predicates are consequently expected to hold for histories ending with output from "this" object, in contrast to the assumptions that should hold for histories ending with input. Thus, interface behavior is specified following an input/output-driven assumption guarantee paradigm.

4.2   Internal Interfaces

As explained in Section 3, the internal structure of the **SoftwareBus** consists of a portmapper with a set of data servers. We now consider interfaces for the portmapper and the data servers in OUN.

The interface **SB_Portmapper** is similar to SB_SoftwareBusConnections. Let p be an OUN object which offers the SB_Portmapper interface (i.e. p is the portmapper). Let h be the history of p. The sequence of calls that we expect from a data server d to the portmapper p can be described by a predicate:

$correctComSeq'(d, p, h) =$
h **prp** $[d{\hookleftarrow}p.\mathrm{pm\_initialize}(\_; \_)\ [d{\hookleftarrow}p.\mathrm{pm\_c\_a}(\_, \_; \_)\ d{\hookleftarrow}p.\mathrm{pm\_d\_a}(\_, \_)]^*$
$\quad d{\hookleftarrow}p.\mathrm{pm\_exit}(\_)]^*$

The following predicates on the history of the portmapper are used to determine whether an application a is registered in the **SoftwareBus** system and whether the application a_1 has a logical connection to a_2, respectively.

$up'(a, p, h) =$
$\exists d : h/\ \{d{\hookleftarrow}p.\mathrm{pm\_initialize}(n; a), d{\hookleftarrow}p.\mathrm{pm\_exit}(a)\}$
$\quad$ **ptn** $[d{\hookleftarrow}p.\mathrm{pm\_initialize}(n; a)\ d{\hookleftarrow}p.\mathrm{pm\_exit}(a)]^*\ d{\hookleftarrow}p.\mathrm{pm\_initialize}(n; a).$

$connection'(a_1, a_2, p, h) =$
$\exists d : h/\ \{d{\hookleftarrow}p.\mathrm{pm\_c\_a}(a_1, \_; a_2), d{\hookleftarrow}p.\mathrm{pm\_d\_a}(a_1, a_2)\}$
$\quad$ **ptn** $[d{\hookleftarrow}p.\mathrm{pm\_c\_a}(a_1, \_; a_2)\ d{\hookleftarrow}p.\mathrm{pm\_d\_a}(a_1, a_2)]^*\ d{\hookleftarrow}p.\mathrm{pm\_c\_a}(a_1, \_; a_2).$

In the **SoftwareBus** system, applications connect and disconnect to each other. Two applications should not attempt to connect unless both are registered with the portmapper. Also, two applications should not attempt to disconnect unless they already have an open connection. This can be expressed by a predicate on the history of the portmapper as follows.

$cn'(p, \varepsilon) =$**true**
$cn'(p, h \vdash d{\leftarrow}p.\mathrm{pm\_c\_a}(a_1, \_; a_2)) = cn'(p, h) \wedge up'(a_1, p, h) \wedge up'(a_2, p, h)$
$cn'(p, h \vdash d{\leftarrow}p.\mathrm{pm\_d\_a}(a_1, a_2)) = cn'(p, h) \wedge connection'(a_1, a_2, p, h)$
$cn'(p, h \vdash \mathrm{others}) = cn'(p, h)$

The expected behavior of the data servers in the environment becomes the assumption predicate of the SB_Portmapper interface. The correct transmittal of references is the responsibility of the portmapper. Hence, using the predicates defined above, the interface SB_Portmapper can be specified as follows:

```
interface SB_Portmapper
begin
    with SB_DataServer
        [operations as in the UML specification]
        asm correctComSeq'(caller,this, h)
        inv cn'(this, h)
end
```

SB_DataServer is similar to SB_SoftwareBusData and is omitted here.

5   Adding Robustness to the Portmapper

The **SoftwareBus** system, as specified in the previous sections, is clearly prone to errors. In particular, the **SoftwareBus** has a dynamic structure where user applications can join or exit the system at any time and objects can be (remotely) created, modified, and deleted. This may cause difficulty as previously valid object or application names and references may no longer be available to the environment. Of primary interest is the robustness of the portmapper, on which the entire system depends. We want to remove situations that may cause deadlock in the portmapper, to ensure that the communication framework is operative even when user applications have deadlocked. (In open distributed systems like the **SoftwareBus**, the robustness of user applications is outside our control.) Possible deadlocks in the portmapper will be avoided by issuing *exceptions* in response to method calls from user applications when regular behavior is out of place. In this section, we consider modifications of the specifications that make the portmapper more robust.

We will follow the methodology outlined in [13], where several refinement relations are proposed for a stepwise development of OUN specifications with regard to fault-tolerance. The relations ensure that, after appropriate manipulation of the traces, the behavior of the intolerant specification is recovered. The exact relation required in each case depends on how the safety and liveness properties of the intolerant specification should be preserved. (In this paper, only safety properties are considered.) The occurrence of a fault is represented in the formalism by a special event, replacing the usual completion event and thus acting as an error message in response to a method call. Upon receipt of the error message, the calling object may choose its course of action. In the syntax of OUN interfaces, the keyword **throws** precedes the fault classes that are handled by an exceptional completion event.

In the specification of the portmapper, consider the following exceptions:

- $F1$: An application tries to register to the system with a name that is in use.
- $F2$: An application tries to connect to another, unavailable application.
- $F3$: An application tries to close a connection that is not open.

We refer to these error situations as fault classes $F1$, $F2$, and $F3$, respectively. In all three cases, the portmapper should return an exceptional completion event in response to the erroneous method call and continue as if the fault had not occurred. We now modify the interface of the portmapper accordingly.

Inside the **SoftwareBus**, data servers register user applications with the portmapper. Let $in\_use(h)$ denote a function on the history of the portmapper that calculates the set of application names currently in use for **SoftwareBus** applications. A fault of class $F1$ occurs when an application name a is already in use by a user application at the invocation of $pm\_initialize(a)$. If $x \leftarrow y.m(i_1, \ldots, i_n; \ldots)$ is a completion event in response to an invocation of a method m with inputs $i_1, \ldots, i_n$ and F is a fault class, let $x \leftarrow y.m_F(i_1, \ldots, i_n)$ denote the F-exception event raised in response to this invocation of m. Let

$reg(h)$ express that $F1$ exception events are issued correctly, where h is the history of the portmapper:

$$reg(h \vdash d{\leftarrow}p.\text{pm\_initialize}(a; \_)) = a \notin in\_use(h) \land reg(h)$$
$$reg(h \vdash d{\leftarrow}p.\text{pm\_initialize}_{F1}(a)) = a \in in\_use(h) \land reg(h)$$
$$reg(h \vdash others) = reg(h)$$

Here, different completion events are issued in response to calls to pm_initialize (a), depending on whether the name a is currently used in the system or not.

Next, we specify when exception events for fault classes $F2$ and $F3$ should be issued. If a_1 attempts to connect to a_2, the portmapper should respond by an $F2$ exception when $\neg up(a_2, h)$ (where h is the current history). Similarly, an $F3$ exception should be issued in response to an attempt to disconnect a non-existing connection. Let cn'' modify the cn' predicate:

$$cn''(p, \varepsilon) = \textbf{true}$$
$$cn''(p, h \vdash a_1{\leftarrow}p.\text{pm\_c\_a}(\_, a_2; \_)) = up(a_2, h) \land cn''(p, h)$$
$$cn''(p, h \vdash a_1{\leftarrow}p.\text{pm\_c\_a}_{F2}(\_, a_2; \_)) = \neg up(a_2, h) \land cn''(p, h)$$
$$cn''(p, h \vdash a_1{\leftarrow}p.\text{pm\_d\_a}(\_, a_2)) = connection'(a_1, a_2, p, h) \land cn''(p, h)$$
$$cn''(p, h \vdash a_1{\leftarrow}p.\text{pm\_d\_a}_{F3}(\_, a_2)) = \neg connection'(a_1, a_2, p, h) \land cn''(p, h)$$
$$cn''(p, h \vdash others) = cn''(p, h)$$

The predicates cn'' and reg regulate *output* from the portmapper, so together they become the invariant of the robust portmapper interface. We will now adapt the assumption of **SB_Portmapper** to handle exceptional completion events. We assume that for initialization and for opening connections, an application can attempt to repeat a call that fails. Define the new assumption predicate:

$$correctComSeq''(a, p, h) =$$
$$h \ \textbf{prp} \ [a{\leftrightarrow}p.\text{pm\_initialize}_{F1}(\_; \_)^* \ a{\leftrightarrow}p.\text{pm\_initialize}(\_; \_)$$
$$[a{\leftrightarrow}p.\text{pm\_c\_a}_{F2}(\_, \_; \_)^* \ a{\leftrightarrow}p.\text{pm\_c\_a}(\_, \_; \_)$$
$$a{\leftrightarrow}p.\text{pm\_d\_a}(\_, \_) \ a{\leftrightarrow}p.\text{pm\_d\_a}_{F3}(\_, \_)^*]^*$$
$$a{\leftrightarrow}p.\text{pm\_exit}()]^*$$

With these modified predicates, we specify the robust portmapper interface:

```
interface SB_RobustPortmapper
begin
   with SB_DataServer
      opr  pm_initialize(; object_ref ) throws F1
      opr  pm_exit( )
      opr  pm_c_a( user_ref, server_name; server_ref ) throws F2
      opr  pm_d_a( user_ref, server_ref ) throws F3
   asm correctComSeq''(caller, this, h)
   inv cn''(this, h) ∧ reg(h)
end
```

Ignoring failed method calls in the **SB_RobustPortmapper** interface, i.e. exception events and the initiation events that correspond to them, we obtain the intolerant interface **SB_Portmapper**. In this sense, the robust portmapper interface is a fault-tolerant refinement of the intolerant portmapper [13]. If we adapt the data servers to the considered fault classes, faults can to some degree be kept within the **SoftwareBus**, without penetrating to the outside, which gives us a certain fault transparency for the **SoftwareBus** system. The robust portmapper tolerates possibly incorrect and deadlocked user applications and the communication framework per se remains operational.

6   Discussion

In this paper, we consider how to combine graphical and formal specification notations to develop a dynamic communication framework. We study a simplified version of the OECD **SoftwareBus** system [2], focusing on the basic infrastructure needed to exchange data between applications. Our study does not cover all the operations and functionality needed for actual applications. The OECD **SoftwareBus** provides this communication functionality using specially designed methods for remote creation, modification, and deletion of objects and classes, which can be captured with the methodology outlined in this paper.

Our approach starts with graphical specifications in UML and we develop a formal specification of the **SoftwareBus** system, concentrating on the central aspects of communication and openness. UML interface specifications are extended into the textual specification language OUN by predicates on traces, in order to enable formal reasoning about behavior. OUN interface behavior relies on explicit communication histories rather than state variables. We illustrate various ways of extracting information from the traces by predicates and patterns that mimic a graphical specification style. In the case study, OUN is used to capture dynamic system behavior, such as initialization of new user applications, connections between applications that open or close, and applications that exit the **SoftwareBus** system, by means of these predicates. Hence, the formalism lets us capture the flexibility of the **SoftwareBus** system in a rigorous way.

OUN supports formal development of specifications, syntactically by means of interface inheritance and semantically by means of refinement. In the case study, more complete specifications of the object interfaces can be obtained through (multiple) inheritance [12]. With our design, the data servers are of particular interest, forming the junction between the external and internal views of the system. The data servers communicate with local user applications, the portmapper, and with remote user applications connected to the **SoftwareBus**. Through inheritance, we can combine behaviors that are captured in different interfaces. Also, OUN provides us with an incremental approach to system robustness [13], as illustrated in the case study.

The development process proposed here is based on a formalization of UML specifications, rather than a formalization of UML itself. The advantage of using UML constructs for specification is that these constructs are intuitive, commonly accepted, and used in industrial software development. UML constructs are important to describe initial software requirements, normally a result of discussions between users and systems analysts (or software engineers). Extending UML interface specifications, we obtain specifications in OUN that capture dynamic aspects not easily expressible in UML or OCL [27]. Although OCL extends UML with object invariants and pre- and postconditions for methods, precise specification of output from objects is still difficult to capture in OCL as the language expresses constraints on object attributes and not on communication events [15]. OCL, as well as other object-oriented formalisms such as Object-Z [25], Maude [18], and temporal logic-based approaches such as TLA [17], specify components by an abstract implementation using state variables. For open distributed systems, it is perhaps better to perceive the behavior of a component as locally determined by its interaction with the environment [1]. In OUN, interface specification is based on the observable behavior of black-box components.

We are recommended to specify open distributed systems by means of object orientation and multiple viewpoints [9]. Both UML and OUN support these features. OUN is object-oriented, including notions of inheritance and object identity, in contrast to process algebras like CSP [8], the π-calculus [19], LOTOS [4], and Actors [1]. As UML and OCL lack a formally defined semantics and proof system, OUN is a suitable supplement for formal reasoning, with precise notions of composition and refinement.

Our approach relies on PVS [22] as a tool for consistency checking and verification of specifications. Basic modeling constructs and conditions of UML class diagrams can be expressed in the PVS specification language in terms of functions and abstract data types [3]. For further system development, OUN specifications are translated into PVS in order to formally verify the correctness of development steps. As OUN notions of composition and refinement are expressed in PVS, OUN syntax can be translated into PVS in terms of trace sets to take advantage of the PVS theorem proving facilities [11]. A framework for the consistency check was described in [26] where software specification is done within a system development environment which integrates Rational Rose (a tool supporting UML from Rational Software Corporation) and the PVS toolkit in order to cover the software development process from specification of system requirements, system design, and verification, to code generation. Code generation facilities for OUN specifications are currently under development.

7   Conclusion

This paper proposes an approach to the specification of open distributed systems, based on a combination of UML and OUN specification techniques. To illustrate the approach, we develop parts of a specification of an open communication framework where data and resources are exchanged between applications and where applications connect and disconnect over time. In the development process, graphical UML constructs are used to specify interfaces, classes, and their relations. Class diagrams in UML are expanded into OUN interface specifications by restricting the implicit history variables of communication calls. With first-order predicates for assumption and invariant clauses, we specify the observable behavior of components. OUN permits formal reasoning about system development and captures certain forms of openness by textual analysis, as shown in the case study.

For the development of open distributed systems, OUN is well-suited as a complement to UML. UML is the de facto industry standard and uses intuitive graphical notation, but it lacks the formalization necessary for rigorous system development and the concepts needed to capture the dynamic aspects of reactive systems. In OUN, reasoning is both compositional and incremental. Software units can be written, formally analyzed, and modified independently, while we have control of the maintenance of earlier proven results. The formalism lets us capture dynamic behavior that is not easily handled in UML.

Acknowledgments

This work is a part of the ADAPT-FT project. The authors thank H. Jokstad and E. Munthe-Kaas for discussions, suggestions, and helpful comments.

References

1. G. A. Agha, I. A. Mason, S. F. Smith, and C. L. Talcott. A foundation for actor computation. *Journal of Functional Programming*, 7(1):1–72, Jan. 1997.
2. T. Akerbæk and M. Louka. The software bus, an object-oriented data exchange system. Technical Report HWR-446, OECD Halden Reactor Project, Institute for Energy Technology, Norway, Apr. 1996.
3. D. B. Aredo, I. Traore, and K. Stlen. Towards a formalization of UML class structure in PVS. Research Report 272, Dept. of Informatics, Univ. of Oslo, 1999.
4. T. Bolognesi and E. Brinksma. Introduction to the ISO specification language LOTOS. *Computer Networks and ISDN Systems*, 14(1):25–59, 1987.
5. G. Booch. *Object-Oriented Analysis and Design with Applications*. Benjamin-Cummings, Redwood City, CA, 1991.
6. G. Booch, J. Rumbaugh, and I. Jacobson. *The Unified Modeling Language User Guide*. Addison-Wesley, Reading, Massachusetts, USA, 1999.
7. J. Eiler. Critical safety function monitoring: an example of information integration. In *Proceedings of the Specialists' Meeting on Integrated Information Presentation in Control Rooms and Technical Offices at Nuclear Power Plants (IAEA-I2-SP-384.38)*, pages 123–133, Stockholm, Sweden, May 2000.
8. C. A. R. Hoare. *Communicating Sequential Processes*. International Series in Computer Science. Prentice Hall, Englewood Cliffs, NJ, 1985.
9. ITU Recommendation X.901-904 ISO/IEC 10746. *Open Distributed Processing - Reference Model parts 1–4*. ISO/IEC, July 1995.
10. I. Jacobson, M. Christerson, P. Jonsson, and G. Övergaard. *Object-Oriented Software Engineering: A Use Case Driven Approach*. Addison-Wesley, 1992.
11. E. B. Johnsen and O. Owe. A PVS proof environment for OUN. Research Report 295, Department of informatics, University of Oslo, 2001.
12. E. B. Johnsen and O. Owe. A compositional formalism for object viewpoints. In *Proc. 5th International Conference on Formal Methods for Open Object-Based Distributed Systems (FMOODS 2002)*. Kluwer Academic, 2002. To appear.

13. E. B. Johnsen, O. Owe, E. Munthe-Kaas, and J. Vain. Incremental fault-tolerant design in an object-oriented setting. In *Proceedings of the Asian Pacific Conference on Quality Software (APAQS'01)*. IEEE press, Dec. 2001.
14. G. Kahn. The semantics of a simple language for parallel programming. In J. L. Rosenfeld, editor, *Information Processing 74: Proceedings of the IFIP Congress 74*, pages 471–475. IFIP, North-Holland Publishing Co., Aug. 1974.
15. A. Kleppe and J. Warmer. Extending OCL to include actions. In A. Evans, S. Kent, and B. Selic, editors, *Proceedings of UML 2000*, volume 1939 of *Lecture Notes in Computer Science*, pages 440–450, York, UK, Oct. 2000. Springer-Verlag.
16. F. Kostiha. Establishment of an on-site infrastructure to facilitate integration of software applications at Dukovany NPP. In *Proceedings of the Specialists' Meeting on Integrated Information Presentation in Control Rooms and Technical Offices at Nuclear Power Plants (IAEA-I2-SP-384.38)*, Stockholm, Sweden, May 2000.
17. L. Lamport. The temporal logic of actions. *ACM Transactions on Programming Languages and Systems*, 16(3):872–923, May 1994.
18. J. Meseguer. Conditional rewriting logic as a unified model of concurrency. *Theoretical Computer Science*, 96:73–155, 1992.
19. R. Milner. *Communicating and Mobile Systems: the π-Calculus*. Cambridge University Press, May 1999.
20. Object Management Group. *UML Language Specification, version 1.4*, Sept. 2001.
21. O. Owe and I. Ryl. OUN: a formalism for open, object oriented, distributed systems. Research Report 270, Dept. of informatics, Univ. of Oslo, Aug. 1999.
22. S. Owre, J. Rushby, N. Shankar, and F. von Henke. Formal verification for fault-tolerant architectures: Prolegomena to the design of PVS. *IEEE Transactions on Software Engineering*, 21(2):107–125, Feb. 1995.
23. D. L. Parnas and Y. Wang. The trace assertion method of module interface specification. Technical Report 89-261, Department of Computing and Information Science, Queen's University at Kingston, Kingston, Ontario, Canada, Oct. 1989.
24. J. Rumbaugh, M. Blaha, W. Premerlani, F. Eddy, and W. Lorensen. *Object-oriented Modeling and Design*. Prentice Hall, Englewood Cliffs, New Jersey, 1991.
25. G. Smith. *The Object-Z Specification Language*. Advances in Formal Methods. Kluwer Academic Publishers, 2000.
26. I. Traore, D. B. Aredo, and K. Stlen. Formal development of open distributed systems: Towards an integrated framework. In *Proc. Workshop on Object-Oriented Specification Techniques for Distributed Systems and Behaviours (OOSDS'99)*, Paris, France, Sept. 1999.
27. J. Warmer and A. Kleppe. *The Object Constraint Language: Precise Modeling with UML*. Object Technology Series. Addison-Wesley, 1999.

Translations between Textual Transition Systems and Petri Nets

Katerina Korenblat, Orna Grumberg, and Shmuel Katz

Computer Science Department
The Technion
Haifa, Israel
{orna,katz}@cs.technion.ac.il

Abstract. Translations between models expressed in textual transition systems and those expressed in structured Petri net notation are presented, in both directions. The translations are *structure-preserving*, meaning that the hierarchical structure of the systems is preserved. Furthermore, assuming non-finite data has been abstracted out of the textual transition system, then translating one model to another and then back results in a model which is identical to the original one, up to renaming and the form of Boolean expressions. Due to inherent differences between the two notations, however, some additional information is required in order to obtain this identity. The information is collected during the translation in one direction and is used in the translation back.

Our translation is also *semantics-preserving*. That is, the original model and the translated model are bisimulation equivalent, assuming non-finite data is abstracted. Thus, the translation preserves all temporal properties expressible in the logic CTL*.

The translations are both more generally applicable and more detailed than previously considered. They are shown both for individual modules, with a collection of transitions, and for a structured system, where modules are combined in different ways.

Keywords: model translations, Petri nets, textual transition systems, structure and semantics preservation.

1 Introduction

In order to use different verification tools for different properties of a model, it has become common to translate among notations. Here we show how such translations can be done for the very different paradigms of textual transition systems as seen in [9] and a structured version of Petri nets, as seen in, e.g., [12]. Textual transition systems are particularly suitable for a high level description of programs and can be verified using the temporal-logic verifier STeP [2]. Petri nets, on the other hand, are suitable for the analysis of the control flow of concurrent protocols. For each paradigm we suggest a translation both for a flat, simple version, and for a structured one. Rather than considering the translation as an internal prelude to activating a tool, we emphasize the optimizations that

M. Butler, L. Petre, and K. Sere (Eds.): IFM 2002, LNCS 2335, pp. 339–359, 2002.
© Springer-Verlag Berlin Heidelberg 2002

are possible in order to obtain a result natural in the target notation, and which has easy traceability back to the source. This is important, for example, in order to allow errors discovered in the target model to be traced back to the corresponding error in the source.

After briefly presenting the two notations for expressing models, we show our algorithms for translating from a textual transition system to a Petri net, and then for translation in the opposite direction. We do assume that data manipulations of non-finite state variables (e.g., integer variables) have been abstracted away from the textual transition systems. It is important to note that the notion of 'transition' is fundamentally different for the two notations. A textual transition represents an entire family of connections between states to which the transition is applicable and the ones after the transition, expressed as a predicate or assignments relating the state before and the one after. A Petri net transition also applies to many configurations of tokens in the system (called a *marking*) that traditionally are associated with the states, namely all those for which the input places of the transition have tokens. These are transformed to a configuration where the output places have tokens, while the rest of the system configuration is unchanged. Thus both of these notions of 'transition' differ from a single edge connecting one full system state to another, in a state transition diagram or Kripke structure, even though those too are called 'transition systems'.

The translations must connect these concepts, and also treat the different concepts of modularity and synchronization supported by each. We also show that additional information from a translation in one direction can be used to help in traceability or to improve the quality of a translation back in the other direction. This is especially useful when a system has been translated, the result has been slightly modified, and it is then translated back to the original notation. Using the additional information can yield a result which has a similar structure to the original. The additional information is shown to be "complete" relative to the abstraction of variables from the textual transition notation mentioned above. That is, if a model is translated to another and then immediately translated back, then based on the additional information the same model is obtained, up to renaming and changing the form of Boolean expressions.

Our translation is also *semantics-preserving* under data abstraction. That is, the original model and the translated model are bisimulation equivalent. Thus, the translation preserves all temporal properties expressible in the logic CTL*.

The translations seen in this paper are abstractions of the operation of actual compilers that are part of the VeriTech framework [7] for translating among specification and verification tools. The textual transition system notation is similar to the core notation of VeriTech, that is used as an intermediate notation in translating among diverse tools.

1.1   Related Works

The problem of translating a specification given in terms of one formal model to others has been considered for many formalisms. The most general frameworks for this are the VeriTech project [7] and the SAL project [1]. Below we consider translations related specifically to Petri net models. Often translations to Petri nets arise from the task of transforming an input language of some task-oriented Petri net model [3], [8]. Translations of Petri Nets to formalisms that provide additional analysis possibilities appear in [16], [6], [14].

Several papers considered the relationship between various classes of Petri nets and explicit state transition systems. In [10] behaviour preserving transformations were shown between elementary transition systems and elementary net systems. In [15] the existence of an ST-bisimilar Petri net is proved for an arbitrary asynchronous transition system. There are works (see, for example [17], [11]) characterizing classes of explicit state transition systems generated by different classes of Petri Nets. The idea of those translations is to extract a set of events available in a state of the model and to simulate this set explicitly in terms of the other model. Those works focus on an extraction of classes of the models which somehow correspond. On the other hand, our task in this paper is to give a structured correspondence between wider classes of Petri nets and textual transition systems (that are closer to programs than are explicit state transition systems).

In [6] a translator is presented from Petri nets to the language PROMELA of the verification tool SPIN. A place in a Petri net is translated to a variable (expressing a number of tokens in the corresponding place) in PROMELA, and a transition in a Petri net is translated to a rule for changing variable values, corresponding to the transition firing. A similar method is used in [16] for a translation of safe Petri nets to textual transition systems. Our translation establishes correspondences among transitions in Petri nets and transitions in textual transition systems in a similar way to theirs, although we attempt to optimize the result. Moreover, we also give a translation in the other direction.

Since the concept of modularity used in Petri nets is quite different from that accepted in other formalisms, most existing translations deal with nonmodular Petri nets. A translator that does refer to the compositional structure of the model is suggested in [13]. There a SA/RT specification model is translated to a class of Petri nets that does allow composing subnets through external places. Since the modularity in textual transition systems allows additional possibilities, we use a more powerful Object Oriented Petri net model, and show a correspondence between modularity of the models in both directions.

2 Preliminaries

2.1 Textual Transition Systems

The textual transition system notation (denoted TTS in the continuation) is similar to the one described in [9], but extended to treat various degrees of synchronization among modules. A *transition* t is a state transformer with an enabling condition, denoted *enable*(t), defining the set of states for which it is applicable, and assignments, denoted *assign*(t), that relate the state before the transition to the state afterwards. A *basic module* has a header with the module name followed by formal parameters within parentheses, locally declared variables, and a set of named transitions. A *composed module* has a header as above, and local variables, but contains instantiations of other modules, with actual parameters in place of formal ones, and with composition operators between them. Modules can be composed asynchronously (using ||| as in Lotos), synchronously (using ||) and partially synchronously, by listing pairs of transitions that must synchronize, between | delimiters. Thus a typical partial synchronization would appear as $M1(a, b)|(t, s)|M2()$ where t and s are the names of transitions in $M1$ and $M2$, respectively (see Figure 6.2 for a richer example).

Two transitions that are synchronized are equivalent to a single 'product' transition defined by taking the conjunction of their enabling predicates, and the union of their sets of assignments. A module composed asynchronously from instantiations of two submodules is equivalent to a basic module with the union of the transitions in the components. One with synchronous composition is equivalent to taking the cross product of the transitions in the components, while a partial synchronization is equivalent to taking the cross product of those that synchronize and the union of the rest.

2.2   Object Oriented Petri Nets

In this paper we use as a Petri net model a combination of object-oriented concepts and standard place/transition Petri nets. The approach chosen for expressing the structuring primitives and composing mechanisms is from [5], [4], restricted to the case of safe place/transition Petri nets. Inheritance is out of our scope since there is no analogous concept in textual transition systems.

First, we define a *safe Petri net* as a structure $N = (P, T, F, m_0)$, where P and T are disjoint sets of *places* and *transitions*, respectively; $F \subseteq (P \times T) \cup (T \times P)$; and $m_0 \subseteq P$ is the *initial marking* of N. A *marking* of N is the set of its places which contain tokens. A place p is a *preplace* of a transition t (written $p \in \bullet t$) if $(p, t) \in F$. It is a *postplace* of t (written $p \in t \bullet$) if $(t, p) \in F$. A transition t is *enabled* at a marking m if $\bullet t \subseteq m$ and $t \bullet \cap (m \setminus \bullet t) = \emptyset$, i.e. all preplaces of t contain a token and all postplaces of t that are not preplaces of t do not contain a token. A marking m' is obtained by *firing* of enabled transition t from m if $m' = (m \setminus \bullet t) \cup t \bullet$, i.e. in a firing of a transition tokens move from preplaces of the transition to its postplaces. A marking is *reachable* if it is obtained from the initial marking by firing a sequence of transitions.

A *PN-class* is characterized by a safe Petri net, a set of interfaces, a set of class instance holders referring to other classes, and a set of arcs connecting interfaces with places, transitions or other interfaces outside of the class. Directed and undirected interfaces are distinguished. For the first ones only interface-to-place and transition-to-interface arcs are allowed. We define a *basic PN-class* as a PN-class which does not refer to other classes. A place from a PN-class is an *input place* of this class if there is an arc from some interface of the PN-class to this place. We denote places, transitions and interfaces by *net elements*.

Petri net models are presented as communicating PN-class instances and net elements. Class instances communicate by sending and receiving tokens to and from one another. They are hierarchically structured, i.e. they may contain other class instances.

If a Petri net model is obtained from a translation of a transition system model using our TTS→PN-translation then we assume the following agreements on net element names.

- Two places constructed from one boolean variable are called by the same name superscripted by $'0'$ and $'1'$.
- Several places that correspond to one program counter are called by the same name, beginning with &, and extended with the program counter values.
- Several PN-transitions that correspond to one TTS-transition are called by the same name with different superscripts.
- A pair of input and output interfaces used for connection with the same outside place are called by the same name with prefixes $In\_$ and $Out\_$, respectively.

3   Translating Transition Systems to Petri Nets

3.1   Basic Issues of the Translation

Each transition system model can be translated into a Petri net model. There are two styles of translation. The first one constructs a flat Petri net in which we lose information about the modularity of the transition system model. The second style translates a transition system model to a hierarchical Petri Net (for instance, the Petri net model described above) that keeps the original modular structure of the model. Note that for an arbitrary transition system model, a single module representation can be constructed using the semantics of transition systems. Then the translation of a transition system model to a flat Petri net is a special case of the modular translation which will be described below.

The main stages of the translation from transition systems to Petri Nets involve translating a basic TTS-module, and representing the modular structure of a transition system model. In the first stage, we associate internal variables of the TTS-module with places and external variables (including parameters) with interfaces; transitions from the TTS-module are associated with transitions in the corresponding PN-class (in a way to be described later).

In treating the modularity, an instantiation of a TTS-module is translated to an instance of the corresponding PN-class whose interfaces are connected with outside places produced for the external variables and actual parameters of the TTS-module. Asynchronous composition of two TTS-modules is translated to a PN-class consisting of the instances of the PN-subclasses corresponding to those TTS-modules. To represent partial synchronization we extend the set of interfaces of the corresponding synchronized PN-classes with new interfaces which correspond to preplaces/postplaces of the synchronized PN-transitions. Synchronous composition of two TTS-modules is translated as a partial synchronization between those TTS-modules in which all transitions are synchronized.

Explicit control constructions, allowed in other model notations, can be expressed in transition systems by program counters. To translate them to Petri Nets we produce a special place for each value of each of the program counters. Moving a token through these places gives the required control order.

Below we explain the translation outlined above in greater detail.

3.2   Representation of Variables

To translate a variable of an enumerated type we can produce a place for each variable value and obtain a place/transition net. In this paper we consider in detail the translation of a boolean variable to a pair of places. We also give a brief description of an extension of this technique for a variable of an enumerated type by showing how to handle the program counters.

An unbounded (e.g., integer) variable is abstracted before the translation to a boolean one which is identically equal to *true*. Note that in transition system models an uninitialized variable is given some arbitrary initial value and from then on it is always defined. Therefore, an abstracted variable can be considered as a resource which is always present and whose value is not considered. We mark a fully abstracted variable with the label *'abs'* to show that it is obtained by abstraction of a variable of a more powerful type.

Usually a boolean variable is translated to a pair of places corresponding to its values. At any state of the constructed Petri net we have exactly one token in this pair of places which represents a concrete value of the variable. However, there exists a class of boolean variables which we can represent by one place and interpret its *true*-value as the presence of a token in the place, and its *false*-value as the absence of a token. We can identify this class as the set of variables whose old and new values cannot be *false* simultaneously in any TTS-transition where the variable appears. In the continuation, such variables are marked with the label *'tkn'*. As will be shown in Section 4 when we translate a Petri net model to a transition systems representation, for each place we obtain a variable from this class if we do not translate it in a special way due to some name agreements.

Thus we have a transition system model with boolean variables some of which are labeled with *'abs'* or *'tkn'*. Consider a variable v. In the general case (there is no label for v), we represent v as a pair of places v^1 and v^0 for *true* and *false* values of v, respectively. If v is marked with *'abs'* we translate it to the place v^1 which always contains a token. If v is marked with *'tkn'* we translate it to the place v which contains a token iff $v = true$.

We say that an initial value of a variable is *necessary* if there is an execution of the transition system model in which the variable is used before its value is assigned by the noninitialized part of the model. For each variable which is not initialized but whose initial value is necessary, we model nondeterministic choice of its initial value in the following way. For a boolean variable v without a label we add to the Petri net model an additional place $INIT\_v$ containing a token in the initial marking. A place v^i obtains a token from $INIT\_v$ through the corresponding transition $INIT\_v^i$ (see Fig. 3.1a). For a boolean variable labeled with *'tkn'* we produce a construction analogous to the previous case except that a

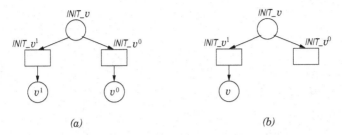

Fig. 3.1. Modeling of nondeterministic choice of the initial value of v

place v^0 does not exist (see Fig. 3.1b). So there is an option of throwing away the initializing token. For an abstracted variable its concrete value is not considered and we can initialize it by putting a token in the corresponding place.

We refer to parameters and external variables of the TTS-module as *external identifiers*. An external identifier of the TTS-module is translated to interfaces of the corresponding PN-class just as an internal variable is translated to places. In a Petri net model, input, output, and undirected interfaces are distinguished. A variable with a label $'abs'$ is translated to an undirected interface. For a variable of other types we produce an input interface if the corresponding variable value is used in the module and an output interface if the corresponding variable value is produced in the module. Name agreements for an interface are the same as for a place, however if we need both input and output interfaces for an external identifier we add $'In\_'$ and $'Out\_'$ prefixes to their names to distinguish them.

3.3 Representation of TTS-Transitions

Since a notion of a transition exists in both models, we will distinguish between TTS-transitions and PN-transitions.

When a variable is represented in Petri Nets by several places, any change of its value has to be expressed explicitly by firing of some PN-transition with its old value as an input and the new value as an output. So we need a separate PN-transition for each valuation of variables appearing in a TTS-transition. For each TTS-transition we want a small number of PN-transitions. To reduce the number of PN-transitions we transform the *enable*-part of the TTS-transition to disjunctive normal form and translate a part of the transition corresponding to each disjunct as a separate PN-transition. For example, if we translate the TTS-transition t from Figure 3.2 directly we will obtain a PN-transition for each of the seven valuations of variables x, y, z and a that satisfy the enabling condition. Using the disjunctive normal form $(a \wedge x) \vee (a \wedge y) \vee (a \wedge !z)$ we can consider only three PN-transitions for the valuations corresponding to each disjunct.

Fix a TTS-transition t. Below we consider the case in which all variables are local. The case of external variables of the translated TTS-module is obtained by using interfaces for the variables instead of places.

A set of *conditions* of a TTS-transition t (written $Cond(t)$) is the set of disjuncts from the disjunctive normal form of the *enable*-part of t. For each

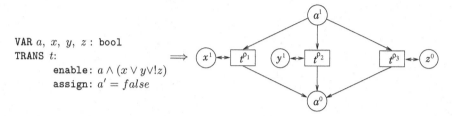

VAR a, x, y, z : bool
TRANS t:
    enable: $a \wedge (x \vee y \vee !z)$
    assign: $a' = false$

Fig. 3.2. Translation of a TTS-transition t

condition c from $Cond(t)$ and a valuation ρ of variables of $c \cup assign(t)$ and their primed version satisfying $enable(t)$, we construct a PN-transition t^ρ in the following way. Let us denote by $Obtained^{t^\rho}$ ($Lost^{t^\rho}$) the set of places corresponding to new (old) values of variables which are changed in t. A set of places corresponding to variables which are used in t but do not change their values is denoted by $Used^{t^\rho}$. Let us characterize these sets for different types of variables in a formal way. Consider a variable v such that $\rho(v) = val$ and $\rho(v') = val'$. If $val = val'$, we put the place corresponding to this value in $Used^{t^\rho}$. Consider the case where a value of v is changed. If v is not labeled, the place corresponding to val belongs to $Lost^{t^\rho}$ and the place corresponding to val' belongs to $Obtained^{t^\rho}$. If v is labeled with $'tkn'$ then the corresponding place belongs to $Obtained^{t^\rho}$ if $val = false$, or to $Lost^{t^\rho}$ if $val = true$. Since after abstraction we obtain a variable which is always $true$, a place corresponding to an abstracted variable always belongs to $Used^{t^\rho}$.

Now we can construct t^ρ as a PN-transition with a set of preplaces $Lost^{t^\rho} \cup Used^{t^\rho}$ and a set of postplaces $Obtained^{t^\rho} \cup Used^{t^\rho}$ (see Fig. 3.3).

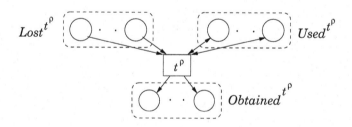

Fig. 3.3. Construction of a PN-transition

As was shown before, the TTS-transition t from Figure 3.2 is translated to three PN-transitions t^{ρ_1}, t^{ρ_2}, t^{ρ_3}, where ρ_1 : $a=true$, $a'=false$, $x=true$, $x'=true$; ρ_2 : $a=true$, $a'=false$, $y=true$, $y'=true$; and ρ_3 : $a=true$, $a'=false$, $z=false$, $z'=false$. As an example we construct t^{ρ_1} as follows. Since $\rho_1(a) \neq \rho_1(a')$, the place a^1 corresponding to $\rho_1(a)$ belongs to $Lost^{t^{\rho_1}}$ and the place a^0 corresponding to $\rho_1(a')$ belongs to $Obtained^{t^{\rho_1}}$. Since $\rho_1(x) = \rho_1(x')$, the place x^1 corresponding to $\rho_1(x)$ belongs to $Used^{t^{\rho_1}}$.

```
VAR  a : int [a : boolean +' abs']
     &PC : int INIT 1
TRANS t₁:
     enable: &PC = 1
     assign: a' = a + 1 [a' = true]
             &PC' = 2
TRANS t₂:
     enable: &PC = 2
     assign: a' = 0 [a' = true]
TRANS t₃:
     assign: &PC' = 3
```

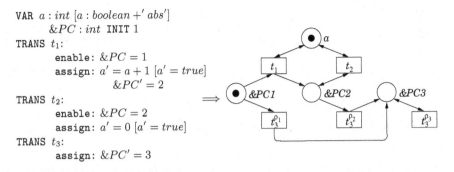

Fig. 3.4. Treating program counters (ρ_1: $\&PC = 1$; ρ_2: $\&PC = 2$; ρ_3: $\&PC = 3$)

Let us consider now the translation of program counters. To express the order of execution among PN-transitions defined by a program counter we produce a special place for each possible value of the program counter. When we translate a transition with a program counter we cannot produce a token on the place for its current value without removing a token from the place for its previous value because a program counter can have no more than one value. We assume that program counters are always initialized. Obviously, a place corresponding to the initial value of the program counter contains a token in the initial state.

As was done for boolean variables, we construct for each value of a program counter in a TTS-transition a separate PN-transition. Given a TTS-transition and a program counter with known old and new values in it, to express the change of the program counter value in the constructed PN-transition we add the place corresponding to the old value of the program counter to its input, and the place corresponding to the new one to its output. Note that a TTS-transition in which the program counter appears only in the *assign*-part is equivalent to a version of that transition with a disjunction over all possible values of the program counter in the *enable*-part.

The translation of a program counter is illustrated in Fig. 3.4. We produce a place a for a fully abstracted variable a (a result of abstraction is shown in the brackets), and places $\&PC1$, $\&PC2$, $\&PC3$ for the corresponding values of $\&PC$. For the TTS-transition t_3 we have three possible values of $\&PC$ and three PN-transitions $t_3^{\rho_1}$, $t_3^{\rho_2}$ and $t_3^{\rho_3}$, respectively. In the TTS-transition t_2, $\&PC$ is not assigned, therefore a token is returned to the place $\&PC2$ after the execution of the PN-transition t_2.

3.4 Translation of Modular Structure

In this section we translate an arbitrary TTS-module to a PN-class assuming that its variables are translated to places and interfaces as shown before, and for each submodule the corresponding PN-class is already produced. We need to show how an instantiation of a submodule induces arcs connecting the interfaces of the corresponding subclass with net elements outside of this subclass. To finish the

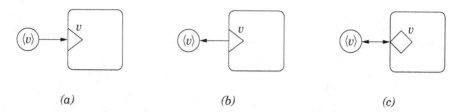

(a)   (b)   (c)

Fig. 3.5. Representing the connection between interfaces and their actual values

translation we must also show how the different composition operations influence the connection between the produced instances of subclasses.

Given a TTS-module m and an external identifier v in it, an instantiation of m uses a corresponding actual parameter of m, if v is a parameter, or v itself, otherwise, which will be denoted by $\langle v \rangle$. We first describe the construction of arcs connecting a PN-class with its outside in the case of variables labeled with $'tkn'$. As shown in Section 3.2, variables v and $\langle v \rangle$ are translated to the interface v and a place $\langle v \rangle$. If v is an input interface we have an arc $(\langle v \rangle, v)$ (see Fig. 3.5a), and if v is an output interface we have an arc $(v, \langle v \rangle)$ (see Fig. 3.5b).

In the case of variables labeled with $'abs'$, as shown in Section 3.2, variables v and $\langle v \rangle$ are translated to the undirected interface v^1 and a place $\langle v \rangle^1$. Then we have a bidirectional arc $(v^1, \langle v \rangle^1)$ (see Fig. 3.5c).

An asynchronous composition of two TTS-modules is represented in a Petri net model as a class consisting of the instances of classes corresponding to these modules. Next we consider the translation of partial synchronization of two TTS-modules. Given a PN-transition t from class N^m, a new class $N^m \backslash t$ is constructed as the class containing all PN-transitions of N^m besides t and additional input (output) interfaces for preplaces (postplaces) of t. A partial synchronization $m_1 | (t_1, t_2) | m_2$ is represented as a class consisting of instances of classes $N^{m_1} \backslash t_1$ and $N^{m_2} \backslash t_2$ connected with the new PN-transition $t_1 t_2$ from $N^{m_1 | (t_1, t_2) | m_2}$ in the following way: $t_1 t_2$ connects to interfaces corresponding to local variables used in the TTS-transition t_i and to places corresponding to external identifiers used in the TTS-transition t_i. To illustrate partial synchronization consider Fig. 3.6.

Note that if some external identifiers have different (old or new) values in the TTS-transitions t_1 and t_2, the corresponding synchronized transition does not exist. So we construct a synchronized transition $t_1 t_2$ only in cases where the original and obtained values in t_1 and t_2 coincide.

A full synchronization can be considered as a partial synchronization of all combinations of transitions from the synchronized TTS-modules.

4   Translating Petri Nets to Transition Systems

4.1   Representation of Elements of a PN-Class

In this section we show how a Petri net model can be translated to a transition system model. Similarly to the other direction, there are two important aspects

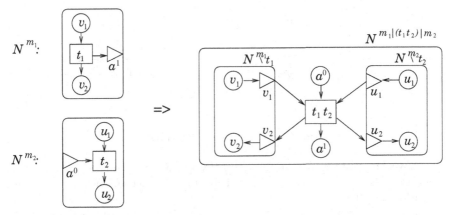

Fig. 3.6. Translation of partial synchronization

of the translation. The first is the construction of basic TTS-modules for basic PN-classes, and the second is the representation of structured PN-classes. To construct a basic TTS-module corresponding to a given basic PN-class we translate its places to variables, interfaces to either external variables or parameters and PN-transitions to TTS-transitions.

To design the translation of a basic PN-class N^m, we first consider the translation of its interfaces. We use the following criterion for deciding which interfaces will be represented by parameters of m and which by external variables: If in all instantiations of N^m the interface is connected with outside places that correspond to the same variable, then the interface is translated to an external variable. Otherwise, the interface is translated to a formal parameter of m and the name of this parameter agrees with the name of the interface.

For places in N^m we produce internal variables in m except for input places. Places with the prefix & (corresponding to a program counter) will be translated in a special way, described later. For places v^1, v^0 from N^m we produce a boolean variable v in m which is initialized with 1 if there exists an initial token in the place v^1 and with 0 – otherwise. In the same way we can translate a pair of places which contain exactly one token in any state of the net (this pair of places forms a *place invariant*). However, here the choice of which place represents '1' and which '0' is arbitrary. The initialization of the corresponding variable is defined according to this choice.

Consider now a place v in N^m that has no superscript and is not a part of a place invariant. We produce a boolean variable v in m with the label $'tkn'$ which indicates that the value of the variable is to be interpreted as the presence of a token in the place. We initialize such a variable with *true* if the corresponding place contains a token in the initial marking, and with *false* – otherwise.

An input place is translated to an external variable if it can receive a token only through one arc. It is translated to a parameter, otherwise. In both cases it will be handled like any other place when the PN-class containing N^m will be translated.

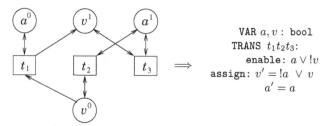

Fig. 4.1. Translation of PN-transitions

Next we consider the translation of PN-transitions. We refer to transitions that are connected with places only. Transitions connected with interfaces are translated in the same way.

A possible approach is to translate each PN-transition to a TTS-transition in which all variables are defined. Another approach is to identify a set of PN-transitions which can be represented by one TTS-transition under different valuations of its variables. Such a set will be translated to a single TTS-transition. The advantage of the latter approach is that the resulting system is more concise. Furthermore, if such a set of PN-transitions is the result of the TTS→PN-translation, then this approach results in a model which has a greater resemblance to the original transition system.

We therefore follow the second approach. For this purpose we introduce the notion of *generalized transition* which is a set of PN-transitions with the same set of variables produced for their input and output places. A set of PN-transitions obtained from one TTS-transition in a preceding TTS→PN-translation is also considered as a generalized transition. Recall that all PN-transitions in this set have the same name with different superscripts and are therefore easy to identify.

As an example of a generalized transition, consider the PN-transitions t_1, t_2 and t_3 (see Fig. 4.1). Note that $\bullet t_1 = \{a^0, v^0\}$, $\bullet t_2 = \{a^1, v^0\}$, $\bullet t_3 = \{a^1, v^1\}$. These sets of places correspond to the set of variables $\{a, v\}$. Similarly, the outputs of t_1, t_2 and t_3 correspond to the set of variables $\{a, v\}$. Thus, $\{t_1, t_2, t_3\}$ is a generalized transition.

Given a generalized transition $T = \{t_1, \ldots, t_n\}$, we construct the TTS-transition t^T as follows. First we construct an enabling predicate for each t_j in T. The *enable*-part of t^T is the disjunction of all these enabling predicates. Then we construct the *assign*-part of t^T. For each variable v, corresponding to a preplace or a postplace of some t_j in T, the *assign*-part defines the value of v after the execution of t^T.

Given a PN-transition t_j from T, the enabling predicate for t_j is the conjunction of the following conditions: For each place p connected with t_j, that has a variable v corresponding to it, if p is an input place with a superscript 1 (0) the condition is v ($!v$, respectively); if p is an input place without superscript the condition is v; if p is an output place without superscript which is not an input place the condition is $!v$. The reason for the latter case is that we deal with safe Petri nets in which a transition is not enabled if one of its output places contains a token.

We now show how to construct the *assign*-part. Given a PN-transition t_j from T and a place v without superscript connected with t_j, the *assign*-part of t^T contains the assignment $v' = true$ if v is an output place and $v' = false$ if v is not an output place. This definition is motivated by the fact that output places receive a token after the execution of the transition while input places lose their token.

Consider now the case in which v is a variable with a superscript which corresponds to an output place of a PN-transition from T. Suppose that each set of input places determines a unique value of v in T. For each t_j from T we construct a formula $f^{t_j} = f_1^{t_j} \rightarrow f_2^{t_j}$, where $f_1^{t_j}$ is the conjunction of variables or their negations corresponding to the input places of t_j, and $f_2^{t_j}$ is the value of v in t_j. The formula f^T is defined as the conjunction of f^{t_j} for each t_j from T, and the *assign*-part of t^T contains the assignment $v' = f^T$. To simplify the *assign*-part it is sometimes useful to conjunct it with the enabling condition of t^T. Note that this conjunction never changes the values calculated by the transition since the transition is executed only when it is enabled.

Next we handle a generalized transition T which, for some input values can produce two different new values for some variable v. For each maximal subset T' of T, which contains only one new value of v we construct a formula $f^{T'}$ as shown above. Since in textual transition systems a nondeterministic choice is possible only for variables and constant values, if there is a set T' for which $f^{T'}$ cannot be expressed by a variable or a constant value then we translate each T' to a separate TTS-transition. Otherwise, the *assign*-part of t^T defines the new value of v by a nondeterministic choice among the formulas $f^{T'}$ for each subset T' of T containing only one new value of v.

The following example demonstrates the translation of the generalized transition $T = \{t_1, t_2, t_3\}$ (see Fig. 4.1). Since for each input of T there is only one new value for v and a, T is translated to one TTS-transition. We construct the TTS-transition $t_1 t_2 t_3$ as follows: for t_1 we have the enabling predicate $!a \wedge !v$, for t_2 $a \wedge !v$, and for t_3 $a \wedge v$. Combining the three predicates by disjunction and applying some simplifications we obtain the *enable*-part of $t_1 t_2 t_3$: $a \vee !v$.

To construct an *assign*-part of $t_1 t_2 t_3$ we write the relationship between the input valuations and the output values of v: $((!a \wedge !v) \rightarrow true) \wedge ((a \wedge !v) \rightarrow false) \wedge ((a \wedge v) \rightarrow true) \equiv !a \vee v$ and of a: $((!a \wedge !v) \rightarrow false) \wedge ((a \wedge !v) \rightarrow true) \wedge ((a \wedge v) \rightarrow true) \equiv a \vee v$. Conjuncting this expression with the *enable*-part we obtain: $(a \vee v) \wedge (a \vee !v) \equiv a$. Therefore the *assign*-part of $t_1 t_2 t_3$ will be $v' = !a \vee v$ and $a' = a$.

We will now describe the translation of places corresponding to program counters. Note that in a Petri net any control structure is expressed by moving tokens and no program counters are used. However, a Petri net can contain places of a special form which have been introduced in the translation of program counters from a transition system model. In back-translation of a Petri net with such places, we restore the program counters in the following way. A set of places of the form $\&PCi$ corresponds to the program counter $\&PC$ in a transition system model. Fix a PN-transition t^{PN} connected with one of the places $\&PCi$,

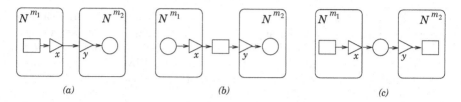

Fig. 4.2. Types of connection among PN-classes

and a TTS-transition t^{TTS} obtained from t^{PN}. For any input place $\&PCi$ of t^{PN} we add the conjunct $\&PC = i$ to the *enable*-part of t^{TTS}, and for any output place $\&PCi$ of t^{PN} we add an assignment $\&PC' = i$ to the *assign*-part of t^{TTS}. For a generalized transition we obtain the *enable*- and *assign*-parts for separate transitions as above and compose them as in the case of usual places.

If the TTS→PN-translation handles enumerated-type variables similarly to program counters, then the back PN→TTS-translation can handle enumerated-type variables in the same way.

4.2 Composing Structured Classes

In the translation of a structured PN-class, first we find PN-transitions of a special form which are used for synchronization of different subnets. Such PN-transitions will be used for the construction of partial synchronization in the transition system model. Bellow we refer to a PN-transition in a PN-class as a *synchronized transition* if it is connected with interfaces of more than one subclass.

Since the structure of a TTS-module has to be homogeneous (i.e., it cannot mix submodules with simple transitions), in a PN-class N^m which contains both subclasses and net elements we extract an additional subclass N^{m_add} and translate it to a separate submodule m_add. N^{m_add} consists of all transitions appearing in N^m except for the synchronized ones, and all places appearing in N^m except for places connected with interfaces.

A PN-class can contain component holders that refer to other PN-classes. During class instantiation each component holder is replaced by an instantiation of the PN-class it refers to. Thus, to construct a TTS-module corresponding to a structured PN-class we need to translate instances of subclasses and relations among them. Here we consider three types of connections among PN-classes in a Petri net model (see Fig. 4.2):

(a) an output transition of one PN-class connects to an input place of another;
(b) PN-classes are connected through an external synchronized transition;
(c) PN-classes are connected through an external place.

Connections are translated together with the translation of instances of PN-classes. An instance of a PN-class is translated to an instantiation of the corresponding TTS-module, whose actual parameters are determined by the connec-

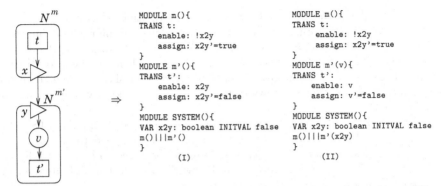

```
MODULE m(){                    MODULE m(){
TRANS t:                       TRANS t:
    enable: !x2y                   enable: !x2y
    assign: x2y'=true             assign: x2y'=true
}                              }
MODULE m'(){                   MODULE m'(v){
TRANS t':                      TRANS t':
    enable: x2y                    enable: v
    assign: x2y'=false             assign: v'=false
}                              }
MODULE SYSTEM(){               MODULE SYSTEM(){
VAR x2y: boolean INITVAL false VAR x2y: boolean INITVAL false
m()|||m'()                     m()|||m'(x2y)
}                              }
        (I)                            (II)
```

Fig. 4.3. Translation of the connection of type (a) using an external variable x2y (I), or a parameter v with the actual value x2y (II)

tions to the given PN-class. Below we describe the translation of the different types of connections.

In case (a) we produce an additional external variable for the arc connecting the interfaces of two submodules. We use it in the submodules instead of the variables produced for the interfaces and instead of the input places connected to these interfaces (see Fig. 4.3(I)). Another possible translation is to use the external variable as an actual parameter of the submodules connected by the given interfaces (see Fig. 4.3(II)).

In case (b) we translate two subnets connected through a synchronized transition to a partial synchronization between two TTS-submodules corresponding to the given subnets. We now show how to produce a synchronized pair of TTS-transitions corresponding to a synchronized PN-transition. If we have no extra information we translate all places connected to a synchronized transition as external variables. We then construct a TTS-transition for the synchronized PN-transition using these external variables. This TTS-transition is added to each of the submodules and used in a synchronization pair. If there is extra information available, we can more meaningfully divide a synchronized transition to a pair of separate PN-transitions belonging to the synchronized subclasses. The extra information can be obtained from an analysis of the model or from a previous TTS→PN-translation, and is discussed further in the following section.

In case (c), if an interface of either N^{m_1} or N^{m_2} is translated as a parameter, we translate the outside place connected with the interface to be an external variable. This variable is then used as the actual parameter of the TTS-module m_1 or m_2, respectively. Otherwise, in both m_1 and m_2 we use the external variable corresponding to the intermediate place instead of the variables produced for the interfaces connected with this place.

5 Additional Information

When we apply a translation in one direction, slightly change the system, and then apply a translation in the other direction it would be desirable to obtain a system similar to the original. However some information is lost in the process of translation. This information can be saved as additional information outside of the constructed model and can later be used in a back translation. One way to keep the additional information is by adding labels to elements of the constructed model and by using a number of name agreements. It should be noted that if additional information is not available, some of it can be retrieved by an analysis of the model.

We first describe the additional information collected during the TTS→PN-translation. Recall that the TTS→PN-translation is applied to an abstracted transition system model in which variables are restricted to be either fully abstracted or defined over finite domain. Below we assume that all finite domains are boolean, except those of program counters.

(PLC) When a boolean variable v is translated to a pair of places, the places are names v^1 and v^0 to denote *true* and *false* values of v.

(ABS) For a fully abstracted variable, the corresponding place is labeled $'abs'$.

(TR) A TTS-transition is usually translated to several PN-transitions. Their names are the name of the TTS-transition with different superscripts.

(PAR) When an external identifier (a parameter or an external variable) is translated to an interface, the interface is labeled by $'par'$ if the external identifier is a parameter.

(SYN) When a pair of synchronized transitions (each from a different TTS-module) is translated to one PN-transition, the arcs connected to the PN-transition are each labeled by the name of the TTS-module it came from.

(PC) A program counter $\&PC$ is translated to a set of places, one for each of its values. The place corresponding to the value i will be named $\&PCi$.

The additional information from the PN→TTS-translation is:

(TKN) When a place is translated to a variable, we label the variable by $'tkn'$ to denote that its values can be interpreted as the presence of a token, i.e., its *false*-value is never used in an enabling condition of a TTS-transition without being changed.

(ADD) When a class N^m consists of net elements as well as subclasses, the net elements are translated as a separate subclass. The corresponding TTS-module is labeled by $'add'$ to indicate that it should not be translated back as a separate subclass.

(VarMv) When translating an input place of some PN-class as an external variable of the corresponding TTS-module, we label the external variable by $'input'$ to indicate that it belongs to the PN-class.

As shown in Section 7, the suggested additional information is "complete" in the sense that applying two translations in a row results in the original model, up to renaming.

6   Example

As an example we consider an Alternating Bit Protocol. Let us translate its Petri net representation (Fig. 6.1) to a transition system model (Fig. 6.2). First we translate basic PN-classes. For the PN-class *SENDER* with interfaces *new*, *next*, *mes* and *ack* we produce a TTS-module SENDER with parameters new, next. For arcs *(mes, mes)*, *(ack, ack)* joining PN-classes *SENDER* and *RECEIVER* we produce external variables m and a which are used in the translation of these PN-classes instead of the variables produced for the interface *mes* and the input place *sent_mes* (an interface *ack* and an input place *sent_ack*, respectively). For the internal place *old* we produce a boolean variable old initialized with *false*.

The PN-class *ALTERNATIVE* consists of an instance of the PN-class *SENDER* and an instance of the PN-class *RECEIVER*. It is translated to the TTS-module ALTERNATIVE with parameters corresponding to the interfaces of *ALTERNATIVE* and the internal variables m and a representing arcs between those two subclasses. The instance of *SENDER* is translated to an instantiation of SENDER with the actual parameters new_mes, next_mes. These parameters correspond to the interfaces *new_mes* and *next_mes* of *ALTERNATIVE* that are connected with interfaces *new* and *next* of *SENDER*. The instance of *RECEIVER* is translated analogously, and the obtained two module instantiations are composed by asynchronous composition operation.

The Petri net model consists of two instances of the PN-class *ALTERNATIVE* connected through external places *ack_bit0*, *ack_bit1*, *mes_bit0*, and *mes_bit1*. These places are translated to the global variables with the same names. ack_bit0 and mes_bit0 are initialized with *true* because the corresponding places contain tokens. We translate the Petri net model to an asynchronous composition of two instantiations of the TTS-module ALTERNATIVE using the obtained global variables as actual parameters.

Next we translate the transition system representation of the Alternating Bit Protocol (Fig. 6.2) to a Petri net model, without using additional information. The changed part is shown in Figure 6.3 by bold lines. Note that all variables of the transition system model can be labeled with *'tkn'* because they originate from Petri net places. We now explain the translation of the basic TTS-module SENDER. Its internal variable old is translated to the place *old*. The parameters new, next and external variables a, m are translated to input interfaces *new*, *a* and output interfaces *next*, *m*.

The TTS-module ALTERNATIVE is translated to the PN-class *ALTERNATIVE* consisting of an instance of the PN-class *SENDER* and an instance of the PN-class *RECEIVER* which are connected with places *mes* and *ack* and with the interfaces of *ALTERNATIVE*. The TTS-module *SYSTEM* is translated analogously to *ALTERNATIVE*.

The only difference between the original Petri net model and the one obtained after two translations is that the places *sent_mes* and *sent_ack* have been moved outside of the PN-classes *RECEIVER* and *SENDER*, respectively. In addition, some of the places and interfaces are named differently. Using the additional information (VarMv) will result in moving places *m* and *a* into the subclasses of

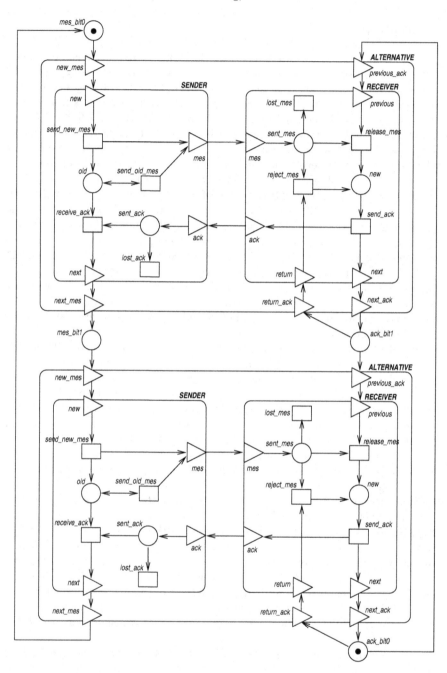

Fig. 6.1. Petri Net representation of Alternating Bit Protocol

```
HOLD_PREVIOUS
VAR mes_bit0: boolean INITVAL true
 mes_bit1: boolean INITVAL false
 ack_bit0: boolean INITVAL true      MODULE RECEIVER(previous, next, return){
 ack_bit1: boolean INITVAL false       VAR new: boolean INITVAL false
                                       TRANS release_mes:
MODULE SENDER(new, next){              enable: m /\ previous /\ !new
VAR old: boolean INITVAL false         assign: new'=true
TRANS send_new_mes:                            m'=false
    enable: new /\ !old /\ !m               previous'=false
    assign: old'=true              TRANS reject_mes:
            m'=true                    enable: m /\ return /\ !new
            new'=false                 assign: new'=true
TRANS send_old_mes:                            m'=false
    enable: old /\ !m                          return'=false
    assign: m'=true                TRANS send_ack:
            old'=true                  enable: new /\ !next /\ !a
TRANS receive_ack:                     assign: a'=true
    enable: a /\ old /\ !next                   next'=true
    assign: next'=true                         new'=false
            a'=false               TRANS lost_mes:
            old'=false                 enable: m
TRANS lost_ack:                        assign: m'=false
    enable: a                    }
    assign: a'=false
}
MODULE ALTERNATIVE(new_mes, next_mes, previous_ack, next_ack, return_ack){
VAR m: boolean INITVAL false
    a: boolean INITVAL false
(SENDER(new_mes, next_mes)|||RECEIVER(previous_ack, next_ack, return_ack))
}
MODULE SYSTEM(){
(ALTERNATIVE(mes_bit0, mes_bit1, ack_bit0, ack_bit1, ack_bit1)|||
 ALTERNATIVE(mes_bit1, mes_bit0, ack_bit1, ack_bit0, ack_bit0))
}
```

Fig. 6.2. Transition systems representation of Alternating Bit Protocol

the PN-class *ALTERNATIVE*. Thus, the new Petri net model will be identical to the original one (up to renaming of net elements).

7   Correctness

Given a Petri net model N with a set of places P^N, the Kripke structure of N is a four tuple $\mathcal{M}(N) = (M^N, m_0^N, R^N, L^N)$, where

- $M^N \subseteq 2^{P^N}$ is the set of reachable markings of N;
- m_0^N is the initial marking of N;

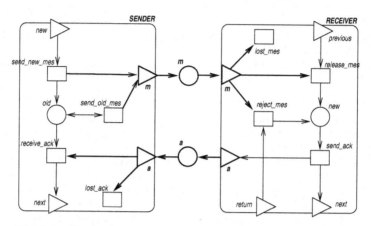

Fig. 6.3. Changed part from Figure 6.1 after translation from TTS

- $R^N \subseteq M^N \times M^N$ is a transition relation such that $(m, m') \in R^N$ if m' is obtained from m by firing a transition of N;
- $L^N : M^N \to 2^{P^N}$ is the identity function.

Let TS be a textual transition system with a set of variables Var extended with labels from the set $\{'tkn', \, 'abs', \, 'PC'\}$. Let $P(Var)$ be the set of places corresponding to variables in Var. Such a correspondence is obtained by both TTS→PN- and PN→TTS-translations. The Kripke structure of TS is a four tuple $\mathcal{M}(TS) = (S^{TS}, \, S_0^{TS}, \, R^{TS}, \, L^{TS})$, where

- S^{TS} is the set of reachable states of TS;
- S_0^{TS} is the set of initial states of TS;
- $R^{TS} \subseteq S^{TS} \times S^{TS}$ is a transition relation such that $(s, s') \in R^{TS}$ if s' is obtained from s after the execution of some TTS-transition;
- $L^{TS} : S^{TS} \to 2^{P(Var)}$ is a function labeling a state of TS with the set of places corresponding to variable values in the state. The precise definition is omitted due to lack of space.

Note that the labeling of the Kripke structure of TS is not standard since it is labeled by places of Petri nets rather than by values of the variables. This is done in order for the Kripke structures of TS and N to be comparable by the bisimulation preorder.

Theorem 1. *Given a textual transition system TS in which all variables are initialized, and a Petri net model N obtained from TS by the TTS→PN-translation, the Kripke structures $\mathcal{M}(TS)$ and $\mathcal{M}(N)$ are bisimulation equivalent.*

Theorem 2. *If the TTS→PN-translation is applied to a textual transition system TS, yielding a Petri net model N, and the PN→TTS-translation is then applied to N, using the additional information (PAR), (PLC), (PC), (TR), and (SYN), then the resulting model is identical to TS up to naming of variables and transitions and the form of boolean conditions.*

Similar theorems hold also for the translations in the other direction.

References

1. Saddek Bensalem, Vijay Ganesh, Yassine Lakhnech, César Muñoz, Sam Owre, Harald Rueß, John Rushby, Vlad Rusu, Hassen Saïdi, N. Shankar, Eli Singerman, and Ashish Tiwari. An overview of SAL. In C. Michael Holloway, editor, *LFM 2000: Fifth NASA Langley Formal Methods Workshop*, pages 187–196, Hampton, VA, June 2000. Available at http://shemesh.larc.nasa.gov/fm/Lfm2000/Proc/.
2. N. Bjorner, A. Browne, E. Chang, M. Colon, A. Kapur, Z. Manna, H.B. Simpa, and T.E. Uribe. Step: The stanford temporal prover - user's manual. Technical Report STAN-CS-TR-95-1562, Department of Computer Science, Stanford University, November 1995.
3. B. Eichenauer and M. Zelm. Transformation of cimosa-models into petrinet-models with pace. Technical report, 1999. http://www.ibepace.com.
4. R. Esser. *An Object Oriented Petri Net Approach to Embedded System Design*. Phd dissertation, ETH Zurich, 1996.
5. R. Esser, J.W. Janneck, and M. Naedele. Using an object-oriented petri net tool for heterogeneous systems design: A case study. In *Proceedings of Algorithmen und Werkzeuge fur Petrinetze*, 1997.
6. B. Grahlmann and C. Pohl. Profiting from spin in pep. In *Proceedings of the SPIN'98 Workshop*, 1998.
7. S. Katz and O. Grumberg. A framework for translating models and specifications. In *Third international conference on Integrated Formal Methods (IFM'02)*, Turku, Finland, May 2002.
8. P. Kemper. Logistic process models go petri nets. In S. Philippi, editor, *Fachberichte Informatik, No. 7-2000: 7. Workshop Algorithmen und Werkzeuge fur Petrinetze, 2.-3*, pages 69–74. Universitatt Koblenz-Landau, Institut fur Informatik, 2000.
9. Z. Manna and A. Pnueli. *The Temporal Logic of Reactive and Concurrent Systems: Specification*. Springer-Verlag, 1992.
10. M. Nielsen, G. Rozenberg, and P.S. Thiagarajan. Elementery transition systems. *Theoretical Computer Science*, 96:3–33, 1992.
11. M. Pietkiewicz-Koutny. Transition systems of elementary net systems with inhibitor arcs. In P. Azma and G. Balbo, editors, *18th International Conference on Application and Theory of Petri Nets*, volume 1248 of *LNCS*, pages 310–327. Springer-Verlag, 1997.
12. W. Reisig. *Elements of Distributed Algorithms- Modeling and Analysis with Petri Nets*. Springer-Verlag, 1998.
13. L. Shi and P. Nixon. An improved translation of sa/rt specification model to high-level timed petri nets. In *FME'96: Industrial Benefit and Advances in Formal Methods*, volume 1051 of *LNCS*, pages 518–537. Springer-Verlag, 1996.
14. R. Sisto and A. Valenzano. Mapping petri nets with inhibitor arcs onto basic lotos behaviour expressions. *IEEE Transactions on Computers*, 44(12):1361–1370, 1995.
15. W. Vogler. Concurrent implementation of asynchronous transition systems. In *Application and Theory of Petri Nets 1999, 20th International Conference, ICATPN'99*, volume 1630 of *LNCS*, pages 284–303. Springer-Verlag, 1999.
16. G. Wimmel. A bdd-based model checker for the pep tool. Technical report. Project Report 1997, http://theoretica.Informatik.Uni-Oldenburg.DE/ pep.
17. G. Winskel and M. Nielsen. Models for concurrency. In S. Abramskky, D. Gabbay, and T.S.E. Maibaum, editors, *Handbook of Logic in Computer Science*, volume 4, pages 1–148. 1995.

Specification and Proof of Liveness Properties under Fairness Assumptions in B Event Systems

Héctor Ruíz Barradas[1,*] and Didier Bert[2]

[1] Universidad Autónoma Metropolitana Azcapotzalco, México D.F., México
hrb@correo.azc.uam.mx, Hector.Ruiz@imag.fr
[2] Laboratoire Logiciels, Systèmes, Réseaux - LSR-IMAG - Grenoble, France
Didier.Bert@imag.fr

Abstract. We present a proposal of specification and proof of liveness properties in B event systems under fairness assumptions. We give proof obligations in order to prove basic progress properties in B event systems under two types of assumptions: minimal progress and weak fairness. We define proof obligations in terms of weakest preconditions, which allow us to prove basic liveness properties as usual B proof obligations. We suggest the use of UNITY "Leads To" operator to specify more general liveness properties. In this way, we integrate the UNITY logic in the specification and proof of B event systems.

1 Introduction

Specification of distributed systems in a B framework has been investigated since several years [2,6]. The main results of this research activity were the introduction of guarded commands (events) for the specification of the abstract level and the event refinement. The specification of liveness properties in B event systems has been studied in different ways. In [10] there was a proposal for specifying liveness properties in B with TLA$^+$ formulae, but no proof obligations were proposed to claim that these properties hold. The first serious proposal was presented in [3], where the proof obligations for these properties are given in a way similar to loop termination. In [9] liveness properties are specified by PLTL formulae and model checking is used in order to verify these properties. In [8], the authors introduce fairness assumptions in order to verify by model checking liveness properties. In this paper, we propose a different way for the specification of liveness properties in B event systems. We integrate the UNITY logic [7] in the specification and proof of liveness properties. Moreover fairness assumptions can be expressed as proof obligations. In the following paragraphs, we illustrate by an example, the motivations for our work.

Let *Phils* be a B event system as defined in [3]. The state of *Phils* is represented by the variable *phils* of type $PHIL \rightarrow STATE$. $PHIL$ is a given set representing the set of philosophers (processes) and $STATE = \{TT, HH, EE\}$

---

* In sabbatical year at Laboratoire Logiciels, Systèmes, Réseaux, Grenoble, France.

denotes the state *thinking, hungry* or *eating* of each philosopher. We use the following sets in this paper:

$$Thk = phils^{-1}[\{TT\}], \ Hgy = phils^{-1}[\{HH\}] \text{ and } Etg = phils^{-1}[\{EE\}]$$

The events in *Phils* system are:

EVENTS

$hgy \;\hat{=}\;$ ANY p WHERE $p \in PHIL \wedge p \in Thk$ THEN $phils(p) := HH$ END ;

$eat \;\hat{=}\;$ ANY p WHERE $p \in PHIL \wedge p \in Hgy$ THEN $phils(p) := EE$ END ;

$thk \;\hat{=}\;$ ANY p WHERE $p \in PHIL \wedge p \in Etg$ THEN $phils(p) := TT$ END

END

We are interested in the specification and proof of liveness properties of style *P LeadsTo Q* where *P* and *Q* are predicates on system states. The informal meaning of this expression is: "if predicate *P* ever becomes true, then the system state will change eventually to another state where predicate *Q* is true". In particular, we would like to specify and prove that any hungry philosopher will eat eventually.

In this system, we have not any useful information to claim that any hungry philosopher will eat eventually. In order to guarantee that the property holds, a classical way is to introduce control variables to specify an abstract scheduler [4,3] and then, define a variant, but the specification then becomes overcomplicated at this level of abstraction.

To specify and prove liveness properties, and at the same time, to maintain a high level of abstraction in the specification of a B systems, we propose the use of fairness assumptions in the specification. These suppositions will allow us to claim that a particular event will be activated when it is enabled under certain fairness conditions.

In this paper, we present a way to specify and prove liveness properties under fairness assumptions in the context of B systems. In the next Section we present our proposal: we introduce the logic that motivates our work, then we show the specification of liveness properties and finally we give the proof obligations needed to prove these properties under two different fairness constraints. Section 3 shows how we prove that the property holds, using the given proof obligations. Section 4 exemplifies the way that we can use fairness constraints in order to refine a B event system. Finally, in the last Section, we give our conclusion and we reveal our future work.

2   Liveness Properties

We propose a specification approach of liveness properties in B event systems, similar to the style of the UNITY formalism [7]. This formalism is a proposal of parallel programming independent of a particular computer architecture. It is made of a computational model and a proof system. The safety and liveness properties of an algorithm are specified using a particular temporal logic then, a UNITY program is derived by stepwise refinements of the specification. The correctness of the refinements must be proved at each step, using theorems of the proof system. In a final step, the derived program is mapped to a particular computer architecture in a informal way.

This section is made up of three parts. In the first part we introduce the main concerns needed in the specification of liveness properties in UNITY formalism. In the second part we present how to specify and prove *basic* liveness properties in the context of B event systems. Finally, in the last part, we show how to integrate the UNITY proof system to compose basic liveness properties in order to specify and prove *general* liveness properties.

2.1   Liveness Properties in UNITY

In the logic programming of UNITY, there are two relations to specify progress properties[1]: "Ensures" relation, denoted by *ensures* and "Leads To" relation, denoted by $\leadsto$ [2].

The most basic progress property in a program is given by: p *ensures* q, where p and q are predicates on the program states. The informal meaning of this property is: "if p holds at some point in the computation, p holds as long as q does not hold, and eventually q holds".

In general, progress properties are specified by "Leads To" relations. To claim that the property $p \leadsto q$ holds in a program, that property must be derived by a finite number of applications of the following rules:

- Basic rule:

$$\frac{p \ ensures \ q}{p \leadsto q}$$

- Transitivity :

$$\frac{p \leadsto r, r \leadsto q}{p \leadsto q}$$

- Disjunction :

$$\frac{(\forall m \cdot m \in M \Rightarrow p(m) \leadsto q)}{(\exists m \cdot m \in M \land p(m)) \leadsto q}$$

for any set M.

The definition of *ensures* relation depends on a certain fairness assumption [11]. We take from that work two definitions of *ensures* relation under the fairness assumptions of: Minimal Progress (MP) and Weak Fairness (WF). In a system with a MP fairness assumption, if some event is enabled at each step of the execution, some enabled event is selected for execution; if two or more statements are enabled in a given state, the selection of the statement enabled for execution

---

[1] In [7], liveness properties are referenced as "progress properties".
[2] In [7], the "Leads To" relation is denoted by $\mapsto$.

is non-deterministic. On the other hand, if we have a WF fairness assumption in a system, each continuously enabled event is infinitely often selected for execution.

We note that the MP fairness definition corresponds to a supposition where we have no guarantee about the execution of enabled events; an event can be always enabled and never be executed. MP fairness assumption is the original approach in [3] and WF assumption is the approach in the original proposal of UNITY in [7].

Under MP fairness assumption, the definition of *ensures* relation is:

$$p \ ensures \ q \equiv (\forall t \cdot (p \wedge \neg q \wedge grd.t \Rightarrow wp.t.q)) \wedge (\exists s \cdot (p \wedge \neg q \Rightarrow grd.s))$$

where the bound variables t and s are respectively universally and existentially quantifies over all statements of a program. $grd.t$ denotes the guard of t and $wp.t.q$ is the weakest precondition of t with respect to q. With this definition, in order to guarantee that a program establishes any q predicate while the program is in a state satisfying p, every statement of the program must be able to establish q and at any state of a computation, a statement must be enabled.

However, if a WF fairness assumption is considered, the definition of *ensures* relation is:

$$p \ ensures \ q \equiv (\forall t \cdot (p \wedge \neg q \Rightarrow wp.t.(p \vee q))) \wedge (\exists s \cdot (p \wedge \neg q \Rightarrow wp.s.q \wedge grd.s))$$

With this definition, whenever a statement of the program is executed in a state where p holds, it must be able to preserve p or establish q, and the program must have an enabled statement which must establish q.

The proof system of UNITY has a rich variety of theorems about relations *ensures* and "Leads To". These theorems are used in the proof of several properties of UNITY programs and can be seen in [7]. In this paper we use the induction theorem and the inductive definition of "Leads To" relation in the proof of liveness properties in B event systems.

2.2   Integrating Basic Liveness Properties in B

Basic liveness properties are properties that a system guarantees by an atomic action. We specify basic liveness properties by *ensures* relations. To specify basic progress properties in a B event system, we propose the use of two new clauses in a B component (SYSTEM or REFINEMENT): FAIRNESS and MODALITIES[3]. We specify: FAIRNESS MP or FAIRNESS WF to indicate that we consider a minimal progress or weak fairness assumption respectively in the system. For each property P *ensures* Q that we need to specify, we write P ENSURES Q in a MODALITIES clause; as in the invariant, several such properties are separated by a $\wedge$ operator.

The proof obligations that we propose are inspired by the corresponding definitions of *ensures* relation under MP or WF assumptions presented in the previous subsection. We consider a B event system Sys with invariant I. Let E be the set of events in Sys, the corresponding proof obligations are:

---

[3] In fact the MODALITIES clause was introduced in [3] but with a different meaning.

	ANTECEDENT	CONSEQUENT
MP0	$I \wedge P \wedge \neg Q \Rightarrow [\![_{e \in E}\ e]\ Q$	P ENSURES Q
MP1	$I \wedge P \wedge \neg Q \Rightarrow grd([\![_{e \in E}\ e)$	
WF0	$I \wedge P \wedge \neg Q \Rightarrow [\![_{e \in E}\ e]\ (P \vee Q)$	P ENSURES Q
WF1	$I \wedge P \wedge \neg Q \Rightarrow \langle [\![_{e \in E}\ e \rangle\ Q$	

where $[e]\ R$ is the weakest precondition of e w.r.t. R, $[\![_{e \in E}\ e$ is the choice notation over a set E introduced in appendix A.2 in [3], $grd(e)$ is the guard of event e: $grd(e) \equiv \neg[e]\ false$ and $\langle e \rangle\ R$ is defined by: $\langle e \rangle\ R \equiv \neg[e]\ \neg R$.

In order to analyze these proof obligations we consider that x is the (list of) state variable(s) of system Sys of type T and that any event e in E terminates: $[e]\ true \equiv true$. According to [1] we can express any event e in the generalized substitution language by its normalized form:

$$e \mathrel{\widehat{=}} @x' \cdot ((x, x') \in \mathsf{rel}(e) \Longrightarrow x := x') \tag{1}$$

where $\mathsf{rel}(e)$ is a binary relation expressing the dynamics of the substitution since it relates the before-value to the corresponding after-values of x; $\mathsf{rel}(e)$ is defined by $\{(x, x') \mid (x, x') \in T \times T \wedge \neg[e]\ x \neq x'\}$. System Sys transforms the initial value of x, by successive application of events in E. As the set of events E is finite, we can represent the choice of events by the bounded choice construction $[\![_{e \in E}\ e$. Since the state variable is the same for any event in E, using the normal form (1) of the events in Sys, the expression $[\![_{e \in E}\ e$ can be rewritten as follows:

$$[\![_{e \in E}\ e = @x' \cdot (\exists e \cdot (e \in E \wedge (x, x') \in \mathsf{rel}(e)) \Longrightarrow x := x') \tag{2}$$

The successive transformations of x by the repeated application of events from E can be regarded as an execution sequence $\sigma_0, \sigma_1, \ldots$, where each σ_i is a state (value) of x. σ_0 is an initial state as described in the initialization clause of Sys. For each σ_i and σ_{i+1} in any execution sequence, there is an event e in Sys such that $(\sigma_i, \sigma_{i+1}) \in \mathsf{rel}(e)$.

Using equality (2) we give the following equivalence for any predicate R where x' is not free:

$$[[\![_{e \in E}\ e]\ R \equiv \forall (x', e) \cdot (e \in E \wedge (x, x') \in \mathsf{rel}(e) \Rightarrow [x := x']\ R) \tag{3}$$

We use this equivalence so as to analyze the proof obligations of P ENSURES Q, where P and Q do not contain x' as free variable.

The proof obligations MP0 is rewritten as follows using equivalence (3):

$$I \wedge P \wedge \neg Q \Rightarrow \forall (x', e) \cdot (e \in E \wedge (x, x') \in \mathsf{rel}(e) \Rightarrow [x := x']\ Q)$$

We demonstrate with MP0 that any event in Sys establishes Q. The proof is done under the assumption $P \wedge \neg Q$. We prove that for any event e in Sys and for any value x' assigned to x after execution of e, $[x := x']$ Q holds. We note that in this proof, we assume that there is an event e and a value x' such that $(x, x') \in \mathsf{rel}(e)$ holds, that is, an event with enabled guard. The existence of such event and value is proved with MP1 proof obligation, which is rewritten as follows using equivalence (3):

$$I \wedge P \wedge \neg Q \Rightarrow \exists(x', e) \cdot (e \in E \wedge (x, x') \in \mathsf{rel}(e))$$

The proof of MP1 guarantees that under the assumption $P \wedge \neg Q$ there is an event e and a value x' which enable the guard of e. In this way, for any states σ_i and σ_{i+1} in any execution sequence, if $P \wedge \neg Q$ holds in state σ_i, then Q holds in state σ_{i+1}.

The proof obligation WF0 is rewritten as follows using equivalence (3):

$$(I \wedge P \wedge \neg Q \Rightarrow \forall(x', e) \cdot (e \in E \wedge (x, x') \in \mathsf{rel}(e) \Rightarrow [x := x'] (P \vee Q)))$$

We prove with WF0, under the assumption of the invariant, that any event in Sys, executed in a state where $P \wedge \neg Q$ holds and assuming its guard enabled, maintains P or establishes Q after its execution. With this proof, we guarantee that any event executed in a state where $P \wedge \neg Q$ holds, maintains P while Q does not hold. However we have no guarantee about the establishment of Q. Proof obligation WF1 guarantees the existence of an enabled event which establishes Q. This proof obligation is rewritten as follows using the equivalence (3):

$$I \wedge P \wedge \neg Q \Rightarrow \exists(x', e) \cdot (e \in E \wedge (x, x') \in \mathsf{rel}(e) \wedge [x := x'] Q)$$

Indeed, as we can see, this proof obligation guarantees the existence of certain enabled event e in a state where $P \wedge \neg Q$ holds and a value x' calculated by e, such that $[x := x']$ Q holds after execution of e. As for MP1, the guard (firing condition) contains the existence of the event e and of the value x' such that the postcondition holds. The guarantee of execution of such an event e is given by the weak fairness assumption: "each continuously enabled event is infinitely often selected for execution". In terms of execution sequences, proof obligations WF0, WF1 and the weak fairness assumption, guarantee that for any state σ_i in an execution sequence, if $P \wedge \neg Q$ holds, then there is a state σ_j, with $j > i$, where Q holds, and for any state σ_k, $i \leq k < j$, $P \wedge \neg Q$ holds. Moreover, for any state σ_k, the guard of the event executed in σ_j must be enabled. This last condition means that we cannot use WF1 proof obligation in order to demonstrate the existence of certain event which establishes Q when the guard of such event is *not* continuously enabled. In this case, we need to use a strong fairness assumption.

As we can see in equality (2), the choice among events in E can be considered as a single unbounded choice. This unbounded choice describes a family of events $\epsilon(x')$ for each x' in $\mathcal{T}$:

$$\epsilon(x') = \exists e \cdot (e \in E \wedge (x, x') \in \mathsf{rel}(e)) \Longrightarrow x := x' \tag{4}$$

The system Sys selects for execution an event $\epsilon(x')$ for a certain x' in a non deterministic way. Each event $\epsilon(x')$ updates the state variable x' in a deterministic way. In our approach, we do not distinguish between non-determinism at the event level or in the event bodies as it is done in [5]. As we have seen, the non-deterministic choice at the event level $[\![_{e\in E}\ e$ is regarded as a non-deterministic choice among events $\epsilon(x')$. This fact is guaranteed by the equivalence:

$$[\![_{e\in E}\ e]\ R \equiv [\![_{x'\in T}\ \epsilon(x')]\ R \tag{5}$$

for any R where x' is not free. We reason about the fair choice of events in the family of events $\epsilon(x')$, but we specify our systems as a bounded choice of events $[\![_{e\in E}\ e$.

2.3 Integrating General Liveness Properties in B

Considering a minimal progress assumption, if $P \wedge \neg Q$ holds in a certain state σ_i of an execution sequence, then Q holds in state σ_{i+1} . However, if we consider a weak fairness assumption, we cannot ensure that Q will be *true* in state σ_{i+1}, but we can ensure that Q holds in a certain state σ_j where $j > i$. In any way, Q is established in an atomic way, in a transition from state σ_{j-1} to state σ_j. So, properties of style P ENSURES Q guarantee that a system transfers from a state where P holds to another state where Q holds.

Moreover, we can specify and prove more general liveness properties in a system by composing basic liveness properties. For that, we use the "Leads To" relation. A property $P \rightsquigarrow Q$ guarantees that a system will be in a state where Q holds if it is in a state where P holds. In terms of execution sequences, if P holds in a certain state σ_i, the system transfers to a state σ_j, $j \geq i$, where Q holds. However, we do not know if P is preserved in states σ_k for $i \leq k \leq j$. This is the main difference between the relations "Leads To" and *ensures*.

In order to prove that a property $P \rightsquigarrow Q$ holds in a B event system, we must be able to demonstrate that this property is derived by a finite number of applications of the rules defined by the UNITY theory:

	ANTECEDENT	CONSEQUENT
BRL	P ENSURES Q	$P \rightsquigarrow Q$
TRA	$P \rightsquigarrow R,\ R \rightsquigarrow Q$	$P \rightsquigarrow Q$
DSJ	$\forall m \cdot (m \in M \Rightarrow P(m) \rightsquigarrow Q)$	$\exists m \cdot (m \in M \Rightarrow P(m)) \rightsquigarrow Q$

We remark two important facts about definition of "Leads To":

1. Definition of "Leads To" relation does not depend on fairness assumptions.
2. Liveness properties can be specified and proved without definition of a variant.

So as to reason about liveness properties, we incorporate the proof system of UNITY in the framework of B event systems. We can use all theorems in [7] concerning *ensures* and "Leads To" relations in the proof of several properties of B event systems. We present only one rule of the proof system: "The Induction Principle" for "Leads to":

	ANTECEDENT	CONSEQUENT
IND	$\forall v \cdot (P \wedge V = v \rightsquigarrow P \wedge V < v \vee Q)$	$P \rightsquigarrow Q$

Informally, this rule indicates that in any state where P holds and the variant value is v, over a well founded set, if we prove that the execution of a program changes into a state where P holds but the value of the variant is lower than v or Q holds, then we claim that $P \rightsquigarrow Q$ holds in the system. As we can see, rule IND is very similar to the proof obligations for modalities introduced in [3]. However, we have several ways to prove the antecedent of rule IND. In the examples of this paper, we prove the antecedent of rule IND by the proof of $\mathcal{P}$ ENSURES $\mathcal{Q}$ where $\mathcal{P} \equiv P \wedge V = v$ and $\mathcal{Q} \equiv P \wedge V < v \vee Q$. In turn, this *ensures* property is proved by the proof obligations under MP or WF assumptions. By application of rule BRL we get the antecedent of rule IND, and then the proof of $P \rightsquigarrow Q$. We remark that the specification and proof of liveness properties with "Leads To" relation are given in the framework of the proof system of UNITY, and the proof of properties with *ensures* relation is given in a B framework.

3   Examples of Liveness Properties and Their Proofs

We show how to use fairness assumptions so as to specify and prove liveness properties in B event systems. We present in the first subsection the specification and proof of liveness properties under minimal progress assumption and, in the second one, under weak fairness assumption.

In the proofs of this paper, we weaken the antecedent of proof obligations MP0, MP1, WF0 and WF1. Instead of $P \wedge \neg Q$ in the antecedents of these proof obligations, we only write P. We name these proof obligations: "simplified proof obligations". In fact, the simplified proof obligations are stronger than MP0, MP1, WF0 and WF1. Moreover, we do not write explicitly the invariant of the system in the proof obligations; all the proofs are done under the assumption of the invariant.

3.1   Minimal Progress Assumption

Let us consider a minimal progress fairness assumption in the system *Phils* presented in Section 1. Under this fairness constraint, we do not have any guarantee concerning the firing of events. We cannot claim that the property

$$p \in Hgy \rightsquigarrow p \in Etg$$

holds in *Phils* for any p in *PHIL*.

As an example of specification and proof of liveness property, using a minimal progress assumption, we consider the system *PhilSeq*. This system has a pointer which indicates the philosopher that may change its state. The pointer continuously increases modulo $\mathsf{card}(PHIL)$, giving in this way a sequential behavior to the system. *PhilSeq* has the same variable *phils* that *Phils* and the pointer is modeled by variable ix of type $0..\mathsf{card}(PHIL) - 1$ initialized to 0. We use the constant function idx of type $PHIL \rightarrowtail 0..\mathsf{card}(PHIL) - 1$ to assign a number to each philosopher. The events of *PhilSeq* are:

EVENTS

$hgy \;\widehat{=}\;$ ANY p WHERE $p \in PHIL \wedge p \in Thk \wedge idx(p) = ix$ THEN

$\qquad phils(p), ix := HH, (ix + 1) \bmod \mathsf{card}(PHIL)$ END ;

$eat \;\widehat{=}\;$ ANY p WHERE $p \in PHIL \wedge p \in Hgy \wedge idx(p) = ix$ THEN

$\qquad phils(p), ix := EE, (ix + 1) \bmod \mathsf{card}(PHIL)$ END ;

$thk \;\widehat{=}\;$ ANY p WHERE $p \in PHIL \wedge p \in Etg \wedge idx(p) = ix$ THEN

$\qquad phils(p), ix := TT, (ix + 1) \bmod \mathsf{card}(PHIL)$ END

END

We show that the property $p \in Hgy \wedge ix = idx(p) \rightsquigarrow p \in Eat$ holds in *PhilSeq* for any $p \in PHIL$ assuming a minimal progress fairness constraint. This property is deduced from application of BRL rule to the property

$$p \in Hgy \wedge ix = idx(p) \text{ ENSURES } p \in Etg \qquad\qquad (6)$$

In order to prove (6), the following proof obligations must hold in *PhilSeq*:

- MP0: $p \in Hgy \wedge ix = idx(p) \wedge \neg(p \in Etg) \Rightarrow [hgy \;[\!]\; eat \;[\!]\; thk]\, p \in Etg$
- MP1: $p \in Hgy \wedge ix = idx(p) \wedge \neg p \in Etg \Rightarrow grd(hgy \;[\!]\; eat \;[\!]\; thk]\, p \in Etg)$

Case MP0. For event hgy, we have $x \in Thk \wedge ix = idx(x)$, where x is universally quantified over *PHIL*, for the antecedent of $[hgy]\, p \in Etg$ and $p \in Hgy \wedge ix = idx(p)$ for the antecedent of the proof obligation. From the conjunction of these predicates we deduce $p = x$ and therefore $p \in Hgy \wedge x \in Thk$ is false; the antecedent of MP0 is false and consequently, MP0 holds. The proof for event thk is similar. For event eat, from the antecedent of the proof obligation we deduce $p = x$, and therefore the consequent $(phils \vartriangleleft \{x \mapsto EE\})(p) = EE$ holds. MP1 is proved by observing that the antecedent of the proof obligation implies the guard of event eat. □

In fact, we can prove in *PhilSeq* a stronger property: $p \in Hgy \rightsquigarrow p \in Eat$. So as to prove this property, we use the induction principle for "Leads To". In order to apply that rule, we define the variant $V(i, p)$ as a distance between a philosopher p and the pointer ix:

$$V(i, p) = \begin{cases} 0 & \text{if } i = idx(p) \\ idx(p) - i & \text{if } i < idx(p) \\ \mathsf{card}(PHIL) - i + idx(p) & \text{if } i > idx(p) \end{cases}$$

Now we can prove, for any $p \in PHIL$ and $n \in \mathbb{N}$, that the property

$$p \in Hgy \wedge V(ix, p) = n \text{ ENSURES } p \in Hgy \wedge V(ix, p) < n \vee p \in Etg \qquad (7)$$

holds in *PhilSeq*. Then, using BRL rule we prove the antecedent of IND rule:

$$\frac{\forall n \cdot (p \in Hgy \wedge V(ix, p) = n \leadsto (p \in Hgy \wedge V(ix, p) < n) \vee p \in Etg)}{p \in Hgy \leadsto p \in Etg}$$

and finally by application of this rule, we conclude that $p \in Hgy \leadsto p \in Etg$ holds in *PhilSeq*.

The proof obligations MP0 and MP1 for property (7) are:

$$p \in Hgy \wedge V(ix, p) = n \Rightarrow [hgy \, [] \, eat \, [] \, thk] \, (p \in Hgy \wedge V(ix, p) < n \vee p \in Etg)$$

and

$$p \in Hgy \wedge V(ix, p) = n \Rightarrow grd(hgy) \vee grd(eat) \vee grd(thk)$$

respectively. The proof of MP0 is by case analysis. When $ix = idx(p)$ holds, the proof is similar to the proof of MP0 for property (6). When $ix \neq idx(p)$ holds, the proof is reduced to $V(ix, p) = n \Rightarrow V((ix + 1 \bmod \mathsf{card}(PHIL)), p) < n$. This predicate follows from definition of $V(ix, p)$. So as to prove MP1, we deduce from the invariant: $\exists s \cdot (s \in STATE \wedge ix = p \wedge phils(p) = s)$ for any p in *PHIL*. From this predicate, we conclude that there is a guard in the events of *PhilSeq* which is true for each value of s. Hence, MP1 holds. $\square$

PhilSeq imposes strong constraints in the specification of the system. The variable ix has the role of a scheduler who indicates the next process to execute. All processes change their state in a sequential way. We chose this specification in order to give a simple variant V. Now, we present a little different system, it enables execution of events hgy and thk in any interleaved way, but it imposes a sequential execution of event eat among different philosophers. This system is named *PhilSeqP* and its events are:

EVENTS

$\quad hgy \mathrel{\widehat{=}}$ ANY p WHERE $p \in PHIL \wedge p \in Thk$ THEN $phils(p) := HH$ END ;

$\quad eat \mathrel{\widehat{=}}$ ANY p WHERE $p \in PHIL \wedge p \in Hgy \wedge idx(p) = ix$ THEN

$\qquad phils(p), ix := EE, (ix + 1) \bmod \mathsf{card}(PHIL)$ END ;

$\quad thk \mathrel{\widehat{=}}$ ANY p WHERE $p \in PHIL \wedge p \in Etg$ THEN $phils(p) := TT$ END

END

In order to guarantee the progress in *PhilSeqP* we need a variant function. We cannot use the same variant V as in system *PhilSeq* because V is not decremented by events hgy and thk. We define a new variant V':

$$V' = [V(ix, p), \mathsf{card}(Etg), \mathsf{card}(Thk)]$$

where p is universally quantified over *PHIL*. This variant is decremented under a lexicographic order $\prec$. Now we can prove that the property:

$$p \in Hgy \wedge [V(ix, p), \mathsf{card}(Etg), \mathsf{card}(Thk)] = [n, e, t] \text{ ENSURES}$$
$$p \in Hgy \wedge [V(ix, p), \mathsf{card}(Etg), \mathsf{card}(Thk)] \prec [n, e, t] \vee p \in Etg \qquad (8)$$

holds in system *PhilSeqP*. In this property the variables are universally quantified, p over *PHIL* and n, e and t over $\mathbb{N}$. Applying BRL rule to (8) and then IND, we prove that $p \in Hgy \rightsquigarrow p \in Etg$ holds in *PhilSeqP*.

The simplified proof obligations for the proof of property (8) are:

- MP0: for any event *ev* in *PhilSeqP*

$$p \in Hgy \wedge [V(ix,p), \mathsf{card}(Etg), \mathsf{card}(Thk)] = [n,e,t] \Rightarrow$$
$$[ev]\, p \in Hgy \wedge [V(ix,p), \mathsf{card}(Etg), \mathsf{card}(Thk)] \prec [n,e,t] \vee p \in Etg$$

- MP1: for some event *ev* in *PhilSeqP*

$$p \in Hgy \wedge [V(ix,p), \mathsf{card}(Etg), \mathsf{card}(Thk)] = [n,e,t] \Rightarrow grd(ev)$$

Comments: We first explain the proof of MP0. The events *hgy* and *thk* do not modify $V(ix,p)$. Event *hgy* decreases $\mathsf{card}(Thk)$ and event *thk* diminishes $\mathsf{card}(Etg)$. The decrement of $\mathsf{card}(Etg)$ and the increment of $\mathsf{card}(Thk)$ by event *thk* decreases the variant V' in the lexicographic order. The proof of the decrement of distance $V(ix,p)$ by event *eat* is the same proof as in system *PhilSeq*. The proof of MP1 is done by case analysis. We suppose that $Thk \neq \{\}$ and $Etg \neq \{\}$ holds; it implies the guards of *hgy* or *thk* respectively. Then, we suppose $Thk = Etg = \{\}$; this supposition and the types of *ix* and *phils* are sufficient to prove the guard of *hgy*.   □

3.2   Weak Fairness Assumption

Let us consider again the system *Phils*, but under a weak fairness assumption. In this case, we do not need to modify the system in order to guarantee a certain liveness property as we did with the systems *PhilSeq* or *PhilSeqP*. We show how a weak fairness assumption is sufficient to prove that the property $p \in Hgy \rightsquigarrow p \in Etg$ holds in *Phils*.

Under a weak fairness assumption, the following property holds in system *Phils*:

$$p \in Hgy \text{ ENSURES } p \in Etg \tag{9}$$

We obtain the proof of $p \in Hgy \rightsquigarrow p \in Etg$ by application of BRL rule to this property. The proof obligations that we need to discharge the proof of property (9) are

- WF0: $p \in Hgy \wedge \neg p \in Etg \Rightarrow [hgy \,[\!]\, eat \,[\!]\, thk]\, (p \in Hgy \vee p \in Etg)$
- WF1: $p \in Hgy \wedge \neg p \in Etg \Rightarrow \langle hgy \,[\!]\, eat \,[\!]\, thk \rangle\, p \in Etg$

Proof of WF0. The following predicates hold in *Phils*: $p \in Hgy \Rightarrow [hgy \,[\!]\, thk]\, p \in Hgy$ and $p \in Hgy \Rightarrow [eat]\, p \in Hgy \vee p \in Etg$; WF0 follows from it. In order to prove WF1 we prove $p \in Hgy \Rightarrow \langle eat \rangle\, p \in Etg$. This predicate is rewritten as:

$$p \in Hgy \Rightarrow \exists x \cdot (x \in PHIL \wedge x \in Hgy \wedge p \in (phils \vartriangleleft \{x \mapsto EE\})^{-1}[\{EE\}])$$

which holds trivially and then WF1 holds.   □

We do not need a variant in the system *Phils* with a weak fairness assumption in order to prove the liveness property $p \in Hgy \rightsquigarrow p \in Etg$. However, in general, the use of a variant is a powerful mechanism to prove liveness properties. A weak fairness assumption enable us to specify a system in a more abstract way, without considering a particular scheduling of events. In the next paragraphs we combine a weak fairness assumption and a variant in order to prove a liveness property in a more complex situation.

In the system *Phils*, even if we consider a weak fairness assumption, we have not a fair politic in the transition from state *hungry* to state *eating* for any philosopher. A philosopher can transit to state *eating* many times and in the meantime, another philosopher may wait in a *hungry* state an unspecified amount of time. To solve this problem, we present a solution, inspired from [7], which introduces a dynamic priority among the philosophers in a *hungry* state.

We specify the system *PhilPri* where each philosopher p in a *hungry* state may transit to state *eating* only if its neighbors in state *hungry* have lower priority than p. In order to prevent p from arriving to state *hungry* and then transit to state *eating* again, p drops its priority when it arrives to state *eating*.

The neighborhood among the philosophers is represented by a constant relation ngb of type $PHIL \leftrightarrow PHIL$. This is a symmetric $(ngb = ngb^{-1})$ and non-reflexive relation $(\mathrm{id}(PHIL) \cap ngb = \{\})$. This relation symbolizes an unordered graph, where two philosophers p and q are neighbors if and only if $(p, q) \in ngb$.

The priority among philosophers is represented by a relation pr of type $PHIL \leftrightarrow PHIL$. pr represents an acyclic graph which is obtained from ngb by assigning a direction to each edge in ngb. The graph depicted by pr represents a partial order among philosophers. Thus, the invariant contains $pr \cup pr^{-1} = ngb$ and $pr \cap pr^{-1} = \{\}$. We say that a philosopher p has priority over a philosopher q if and only if $(q, p) \in pr$.

In order to formally specify that the graph represented by pr is acyclic, we define the set $\mathcal{P}r(p, r)$ as the set of philosophers which have a higher priority than p in the graph r. The inductive definition of $\mathcal{P}r(p, r)$ is:

$$r[\{p\}] \subseteq \mathcal{P}r(p, r) \wedge$$
$$r[\mathcal{P}r(p, r)] \subseteq \mathcal{P}r(p, r) \wedge$$
$$\forall s.(s \in \mathbb{P}(PHIL) \wedge r[\{p\}] \subseteq s \wedge r[s] \subseteq s \Rightarrow \mathcal{P}r(p, r) \subseteq s)$$

From this inductive definition, the recursive definition of $\mathcal{P}r(p, r)$ follows:

$$\mathcal{P}r(p, r) = r[\{p\}] \cup r[\mathcal{P}r(p, r)]$$

Now we can state that pr is an acyclic graph if and only if $p \notin \mathcal{P}r(p, pr)$, for any p in *PHIL*. The initial value of pr is *PRI*, which is obtained from ngb $(PRI \cup PRI^{-1} = ngb)$. *PRI* has no cycle $(\forall p \cdot (p \in PHIL \Rightarrow p \notin \mathcal{P}r(p, PRI)))$ and it is asymmetric $(PRI \cap PRI^{-1} = \{\})$.

Any philosopher p in a *hungry* state can transit to an *eating* state only if he has a higher priority than his neighbors in state *hungry*. We define the predicate $top(p)$ which denotes the condition of the transition:

$$top(p) \equiv pr[\{p\}] \cap Hgy = \{\}$$

When the philosopher p changes to state *eating*, its priority drops. Any philosopher in an *eating* state has lower priority than its neighbors in *hungry* state. In order to describe this change in the priority graph, pr is changed to:

$$(pr \rhd \{p\}) \cup \{p\} \times ngb[\{p\}]$$

In this case, the direction of any arrow which is directed to p is inverted, and then p looses its priority among its neighbors. We present now the events of system *PhilPri*:

EVENTS

$hgy \mathrel{\widehat{=}}$ ANY p WHERE $p \in PHIL \land p \in Thk$ THEN $phils(p) := HH$ END ;

$eat \mathrel{\widehat{=}}$ ANY p WHERE $p \in PHIL \land p \in Hgy \land top(p)$ THEN

$\quad phils(p), pr := EE, (pr \rhd \{p\}) \cup \{p\} \times ngb[\{p\}]$ END ;

$thk \mathrel{\widehat{=}}$ ANY p WHERE $p \in PHIL \land p \in Etg$ THEN $phils(p) := TT$

END

As we have done in the previous examples, we specify that any philosopher in *hungry* state, eventually goes to a *eating* state. We cannot guarantee that the property $p \in Hgy$ ENSURES $p \in Etg$ holds in *PhilPri*, because we cannot prove that $top(p)$ holds when p is in state *hungry*. We need again a variant in order to prove that $p \in Hgy \rightsquigarrow p \in Etg$ holds in *PhilPri*. The variant must be decremented by the system, however as we have a weak fairness assumption, the proof obligations do not need that any event decrements the variant, we need only one event does so.

From the inductive definition of set $\mathcal{P}r(p, pr)$ we can prove that the set of philosophers with higher priority than p in a state where pr is modified according to the given rule, is a subset of the set of philosophers with higher priority than p in a given state pr: $p \neq q \Rightarrow \mathcal{P}r(p, pr \rhd \{q\} \cup \{q\} \times ngb[\{q\}]) \subseteq \mathcal{P}r(p, pr)$. So we propose $\mathsf{card}(\mathcal{P}r(p, pr))$ as the variant for this proof.

Now we can argue that the property

$$p \in Hgy \land \mathsf{card}(\mathcal{P}r(p, pr)) = n \text{ ENSURES } p \in Hgy \land \mathsf{card}(\mathcal{P}r(p, pr)) < n \lor p \in Etg$$

holds in *PhilPri* and by application of BRL and IND rules, we deduce that $p \in Hgy \rightsquigarrow p \in Etg$ holds in *PhilPri*.

The simplified proof obligations for this property are:

– WF0: for any event ev in *PhilPri*,

$\quad p \in Hgy \land \mathsf{card}(\mathcal{P}r(p, pr)) = n \Rightarrow [ev]\ (p \in Hgy \land \mathsf{card}(\mathcal{P}r(p, pr)) = n \lor$
$\quad p \in Hgy \land \mathsf{card}(\mathcal{P}r(p, pr)) < n \lor p \in Etg)$

– WF1: for some event ev in *PhilPri*,

$\quad p \in Hgy \land \mathsf{card}(\mathcal{P}r(p, pr)) = n \Rightarrow \langle ev \rangle\ (p \in Hgy \land \mathsf{card}(\mathcal{P}r(p, pr)) < n \lor p \in Etg)$

In the proofs of WF0 and WF1 we use properties of acyclic graphs. The inductive definition of set $Pr(p, pr)$ allows us to prove these properties. In fact, the inductive definition of set $Pr(p, pr)$ is the image of $\{p\}$ under the transitive closure of relation pr ($Pr(p, pr) = pr^+[\{p\}]$). However the explicit axiomatization of the properties of the transitive closure allow us to prove mechanically all the proof obligations[4].

4   Refinement under Fairness Assumptions

In this section, we present the way we use fairness assumptions in the refinement of a B system. In the first part, we motivate by an example the specification of liveness properties in the refinement of a system in order to guarantee a certain progress condition proved in its abstraction. In that example, which seems a correct refinement, we are not able to prove a liveness property proved in its abstraction, without a fairness assumption (minimal progress or weak fairness). In the second part, we develop our example, and we show the refinement of a system, which preserves the liveness property proved in its specification under minimal progress and weak fairness assumption. Finally we give some comments about the refinement of liveness properties.

4.1   Unfair Refinement

We consider a refinement, named *PhilNotFair*, of system *Phils*. In *PhilNotFair* we introduce a new event named *srv*. This event models a central server, which assigns a token to one philosopher in state *hungry*. The event *eat* of *Phils* is refined in order to change the state of a philosopher p from *hungry* to *eating* only if p has the token, and the event *thk* is refined so as to change the state of a philosopher p from *eating* to *thinking* and to release the token.

We retain in *PhilNotFair* the variable *phils* which records the state of each philosopher and we add the variable *tk* of type $PHIL \rightarrow BOOL$. *tk* records the philosopher who has assigned the token. For any p in *PHIL*, $tk(p)$ is initialized to *false*. The set *Tk* is equal to $tk^{-1}[\{true\}]$; it represents the set of philosophers which have assigned a token. For the sake of simplicity, *Tk* is defined as a singleton ($\mathsf{card}(Tk) \leq 1$). The events of *PhilNotFair* are as follow:

EVENTS

    $hgy \mathrel{\widehat{=}}$ ANY p WHERE $p \in PHIL \wedge p \in Thk$ THEN $phils(p) := HH$ END ;

    $eat \mathrel{\widehat{=}}$ ANY p WHERE $p \in PHIL \wedge p \in Hgy \wedge p \in Tk$ THEN $phils(p) := EE$ END ;

    $thk \mathrel{\widehat{=}}$ ANY p WHERE $p \in PHIL \wedge p \in Etg$ THEN $phils(p), tk(p) := TT, false$ END ;

    $srv \mathrel{\widehat{=}}$ ANY p WHERE $p \in PHIL \wedge p \in Hgy \wedge Tk = \{\}$ THEN $tk(p) := true$ END

END

---

[4] All the proofs of dynamic properties of this paper have been expressed as assertions and carried out, automatically or interactively, with Atelier B.

We can prove that the concrete events of *PhilNotFair* are correct refinements of the abstract events of *Phils*. As it is stated in [3], we have that the new event *srv* cannot take control forever since it decrements the variant $1 - \mathsf{card}(Tk)$. System *PhilNotFair* is deadlock free: $true \Rightarrow grd(hgy) \vee grd(eat) \vee grd(thk) \vee grd(srv)$. In order to prove it, we reason by case analysis. We have trivially that $Thk \neq \{\} \Rightarrow grd(hgy)$ and $Thk = \{\} \wedge Etg \neq \{\} \Rightarrow grd(thk)$. If we consider that $Thk = \{\} \wedge Etg = \{\}$ holds, we then have $Hgy = PHIL$. Now we suppose that $Tk = \{\}$ holds. From $Hgy = PHIL \wedge Tk = \{\}$ we conclude $grd(srv)$. Finally, we have that $Hgy = PHIL \wedge Tk \neq \{\} \Rightarrow grd(eat)$ holds, and we have the proof of deadlock freeness in *PhilNotFair*.   □

However the system *PhilNotFair* does not preserve the property $p \in Hgy \rightsquigarrow p \in Etg$ that we proved in system *Phils* under a weak fairness assumption in section 3.2. Even if we consider a weak fairness assumption, we cannot prove that $p \in Hgy \rightsquigarrow p \in Etg$ holds in *PhilNotFair*. We can claim, by the weak fairness assumption, that the event *srv* will be infinitely often executed if it is continuously enabled, but we cannot ensure that the token will be assigned to a particular philosopher by the unbounded choice substitution. A philosopher may stay in *hungry* state forever. In order to support this claim, we can consider the family of events $\epsilon(phils', tk')$ as presented in equality (4) in section 2.2. For the sake of simplicity, we consider a state with five philosophers, all philosophers are in state *hungry* and the token is not assigned. The vector $\langle H, H, H, H, H \rangle$ represents the state of variable *phils* and the vector $\langle F, F, F, F, F \rangle$ the state of the variable *tk*. We consider only two events of the family: $\epsilon(\langle H, H, H, H, H \rangle, \langle F, F, F, F, T \rangle)$ and $\epsilon(\langle H, H, H, H, H \rangle, \langle T, F, F, F, F \rangle)$. These events model the assignment of the token by *srv*; the first event assigns to the philosopher number five, and the second event to the number one. In the current state, the guards of the two events are enabled. When any of these events is executed, the change of state disables the guard of the two events. The guard of an event may be often enabled and disabled and it is not continuously enabled as it is required by the weak fairness assumption. In order to be able to analyze this case, we need a strong fairness assumption.

By this simple example, we demonstrate the importance of formally specifying liveness properties in a refinement, if we want to prove a certain progress condition. In the next section we present a refinement of system *Phils*, very close to system *PhilNotFair*, that preserves the liveness property $p \in Hgy \rightsquigarrow p \in Etg$.

4.2   Fair Refinement

In order to guarantee that any philosopher in state *hungry* will be in state *eating* eventually, we specify a system with a sequence which records each philosopher that changes to state *hungry*. In this way, the token is assigned to the first philosopher in the sequence.

We specify a fair refinement of system *Phils* named *PhilFair*. The state variables of this system are similar to the variables of system *PhilNotFair*. The only difference is the sequence *sq*. We define *sq* as an injective sequence of philosophers ($sq \in \mathsf{iseq}(PHIL)$) with an initially empty value. The range of *sq* is the set of philosophers in *hungry* state ($Hgy = \mathsf{ran}(sq)$). We retain the variable tk of type $PHIL \rightarrow BOOL$; for any p in $PHIL$, $tk(p)$ is initialized to *false*. If a philosopher p has assigned the token, then $tk(p) = true$. The set Tk is defined as a singleton ($\mathsf{card}(Tk) \leq 1$); if it is not empty, it contains the philosopher which has assigned the token ($Tk = tk^{-1}[\{true\}]$). The token is assigned to the first philosopher in the sequence ($Hgy \cap Tk \subseteq \{\mathsf{first}(sq)\}$). The philosopher in *eating* state is the only philosopher who has the token ($Etg \subseteq Tk$). Finally, any philosopher in state *thinking* has no token ($Tk \subseteq PHIL - Thk$). The events of *PhilFair* are the following:

EVENTS

$hgy \triangleq$ ANY p WHERE $p \in PHIL \wedge p \in Thk$ THEN

   $phils(p), sq := HH, sq \leftarrow p$ END ;

$eat \triangleq$ ANY p WHERE $p \in PHIL \wedge p \in Hgy \wedge p \in Tk$ THEN

   $phils(p), sq := EE, \mathsf{tail}(sq)$ END ;

$thk \triangleq$ ANY p WHERE $p \in PHIL \wedge p \in Etg$ THEN

   $phils(p), tk(p) := TT, false$ END ;

$srv \triangleq$ SELECT $sq \neq [] \wedge Tk = \{\}$ THEN $tk(\mathsf{first}(sq)) := true$ END

END

Each concrete event of *PhilFair* refines the corresponding abstract events. As we do with system *PhilNotFair*, we can prove that the new event srv does not take control forever and that the system is deadlock free. However, we show in the following paragraphs, that these proofs (deadlock and livelock freeness) are also obtained as an outcome of the proof that a certain basic progress property holds under minimal progress or weak fairness assumption.

Refinement under a Minimal Progress Assumption. Under a minimal progress assumption, we know that in order to establish a basic progress property P ENSURES Q, the given proof obligations state that any event in the system must establish Q. We cannot ensure that any event will establish $p \in Etg$ if it starts its execution in a state where $p \in Hgy$ holds, but we can ensure that any event decrements a variant. The variant that we give for this example is a sequence of four natural numbers which is decremented in a lexicographic order $\prec$. In order to describe this variant, we define the function fr of type $\mathsf{iseq}(PHIL) \rightarrow \mathbb{N}$ as $fr(sq) = \mathsf{card}(PHIL) - \mathsf{size}(sq)$; this function gives the number of free places in sq. The variant that we give for *PhilFair* is:

$$V(p, sq, Etg, Tk) = [sq^{-1}(p), fr(sq), \mathsf{card}(Etg), 1 - \mathsf{card}(Tk)]$$

Now, we state that the following property holds in *PhilFair*

$$p \in Hgy \wedge [sq^{-1}(p), fr(sq), \mathsf{card}(Etg), 1 - \mathsf{card}(Tk)] = [n, f, e, t] \text{ ENSURES}$$
$$p \in Hgy \wedge [sq^{-1}(p), fr(sq), \mathsf{card}(Etg), 1 - \mathsf{card}(Tk)] \prec [n, f, e, t] \vee p \in Etg \quad (10)$$

where n, f, e and t are universally quantified over $\mathbb{N}$. By applying BRL and IND rules to this property, we have that $p \in Hgy \rightsquigarrow p \in Etg$ holds in *PhilFair*.

In order to demonstrate this property, we need to prove the corresponding simplified proof obligations:

– MP0 for any event ev in *PhilFair*

$$p \in Hgy \wedge [sq^{-1}(p), fr(sq), \mathsf{card}(Etg), 1 - \mathsf{card}(Tk)] = [n, f, e, t] \Rightarrow$$
$$[ev] \, (p \in Hgy \wedge [sq^{-1}(p), fr(sq), \mathsf{card}(Etg), 1 - \mathsf{card}(Tk)] \prec [n, f, e, t] \vee p \in Etg)$$

– MP1 for some event ev in *PhilFair*

$$p \in Hgy \wedge [sq^{-1}(p), fr(sq), \mathsf{card}(Etg), 1 - \mathsf{card}(Tk)] = [n, f, e, t] \Rightarrow grd(ev)$$

The proof of MP0 is done by analyzing what elements of the variant are modified. Event hgy does not modify the position of any philosopher in the sequence. However, it decrements the number of free places in sq. In this way $p \in Hgy \wedge [sq^{-1}(p), fr(sq)] = [n, f] \Rightarrow [hgy] \, (p \in Hgy \wedge [sq^{-1}(p), fr(sq)] \prec [n, f])$ holds and MP0 holds for event eat. Event eat decrements the position of philosopher p in the sequence or establish $p \in Etg$. From it, we have that $p \in Hgy \wedge sq^{-1}(p) = n \Rightarrow [eat] \, (p \in Hgy \wedge sq^{-1}(p) < n \vee p \in Etg)$ holds and then MP0 for event eat holds. Event thk does not modify the sequence, but it decrements the number of philosophers in state *eating*, therefore $p \in Hgy \wedge \mathsf{card}(Etg) = e \Rightarrow [thk] \, (p \in Hgy \wedge \mathsf{card}(Etg) < e)$ holds and then MP0 holds for this event. Finally event srv does not modify neither sq nor $\mathsf{card}(Etg)$, but it decrements $1 - \mathsf{card}(Tk)$ and therefore MP0 holds. The proof of MP1 is done in the same way as we do for the proof of deadlock freeness in system *PhilNotFair*.

$\square$

In the proof of property $p \in Hgy \rightsquigarrow p \in Etg$ under a minimal progress assumption, we proved with MP0 that the new event srv does not take control forever because it decrements $1 - \mathsf{card}(Tk)$, and with MP1 that the system is deadlock free. These proofs are the same as for system *PhilNotFair*, but with MP0 and MP1 we have also the proof that the refinement preserves the progress property specified in its abstraction.

Refinement under a Weak Fairness Assumption. Under a weak fairness assumption, in order to prove that a basic progress property P ENSURES Q holds, we must demonstrate that any event in the system establishes $P \vee Q$ if it is executed in a state where $P \wedge \neg Q$ holds. As we cannot guarantee that $p \in Hgy$ ENSURES $p \in Etg$ holds in *PhilFair*, we need a variant to bound the number of state transitions that a philosopher in state *hungry* must wait in order to change to state *eating* as we do in system *PhilNotFair*. However, by the weak fairness assumption, we do not need that any event decrements the variant; WF1 requires that some event decrements it. The weak fairness assumption gives us the possibility of specify a variant simpler than the variant used in *PhilFair* with MP assumption. In this case, the variant corresponds to the position of philosopher p in the sequence sq. Now we claim that the property:

$$p \in Hgy \wedge sq^{-1}(p) = n \rightsquigarrow p \in Hgy \wedge sq^{-1}(p) < n \vee p \in Etg \tag{11}$$

holds in *PhilFair*. By applying BRL and IND rules to this property, we conclude that $p \in Hgy \leadsto p \in Etg$ holds in *PhilFair* under a weak fairness assumption.

Property (11) follows from the following basic progress properties:

$$P \wedge Etg = \{\} \wedge Tk \neq \{\} \text{ ENSURES } Q \tag{12}$$

$$P \wedge \neg (Etg = \{\} \wedge Tk \neq \{\}) \text{ ENSURES } P \wedge Etg = \{\} \tag{13}$$

$$P \wedge Etg = \{\} \wedge Tk = \{\} \text{ ENSURES } P \wedge Etg = \{\} \wedge Tk \neq \{\} \tag{14}$$

where $P \equiv p \in Hgy \wedge sq^{-1}(p) = n$ and $Q \equiv p \in Hgy \wedge sq^{-1}(p) < n \vee p \in Etg$, by applying BRL, TRA and DSJ rules:

1. $P \wedge Etg = \{\} \wedge Tk \neq \{\} \leadsto Q$; BRL to (12)
2. $P \wedge \neg(Etg = \{\} \wedge Tk \neq \{\}) \leadsto P \wedge Etg = \{\}$; BRL to (13)
3. $P \wedge Etg = \{\} \wedge Tk = \{\} \leadsto P \wedge Etg = \{\} \wedge Tk \neq \{\}$; BRL to (14)
4. $P \wedge Etg = \{\} \wedge Tk = \{\} \leadsto Q$; TRA to 3,1
5. $P \wedge Etg = \{\} \leadsto Q$; DSJ to 4,1
6. $P \wedge \neg(Etg = \{\} \wedge Tk \neq \{\}) \leadsto Q$; TRA to 2,5
7. $P \leadsto Q$; DSJ to 1,6

The basic progress properties are proved with WF0 and WF1 proof obligations. We must notice that not any of the basic progress properties holds in *PhilFair* under a minimal progress assumption.

If we consider a weak fairness assumption in a refinement of a system, and we prove that P ENSURES Q holds in that refinement, we know that any event does establish $P \vee Q$ when it is executed in a state where $P \wedge \neg Q$ holds (WF0) and that some event must have its guard enabled in a state satisfying $P \wedge \neg Q$ and moreover it does establish Q (WF1). By the weak fairness assumption, we have that any event with a continuously enabled guard, will be executed infinitely often and this includes the new events in a refinement. So, if the guard of an event is continuously enabled, we cannot have a deadlock in the system. Proof obligation WF1 ensures that there is always an event with enabled guard in any state where $P \wedge \neg Q$ holds, and therefore the system is deadlock free in these states. In the other hand, if two or more events have their guard enabled, by the weak fairness assumption, a particular event cannot take control forever, and we do not need to prove that the new events in a refinement decrements a variant in order to bound their execution.

4.3 On the Refinement of Liveness Properties

In our proposed approach, liveness properties are classified as basic progress properties or general liveness properties. In this paragraph we give some hints about the preservation of those properties when an abstract system A with n abstract events a_i is refined into a concrete system C with n concrete events c_i and m new events h_j, such that each concrete event c_i refine the abstract event a_i.

Basic progress properties are specified as properties of style P ENSURES Q. Under minimal progress fairness assumptions, proof obligations MP0 and MP1 guarantee that such a property holds in system A. In order to preserve the property in the concrete system C, MP0 and MP1 must hold in it. However, to reduce the overhead of the proof, we can see that the concrete events c_i already satisfy MP0, as they are refinements of the abstract events a_i. So, we must only prove that MP0 holds for the new events h_j. On the other hand, as the guards of the concrete events c_i are stronger than the guards of the abstract events a_i, we need to prove that there is an enabled guard, when the system is in a state where $P \wedge \neg Q$ holds. In a similar way, under a weak fairness assumption, if we proved that P ENSURES Q holds in the abstract system, WF0 proof obligations are preserved by the concrete events c_i and we need to prove that WF0 holds for the new events h_j. Proof obligation WF1 must be reproved because the guards of the concrete events are stronger than the guards of the abstract events.

If we proved a property of style $P \rightsquigarrow Q$ in the abstract system, this property was derived from one or several basic liveness properties by the way of UNITY rules. So, we need to assert that each used basic liveness property is preserved in the concrete system in order to guarantee the preservation of the general liveness property. Then, the proof of the preservation of the asserted basic liveness properties follows from the hints given in the paragraph above.

5   Conclusion

In this paper we presented a proposal of specification and proof of liveness properties in B event systems under fairness assumptions. We gave proof obligations in order to prove basic progress properties in B event systems under two types of assumptions: minimal progress and weak fairness. We defined proof obligations in terms of weakest preconditions of substitutions, which allow us to prove basic liveness properties in a B framework. We suggested the use of $\rightsquigarrow$ operator to specify more general liveness properties. In this way, we integrated the UNITY logic in the specification and proof of B event systems.

With our approach, we combine basic progress properties in order to prove more general liveness properties, instead of using model checking techniques as it is proposed in [8]. Moreover, the proof of liveness properties is not necessarily given by proving the decrement of a variant, in a way similar to a loop termination, as it is proposed in [3]. We dispose of the UNITY system rules, which provides a variety of theorems, which can be used in the study and proof of properties in B event systems.

We claim the use of weak fairness assumptions in order to have abstract specifications without the introduction of schedulers. We show by some examples, how the specification of a B event system under weak fairness assumption is simpler than the specification under minimal progress assumption. Analyzing these examples, we conclude that the proof of liveness properties under weak fairness assumptions is simpler than the proof under minimal progress assumptions. However, when we refine a system, and we are close to its implementation, a minimal progress assumption is more realistic. The proof obligations for liveness properties under minimal progress assumptions are a guarantee of the preservation of progress in the low level of abstraction.

There are several directions in our future research work. We need to improve our study of refinement of liveness properties under fairness assumptions. From a theoretical point of view, we would like to study strong fairness assumptions in order to have specifications that are more abstract. The composition of liveness and safety properties is a main concern in the modularization of proofs in B event systems. From a practical point of view, in order to well assess the benefits of our proposal, we need to apply it to real case studies. Another issue is to enhance the support tools of B, to generate the proposed proof obligations and to integrate a UNITY like deduction system.

References

1. J.-R. Abrial. *The B-Book, Assigning Programs to Meanings.* Cambridge University Press, 1996.
2. J.-R. Abrial. Extending B Without Changing it (for Developing Distributed Systems). In *First B Conference*, pages 169–190. Nantes, november 1996.
3. J.-R. Abrial and L. Mussat. Introducing Dynamic Constraints in B. In *B'98: Recent Advances in the Development and Use of the B Method, LNCS 1393*, pages 83–128. Springer-Verlag, april 1998.
4. Krzysztof R. Apt and Ernst-Rüdiger Olderog. *Verification of Sequential and Concurrent Programs.* Graduate texts in computer science. Springer-Verlag, second edition edition, 1997.
5. R. J. R. Back and Q. W. Xu. Fairness in action systems. Reports on Computer Science & Mathematics 159, Åbo Akademi, 1995.
6. M. Butler and M. Waldén. Distributed System Development in B. In *First B Conference*, pages 155–168. Nantes, november 1996.
7. K. Mani Chandy and Jayadev Misra. *Parallel Program Design A Foundation.* Addison-Wesley, 1988.
8. S. Chouali F. Bellegarde and J. Julliand. Verification of Dynamic Constraints for B Event Systems under Fairness Assumptions . In *ZB 2002 International Conference, LNCS 2272*, pages 481–500. Springer-Verlag, january 2002.
9. P.-A. Masson J. Julliand and H. Mountassir. Vérification par model-checking modulaire des propriétés dynamiques introduites en B. *Technique et science informatique*, 20(7), 2001.
10. D. Méry. Machines Abstraites Temporelles Analyse Comparative de B et TLA$^+$. In *First B Conference*, pages 191–220. Nantes, november 1996.
11. Josyula Ramachandra Rao. *Extensions of the UNITY Methodology.* Number 908 in Lectures Notes in Computer Science. Springer, 1995.

Minimally and Maximally Abstract Retrenchments

C. Jeske, R. Banach

Computer Science Dept., Manchester University, Manchester, M13 9PL, U.K.

jeskec@cs.man.ac.uk, banach@cs.man.ac.uk

Abstract. The drawbacks of using reı nement alone in the construction of speciı cations from simple abstract models is used as the spur for the introduction of retrenchment — a method based on the main ideas of reı nement but one which is more liberal in character. The basics of the retrenchment mechanism are reviewed in preparation for exploring its integration with reı nement. The particular aspect of integration investigated in this paper is the factorisation of a retrenchment step from an abstract to a concrete model into a refinement followed by a retrenchment. The objective is to engineer a system which is at the level of abstraction of the concrete model, but is reı nable from the abstract one. The construction given here solves the problem in a universal manner, there being a canonical factorisation of the original retrenchment into an I/O-filtered refinement to the universal system followed by a retrenchment. The universal property arises from the fact that the refinement component of any similar factorisation is refinable to the universal system. An idempotence property supports the claim that the construction is at the correct level of abstraction. A synopsis of an earlier result which factorised a retrenchment step into a canonical retrenchment to a universal system followed by a reı nement is presented. A reı nement relationship is then shown to exist between the two universal systems. Finally, the consequences of including termination criteria are brieı y explored.

Keywords. Reı nement, Retrenchment, Integration.

1 Introduction

Reı nement is a well established technique for the formal construction of software. Of the many variants which can be found in the literature, the reı nement calculus as exempliı ed by Back and von Wright [2] and Morgan [14], is concerned with the application of correctness-preserving transformations which convert an abstract and possibly non-executable speciı cation of some program into efı cient executable code. Alternatively, in reı nement methods like B [1], VDM [11] and Z [18], the notion of reı nement is less calculational. Here, each reı nement step involves writing a yet more concrete version of the original speciı cation, typically by the addition of more detail into the development. To ensure that the result of each step meets the requirements of the original speciı cation, the developer is required to show that certain proof obligations (POs) hold at each stage. It is this latter process for which the term reı nement will be used in the remainder of this paper. For a tutorial on reı nement calculi and methods consult [12].

The ability to steadily incorporate detail has resulted in refinement being used not only in the implementation of speciı cations but also as a tool in the construction of the speciı cations themselves. However, when the method is applied to realistic systems, it often suffers from shortcomings which at best make the development of the speciı cation awkward, and at worst can mean that large parts of the process cannot be controlled by the reı nement mechanism. In particular, if we look at the construction of systems

M. Butler, L. Petre, and K. Sere (Eds.): IFM 2002, LNCS 2335, pp. 380–399, 2002.

which are entirely discrete in character, we sometimes ı nd that the use of reı nement imposes an unnatural decomposition on the development, with the technique obstructing the gradual construction of the speciı cation in an intelligible and clear manner. For problems which start life as models expressed using continuous mathematics, the situation is more severe. The need to move from the continuous to the discrete domain means refinement is usually unable to relate most of the models in the development, thus excluding large parts of the process from the advantages of a formal approach. In the light of these difı culties, a more ı exible speciı cation tool called retrenchment was ı rst put forward in [4], and further developed in [5, 6, 7]. Although based on the main ideas of reı nement, it is more liberal in character, and is intended to be able to relate pairs of models that arise naturally in the design process, or occur as a result of standard engineering methods, and which cannot be related by reı nement.

The ability to accommodate accepted engineering practice is an important one. To expect engineers to abandon tried and tested procedures is unrealistic and any attempts to impose an unnatural development strategy are likely to result in rejection. Unfortunately, attempts to shoehorn established design methods into the framework of the refinement mechanism often result in just such a strategy. The aim of retrenchment is therefore not to disrupt current discipline but to enable speciı cations to be developed in a manner which is in harmony with established engineering or designer intuition.

The more liberal nature of retrenchment arises from its less demanding POs, whose structure has been inı uenced by the intention to facilitate the smooth integration of retrenchment with its reı nement precursor. The integration of these two techniques is the topic of this paper, which builds on the work in [3], and examines a further way in which a reı nement and retrenchment step can be combined.

Let us suppose we have a retrenchment from an abstract to a concrete model. Given such a step, the work carried out in [3] addressed the problem of ı nding a system which reı ected at the abstract level the detail which had been incorporated into the concrete model. The solution presented was a universal construction at the level of abstraction of the abstract model, but which was reı nable to the concrete one. Following on from this result, the goal of the work presented in this paper is to construct a system which is at the level of abstraction of the concrete model but is reı nable from the abstract one. The solution given here is a universal system which is at the required level of abstraction.

Such constructions serve to integrate retrenchment and reı nement and show that the two techniques are not incompatible with one another. For those charged with the responsibility of building system speciı cations, this issue is an important one. To accept retrenchment into the fold of formal development methods, they need to be secure in the knowledge that the use of retrenchment will not split the development process into incompatible and irreconcilable paths.

The remainder of this paper is organised as follows. Section 2 touches on the drawbacks of using reı nement as the sole means to develop detailed speciı cations from simple abstract models. This serves as the motivation for retrenchment, the basics of which are presented in Section 3. Section 4 deﬁnes I/O-ﬁltered reﬁnements, a particular form of reﬁnement which facilitates its integration with retrenchment. The heart of this paper is Section 5, which looks at the canonical factorisation of a retrenchment step into a reﬁnement followed by a retrenchment. That this construction is idempotent is shown in Section 6. Section 7 brieﬂy outlines an earlier result which looked at factorising a retrenchment step into a canonical retrenchment followed by a reﬁnement. Section 8 considers an alternative approach to requirements validation. Section 9 shows that there is a reﬁnement relationship between the intermediate systems constructed in the two factorisations. In the penultimate section the results presented so far are extended to a total correctness setting. Finally, Section 11 concludes.

Notation. In the sequel we will view systems from a set theoretic and relational viewpoint, which we discuss using a logical meta-notation. Thus a predicate *is* just a notation for a set etc.

2   Some Drawbacks of Refinement

We shall use the forward simulation method of proving reﬁnement, since almost all applications of reﬁnement are of this kind. For a comprehensive discussion of both forward and backward simulation see [10].

We introduce a small example which nicely illustrates the kinds of problems that can be experienced when using reﬁnement as the sole tool for constructing a speciﬁcation. Consider a system whose state u is a set of NATs, and which has an operation $AddEl(i)$ to add an element i to the set. Its description (in a suitable syntactic framework) will be our idealised abstract model. At a more concrete level, we model sets of NATs by injective sequences of NATs, so $u = \{1, 2, 3\}$ would correspond to $w = [1, 2, 3]$, or $w = [2, 1, 3]$, or to any of the other four possible serialisations. It follows that the retrieve relation, $G(u, w)$, which associates corresponding abstract and concrete states, has the form $u = \operatorname{ran}(w)$. At this more concrete level we also wish to take account of a practical aspect of the system and limit the maximum length of the sequence to 10. Thus not all sets have concrete representations. The concrete $AddEl(i)$ operation must test the length of the sequence and for the prior presence of i. If the length of the sequence is less than 10, we can model the addition of a new element by, for example, appending the new integer to the end of the sequence. But what are we to do when the length of the sequence is at its maximum? Clearly, appending a new element in this case is not an option since this would violate the bound on the length of w. Now, for the concrete $AddEl(i)$ to be a reﬁnement of the abstract one the following PO must hold:

$$G(u, w) \wedge stp_{AddEl_C}(w, i, w') \implies (\exists\, u' \bullet stp_{AddEl_A}(u, i, u') \wedge G(u', w')) \tag{2.1}$$

where $stp_{AddEl_C}(w, i, w')$ is the transition or step relation of the concrete $AddEl$ (similarly for the abstract one), and primes indicate the after-state. Examining (2.1) we see that whenever the concrete operation can make a step, the abstract operation must be able to make some matching step. Thus simply doing nothing, i.e. modelling this situation with a *skip*, is not an alternative since an element will still be added at the abstract level. The only other plausible choice would be for the concrete operation to output an error message, but this would also fail because (2.1) does not allow a change in the I/O signature. Even if the concrete operation did something else within its constraints, it could not tie up with the abstract operation, which would produce a set of cardinality 11.

The above demonstrates one very simple situation in which reı nement fails to adequately describe a desirable development step. A similar but more detailed example can be found in [8]. For systems involving continuous variables the shortcomings of reı nement are discussed in [15] which looks at the speciı cation of a program for dose calculation in radiotherapy. In the following section we introduce retrenchment, and show how it effortlessly overcomes the problem encountered above with reı nement.

3 Retrenchment

To make progress we will need to talk about abstract and concrete systems, which we shall call *Abs* and *Conc* respectively. Each system will be described by a state space and a set of operation names. Individual operations will be deı ned by a transition or step relation and will have their own input and output spaces. For the present we shall work in a partial correctness framework, thus the transition relations will only consist of steps which initialise and terminate successfully. Refer once more to [10] for one approach to partial and total correctness in a relational setting.

For *Abs* the state space will be denoted by U with typical element u. Ops_A will be the set of operation names with Op_A designating a typical operation. For each Op_A the input and output spaces will be I_{Op_A} and O_{Op_A} with i and o representing typical elements respectively. We will miss out the subscripts on i and o, since it will be clear from the context as to the Op_A to which they belong. A typical Op_A transition will be depicted by u -(i, Op_A, o)-› u', where u and u' are the before- and after- states, and i and o are the input and output values. The set of such steps will form the transition or step relation $stp_{Op_A}(u, i, u', o)$. $Init_A(u')$ is the predicate that will represent the initialisation operation which will set the state to some initial value u'.

The set up for the concrete system *Conc* parallels that for *Abs*. The state space will be W with typical element w. Inputs and outputs are $k \in K$ and $q \in Q$ respectively. The operation names are $Op_C \in Ops_C$, and for each Op_C the transition relation is $stp_{Op_C}(w, k, w', q)$, with typical transition w -(k, Op_C, q)-› w'. The initialisation operation is $Init_C(w')$.

Unlike with reı nement, *Conc* is permitted to have additional operations and so $Ops_A \subseteq Ops_C$. Corresponding abstract and concrete states will be related by the familiar retrieve relation $G(u, w)$. In addition, for each $Op_A \in Ops_A$, there is a within relation $P_{Op}(i, k, u, w)$ and a concedes relation $C_{Op}(u', w', o, q; i, k, u, w)$. These combine to give the proof obligations for retrenchment. First, there is the initialisation PO (Init PO), which is the same as for reı nement. Thus:

$$Init_C(w') \Rightarrow (\exists u' \bullet Init_A(u') \wedge G(u', w')) \tag{3.1}$$

Second, each pair of related operations must satisfy the operation PO (Op PO):

$$G(u, w) \wedge P_{Op}(i, k, u, w) \wedge stp_{Op_C}(w, k, w', q) \Rightarrow$$
$$(\exists\, u', o \bullet stp_{Op_A}(u, i, u', o) \wedge (G(u', w') \vee C_{Op}(u', w', o, q; i, k, u, w))) \quad (3.2)$$

Notice that the within relation is concerned with both before-states and input values and so enables a change in input signature as well as mixing of input and state information. This allows, for example, information which formed part of the state at one level, to be remodelled as input at the next. What is more, appearing as a conjunct in the antecedent, the within relation strengthens the retrieve relation in before-states and so can be used to restrict the relationship between adjoining levels of abstraction. The concedes relation is mainly concerned with after-states and output values, but may involve before-states and inputs for greater 1 exibility; the punctuation used in C_{Op} is intended to emphasise this view. Thus, in particular, the concedes relation allows change of output signature and mingling of output and state. More importantly, it admits weakening of the retrieve relation in after-states by being a disjunct to it, and it is especially this aspect which allows the expression of non-refinement like behaviour. The added flexibility provided by the within and concedes relations therefore introduces the possibility of relating models which cannot be related by rei nement.

Let us return to the example in Section 2 and see how the proposed development step can be captured formally by the retrenchment mechanism. We have $\mathsf{Ops}_A = \mathsf{Ops}_C = \{Init, AddEl\}$, $\mathsf{U} = \mathsf{P(NAT)}$, $\mathsf{W} = \mathsf{iseq(NAT)}$, $\mathsf{I}_{AddEl} = \mathsf{K}_{AddEl} = \mathsf{NAT}$, $\mathsf{O}_{AddEl} = \varnothing$, and Q_{AddEl} will depend on how we dei ne the concrete $AddEl$ operation. In the simple case in which $AddEl_C$ performs a *skip* when the length of the sequence is at maximum, $\mathsf{Q}_{AddEl} = \varnothing$, otherwise it contains an overı ow message; we concentrate on the former.

To describe the *skip* case fully, we need to give the within and concedes relations for $AddEl(i)$. Some examples follow, the 1 rst three in order of increasing strength:

1. $P_1 = \textit{true}$, $C_1 = (i \notin u \Rightarrow w' = w)$
2. $P_2 = \textit{true}$, $C_2 = (i \notin u \wedge w' = w)$
3. $P_3 = \textit{true}$, $C_3 = (|u| = 10 \wedge i \notin u \wedge w' = w)$
4. $P_4 = (|u| \le 10)$, $C_4 = (i \notin u \wedge w' = w)$
5. $P_5 = (|u| < 10 \vee (|u| = 10 \wedge i \in u))$, $C_5 = \textit{false}$

Notice how examples 4 and 5 use the within clause to exclude certain situations from consideration. In example 5 for instance, the antecedent of the Op PO will be false when $|u| = 10 \wedge i \notin u$, and thus the PO will hold trivially, permitting us to dei ne different behaviour for the concrete system: it can do a *skip* and not add an eleventh element to the sequence. In the 1 rst three examples, the concedes clause is used to allow the concrete system to exhibit different behaviour. All three clauses will be true if the concrete system performs a *skip* when the eleventh element is added in the abstract system. Note also that example 5 describes fewer corresponding pairs of steps than the others, since the cases for which $|u| = 10 \wedge i \notin u$ are not in the scope of the relationship between the two models. In fact the triviality of the concedes relation here means that example

5 is describing a particular kind of refinement, and shows that by suitably restricting one's focus a reı nement can often be found lurking inside a retrenchment. This point of view is explored in [6, 7].

Retrenchment is not the only approach in the literature which attempts to address the restrictive nature of refinement. For example, work in [9, 19] extends refinement by permitting a change in I/O signature across a development step. Other proposals include Liu's notion of evolution [13]. Development steps which cannot be described by reı nement, are incorporated by demanding that the pre- and post- conditions of the abstract specıı cation in the development step be semantically equivalent to subformulae of the pre- and post- conditions at the more concrete level. Now, since Q is a subformula of $(P \wedge Q) \vee (P \wedge \neg Q)$, and the latter is equivalent to P, we can go from any Q to any P and so can relate any two models. Evolution, like retrenchment, is a weakening of reı nement. This too is true of Smith's approach which he calls realisation [16, 17]. In [16] Smith voices concerns similar to our own. A development route which for pragmatic or methodological reasons starts out with an idealised abstract model, often cannot relate all the intermediate steps using refinement. Smith defines realisation rules which allow a specıı cation to be transformed to one with different functionality in such a way that properties of the resulting specification can be derived from those of the transformed one.

4   I/O-Filtered Refinements

Here we deı ne a particular type of reı nement, I/O-ı ltered reı nement, which allows for the easier integration of retrenchment and reı nement steps. I/O-ı ltered reı nement allows for a change in I/O signature thus reı ecting a feature available in retrenchment but prohibited in classical reı nement.

We will use the abstract and concrete systems *Abs* and *Conc* set up earlier. For an I/O-filtered refinement $Ops_A = Ops_C$, and the relationship between the two levels *Abs* and *Conc* is specified by the retrieve relation $G(u, w)$, and for each $Op \in Ops_A$, a within relation $R_{Op}(i, k)$ and a nevertheless relation $V_{Op}(o, q)$. All three relations are constrained to be total on their first components and surjective on their second; i.e. they are relations S satisfying ı rstly $\forall a \exists b \bullet S(a, b)$ and secondly $\forall b \exists a \bullet S(a, b)$. Notice that unlike in retrenchment, these relations set apart the states, inputs and outputs. The Init PO for I/O-filtered refinement is the same as (3.1), while the Op PO has the form:

$$G(u, w) \wedge R_{Op}(i, k) \wedge stp_{Op_C}(w, k, w', q) \Rightarrow$$
$$(\exists\, u', o \bullet stp_{Op_A}(u, i, u', o) \wedge G(u', w') \wedge V_{Op}(o, q)) \tag{4.1}$$

Observe that the structure of this PO corresponds more closely to that found in retrenchment, with operation inputs being dealt with in the antecedent while outputs appear in the consequent. However, note that in contrast to the retrenchment case, the relation involving outputs appears as a conjunct.

5   Minimally Abstract Retrenchments

In this section we tackle the problem of decomposing the retrenchment from *Abs* to *Conc* into a reı nement followed by a retrenchment. The objective is to engineer a system *Univ*, which is at the level of abstraction of the concrete model, but is reı nable from the abstract one. That *Univ* is indeed at the desired level is supported by showing that, within a class of systems, *Univ* has appropriate universal properties. Specıı cally, that for any system *Xtra* in the class achieving a similar factorisation, there is an I/O-ı ltered refinement from *Xtra* to *Univ*. We shall also show that for any other system *Univ** which has the same properties as *Univ*, *Univ* and *Univ** are mutually I/O-ı ltered interreı nable. This interreı nability demonstrates an equivalence between the two systems. These ideas are made precise in Theorem 5.1 below.

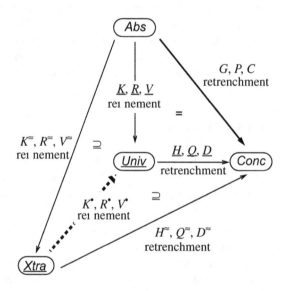

Figure 5.1:   Canonical factorisation of the retrenchment from *Abs* to *Conc* into a reı nement followed by a retrenchment.

Theorem 5.1 Let there be a retrenchment as above from *Abs* to *Conc*. Then (see Figure 5.1):

(1)   There is a universal system *Univ*, which satisfies properties (U1) to (U5) below, such that there is an I/O-filtered refinement from *Abs* to *Univ* and a retrenchment from *Univ* to *Conc* whose composition is the given retrenchment.

(2)   Whenever there is a system *Xtra* which satisfies (X1) to (X5) below, and there is an I/O-filtered refinement from *Abs* to *Xtra* and a retrenchment from *Xtra* to *Conc* whose composition is the given retrenchment, then there is an I/O-filtered

refinement from $\underline{Xtra}$ to $\underline{Univ}$ such that $\underline{K} \Rightarrow K^{\approx};K^{\bullet}$, $\underline{R} \Rightarrow R^{\approx};R^{\bullet}$, $\underline{V} \Rightarrow V^{\approx};V^{\bullet}$, and $H^{\approx} \Rightarrow K^{\bullet};\underline{H}$, $Q^{\approx} \Rightarrow (K^{\bullet} \wedge R^{\bullet});\underline{Q}$, $D^{\approx} \Rightarrow (K'' \wedge V^{\bullet} \wedge R^{\bullet} \wedge K^{\bullet});\underline{D}$.

(3) Whenever a system $\underline{Univ}^{*}$ has properties (1) and (2) above of $\underline{Univ}$, then the transitions of $\underline{Univ}$ and $\underline{Univ}^{*}$ are mutually I/O-filtered interrefinable.

To prove part (1) of the theorem, we begin by describing the construction of $\underline{Univ}$. The operation names set of $\underline{Univ}$ is $\mathrm{Ops_U}$ with elements $Op_{\underline{U}}$. The state space is $\underline{V}$ with elements $\underline{v}$, inputs are $\underline{i} \in \underline{J}$ and outputs $\underline{p} \in \underline{P}$. These are all assembled from the Abs and $Conc$ systems as follows.

Firstly $\mathrm{Ops_U} = \mathrm{Ops_A}$ as $\underline{Univ}$ is rei nable from Abs. The spaces are $\underline{V} = U \times W$, $\underline{J} = I \times K$ and $\underline{P} = O \times Q$. We can now give the transitions of $\underline{Univ}$. For each operation $Op_{\underline{U}}$ a typical transition is $\underline{v}$ -$(\underline{i}, Op_{\underline{U}}, \underline{p})$-> $\underline{v}'$ or more explicitly:

$$(u, w) \text{ -}((i, k), Op_{\underline{U}}, (o, q)) \text{-> } (u', w') \tag{5.1}$$

iff u, i, u', o, w, k, w', q satisfy:

$$G(u, w) \wedge P_{Op}(i, k, u, w) \wedge stp_{Op_A}(u, i, u', o) \wedge stp_{Op_C}(w, k, w', q) \wedge$$
$$(G(u', w') \vee C_{Op}(u', w', o, q; i, k, u, w)) \tag{5.2}$$

Finally, the initialisation operation $Init_{\underline{U}}(\underline{v}')$ assigns any value (u', w') to $\underline{v}'$ such that $Init_A(u') \wedge Init_C(w') \wedge G(u', w')$ holds.

Next, we need to set up the I/O-filtered refinement from Abs to $\underline{Univ}$ and the retrenchment from $\underline{Univ}$ to $Conc$. This is done by dei ning the constituent relations and proving that the relevant POs are satisi ed. We will then show that the composition of this I/O-1 ltered rei nement and new retrenchment gives the original retrenchment.

The data for the I/O-1 ltered rei nement consists of the retrieve, within and nevertheless relations. The retrieve relation is:

$$\underline{K}(u, \underline{v}) = (\underline{v} = (u, w)) \tag{5.3}$$

For an operation Op the within relation is:

$$\underline{R}_{Op}(i, \underline{j}) = (\underline{j} = (i, k)) \tag{5.4}$$

and the nevertheless relation is:

$$\underline{V}_{Op}(o, \underline{p}) = (\underline{p} = (o, q)) \tag{5.5}$$

The constituent relations of an I/O-1 ltered rei nement must be total and surjective and it is evident that these relations satisfy this requirement.

We now need to show that the rei nement POs hold for the above dei nitions. The Init PO is

$$Init_{\underline{U}}(\underline{v}') \Rightarrow (\exists u' \bullet Init_A(u') \wedge \underline{K}(u', \underline{v}')) \tag{5.6}$$

Assuming the antecedent we have $Init_{\underline{U}}(\underline{v}')$ which, by dei nition, assigns a value (u', w') to $\underline{v}'$ such that $Init_A(u')$ holds. For this assignment $\underline{K}(u', \underline{v}')$ also holds, and so for any initial $\underline{v}'$ there is a u' as required.

For the Op PO we have to show that:

$$\underline{K}(u, \underline{v}) \wedge \underline{R}_{Op}(\underline{i}, \underline{j}) \wedge stp_{Op_U}(\underline{v}, \underline{i}, \underline{v}', \underline{p}) \Rightarrow$$
$$(\exists\, u', o \bullet stp_{Op_A}(u, i, u', o) \wedge \underline{K}(u', \underline{v}') \wedge \underline{V}_{Op}(o, \underline{p})) \tag{5.7}$$

Let us assume the antecedents. Thus we have $stp_{Op_U}(\underline{v}, \underline{i}, \underline{v}', \underline{p})$, the deı nition of which gives, amongst other things, $stp_{Op_A}(u, i, u', o)$ where $\underline{v}' = (u', w')$ and $\underline{p} = (o, q)$. For these values $\underline{K}(u', \underline{v}')$ and $\underline{V}_{Op}(o, \underline{p})$ both hold and therefore the consequent holds. We are done.

The retrenchment is deı ned by the retrieve, within and concedes relations. The retrieve relation is:

$$\underline{H}(\underline{v}, w) = (\underline{v} = (u, w) \wedge G(u, w)) \tag{5.8}$$

For an operation Op the within relation is:

$$\underline{Q}_{Op}(\underline{j}, k, \underline{v}, w) = (\underline{j} = (i, k) \wedge \underline{v} = (u, w) \wedge P_{Op}(i, k, u, w)) \tag{5.9}$$

and the concedes relation is deı ned as:

$$\underline{D}_{Op}(\underline{v}', w', \underline{p}, q; \underline{j}, k, \underline{v}, w) = (\underline{v}' = (u', w') \wedge \underline{p} = (o, q) \wedge \underline{j} = (i, k) \wedge$$
$$\underline{v} = (u, w) \wedge C_{Op}(u', w', o, q; i, k, u, w)) \tag{5.10}$$

We now turn to the matter of showing that the retrenchment POs are valid. This time the Init PO is:

$$Init_C(w') \Rightarrow (\exists\, \underline{v}' \bullet Init_U(\underline{v}') \wedge \underline{H}(\underline{v}', w')) \tag{5.11}$$

We assume $Init_C(w')$. For this initial w', Init PO (3.1) of the original retrenchment says that there is an initial u' such that $Init_A(u')$ and $G(u', w')$ hold. By combining this u' with the w', we get a $\underline{v}'$ for which $Init_U(\underline{v}')$ holds. Then, using (5.8), we obtain $\underline{H}(\underline{v}', w')$. This completes the proof.

For the operation PO we have to show:

$$\underline{H}(\underline{v}, w) \wedge \underline{Q}_{Op}(\underline{j}, k, \underline{v}, w) \wedge stp_{Op_C}(w, k, w', q) \Rightarrow$$
$$(\exists\, \underline{v}', \underline{p} \bullet stp_{Op_U}(\underline{v}, \underline{j}, \underline{v}', \underline{p}) \wedge (\underline{H}(\underline{v}', w') \vee \underline{D}_{Op}(\underline{v}', w', \underline{p}, q; \underline{j}, k, \underline{v}, w))) \tag{5.12}$$

We assume the antecedents. Using the deı nitions of $\underline{H}(\underline{v}, w)$ and $\underline{Q}_{Op}(\underline{j}, k, \underline{v}, w)$ we obtain $G(u, w)$ and $P_{Op}(i, k, u, w)$ where $\underline{v} = (u, w)$ and $\underline{j} = (i, k)$. These, and $stp_{Op_C}(w, k, w', q)$, make up the antecedents of the **Abs** to **Conc** retrenchment Op PO (3.2), so we know there are u', o such that $stp_{Op_A}(u, i, u', o) \wedge (G(u', w') \vee C_{Op}(u', w', o, q; i, k, u, w))$ holds. We now have all the pieces we need to use (5.2) to get $stp_{Op_U}(\underline{v}, \underline{j}, \underline{v}', \underline{p})$, with $\underline{v}' = (u', w')$ and $\underline{p} = (o, q)$.

We are left with showing $\underline{H}(\underline{v}', w') \vee \underline{D}_{Op}(\underline{v}', w', \underline{p}, q; \underline{j}, k, \underline{v}, w)$. Now, $G(u', w') \vee C_{Op}(u', w', o, q; i, k, u, w)$ is true. So ı rst suppose $G(u', w')$ holds. Then since $\underline{v}' = (u', w')$, (5.8) says $\underline{H}(\underline{v}', w')$ is true and so $\underline{H}(\underline{v}', w') \vee \underline{D}_{Op}(\underline{v}', w', \underline{p}, q; \underline{j}, k, \underline{v}, w)$ must also be true. If on the other hand $C_{Op}(u', w', o, q; i, k, u, w)$ is true, then as $\underline{v}' = (u', w')$, $\underline{p} = (o, q)$, $\underline{j} = (i, k)$ and $\underline{v} = (u, w)$, (5.10) gives $\underline{D}_{Op}(\underline{v}', w', \underline{p}, q; \underline{j}, k, \underline{v}, w)$ from which we once more obtain $\underline{H}(\underline{v}', w') \vee \underline{D}_{Op}(\underline{v}', w', \underline{p}, q; \underline{j}, k, \underline{v}, w)$. This completes the proof.

Finally we need to deﬁne the composition of the I/O-ﬁltered reﬁnement and retrenchment just constructed. We deﬁne the composition to be a retrenchment for which the component relations are constructed as follows. The retrieve relation is:

$$G(u, w) = (\underline{K};\underline{H})(u, w) = (\exists\, \underline{v} \bullet \underline{K}(u, \underline{v}) \wedge \underline{H}(\underline{v}, w)) \tag{5.13}$$

The within relation has the form:

$$P_{Op}(i, k, u, w) = ((\underline{K} \wedge R_{Op});Q_{Op})(i, k, u, w) =$$
$$(\exists\, \underline{v}, j \bullet \underline{K}(u, \underline{v}) \wedge \underline{R}_{Op}(i, j) \wedge Q_{Op}(j, k, \underline{v}, w)) \tag{5.14}$$

and the concedes relation is deﬁned as:

$$C_{Op}(u', w', o, q; i, k, u, w) =$$
$$((\underline{K}' \wedge \underline{V}_{Op} \wedge R_{Op} \wedge \underline{K});\underline{D}_{Op})(u', w', o, q; i, k, u, w) =$$
$$(\exists\, \underline{v}', \underline{p}, j, \underline{v} \bullet \underline{K}(u', \underline{v}') \wedge \underline{V}_{Op}(o, \underline{p}) \wedge \underline{R}_{Op}(i, j) \wedge \underline{K}(u, \underline{v}) \wedge$$
$$\underline{D}_{Op}(\underline{v}', w', \underline{p}, q; j, k, \underline{v}, w)) \tag{5.15}$$

It is easy to show that these deﬁnitions do indeed recover the relations of the original retrenchment. Consider the definition for $G(u, w)$. (5.8) and (5.3) fix $\underline{v}$ to (u, w) for which (5.8) holds only if G holds. Similar arguments apply to the equalities for P and C.

We now state and prove properties (U1) to (U5) of _Univ_ mentioned in Theorem 5.1. Thus:

$$G(u, w) \wedge \underline{K}(u, (u, w)) \Rightarrow \underline{H}((u, w), w) \tag{U1}$$

$$P_{Op}(i, k, u, w) \wedge \underline{K}(u, (u, w)) \wedge \underline{R}_{Op}(i, (i, k)) \Rightarrow Q_{Op}((i, k), k, (u, w), w) \tag{U2}$$

$$C_{Op}(u', w', o, q; i, k, u, w) \wedge \underline{K}(u', (u', w')) \wedge \underline{V}_{Op}(o, (o, q)) \wedge$$
$$\underline{R}_{Op}(i, (i, k)) \wedge \underline{K}(u, (u, w)) \Rightarrow$$
$$\underline{D}_{Op}((u', w'), w', (o, q), q; (i, k), k, (u, w), w) \tag{U3}$$

$$(G(u', w') \vee C_{Op}(u', w', o, q; i, k, u, w)) \wedge$$
$$(\underline{H}((u', w'), w') \vee \underline{D}_{Op}((u', w'), w', (o, q), q; (i, k), k, (u, w), w)) \Rightarrow$$
$$\underline{K}(u', (u', w')) \tag{U4}$$

$$stp_{Op_C}(w, k, w', q) \wedge G(u, w) \wedge P_{Op}(i, k, u, w) \wedge$$
$$stp_{Op_A}(u, i, u', o) \wedge (G(u', w') \vee C_{Op}(u', w', o, q; i, k, u, w)) \wedge$$
$$\underline{H}((u, w), w) \wedge Q_{Op}((i, k), k, (u, w), w) \wedge stp_{Op_U}((u, w), (i, k), (u', w'), (o, q)) \wedge$$
$$(\underline{H}((u', w'), w') \vee \underline{D}_{Op}((u', w'), w', (o, q), q; (i, k), k, (u, w), w)) \Rightarrow$$
$$\underline{V}_{Op}(o, (o, q)) \tag{U5}$$

To demonstrate that these properties hold is easy. (U1) to (U3) are an immediate consequence of (5.8) to (5.10) respectively. (U4) and (U5) are both trivially true since $\underline{K}(u', (u', w'))$ and $\underline{V}_{Op}(o, (o, q))$ hold by deﬁnition. It will become clear why these properties are of interest later. This completes the proof for part (1) of the theorem.

We move on to part (2). Assume an I/O-1 ltered rei nement from **Abs** to <u>**Xtra**</u> given by retrieve relation $K^\approx$, within relations $R^\approx{}_{Op}$, and nevertheless relations $V^\approx{}_{Op}$; and a retrenchment from <u>**Xtra**</u> to **Conc** given by retrieve relation $H^\approx$, within relations $Q^\approx{}_{Op}$, and concedes relations $D^\approx{}_{Op}$. Let the state, input and output spaces of <u>**Xtra**</u> be given by $v^\approx \in V^\approx, j^\approx \in J^\approx, p^\approx \in P^\approx$. Let $Init_X$ and stp_{Op_X} be the initialisation and step predicates for <u>**Xtra**</u>. Lastly, let <u>**Xtra**</u> have properties (X1) to (X5):

$$G(u, w) \wedge K^\approx(u, v^\approx) \implies H^\approx(v^\approx, w) \tag{X1}$$

$$P_{Op}(i, k, u, w) \wedge K^\approx(u, v^\approx) \wedge R^\approx{}_{Op}(i, j^\approx) \implies Q^\approx{}_{Op}(j^\approx, k, v^\approx, w) \tag{X2}$$

$$
\begin{aligned}
&C_{Op}(u', w', o, q; i, k, u, w) \wedge K^\approx(u', v^{\approx\prime}) \wedge V^\approx{}_{Op}(o, p^\approx) \wedge \\
&R^\approx{}_{Op}(i, j^\approx) \wedge K^\approx(u, v^\approx) \implies \\
&\qquad D^\approx{}_{Op}(v^{\approx\prime}, w', p^\approx, q; j^\approx, k, v^\approx, w)
\end{aligned}
\tag{X3}
$$

$$
\begin{aligned}
&(G(u', w') \vee C_{Op}(u', w', o, q; i, k, u, w)) \wedge \\
&(H^\approx(v^{\approx\prime}, w') \vee D^\approx{}_{Op}(v^{\approx\prime}, w', p^\approx, q; j^\approx, k, v^\approx, w)) \implies \\
&\qquad K^\approx(u', v^{\approx\prime})
\end{aligned}
\tag{X4}
$$

$$
\begin{aligned}
&stp_{Op_C}(w, k, w', q) \wedge G(u, w) \wedge P_{Op}(i, k, u, w) \wedge \\
&stp_{Op_A}(u, i, u', o) \wedge (G(u', w') \vee C_{Op}(u', w', o, q; i, k, u, w)) \wedge \\
&H^\approx(v^\approx, w) \wedge Q^\approx{}_{Op}(j^\approx, k, v^\approx, w) \wedge stp_{Op_X}(v^\approx, j^\approx, v^{\approx\prime}, p^\approx) \wedge \\
&(H^\approx(v^{\approx\prime}, w') \vee D^\approx{}_{Op}(v^{\approx\prime}, w', p^\approx, q; j^\approx, k, v^\approx, w)) \implies \\
&\qquad V^\approx{}_{Op}(o, p^\approx)
\end{aligned}
\tag{X5}
$$

To prove part (2), we must show that there is an I/O-1 ltered rei nement from <u>**Xtra**</u> to <u>**Univ**</u>. To this end we now dei ne relations $K^\bullet$, $R^\bullet{}_{Op}$, $V^\bullet{}_{Op}$, indicate that they satisfy the stated inclusions, and prove that they are the retrieve, within and nevertheless relations of the desired rei nement. Thus:

$$K^\bullet(v^\approx, \underline{v}) = (\exists u \bullet \underline{K}(u, \underline{v}) \wedge K^\approx(u, v^\approx)) \tag{5.16}$$

$$R^\bullet{}_{Op}(j^\approx, \underline{j}) = (\exists i \bullet \underline{R}_{Op}(i, \underline{j}) \wedge R^\approx{}_{Op}(i, j^\approx)) \tag{5.17}$$

$$V^\bullet{}_{Op}(p^\approx, \underline{p}) = (\exists o \bullet \underline{V}_{Op}(o, \underline{p}) \wedge V^\approx{}_{Op}(o, p^\approx)) \tag{5.18}$$

Observe that $K^\bullet$ is total and surjective since both $\underline{K}$ and $K^\approx$ are total and surjective. Similarly, $R^\bullet{}_{Op}$ and $V^\bullet{}_{Op}$ are also total and surjective. Given the above dei nitions, establishing that $\underline{K} \implies K^\approx; K^\bullet$, $\underline{R} \implies R^\approx; R^\bullet$, $\underline{V} \implies V^\approx; V^\bullet$, and $H^\approx \implies K^\bullet; \underline{H}$, $Q^\approx \implies (K^\bullet \wedge R^\bullet); \underline{Q}$, $D^\approx \implies (K^{\bullet\prime} \wedge V^\bullet \wedge R^\bullet \wedge K^\bullet); \underline{D}$ all hold is straightforward and details have therefore been omitted.

We move on to the initialisation PO. We need to show

$$Init_{\underline{U}}(\underline{v}') \implies (\exists v^{\approx\prime} \bullet Init_{\underline{X}}(v^{\approx\prime}) \wedge K^\bullet(v^{\approx\prime}, \underline{v}')) \tag{5.19}$$

We assume the antecedent, and so from the deﬁnition of $Init_U(\underline{v}')$ we know $Init_C(w')$ and $G(u', w')$ both hold with $\underline{v}' = (u', w')$. Now, as $Init_C(w')$ is true, the PO for the retrenchment from __Xtra__ to *Conc*,

$$Init_C(w') \Rightarrow (\exists\, v^{\approx\prime} \bullet Init_X(v^{\approx\prime}) \wedge H^{\approx}(v^{\approx\prime}, w')) \tag{5.20}$$

gives $Init_X(v^{\approx\prime})$, this being one of the desired consequents, and also $H^{\approx}(v^{\approx\prime}, w')$. This, together with the $G(u', w')$ above, gives $K^{\approx}(u', v^{\approx\prime})$ by (X4), and thus since $\underline{K}(u', \underline{v}')$ obviously holds, (5.16) says the other consequent $K^{\bullet}(v^{\approx\prime}, \underline{v}')$ must also be true. We are done.

All that remains is to show the operation PO:

$$K^{\bullet}(v^{\approx}, \underline{v}) \wedge R^{\bullet}_{Op}(j^{\approx}, \underline{i}) \wedge stp_{Op_U}(\underline{v}, \underline{i}, \underline{v}', \underline{p}) \Rightarrow$$
$$(\exists\, v^{\approx\prime}, p^{\approx} \bullet stp_{Op_X}(v^{\approx}, j^{\approx}, v^{\approx\prime}, p^{\approx}) \wedge K^{\bullet}(v^{\approx\prime}, \underline{v}') \wedge V^{\bullet}_{Op}(p^{\approx}, \underline{p})) \tag{5.21}$$

is satisﬁed. As usual we assume the antecedents. Therefore $stp_{Op_U}(\underline{v}, \underline{i}, \underline{v}', \underline{p})$ is true and so (5.2) says $G(u, w)$, $P_{Op}(i, k, u, w)$ and $stp_{Op_C}(w, k, w', q)$, where $\underline{v} = (u, w)$, $\underline{i} = (i, k)$, $\underline{v}' = (u', w')$ and $\underline{p} = (o, q)$, are true as well. The antecedent $K^{\bullet}(v^{\approx}, \underline{v})$ gives $K^{\approx}(u, v^{\approx})$, and since we have $G(u, w)$, (X1) implies that $H^{\approx}(v^{\approx}, w)$ holds. The remaining antecedent $R^{\bullet}_{Op}(j^{\approx}, \underline{i})$ gives $R^{\approx}_{Op}(i, j^{\approx})$, which together with the $P_{Op}(i, k, u, w)$ and the $K^{\approx}(u, v^{\approx})$ we already have furnish $Q^{\approx}_{Op}(j^{\approx}, k, v^{\approx}, w)$ via (X2).

So we have established that $H^{\approx}(v^{\approx}, w)$ and $Q^{\approx}_{Op}(j^{\approx}, k, v^{\approx}, w)$ both hold. Combining these with the $stp_{Op_C}(w, k, w', q)$ mentioned above, gives the antecedents of the __Xtra__ to *Conc* retrenchment:

$$H^{\approx}(v^{\approx}, w) \wedge Q^{\approx}_{Op}(j^{\approx}, k, v^{\approx}, w) \wedge stp_{Op_C}(w, k, w', q) \Rightarrow$$
$$(\exists\, v^{\approx\prime}, p^{\approx} \bullet stp_{Op_X}(v^{\approx}, j^{\approx}, v^{\approx\prime}, p^{\approx}) \wedge (H^{\approx}(v^{\approx\prime}, w') \vee$$
$$D^{\approx}_{Op}(v^{\approx\prime}, w', p^{\approx}, q; j^{\approx}, k, v^{\approx}, w))) \tag{5.22}$$

From this we obtain one of the consequents we want, namely $stp_{Op_X}(v^{\approx}, j^{\approx}, v^{\approx\prime}, p^{\approx})$, and in addition $H^{\approx}(v^{\approx\prime}, w') \vee D^{\approx}_{Op}(v^{\approx\prime}, w', p^{\approx}, q; j^{\approx}, k, v^{\approx}, w)$. Next, we notice that the deﬁnition of $stp_{Op_U}(\underline{v}, \underline{i}, \underline{v}', \underline{p})$ also gives $G(u', w') \vee C_{Op}(u', w', o, q; i, k, u, w)$. Therefore, because we have $H^{\approx\prime} \vee D^{\approx}_{Op}$, we can use (X4) to conclude that $K^{\approx}(u', v^{\approx\prime})$ is true. Then, as $\underline{K}(u', \underline{v}')$ also holds, we can get $K^{\bullet}(v^{\approx\prime}, \underline{v}')$ by applying (5.16).

Our last task is to demonstrate that the ﬁnal consequent, $V^{\bullet}_{Op}(p^{\approx}, \underline{p})$, holds. From the preceding steps we already know that $G(u, w) \wedge P_{Op}(i, k, u, w)$, $stp_{Op_C}(w, k, w', q)$, $G(u', w') \vee C_{Op}(u', w', o, q; i, k, u, w)$, $H^{\approx}(v^{\approx}, w) \wedge Q^{\approx}_{Op}(j^{\approx}, k, v^{\approx}, w)$, $stp_{Op_X}(v^{\approx}, j^{\approx}, v^{\approx\prime}, p^{\approx})$ and $H^{\approx}(v^{\approx\prime}, w') \vee D^{\approx}_{Op}(v^{\approx\prime}, w', p^{\approx}, q; j^{\approx}, k, v^{\approx}, w)$ all hold. Recalling that $stp_{Op_U}(\underline{v}, \underline{i}, \underline{v}', \underline{p})$ also gives $stp_{Op_A}(u, i, u', o)$, provides the missing piece we need to be able to use (X5) and so get $V^{\approx}_{Op}(o, p^{\approx})$. From here it is a simple step to obtain $V^{\bullet}_{Op}(p^{\approx}, \underline{p})$, since (5.18) says that all we now require is $\underline{V}(o, \underline{p})$ which, because $\underline{p} = (o, q)$, deﬁnitely holds. We are done. We have now proved part (2) of the theorem.

It remains to prove part (3). Given that __Univ*__ has the same properties as __Univ__, and noting that properties (U1) to (U5) of __Univ__ correspond to (X1) to (X5) of __Xtra__, means there will be an I/O-filtered refinement from _Univ_ to _Univ*_ and an I/O-filtered refinement from _Univ*_ to _Univ_. This completes the proof of Theorem 5.1. ☺

Note that the mutual interreı nability in part (3) is not isomorphism in the conventional set theoretical sense; the mutual interreı nability established here amounts to a much looser notion of equivalence of systems.

To conclude this section let us examine the structure of _Univ_ in the context of our running example. The state space of the _Univ_ is the Cartesian product of the state spaces of the abstract and concrete systems. Thus individual states will be ordered pairs of sets and sequences, e.g. ({2, 4, 6}, [2, 4, 6]} and ({9, 12}, [5]).

As for the transitions of the universal system, (5.2) tells us that these will consist of corresponding pairs of abstract and concrete transitions, i.e. those for which G, P_{Op} and $G' \vee C_{Op}$ hold. Thus for nonboundary cases, _Univ_ will undergo transitions which look like:

$$({\{2, 4, 6\}, [2, 4, 6]}) \text{ -}((8, 8), AddEl)\text{-> } (\{2, 4, 6, 8\}, [2, 4, 6, 8])$$

For the boundary steps on the other hand (where the concrete operation performs a _skip_), instances look like:

$$(\{1..10\}, [1..10]) \text{ -}((11, 11), AddEl)\text{-> } (\{1..11\}, [1..10])$$

and we see clearly why the general product structure is needed for the universal state space; evidently [1..10] can never be a serialisation of {1..11}.

6 Idempotence

One of the aims in the preceding section was to construct _Univ_ so that it was at the level of abstraction of _Conc_ but refinable from _Abs_. We showed that for any other similar factorisation, the refinement component was refinable to _Univ_. In this section we provide further evidence indicating that _Univ_ is at a low enough level. Specifically, we show that applying the universal construction to the _Univ_ to _Conc_ retrenchment itself, yields a system, _UUniv_, which in essence is no different from that of _Univ_.

Based on (5.1), which deı nes the transitions of the universal system, the transitions of _UUniv_ look like $((u, w), w) \text{ -}(((i, k), k), Op_{UU}, ((o, q), q))\text{-> } ((u', w'), w')$ for which

$$\underline{H}((u, w), w) \wedge \underline{Q}_{Op}((i, k), k, (u, w), w) \wedge stp_{Op_{U}}((u, w), (i, k), (u', w'), (o, q)) \wedge$$
$$stp_{Op_{C}}(w, k, w', q) \wedge (\underline{H}((u', w'), w') \vee \underline{D}_{Op}((u', w'), w', (o, q), q; (i, k), k, (u', w), w))$$

must hold. Substituting for $\underline{H}$, $\underline{Q}_{Op}$, $\underline{D}_{Op}$, $stp_{Op_{U}}$ in the above gives (5.2) which deı nes the _Univ_ transitions $(u, w) \text{ -}((i, k), Op_{U}, (o, q))\text{-> } (u', w')$. Thus the set of _UUniv_ transitions is isomorphic to those of _Univ_ since having an extra copy of the concrete transition in _UUniv_ is isomorphic to having just the one copy in the corresponding _Univ_ transition.

Note that the reı nements from _Abs_ to _Univ_ and _Univ_ to _UUniv_ will compose to give a reı nement from _Abs_ to _UUniv_. Thus by Theorem 5.1 _Univ_ and _UUniv_ are equivalent and so at the same level of abstraction. All this supports our claim that _Univ_ is at a low enough level.

7 Maximally Abstract Retrenchments

Here we reproduce some material from [3] in order to lay the necessary groundwork for subsequent sections. The concern in loc. cit. was to construct a universal system _Univ_ which was at the level of _Abs_ but was reı nable to _Conc_ (see Figure 7.1). The universality of the construction arises from the fact that there is a reı nement from _Univ_ to the

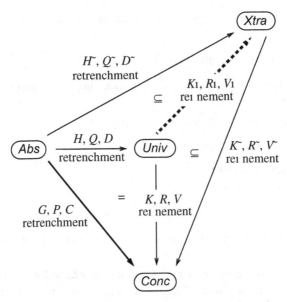

Figure 7.1: Canonical factorisation of the retrenchment from _Abs_ to _Conc_ into a retrenchment followed by a reı nement.

retrenchment component of any similar factorisation. Theorem 7.1 below describes these ideas in more detail.

Theorem 7.1 Let there be a retrenchment from the _Abs_ to _Conc_. Then

(1) There is a universal system _Univ_ such that there is a retrenchment from _Abs_ to _Univ_ and an I/O-filtered refinement from _Univ_ to _Conc_ whose composition is the given retrenchment.

(2) Whenever there is a system _Xtra_ and a retrenchment from _Abs_ to _Xtra_ and an I/O-filtered refinement from _Xtra_ to _Conc_ whose composition is the given retrenchment, then there is an I/O-filtered refinement from _Univ_ to the concrete core bound

transitions of $Xtra^1$; such that $H^\frown \Rightarrow H;K_1$, $\quad Q^\frown \Rightarrow Q;R_1{\wedge}K_1$, $\quad D^\frown \Rightarrow$ $D;K_1'{\wedge}V_1{\wedge}R_1{\wedge}K_1$, and such that $K \Rightarrow K_1;K^\frown$, $R \Rightarrow R_1;R^\frown$, $V \Rightarrow V_1;V^\frown$.

(3) Whenever a system $Univ^*$ has properties (1) and (2) above of $Univ$, then the concrete core bound transitions of $Univ$ and $Univ^*$ are mutually I/O-filtered interrefinable.

We now describe the structure of $Univ$. The operation names set of $Univ$ is Ops_U with elements Op_U. The state space is V with elements v, inputs are $j \in$ J and outputs $p \in$ P. These are all constructed from Abs and $Conc$ as follows.

Firstly, $Ops_U = Ops_C$. The spaces are V = U $\times$ W, J = I $\times$ K and P = O $\times$ Q. To give the transitions of $Univ$ we observe that Ops_U decomposes as $Ops_U = Ops_A \cup (Ops_U - Ops_A)$.

For an operation $Op_U \in (Ops_U - Ops_A)$, we have a transition v -(j, Op_U, p)-> v' or more explicitly:

$$(u, w) \text{ -}((i, k), Op_U, (o, q))\text{-> } (u', w') \tag{7.1}$$

for arbitrary values u, i, o, u', w, k, q, w'; so the non-Op_A transitions of $Univ$ form a universal relation.

For an $Op_A \in Ops_A$, a transition is v -(j, Op_A, p)-> v' or:

$$(u, w) \text{ -}((i, k), Op_A, (o, q))\text{-> } (u', w') \tag{7.2}$$

iff u, i, o, u', w, k, q, w' satisfy:

$$G(u, w) \wedge P_{Op}(i, k, u, w) \Rightarrow$$
$$stp_{Op_A}(u, i, u', o) \wedge (G(u', w') \vee C_{Op}(u', w', o, q; i, k, u, w)) \tag{7.3}$$

Last, $Init_U(v')$ in $Univ$ assigns any value (u', w') to v' such that $Init_A(u') \wedge G(u', w')$ holds.

Finally, we give the data for the retrenchment from Abs to $Univ$ and the I/O-1 ltered rei nement from $Univ$ to $Conc$. The component relations of the retrenchment were de-1 ned as follows. The retrieve relation had the form:

$$H(u, v) = (v = (u, w) \wedge G(u, w)) \tag{7.4}$$

For each operation Op the within relation was:

$$Q_{Op}(i, j, u, v) = (j = (i, k) \wedge v = (u, w) \wedge P_{Op}(i, k, u, w)) \tag{7.5}$$

while the concedes relation looked like:

$$D_{Op}(u', v', o, p; i, j, u, v) =$$
$$(v' = (u', w') \wedge p = (o, q) \wedge j = (i, k) \wedge v = (u, w) \wedge$$
$$C_{Op}(u', w', o, q; i, k, u, w)) \tag{7.6}$$

---

1. The concrete core bound transitions of $Xtra$ (resp. $Univ$, $Univ^*$) are those transitions which are related by the Abs to $Xtra$ (resp. $Univ$, $Univ^*$) retrenchment to transitions in Abs.

For the I/O-filtered refinement, the retrieve relation K, and for each Op, the within relation R_{Op} and nevertheless relation V_{Op}, were defined as projection functions onto the second component:

$$K(v, w) \;=\; (v = (u, w)) \tag{7.7}$$

$$R_{Op}(j, k) \;=\; (j = (i, k)) \tag{7.8}$$

$$V_{Op}(p, q) \;=\; (p = (o, q)) \tag{7.9}$$

8   Requirements Validation

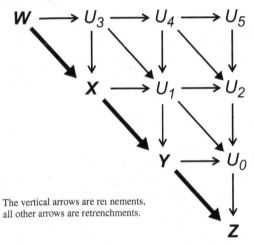

The vertical arrows are rei nements,
all other arrows are retrenchments.

Figure 8.1: Requirements Validation. Lifting the system Z to the level of abstraction of W.

The constructions discussed in this paper present an alternative approach for validating that all the requirements of a system have been taken into account. Let us suppose we have a development consisting of a series of retrenchment steps from a system W to a system Z as shown in Figure 8.1. Then it is possible to decompose the retrenchment from Y to Z and construct a system U_0 which is at the level of abstraction of Y but expresses the detail in Z. Similarly we can construct new systems U_1 and U_3 which are at the level of X and W respectively. Now, the rei nement from U_1 to Y and the retrenchment from Y to U_0 compose to give a retrenchment from U_1 to U_0. This new retrenchment can itself be factorised to give the system U_2 which will be at the level of X. Continuing this process will eventually result in the construction of U_5, which expresses the detail introduced in Z, but is itself at the abstract level of W. Since rei nements compose, the POs of the single rei nement from U_5 to Z can be used to validate that all the requirements of the starting system W have been fulı lled. In [3], the author argued that although it is unlikely that developers would be disposed to carrying out requirements validation in this way, such a possibility admits the opportunity of being able to view the problem from a different perspective which is always beneı cial.

9 The Other Diagonal

In this section we show that the systems *Univ* and *Univ* are related by an I/O-ı ltered reı nement for the cases where $Ops_U = Ops_{\underline{U}}$ (see Figure 9.1). First we deı ne the re-

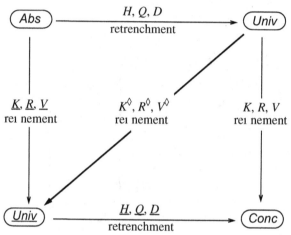

Figure 9.1: A reı nement from *Univ* to *Univ*.

lations $K^{\Diamond}$, $R^{\Diamond}_{Op}$ and $V^{\Diamond}_{Op}$, and then show that they are the retrieve, within and nevertheless relations of the required refinement. Thus:

$$K^{\Diamond}(v, \underline{v}) = (v = \underline{v}) \tag{9.1}$$

$$R^{\Diamond}_{Op}(j, \underline{j}) = (j = \underline{j}) \tag{9.2}$$

$$V^{\Diamond}_{Op}(p, \underline{p}) = (p = \underline{p}) \tag{9.3}$$

and we see that they are all both total and surjective since each one is a relation between corresponding ordered pairs.

As usual we commence with the Init PO:

$$Init_{\underline{U}}(\underline{v}') \Rightarrow (\exists v' \bullet Init_U(v') \wedge K^{\Diamond}(v', \underline{v}')) \tag{9.4}$$

Suppose the antecedent holds. From the definition of $Init_{\underline{U}}(\underline{v}')$ we know $Init_A(u') \wedge G(u', w')$, where $\underline{v}' = (u', w')$, holds. Setting $v' = \underline{v}'$, it follows from the definition of $Init_U(v')$ that it holds too. Lastly, for this assignment, from (9.1) we also know that $K^{\Diamond}(v', \underline{v}')$ is true. Hence for any initial $\underline{v}'$ there is a v' as required.

Next, we focus on the Op PO, namely:

$$K^{\Diamond}(v, \underline{v}) \wedge R^{\Diamond}{}_{Op}(j, \underline{j}) \wedge stp_{Op_U}(\underline{v}, \underline{j}, \underline{v}', \underline{p}) \Rightarrow$$
$$(\exists\, v', p \bullet stp_{Op_U}(v, j, v', p) \wedge K^{\Diamond}(v', \underline{v}') \wedge V^{\Diamond}{}_{Op}(p, \underline{p})) \tag{9.5}$$

Assume the antecedents. Knowing $stp_{Op_U}(\underline{v}, \underline{j}, \underline{v}', \underline{p})$, (5.2) says that $G(u, w) \wedge P_{Op}(i, k, u, w)$ and $stp_{Op_A}(u, i, u', o)$ and $G(u', w') \vee C_{Op}(u', w', o, q; i, k, u, w)$ all hold, with $\underline{v}' = (u', w')$, $\underline{p} = (o, q)$, $\underline{j} = (i, k)$ and $\underline{v} = (u, w)$. Furthermore, from $K^{\Diamond}$ and (9.1) we get $v = \underline{v}$, while $R^{\Diamond}$ and (9.2) gives $j = \underline{j}$. Now let $v' = \underline{v}'$ and $p = \underline{p}$, then we obtain $stp_{Op_U}(v, j, v', p)$ via (7.3). Finally, for the given assignments, $K^{\Diamond}(v', \underline{v}')$ follows from (9.1) and $V^{\Diamond}{}_{Op}(p, \underline{p})$ from (9.3). Therefore there are v', p for which the consequent of (9.5) is true. We are done. ☺

Notice that the direction of the reı nement supports our assertion that _Univ_ is more concrete in character than _Univ_. Moreover, there is no reı nement in the other direction, since it is not possible to derive stp_{Op_C}, and thus stp_{Op_U}, from the assumptions we would have in that case. This is exactly as it should be, for otherwise the systems would be equivalent and so could not be at different levels of abstraction. Also, the presence of $stp_{Op_C}(w, k, w', q)$ only in the deı nition of _Univ_ transitions, can be regarded as a further expression of _Univ_'s more concrete nature.

10 Termination

So far we have considered reı nement steps which preserve partial correctness. To extend our discussion to the total correctness arena, we now assume that for each operation Op there is a termination predicate trm_{Op} (in before-states and inputs), which holds for those steps for which termination is guaranteed. In the majority of reı nement methodologies, the structure of the POs is such that trm_{Op} for an abstract operation implies trm_{Op} for the corresponding concrete operation. The upshot of this is that the inclusion of the termination aspects of operations ensures the preservation of properties between levels of abstraction. In retrenchment the direction of the trm_{Op} dependency is reversed allowing a retrenchment step to only preserve chosen properties of the more abstract model. Returning to our original retrenchment from _Abs_ to _Conc_, we therefore ı nd that the termination PO has the form:

$$G(u, w) \wedge P_{Op}(i, k, u, w) \wedge trm_{Op_C}(w, k) \Rightarrow trm_{Op_A}(u, i) \tag{10.1}$$

To include termination aspects in the construction given in Section 5, we augment the structure of _Univ_ with the termination predicate:

$$trm_{Op_U}(\underline{v}, \underline{j}) = (\exists\, u, i \bullet \underline{K}(u, \underline{v}) \wedge \underline{R}_{Op}(i, \underline{j})) \tag{10.2}$$

and this must satisfy the corresponding reı nement and retrenchment termination POs:

$$\underline{K}(u, \underline{v}) \wedge \underline{R}_{Op}(i, \underline{j}) \wedge trm_{Op_A}(u, i) \Rightarrow trm_{Op_U}(\underline{v}, \underline{j}) \tag{10.3}$$

$$\underline{H}(\underline{v}, w) \wedge \underline{Q}_{Op}(\underline{j}, k, \underline{v}, w) \wedge trm_{Op_C}(w, k) \Rightarrow trm_{Op_U}(\underline{v}, \underline{j}) \tag{10.4}$$

That this is indeed the case is easy to establish. Taking (10.3) 1 rst and assuming the antecedents, we have a u and an i such that $\underline{K}(u, \underline{v}) \wedge \underline{R}_{Op}(i, \underline{i})$ holds. Therefore $trm_{Op_U}(\underline{v}, \underline{i})$ holds and we are done. Proceeding on to (10.4), from the antecedents $\underline{H}(\underline{v}, w)$ and $\underline{Q}_{Op}(\underline{i}, k, \underline{v}, w)$, using (5.8) and (5.9), we know $\underline{v} = (u, w)$ and $\underline{i} = (i, k)$. For these values $\underline{K}(u, \underline{v})$ and $\underline{R}_{Op}(i, \underline{i})$ clearly hold, so we can apply (10.2) to get $trm_{Op_U}(\underline{v}, \underline{i})$.

All that remains is to show that the termination PO for the rei nement from *Xtra* to *Univ* holds. The PO says:

$$K^\bullet(v^\approx, \underline{v}) \wedge R^\bullet{}_{Op}(\underline{j}^\approx, \underline{i}) \wedge trm_{Op_X}(v^\approx, \underline{j}^\approx) \;\Rightarrow\; trm_{Op_U}(\underline{v}, \underline{i}) \tag{10.5}$$

Given the antecedents, $K^\bullet(v^\approx, \underline{v})$ and (5.16) gives $\underline{K}(u, \underline{v})$ with $\underline{v} = (u, w)$, while $R^\bullet{}_{Op}(\underline{j}^\approx, \underline{i})$ and (5.17) provide $\underline{R}_{Op}(i, \underline{i})$ with $\underline{i} = (i, k)$. Since $\underline{K}$ and $\underline{R}_{Op}$ hold, (10.2) is satisi ed, giving $trm_{Op_U}(\underline{v}, \underline{i})$. We are done.

To complete the picture, we will also demonstrate that the termination PO for the re-1 nement from *Univ* to *Univ* holds. The PO in this case reads:

$$K^\Diamond(v, \underline{v}) \wedge R^\Diamond{}_{Op}(\underline{j}, \underline{i}) \wedge trm_{Op_U}(v, j) \;\Rightarrow\; trm_{Op_U}(\underline{v}, \underline{i}) \tag{10.6}$$

Once again, to confirm this is straightforward. As usual we assume the antecedents. For the chosen values of $\underline{v}$ and $\underline{i}$, say (u, w) and (i, k), (5.3) and (5.4) say $\underline{K}(u, \underline{v})$ and $\underline{R}_{Op}(i, \underline{i})$ are true, which means $trm_{Op_U}(\underline{v}, \underline{i})$ must also be true. ☺

Space restrictions prevent us from developing these results further, but we have laid the foundations from which a more detailed analysis of the termination aspects can be made. Finally, we take this opportunity to make a correction to the earlier work on maximally abstract retrenchments [3], and note that in Section 8 the termination PO for the rei nement from *Univ* to *Xtra* can only be established by restricting the universality result to situations in which the relations $K^\sim$, $R^\sim{}_{Op}$ and $V^\sim{}_{Op}$ of the rei nement from *Xtra* to *Conc* are functions. The main result presented in that paper is not affected by the introduction of this constraint.

11 Conclusion

This paper has shown how a retrenchment step can be factorised into a canonical I/O-1 ltered rei nement to a universal system followed by a retrenchment. Within the class of systems whose properties we stated, the universal character of the aforementioned system arises from the fact that for all other similar factorisations whose intermediate system belongs to the same class, there is a rei nement from the intermediate system to the universal model. The objective was for the universal system to be at the concrete level, and in support of this claim, in addition to the universality result, we showed that the construction of the universal system was idempotent.

Furthermore, given the maximal and minimal factorisations discussed in this paper, we proved in Section 9 that for a given retrenchment step, there was also an I/O-1 ltered rei nement from the universal system at the abstract level to the universal system at the concrete one (if we assume *Conc* has no additional operations, i.e. $\mathsf{Ops}_A = \mathsf{Ops}_C$). Finally, we briei y explored the effect of extending the partial correctness framework to a total correctness setting by including guaranteed termination predicates in our models.

The principal purpose of all this activity is to integrate retrenchment with rei nement, and this has been achieved to the degree outlined in the preceding sections. It is important to demonstrate that rei nement and retrenchment work well together, thus encouraging the joint use of the two techniques in the construction of complex industrial scale specifications. Moreover, the adoption of retrenchment into the developer's armoury will enable formality to be introduced earlier in the development hierarchy than is possible by the use of rei nement alone.

References

[1]   Abrial J. R. *The B-Book: Assigning Programs to Meanings.* C.U.P., 1996.

[2]   Back R. J. R., von Wright J. *Refinement Calculus: A Systematic Introduction.* Springer, 1998.

[3]   Banach R. Maximally Abstract Retrenchments. In *Proc. IEEE ICFEM-00*, pages 133-142. IEEE Computer Society Press, 2000.

[4]   Banach R., Poppleton M. Retrenchment: An Engineering Variation on Rei nement. In Bert (ed.), *Proc. B-98*, LNCS **1393**, 129-147. Springer 1998. See also UMCS Technical Report UMCS-99-3-2, http://www.cs.man.ac.uk/cstechrep

[5]   Banach R., Poppleton M. Retrenchment and Punctured Simulation. In Araki, Galloway, Taguchi (eds.), *Proc. IFM-99*, pages 457-476. Springer 1999.

[6]   Banach R., Poppleton M. Sharp Retrenchment, Modulated Rei nement and Simulation. *Formal Aspects of Computing*, **11**, 498-540, 1999.

[7]   Banach R., Poppleton M. Retrenchment, Rei nement and Simulation. In Bowen, Dunne, Galloway, King (eds.), *Proc. ZB-00*, LNCS **1878**, 304-323. Springer, 2000.

[8]   Banach R., Poppleton M. Engineering and Theoretical Underpinnings of Retrenchment. To be submitted. Available at: http://www.cs.man.ac.uk/~banach/some.pubs/Retrench.Underpin.ps.gz

[9]   Boiten E., Derrick J. IO-Rei nement in Z. In *Third BCS-FACS Northern Formal Methods Workshop.* Ilkley, U.K. 1998.

[10]   de Roever W.-P., Engelhardt K. *Data Refinement: Model-Oriented Proof Methods and their Comparison.* Cambridge University Press, 1998.

[11]   Jones C. B. *Systematic Software Development Using VDM*, 2nd ed. Prentice Hall, 1990.

[12]   Litteck H.J., Wallis P.J.L. Rei nement Methods and Rei nement Calculi. *Software Engineering Journal* **7**(3), 219-229, 1992.

[13]   Liu S. Evolution: A More Practical Approach than Rei nement for Software Development. In *Proc. ICECCS-97*, pages 142-151. IEEE, 1997.

[14]   Morgan C. *Programming from Specifications*, 2nd ed. Prentice Hall, 1994.

[15]   Poppleton M., Banach R. Retrenchment: Extending Rei nement for Continuous and Control Systems. In *Proc. IWFM'00*, Springer Electronic Workshop in Computer Science Series, http://ewic.org.uk/ewic. Springer, 2000.

[16]   Smith G. Stepwise Development from Ideal Specii cations. In Edwards (ed.), *Aus. Comp. Sci. Conf.* **22**(1), 227-233. IEEE Computer Society, 2000.

[17]   Smith G., Fidge C. Incremental Development of Real-Time Requirements: The Light Control Case Study. JUCS **6**, 704-730, 2000.

[18]   Spivey J. M. *The Z Notation: A Reference Manual*, 2nd ed. Prentice Hall, 1993.

[19]   Stepney S., Cooper D., Woodcock J. More Powerful Z Data Rei nement: Pushing the State of the Art in Industrial Rei nement. In Bowen, Fett, Hinchey (eds.), *Proc. ZUM'98*, LNCS **1493**, 284-307. Springer, 1998.

Author Index

Lecture Notes in Computer Science

For information about Vols. 1–2255
please contact your bookseller or Springer-Verlag